HOW TO DESIGN AND EVALUATE RESEARCH IN EDUCATION

HOW TO DESIGN AND EVALUATE RESEARCH

JACK R. FRAENKEL

San Francisco State University

NORMAN E. WALLEN

San Francisco State University

IN EDUCATION

McGRAW-HILL PUBLISHING COMPANY

New York   St. Louis   San Francisco   Auckland   Bogotá   Caracas
Hamburg   Lisbon   London   Madrid   Mexico   Milan   Montreal   New Delhi
Oklahoma City   Paris   San Juan   São Paulo   Singapore   Sydney
Tokyo   Toronto

This book was developed by Lane Akers, Inc.

How to Design and Evaluate Research in Education

1 2 3 4 5 6 7 8 9 0   DOW DOW   8 9 4 3 2 1 0 9

ISBN   0-07-557212-5

This book was set in Galliard by Monotype Composition Company.
The editors were Lane Akers and Lauren Shafer;
the designer was Harry Rinehart;
the production supervisor was Birgit Garlasco.
R. R. Donnelley & Sons Company was printer and binder.

Cover painting: Arlene Erdich, "Broken Images".

CKC
370.78
c.1
6/16

Library of Congress Cataloging-in-Publication Data

Fraenkel, Jack R., (date).
   How to design and evaluate research in education / Jack R. Fraenkel,
Norman E. Wallen.
     p.   cm.
   Includes bibliographical references.
   ISBN 0-07-557212-5 (Text).—ISBN 0-07-021770-X (Instructor's
manual)
   1. Education—Research—Methodology.   2. Education—Research—
Evaluation.   3. Proposal writing in educational research.
I. Wallen, Norman E.   II. Title.
LB1028.F665   1990
370'.78—dc20   89-35980

ABOUT THE AUTHORS

JACK R. FRAENKEL is currently Professor of Interdisciplinary Studies in Education and Director of the Research and Development Center, College of Education, San Francisco State University. He received his Ph.D. from Stanford University, and has taught courses in research methodology for more than twenty years. His current work centers around advising and assisting faculty and students in the generation and development of research endeavors.

NORMAN E. WALLEN is also Professor of Interdisciplinary Studies in Education at San Francisco State University, where he has taught since 1966. An experienced researcher, he has taught courses in statistics and research design to Master's and Doctoral students for many years. His current work focuses on strategies for the recruitment and retention of at-risk students.

TO MARGE AND LINA

Contents
in Brief

CONTENTS

Three   VARIABLES AND HYPOTHESES   34

Four   REVIEWING THE LITERATURE   46

Five   SAMPLING   66

Fourteen   **CAUSAL-COMPARATIVE
RESEARCH   304**

Fifteen   **SURVEY
RESEARCH   330**

Sixteen **QUALITATIVE RESEARCH 366**

Seventeen **HISTORICAL RESEARCH 410**

PREFACE

How to Design and Evaluate Research in Education is directed to students taking their first course in educational research. Because this field continues to grow so rapidly with regard to both the knowledge it contains and the methodologies it employs, the authors of any introductory text are forced to carefully define their goals as a first step in deciding what to include in their book. In our case, we continually kept three main goals in mind. We wanted to produce a text that would:

1. Provide students with the basic information needed to understand the research process, from idea formulation through data analysis and interpretation.
2. Enable students to use this knowledge to design their own research investigation on a topic of personal interest.
3. Permit them to read and understand the literature of educational research.

The first two goals are intended to satisfy the needs of those students who must plan and carry out a research project as part of their course requirements. The third goal is aimed at students whose course requirements include learning how to read and understand the research of others. Many instructors, ourselves included, build all three goals into their courses, since each one seems to reinforce the others. It is hard to read and fully comprehend the research of others if you have not yourself gone through the process of designing and evaluating a research project. Similarly, the more you read and evaluate the research of others, the better equipped you will be to design your own meaningful and creative research. In order to achieve the above goals, we have developed a book with the following characteristics.

CONTENT COVERAGE

Goal one, to provide students with the basic information needed to understand the research process, has resulted in a four-part book plan.

Part One (Chapter One) introduces students to the nature of educational research, briefly overviews each of the six methodologies discussed later in the text, and presents an overview of the research process.

Part Two (Chapters Two–Eleven) discusses the basic concepts and procedures that must be understood before one can engage in, or even plan to do, research intelligently, including variables, definitions, sampling, instrumentation, validity, reliability, and data collection and analysis. These and other concepts are covered thoroughly, clearly, and relatively simply. The emphasis throughout is to show students, by means of clear and appropriate examples, how to set up a research study in an educational setting on a question of interest and importance.

Part Three (Chapters Twelve–Seventeen) describes and illustrates the methodologies most commonly used in educational research. Many key concepts presented in Part Two are considered again in these chapters in order to illustrate their application to each methodology. Finally, each methodology chapter concludes with a carefully chosen study from the published research literature. Each study is analyzed by the authors with regard to both its strengths and weaknesses. Students are shown how to read and critically analyze a study they might find in the literature.

Part Four (Chapter 18) concludes the book by showing how to prepare a research proposal/report (involving a methodology of choice) that builds on the concepts and examples developed and illustrated in the previous chapters.

RESEARCH EXERCISES

In order to achieve our second goal of helping students learn to apply their knowledge of basic processes and methodologies, we organized the chapters in the same order that students normally follow in developing a research proposal or conducting a research project. Then we concluded each chapter with a research exercise that includes a fill-in problem sheet. These exercises allow students to apply their understanding of the major concepts of each chapter. When completed, these accumulated problem sheets will have led students through the step-by-step processes involved in designing their own research projects. Although this step-by-step development requires some revision of their work as they learn more about the research process, the gain in understanding that results as they slowly see their proposal develop "before their eyes" justifies the extra time and effort involved.

ACTUAL RESEARCH STUDIES

Our third goal, to enable students to read and understand the literature of educational research, has led us to conclude each of the Part Three methodology chapters with a published study that illustrates a particular research method. At the end of each study we analyze its strengths and weaknesses and offer suggestions as to how it might be improved. Similarly, we conclude the book with a student research proposal that we have critiqued with marginal comments. This annotated proposal has proved an effective means of helping students understand both good and questionable research practices.

STYLE OF PRESENTATION

Because students are typically anxious regarding the content of research courses, we have taken extraordinary care not to overwhelm them with dry, abstract discussions. More than any text to date, our presentations are laced with clarifying examples and with summarizing charts, tables, and diagrams. Our experience in teaching research courses for more than twenty years has convinced us that there is no such thing as having "too many" examples in a basic text.

In addition to the many examples and illustrations that are embedded in our (we hope) informal writing style, we have built the following pedagogical features into the book: 1) lists of chapter-opening learning objectives; 2) end-of-chapter summaries and discussion questions; and 3) an extensive end-of-book glossary.

ACKNOWLEDGMENTS

Many organizations and individuals graciously gave us permission to reprint their materials in this book, and we thank them accordingly. We are grateful to the Literary Executor of the late Sir Ronald A. Fisher, F.R.S., to Dr. Frank Yates, F.R.S., and to Longman Group Ltd. London, for permission to reprint Tables II and VII from their book *Statistical Tables for Biological, Agricultural and Medical Research* (6th edition, 1974). We thank the editors and staff at McGraw-Hill Publishing Company for their efforts in turning the manuscript into a finished product: Lane Akers for his support and encouragement, Lauren Shafer for shepherding the book through production, and a special word of thanks to the copyeditor, Cynthia Garver, who called our attention to many places in the manuscript that needed clarification, and who offered a number of helpful suggestions for such clarification. Also, we wish to thank the reviewers, Professors Paul Dixon, Kent State University, Noreen Michael, University of Kansas, William Ware, University of North Carolina, and especially Enoch Sawin of San Francisco State University, whose unusually thorough reviews of the manuscript in various preliminary forms led to innumerable improvements. Finally, we are grateful to our students over the years, for all they have taught us.

Jack R. Fraenkel
Norman E. Wallen

HOW TO DESIGN AND EVALUATE RESEARCH IN EDUCATION

Part One

INTRODUCTION TO RESEARCH

Chapter One

THE NATURE OF EDUCATIONAL RESEARCH

Educational research takes many forms. In this chapter we introduce you to the subject of educational research and explain why knowledge of various types of research can be of value to educators. Because research is but one way to obtain knowledge, we describe several other ways and compare the strengths and weaknesses of each. We also give a brief overview of several research methodologies used in education to set the stage for a more extensive discussion of them in later chapters.

Objectives

Reading this chapter should enable you to:

- *Explain* what is meant by the term "educational research" and *give two examples* of the kinds of topics educational researchers might investigate
- *Explain* why a knowledge of scientific research methodology can be of value to educators
- *Name* and *give an example* of four ways of knowing other than the method used by scientists
- *Explain* what is meant by the term "scientific method"
- *Give an example* of six different types of research methodologies used by educational researchers
- *Describe* briefly the basic components involved in the research process

---

Some Examples of Educational Concerns

- A high school principal in San Francisco wants to improve the morale of her faculty.
- The director of the gifted student program in Denver would like to know what happens during a typical week in an English class for advanced placement students.
- An elementary school counselor in Boise wishes she could get more students to "open up" to her about their worries and problems.
- A tenth grade biology teacher in Atlanta wonders if discussions are more effective than lectures in motivating students to learn biological concepts.
- A physical education teacher in Tulsa wonders if ability in one sport correlates with ability in other sports.

- A seventh grade student in Philadelphia asks her counselor what she can do to improve her study habits.
- The president of the local PTA in Little Rock, parent of a sixth grader at Cabrillo School, wonders how she can get more parents involved in school-related activities.

Each of the above examples, although fictional, represents a typical sort of question or concern facing many of us in education today. Together, these examples suggest that teachers, counselors, administrators, parents, and students continually need information to do their jobs. Teachers need to know what kinds of materials, strategies, and activities best help students learn. Counselors need to know what problems hinder or prevent students from learning and how to help them with these problems. Administrators need to know how to provide a happy and

3

productive learning environment. Parents need to know how to help their children succeed in school. Students need to know how to study to learn as much as they can.

Why Research Is of Value

How can educators, parents, and students obtain the information they need? Many ways of obtaining information, of course, exist. One can consult experts, review books and articles, question or observe colleagues with relevant experience, examine one's own experience in the past, or even rely on intuition. All these approaches suggest possible ways to proceed, but the answers they provide are not always reliable. Experts may be mistaken; source documents may contain no insights of value; colleagues may have no experience in the matter; one's own experience or intuition may be irrelevant or mistaken.

This is why a knowledge of scientific research methodology can be of value. The scientific method provides us with another way of obtaining information—information that is as accurate and reliable as we can get. Let us compare it, therefore, with some of the other ways of knowing that exist.

Ways of Knowing

SENSORY EXPERIENCE

We see, we hear, we smell, we taste, we touch. Most of us have seen the fireworks on the Fourth of July, heard the whine of a jet airplane's engines overhead, smelled a rose, tasted chocolate ice cream, and felt the wetness of a rainy day. The data we take in from the world through our senses is the most immediate way we have of knowing something. Using sensory experience as a means of obtaining information, the director of the gifted student program mentioned above, for example, might visit an advanced placement English class to see and hear

what happens during a week or two of the semester.

Sensory data, to be sure, can be refined. Seeing the temperature on an outdoor thermometer can refine our knowledge of how cold it is; a top-quality stereo system can help us hear Beethoven's Fifth Symphony with greater clarity; smell, taste, touch—all can be enhanced, and usually need to be. Many experiments in sensory perception have revealed that we are not always wise to trust our senses too completely. Our senses can (and often do) deceive us: The gunshot we hear becomes a car backfiring; the water we see in the road ahead is but a mirage; the chicken we thought we tasted turns out to be rabbit.

Sensory knowledge is undependable. Sensory knowledge is also incomplete. The data we take in through our senses do not account for all (or even most) of what we seem to feel is the range of human knowing. To obtain reliable knowledge, therefore, we cannot rely on our senses alone but must check what we think we know with other sources.

AGREEMENT WITH OTHERS

One such source is the opinions of others. Not only can we share our sensations with others, but also we can check on the accuracy and authenticity of these sensations: Does this soup taste salty to you? Isn't that John over there? Did you hear someone cry for help? Smells like mustard, doesn't it?

Obviously this is a great advantage. Checking with others on whether they see or hear what we do can help us discard what is untrue and manage our lives more intelligently by focusing on what is true. If, while hiking in the country, I do not hear the sound of an approaching automobile but several of my companions do, I am likely to proceed with caution. All of us frequently discount our own sensations when others report that we are missing something or "seeing" things incorrectly. Using agreement with others as a means of obtaining information, the tenth grade biology teacher in Atlanta, for example, might check with her colleagues to see if they find discussions more effective than lectures in motivating their students to learn.

The problem with such common knowledge is that it, too, can be wrong. A majority vote of a committee is no guarantee of the truth. My friends might be wrong about the presence of an approaching automobile, or the automobile they hear may be moving away from rather than coming toward us. Two groups of eyewitnesses to an accident may disagree as to which driver was at fault. Hence, we need to consider some additional ways to obtain reliable knowledge.

EXPERT OPINION

Perhaps there are particular individuals we should consult. Experts in their field. People who know a great deal about what we are interested in finding out. We are likely to believe a noted heart specialist, for example, if he says that Uncle Charlie has a bad heart. Surely, a Ph.D. in economics knows more than most of us do about what makes the economy tick. And shouldn't we believe our family dentist if he tells us that back molar has to be pulled? To use expert opinion as a means of obtaining information, perhaps the physical education teacher in Tulsa we mentioned should inquire of a noted authority in the physical education field whether or not ability in one sport correlates with ability in another.

Well, maybe. It depends on the credentials of the experts and the nature of the question about which they are being consulted. For experts, like all of us, can be mistaken. For all their study and training, what experts know is still based primarily on what they have learned from reading and thinking, from listening to and observing others, and from their own experience. No expert, however, has studied or experienced all there is to know in a given field, and thus can never be totally sure. All any expert can do is give us an opinion based on what he or she knows, and no matter how much this is, it is never all there is to know. Let us consider, then, another way of knowing—logic.

LOGIC

We also know things logically. Our intellect—the capability we have to reason things out—allows us to use sensory data to develop a new kind of knowledge. Consider the famous syllogism:

All human beings are mortal.
Sally is a human being.
Therefore, Sally is mortal.

To assert the first statement (called the major premise), we need only generalize from our experience about the mortality of individuals. We have never experienced anyone who was not mortal, so we state that all human beings are. The second statement (called the minor premise) is based entirely on sensory experience. We come in contact with Sally and classify her as a human being. We don't have to rely on our senses, then, to know that the third statement (called the conclusion) must be true. Logic tells us it is. As long as the first two statements are true the third statement must be true.

Take the case of the counselor in Philadelphia who is asked to advise her counselee on how to improve her study habits. Using logic, she might present the following argument: Students who take notes on a regular basis in class find that their grades improve; if you will take notes on a regular basis, then your grades should improve as well.

This is not all there is to logical reasoning, of course, but it is enough to give you an idea of another way of knowing. There is a fundamental danger in logical reasoning of which we need to be aware, however: It is only when the major and minor premises of a syllogism are *both* true that the conclusion is guaranteed to be true. If either of the premises are false, the conclusion may or may not be true.*

There is still another way of knowing to consider—the method of science. We turn to it next.

---

* In the note-taking example, the major premise (all students who take notes on a regular basis in class improve their grades) is probably *not* true.

THE SCIENTIFIC METHOD

When many people hear the word "science," they think of things like white coats, laboratories, test tubes, or space exploration. Scientists are people who know a lot and the term "science" suggests a tremendous body of knowledge. What we are interested in here, however, is science as a method of knowing. It is the **scientific method** that is important to researchers.

What is this method? Essentially it involves the testing of ideas in the public arena. Almost all of us humans are capable of making connections—of seeing relationships and associations—among the sensory data we experience. Most of us then identify these connections as "facts"—items of knowledge about the world in which we live. We may speculate, for example, that our students may be less attentive in class when we lecture than when we engage them in discussion. A physician may guess that people who sleep between six to eight hours each night will be less anxious than those who sleep more or less than that amount. A counselor may feel that students read less than they used to because they spend most of their free time watching television. But in each of these cases, we do not really know if what we think is true. What we are dealing with are only guesses or hunches, or as scientists would say, hypotheses.

What we must now do is put each of these guesses or hunches to a rigorous test to see if they hold up under more controlled conditions. To investigate our speculation on attentiveness scientifically, we can observe carefully and systematically how attentive our students are when we lecture and when we hold a class discussion. The physician can count the number of hours slept by various individuals, then measure and compare their respective anxiety levels. The counselor can compare the reading habits of students who watch different amounts of television.

Such investigations, however, do not constitute science unless they are made public. This means that all aspects of the investigation are described in sufficient detail so the study can be repeated by any who question the results—provided, of course, that those interested possess the necessary competence and resources. Private procedures, speculations, and conclusions are not scientific until they are made public.

There is nothing very mysterious, then, about how scientists work in their quest for reliable knowledge. In reality, many of us proceed this way when we try to reach an intelligent decision about a problem that is bothering us. These procedures can be boiled down into five distinct steps.

- First, there is a problem of some sort—some disturbance in our lives that disrupts the normal or desirable state of affairs. Something is bothering us. For most of us who are not scientists, it may be a tension of some sort, a disruption in our normal routine. To the professional scientist, it may be an unexplained discrepancy in one's field of knowledge, a gap to be closed.
- Second, steps are taken to define the problem more precisely, to become more clear about exactly what the problem is. For example, we may find that we are having trouble explaining certain ideas to our students. The scientist may face the far more complex problem of determining the cause of cancer.
- Third comes an attempt to search out every potential solution to the problem imaginable. All ideas are grist for the mill here. One's imagination is allowed, even encouraged, to run free. Any guess, any hunch, any idea is food for thought. This is absolutely crucial. After all, it is impossible even to consider, let alone evaluate, an idea unless it is thought of first! It is for this reason that scientists defend the right to think freely with such passion. For freedom of thought—the freedom to propose and consider *any* idea, even those that some people feel are quite outrageous—is absolutely essential to the scientific method. Letting other students teach their peers may seem a ridiculous solution to some, but it is one possibility to be considered. That lack of exercise may contribute to cancer is perhaps un-

likely, but it should not be dismissed out-of-hand.

- The fourth step is to project the consequences of each of the possible solutions we have conceived. If we were to do such-and-such, what would happen? Letting other students teach their peers might result in more noise in the classroom, cause some students to be even more confused, and make the class more difficult to control, but many students who are now having trouble learning might be helped. Suggesting that lack of exercise is a cause of cancer may bring ridicule from scientific colleagues and be hard to investigate, but it is an idea that can be studied.

- Fifth and finally, we test our solutions to see what consequences actually do result. We try out our idea of having students teach students; we also try out any other promising solutions we have. Likewise, scientists propose and test each of their hunches. They design experiments, prepare exercise routines, administer them under controlled conditions, and see how individuals under different routines react. In short, they try out each of their hypotheses to get at the consequences, to see what happens. Notice that all this testing, however, is done publicly. There is nothing private about it. The value of scientific research is that its results can be replicated (repeated) by anyone who is interested in doing so.

The general order of the scientific method, then, is as follows:

Identification of a Problem

↓

Definition of the Problem

↓

Formulation of Hypotheses

↓

Projection of Consequences

↓

Testing of Hypotheses

This is not to say that all (or even most) scientists routinely proceed through each of the steps in this order to arrive at a solution to the problems they are investigating. Often, in fact, a problem may grow out of a perceived consequence. A scientist may notice something happening (a consequence), wonder why it does, and decide to try and find out. The essential point is that scientists are curious folk—they are intrigued by problems and puzzles—and spend much of their professional lives trying to solve them. The essence of all research endeavors lies in this curiosity—this desire to find out why people do the things they do, as well as whether or not certain ways of doing things work better than other ways.

Types of Research

All of us engage in actions that have some of the characteristics of formal research, although perhaps we do not realize this at the time. We try out new methods of teaching, new materials, new textbooks. We compare what we did this year with what we did last year. Teachers frequently ask students and colleagues their opinions about school and classroom activities. Counselors interview students, faculty, and parents about school activities. Administrators hold regular meetings to gauge how the faculty feels about various issues. School boards query administrators, administrators query teachers, teachers query students and each other.

We observe, we analyze, we question, we hypothesize, we evaluate. But rarely do we do these things systematically. Rarely do we observe under controlled conditions. Rarely are our instruments as accurate and reliable as they might be. Rarely do we use the variety of research techniques and methodologies that are at our disposal.

The term "research" means any sort of "careful, systematic, patient study and investigation in some field of knowledge, undertaken to discover or establish facts and principles."[1]

There are many methodologies that fit this definition. If we learn how to use more of these methodologies where they are appropriate and if we can become more scientific in our research efforts, we can obtain more reliable information upon which to base our educational decisions. Let us look, therefore, at some of the research methodologies we might use.

EXPERIMENTAL RESEARCH

Experimental research is the most rigorous of scientific methods. Because the researcher actually establishes different treatments and then studies their effects, results of this type of research lead to the most clear-cut interpretations.

Suppose a history teacher is interested in the following question: "How can I most effectively teach important concepts (such as democracy or colonialism) to my students?" The teacher might compare the effectiveness of two or more methods of instruction (usually called the *independent variable*) in promoting the learning of historical concepts. After systematically assigning students to contrasting forms of history instruction (such as inquiry, case studies, illustrated lectures, programmed units, and small group discussions), the teacher could compare the effects of these contrasting methods by testing students' conceptual knowledge. Student learning could be assessed by an objective test or some other measuring device. The scores on the test (usually called the *dependent variable*), if they differ, would give some idea of the effectiveness of the various methods. A simple graph could be plotted to show the results, as illustrated in Figure 1.1.

In the simplest sort of experiment, there are two contrasting methods to be compared and an attempt is made to control for all other **(extraneous) variables,** such as student ability level, age, grade level, time, materials, teacher characteristics, etc., that might affect the outcome under investigation. Methods of such control could include holding the classes during the same or closely related periods of time, using the same materials in both groups, comparing

FIGURE 1.1

Example of Results of Experimental Research: Effect of Method of Instruction on History Test Scores[a]

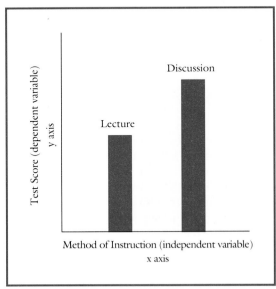

[a] Many of the examples of data presented throughout this text, including that shown in Figure 2.1, are hypothetical. When actual data are shown, the source is indicated.

students of the same age and grade level, and so on.

Of course, we want to have as much control as possible over the assignment of individuals to the various treatment groups, to ensure the groups are similar. But in most schools, systematic assignment of students to treatment groups is difficult, if not impossible, to achieve. Nevertheless, useful comparisons are still possible. You might wish to compare the effect of different teaching methods (lectures vs. discussion, for example) on student achievement or attitudes in two or more *intact* history classes in the same school. If a difference exists between the classes in terms of what is being measured, this result can suggest how the two methods compare, even though the exact causes of the difference would be somewhat in doubt. We discuss various kinds of experimental research in Chapter Twelve.

CORRELATIONAL RESEARCH

Another type of research is done to determine relationships among two or more variables; this is called **correlational research.** This type of research can help us make more intelligent predictions.

For instance, could a math teacher predict which sorts of individuals are likely to have trouble learning the subject matter of algebra? If we could make fairly accurate predictions in this regard, then perhaps we could suggest some corrective measures for teachers to use to help such individuals so that large numbers of "algebra-haters" are not produced.

How do we do this? First, we need to collect various kinds of information on students that we think is related to their achievement in algebra. Such information might include their performance on a number of tasks logically related to the learning of algebra (such as computational skills, ability to solve word problems, understanding of math concepts, and so on), their verbal abilities, study habits, aspects of their backgrounds, their early experiences with math courses and math teachers, the number and kinds of math courses they've taken, and anything else that might conceivably point up how those students who do well in math differ from those who do poorly.

We then examine the data to see if any relationships exist between some or all of these characteristics and subsequent success in algebra. What do those who learn math easily seem to have in common? What do they seem to be doing that those who have trouble learning math seem to ignore or avoid? What do they apparently not do? Such information can assist us to predict more accurately the likelihood of learning difficulties for certain types of students in algebra courses. It even may suggest some things to try out with different groups of students to help them learn.

In short, correlational research seeks to investigate whether one or more relationships of some type exist. The approach requires no manipulation or intervention on the part of the researcher other than that required to adminis-ter the instrument(s) necessary to collect the data desired. In general, this type of research would be undertaken when one wants to look for and describe relationships that may exist among naturally occurring phenomena, without trying in any way to alter these phenomena. We talk more about correlational research in Chapter Thirteen.

CAUSAL-COMPARATIVE RESEARCH

Another type of research is intended to determine the cause for or the consequences of differences between groups of people; this is called **causal-comparative research.** Suppose a teacher wants to determine whether students from single-parent families do more poorly in her course than students from two-parent families. To investigate this question experimentally, the teacher would systematically select two groups of students and then assign each a single- or two-parent family—which is clearly impossible (not to mention immoral!).

To test this question using a causal-comparative design, the teacher might compare two groups of students who already belong to one or the other type of family to see if they differ in their achievement. Suppose the groups do differ. Can the teacher conclude that the difference in family situation produced the difference in achievement? Alas, no. The teacher can conclude that a difference does exist but cannot say what caused the difference.

Interpretations of causal-comparative research are limited, therefore, because the researcher cannot say whether a particular factor is a cause or a result of the behavior(s) observed. In the example presented here, the teacher would not know (1) if any perceived difference in achievement between the two groups was due to the difference in home situation, (2) if the parent status was due to the difference in achievement between the two groups (although this seems unlikely), or (3) if some unidentified factor was at work. Nevertheless, despite problems of interpretation, causal-comparative studies are of value in identifying *possible* causes of observed variations in the behavior patterns of students. We discuss causal-comparative research in Chapter Fourteen.

SURVEY RESEARCH

Another type of research obtains data to determine specific characteristics of a group. This is called **survey research.** Take the case of a high school principal who wants to find out how his faculty feels about his administrative policies. What do they like about his policies? What do they dislike? Why? Which policies do they like the best or least?

These sorts of questions can best be answered through a variety of survey techniques that measure faculty attitudes toward the policies of the administration. A *descriptive survey* involves asking the same set of questions (often prepared in the form of a written questionnaire or ability test) to a large number of individuals either by mail, by telephone, or in person. When answers to a set of questions are solicited in person, the research is called an *interview*. Responses are then tabulated and reported, usually in the form of frequencies or percentages of those who answer in a particular way to each of the questions.

The difficulties involved in survey research are mainly twofold: (1) ensuring that the questions to be answered are clear and not misleading and (2) getting a sufficient number of the questionnaires completed and returned so that meaningful analyses can be made. The big advantage of survey research is that it has the potential to provide us with a lot of information obtained from quite a large sample of individuals.

If more details about particular questions in a survey are desired, the principal (or someone else) can conduct personal interviews with faculty. The advantages of an interview (over a questionnaire) are that open-ended questions (those requiring a response of some length) can be used with greater confidence, particular questions of special interest or value can be pursued in depth, follow-up questions can be asked, and items that are unclear can be explained. We discuss survey research in Chapter Fifteen.

QUALITATIVE RESEARCH

In all the examples presented so far, the questions being asked involve *how well, how much,* or *how accurately* different learnings, attitudes, or ideas exist or are being developed. Possibilities for research included experimental comparisons between alternative methods of teaching history, an investigation of relationships between mathematics achievement and various "predictors," an assessment of relative achievement among single-parent and two-parent students, and a survey of faculty members about their feelings toward administrative policy.

Researchers might wish to obtain a more complete picture of the educational process, however, than answers to the above questions provide. A department chairperson, for example, might be interested in knowing more than just how well, how much of, or how accurately something is done. He or she may want to obtain a more wholistic picture of what goes on in a particular situation or setting. When this is the case, some form of **qualitative research** is called for.

Consider the subject of physical education. Just how do physical education teachers teach their subject? What kinds of things do they do as they go about their daily routine? What sorts of things do students do? In what kinds of activities do they engage? What are the explicit and implicit rules of the game that exist in PE classes which seem to help or hinder the process of learning?

To gain some insight into these concerns, an **ethnographic study** can be conducted. The emphasis in this type of research is on documenting or portraying the everyday experiences of individuals by observing and interviewing them and relevant others. An elementary classroom, for example, might be observed on as regular a basis as possible, and the students and teacher involved might be interviewed in an attempt to describe, as fully and as richly as possible, what goes on in that classroom. Descriptions (a better word might be "portrayals") might depict the social atmosphere of the classroom; the intellectual and emotional experiences of students; the manner in which the teacher acts toward and reacts to students of different ethnicities, sexes, or abilities; how the "rules" of the class are learned, modified and enforced; the kinds of questions asked by the teacher and students; and so forth. The data could include detailed prose descriptions by students of classroom activities, audiotapes of pupil-student conferences, videotapes of classroom discussions, examples of teacher lesson plans and student work, sociograms depicting "power" relationships in the classroom, and flowcharts illustrating the direction and frequency of certain types of comments (for example, the kinds of questions asked by teacher and students to one another and the responses that different kinds produce).

Qualitative research also lends itself well to a detailed study of one or a few individuals. Sometimes much can be learned from studying just one individual (such as a student who is able to learn a second language rather easily). This is called a **case study.** Sometimes documents rather than individuals or classes are observed and analyzed. This type of research is known as **content analysis.** It is just what its name implies—the analysis of the written or visual contents of a document. We discuss these types of research in Chapter Sixteen.

HISTORICAL RESEARCH

You are already probably familiar with **historical research**: Some aspect of the past is studied, either by perusing documents of the period or by interviewing individuals who lived during the time. An attempt is then made to reconstruct as accurately as possible what happened during that time and to explain why it did.

For example, a curriculum coordinator in a large urban school district might want to know what sorts of arguments have been made in the past as to what should be included in the social studies curriculum for grades K–12. She could read what various social studies and other curriculum theorists have written on the topic and then compare the positions they espoused. The major problems in historical research are making sure that the documents or individuals really did

come from (or live during) the period under study, and once this is established, ascertaining that what the documents/individuals say is true. We discuss historical research in more detail in Chapter Seventeen.

ALL HAVE VALUE

It must be stressed that each of the research methodologies described so briefly above has value for us in education. Each constitutes a different way of inquiring into the realities that exist within our classrooms and schools and into the minds and emotions of teachers, counselors, administrators, parents, and students. Each represents a different tool for use in trying to understand what goes on, and what works, in schools. It is inappropriate to consider any one or two of these approaches as superior to any of the others. The effectiveness of a particular methodology depends in large part on the nature of the research question one wants to ask and the specific context within which the particular investigation is to take place. We need to gain insights into what goes on in education from as many perspectives as possible, and hence we need to construe research in broad rather than narrow terms.

As far as we are concerned, research in education should ask a variety of questions, move in a variety of directions, encompass a variety of methodologies, and use a variety of tools. Different research orientations, perspectives, and goals should not only be allowed, but encouraged. The intent of this book is to help you learn how and when to use several of these methodologies.

General Research Types

It is useful to consider the various research methodologies we have described as falling within one or more general research categories—descriptive, associational, or intervention-type studies. **Descriptive studies** describe a given state of affairs as fully and carefully as possible.

One of the best examples of descriptive research is found in biology, where each variety of plant and animal species is meticulously described and information is organized into useful taxonomic categories, as is done so thoroughly in botany and zoology.

In educational research, the primary descriptive methodology is the survey, as when researchers summarize the characteristics (abilities, preferences, behaviors, and so on) of individuals or groups, or (sometimes) physical environments (such as schools), or, as in some historical studies, changes in any of these over time. Examples of descriptive studies in education include identifying the achievements of various groups of students; describing the behaviors of teachers, administrators, or counselors; describing the attitudes of parents; and describing the physical capabilities of schools. The description of phenomena is the starting point for all research endeavors.

Descriptive research, in and of itself, however, is not very satisfying, since most researchers want to have a more complete understanding of people and things. This requires a more detailed analysis of the various aspects of phenomena and their interrelationships. Advances in biology, for example, have come about, in large part, as a result of the categorization of descriptions and the subsequent determination of relationships among these categories.

Educational researchers also want to do more than simply describe situations or events. They want to know how (or if), for example, differences in achievement are related to such things as teacher behavior, student diet, student interests, or parental attitudes. By investigating such possible relationships, researchers are able to understand phenomena more completely. Furthermore, the identification of relationships enables the making of predictions. If researchers know that student interest is related to achievement, for example, they can predict that students who are more interested in a subject will demonstrate higher achievement in that subject than students who are less interested. Research that investigates relationships is often referred to as **associational research.** Correlational and causal-comparative methodologies are the principal examples of associational research. Examples of associational studies include studying relationships (a) between achievement and attitude, between childhood experiences and adult characteristics, or between teacher characteristics and student achievement—all of which are correlational studies; and (b) between methods of instruction and achievement (comparing students who have been taught by each method), or between gender and attitude (comparing attitudes of males and females)—both of which are causal-comparative studies.

As useful as associational studies are, they too are ultimately unsatisfying because they do not permit researchers to "do something" to influence or change outcomes. Simply determining that student interest is predictive of achievement does not tell us how to change or improve either interest or achievement, although it does suggest that increasing interest would increase achievement. To find out whether something will influence or have an effect on something else, researchers need to conduct some form of intervention study.

In **intervention studies,** a particular method or treatment is introduced to influence one or more outcomes. Such studies enable researchers to assess, for example, the effectiveness of various teaching methods, curriculum models, classroom arrangements, and other efforts at influencing the characteristics of individuals or groups. Intervention studies can also contribute to general knowledge by confirming (or failing to confirm) theoretical predictions (for instance, that abstract concepts can be taught to young children). The primary methodology used in intervention research is the experiment.

Some types of educational research may combine these three general approaches. Although historical and qualitative research methodologies are primarily descriptive in nature, at times they may be associational if the investigator examines relationships. A descriptive historical study of college entrance requirements over time that examines the relationship between those requirements and achievement in mathematics is also associational. An ethnographic study that describes in detail the daily activities of an inner-city high school and also finds a relationship between media attention and teacher morale in the school is both descriptive and associational. An investigation of the effects of different teaching methods on concept learning that also reports the relationship between concept learning and gender is an example of a study that is both an intervention and an associational-type study.

A Brief Overview of the Research Process

Regardless of methodology, all researchers engage in a number of similar activities. Almost all research plans include, for example, a problem statement, a hypothesis, definitions, a literature review, a sample of subjects, tests or other measuring instruments, a description of procedures to be followed, including a time schedule, and a description of intended data analyses. We deal with each of these components in some detail throughout this book, but we want to give you a brief overview of them before we proceed.

Figure 1.2 presents a schematic of the research components. The solid-line arrows indicate the sequence in which the components are usually presented and described in research proposals and reports. They also indicate a useful sequence for planning a study (that is, thinking about the research problem, followed by the hypothesis, followed by the definitions, and so forth). The broken-line arrows indicate the most likely departures from this sequence (for example, consideration of instrumentation sometimes results in changes in the sample). The nonlinear pattern is intended to point out that, in practice, the process does not necessarily follow this precise sequence. In fact, experienced researchers often consider many of these components simultaneously as they develop their research plan.

Statement of the Research Problem. The problem of a study sets the stage for everything else. The **problem statement** should be accompanied by a description of the background of the problem (what factors caused it to be a problem in the first place) and a rationale or

FIGURE 1.2

The Research Process

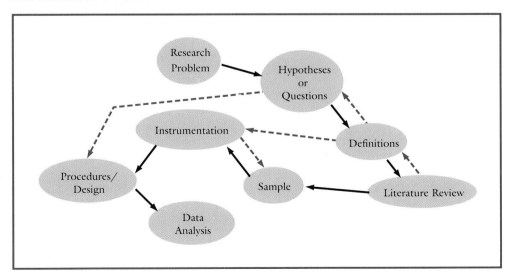

justification for studying it. Any legal or ethical ramifications related to the problem should be discussed and resolved.

Formulation of an Exploratory Question or a Hypothesis.   Research problems are usually stated as questions, and often as hypotheses. A **hypothesis** is a prediction, an explanation of why certain results or outcomes are expected to occur. The hypotheses of a study should clearly indicate any relationships expected between the **variables** (the factors, characteristics, or conditions) being investigated and be so stated that they can be tested within a reasonable period of time. Not all studies are hypothesis-testing studies, but many are.

Definitions.   All key terms in the problem statement and hypothesis should be defined as clearly as possible.

Review of the Related Literature.   Other studies related to the research problem should be located and their results briefly summarized. The **literature review** (of appropriate journals, reports, monographs, etc.) should shed light on what is already known about the problem and should indicate logically why the proposed study would be an extension of this prior knowledge.

Sample.   The subjects (the **sample**) of the study should be identified, and the larger group, or **population** (to whom results are to be gen-eralized) should be clearly identified. The sampling plan (the procedures by which the subjects will be selected) should be described.

Instrumentation.   Each of the measuring **instruments** that will be used to collect data from the subjects should be described in detail and a rationale should be given for their use.

Procedures.   The actual procedures of the study—what the researcher will do (what, when, where, how, and with whom) from beginning to end, in the order in which they will occur, should be spelled out in detail, along with any special arrangements if they are needed. The procedures section of a research plan should be as detailed as possible. A realistic time schedule outlining when various tasks are to be started, along with expected completion dates, should also be provided. All materials (e.g., textbooks) and/or equipment (e.g., computers) that will be used in the study should also be described. The general design or methodology (e.g., an exper-iment or a survey) to be used should be stated. In addition, possible sources of bias should be identified and how they will be controlled should be explained.

Data Analysis.   The statistical techniques, both descriptive and inferential, to be used to analyze the data should be described. The com-parisons to be made to answer the research question should be made clear.

Main Points of Chapter One

- There are many ways to obtain information, including sensory experience, agreement with others, expert opinion, logic, and the scientific method.
- The scientific method is considered by researchers the most likely way to produce reliable and accurate knowledge.
- The scientific method involves answering questions through systematic and public accumulation of knowledge.
- Some of the most commonly used scientific research methodologies in education include experimental research, correlational research, causal-comparative research, survey research, qualitative research, and historical research.
- Experimental research involves manipulating conditions and studying effects.

- Causal-comparative research involves comparing known groups who have had different experiences to determine possible causes or consequences of group membership.
- Correlational research involves studying relationships among variables within a single group.
- Survey research involves describing the characteristics of a group by means of such instruments as interview schedules, questionnaires, and tests.
- Qualitative research involves obtaining a wholistic picture of what goes on in a particular situation or setting. Three of the most common forms of qualitative research are ethnographic research, case studies, and content analyses.
- Historical research involves studying some aspect of the past.
- Each of the research methodologies described constitutes a different way of inquiring into reality and is thus a different tool to use in understanding what goes on in education.
- Individual research methodologies can be classified into general research types. Descriptive studies describe a given state of affairs. Associational studies investigate relationships. Intervention studies assess the effects of a treatment or method on outcomes.
- Almost all research plans include a problem statement, an exploratory question or hypothesis, definitions, a literature review, a sample of subjects, instrumentation, a description of procedures to be followed, a time schedule, and a description of intended data analyses.

For Discussion

1. Listed below are several research questions. What methodology do you think would be the most appropriate to investigate each?
    a. What do students think are the least popular courses in the high school curriculum, and why?
    b. How do parents feel about the elementary school counseling program?
    c. How can Tom Adams be helped to learn to read?
    d. Do students who have high scores on reading tests also have high scores on writing tests?
    e. Does team teaching help or hinder student learning?
    f. What sorts of activities work best with slow learners?
    g. What effect does the gender of a counselor have on his or her receptivity by counselees?
    h. In what ways were the kinds of bills passed into law during the administrations of Richard Nixon and Ronald Reagan similar and different?

2. Can any of the above questions be investigated other than scientifically? If so, which ones? How?

3. Can you think of some other ways of knowing besides those mentioned in this chapter? What are they? What, if any, are the limitations of these methods?

4. What other questions, besides those mentioned in the text, can you suggest that would not lend themselves to scientific research?

5. Many people seem to be uneasy about the idea of research, particularly research in schools. How would you explain this?

Note

1. *Webster's new world dictionary of the American language*, Second College Edition. (1984). New York: Simon and Schuster. p. 1208.

Research Exercise One:
What Kind of Research?

Think of a research idea or problem you would like to investigate. Using Problem Sheet 1, briefly describe the problem in a sentence or two. Then indicate the type of research methodology you would use to investigate this problem.

1. A possible topic or problem I am thinking of researching is: _____

_____

_____

_____

2. The type of research that seems most appropriate to this topic or problem is: (*circle one*)

    a. An experiment.

    b. A correlational study.

    c. A causal-comparative study.

    d. A survey using a written questionnaire.

    e. A survey using interviews of several individuals.

    f. An ethnographic study.

    g. A case study.

    h. A content analysis.

    i. A historical study.

Part Two

THE BASICS
OF EDUCATIONAL
RESEARCH

Chapter Two

THE RESEARCH PROBLEM

A research problem is the focus of a research investigation. It is exactly what its name implies—a problem that a researcher wishes to investigate. Research problems are frequently stated as research questions. In this chapter, we discuss the nature of research questions and describe some of their characteristics. We also provide some ways to clarify unclear terms in research questions. Lastly, we present a number of ethical principles important for researchers to consider.

Objectives

- *Give some examples* of potential research problems in education
- *Formulate* a research question
- *Distinguish* between researchable and nonresearchable questions
- *Name* five characteristics that good research questions possess
- *Describe* three ways to clarify unclear research questions
- *Give an example* of an operational definition and *explain* how such definitions differ from other kinds of definitions
- *Describe* briefly what is meant by "ethical" research
- *Describe* briefly three important ethical principles recommended for researchers to follow
- *Explain* what is meant, in research, by the term "relationship" and *give an example* of a research question that involves a relationship

What Is a Research Problem?

A research problem is exactly that—a problem that someone would like to research. A problem can be anything that a person finds unsatisfactory or unsettling, a difficulty of some sort, a state of affairs that needs to be changed, anything this is not working as well as it might. Problems involve areas of concern to researchers as educators, conditions they want to improve, difficulties they want to eliminate, questions for which they seek answers.

Research Questions

Usually a research problem is initially posed as a question, which serves as the focus of the researcher's investigation. The following list of examples of possible research questions in education also gives an appropriate methodology in parentheses. Although there are other possible methodologies that might be used, we consider those given here as particularly suitable.

- Does client-centered therapy produce more satisfaction in clients than does traditional therapy? (experimental research)
- Are the descriptions of people in social studies textbooks biased? (content analysis research)
- What goes on in an elementary school classroom during an average week? (ethnographic research)
- Do teachers behave differently toward students of different genders? (causal-comparative research)
- How can we predict which students might have trouble learning certain kinds of subject matter? (correlational research)

- How do parents feel about the school counseling program? (survey research)
- How can a principal improve faculty morale? (interview research)

What all these questions have in common is that we can collect data of some sort to answer them (at least in part). That's what makes them researchable. For example, a researcher can measure satisfaction on the part of clients who receive different methods of therapy. Or researchers can observe and interview in order to describe the functioning of an elementary school classroom. To repeat, then, what makes these questions researchable is that some sort of information *can* be collected to answer them.

There are other kinds of questions, however, about which information *cannot* be collected. Here are two examples.

- Should philosophy be included in the high school curriculum?
- What is the meaning of life?

Why can't these questions be researched? What is there about them that prevents us from collecting information to answer them? The answer is both simple and straightforward: Both questions are, in the final analysis, not researchable. There is no way to collect information to answer either question.

The first question is a question of *value*—it implies notions of right and wrong, proper and improper and therefore does not have any **empirical** (or observable) referents. There is no way to deal, empirically, with the verb "should." How can we empirically determine whether or not something "should" be done? What data could we collect? There is no way for us to proceed. However, if the question is changed to "Do people *think* philosophy should be included in the high school curriculum?" it becomes researchable. Why? Because now we can collect data to help us answer the question.

The second question is *metaphysical* in nature—that is, beyond the physical, transcendental. Answers to this sort of question lie beyond the accumulation of information.

Here are more research questions. Which ones (if any) do you think are researchable?

1. Is God good?
2. Are children happier when taught by a teacher of the same gender?
3. Does high school achievement influence the academic achievement of university students?
4. What is the best way to teach grammar?
5. What would schools be like today if World War II had not occurred?

We hope you identified questions 2 and 3 as the two that are researchable. Questions 1, 4, and 5, as stated, cannot be researched. Question 1 is another metaphysical question, and, as such, does not lend itself to empirical research (we could ask people if they believe God is good, but that would be another question). Question 4 asks for the "best" way to do something. Think about this one for a moment. Is there any way we can determine the *best* way to do anything? To be able to determine this, we must examine *every* possible alternative, and a moment's reflection brings us to the realization that this can never be accomplished. How would we ever be sure that all possible alternatives have been examined? Question 5 requires the creation of impossible conditions. We can, of course, investigate what people *think* schools would be like.

Characteristics of Good Research Questions

Once a research question has been formulated, researchers want to turn it into as good a question as possible. Good research questions possess four essential characteristics.

1. The question is *feasible* (i.e., it can be investigated without an undue amount of time, energy, or money).
2. The question is *clear* (i.e., most people would agree as to what the key words in the question mean).
3. The question is *significant* (i.e., it is worth

investigating because it will contribute important knowledge about the human condition).
4. The question is *ethical* (i.e., it will not involve physical or psychological harm or damage to human beings, or to the natural or social environment of which they are a part).

Let us discuss each of these characteristics in a bit more detail.

RESEARCH QUESTIONS SHOULD BE FEASIBLE

An important issue in designing research studies is that of feasibility. A feasible question is one that can be investigated with available resources. Some questions (such as those involving space exploration, for example, or the study of the long-term effects of special programs, like Head Start) require a great deal of time and money; others require much less. Unfortunately, the field of education, unlike medicine, business, law, agriculture, pharmacology, or the military, has never established an ongoing research effort tied closely to practice. Most of the research that is done in schools or other educational institutions is likely to be done by "outsiders," often university professors and their students, and usually only if funded by temporary grants. Thus, lack of feasibility often seriously limits research efforts. Two examples of research questions, one feasible and one not-so-feasible, are the following.

> *Feasible:* How do the students at Oceana High School feel about the new guidance program recently instituted in the district?
> *Not-so-feasible:* What would be the effect on achievement of giving each student his or her own microcomputer to use for a semester?

RESEARCH QUESTIONS SHOULD BE CLEAR

Since the research question is the focus of a research investigation, it is particularly impor-

tant that the question is clear. What exactly is being investigated? Let us consider two examples of research questions that are not clear enough.

Example 1. "Is a humanistically oriented classroom effective?" Although the phrase "humanistically oriented classroom" may seem quite clear, many people may not be sure exactly what it means. If we ask, "What *is* a humanistically oriented classroom?" we begin to discover that it is not as easy as we might have thought to describe its essential characteristics. What happens in such classrooms that is different from what happens in other classrooms? Do teachers use certain kinds of strategies? Do they lecture? In what sorts of activities do students participate? What do such classrooms look like—how is the seating arranged, for example? What kinds of materials are used? Is there much variation to be found from classroom to classroom in the strategies employed by the teacher or in the sorts of activities in which students engage? Do the kinds of materials available and/or used vary?

Another term in this question is also ambiguous. What does the term "effective" mean? Does it mean "results in increased academic proficiency," "results in happier children," "makes life easier for teachers," or "costs less money"? Maybe it means all these things and more.

Example 2. "How do teachers feel about special classes for the educationally handicapped?" The first term that needs clarification is "teachers." What age group does this involve? What level of experience (i.e., are probationary teachers, for example, included)? Are teachers in both public and private schools included? Are teachers throughout the nation or only in a specific locality included? Does the term refer to teachers who do not teach special classes as well as those who do?

The phrase "feel about" is also ambiguous. Does it mean opinions? emotional reactions? Does it suggest actions? Or what? The terms "special classes" and "educationally handicapped" also need to be clarified. An example of a legal definition of an educationally handicapped student is:

A minor who, by reason of marked learning or behavioral disorders, is unable to adapt to a normal classroom situation. The disorder must be associated with a neurological handicap or an emotional disturbance and must not be due to mental retardation, cultural deprivation, or foreign language problems.

Note that this definition itself contains some ambiguous words, such as "marked learning disorders," which lend themselves to a wide variety of interpretations. This is equally true of the term "cultural deprivation," which is not only ambiguous but also often offensive to members of ethnic groups to whom the term is frequently applied.

As we begin to think about these (or other) questions, it appears that terms which seemed at first glance to be words or phrases that everyone would easily understand are really quite complex, and far more difficult to define than we might originally have thought.

This is true of many current educational concepts and methodologies. Consider such terms as "core curriculum," "client-centered counseling," "activity learning," and "effective management." What do such terms mean? If you were to ask a sample of five or six teachers, counselors, or administrators that you know, you probably would get several different definitions. Although such ambiguity is often valuable in some circumstances and for certain purposes, it represents a problem to investigators of a research question. Researchers have no choice but to be specific about the terms used in a research question, to define precisely what is to be studied. In making this effort, researchers gain a clearer picture of how to proceed with an investigation, in fact, sometimes deciding to change the very nature of the research. How, then, might the clarity of a research question be improved?

Defining Terms. There are essentially three ways to clarify important terms in a research question. The first is to use a **constitutive definition**—i.e., to use what is often referred to as the *dictionary approach*. Researchers simply use other words to say more clearly what is meant.

Thus, the term "humanistic classroom" might be defined as:

A classroom in which: (a) the needs and interests of students have the highest priority; (b) students work on their own for a considerable amount of time in each class period; and (c) the teacher acts as a guide and a resource person rather than an informant.

Notice, however, that this definition is still somewhat unclear, since the words being used to explain the term "humanistic" are themselves ambiguous. What does it mean to say that the "needs and interests of students have the highest priority"? or that "students work on their own"? What is a "considerable amount" of each class period? What does a teacher do when acting as a "guide" or a "resource person"? Further clarification is needed.

Researchers in communication have demonstrated just how difficult it is to be sure that the message sent is the message received. It is probably true that none of us ever completely understands the meaning of terms used to communicate with us. That is, we can never be certain that the message we receive is the one the sender intended. Some years ago, one of the leaders in our field is said to have become so depressed by this idea that he quit talking to his colleagues for several weeks. A more constructive approach is simply to do the best we can. We must try to explain our terms to others. While most researchers try to be clear, there is no question that some do a much better job than others.

Another important point to remember is that often it is a term or phrase that needs to be defined rather than only a single word. For example, the term "nondirective therapy" will surely not be clarified by precise definitions of "nondirective" and "therapy," since it has a more specific meaning than the two words defined separately would convey. Similarly, such terms as "learning disability," "bilingual education," "interactive video," and "home-centered health care" need to be defined as linguistic wholes.

Here are three definitions of the term "motivated to learn." Which do you think is the clearest?

1. Works hard.
2. Is eager and enthusiastic.
3. Sustains attention to a task.*

As you have seen, the dictionary approach to clarifying terms has its limitations. A second possibility is to clarify *by example*. Researchers might think of a few humanistic classrooms with which they are familiar and then try to describe as fully as possible what happens in these classrooms. Usually we suggest that people observe such classrooms to see for themselves how they differ from other classrooms. This approach also has its problems, however, since our descriptions may still not be as clear to others as they would like.

Thus, a third method of clarification is to define important terms operationally. **Operational definitions** require that researchers specify the actions or operations necessary to measure or identify the term. For example, here are two possible operational definitions of the term "humanistic classroom."

1. Any classroom *identified* by specified experts as constituting an example of a humanistic classroom.
2. Any classroom *judged* (by an observer spending at least one day per week for four to five weeks) to possess all the following characteristics:
   a. no more than three children working with the same materials at the same time;
   b. the teacher never spending more than twenty minutes per day addressing the class as a group;
   c. at least half of every class period open for students to work on projects of their own choosing at their own pace;
   d. several (more than three) sets of different kinds of educational materials available for every student in the class to use;
   e. nontraditional-type seating—students sit

in circles, small groupings of seats, or even on the floor to work on their projects;
   f. frequent (at leat two per week) discussions of ideas in which students are encouraged to give their viewpoints about topics being read about in their textbooks.

The above listing of characteristics and behaviors may be a quite unsatisfactory definition of a humanistic classroom to many people (and perhaps to you). But it is considerably more specific (and thus clearer) than the definition with which we began.* Armed with this definition (and the necessary facilities), researchers could decide quickly whether or not a particular classroom matched the definition and, hence, qualified as an example of a humanistic classroom to include in a research investigation.

Defining terms operationally is a helpful way to clarify their meaning. Operational definitions are useful tools and should be mastered by all students of research. Remember that the operations or activities necessary to measure or identify the term must be specified. Which of the following possible definitions of the term "motivated to learn mathematics" do you think are operational?

1. As shown by enthusiasm in class.
2. As judged by the student's math teacher using a rating scale.
3. As measured by the "Math Interest" questionnaire.
4. As shown by attention to math tasks in class.
5. As reflected by achievement in mathematics.
6. As indicated by enrollment in mathematics electives.
7. As shown by effort expended in class.
8. As demonstrated by number of optional assignments completed.
9. As demonstrated by reading math books outside class.

---

* We judge 3 to be the clearest, followed by 1 and then 2.

* This is not to say that this list would not be improved by making the guidelines even more specific. These characteristics, however, do meet the criterion for an operational definition—they specify the actions researchers need to take to measure or identify the variable being defined.

10. As observed by teacher aides using the "Mathematics Interest" Observation Record.*

The importance of researchers being clear about the terms in their research questions cannot be overstated. It is very difficult to proceed with plans for the collection and analysis of data if researchers do not know exactly what kind of data to look for. And researchers will not know what to look for if they are unclear about the meaning of the key terms in the research question.

RESEARCH QUESTIONS SHOULD BE SIGNIFICANT

Research questions also should be *worth* investigating. In essence, we need to consider whether a question is worth spending time and energy (and often money) on to get an answer. What, we might ask, is the value of investigating a particular question? In what ways will it contribute to our knowledge about education? to our knowledge of human beings? Is such knowledge important in some way? If so, how? These questions ask researchers to think about why a research question is worthwhile, that is, important or significant.

It probably goes without saying that a research question is of interest to the person who asks it. But is interest alone sufficient justification for an investigation? For some people, the answer is a clear "yes!" They say that any question that someone sincerely wants an answer to is worth investigating. Others, however, say that personal interest, in and of itself, is insufficient as a reason for investigating a question. Too often, they point out, personal interest can result in the pursuit of trivial or insignificant questions. Since most research efforts require some (and often a considerable) expenditure of time, energy, materials, money, and/or other resources, it is easy to appreciate

the point of view that some useful outcome or payoff should be forthcoming as a result of the research. The investment of oneself and others in a research enterprise should contribute some knowledge of value to the field of education.

Generally speaking, most researchers do not believe that research efforts based primarily on personal interest alone warrant investigation. Furthermore, there is some reason to question a "purely curious" motive on psychological grounds. Most questions probably have some degree of hidden motivation behind them, and, for the sake of credibility, these reasons should be made explicit.

One of the most important tasks for any researcher, therefore, is to think through the value of the intended research before too much preliminary work is done. There are three important questions to ask about a research question.

1. How might answers to this question advance knowledge in my field?
2. How might answers to this question improve educational practice?
3. How might answers to this question improve the human condition?

As you think about possible questions that might be researched, therefore, ask yourself: "Why would it be important to answer this question?" Does the question have implications for the improvement of practice? for administrative decision making? for program planning? Is there an important issue that can be illuminated to some degree by a study of this question? Is it related to a current theory that I have doubts about or would like to substantiate? Thinking through possible answers to these questions can help us judge the significance of a potential research question.

Ethics and Research

In addition to feasibility, clarity, and significance, researchers need to consider the ethics

---

* The operational definitions are 2, 3, 6, 8, and 10. The nonoperational definitions are 1, 4, 5, 7 and 9, because the activities or operations necessary for identification of the behavior have not been specified.

of their research. The basic question to ask in this regard is, "Will any physical or psychological harm come to anyone as a result of my research?" Naturally, no researcher wants this to happen to any of the subjects in a research study. Since this is such an important (and often overlooked) issue, we need to discuss it in some detail.

In a somewhat larger sense, ethics also refers to questions of right and wrong. By behaving ethically, a person is doing what is right. But what does it mean to be "right" as far as research is concerned?

Webster's New World Dictionary defines ethical (behavior) as "conforming to the standards of conduct of a given profession or group." What researchers consider to be ethical, therefore, is largely a matter of agreement among them. The Committee on Scientific and Professional Ethics of the American Psychological Association has published a list of ethical principles for the conduct of research with human subjects. We have substituted the word "educator" for the word "psychologist" in their statement. Please read this statement carefully and think about what it suggests.

A Statement of Ethical Principles

The decision to undertake research rests upon a considered judgment by the individual educator about how best to contribute to science and human welfare. Having made the decision to conduct research, the educator considers alternative directions in which research energies and resources might be invested. On the basis of this consideration, the educator carries out the investigation with respect and concern for the dignity and welfare of the people who participate and with cognizance of federal and state regulations and professional standards governing the conduct of research with human participants.

a. In planning a study, the investigator has the responsibility to make a careful evaluation of its ethical acceptability. To the extent that the weighing of scientific and human values suggests a compromise of any principle, the investigator incurs a correspondingly serious obligation to seek ethical advice and to observe stringent safeguards to protect the rights of human participants.

b. Considering whether a participant in a planned study will be a "subject at risk" or a "subject at minimal risk," according to recognized standards, is of primary ethical concern to the investigator.

c. The investigator always retains the responsibility for ensuring ethical practice in research. The investigator is also responsible for the ethical treatment of research participants by collaborators, assistants, students, and employees, all of whom, however, incur similar obligations.

d. Except in minimal-risk research, the investigator establishes a clear and fair agreement with research participants, prior to their participation, that clarifies the obligations and responsibilities of each. The investigator has the obligation to honor all promises and commitments included in that agreement. The investigator informs the participants of all aspects of the research that might reasonably be expected to influence willingness to participate and explains all other aspects of the research about which the participants inquire. Failure to make full disclosure prior to obtaining informed consent requires additional safeguards to protect the welfare and dignity of the research participants. Furthermore, research with children or with participants who have impairments that would limit understanding and/or communication requires special safeguarding procedures.

e. Methodological requirements of a study may make the use of concealment or deception necessary. Before conducting such a study, the investigator has a special responsibility to: (i) determine whether the use of such techniques is justified by the study's prospective scientific, educational, or applied value; (ii) determine whether alternative procedures are available that do not use concealment or deception, and (iii) ensure that the participants are provided with sufficient explanation as soon as possible.

f. The investigator respects the individual's freedom to decline to participate in or to withdraw from the research at any time. The obligation to protect this freedom requires careful thought and consideration when the investigator is in a position of authority or influence over the participant. Such positions of authority include, but are not limited to, situations in which research participation is required as part of employment or in which the participant is a student, client, or employee of the investigator.

g. The investigator protects the participant from physical and mental discomfort, harm, and danger that may arise from research procedures. If risks of such consequences exist, the investigator informs the participant of that fact. Research procedures likely to cause serious or lasting harm to a participant are not used unless the failure to use these procedures might expose the participant to risk of greater harm, or unless the research has great potential benefit and fully informed and voluntary consent is obtained from each participant. The participant should be informed of procedures for contacting the investigator within a reasonable time period following participation should stress, potential harm, or related questions or concerns arise.

h. After the data are collected, the investigator provides the participant with information about the nature of the study and attempts to remove any misconceptions that may have arisen. Where scientific or humane values justify delaying or withholding this information, the investigator incurs a special responsibility to monitor the research and to insure that there are no damaging consequences for the participant.

i. Where research procedures result in undesirable consequences for the individual participant, the investigator has the responsibility to detect and remove or correct these consequences, including long-term effects.

j. Information obtained about a research participant during the course of an investigation is confidential unless otherwise agreed upon in advance. When the possibility exists that others may obtain access to such information, this possibility, together with the plans for protecting confidentiality, is explained to the participant as part of the procedure for obtaining informed consent.[1]

The above statement of ethical principles suggests three very important issues that every researcher should address—the protection of participants from harm, the ensuring of confidentiality of research data, and the question of deception of subjects. How can these issues be addressed, and how can the interests of the subjects involved in research be protected?

PROTECTING PARTICIPANTS FROM HARM

Perhaps the most important ethical consideration of all, it is a fundamental responsibility of every researcher to do all in his or her power to ensure that participants in a research study are protected from physical or psychological harm, discomfort, or danger that may arise due to research procedures. Any sort of study that is likely to cause lasting, or even serious, harm or discomfort to any participant should not be conducted, unless the research has the potential to provide information of extreme benefit to human beings. Even when this may be the case, participants should be fully informed of the dangers involved and in no way required to participate.

A further responsibility in protecting individuals from harm is obtaining the consent of individuals who may be exposed to any risk. Fortunately, almost all educational research involves activities that are within the customary, usual procedures of schools or other agencies and as such involve little or no risk. Legislation recognizes this by specifically exempting most categories of educational research from formal review processes.[2] Nevertheless, researchers should carefully consider whether there is any likelihood of risk involved and, if there is, provide full information followed by formal consent by participants (or their guardians). Three important ethical questions to ask about harm in any study are:

1. Could people be harmed (physically or psychologically) during the study?
2. If so, could the study be conducted in another way to find out what the researcher wants to know?

3. Is the information that may be obtained from this study so important that it warrants possible harm to the participants?

These are difficult questions, and they deserve discussion and consideration by all researchers.

ENSURING CONFIDENTIALITY OF RESEARCH DATA

Once the data in a study have been collected, researchers should make sure that no one else (other than perhaps a few key research assistants) has access to the data. Whenever possible, the names of the subjects should be removed from all data collection forms. This can be done by assigning a number or letter to each form, or, if possible, subjects can be asked to furnish information anonymously. Ideally, not even the researcher should be able to link the data to a particular subject. Sometimes, however, it is important to the study to identify individual subjects. When this is the case, the linkage system should be carefully guarded.

All subjects should be assured that any data collected from or about them will be held in confidence. The names of individual subjects should never be used in any publications that describe the research. And all participants in a study should always have the right to withdraw from the study or to request that data collected about them not be used.

SHOULD SUBJECTS BE DECEIVED?

The issue of deception is particularly troublesome. Many studies cannot be carried out unless some deception of subjects takes place. It is often difficult to find naturalistic situations in which certain behaviors occur frequently. For example, a researcher may have to wait a long time for a teacher to reinforce students in a certain way. It may be much easier for the researcher to observe the effects of such reinforcement by employing the teacher as a confederate.

Sometimes it is better to deceive subjects than to submit them to pain or trauma, as investigating a particular research question might require. The famous Milgram study of obedience is a good example.[3] In this study, subjects were ordered to give increasingly severe electric shocks to another subject whom they could not see sitting behind a screen. What they did not know was that the individual to whom they thought they were administering the shocks was a confederate of the experimenter, and no shocks were actually being administered. The dependent variable was the level of shock subjects administered before they refused to administer any more. Out of a total of forty subjects who participated in the study, twenty-six followed the "orders" of the experimenter and (so they thought) administered the maximum shock possible of 450 volts! Even though no shocks were actually administered, publication of the results of the study produced widespread controversy. Many people felt the study was unethical. Others argued that the importance of the study and its results justified the deception. Notice that the study raises questions about not only deception but also harm since some participants could have suffered emotionally from later consideration of their actions.

Perhaps the most serious problem involving deception is what it may ultimately do to the reputation of the scientific community. If people in general begin to think of scientists and researchers as liars, or as individuals who misrepresent what they are about, the overall image of science may suffer. Fewer and fewer people will be willing to participate in research investigations. As a result, the search for reliable knowledge about our world may be impeded.

Research Questions Should Investigate Relationships

There is an additional characteristic that good research questions often possess. They frequently (but not always) suggest a relationship of some sort to be investigated. (We discuss the reasons for this in Chapter Three.) A suggested relationship means that two qualities or characteristics are tied together or connected in some way. Are motivation and learning related? If so, how? What about age and attractiveness? speed and weight? height and strength? a principal's administrative policies and faculty morale?

It is important to understand how the term "relationship" is used in research, since the term has other meanings in everyday life. When researchers use the term "relationship," they are not referring to the nature or quality of an association between people, for example. What we and other researchers mean is perhaps best clarified visually. Look for example, at the data in parts A and B in Figure 2.1. What do you notice?

The hypothetical data in part A show that out of a total of thirty-two individuals, sixteen

were Republicans and sixteen were Democrats. It also shows that half were male and half were female. Part B shows the same breakdown by party affiliation. What is different in the two figures is that there is no association or relationship between gender and political party shown in part A, whereas there is a very strong relationship between these two factors shown in part B. We can express the relationship in B by saying that males tend to be Republicans while females tend to be Democrats. We can also express this relationship in terms of a prediction. Should another female join the group in part B, we would predict she would be a Democrat since fourteen of the previous sixteen females are Democrats.

FIGURE 2.1

*Illustration of Relationship between Voter Gender
and Party Affiliation*

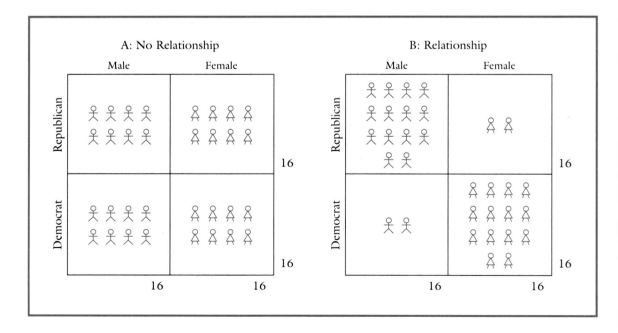

Main Points of Chapter Two

- Many research problems are stated as questions.
- The essential characteristic of a researchable question is that there is some sort of information that can be collected in an attempt to answer the question.
- Good research questions have four essential characteristics: They are feasible, clear, significant, and ethical.
- An additional characteristic of good research questions is that they often (but not always) suggest a relationship to be investigated.
- Three commonly used ways to clarify ambiguous or unclear terms in a research question involve the use of constitutive (dictionary-type) definitions, definition by example, and operational definitions.
- A constitutive definition uses additional terms to clarify meaning.
- An operational definition describes how examples of a term are to be measured or identified.
- There are a number of ethical principles of which all researchers should be aware and apply in their investigations.
- The basic ethical question for all researchers to consider is, "Will any physical or psychological harm come to anyone as a result of my research?"
- All subjects in a research study should be assured that any data collected from or about them will be held in confidence.
- The term "deception," as used in research, refers to misinforming the subjects of a study as to some or all aspects of the research topic.
- The term "relationship," as used in research, refers to a connection or association between characteristics.

For Discussion

1. Listed below are a series of questions. Think how a researcher could collect information (from friends, colleagues, students, or others) to help answer each question, at least in part. Could data be collected on all of these questions? If so, how? If not, why not?
   a. Does client-centered or traditional therapy produce more satisfaction in clients?
   b. How might staff morale be improved?
   c. Should psychology be required of all students in graduate school?
   d. Do students learn more from a teacher of the same gender?

2. What relationship (if there is one) is suggested in each of the above questions?

3. Here are three descriptions of ideas for research. Which (if any) might have some ethical problems? Why?
   a. A researcher is interested in investigating the effects of diet on physical development. He designs a study in which two groups are to be compared. Both groups are composed of 11 year olds. One group is to be given an enriched diet, high in vitamins, that has been shown to have a strengthening effect on laboratory animals. A second group is not to be given this diet. The groups are to be selected from all the 11

year olds in an elementary school near the university where the researcher teaches.

b. A researcher is interested in the effects of music on attention span. She designs an experimental study in which two similar high school government classes are to be compared. For a five-week period, one class has classical music played softly in the background as the teacher lectures and holds class discussions on the Civil War (the period of history the class is studying during this time). The other class studies the same material and participates in the same activities as the first class, but does not have any music played during the five weeks.

c. A researcher is interested in the effects of drugs on human beings. She asks for subjects from the warden of the local penitentiary to participate in an experiment. The warden assigns several prisoners to participate in the experiment, but does not tell them what it is about. The prisoners are injected with a number of drugs whose effects are unknown. Their reactions to the drugs are then described in detail by the researcher.

4. Here are three examples of research questions. How would you rank them (1 = highest) for clarity? For significance? Why?

a. How many students in the sophomore class signed up for a course in driver training this semester?

b. Why do so many students in the district say they dislike English?

c. Is inquiry or lecture more effective in teaching social studies?

5. Are there any research questions that should *not* be investigated in schools? If so, why not?

Notes

1. Committee on Scientific and Professional Ethics and Conduct. (1981). Ethical principles of psychologists. *American Psychologist, 36,* 633–638. Copyright 1981 by the American Psychological Association. Reprinted by permission.

2. Family Educational Rights and Privacy Act (also known as the Buckley Amendment) of 1974.

3. S. Milgram. (1967). Behavioral Study of Obedience. *Journal of Abnormal and Social Psychology, 67,* 371–378.

Research Exercise Two:
The Research Question

Using Problem Sheet 2, restate the research problem you listed in Research Exercise One in a sentence or two, and then formulate a research question that relates to this problem. Now list all the key terms in the question that you think are not clear and need to be defined. Define each of these terms both constitutively and operationally. State why you think your question is an important one to study and identify any possible ethical problems in carrying out such a study. How might such problems be remedied?

1. My (restated) research problem is: _____
_____

2. My research question is: _____
_____

3. The following are the key terms in the problem or question that are not clear and which need to be defined:

    a. _____   d. _____

    b. _____   e. _____

    c. _____   f. _____

4. Here are my constitutive definitions of these terms: _____
_____
_____

5. Here are my operational definitions of these terms:
_____
_____
_____

6. My justification for investigating this question/problem (why I would argue that it is an important question to investigate) is as follows:
_____
_____
_____

7. Does this research pose any ethical problems? Yes _____ No _____. If so, what are they?
_____
_____

    How can they be remedied? _____
_____

33

Chapter Three

VARIABLES AND HYPOTHESES

One of the most important concepts in research is the concept of variable. Many kinds of variables exist, and much educational research involves looking for relationships among variables. In this chapter, several kinds of variables are described and discussed. In addition, the concept of hypothesis is discussed, since many hypotheses express relationships between variables. Research questions, in fact, are often restated as hypotheses.

- *Explain* what is meant by the term "variable" and *name* five variables that might be investigated by educational researchers
- *Explain* how a variable differs from a constant
- *Distinguish* between a quantitative and a categorical variable
- *Explain* how independent and dependent variables are related
- *Explain* what an hypothesis is and *formulate* two hypotheses that might be investigated in education
- *Name* two advantages and two disadvantages of stating research questions as hypotheses
- *Distinguish* between directional and nondirectional hypotheses and *give an example* of each

Importance of Studying Relationships

We mentioned in Chapter Two that an important characteristic of many research questions is that they suggest a relationship of some sort to be investigated. Not all research questions, however, suggest relationships. Sometimes researchers are interested only in obtaining descriptive information to find out how people think or feel or to describe how they behave in a particular situation. Other times the intent is to describe a particular program or activity. Such questions also are worthy of investigation. As a result, researchers may ask questions like the following.

- How do the parents of the sophomore class feel about the counseling program?
- What changes would the staff like to see instituted in the curriculum?

- Has the number of students enrolling in college preparatory as compared to non-college preparatory courses changed over the last four years?
- How does the new reading program differ from the one used in this district in the past?
- What does an inquiry-oriented social studies teacher do?

Notice that no relationship is suggested in these questions. The researcher simply wants to identify characteristics, behaviors, feelings, or thoughts. Such information is often necessary to obtain as a first step in designing other research or to make educational decisions of some sort.

The problem with purely descriptive research questions is that answers to them do not help us understand why people feel or think or behave a certain way, why programs possess certain characteristics, why a particular strategy is to be used at a certain time, and so forth. We may learn what happened, or where or when (and even how) something happened, but not why it happened. As a result, our understanding of a situation, group, or phenomenon is limited. For this reason scientists consider research questions that suggest relationships to be investigated extremely important, because the answers to them help explain the nature of the world in which we live. We learn to understand the world by learning to explain how parts of it are related. We begin to detect *patterns* or connections between the parts.

Variables

WHAT IS A VARIABLE?

At this point, it is important to introduce the idea of variables, since a relationship is a statement about variables. What is a variable? A **variable** is a concept—a noun that stands for variation within a class of objects, such as chair, gender, eye color, achievement, motivation, or running speed. Even "spunk," "style," and "lust for life" are variables. Notice that the individual members in the class of objects, however, must differ—or vary—to qualify the class as a variable. If all members of a class are identical, we do not have a variable. Such characteristics are called **constants,** since the individual members of the class are not allowed to vary, but rather are held constant. In any study, some characteristics will be variables, while others will be constants.

An example may make this distinction clearer. Suppose a researcher is interested in studying the effects of reinforcement on student achievement. The researcher systematically divides a large group of students, all of whom are ninth graders, into three smaller subgroups. She then trains the teachers of these subgroups to reinforce their students in different ways (one gives verbal praise, the second gives monetary rewards, the third gives extra points) for various tasks the students perform. In this study, "reinforcement" would be a variable (it contains three variations), while the grade level of the students would be a constant.

Notice that it is easier to see what some of these concepts stand for than others. The concept of "chair," for example, stands for the many different objects that possess legs, a seat, and a back that we sit on. Furthermore, different observers would probably agree as to what represent examples of chairs. It is not so easy, however, to see what a concept like "motivation" stands for, or to get agreement as to what it means. The researchers must be specific here—they must define "motivation" as clearly as possible. They must do this so that it can be measured or manipulated. We cannot meaningfully measure or manipulate a variable if we cannot define it. As we mention above, much educational research involves looking for a relationship among variables. But what variables?

There are many variables "out there" in the real world that can be investigated. Obviously, we can't investigate them all. So we must choose. Researchers choose certain variables to investigate because they have a suspicion that these variables are somehow related and that if they can discover the nature of this relationship, it can help us make more sense out of the world in which we live.

QUANTITATIVE VERSUS CATEGORICAL VARIABLES

Variables can be classified in several ways. One way is to distinguish between quantitative and categorical variables. **Quantitative variables** exist in some degree (rather than all or none) along a continuum from "less" to "more," and we can assign numbers to different individuals or objects to indicate how much of the variable they possess. An obvious example is height (John is 6′ tall and Sally is 5′4″.) or weight (Mr. Adams weighs only 150 lbs. and his wife 140 lbs., but their son tips the scales at an even 200 lbs.). We can also assign numbers to various individuals to indicate how much "interest" they have in a subject, with a "5" indicating very much interest, a "4" much interest, a "3" some interest, a "2" little interest, a "1" very little interest, down to a "0" indicating no interest in the subject. If we can assign numbers in this way, we have the variable "interest."

Quantitative variables can be often (but not always) subdivided into smaller and smaller units. "Length," for example, can be measured in miles, yards, feet, inches, or in whatever subdivision of an inch is needed. By way of contrast, **categorical variables** do not vary in degree, amount, or quantity but are qualitatively different. Examples include eye color, gender, religious preference, occupation, position on a baseball team, and most kinds of research "treatments" or "methods." For example, if a researcher wished to compare computerized and noncomputerized classrooms, the variable involved would be the presence or absence of computers. This is a categorical variable—a classroom is either one or the other—either computerized or noncomputerized, not somewhere on a continuum between being computerized and not being computerized. All members within each category of this variable are considered the same.

Can "teaching method" be considered a variable? Yes, it can. Suppose a researcher is interested in studying teachers who use different methods in teaching. The researcher locates one teacher who lectures exclusively, another who buttresses her lectures with slides and filmstrips, and a third who uses the case study method and lectures not at all. Does the teaching method "vary"? It does. You may need to practice thinking of differences in methods, or in groups of people (teachers compared to administrators, for example) as variables, but mastering this idea is extremely useful in learning about research.

Now, here are several variables. Which ones are quantitative variables and which ones are categorical variables?

1. type of automobile owned
2. learning ability
3. ethnicity
4. cohesiveness
5. heartbeat rate
6. gender*

Most research in education studies the relationship between either (a) two (or more)

quantitative variables, (b) one categorical and one quantitative variable, or (c) two or more categorical variables. Here are some examples of each:

(a) *Two quantitative variables:*
- Age and amount of interest in school
- Reading achievement and mathematics achievement
- Classroom humanism and student motivation
- Amount of time watching television and aggressiveness of behavior
(b) *One categorical and one quantitative variable:*
- Method used to teach reading and reaching achievement
- Counseling approach and level of anxiety
- Nationality and liking for school
- Student gender and amount of praise given by teachers
(c) *Two categorical variables:*
- Ethnicity and father's occupation
- Gender of teacher and subject taught
- Administrative style and college major
- Religious affiliation and political party membership

Sometimes researchers have a choice of whether to treat a variable as quantitative or categorical. It is not uncommon, for example, to find studies in which a variable such as "anxiety" is studied by comparing a group of "high-anxiety" students to a group of "low-anxiety" students. This treats anxiety as though it were a categorical variable. While there is nothing really wrong with doing this, there are three reasons why it is preferable in such situations to treat the variable as quantitative.

1. Conceptually, we consider variables such as anxiety to be a matter of degree in people, not a matter of "either-or."
2. Collapsing the variable into two (or even several) categories eliminates the possibility of using more detailed information about the variable since differences among individuals within a category are ignored.

---

* 1, 3, and 6 represent categorical variables; 2, 4, and 5 represent quantitative variables.

3. The dividing line between groups (for example, between individuals of high, middle, and low anxiety) is almost always arbitrary (that is, lacking in any defensible rationale).

MANIPULATED VERSUS OUTCOME VARIABLES

Whenever researchers set up an experiment along the lines of the examples described in Chapter One, in which there are two or more experimental conditions, they *create* a variable. Suppose, for example, that a researcher decides to investigate the effect of different amounts of reinforcement on reading achievement and systematically assigns students to three different groups. One group is praised continuously every day during their reading session; the second group is told simply to "keep up their good work"; while the third group is told nothing at all. The researcher, in effect, *manipulates* the conditions in the experiment, thereby creating the variable "amount of reinforcement." Whenever experimental conditions are set up by a researcher, one or more variables are created. Such variables are called **experimental variables** or **manipulated variables** or **treatment variables.**

Generally speaking, most studies in education with one quantitative and one categorical variable are studies comparing different methods or treatments. In such studies, the different methods or treatments represent a categorical variable. Often the other variable, the quantitative one, is referred to as an "outcome variable."*

The reason is rather clearcut. The investigator, after all, is interested in the effect of the differences in method on one or more outcomes (such as the achievement of students, their motivation, interest, and so on). An outcome is a result of some sort, an observed behavior, product, or condition of an organism that has been stimulated in some way. Since such outcomes

vary for different people, in different situations, and under different conditions, they are often called *outcome variables*. All the following can be examples of outcome variables:

- the amount of uneasiness that applicants for a position express in an interview;
- how anxious students are before an examination;
- neatness;
- the "openness" of a classroom;
- how disruptive students are in a history class;
- the ability of people to express themselves in writing;
- fluency in a foreign language;
- teacher-student rapport.

Notice two things about each of the above examples. First, each represents a possible result or outcome of some sort that can be produced by something else. In a methods study, researchers are interested in the effect of different methods on a particular outcome or outcomes. They are never completely certain as to what it is, exactly, that produces these outcomes, however. Thus, the level of anxiety students feel before an examination may be caused by their previous performance on similar exams, the amount of studying they have done in preparation for the exam, how important a good grade on the exam is to them, or any one of several other factors in addition to the methods being studied. The "disruptiveness" of students in a history class may be due to their disrespect for the teacher, the teacher's failure to discipline them for past disruptions, their inability to do as the teacher requests, bad feelings among several students, and so forth.

This is why research is necessary. Many outcomes like the above are not very well understood by educators. Researchers have designed studies not only to understand better the nature of these (and other) outcomes, but also to gain insight into what causes them. (We shall look at some examples of such studies in later chapters.)

The second thing to notice about each of

---

* It is also possible for an outcome variable to be categorical. For example, the variable "college completion" could be divided into the categories of "dropouts" and "college graduates."

the examples above is that the amount or degree of each can vary in different situations or under different conditions. Not all people have the same degree of fluency in Spanish, for example. The amount of rapport that exists between teachers and students varies for different teachers with different students, and vice-versa. Neatness, expressiveness, anxiety—such qualities are possessed in varying amounts by different people. That is why they can be considered quantitative variables.

Let's check your understanding. Suppose a researcher plans to investigate the following question: "Will students who are taught by a team of three teachers learn more science than students taught by one individual teacher?" What is the outcome variable in this question?*

INDEPENDENT VERSUS DEPENDENT VARIABLES

Two other terms for variables that are frequently mentioned in the literature are independent and dependent variables. Examples of **independent variables** are the treatment or manipulated variables referred to previously: those variables the investigator chooses to study (and often manipulate) in order to assess their possible effect(s) on one or more other variables. An independent variable is presumed to have an effect on, to influence somehow, another variable. The variable that the independent variable is presumed to affect is called the **dependent** (or outcome) **variable**. In common-sense terms, the nature of the dependent variable "depends on" what the independent variable does to it, how it affects it. Not all independent variables are manipulated. A researcher studying the relationship between childhood success in mathematics and adult career choice is likely to refer to the former as the independent variable and subsequent career choice as the dependent variable, even though success is not manipulated.

It is possible to investigate more than one independent (and also more than one dependent) variable in a study. For simplicity's sake, how-

ever, we present examples in which only one independent and one dependent variable are involved.

The relationship between independent and dependent variables can be portrayed graphically as follows.

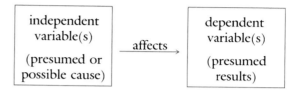

Look again at the research question about team teaching that we mentioned earlier: "Will students who are taught by a team of three teachers learn more science than students taught by one individual teacher?" What are the independent and the dependent variables in this question?*

Notice that there are two conditions (sometimes called levels) in the independent variable— "three teachers" and "one teacher." Also notice that the dependent variable is not "science learning," but "amount of science learning." Can you see why?

EXTRANEOUS VARIABLES

A basic problem in research is that there are many possible independent variables that could have an effect on the dependent variables. Once researchers have decided which variables to study, they must be concerned about the influence or effect of other variables that exist. Such variables are usually called "extraneous variables." The task is to control these extraneous variables somehow to eliminate or minimize their effect.

Extraneous variables are independent variables that have not been controlled. Look again at the research question about team teaching presented above. What might be some other

---

* The outcome variable is *amount of science learning.*

* The independent variable is the *number of teachers,* and the dependent variable is the *amount of science learning.* Notice, again, that the dependent variable is also the outcome variable in this study.

variables that could have an effect on the learning of students in a classroom situation?

There are many possible extraneous variables that might have an effect on student learning here. The personality of the teachers involved is one possibility. The intelligence level of the students is another. Time of day the classes are taught, nature of the subject taught, textbooks used, type of learning activities the teachers employ, and teaching methods—all are possible other variables that could affect learning. Such variables would probably be extraneous variables in this study.

One way to control extraneous variables is to hold them constant. For example, if a researcher were to include only girls as the subjects of a study, she would be controlling the variable of a gender. We would say that the gender of the subjects does not vary; it would be a constant in this study.

Researchers must continually think about how they might control the possible effect(s) of extraneous variables. We will discuss how to do this in some detail in Chapter Eleven, but for now you need to make sure you understand the difference between independent and dependent variables and to be aware of possible extraneous variables. Try your hand at the following question: What are the variables? "Will students who are taught history by a teacher of the same gender like the subject more than students taught by a teacher of a different gender?"*

Hypotheses

WHAT IS AN HYPOTHESIS?

A research question is often restated as an hypothesis. An **hypothesis** is, simply put, a prediction of some sort regarding the possible

---

* The dependent variable is *liking for history*, the independent variable is the *gender of the teacher*. Possible extraneous variables include the *personality* and *ability* of the teacher(s) involved; the *personality* and *ability level* of the students; the *materials*, such as textbooks, etc.; the *style of teaching*; *ethnicity* and/or *age* of the teacher and students; and others. The researcher would want to control as many of these variables as possible.

outcomes of a study. For example, here is the previous research question followed by its restatement in the form of an hypothesis:

> *Question:* Will students who are taught history by a teacher of the same gender like the subject more than students taught by a teacher of a different gender?
> *Hypothesis:* Students taught history by a teacher of the same gender will like the subject more than students taught history by a teacher of a different gender.

Here are two more examples of research questions followed by the restatement of each as an hypothesis:

> *Question:* Is rapport with clients different with counselors using client-centered therapy than with those using behavior-modification therapy?
> *Hypothesis:* Counselors who use a client-centered therapy approach will have a greater rapport with their clients than counselors who use a behavior-modification approach.

> *Question:* How do teachers feel about special classes for the educationally handicapped?
> *Hypothesis:* Teachers believe that students attending special classes for the educationally handicapped are thereby stigmatized.

or

Teachers believe that special classes for the educationally handicapped will help such students improve their academic skills.

ADVANTAGES OF STATING RESEARCH QUESTIONS AS HYPOTHESES

Stating questions as hypotheses has both advantages and disadvantages. What are some of the advantages? First, an hypothesis forces us to think more deeply about the possible outcomes of a study. Restating a question as an hypothesis can lead to a more sophisticated understanding of what the question implies and exactly what variables are involved. Often, as in the case of the third example above, when more than one hypothesis seems to suggest itself, we are forced to think more carefully about what we really want to investigate.

A second advantage of restating questions as hypotheses involves a philosophy of science. The rationale underlying this philosophy is as follows: If one is attempting to build a body of knowledge in addition to answering a specific question, then stating hypotheses is a good strategy because it enables one to make specific predictions based on prior evidence or theoretical argument. If these predictions are borne out by subsequent research, the entire procedure gains both in persuasiveness and efficiency. A classic example is Albert Einstein's theory of relativity. Many hypotheses were formulated as a result of Einstein's theory, which were later verified through research. As more and more of these predictions were shown to be fact, they not only became useful in their own right but also they provided increasing support for the original ideas in Einstein's theory, which generated the hypotheses in the first place.

Lastly, restating a research question as an hypothesis helps us see if we are, or are not, investigating a relationship. If not, we may possibly see a need to formulate one.

DISADVANTAGES OF STATING RESEARCH QUESTIONS AS HYPOTHESES

Essentially, the disadvantages of stating research questions as hypotheses are twofold. First, stating an hypothesis may lead to a **bias,** either conscious or unconscious, on the part of the researcher. Once investigators state an hypothesis, they may be tempted to arrange the procedures or manipulate the data in such a way as to bring about a desired outcome.

This is probably more the exception than the rule. Researchers are assumed to be intellectually honest—although there are some famous exceptions. All studies should be subject to peer review; in the past, a review of suspect research has, on occasion, revealed such inadequacies of method that the reported results were cast into doubt. Furthermore, any particular study can be replicated to verify the findings of the study. Unfortunately, few educational research studies are repeated, so this "protection" is somewhat of an illusion. A dishonest investigator stands a fair chance of getting away with falsifying results. Why would a person deliberately distort one's findings? Probably because professional recognition and financial reward accrue to those who publish important results.

Even for the great majority of researchers who are honest, however, commitment to an hypothesis may lead to distortions that are unintentional and unconscious. But it is probably unlikely that any researcher in the field of education is ever totally disinterested in the outcomes of a study; therefore her attitudes and/or knowledge may favor a particular result. For this reason, we think it is desirable for researchers to make their predilections known regarding an hypothesis so that they are clear to others interested in their research. This also allows investigators to take steps to ensure (as much as possible) against their personal biases.

The second disadvantage of stating hypotheses is that focusing attention on an hypothesis may prevent researchers from noticing other phenomena that might be important to study. For example, deciding to study the effect of a "humanistic" classroom on student motivation might lead a researcher to overlook its effect on such characteristics as sex-typing or decision making, which would be quite noticeable to another researcher who was not focusing on just motivation. This seems to be a good argument for ensuring that not all research be directed toward hypothesis testing.

Consider the example of a research question presented earlier in this chapter. The question was, "How do teachers feel about special classes for the educationally handicapped?" We offered two (of many possible) hypotheses that might flow out of this question: (1) "Teachers believe that students attending special classes for the educationally handicapped are thereby stigmatized" and (2) "Teachers believe that special classes for the educationally handicapped will help such students improve their academic skills." Both these hypotheses implicitly suggest a comparison between special classes for the educationally handicapped and some other kind of arrangement. Thus, the relationship to be investigated is between teacher beliefs and type of class. Notice that it is important to compare what teachers think about special classes with their beliefs about other kinds of arrangements. If researchers looked only at teacher opinions about special classes without also identifying their views about other kinds of arrangements, they would not know if their beliefs about special classes were in any way unique or different.

SIGNIFICANT HYPOTHESES

As we begin to think about possible hypotheses suggested by a research question, we begin to see that some of them are more significant than others. What do we mean by "significant"? Simply that some may lead to more useful knowledge. Compare, for example, the following pairs of hypotheses. Which hypothesis in each pair would you say is more significant?

Pair 1
a. Second graders like school less than they like watching television.
b. Second graders like school less than first graders but more than third graders.

Pair 2
a. Most students with academic disabilities prefer being in regular classes than in special classes.
b. Students with academic disabilities will have more negative attitudes about themselves if they are placed in special classes than if they are placed in regular classes.

Pair 3
a. Counselors who use client-centered therapy procedures get different reactions from counselees than do counselors who use traditional therapy procedures.
b. Counselees who receive client-centered therapy express more satisfaction with the counseling process than do counselees who receive traditional therapy.

In each of the three pairs, we think that the second hypothesis is more significant than the first since in each case (in our judgment) not only is the relationship to be investigated clearer and more specific but also investigation of the hypothesis seems more likely to lead to a greater amount of knowledge. It also seems to us that the information to be obtained will be of more use to people interested in the research question.

DIRECTIONAL VERSUS NONDIRECTIONAL HYPOTHESES

Let us make a distinction between directional and nondirectional hypotheses. A **directional hypothesis** is one in which the specific direction (such as higher, lower, more, less, and so on) that a researcher expects to emerge in a relationship is indicated. The particular direction expected is based on what the researcher has found in the literature, from personal experience, or the experience of others. The second hypothesis in each of the three pairs above is a directional hypothesis.

Sometimes it is difficult to make specific predictions. If a researcher suspects that a relationship exists, but has no basis for predicting the direction of the relationship, she cannot make a directional hypothesis. A **nondirectional hypothesis** does not make a specific prediction about what direction the outcome of a study will take. The above three hypotheses, in nondirectional form, would be stated as follows:

Nondirectional hypothesis for 1b: First, second, and third graders will feel differently toward school.
Nondirectional hypothesis for 2b: There will be a difference between the scores on an

attitude measure of students with academic disabilities placed in special classes and such students placed in regular classes.

Nondirectional hypothesis for 3b: There will be a difference in expression of satisfaction with the counseling process between students who receive client-centered therapy and students who receive traditional therapy.

Both directional and nondirectional hypotheses appear in the literature of research, and you should learn to recognize each when you see them.

Main Points of Chapter Three

- A variable is any characteristic or quality that varies among the members of a particular group.
- A constant is any characteristic or quality that is the same for all members of a particular group.
- Several kinds of variables are studied in educational research, the most common being independent and dependent variables.
- An independent variable is a variable presumed to affect or influence other variables.
- A dependent (or outcome) variable is a variable presumed to be affected by one or more independent variables.
- A quantitative variable is a variable that varies in amount or degree, but not in kind.
- A categorical variable is a variable that varies only in kind, not in degree or amount.
- An extraneous variable is an independent variable that may have unintended effects on a dependent variable in a particular study.
- The term "hypothesis" as used in research refers to a prediction of results made before a study commences.
- A significant hypothesis is one that is likely to lead, if it is supported, to a greater amount of important knowledge than a nonsignificant hypothesis.
- Stating a research question as a hypothesis has both advantages and disadvantages.
- A directional hypothesis is a prediction about the specific nature of a relationship—e.g., whether the outcome will be an increase or a decrease.
- A nondirectional hypothesis is a prediction that a relationship exists without specifying its exact nature—e.g., that a change will occur without indicating whether it will be up or down.

For Discussion

1. Here are several research questions. Which ones suggest relationships?
   a. How many students are enrolled in the sophomore class this year?
   b. As the reading level of a text passage increases, does the number of errors students make in pronouncing words in the passage increase?
   c. Do individuals who see themselves as socially "attractive" expect their romantic partners also to be (as judged by others) socially attractive?
   d. What does the faculty dislike about the new English curriculum?

    e. Who is the brightest student in the senior class?

    f. Will students who score above the 90th percentile on a standardized reading test also score above the 90th percentile on a standardized writing test?

    g. Which political party contains the most Protestants—Democrat or Republican?

2. What kinds of variables can you identify in each of the above questions?

3. See if you can restate each of the questions in #1 as (a) a directional hypothesis and (b) a nondirectional hypothesis.

4. How would you rank the questions in #1 in terms of significance? Why?

5. Listed below are a number of variables. Which ones are quantitative and which ones are categorical?

    a. Religious preference.

    b. Neatness.

    c. Eye color.

    d. Curiosity.

    e. Writing ability.

    f. Jumping ability.

    g. Fluency in Spanish.

    h. Test anxiety.

    i. Grade level.

    j. Appreciation of classical music.

    k. Mathematics ability.

    l. Judged essay quality.

6. What might cause a researcher to state a directional hypothesis rather than a nondirectional hypothesis? What about the reverse?

7. Are there any variables that researchers should *not* study? Explain.

Research Exercise Three:
The Research Hypothesis

Formulate a testable hypothesis related to the research question you developed in Research Exercise Two. Using Problem Sheet 3, state the hypothesis in a sentence or two. Check to see if it suggests a relationship between at least two variables. If it does not, revise it so that it does. Now name these variables, and then indicate which is the independent variable and which is the dependent variable. Last, list as many extraneous variables as you can think of that might affect the results of your study.

1. The hypothesis I wish to investigate is: _____
   _____

2. This hypothesis suggests a relationship between at least two variables. They are: _____
   and _____

3. More specifically, the variables in my study are:

   a. dependent _____

   b. independent _____

4. Possible extraneous variables that might affect my results include:

   a. _____   d. _____

   b. _____   e. _____

   c. _____

Chapter Four

REVIEWING
THE LITERATURE

Before planning the details of a study, researchers usually dig into the literature to find out what has been written about the topic they are interested in investigating. Both the opinions of experts in the field and other research studies are of interest. Such reading is referred to as a "review of the literature." In this chapter, we describe in detail the steps researchers go through in conducting a literature review.

- *Describe* briefly why a literature review is of value
- *Name* the steps a researcher goes through in conducting a review of the literature
- *Describe* briefly the kinds of information contained in a general reference and *give an example* of such a source
- *Explain* the difference between a primary and a secondary source and *give an example* of each type
- *Explain* what is meant by the phrase "search term" and how such terms are used in literature searches
- *Conduct* both a manual and a computer search of the literature on a topic of interest to you and *write* a summary of your review

The Value of a Literature Review

A **literature review** is helpful in two ways. It not only helps researchers glean the ideas of others interested in a particular research question, but it also lets them see what the results of other (similar, or related) studies of the question have been. A detailed literature review, in fact, is usually required of master's and/or doctoral students when they complete a thesis. Researchers then weigh information from a literature review in the light of their own concerns and situation. Thus, there are two important points here. Researchers need not only to be able to locate other work dealing with their problems but also to be able to evaluate this work in terms of its relevance to the research question of interest.

Types of Sources

Researchers need to be familiar with three basic types of sources as they begin to search for information related to the research question.

1. *General references* are the sources researchers refer to first. In effect, they tell where to look to locate other sources, such as articles, monographs, books, and other documents, that deal directly with the research question. Most general references are either *indexes,* which list the author, title, and place of publication of articles and other materials on education, or **abstracts,** which give a brief summary of various publications, as well as their author, title, and place of publication. An index frequently used by researchers in education is *Current Index to Journals in Education*. A commonly used abstract is *Psychological Abstracts*.

47

2. **Primary sources** are publications in which individuals who do research report the results of their studies. Authors communicate their findings directly to readers. Most primary sources in education are journals, such as the *Journal of Educational Research* or the *Journal of Research in Science Teaching*. These journals are usually published monthly or quarterly, and the articles in them typically report on a particular research study.

3. **Secondary sources** refer to publications in which authors describe the work of others. The most common secondary sources in education are textbooks. A textbook in educational psychology, for example, may describe several studies that have been done in psychology as ways of illustrating various ideas and concepts. Other commonly used secondary sources include educational encyclopedias, research reviews, and yearbooks.

Researchers who seek information on a given topic would refer first to one or more general references to locate primary and secondary sources of value. For a quick overview of the problem at hand, secondary sources are probably the best bet. For detailed information about the research that others have done, primary sources should be consulted.

Steps Involved in a Literature Search

Several steps are involved in a literature review.

1. Define the research problem as precisely as possible.
2. Peruse relevant secondary sources.
3. Select and peruse one or two appropriate general reference works.
4. Formulate search terms (key words or phrases) pertinent to the problem or question of interest.
5. Search the general references for relevant primary sources.
6. Obtain and read relevant primary sources; note and summarize key points in the sources.

Let us consider each of these steps in some detail.

DEFINE THE PROBLEM AS PRECISELY AS POSSIBLE

The first thing a researcher needs to do is to state the research question as specifically as possible. General questions like "What sorts of teaching methods work well in the classroom?" or "How can a principal be a more effective leader?" are too fuzzy to be of much help when one starts to look through a general reference. The question of interest should be narrowed down to a specific area of concern. More specific questions, therefore, might be "Is discussion more effective than slide-tape presentations in motivating students to learn social studies concepts?" or "What sorts of strategies do principals judged effective by their staffs use to improve faculty and staff morale?" A serious effort should be made to state the question so that it focuses on the specific issue for investigation.

PERUSE ONE OR TWO SECONDARY SOURCES

Once the research question has been stated in specific terms, it is a good idea to look through one or two secondary sources to get an overview of previous work that has been done on the problem. This needn't be a monumental chore nor take an overly long time. The main intent is to get some idea of what is already known about the problem of which the question is a part and of some of the other questions that are being asked. Researchers may also get an idea or two about how to revise or improve the research question. Here are some of the most commonly used secondary sources in education.

Encyclopedia of Educational Research (current edition): Contains brief summaries of over 300 topics in education. Excellent source for getting a brief overview of the problem.

Handbook of Research on Teaching: Contains longer articles on various aspects of teaching. Most are written by educational researchers who specialize in the topic on which they are writing. Includes extensive bibliographies.

National Society for the Study of Education (NSSE) Yearbooks: Published every year, these yearbooks deal with recent research on various topics. Each book usually contains from ten to twelve chapters dealing with various aspects of the topic. The society also publishes a number of volumes on contemporary educational issues that deal in part with research on various topics. A list of these volumes can be found in the back of the most recent yearbook.

Review of Educational Research: Published four times a year, this is a journal that contains reviews of research on various topics in education. Includes extensive bibliographies.

Review of Research in Education: Published yearly, each volume contains surveys of research on important topics written by leading educational researchers.

Subject Guide to Books in Print (most recent edition): Each of the above sources contain reviews of research on various topics of importance in education. There are many topics, however, that have not been the subjects of a recent review. If a research question deals with such a topic, the best chance for locating information discussing research on the topic lies in recent books or monographs on the subject. The best source for identifying books that might discuss research on a topic is the current edition of *Books in Print.* Other places to look for new books on your topic are the card catalog* (Figure 4.1) and the curriculum department (for text-

*Card catalogs may soon be a thing of the past. Most universities are converting the information in their card catalogs into a computer database. In the near future, rather than scanning through a number of cards, you will simply ask the computer to call up on screen the bibliographic data of the particular sources in which you are interested.

FIGURE **4.1**

Sample Card from University Card Catalog

```
                    San Francisco State University.
                       Masters Theses Collection--Degree
                       in Social science.
      AS
      36          Fraenkel, Jack R.
      1965           A comparison of achievement between
      .F73x        students taught by a teaching team and
                    students taught in traditional classes
                    on a standardized examination in United
                    States history / by Jack R. Fraenkel.
                    --1965.
                       iv, 61 leaves ; 29 cm.
                       Typescript.
                       Thesis (M.A.)--San Francisco State
                    College.
                       Bibliography: leaves 42-44.
                       1. Teaching teams.  2. United States
                    --History--Study and teaching.   I. San
                    Francisco State University. Masters
                    Theses Collection--Degree in
                    Social science.   II. Title

      CSfSt    16 APR 80   6211387   CSFant
```

books) in the library. *Education Index* and *Psychological Abstracts* also list newly published professional books in their fields.

SELECT THE APPROPRIATE GENERAL REFERENCES

After reading in a secondary source to get a more informed overview of the problem, researchers should have a clearer idea of exactly what to investigate. At this point it is a good idea to look again at the research question to see if it needs to be rewritten in any way to make it more focused. Once satisfied, researchers can select one or two general references to help identify particular journals or other primary sources related to the question.

There are many general references a researcher can consult. Here is a listing of the ones most commonly used in education.

Education Index: Published monthly. Indexes articles from over 300 educational publications, but only gives bibliographical data (author, title, and place of publication). For this reason, *Current Index to Journals in Education,* or CIJE (see next page), is preferred by most educational

FIGURE 4.2

Part of a Page from **Education Index**

Group work

See also
Parents—Counseling services
Self help groups
Sensitivity training
Social group work

Adjustment to divorce: three components to assist children. R. G. Cantrell. bibl *Elem Sch Guid Couns* 20:163-73 F '86

Child, adult-interactional, and socioeconomic setting events as predictors of parent training outcome. J. E. Dumas. bibl *Educ Treat Child* 7:351-63 Fall '84

Circle of friends. G. J. Krysiak. *Sch Couns* 33:47-9 S '85

Coping with family change: a model for therapeutic group counselling with children and adolescents. R. Freeman and B. Couchman. bibl *Sch Guid Work* 40:44-50 My '85

Counseling children of divorce. R. K. Goldman and M. J. King. bibl *Sch Psychol Rev* 14 no3:280-90 '85

A curative factor framework for conceptualizing group counseling. M. Waldo. bibl *J Couns Dev* 64:52-8 S '85

Dual-career families: terminology, typologies, and work and family issues. C. C. Cherpas. bibl *J Couns Dev* 63:616-20 Je '85

The effect of small-group counseling on underachievers. M. Bland and P. Melang. *Elem Sch Guid Couns* 20:303-5 Ap '86

The effects of classroom meetings on self-concept and behavior. S. N. Sorsdahl and R. P. Sanchc. bibl *Elem Sch Guid Couns* 20:49-56 O '85

The effects of group and individual vocational counseling on career indecision and personal indecisiveness. S. E. Cooper. bibl *J Coll Stud Pers* 27:39-42 Ja '86

Engaging non-attending family members in marital and family counseling: ethical issues. S. A. Wilcoxon. bibl *J Couns Dev* 64:323-4 Ja '86

Group applications of hypnosis for college students. P. A. Payne and G. H. Friedman. bibl *J Coll Stud Pers* 27:154-60 Mr '86

Group counseling—it works! M. M. Omizo and S. A. Omizo. *Acad Ther* 21:367-9 Ja '86

A group for teaching job interview skills to international students. F. B. Wortham. *J Coll Stud Pers* 27:179-81 Mr '86

Source: *Education Index,* July 1985–June 1986, p. 321. Reprinted by permission of H. W. Wilson Co., Bronx, New York.

researchers doing a literature search on a topic in education. Figure 4.2 illustrates part of a page listing under the topic of "Counseling" in *Education Index.*

Psychological Abstracts: Published monthly by the American Psychological Association. Covers over 900 journals, reports, monographs, and other documents (including books and other secondary sources). Abstracts (brief summaries of articles) are presented in addition to bibliographical data. Although there is considerable overlap with CIJE, *Psych Abstracts* (as it is often called) usually gives a more thorough coverage of psychological than educational topics. It should definitely be consulted for any topic dealing with some aspect of psychology.

Resources in Education (RIE): Published monthly by the Educational Resources Information Center (ERIC), these volumes report on all sorts of documents researchers could not find elsewhere. The monthly issues of RIE review speeches given at professional meetings, documents published by state departments of education, final reports of federally funded research projects, reports from school districts, commissioned papers written for government agencies, and other published and unpublished documents. Bibliographic data are provided on all documents, and also an abstract (usually) of the document. Many reports that would otherwise never be published are reported in RIE, which makes this an especially valuable resource. RIE should always be consulted, regardless of the nature of a research topic (Figure 4.3).

Current Index to Journals in Education (CIJE): Also published monthly by ERIC, this index covers what RIE does not—journal articles. Abstracts of articles from almost 800 publications, including many from foreign countries, are provided (Figure 4.4). Since the coverage is so thorough, a search of RIE and CIJE should be sufficient, for most research problems in education, to locate most of the relevant references.

Sociological Abstracts: Published five times a year, this source is similar in format to *Psych Abstracts.* It provides bibliographic data plus abstracts. It is worth consulting if the topic involves some aspect of sociology or social psychology.

Exceptional Child Education Resources (ECER): Published quarterly by The Council for Exceptional Children. It provides information about exceptional children from over 200 journals. Using a format similar to CIJE, it provides author, subject, and title indexes. It is worth

FIGURE 4.3

Excerpt from RIE

ED 276 643   SO 017 565
Shoemaker, Rebecca S.
The Constitution and Citizenship Education.
Spons Agency—Indiana Committee for the Humanities, Indianapolis; Social Studies Development Center, Bloomington, Ind.
Pub Date—86
Note—16p.; Paper presented at a Rountable Meeting on the Constitution in the Education of Citizens (Evansville, IN, September 25, 1986).
Pub Type—Opinion Papers (120)—Speeches/Meeting Papers (150)
EDRS Price - MF01/PC01 Plus Postage.
Descriptors—Citizen Participation, *Citizenship Education, Community Education, Critical Thinking. Elementary Secondary Education, Governmental Structure, Political Influences, *Political Issues, *Social Studies, *Values Education
Identifiers—Power, *United States Constitution
    The paper takes the position that the study and understanding of the United States Constitution should be a critical part of citizenship education, especially as its Bicentennial approaches. Several factors suggest that the Constitution has become the most durable document of its kind in history, and that its teaching should be centered in both the school and the community. It is proposed that the teaching of citizenship education could be addressed through three topics: (1) principles, including federalism, separation of powers, checks and balances, the concept of limited government, and the distinction between a democracy and a republic; (2) issues, including judicial review, the power struggle between states and the national government, civil liberties, changing the document, and other controversial subjects; and (3) values, such as representative government, respect for rights, divided responsibilities, and tradition. (TRS)

FIGURE 4.4

Sample Entries from Current Index to Journals in Education (CIJE)

EJ 343 588   CS 733 294
The Best Teaching: Intuition Isn't Enough. Abshire, Gary M. *Clearing House;* v60 n2 p59-61 Oct 1986 (Reprint: UMI)
Descriptors: *Teacher Effectiveness; *Teacher Qualifications; *Teaching Methods; *Teacher Role; *Teacher Education; Teacher Student Relationship; Material Development; Elementary Secondary Education

Discusses factors, beyond intuition, that produce optimal teaching: written objectives; organization of exhaustive research; selective rearrangement of subject matter; well-timed distribution of course syllabus and other handouts; planning of lesson presentation, conclusion, classroom activities and outside assignments; sensitivity to level, time factor, environment, student participation, and an open mind. (JK)

EJ 343 589   CS 733 295
Improving Learning through Student Questioning. Perez, Samuel A. *Clearing House;* v60 n2 p63-65 Oct 1986 (Reprint: UMI)
Descriptors: Elementary Secondary Education; *Cognitive Processes; *Reading Comprehension; *Questioning Techniques; *Learning Strategies; Teaching Methods
Identifiers: *Socratic Method

Uses the Socratic method as a point of departure and suggests steps that teachers can take to teach students how to formulate their own questions for better comprehension ability. (JK)

Source: Reprinted from *Current Index to Journals in Education,* January–June 1987, p. 165. Copyright © 1987 by The Oryx Press, 2214 N. Central Ave., Phoenix, AZ 85004. Reprinted by permission.

consulting if a research topic deals with exceptional children, since it covers several journals not searched for in CIJE.

Most doctoral dissertations and many master's theses in education report on original research, and hence are valuable sources for literature reviews.

Dissertation Abstracts International (DAI): The major reference for dissertations, published monthly. DAI contains the abstracts of doctoral dissertations submitted by almost 500 universities in the United States and Canada. There are two sections: Section A contains dissertations

FIGURE 4.5

Excerpt from Dissertation
Abstracts International

TOWARD A GROUNDED THEORY OF BURNOUT AMONG
SUBURBAN, ELEMENTARY SCHOOLTEACHERS
Order No. DA8702636

SIMKINS, MICHAEL BRIAN, ED.D. *University of California, Los Angeles,*
1986. 255pp. Chair: Charlotte Crabtree

Burnout has gained currency as a serious problem in many
professions, teaching among them. The purpose of the study was to
seek a theoretical perspective on teacher burnout which might guide
efforts to control or ameliorate it. In particular, the study sought to
answer three questions: (1) How do teachers themselves define
burnout? (2) Are there different varieties of teacher burnout? (3) What
specific factors account for burnout among teachers?

Because of its suitability for identifying meaningful categories from
qualitative data, the grounded theory approach of Glaser and Strauss
(1967) was selected as the method for the study. The core of this
approach is the constant comparative analysis of data, from which
theory is ''discovered'' and provisionally tested. The primary source of
data were ethnographic interviews held over a period of eighteen
months with twenty-five elementary schoolteachers. These teachers
spoke candidly and at length about their careers in general and about
burnout in particular. Excerpts from their comments were used
extensively in the exposition of the findings.

The study yielded a grounded, substantive theory of teacher
burnout, the key features of which include: (1) a conceptualization of
burnout as a generalized malfunctioning of the reward structure of
teaching; (2) a taxonomy of four varieties of burnout—the Dismayed,
the Nonchalant, the Valiant, and the Miserable—which are contrasted
in terms of teachers' attitudes toward continuing in teaching, the ways
in which they feel shortchanged, how they experience burnout, and
how they cope or contend with the problem; (3) a catalog and
detailed description of twenty factors which appear to contribute to
burnout; and (4) a set of propositions which describe ways in which
the factors influence the development and experience of burnout.
Implications for school leadership personnel and questions for further
research are included.

Source: From *Dissertation Abstracts International–A: Humanities and Social
Sciences, 47,* nos. 11–12, May–June 1987, p. 4032. Reprinted by permission of
University Microfilms International.

in the humanities and the social sciences
and includes education (Figure 4.5). Section B contains dissertations in the physical sciences and engineering and includes
psychology.

Keyword Title Index: Comes with each
monthly issue of DAI. It is just what its
title implies—an alphabetical listing of
key words contained in the titles of the
dissertations included in that issue. In

FIGURE 4.6

Excerpt From
Keyword Index of DAI

COUNSELING
A DEVELOPMENTAL COUNSELING APPROACH TO ALTER
SELF-CONCEPT AND RACIAL PREJUDICE IN
ELEMENTARY CHILDREN—GUYTON, JANE MCCLARY
(ED.D 1987 UNIVERSITY OF ARKANSAS) 105p 48/05A,
p. 1116 DET87-18814
EFFECTS OF DIFFERENT LEVELS OF ACCULTURATION,
COUNSELOR ETHNICITY, AND COUNSELING STRATEGY
ON CLIENT'S PERCEPTIONS OF COUNSELOR
CREDIBILITY AND INFLUENCE (MEXICAN-AMERICAN)—
PONCE, FRANCISCO QUINTANILLA (PH.D. 1987
UNIVERSITY OF CALIFORNIA, SANTA BARBARA) 144p.
48/06A, p. 1399 DET87-19633
THE EFFECTIVENESS OF A CAREER COUNSELING
INTERVENTION, THE HARRINGTON-O'SHEA CAREER
DECISION-MAKING SYSTEM, AS AN AID TO HISPANICS
TO MAKE AND IMPLEMENT APPROPRIATE CAREER
DECISIONS (MCIP)—THOMPSON, DALE WILSON (PH.D.
1987 THE CATHOLIC UNIVERSITY OF AMERICA) 194p.
48/03A, p. 567 DET87-13912
A COMPARATIVE STUDY: THE EFFECT OF TRAINING ON
STUDENTS PERFORMANCE IN CAMPUS
INTERVIEWING (EMPLOYMENT, CAREER
DEVELOPMENT, COUNSELING)—BRANT, MARY BALL
(ED.D. 1987 INDIANA UNIVERSITY) 164p. 48/01A.
p. 56 DET87-08831
THE EFFECT OF RETIREMENT-LEISURE COUNSELING ON
LEISURE AND RETIREMENT ATTITUDE—LANGLIEB,
KENNETH ROGER (PH.D. 1987 KANSAS STATE
UNIVERSITY) 176p. 48/04A, p. 836 DET87-15221

Source: *Comprehensive Dissertation Index 1987.* Social
Sciences and Humanities Supplement, Part I. Reprinted by
permission of University Microfilms International.

looking for dissertations dealing with a
specific topic, researchers identify key
terms (see below) in the research question
and then see if there are any relevant
abstracts listed under these terms in the
Keyword Index (Figure 4.6).

Dissertation Abstracts Ondisc. Many universities now have this computer database
with search software that allows an individual to do a computer search (by
keyword, subject, author, even school!)
of the *Dissertation Abstracts* database. It
includes information on over 900,000
doctoral dissertations and master's theses
in hundreds of subject areas, with some
30,000 new titles being added each year.
We describe how to do a computer search
of the literature later in this chapter.

FORMULATE SEARCH TERMS

Once a general reference work has been
selected, researchers need to formulate some

search terms—descriptor words to use to help locate primary sources. To do this, researchers identify the most important words in the problem statement. Take, for example, the research question "Do students taught by a teaching team learn more than students taught by an individual teacher?" What are the most important words—the key terms—in this question? Remember that a researcher conducts a literature search to find out what other research has been done with regard to, and what others think about, the research question of interest. The key term in this question, therefore, is "teaching team." This term, plus other terms that are similar to it, or synonyms for it, should be listed. Possibilities here, therefore, might include "team teaching," "joint teaching," "cooperative teaching," and the like. These should be listed alphabetically, and then the general reference work consulted to see what articles are listed under these terms. The researcher would then select the articles that seem to bear on his or her topic.

SEARCH THE GENERAL REFERENCES

What is a useful way to search through a general reference work? Although there is no magic formula to follow, the following is one that is used by many researchers in education. Let us use *Education Index* as an example.

1. Find the most recent issue and work backwards. Each of the monthly issues is combined every quarter, and the quarterly issues in turn are combined into a yearly volume. Researchers would need to search through each of the monthly issues for the current quarter, therefore, then the quarterly issues for the current year, and then the yearly volumes for as far back as they wish to go.

2. Look to see if there are any articles listed under each of the search terms in the current issue.

3. List the bibliographical data of pertinent articles on bibliographic cards. If any articles are found that deal with some aspect of the researcher's topic, the author, title, page, publication date, and publication source should be listed on a 3 by 5 (or perhaps larger)* card (Figure 4.7). A separate card should be used for each reference listed. The important thing is to take care to record the bibliographic data completely and accurately. Nothing is more annoying than to

---

* Some researchers prefer 4 by 6 (or 5 by 8) cards so they can later make notes pertaining to the contents of the reference on the same card.

FIGURE 4.7

Sample Bibliographic Card

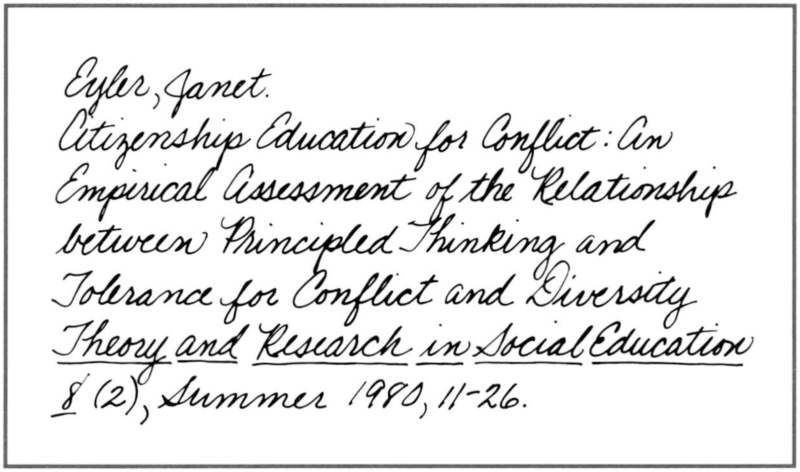

Eyler, Janet.
Citizenship Education for Conflict: An Empirical Assessment of the Relationship between Principled Thinking and Tolerance for Conflict and Diversity Theory and Research in Social Education 8 (2), Summer 1980, 11-26.

find that one has listed a reference incorrectly on a bibliographic card and thus be unable to locate it.

4. Continue looking through other issues. If, after looking through several issues, the researcher finds no articles relevant to the research topic under a particular search term, the term should be dropped from the search list. When enough articles have been gathered to obtain an adequate idea as to what else has been written about the topic, the search can be stopped. How many articles is enough? Again, there is no magic number. It depends on the purpose of the search. To obtain a fairly complete listing of what has been written on a topic, a researcher would need to extend the search over several years. To simply obtain a few articles to get a "feeling" for the kinds of articles that have been written on a topic, it may be necessary to search only a few issues.

***Searching* Psychological Abstracts.** After deciding to search through *Psychological Abstracts,* researchers should turn first to the index volume for a particular year to check for the search terms. Only the subjects of the articles are listed there,

followed by a number. The following is from Volume 73, Subject Index II, January–December 1986, p. 1151, under Motivation:

> motivation and goal setting, skill & confidence in sports
> performance, athletes, 23150.

The number refers to the number of the abstract, which can then be looked up in the appropriate volume of abstracts. There would be found the abstract for the above subject listing (Figure 4.8).

As you can see, the abstracts provided in *Psychological Abstracts* are more informative than just the bibliographic data provided in *Education Index.* Thus it is perhaps somewhat easier to determine if an article is pertinent to a particular topic.

If a topic pertains strictly to education, little is to be gained by searching through *Psychological Abstracts.* If a topic involves some aspect of psychology, however (such as educational psychology), it often is useful to check *Psych Abstracts* as well as *Education Index,* RIE, and CIJE.

***Searching* RIE and CIJE.** Searching through RIE and CIJE is similar to a search in *Psychological Abstracts.* Researchers first go to the *Thesaurus of ERIC Descriptors* (a separate volume) and locate the search terms. These are called descriptors in ERIC. A sample of a thesaurus entry (they are listed alphabetically) is shown in Figure 4.9. A key is provided to show you how ERIC uses the various terms in the descriptor display.

As you can see, other terms are suggested that might be considered for use as additional descriptors. Researchers then look under the relevant descriptors in the Subject Index of RIE and CIJE monthly and cumulative issues to find titles relevant to the topic, which are again listed on note cards as suggested above. Any document abstracted in RIE or CIJE can be ordered from ERIC—the latest issue of RIE tells how to order an ERIC document. Most university libraries, however, maintain a collection of ERIC documents on microfiche (small sheets of microfilm), which are read in a special microfiche viewer.

FIGURE 4.8

Excerpt from **Psychological Abstracts**

> 23150, **Locke, Edwin A. & Latham, Gary P.** (U. Maryland, Coll of Business & Management, College Park) **The application of goal setting to sports.** *Journal of Sport Psychology,* 1985(Sep), Vol 7(3), 205–222.—Reviews clinical and field studies of goal setting. Results indicate that specific, difficult goals lead to better performance than vague or easy goals; short-term goals can help achieve long-term goals; goals affect performance by affecting effort, persistence, and attention and by motivating strategy development; progress feedback is necessary for goal setting to work; goals must be accepted if they are to affect performance; goal attainment is facilitated by a plan of action; and competition is a form of goal setting. Implications of these findings for athletics are discussed. In addition, suggestions are made regarding setting goals for both practice and game situations; setting goals for different elements of athletic skill as well as for strength and stamina; using goals to increase self-confidence; and improving performance by increasing task difficulty independently of goal difficulty. (52 ref)— *Journal abstract.*

Source: *Psychological Abstracts,* 73, pt. 3, p. 2499, July–September 1986. Reprinted by permission of American Psychological Association.

FIGURE 4.9

Sample Thesaurus *Entry,*
Alphabetical Descriptor Display

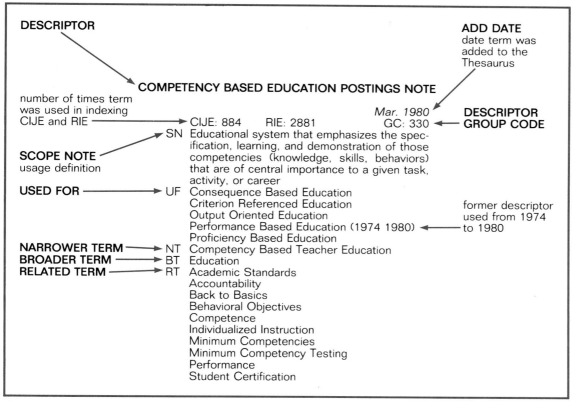

Source: Reprinted from *Thesaurus of ERIC Descriptors,* 11th ed. Copyright © 1986 by The Oryx Press, 2214 N. Central Ave., Phoenix, AZ 85004. Reprinted by permission.

In sum, the abstracts in RIE and *Psychological Abstracts* are presented in more detail than those in CIJE. *Education Index* is less comprehensive than CIJE and gives only bibliographic information, not abstracts. CIJE also covers more journals.

The best strategy for a thorough search is probably as follows.

1. Before 1965—search *Education Index.*
2. From 1966 to 1968—search RIE and *Education Index.*
3. From 1969 to the present—search RIE and CIJE.

OBTAIN PRIMARY SOURCES

After the general references have been searched, researchers will have a pile of bibliographic cards. The next step is to locate each of the sources listed on the cards and then read and take notes on those relevant to the research problem. There are two major types of primary sources to be familiar with in this regard—journals and reports. Although space prevents a complete listing, what follows will give you a pretty good idea of what exists.

Professional Journals. Many journals in education publish reports of research. Some publish articles on a wide range of educational topics, while others limit what they print to a particular specialization, such as social studies education. Most researchers become familiar with the journals in their field of interest, and look them over from time to time. Here is a representative sampling of journals in education.

- *American Educational Research Journal* (Washington, D.C.: American Educational Research Association), 1964–
- *Anthropology and Education Quarterly* (Washington, D.C.: Council on Anthropology and Education), 1970–
- *British Journal of Educational Studies* (London: Faber & Faber)
- *Canadian Education and Research Digest* (Toronto: Canadian Education Association)
- *Child Development* (Chicago: University of Chicago Press, Society for Research in Child Development), 1930–
- *Educational Administration Quarterly* (Columbus, OH: University Council for Educational Administration), 1965–
- *Educational and Psychological Measurement* (Durham, NC.: Educational and Psychological Measurement), 1941–
- *International Journal of Aging and Human Development* (Farmingdale, NY: Baywood Publishing Co.), 1962–
- *International Journal of Behavioral Development* (London: Lawrence Erlbaum Associates, Ltd.), 1978–
- *International Journal of Rehabilitation Research* [Heidelberg, Federal Republic of Germany: College of Education (Pädagogische Hochschule)], 1977–
- *International Review of Education* (Dordrecht, Netherlands: UNESCO Institute for Education), 1954–
- *International Journal of Social Education* (Muncie, IN: Department of History, Ball State University), 1986–
- *Journal of Counseling and Development* (Alexandria, VA: American Association for Counseling and Development), 1922–
- *Journal of Educational Measurement* (Washington, D.C.: National Council on Measurement in Education), 1964–
- *Journal of Educational Psychology* (Washington, D.C.: American Psychological Association), 1910–
- *Journal of Educational Research* (Washington, D.C.: HELDREF Publications), 1920–
- *Journal of Educational Sociology* (New York: Payne Educational Sociology Foundation, New York University), 1927–
- *Journal of Experimental Education* (Washington, D.C.: HELDREF Publications), 1932–
- *Journal of Psychology* (Provincetown, MA: Journal Press), 1935–
- *Journal of Research and Development in Education* (Athens, GA: University of Georgia), 1967–
- *Journal of Research in Mathematics Education* (Reston, VA: National Council of Teachers of Mathematics), 1970–
- *Journal of Research in Music Education* (Vienna, VA: Music Educators National Conference), 1953–
- *Journal of Research in Science Teaching* (New York: National Association for Research in Science Teaching and Association for the Education of Teachers in Science, John Wiley & Sons.), 1962–
- *Journal of School Psychology* (New York: Behavioral Publications), 1962–
- *Journal of Social Psychology* (Provincetown, MA: Journal Press), 1930–
- *Psychological Bulletin* (Washington, D.C.: American Psychological Association), 1904–
- *Psychological Review* (Washington, D.C.: American Psychological Association), 1894–
- *Psychology in the Schools* (Brandon, VT: Clinical Psychology Publishing Co.), 1964–
- *Reading Research Quarterly* (Newark, DE: International Reading Association), 1965–
- *Research in the Teaching of English* (Urbana, IL: National Council of Teachers of English), 1967–

- *Research Quarterly for Exercise and Sport* (Washington, D.C.: American Alliance for Health, Physical Education and Recreation), 1930–
- *School Science and Mathematics* (Tempe, AZ: School Science and Mathematics Association)
- *Sociology and Social Research* (Los Angeles: University of Southern California), 1916–
- *Sociology of Education* (Albany, NY: American Sociological Association), 1927–
- *Theory and Research in Social Education* (Washington, D.C.: National Council for the Social Studies), 1973–

Reports. Many important research findings are first published as reports. Almost all funded research projects produce a final report of their activities and findings when they complete their research. In addition, each year many reports on research activities are published by the United States Government, by state departments of education, by private organizations and agencies, by local school districts, and by professional associations. Furthermore, many individual researchers give a report on their recent work at professional meetings and conferences.

These reports are a valuable source about current research efforts. Most of them are abstracted in the Documents Résumé section of RIE, and ERIC distributes microfiche copies of them to most college and university libraries. Many papers, such as the reports of Presidential Task Forces, national conferences, or specially called professional meetings, are published only as reports. They are usually far more detailed than journal articles and much more up-to-date. Also, they are not copyrighted. Reports are a very valuable source of up-to-date information that could not be obtained anywhere else.

Locating Primary Sources. Most primary source material is located in journal articles and reports, since that is where most of the research findings in education are published. Although the layout of libraries varies, one often is able to go right to the stacks where journals are shelved alphabetically. In some libraries, however, the stacks are closed and one must ask the librarian to get the journals. When this is the case, it is a good idea to prepare call slips for about ten references at a time.

As is almost always the case, some of the references desired will be missing, at the bindery, or checked out by someone else. If an article is particularly important for a researcher to acquire, it often can be obtained directly from the author. Addresses of authors are listed in *Psychological Abstracts* or RIE, but not in *Education Index* or CIJE. Sometimes an author's address can be found in the directory of a professional association, such as the *American Educational Research Association Biographical Membership Directory*, or in *Who's Who in American Education*. If a reprint cannot be obtained directly from the author, it may be possible to obtain it from another library in the area or from interlibrary loan, a service that nearly all libraries provide.

Reading Primary Sources. When the researcher has the journal articles he intends to search gathered together, the review can begin. It is a good idea to begin with the most recent articles and work backward. The reason for this is that most of the more recent articles will have the earlier articles as a foundation and thus can give a quicker understanding of previous work.

How should an article be read? While there is no one perfect way to do this, here are some ideas.

- Read the abstract or the summary first. This will tell whether the article is worth reading in its entirety.
- Record the bibliographic data at the top of a five by eight note card.
- Take notes on the article concentrating on the following points, or photocopy the abstract or summary. Almost all research articles follow the same format. They usually include an abstract; an introductory section that introduces the research problem or question and reviews other related studies; the objectives of the study or the hypotheses to be tested; a description of the research procedures, including the subjects studied, the re-

search design, and the measuring instruments used; the results or findings of the study; a summary (if there is no abstract); and the researcher's conclusions.

- Be as brief as possible in taking notes, yet do not exclude anything that might be important to describe later in the full review.

Some researchers ditto off on note cards the essential steps mentioned above (problem, hypothesis, procedures, findings, conclusions) ahead of time, leaving space to take notes after each step. For each of these steps, the following should be noted.

1. *Problem.* State it clearly.
2. *Hypotheses or objectives.* List them exactly as stated in the article.
3. *Procedures.* List the research methodology used (experiment, case study, and so on), the number of subjects and how they were selected, and the kind of instrument (questionnaire, tally sheet, and so on) used. Make note of any unusual techniques employed.

4. *Findings.* List the major findings. Indicate whether the objectives of the study were obtained or the hypotheses were supported. Often the findings are summarized in a table, which might be xeroxed and pasted to the back of the note card.

5. *Conclusions.* Describe the author's conclusions. Note your disagreements with the author, and the reasons for such disagreement. Note strengths or weaknesses of the study that make the results particularly applicable or limited with regard to your research question.

Figure 4.10 gives an example of a completed note card based on the bibliographic card shown in Figure 4.7.

FIGURE **4.10**

Sample Note Card

Problem: Is there a relationship btwn. principled polit. thinking & tendency to be polit. tolerant?

Hypotheses: Principl. thinkers more likely to: (1) apply principl. of democ. to specific cases than non-principl. thinkers; (2) accept polit. conflict as desirable & legitimate; (3) endorse an active citizenship role; (4) show more polit. involvement than citizens who reason predom. at conventional level.

Procedures: Sample = 135 college fr. & soph. median age 18/19. 2/3 fem. Sampled by classes in requir. gen'l ed. curricul. of small pvt. tchr's. college. Questionnaire study. Rest's Defining Issues Test (DIT) used to identify principled and non-principled thinkers of the 135, 15 Questionnaires discarded due to incomplete. 25 S_s indentif. as P thinkers; 34 as low in such thinking. sex ratio each group was same. Subjects asked respond various items on Q.

Findings: All hypotheses except #4 supported.

Conclusions: Civic tolerance & cognitive moral dvlpmnt. are associated. This intellectual growth is crucial for dvlpmnt. of citizen competence & must be fostered in schools. Tchrs should focus & promote discussions of kinds of conflict which generate controversy in the community. S_s also should be involved in polit. participation experiences in school involving decisions they make, and also in their community outside of school.

A Computer Search of the Literature

A computer search of the literature can be performed in almost all university libraries and most public libraries. Many state departments of education also conduct computer searches, as do some county offices of education and some large school systems. On-line computer terminals are linked to one or more information retrieval systems (such as the Lockheed DIALOG system), which retrieve information from a number of databases. The database most commonly used by educational researchers is ERIC, which can be searched by computer back to 1966. Other databases include *Psychological Abstracts, Exceptional Child Education Resources,* and the *Comprehensive Dissertation Index,* all of which are available in the Lockheed retrieval system. Over 200 databases exist that can be computer searched. Information about them can be obtained from most librarians. There are also a number of commercial information retrieval services that will conduct computer searches for a fee.

Conducting a computer rather than a manual search has a number of advantages. First, it is much faster than a manual search. Second, it is fairly inexpensive. Although the cost of an on-line search will vary with the length and complexity of the search, a typical search of the ERIC database, which includes all references located in RIE and CIJE, can be done for around $25.00 and take less than an hour.* Third, a printout of the search, including abstracts of sources, can be obtained. Fourth, but perhaps most important, more than one descriptor can be searched at the same time. We'll show you an example of this in a moment.

STEPS IN A COMPUTER SEARCH

The steps involved in a computer search are similar to those involved in a manual search, except that much of the work is done by the computer. To illustrate the steps involved, we

can describe an actual search conducted using the ERIC database.

Define the Problem as Precisely as Possible. As for a manual search, the research problem should be stated as specifically as possible so that relevant descriptors can be identified. A broad statement of a problem such as "How effective are questioning techniques?" is much too general. It is liable to produce an extremely large number of references, many of which probably will be irrelevant to the researcher's question of interest. For the purposes of our search, therefore, we posed the following research question: "What sorts of questioning techniques help students understand historical concepts most effectively?"

Decide on the Extent of the Search. The researcher must now decide on the desired number of references to obtain. For a review for a journal article, a researcher might decide to review only twenty to twenty-five fairly recent references. For a more detailed review, such as a master's thesis, perhaps thirty or forty might be reviewed. For a very exhaustive review, as for a doctoral dissertation, as many as 100 or more references might be searched.

Decide on the Database. As we mentioned earlier, many databases are available, but the one most commonly used is ERIC. Descriptors must fit a particular database; some descriptors may not be applicable to different databases, although many do overlap. We used the ERIC database in this example.

Select Descriptors. **Descriptors** are the words the researcher uses to tell the computer what to search for. The selection of descriptors is somewhat of an art. If the descriptor is too general, too many references may be located, many of which are likely to be irrelevant. If the descriptor is too narrow, too few references will be located, and many that might be applicable to the research question may be missed.

Since we used the ERIC database, we selected our descriptors from the *Thesaurus of ERIC Descriptors*. Descriptors can be used sin-

---

* To conduct the search shown in Figure 4.12, we were on-line for some thirty minutes at a cost of $11.93.

gularly or in various combinations to locate references. Certain key words, called "Boolean operators," enable the retrieval of terms in various combinations. The most commonly used Boolean operators are "and" and "or." For example, by asking a computer to search for a single descriptor such as "inquiry," all references containing this term would be selected. By connecting two descriptors with the word "and," however, researchers can narrow the search to locate only the references that contain *both* of the descriptors. Asking the computer to search for "questioning techniques" *and* "history instruction" would narrow the search because only references containing both descriptors would be located. On the other hand, by using the word "or," a search can be broadened, since any references with *either* one of the descriptors would be located. Thus, asking the computer to search for "questioning techniques" *or* "history instruction" would broaden the search because references containing either one of these terms

FIGURE 4.11

Venn Diagrams Showing the Boolean Operators "and" and "or"

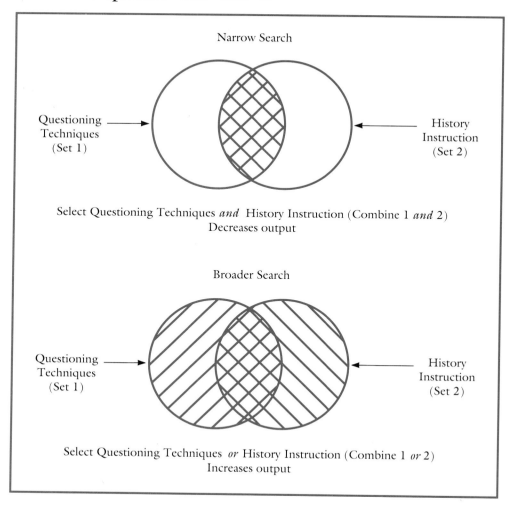

would be located. Figure 4.11 illustrates the results of using these Boolean operators.

All sorts of combinations are possible. For example, a researcher might ask the computer to search for (questioning techniques or inquiry) and (history instruction or civics instruction). For a reference to be selected, it would have to contain *either* the descriptor term "questioning techniques" *or* the descriptor term "inquiry," *as well as either* the descriptor term "history instruction" *or* the descriptor term "civics instruction."

For our search, we chose the following descriptors: questioning techniques, concept teaching, and history instruction.

When we checked the ERIC thesaurus, we found a number of related terms under two of our descriptors that we felt should also be considered. These included "inquiry," "teaching methods," and "learning processes" under "questioning techniques" and "concept formation" and "cognitive development" under "concept teaching." Upon reflection, however, we decided not to include "teaching methods" or "learning

processes" in our search, as we felt these terms were too broad to apply specifically to our research question. We also decided not to include "cognitive development" in our search for the same reason.

Conduct the Search. We were now ready to conduct our search. Figure 4.12 presents a computer printout of the search results.

As you can see, we asked the computer first to search for "questioning techniques" (S1), followed by "history instruction" (S2), followed by a combination (S3) of these two descriptors (note the use of the Boolean operator "and"). This resulted in a total of 2572 references for questioning techniques, 2157 references for history instruction, and 33 for a combination of these two descriptors. We then asked the computer to search just for the descriptor "concept teaching" (S4). This produced a total of 1885 references. Since we were particularly interested in concept teaching as applied to questioning techniques and history instruction, however, we

FIGURE 4.12

Printout of Computer Search

```
File    1:ERIC--66-88/AUG


        Set    Items    Description

? ss questioning techniques and history instruction
        S1     2572    QUESTIONING TECHNIQUES   (METHODS USED FOR CONSTRUCTING
                       AND PRESENTI
        S2     2157    HISTORY INSTRUCTION
        S3       33    QUESTIONING TECHNIQUES AND HISTORY INSTRUCTION


   ss s3 and concept teaching
                 33    S3
        S4     1885    CONCEPT TEACHING
        S5        2    S3 AND CONCEPT TEACHING


? ss (concept formation or concept teaching or inquiry) and s3
        S6     5846    CONCEPT FORMATION
        S7     1885    CONCEPT TEACHING
        S8     5318    INQUIRY (METHOD OR PROCESS OF SEEKING KNOWLEDGE,
                       UNDE . . .)
                 33    S3
        S9       19    (CONCEPT FORMATION OR CONCEPT TEACHING OR INQUIRY) AND S3
```

asked the computer to search for a combination (S5) of these three descriptors (again note the use of the operator "and"). This produced only two references. Since this was much too limited a harvest, we decided to broaden our approach by asking the computer to look for references that included the following combination (S9) of descriptors: ("concept teaching" *or* "concept formation" *or* "inquiry") *and* ("questioning techniques" *and* "history instruction"). This produced a total of 19 references. At this point, we called for a printout of these 19 references and ended our search.

If the initial effort at a search produces too few references, the search can be broadened by using more general descriptors. Thus, we might have used the term "social studies instruction" rather than "history instruction" had we not obtained enough references in our search. Similarly, a search can be narrowed by using more specific descriptors. For example, we might have used the specific descriptor "North American history" rather than the inclusive term "history."

Obtain a Printout of Desired References.
Three printout options are available.

1. Just the title of the reference and its accession number in ERIC (or whatever database is being searched). In ERIC, this is either the EJ or ED number. Here is an example.

```
EJ364977      HE523417
   The Evaluation of a Course in Interviewing
for First Year Medical Students.
```

This option is the least useful of the three, in that titles in and of themselves are often misleading or not very informative. Hence most researchers choose one of the next two options.

2. Complete bibliographic data, the accession number, and a list of descriptors that apply to the particular reference. Only the descriptors preceded by asterisks are listed in the Subject Index. Here is an example.

```
EJ319126      S0514073
   A New Challenge for Clio's Ancient Mask:
Oral Sources for a History of Educational
Institutions.
   Christensen, Lawrence O; Ridley, Jack B.
   Social Studies, u76 n2 p65-68 Mar-Apr 1985
```

```
   Available from UMI
   Language: English
   Document Type: JOURNAL ARTICLE (080);
      PROJECT DESCRIPTION (141)
   Journal Announcement: CIJSEP85
   Target Audience: Teachers; Practitioners
   Descriptors: *Educational History; History
      Instruction;
   Interviews: *Oral History; Questioning
      Techniques; Research Methodology
```

As you can see, this type of printout provides researchers with a better basis for judging the relevance of an article. The third option, however, is the most informative.

3. All the information contained in the second option, plus an abstract of the article if one has been prepared. Here is an example, taken from the printout of our search.

```
EJ354834      S0516549
   Focus Questions: The Engines of Lessons.
   Killoran, James
   Social Science Record, u24 n1 p38-41 Spr
1987
   Available from UMI
   Language: English
   Document Type: JOURNAL ARTICLE (080);
INSTRUCTIONAL MATERIAL (051);
TEACHING GUIDE (052)
   Journal Announcement: CIJSEP87
   Argues that teachers can easily structure
social studies lessons to enhance students'
thinking skills by using carefully structured
focus questions. States that such questions—
often beginning with such words as "is,"
"could," "should," "does," and "can"—go beyond
asking for simple recall of facts or shallow
explanation, to requesting the solution to
problems. Included are two model secondary
level government lessons. (JDH)
   Descriptors: Critical Thinking: Curriculum
Development; *History Instruction;
*Instructional Improvement; Lesson Plans;
*Logical Thinking; *Questioning Techniques;
Secondary Education; *Social Studies; United
States Government (Course)
```

Writing the Literature Review Report

After reading and taking notes on the various sources collected, researchers can prepare the final review. Most literature reviews consist of five parts, as follows:

1. The *introduction* which briefly describes the nature of the research problem and states the research question. The researcher also explains in this section what led him or her to investigate the question, and why it is an important question to investigate.

2. The *body* of the review which briefly reports what others have found or thought about the research problem. Related studies are usually discussed together, grouped under subheads (to make the review easier to read). Major studies are described in more detail, while less important work can be referred to in just a line or two. Often this is done by referring to several studies that reported similar results in a single sentence, somewhat like this: "Several other small-scale studies reported similar results (Adams, 1976; Brown, 1980; Cartright, 1981; Davis, 1985; Frost, 1987)."

3. The *summary* of the review which ties together the main threads revealed in the literature reviewed and presents a composite picture of what is known or thought to date. Findings may be tabulated to give readers some idea of how many other researchers have reported identical or similar findings or have similar recommendations.

4. Any *conclusions* the researcher feels are justified based on the state of knowledge revealed in the literature. What does the literature suggest are appropriate courses of action to take to try to solve the problem?

5. A *bibliography* with full bibliographic data for all sources mentioned in the review. There are many formats that can be used to list references, but the format used by the American Psychological Association (1983) is easy to use.

Main Points of Chapter Four

- The essential steps involved in a review of the literature include: (1) defining the research problem as precisely as possible; (2) perusing the secondary sources; (3) selecting and perusing an appropriate general reference; (4) formulating search terms; (5) searching the general references for relevant primary sources; (6) obtaining and reading the primary sources, and noting and summarizing key points in the sources.
- Researchers need to be familiar with three basic types of sources (general references, primary sources, and secondary sources) in doing a literature review.
- General references are sources a researcher consults to locate other sources.
- Primary sources are those publications in which researchers report the results of their investigations.
- Secondary sources refer to publications in which authors describe the work of others.
- *Education Index* and *CIJE* are two of the most frequently used general references in educational research.
- "Descriptors" are key words researchers use to help locate relevant primary sources.
- There are five essential points (problem, hypotheses, procedures, findings, conclusions) that researchers should record when taking notes on a study.
- Computer searches of the literature have a number of advantages—they are fast, are fairly inexpensive, provide printouts, and enable researchers to search using more than one descriptor at a time.
- The literature review report consists of an introduction, the body of the review, a summary, the researcher's conclusions, and a bibliography.

For Discussion

1. Why might it be unwise for a researcher not to do a review of the literature before planning a study?

2. Many published research articles include only a few references to related studies. How would you explain this? Is this justified?

3. Which do you think are more important to emphasize in a literature review—the opinions of experts in the field or related studies? Why?

4. Which of the secondary sources described in this chapter would be most appropriate to consult on the following topics?
   a. Recent research on social studies education.
   b. A brief overview on new developments in science teaching.
   c. An extensive review of recent and past research on a particular research question.
   d. A survey of recent research on homogeneous grouping.

5. One rarely finds books referred to in literature reviews. Why do you suppose this is so? Is it a good idea?

6. Which of the general references listed in this chapter would you consult on each of the following?
   a. Marriage and family counseling.
   b. Elementary school administration.
   c. Small group discussions.
   d. Deaf children.
   e. A master's thesis on client-centered therapy.
   f. Archery instruction.

Research Exercise Four:
Review of the Literature

Using Problem Sheet 4, again state either your research question or the hypothesis of your study. Then consult an appropriate general reference and list at least three search terms relevant to your problem. Next locate and read three studies related to your question, taking notes as you read on note cards similar to the one shown in Figure 4.10. Attach each of your note cards (one per journal article) to Problem Sheet 4.

PROBLEM SHEET 4
Review of the Literature

1. The question or hypothesis in my study is: _____

_____

_____

_____

2. The general reference(s) I consulted was (were): _____

_____

_____

3. The search terms I used were:

   a. _____

   b. _____

   c. _____

4. The three journals I consulted were:

   a. _____

   b. _____

   c. _____

5. The titles of the studies I read (note cards are attached) were: _____

   a. _____

   b. _____

   c. _____

Chapter Five

SAMPLING

A sample is a group in a research study on which information is obtained. A population is the group to which the results of the study are intended to apply. In almost all research investigations, the sample is smaller than the population, since researchers rarely have access to all the members of the population. In this chapter, we present the idea of sampling from a population. We discuss both random and nonrandom sampling, and describe several different types of sampling designs. Last, we discuss when it is appropriate to generalize the results of a study.

Reading this
chapter should
enable you to:

- *Distinguish* between a sample and a population
- *Explain* what is meant by the term "representative sample"
- *Explain* how a target population differs from an accessible population
- *Explain* what is meant by "random" sampling and *describe* briefly three ways of obtaining a random sample
- *Use* a table of random numbers to select a random sample from a population
- *Explain* what is meant by systematic sampling, convenience sampling, and purposive sampling
- *Explain* how the size of a sample can make a difference in terms of representativeness of the sample
- *Explain* what is meant by the term "external validity"
- *Distinguish* between population generalizability and ecological generalizability and *discuss* when it is (and when it is not) appropriate to generalize the results of a study

---

When we want to know something about a certain group of people, we usually find a few members of the group that we know—or don't know—and study them. After we have finished "studying" these individuals, we usually come to some conclusions about the larger group of which they are a part. Many "common sense" observations, in fact, are based on observations of relatively few people. It is not uncommon, for example, to hear statements such as: "Most female students don't like math"; "You won't find very many teachers voting Republican"; and "Most school superintendents are men."

What Is a Sample?

Most people, we think, base their conclusions about a group of people (students, Republicans, football players, actors, and so on) on the experiences they have with a fairly small number, or **sample,** of individual members. Sometimes such conclusions are an accurate representation of how the larger group of people acts, or what they believe, but often they are not. It all depends on how representative (i.e., how similar) the sample is of the larger group.

One of the most important steps in the research process is to select the sample of individuals who will participate (be observed or questioned) as a part of the study. **Sampling** refers to the process of selecting these individuals.

SAMPLES VERSUS POPULATIONS

A **sample** in a research study refers to any group on which information is obtained. The larger group to which one hopes to apply the results is called the **population.** All 700 (or whatever total number of) students at State University who are majoring in mathematics, for example, constitute a population; fifty of those students constitute a sample. Students who own automobiles make up another population, as do students who live in the campus dormitories. Notice that a group may be both a sample and a population at the same time: All State University students who own automobiles constitute the population of automobile owners at State, yet they also constitute a sample of all automobile owners at state universities in the United States.

When it is possible, researchers would prefer to study the entire population in which they are interested. Usually, however, this is difficult to do. Most populations of interest are large, diverse, and scattered over a large geographic area. Finding, let alone contacting, all the members can be time-consuming, and expensive. For that reason, of necessity, researchers often select a sample to study. Some examples of samples selected from populations are as follows.

- A researcher is interested in studying the effects of diet on the attention span of third grade students in a large city. There are 1500 third graders attending the elementary schools in the city. The researcher selects 150 of these third graders, 30 each in five different schools, as a sample for study.
- An administrator in a large urban high school is interested in determining the opinions of students about a new counseling program that has recently been instituted in the district. There are six high schools and some 14,000 students in the district. From a master list of all students enrolled in the district schools, the administrator selects a sample of 1400 students (350 from each of the four grades, 9–12) to whom he plans to mail a questionnaire asking their opinion of the program.
- The principal of an elementary school district wants to investigate the effectiveness of a new U.S. history textbook used by some of the teachers in the district. Out of a total of twenty-two teachers who are using the text, she selects a sample

of six. She plans to compare the achievement of the students in these teachers' classes with those of another six teachers who are not using the text.

DEFINING THE POPULATION

The first task in selecting a sample is to define the population of interest. In what group, exactly, is the researcher interested? To whom does he or she want the results of the study to apply? The population, in other words, is the group of interest to the researcher, the group to whom the researcher would like to generalize the results of the study. Here are some examples of populations.

- All high school principals in the United States.
- All elementary school counselors in the state of California.
- All students attending Central High School in Omaha, Nebraska, during the academic year 1987–88.
- All students in Mrs. Brown's third grade class at Wharton Elementary School.

The above examples reveal that a population can be any size and that it will have at least one (and sometimes several) characteristic(s) that sets it off from any other population. Notice that a population is always *all* of the individuals who possess a certain characteristic (or set of characteristics).

TARGET VERSUS ACCESSIBLE POPULATIONS

Unfortunately, the actual population (called the **target population**) to which a researcher would really like to generalize is rarely available. The population to which a researcher is *able* to generalize, therefore, is the **accessible population**. The former is one's ideal choice; the latter, one's realistic choice. Consider these examples:

Research problem to be investigated: The effects of computer-assisted instruction on the reading achievement of first and second graders in California.

Target population: All first and second grade children in California.

Accessible population: All first and second grade children in the Laguna Salada elementary school district of Pacifica, California.

Sample: Ten percent of the first and second grade children in the Laguna Salada District in Pacifica, California.

Research question to be investigated: The attitudes of fifth-year teachers-in-training toward their student teaching experience.

Target population: All fifth-year students enrolled in teacher training programs in the United States.

Accessible population: All fifth-year students enrolled in teacher-training programs in the State University of New York.

Sample: 200 fifth-year students selected from those enrolled in the teacher training programs in the State University of New York.

The more narrowly researchers define the population, the more they save on time, effort, and (probably) money, but the more they limit generalizability. It is essential that researchers describe the population and the sample in sufficient detail so interested individuals can determine the applicability of the findings to their own situations. Failure to define in detail the population of interest, and the sample studied, is one of the most common weaknesses of published research reports.

RANDOM VERSUS NONRANDOM SAMPLING

An example of each of the two main types of sampling is as follows.

Random sampling: The dean of a school of education in a large midwestern university wishes to find out how her faculty feel about the sabbatical leave require-

ments currently in operation at the university. She places all 150 names of the school faculty in a hat, mixes them thoroughly, and then draws out the names of 25 individuals to interview.*

Nonrandom sampling: The president of the same university wants to know how his junior faculty feel about a new promotion policy, which he has recently introduced (with the advice of a faculty committee). He selects a sample of 30 from the total faculty of 1000 to talk with. Five faculty members from each of the six schools that make up the university are chosen on the basis of the following criteria: They have taught at the university for less than five years, they are nontenured, they belong to one of the faculty associations on campus, and they have not been a member of the committee that helped the president draft the new policy.

In the first example, 25 names were selected from a hat after all the names had been mixed thoroughly. This is called random sampling because every member of the population (the 150 faculty in the school) presumably had an equal change of being selected. There are more sophisticated ways of drawing a **random sample,** but they all have the same intent—to select a *representative* sample from the population. The basic idea is that the individuals selected are just like the ones who are not selected. One can never be sure of this, of course, but if the sample is selected randomly, and is sufficiently large (more about size in a moment), a researcher should get an accurate view of the larger group. The best way to ensure this is to make sure that no **bias** enters the selection process—that the researcher (or other factors) cannot consciously or unconsciously influence who gets chosen to be in the sample. We'll talk more about how to minimize bias later in this chapter.

In the second example, the president wants representativeness, but not as much as he wants

---

* A better way to do this will be discussed shortly, but this gives you the idea.

to make sure there are certain kinds of faculty in his sample. Thus he has made sure that each of the individuals selected possesses all the criteria mentioned. Each member of the population (the entire faculty of the university) does *not* have an equal chance of being selected; some, in fact, have *no* chance. Hence, this is an example of **nonrandom sampling,** sometimes called "purposive sampling" (see below). Here is another example of a random sample contrasted with a nonrandom sample.

> *Random:* A researcher wishes to conduct a survey of all social studies teachers in a midwestern state to determine their attitudes toward the new state guidelines for teaching history in the secondary schools. There are a total of 725 social studies teachers in the state. The names of these teachers are obtained and listed alphabetically. The researcher then numbers the names on the list from 001 to 725. Using a table of random numbers (see below), which he finds in a statistics textbook, he selects 100 teachers for the sample.
>
> *Nonrandom:* The manager of the campus bookstore at a local university wants to find out how students feel about the services the bookstore provides. Every day for two weeks during her lunch hour, she asks every person who enters the bookstore to fill out a short questionnaire she has prepared and drop it in a box near the entrance before leaving. At the end of the two-week period, she has a total of 235 completed questionnaires.

In the second example, notice that all bookstore users did not have an equal chance of being included in the sample, only those who visited during the lunch hour. That is why the sample is not random.

Random Sampling Methods

After making a decision to sample, researchers try as hard as possible to, in most instances, obtain a sample that is representative of the population of interest—that means they prefer random sampling. The three most common ways of obtaining this type of sample are simple random sampling, stratified random sampling, and cluster sampling. A less common method is two-stage sampling.

SIMPLE RANDOM SAMPLING

A simple **random sample** is one in which each and every member of the population has an equal and independent chance of being selected. If the sample is a large one, it is the best way yet devised by human beings to obtain a sample that is representative of the population from which it has been selected. Let's take an example: Define a population as all eighth grade students in school district Y. Imagine there are 500 such students. If you were one of these students, your chance of being selected is 1 in 500, if the sampling procedure is indeed random. Everyone else has the same chance of being selected.

The larger a random sample is in size, the more likely it is to represent the population. Although there is no guarantee of representativeness, of course, the likelihood of it is greater when researchers use random sampling than when they select any other method. Any differences that exist between the sample and the population should be small and unsystematic. Any differences that do occur are the result of chance rather than bias on the part of the researcher.

The key to obtaining a random sample is to ensure that each and every member of the population has an equal and independent chance of being selected. This can be done by using what is known as a table of random numbers—an extremely large list of numbers that has no order or pattern. Such lists can be found in the back of most statistics books. Table 5.1 illustrates what part of a page of such a book might look like.

For example, to obtain a sample of 200 from a population of 2000 individuals, open the book to any page, select a column of numbers, start anywhere in the column, and begin reading four-digit numbers. (Why four digits? Because the final number 2000 consists of four digits, and we must always use the same number of digits for each person. Person #1 would be identified as 0001; person #2 as 0002; person #635 as 0635; and so forth.) The researcher would then proceed to write down the first 200 numbers in the column that have a value of 2000 or less.

Let us take the first column of four numbers in Table 5.1 as an example. Look at the first number in the column: It is 0117, so #117 in the list of individuals in the population would be selected for the sample. Look at the second number: It is 9123. There is no #9123 in the population. (Because there are only 2000 individuals in the entire population.) So the researcher goes on to the third number: It is 0864, hence #864 in the list of individuals in the population would be chosen. The fourth number in the table of random numbers is 0593, so #593 gets selected. The fifth number is 6662. There is no #6662 in the population, so the researcher goes on to the next number, and so on, until he or she has selected a total of 200 numbers, each representing an individual in the population who will be selected for the sample.

The advantage of random sampling is that it is very likely to produce a representative sample. Its biggest disadvantage is that it is not easy to do. Each and every member of the population must be identified. In most cases, we must be able to contact the individuals selected. In all cases, we must know *who* #117 (for example) is.

Furthermore, simple random sampling is not used if researchers wish to *ensure* that certain subgroups are present in the sample in the same proportion as they are in the population. To do this, researchers must engage in what is known as stratified sampling.

STRATIFIED RANDOM SAMPLING

Stratified random sampling is a process in which certain subgroups, or *strata*, are selected for the sample in the same proportion as they exist in the population. Suppose the director of research for a large school district wants to find

TABLE 5.1

Part of a Table of Random Numbers

011723	223456	222167	032762	062281	565451
912334	379156	233989	109238	934128	987678
086401	016265	411148	251287	602345	659080
059397	022334	080675	454555	011563	237873
666278	106590	879809	899030	909876	198905
051965	004571	036900	037700	500098	046660
063045	786326	098000	510379	024358	145678
560132	345678	356789	033460	050521	342021
727009	344870	889567	324588	400567	989657
000037	121191	258700	088909	015460	223350
667899	234345	076567	090076	345121	121348
042397	045645	030032	657112	675897	079326
987650	568799	070070	143188	198789	097451
091126	021557	102322	209312	909036	342045

out student opinions about a new ninth grade general science textbook the district is considering adopting. She intends to compare the achievement of students using the new book with that of students using the more traditional text the district has purchased in the past. Since she has reason to believe that gender is an important variable that may affect the outcomes of her study, she decides to ensure that the proportion of males and females in the study is the same as in the population. The steps in the sampling process would be as follows.

1. She identifies the target population: all 365 ninth grade students enrolled in general science courses in the district.
2. She finds out that there are 219 females (60 percent) and 146 males (40 percent) in the population. She decides to have a sample made up of 30 percent of the target population (more on sample size in a moment).
4. Using a table of random numbers, she then randomly selects 30 percent *from each strata* of the population, which results in 66 female (30 percent of 219) and 44 male (30 percent of 146) students being selected from these subgroups. The proportion of males and females is the same in both the population and sample—40 and 60 percent (Figure 5.1).

FIGURE **5.1**

Selecting a Stratified Sample

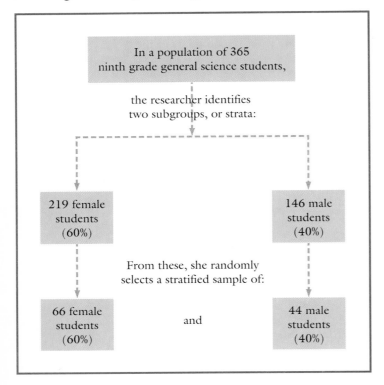

In a population of 365 ninth grade general science students,

the researcher identifies two subgroups, or strata:

219 female students (60%)   146 male students (40%)

From these, she randomly selects a stratified sample of:

66 female students (60%)   and   44 male students (40%)

The advantage of stratified random sampling is that it increases the likelihood of representativeness, especially if one's sample is not very large. It ensures that any key characteristics of individuals in the population are included in the same proportions in the sample. The disadvantage is that it requires still more effort on the part of the researcher.

CLUSTER RANDOM SAMPLING

In both random and stratified random sampling, researchers want to make sure that certain kinds of individuals are included in the sample. But there are times when it is not possible to select a sample of individuals from a population. Sometimes, for example, a list of all members of the population of interest is not available. Obviously, then, simple random or stratified sampling cannot be used. Frequently, researchers cannot select a sample of individuals due to administrative or other restrictions. This is especially true in schools. For example, if a target population were all eleventh grade students within a district enrolled in U.S. history courses, it would be unlikely that the principals of the various high schools would allow the researcher to select a certain number of individual students randomly from each of the eleventh grade U.S. history classes. Even if they would, the time and effort required would make such selection difficult. About the best the researcher could hope for would be to study a number of intact classes, that is, classes already in existence. The selection of groups, or clusters, of subjects rather than individuals is known as **cluster sampling.** Just as simple random sampling is more effective with larger numbers of individuals, so, too, is cluster random sampling more effective with larger numbers of clusters.

Let us consider another example of cluster sampling. The superintendent of a large unified school district in a city on the East Coast wants to obtain some idea of how teachers in the district feel about merit pay. There are 10,000 teachers in all the elementary and secondary schools of the district, and there are fifty schools distributed over a large area. The superintendent does not have the funds to survey all teachers in the district, and he needs the information about merit pay quickly. Instead of randomly selecting a sample of teachers from every school, therefore, he decides to interview all the teachers in selected schools. Each school, then, constitutes a cluster. The superintendent assigns a number to each school, and then uses a table of random numbers to select ten schools (20 percent of the population). All the teachers in the selected schools then constitute the sample. The interviewer questions the teachers at each of these ten schools rather than having to travel to all the schools in the district. If these teachers do represent the remaining teachers in the district, then the superintendent is justified in drawing conclusions about the feelings of the entire population of teachers in his district about merit pay. It is possible that this sample is not representative, of course. Because the teachers to be interviewed all come from a small number of schools in the district, it might be the case that these schools differ in some ways from the other schools in the district, thereby influencing the views of the teachers in those schools with regard to merit pay. The more schools selected, the more likely the findings will be applicable to the population of teachers.

Cluster sampling is similar to simple random sampling except that groups rather than individuals are randomly selected. The advantages of cluster sampling are that it can be used when it is difficult or impossible to select a random sample of individuals, it is often far easier to implement in schools, and it is frequently less time-consuming. Its disadvantage is that there is a far greater chance of selecting a sample that is not representative of the population.

There is a common error with regard to cluster sampling that many beginning researchers make. This is the mistake of randomly selecting only *one* cluster as a sample, and then observing or interviewing all individuals within that cluster. Even if there are a large number of individuals within the cluster, it is the cluster that has been randomly selected, rather than individuals, and hence the researcher is not entitled to draw conclusions about a target population of such individuals. Yet some researchers do draw such conclusions. We repeat, they should not.

TWO-STAGE RANDOM SAMPLING

It is often useful to combine cluster random sampling with individual random sampling. Rather than randomly selecting 100 students from a population of 3000 ninth graders located in 100 classes, the researcher might decide to select 25 classes randomly from the population of 100 classes and then randomly select 4 students from each class. This is much less time consuming than visiting most of the 100 classes (almost all are likely to be included in a simple random sample). Why would this be better than using all the students in four randomly selected classes? (Because four classes are too few to ensure

representativeness, even though they were selected randomly.)

Figure 5.2 on page 74 illustrates the different random sampling methods we have discussed.

Nonrandom Sampling Methods

SYSTEMATIC SAMPLING

In a systematic sample, every *n*th individual in the population list is selected for inclusion in the sample. For example, in a population list of 5000 names, to select a sample of 500, a researcher would select every tenth name on the list until a total of 500 names was chosen. Here is an example of this type of sampling.

The principal of a large middle school (grades 6–8) with 1000 students wants to know how students feel about the new menu in the school cafeteria. She obtains an alphabetical list of all students in the school and selects every tenth student on the list to be in the sample. To guard against bias, she puts the numbers 1 to 10 into a hat, and draws one out. It is a 3. So she selects the students numbered 3, 13, 23, 33, 43, and so on until she has a sample of 100 students to be interviewed.

The above method is technically known as **systematic sampling** *with a random start*. In addition, there are two terms that are frequently used when referring to systematic sampling. The *sampling interval* is the distance between each of the individuals selected for the sample. In the example given above, it was 10. A simple formula to determine it is:

$$\frac{\text{population size}}{\text{desired sample size}}$$

The *sampling ratio* is the proportion of individuals in the population that are selected for the sample. In the example above, it was .10, or 10 percent. A simple way to determine the sampling ratio is:

$$\frac{\text{sample size}}{\text{population size}}$$

FIGURE **5.2**

Random Sampling Methods

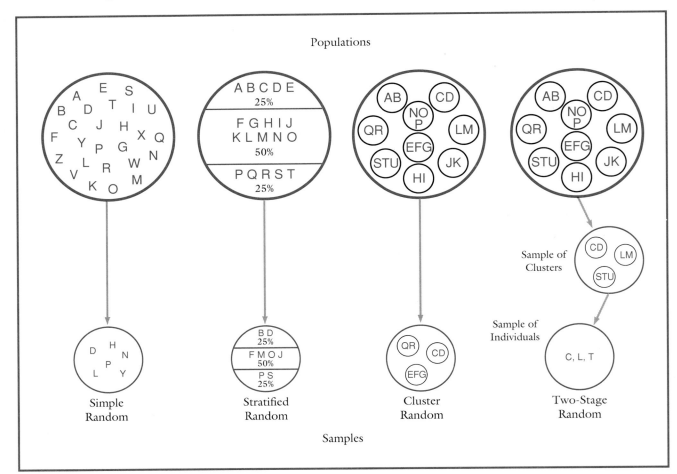

There is a danger in systematic sampling that is sometimes overlooked. If the population has been ordered systematically—that is, if the arrangement of individuals on the list is in some sort of pattern that accidentally coincides with the sampling interval—a markedly biased sample can result. Suppose that the middle school students in the preceding example had not been listed alphabetically, but rather by homeroom, and the homeroom teachers had previously listed the students in their rooms by grade point average, high to low. That would mean that the better students would be at the top of each homeroom list. Suppose also that each home-

room has 30 students. If the principal began her selection of every tenth student with the first or second or third student on the list, her sample would consist of the better students in the school rather than a representation of the entire student body. (Do you see why? Because in each homeroom, the poorest students would be those who were numbered between 24 and 30, and they would never get chosen.)

When planning to select a sample from a list of some sort, therefore, researchers should carefully examine the list to make sure there is no cyclical pattern present. If the list has been arranged in a particular order, researchers should make sure the arrangement will not bias the sample in some way that could distort the results. If such seems to be the case, steps should be taken to ensure representativeness—for example, by randomly selecting individuals from each of the cyclical portions. In fact, if a population list is randomly ordered, a systematic sample drawn from the list is a random sample.

CONVENIENCE SAMPLING

Many times it is extremely difficult (sometimes even impossible) to select either a random or a systematic nonrandom sample. At such times, a researcher will select a convenience sample. A **convenience sample** is a group of individuals who (conveniently) are available for study. Thus a researcher might decide to study two third grade classes at a nearby elementary school because the principal asks for help in comparing the effectiveness of a new spelling textbook. Here are some examples of convenience samples.

- To find out how students feel about food service in the student union at an East Coast university, the manager stands outside the main door of the cafeteria one Monday morning and interviews the first fifty students who walk out of the cafeteria.
- A high school counselor interviews all the students who come to her for counseling about their career plans.
- A news reporter for a local television station asks passersby on a downtown streetcorner their opinions about plans to build a new baseball stadium in a nearby suburb.
- A university professor compares student reactions to two different textbooks in his statistics classes.

In each of the above examples, a certain group of people were chosen for study because they were available. The obvious advantage of this type of sampling is that it is convenient. But just as obviously, it has a major disadvantage in that the sample will quite likely be biased. Take the case of the TV reporter who is interviewing

passersby on the downtown streetcorner. Many possible sources of bias exist. First of all, of course, anyone who is not downtown that day has no chance to be interviewed. Second, those individuals who are unwilling to give their views would not be interviewed. Third, those who agree to be interviewed would probably be individuals who hold strong opinions one way or the other about the stadium. Fourth, depending on the time of day, those who are interviewed quite possibly would be unemployed or have jobs that do not require them to be indoors. And so forth. What possible sources of bias can you find in the other examples? Can you think of some ways that a researcher might reduce or eliminate these biases?

In general, convenience samples cannot be considered representative of any population and should be avoided if at all possible. Unfortunately, sometimes they are the only choice a researcher has. When such is the case, the study should be replicated, that is, repeated, with a number of similar samples to decrease the likelihood that the results obtained were not simply a one-time occurrence. We'll talk more about replication later in the chapter.

PURPOSIVE SAMPLING

On occasion, based on previous knowledge of a population and the specific purpose of the research, investigators use personal judgment to select a sample. Researchers assume they can use their knowledge of the population to judge whether or not a particular sample will be representative. Here are some examples.

- For the past five years, the leaders of the teacher's association in a midwestern school district have represented the views of three-fourths of the teachers in the district on most major issues. This year, therefore, the district administration decides just to interview the leaders of the association rather than to select a sample from all the district's teachers.
- An eighth grade social studies teacher chooses the two students with the highest grade point average in her class; the two whose grade point average falls in the

middle of the class, and the two with the lowest grade point average to find out how her class feels about including a discussion of current events as a regular part of classroom activity. Similar samples in the past have represented the viewpoints of the total class quite accurately.

- A graduate student wants to know how retired people age 65 and over feel about their "golden years." He has been told by one of his professors, an expert on aging and the aged population, that the local Association of Retired Workers is a representative cross section of retired people aged 65 and over. He decides to interview a sample of fifty people who

are members of the association to get their views.

Purposive sampling is different from convenience sampling in that researchers do not simply study whoever is available, but use their judgment to select the sample for a specific purpose. The major disadvantage of purposive sampling is that the researcher's judgment may be in error—he or she may not be correct in estimating the representativeness of a sample. In the first example above, this year's leaders of the teacher's association may hold views markedly different from those of their members. Figure 5.3 illustrates the methods of convenience, purposive, and systematic sampling.

FIGURE 5.3

Nonrandom Sampling Methods

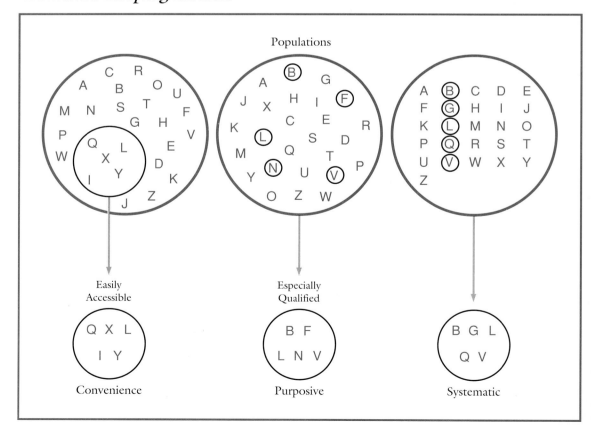

An Illustrative Review of Sampling Methods

Let us illustrate each of the previous sampling methods using the same hypothesis: "Students with low self-esteem demonstrate lower achievement in school subjects."

Target population: All eighth graders in California

Accessible population: All eighth graders in the San Francisco Bay Area (seven counties)

Feasible sample size: $n = 200\text{--}250$

Simple Random Sampling: Identify all eighth graders in all public and private schools in the seven counties (estimated number = 9000). Assign each student a number and then use a table of random numbers to select a sample of 200. The difficulty here is that it is time-consuming to identify every eighth grader in the Bay Area, and to contact (probably) 200 different schools in order to administer instruments to one or two students in those schools.

Cluster Random Sampling: Identify all public and private schools having an eighth grade in the seven counties

$$\frac{9000 \text{ students}}{30 \text{ students/class (estimated)}} = 300 \text{ classes}$$

$$\frac{300 \text{ classes}}{2 \text{ classes/school (estimated)}} = 150 \text{ schools.}$$

Assign each school a number, and then randomly select four schools ($n = 4$ schools $\times$ 2 classes per school $\times$ 30 students per class = 240). Cluster random sampling is much more feasible than simple random sampling to implement, but is limited due to the use of only four schools, even though they are to be selected randomly. For example, the selection of only four schools may exclude the selection of private school students.

Stratified Random Sampling: Obtain data on the number of eighth-grade students in public versus private schools and determine the proportion of each type (e.g., 80% public, 20% private). Determine the number from each type to be sampled: public = 80% (200) = 160; private = 20% (200) = 40. Randomly select these numbers from respective subpopulations of public and private students. Stratification may be used to guarantee that the sample is representative on other variables as well. The difficulty with this method is that stratification requires the researcher know the proportions in each strata of the population, and it also becomes increasingly difficult as more variables are added. Imagine trying to stratify not only on the public-private variable but also (for example) on student ethnicity, gender, and socioeconomic status, and on teacher gender and experience.

Two-Stage Random Sampling: Randomly select twenty-five schools from the population of 150 schools, and then randomly select eight eighth grade students from each school ($n = 8 \times 25 = 200$). This method is much more feasible than simple random sampling and more representative than cluster sampling. It may well be the best choice in this example, but it still requires permission from twenty-five schools and the resources to collect data from each.

Convenience Sampling: Select all eighth graders in four schools where the researcher has accessibility. $n = 30 \times 4 \times 2 = 240$. This method precludes generalizing beyond these four schools, unless a strong argument with supporting data can be made for their similarity to the entire group of 150 schools.

Purposive Sampling: Select eight classes from throughout the seven counties on the basis of demographic data showing that they are representative of all eighth graders. Particular attention must be paid to self-esteem and achievement scores. The problem is that such data are unlikely to be available and, in any case, cannot eliminate possible differences between the sample and the population on other variables—such as teacher attitude and available resources.

Systematic Sampling: Select every 45th student from an alphabetical list for each school

$$\left(\frac{200 \text{ students in sample}}{9000 \text{ students in population}} = \frac{1}{45} \right)$$

This method is as inconvenient as simple random sampling and is likely to result in a biased sample, since the 45th name in each school is apt to be

TABLE 5.2

A Hypothetical Population of 100 Students

Student Number	Sex	School	IQ	Student Number	Sex	School	IQ
01	F	Adams	134	51	M	Beals	110
02	F	Adams	133	52	M	Beals	110
03	F	Adams	130	53	M	Beals	109
04	F	Adams	127	54	M	Beals	108
05	F	Adams	123	55	M	Beals	107
06	M	Adams	123	56	M	Beals	106
07	M	Adams	121	57	M	Beals	101
08	M	Adams	120	58	M	Beals	101
09	F	Adams	119	59	M	Beals	98
10	M	Adams	118	60	M	Beals	97
11	F	Adams	117	61	F	Beals	91
12	F	Adams	117	62	F	Beals	86
13	M	Adams	115	63	F	Beals	83
14	M	Adams	111	64	F	Cortez	137
15	M	Adams	109	65	M	Cortez	136
16	M	Adams	108	66	F	Cortez	133
17	M	Adams	108	67	F	Cortez	130
18	F	Adams	106	68	F	Cortez	128
19	F	Adams	105	69	F	Cortez	125
20	F	Adams	104	70	F	Cortez	125
21	F	Adams	103	71	M	Cortez	122
22	F	Adams	101	72	F	Cortez	121
23	F	Adams	101	73	M	Cortez	118
24	M	Adams	101	74	F	Cortez	118
25	M	Adams	100	75	M	Cortez	113
26	M	Adams	98	76	F	Cortez	113
27	M	Adams	97	77	M	Cortez	111
28	M	Adams	97	78	F	Cortez	111
29	M	Adams	96	79	F	Cortez	107
30	F	Adams	95	80	F	Cortez	106
31	F	Adams	89	81	F	Cortez	106
32	F	Adams	88	82	F	Cortez	105
33	F	Adams	85	83	F	Cortez	104
34	F	Beals	133	84	F	Cortez	103
35	F	Beals	129	85	F	Cortez	102
36	F	Beals	129	86	M	Cortez	102
37	F	Beals	128	87	M	Cortez	100
38	F	Beals	127	88	M	Cortez	100
39	F	Beals	127	89	M	Cortez	99
40	F	Beals	126	90	M	Cortez	99
41	M	Beals	125	91	M	Cortez	99
42	M	Beals	124	92	F	Cortez	98
43	M	Beals	117	93	M	Cortez	97
44	M	Beals	116	94	F	Cortez	96
45	M	Beals	115	95	F	Cortez	95
46	M	Beals	114	96	F	Cortez	93
47	M	Beals	114	97	F	Cortez	85
48	M	Beals	113	98	M	Cortez	83
49	M	Beals	111	99	M	Cortez	83
50	M	Beals	111	100	M	Cortez	81

Parameters: Average: IQ = 109.5. Proportions: M = .50; F = .50. Schools A = .33; B = .30; C = .37

in the last third of the alphabet (remember there are an estimated 60 eighth graders in each school), introducing probable ethnic or cultural bias. An alternative is to select every sixth school from the list of 150 schools (150/6 = 25 schools) and then every sixth student on the list of eighth graders ($n = 60/6 = 10$ students per school). This method results in $n = 25 \times 10 = 250$ students, but it is inferior to random methods because of the possibility of bias inherent in school or student lists, or both. It is also no easier to carry out than random methods.

Sample Size

Drawing conclusions about a population after studying a sample is never totally satisfactory, since researchers can never be sure that their sample is perfectly representative of the population. There are always bound to be some differences between the sample and the population, but if the sample is randomly selected and of sufficient size, these differences are likely to be relatively insignificant and incidental. The question remains, therefore, as to what constitutes an adequate, or sufficient, size for a sample.

Unfortunately, there is no clearcut answer to this question. Suppose a target population consists of 1000 eighth graders in a given school district. Some sample sizes, or course, are obviously too small. Samples with 1 or 2 or 3 individuals, for example, are so small that they cannot possibly be representative. Probably any sample that has less than 20 to 30 individuals within it is too small, since that would only be 2 or 3 percent of the population. On the other hand, a sample can be too large, given the amount of time and effort the researcher must put into obtaining it. In this example, a sample of 250 or more individuals would probably be needlessly large, as that would constitute a quarter of the population. But what about samples of size 50 or 100? Would these be sufficiently large? Would a sample of 200 be too large? At what point, exactly, does a sample stop being too small and become sufficiently large? The best answer is

that a sample should be "as large as the researcher can obtain with a reasonable expenditure of time and energy." This, of course, is not as much help as one would like, but it suggests that researchers should try to obtain as large a sample as they reasonably can.

To illustrate how the size of a sample can make a difference, let us refer to Table 5.2. The data in the table represent information about a population of 100 students (numbered 01 to 100) in three schools, Adams, Beals, and Cortez. In each school, students have been listed in order by their IQ scores from high to low and identified by gender. The **parameters** (summary characteristics) of this population are shown at the bottom of the table.

Let us select a sample of ten from this population. Using the table of random numbers in Appendix A, we selected the following student numbers: 52, 63, 82, 75, 92, 36, 03, 11, 43, and 08. We record the data for each of these students, as shown in Table 5.3. Summarizing the statistics of this sample, we find that there are four males (.40) and six females (.60); three students attending Adams (.30), four students attending Beals (.40), and three students attending Cortez (.30); and an average IQ score of 112.2. Table 5.4 compares these statistics to the population parameters.

As you can see, our sample is not very representative of the population. Where the

TABLE 5.3

Sample #1, Selected from the Population in Table 5.2

Student Number	Sex	School	IQ
52	M	Beals	110
63	F	Beals	83
82	F	Cortez	105
75	M	Cortez	113
92	F	Cortez	98
36	F	Beals	129
03	F	Adams	130
11	F	Adams	117
43	M	Beals	117
08	M	Adams	120

TABLE 5.4

Statistics of Sample #1 Compared to Population Parameters (from Table 5.2)

| | Sex | | School | | | Average |
	Males	Females	A	B	C	IQ
Population	.50	.50	.33	.30	.37	109.5
Sample	.40	.60	.30	.40	.30	112.2

population is evenly divided between males and females, our sample has a proportion of .40 males (40 percent) to .60 females (60 percent). In our sample, only .30 students (30 percent) attend Cortez, as compared to .37 (37 percent) of the population. The average IQ of our sample, 112.2, is 2.7 points above the average IQ of the population.

Let us select another sample and see how it compares, both to the first sample we selected and to the population as a whole. Once again, we use the table of random numbers in Appendix A. This time, we select these numbers: 72, 64, 94, 49, 41, 20, 05, 93, 14, and 99, and record the data for each number, as shown in Table 5.5.

TABLE 5.5

Sample #2, Selected from the Population in Table 5.2

Student Number	Sex	School	IQ
72	F	Cortez	121
64	F	Cortez	137
94	F	Cortez	96
49	M	Beals	111
41	M	Beals	125
20	F	Adams	104
05	F	Adams	123
93	M	Cortez	97
14	M	Adams	111
99	M	Cortez	83

In Table 5.6 these data are compared with the data from sample #1 and from the population. This sample differs considerably from both sample #1 and the population.

What happens if we combine the statistics of samples 1 and 2? Not only is the sample size increased from 10 to 20, but the sample statistics change, as shown in Table 5.7. The statistics of the enlarged sample are more similar to the parameters of the population.

TABLE 5.6

Statistics of Samples #1 and #2 Compared to Population Parameters (from Table 5.2)

| | Sex | | School | | | Average |
	Males	Females	A	B	C	IQ
Population	.50	.50	.33	.30	.37	109.5
Sample #1	.40	.60	.30	.40	.30	112.2
Sample #2	.50	.50	.30	.20	.50	110.8

TABLE 5.7

Combined Sample Statistics Compared to Population Parameters (from Table 5.2)

| | Sex | | School | | | Average |
	Males	Females	A	B	C	IQ
Population	.50	.50	.33	.30	.37	109.5
Both samples	.45	.55	.30	.30	.40	111.5

Let us see what happens if we draw two more samples, again using the table of random numbers in Appendix A. This time our samples are composed of the numbers shown in Table 5.8. Now let us combine the statistics of all four samples. The sample size is now increased to 40, and the sample statistics change, as shown in Table 5.9. This time the average IQ of our combined sample is almost identical to the average IQ of the population. The lesson of the above, we hope, is clear. The larger the sample, the more likely it is to represent the population from which it comes, provided it is randomly selected.

There are a few guidelines that we would suggest with regard to the *minimum* number of subjects needed. For descriptive studies, we think a sample with a minimum number of 100 is essential. For correlational studies, a sample of at least 50 is deemed necessary to establish the existence of a relationship. For experimental and causal-comparative studies, we recommend a minimum of 30 individuals per group, although sometimes experimental studies with only 15 individuals in each group can be defended if they are very tightly controlled; studies using only 15 subjects per group should probably be replicated, however, before too much is made of any findings that occur.

TABLE 5.8

Samples #3 and #4, Selected from the Population in Table 5.2

	Student Number	Sex	School	IQ
#3	83	F	Cortez	104
	37	F	Beals	128
	69	F	Cortez	125
	22	F	Adams	101
	06	M	Adams	123
	36	F	Beals	129
	32	F	Adams	88
	48	M	Beals	113
	14	M	Adams	111
	23	F	Adams	101
#4	56	M	Beals	106
	25	M	Adams	100
	24	M	Adams	101
	11	F	Adams	117
	59	M	Beals	98
	54	M	Beals	108
	84	F	Cortez	103
	31	F	Adams	89
	92	F	Cortez	98
	71	M	Cortez	122

TABLE 5.9

Combined Statistics for all Four Samples Compared to Population Parameters

	Sex		School			Average IQ
	Males	*Females*	*A*	*B*	*C*	
Population	.50	.50	.33	.30	.37	109.5
All four samples	.45	.55	.37	.30	.32	109.6

External Validity: Generalizing from a Sample

As indicated earlier in this chapter, researchers generalize when they apply the findings of a particular study to people or settings that go beyond the particular people or settings used in the study. The whole notion of science is built on the idea of generalizing. Every science seeks to find basic principles or laws that can be applied to a great variety of situations and, in the case of the social sciences, to a great many people. Most researchers wish to generalize their findings to appropriate populations. But when is generalizing warranted? When can researchers say with confidence that what they have learned about a sample is also true of the population? Both the nature of the sample and the environmental conditions—the setting—within which a study takes place must be considered in thinking about generalizability. The extent to which the results of a study can be generalized determines the **external validity** of the study.

POPULATION GENERALIZABILITY

Population generalizability refers to the degree to which a sample represents the population of interest. If the results of a study only apply to the group being studied, and if that group is fairly small or is narrowly defined, the usefulness of any findings is seriously limited. This is why trying to obtain a representative sample is so important. Since the conduct of a study takes a considerable amount of time, energy, and (frequently) money, researchers usually want the results of an investigation to be as widely applicable as possible.

When we speak of representativeness, however, we are referring only to the essential, or *relevant*, characteristics of a population. What do we mean by relevant? Only that the characteristics referred to might possibly be a contributing factor to any results that are attained. For example, if a researcher wished to select a sample of first and second graders to study the effect of reading method on pupil achievement, such

characteristics as height, eye color, or jumping ability would be judged to be irrelevant—that is, we would not expect any variation in them to have an effect on how easily a child learns to read, and hence we would not be overly concerned if those characteristics were not adequately represented in the sample. Other characteristics, such as age, gender, or visual acuity, on the other hand, might (logically) have an effect, and hence should be appropriately represented in the sample.

One aspect of population generalizability that is often overlooked in "methods" or "treatment" studies is that which pertains to the teachers, counselors, administrators, or others who administer the various treatments. We must remember that such studies involve not only a sample of students, clients, or other recipients of the treatments but also a sample of those who implement the various treatments. Thus a study that randomly selects students but not teachers is only entitled to generalize the outcomes to the population of students—*if* taught by the same teachers. To generalize to other teachers, the sample of teachers must also be selected randomly and must be sufficiently large.

Finally, we must remember that the sample in any study is the group about whom data are actually obtained. The best sampling plan is of no value if information is missing on a sizeable portion of the initial sample. Once the sample has been selected, every effort must be made to ensure that the necessary data are obtained on each person in the sample. This is often difficult to do, particularly with questionnaire-type survey studies, but the results are well worth the time and energy expended. Unfortunately, there are no clear guidelines as to how many subjects can be lost before representativeness is seriously impaired. Any researchers who lose over 10 percent of the originally selected sample would be well-advised to acknowledge this limitation and qualify their conclusions accordingly.

Do researchers always want to generalize? The only time researchers are not interested in generalizing beyond the confines of a particular study is when the results of an investigation are of interest only as applied to a particular group of people at a particular time, and where all of the members of the group are included in the study. An example might be the opinions of an elementary school faculty on a specific issue such as whether or not to implement a new math program. This might be of value for decision making or program planning to that faculty, but not to anyone else.

WHEN RANDOM SAMPLING IS NOT FEASIBLE

As we have shown, sometimes it is not feasible or even possible to obtain a random sample. When this is the case, researchers should describe the sample as thoroughly as possible (using, for example, age, gender, ethnicity, socioeconomic status, and so on) so that interested others can judge for themselves the degree to which any findings apply, and to whom and where. This is clearly an inferior procedure compared to random sampling, but sometimes it is the only alternative one has.

There is another possibility when a random sample is impossible to obtain: It is called **replication.** The researcher (or other researchers) repeats the study using different groups of subjects and in different situations. If a study is repeated several times, using different groups of subjects and under different conditions of geography, socioeconomic level, ability, and so on, and if the results obtained are essentially the same in each case, a researcher may have additional confidence about generalizing the findings.

In the vast majority of studies that have been done in education, random samples have not been used. There seem to be two reasons for this. First, there may be insufficient awareness on the part of educational researchers of the hazards involved in generalizing when one does not have a random sample. Second, in many studies it is simply not feasible for a researcher to invest the time, money, or other resources necessary to obtain a random sample. For the results of a particular study to be applicable to a larger group, then, the researcher must argue convincingly that the sample employed, even though not chosen randomly, is in fact representative of the target population. This is diffi-cult, however, and always subject to contrary arguments.

ECOLOGICAL GENERALIZABILITY

Ecological generalizability refers to the degree to which results of a study can be extended to other settings. Researchers must also make clear the nature of the environmental conditions—the setting—under which a study takes place. These conditions must be the same in all important respects in any new situation in which researchers wish to assert that their findings apply. For example, it is not justifiable to generalize from studies on the effects of a new reading program on third graders in a large urban school system to teaching mathematics, even to those students in that system. Research results from urban school environments may not apply to suburban or rural school environments; results obtained with transparencies may not apply to textbooks. What holds true for one subject, or with certain materials, or under certain conditions, or at certain times may not generalize to other subjects, materials, conditions, or times.

An example of inappropriate ecological generalizing occurred in a study which found that a particular method of instruction applied to map reading resulted in greater transfer to general map interpretation on the part of fifth graders in several schools. The researcher accordingly recommended that the method of instruction be used in other content areas, such as mathematics and science, overlooking differences in content, materials, and skills involved, in addition to probable differences in resources, teacher experience, and the like. Improper ecological generalizing such as this remains the bane of much educational research.

Unfortunately, application of the powerful technique of random sampling is virtually never possible with respect to ecological generalizing. While it is conceivable that a researcher could identify "populations" of organization patterns, materials, classroom conditions, and so on and then randomly select a sizeable number of combinations from all possible combinations, the logistics of doing so quickly boggle the mind. Therefore researchers must be cautious about generalizing the results from any one study. Only when outcomes have been shown to be similar through replication across specific environmental conditions can we generalize across those conditions.

Main Points of Chapter Five

- The term "sampling," as used in research, refers to the process of selecting the individuals who will participate (be observed or questioned) in a research study.
- A sample is any group of individuals on when information is obtained.
- The term "population," as used in research, refers to all the members of a particular group. It is the group of interest to the researcher, the group to whom the researcher would like to generalize the results of a study.
- A target population is the actual population to whom the researcher would like to generalize; the accessible population is the population to whom the researcher is entitled to generalize.
- A representative sample is a sample that is similar to the population on all characteristics.
- Sampling may be either random or nonrandom. Random sampling methods include simple random sampling, stratified random sampling, and cluster random sampling. Nonrandom sampling methods include systematic sampling, convenience sampling, and purposive sampling.
- A simple random sample is a sample selected from a population in such a manner that all members of the population have an equal chance of being selected.
- A stratified random sample is a sample selected so that certain characteristics are represented in the sample in the same proportion as they are in the population.
- A cluster random sample is a sample composed of groups rather than individuals.
- A two-stage random sample selects groups randomly and then individuals randomly from these groups.
- A table of random numbers is a table of numbers, listed and arranged in no particular order, that is used to select a random sample.
- A systematic sample is a sample obtained by selecting every nth name in a population.
- A convenience sample is any group of individuals that is conveniently available to be studied.
- A purposive sample is a sample selected because the individuals have special qualifications of some sort.
- Samples should be as large as a researcher can obtain with a reasonable expenditure of time and energy. A recommended minimum number of subjects is 100 for a descriptive study, 50 for a correlational study, and 30 in each group for experimental and causal-comparative studies.
- The term "external validity," as used in research, refers to the extent that the results of a study can be generalized from a sample to a population.
- The term "population generalizability" refers to the extent to which the results of a study can be generalized to a given population of people.

- The term "ecological generalizability" refers to the extent to which the results of a study can be generalized to conditions or settings other than those that prevailed in a particular study.
- When a study is replicated, it is repeated with a new sample and sometimes under new conditions.

For Discussion

1. Listed below are three examples of sampling. One involves simple random sampling, one stratified sampling, and one cluster sampling. Which example involves which method?
   a. Forty pennies are randomly selected from a large jar in which there is to be found $4.00 in pennies.
   b. A random sample of ten airports is surveyed by sending trained interviewers to solicit reactions about air safety from passengers disembarking from arriving airplanes.
   c. A community is found in which the total population consists of individuals with the following religious affiliations: Catholic, 25 percent; Protestant, 50 percent; Jewish, 15 percent; nonaffiliated, 10 percent. The researcher selects a random sample of 100 individuals, made up of 25 Catholics, 50 Protestants, 15 Jews, and 10 nonaffiliated.

2. A team of researchers wants to determine the attitudes of students about the recreational services available in the student union on campus. The team stops the first 100 students they meet on a street in the middle of the campus and asks questions about the union to each of these students. What are some possible ways that this sample might be biased?

3. In 1936, the *Literary Digest*, a popular magazine of the time, selected a sample of voters in the United States and asked the individuals in the sample for whom they would vote in the upcoming election for President— Alf Landon (Republican) or Franklin Roosevelt (Democrat). The magazine editors selected a sample of 2,375,000 individuals from lists of automobile and telephone owners in the United States. On the basis of their findings, the editors predicted that Landon would win by a landslide. In fact, it was Roosevelt who won the landslide victory. What was wrong with the study?

4. Suppose a researcher is interested in studying the effects of music on learning. She obtains permission from a nearby elementary school principal to use the two third grade classes in the school. The ability level of the two classes, as shown by standardized tests, grade point averages, and faculty opinion, is quite similar. In one class, the researcher plays classical music softly every day for a semester. In the other class, no music is played. At the end of the semester, she finds that the class in which the music was played has a markedly higher average in arithmetic than the other class, although they do not differ in any other respect. To what population (if any) might the results of this study be generalized? What, exactly, could the researcher say about the effects of music on learning?

5. When, if ever, might a researcher *not* be interested in generalizing the results of a study? Explain.

6. "The larger a sample, the more justified a researcher is in generalizing from it to a population." Is this statement true? Why or why not?

7. Some people have argued that no population can *ever* be studied in its entirety. Would you agree? Why or why not?

Research Exercise Five:
Sampling Plan

Use Problem Sheet 5 to describe, as fully as you can, your sample—that is, the subjects you will include in your study. Describe the type of sample you plan to use and how you will obtain the sample. Indicate whether or not you expect your study to have population validity: if so, to what population; if not, why it would not. Then indicate whether the study would have ecological validity: if so, to what settings; if not, why it would not.

1. My intended sample (subjects who would participate in my study) consists of (tell who and how many): _____
_____

2. Demographics (characteristics of the sample) are as follows:

    a. age range _____

    b. sex distribution _____

    c. ethnic breakdown _____

    d. location (where are these subjects?) _____

    e. other (describe) characteristics not mentioned above that you deem important (use back if you need more space) _____
    _____
    _____

3. Type of sample: random _____ stratified _____ cluster _____ convenience _____ other (describe)
_____
_____

4. I will obtain my sample by: _____
_____

5. External validity: (I will generalize to the following population):

    a. to what accessible population? _____

    b. to what target population? _____

    c. if not generalizable, why not? _____

6. Ecological validity: (I will generalize to the following settings/conditions):

    a. generalizable to what setting(s)? _____

    b. generalizable to what condition(s)? _____

    c. if not generalizable, why not? _____

87

Chapter Six

INSTRUMENTATION

The collection of data is an extremely important part of all research endeavors, for the conclusions of a study are based on what the data reveal. As a result, the kind(s) of data to be collected, the method(s) of collection to be used, and the scoring of the data need to be considered with care. In this chapter, we define what is meant by "data" and present several types of instruments that can be used to collect data in a research study. We also briefly discuss how to prepare the data for subsequent analysis, and, finally, the different properties that scores are assumed to possess.

Objectives

Reading this chapter should enable you to:

- *Explain* what is meant by the term "data"
- *Explain* what is meant by the term "instrumentation"
- *Name* three ways in which data can be collected by researchers
- *Explain* what is meant by the term "data-collection instrument"
- *Describe* five types of researcher-administered instruments used in educational research
- *Describe* five types of subject-administered instruments used in educational research
- *Explain* what is meant by the term "unobtrusive measures" and *give two examples* of such measures
- *Name* four types of measurement scales and *give an example* of each
- *Name* three different types of scores used in educational research and *give an example* of each
- *Describe* briefly the difference between norm-referenced and criterion-referenced instruments
- *Describe* briefly how to score, tabulate, and code data for analysis

---

What Are Data?

The term **data** refers to the kinds of information researchers obtain on the subjects of their research. Demographic information, such as age, gender, ethnicity, religion, and so on, is one kind of data; scores from a commercially available or researcher-prepared test are another. Responses to the researcher's questions in an oral interview or written replies to a survey questionnaire are other kinds. Essays written by students, grade-point averages obtained from school records, performance logs kept by coaches, anecdotal records maintained by teachers or counselors—all constitute various kinds of data that researchers might want to collect as part of a research investigation. An important decision for every researcher to make during the planning phase of an investigation, therefore, is what kind(s) of data he or she intends to collect. The

device (such as a pencil-and-paper test, a questionnaire, a rating scale, and so on) the researcher uses to collect data is called an **instrument.***

KEY QUESTIONS

The whole process of collecting data is called **instrumentation.** It involves not only the selection or design of the instruments but also the *conditions* under which the instruments will be administered. Several questions arise.

1. *Where* will the data be collected? This question refers to the *location* of the data collection. Where will it be?—in a classroom? a schoolyard? a private home? on the street?

---

* Most, but not all, research requires use of an instrument. In studies where data are obtained exclusively from existing records (grades, attendance, etc.) no instrument is needed.

2. *When* will it be collected? This question refers to the *time* of collection. When is it to take place?—in the morning? afternoon? evening? over a weekend?
3. *How often* are the data to be collected? This question refers to the *frequency* of collection. How many times are the data to be collected?—only once? twice? more than twice?
4. *Who* is to collect the data? This question refers to the *administration* of the instruments. Who is to do this?—the researcher? someone selected and trained by the researcher?

These questions are important because how researchers answer them may affect the data obtained. It is a mistake to think that researchers need only locate or develop a "good" instrument. The data provided by any instrument may be affected by any or all of the preceding considerations. The most highly regarded of instruments will provide useless data, for instance, if administered incorrectly, by someone disliked by respondents, under noisy, inhospitable conditions, or when subjects are exhausted.

All the above questions are important for researchers to answer, therefore, *before* they begin to collect the data they need. A researcher's decisions about location, time, frequency, and administration are always affected by the kind(s) of instrument to be used. And every instrument, no matter what kind, if it is to be of any value, must allow researchers to draw accurate conclusions about the capabilities or other characteristics of the people being studied.

VALIDITY, RELIABILITY, AND OBJECTIVITY

A frequently used (but somewhat old-fashioned) definition of a valid instrument is that it measures what it is supposed to measure. A more accurate definition of **validity** revolves around the defensibility of the inferences researchers make from the data collected through the use of an instrument. An instrument, after all, is a device used to gather data. Researchers then use these data to make inferences about the charac-

teristics of certain individuals.* But to be of any use, these inferences must be correct. All researchers, therefore, want instruments that permit them to draw warranted, or valid, conclusions about the characteristics (ability, achievement, attitudes, and so on) of the individuals they study.

To measure math achievement, for example, a researcher needs to have some assurance that the instrument she intends to use actually does measure such achievement. Another researcher, who wants to know what people think or how they feel about a particular topic, needs assurance that the instrument used will allow him to make accurate inferences. There are various ways to obtain such assurance, and we discuss them in Chapter Seven.

A second consideration is **reliability:** A reliable instrument is one that gives consistent results. If a researcher tested the math achievement of a group of individuals at two or more different times, for example, she should obtain pretty close to the same results each time. This consistency of results would give the researcher confidence that the results accurately represented the achievement of the individuals involved. As with validity, there are a number of procedures that can be used to determine the reliability of an instrument. We discuss several of them in Chapter Seven.

A final consideration is objectivity: **Objectivity** refers to the absence of subjective judgments. Whenever possible, researchers should try to eliminate subjectivity from the judgments they make about the achievement, performance, or characteristics of subjects. Unfortunately, objectivity is probably never attained completely.

We discuss each of these concepts in much more detail in Chapter Seven; in this chapter we look at some of the various kinds of instruments that can be (and often are) used in research and discuss how to find or select them.

---

* Sometimes instruments are used to collect data on other than individuals (such as groups, programs, and environments), but since most of the time we are concerned with individuals in educational research, we use this terminology throughout our discussion.

USABILITY

There are a number of practical considerations every researcher needs to think about. One of these is how easy it will be to use any instrument he or she designs or selects. How long will it take to administer? Are the directions clear? Is it appropriate for the ethnic or other groups to whom it will be administered? How easy is it to score? to interpret the results? How much does it cost? Do equivalent forms exist? Have any problems been reported by others who used it? Does evidence of its reliability and validity exist? And so forth. Getting satisfactory answers to such questions can save a researcher a lot of time and energy and can prevent a lot of headaches.

Means of Classifying Data Collection Instruments

Instruments can be classifed in a number of ways. Here are some of the most useful.

WHO PROVIDES THE INFORMATION?

In educational research there are three general methods available to the researchers for obtaining information. They can get it (a) themselves, with little or no involvement of other people; (b) directly from the subjects of the study; or (c) from others, frequently referred to as *informants,* who are knowledgeable about the subjects. Let us follow a specific example: A researcher wishes to test the hypothesis that inquiry teaching in history classes results in higher level thinking than when such classes are taught by the lecture method. The researcher may elect option (a), in which case she may observe students in the classroom, noting the frequency of study statements indicative of higher level thinking. Or, she may examine existing student records that may include test results and/or anecdotal material she considers indicative of higher level thinking. If she elects option (b),

the researcher is likely to administer tests or request student products (essays, problem sheets) for evidence. She may also decide to interview students using questions designed to get at their thinking about history (or other topics). Finally, if the researcher chooses option (c), she is likely to interview persons (teachers, other students) or ask them to fill out rating scales in which the interviewees assess each student's thinking skills based on their prior experience with the student. Here are examples of each type of method.

1. *Researcher instruments:*
   - A researcher interested in learning and memory development counts the number of times it takes different nursery school children to learn to navigate their way correctly through a maze located in a corner of their school playground. He records his findings on a *tally sheet*.
   - A researcher interested in the concept of "mutual attraction" describes in ongoing *field notes* how the behaviors of people who work together in various settings have been observed to differ.
2. *Subject instruments:*
   - A researcher in an elementary school administers a *weekly spelling test* that requires students to spell correctly the new words learned in class during the week.
   - At a researcher's request, an administrator passes out a *questionnaire* during a faculty meeting which asks the faculty's opinions about the new mathematics curriculum recently instituted in the district.
   - High school English teachers are asked by a researcher to ask their students to keep a *daily log* in which they record their reactions to the plays they read each week.
3. *Informant instruments:*
   - Teachers are asked by a researcher to use a *rating scale* to rate each of their students on their phonic reading skills.
   - Parents are asked by a researcher to keep *anecdotal records* describing the TV characters spontaneously role-played by their preschoolers.

• The president of the student council is interviewed regarding student views on the school's disciplinary code. Her responses are recorded on an *interview schedule*.

WHERE DID THE INSTRUMENT COME FROM?

There are essentially two basic ways for a researcher to acquire an instrument: (a) find and administer a previously existing instrument of some sort, or (b) administer an instrument the researcher has personally developed.

Development of an instrument by the researcher has its problems. Primarily, it is not easy to do. Development of a "good" instrument usually takes a fair amount of time and effort, not to mention a considerable amount of skill.

Selection of an already developed instrument whenever possible, therefore, is preferred. Such instruments are usually developed by experts who possess the necessary skills. There are literally hundreds of such instruments available (some places where such instruments can be found are listed below). Selection of an instrument that has already been developed takes far less time than it does to develop an instrument to measure the same thing. We recommend, therefore, that a strong effort be made to find out if a suitable instrument is already available before trying to develop an instrument of one's own.

Sources for Locating Instruments

Conoley, J. C. & Kramer, J. J. (1989). *The tenth mental measurement yearbook*. Lincoln, Neb.: Buros Institute of Mental Measurements of the University of Nebraska.

Critical reviews of many tests and inventories. Updated periodically.

Mitchell, J. V. (1983). *Tests in print*. Lincoln, Neb.: Buros Institute of Mental Measurements of the University of Nebraska.

Excellent for first attempt at locating an instrument. Updated yearly.

Robinson, S., & Shaver, P. (1976). *Measures of social/psychological attitudes*. Ann Arbor: Institute for Social Research, University of Michigan.

Good for areas indicated.

Simon, A., & Boyer, E. (Eds.) (1970). *Mirrors for behavior*. Philadelphia: Research for Better Schools.

Comprehensive review of many observation instruments.

Sweetland, R. C., & Keyser, D. J. (1986). *Tests*. Kansas City: Test Corporation of America.

Many tests described; readable format.

PAPER AND PENCIL VERSUS PERFORMANCE

Another way to classify instruments is in terms of whether they require a written or marked response or a more general evaluation of performance on the part of the subjects of the study. *Written response–type instruments* include objective (e.g., multiple-choice, true-false, matching, or short answer) tests, short essay examinations, questionnaires, interview schedules, rating scales, and checklists. *Performance-type instruments* include any device designed to measure either a procedure or a product. *Procedures* are ways of doing things, such as mixing a chemical solution, diagnosing a problem in an automobile, writing a letter, solving a puzzle, or setting the margins on a typewriter. *Products* are the end results of procedures, such as the correct chemical solution, the correct diagnosis of auto malfunction, or a properly typed letter. Performance-type instruments are designed to see whether and how well procedures can be followed and to assess the quality of products.

Written-response–type instruments are generally preferred over performance-type instruments, since the use of the latter is frequently quite time-consuming and often requires equipment or other resources that are not readily available. A fairly long period of time would have to be provided to have even a fairly small sample of students (imagine 35!) complete the steps involved in a high school science experiment.

Examples of Data-Collection Instruments

When it comes to *administering* the instruments to be used in a study, either the researchers (or their assistants or other informants) must do it themselves or they must ask the subjects of the study to provide the information desired. Therefore, we group the instruments in the following discussion according to whether or not they are completed by researchers or by subjects. Examples of these instruments include the following:

Who Fills Out the Instrument(s)?

Researcher Completes	Subject Completes
Rating scales	Questionnaires
Interview schedules	Self-checklists
Tally sheets	Attitude scales
Flow charts	Personality (or character) inventories
Performance checklists	Achievement/Aptitude tests
Anecdotal records	Performance tests
Time and motion logs	Projective devices
	Sociometric devices

This distinction, of course, is by no means absolute. Many of the instruments we list might, on a given occasion, be completed by either the researcher(s) or subjects in a particular study.

RESEARCHER-COMPLETED INSTRUMENTS

Rating Scales. A rating is a measured judgment of some sort. When we rate people, we make a jugdment about their behavior or something they have produced. Thus both the behaviors (such as how well a person gives an oral report) and products (such as the actual report itself) of individuals can be rated.

Notice that the terms "observations" and "ratings" are not synonymous. A rating is intended to convey the rater's judgment about an individual's behavior or product. An observation is intended merely to indicate whether a particular behavior is present or absent (see the time and motion log in Figure 6.4). Sometimes, of course, researchers may do both. The activities of a small group engaging in a discussion, for example, can be both observed and rated.

BEHAVIOR RATING SCALES. Behavior rating scales appear in several forms, but those most commonly used ask the observer to circle or mark a point on a continuum to indicate the rating. The simplest of these to construct is a *numerical rating scale:* It provides a series of numbers, with each number representing a particular rating.

Figure 6.1 presents an example of such a scale designed to rate teachers. The problem with this rating scale is that different observers are quite likely to have different ideas about the meaning of the terms that the numbers represent ("excellent," "average," etc.). In other words, the different rating points on the scale are not fully enough described. The same individual,

FIGURE 6.1

Excerpt from a Behavior Rating Scale for Teachers

Instructions: For each of the behaviors listed below, circle the appropriate number, using the following key: 5 = Excellent, 4 = Above Average, 3 = Average, 2 = Below Average, 1 = Poor.

A. Explains course material clearly

    1   2   3   4   5

B. Establishes rapport with students

    1   2   3   4   5

C. Asks high-level questions

    1   2   3   4   5

D. Varies class activities

    1   2   3   4   5

therefore, might be rated quite differently by two different observers. One way to address this problem is to give additional meaning to each number by describing it more fully. For example, in Figure 6.1, the number "5" could be defined as "as among the top five percent of all teachers you have had." In the absence of such definitions, the researcher must either rely on training of respondents or treat the ratings as subjective opinions.

The *graphic rating scale* is an attempt to improve on the vagueness of numerical rating scales. A graphic rating scale describes each of the characteristics to be rated and places them on a horizontal line on which the observer is to place a check. Figure 6.2 presents an example of a graphic rating scale. Here again, this scale would be improved by adding definitions, such as, for example, defining "always" as "95–100 percent of the time," "frequently" as "70–94 percent of the time," and so on.

PRODUCT RATING SCALES.   As we mentioned earlier, researchers may wish to rate products. Examples of products that are frequently rated in education include book reports, maps and charts, diagrams, drawings, notebooks, essays, and creative endeavors of all sorts. Whereas the rating of behaviors must be done at a particular time (when the researcher can observe the behavior), a big advantage of product ratings is that they can be done at any time.* Figure 6.3 presents an example of a scale rating the product "handwriting." To use this scale, an actual sample of the student's handwriting is obtained. It is then moved along the scale until the quality of the handwriting in the sample is most similar to the example shown on the scale.

Interview Schedules.   Interview schedules and questionnaires are basically the same kind of instrument—a set of questions to be answered by the subjects of the study. There are some important differences in how they are administered, however. Interviews are conducted orally, and the answers to the questions are recorded by the researcher (or someone he or she has trained). The advantages of this are that the interviewer can clarify any questions that are obscure and also ask the respondent to expand on answers that are particularly important or revealing. A big disadvantage, on the other hand, is that it takes much longer than the questionnaire to complete. Furthermore, the presence of the researcher may inhibit respondents so that they do not say what they really think.

Figure 6.4 presents an example of a structured interview schedule. Notice in this interview schedule that the interviewers have to do considerable writing, unless the interview is taped. Some interview schedules phrase questions so that the responses are likely to fall in certain categories. This enables the interviewer to check appropriate items rather than transcribe responses. This is sometimes called *pre-coding*. It prevents the respondent from having to wait while the interviewer records a response.

Tally Sheets.   A tally sheet is a device often used by researchers to record the frequency of student behaviors, activities, or remarks. How many high school students follow instructions

FIGURE 6.2

Excerpt from a Graphic Rating Scale

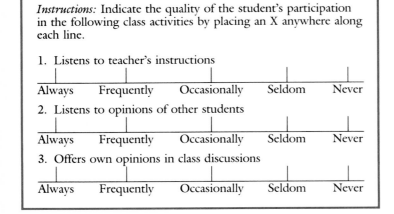

Instructions: Indicate the quality of the student's participation in the following class activities by placing an X anywhere along each line.

1. Listens to teacher's instructions

| Always | Frequently | Occasionally | Seldom | Never |

2. Listens to opinions of other students

| Always | Frequently | Occasionally | Seldom | Never |

3. Offers own opinions in class discussions

| Always | Frequently | Occasionally | Seldom | Never |

---

* Some behavior rating scales are designed to assess behavior over a period of time; for example, how frequently a teacher asks high-level thought questions.

FIGURE 6.3

Example from a Product Rating Scale

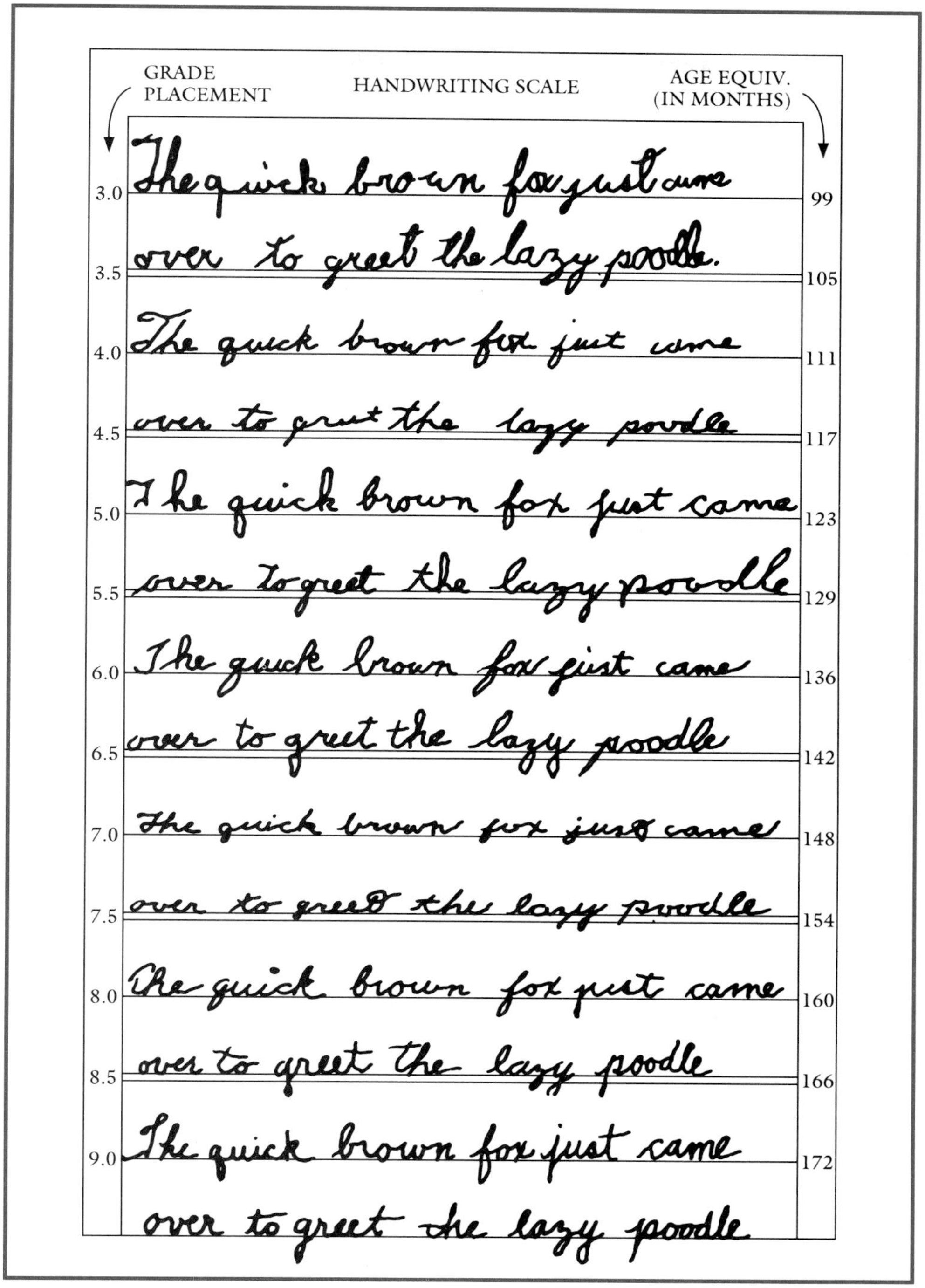

	HANDWRITING SCALE	
GRADE PLACEMENT		AGE EQUIV. (IN MONTHS)

The quick brown fox just came over to greet the lazy poodle.

3.0 — 99
3.5 — 105
4.0 — 111
4.5 — 117
5.0 — 123
5.5 — 129
6.0 — 136
6.5 — 142
7.0 — 148
7.5 — 154
8.0 — 160
8.5 — 166
9.0 — 172

Source: Handwriting scale used in the California Achievement Tests, Form W. (1957). TB/McGraw-Hill, Del Monte Research Park, Monterey, CA 93940. Copyright 1957 by McGraw-Hill.

FIGURE **6.4**

Interview Schedule (for Teachers) Designed to Assess the Effects of a Competency-Based Curriculum in Inner-City Schools

1. Would you rate *pupil academic learning* as excellent, good, fair or poor?
   a. If you were here last year, how would you compare *pupil academic learning* to previous years?
   b. Please give specific examples.

2. Would you rate *pupil attitude toward school generally* as excellent, good, fair or poor?
   a. If you were here last year, how would you compare *pupil attitude toward school generally* to previous years?
   b. Please give specific examples.

3. Would you rate *pupil attitude toward learning* as excellent, good, fair or poor?
   a. If you were here last year, how would you compare *attitude toward learning* to previous years?
   b. Please give specific examples.

4. Would you rate *pupil attitude toward self* as excellent, good, fair or poor?
   a. If you were here last year, how would you compare *pupil attitude toward self* to previous years?
   b. Please give specific examples.

5. Would you rate *pupil attitude toward other students* as excellent, good, fair or poor?
   a. If you were here last year, how would you compare *attitude toward other students* to previous years?
   b. Please give specific examples.

6. Would you rate *pupil attitude toward you* as excellent, good, fair or poor?
   a. If you were here last year, how would you compare *pupil attitude toward you* to previous years?
   b. Please give specific examples.

7. Would you rate *pupil creativity-self expression* as excellent, good, fair or poor?
   a. If you were here last year, how would you compare *pupil creativity-self expression* to previous years?
   b. Please give specific examples.

during fire drills, for example? How many instances of aggression or helpfulness are observed for elementary students on the playground? How often do students in Mr. Jordan's fifth period U.S. history class ask questions? How often do they ask inferential questions? Tally sheets can help researchers answer these kinds of questions.

A tally sheet is simply a listing of various categories of activities or behaviors on a piece of paper. Every time a subject is observed engaging in one of these activities or behaviors, the researcher places a tally in the appropriate category. The kinds of statements that students make in class, for example, often indicate the degree to which they understand various concepts and ideas. The possible category systems that might be devised are probably endless, but Figure 6.5 presents one example.

Flow Charts. A particular type of tally sheet is the participation flow chart. Flow charts are particularly helpful in analyzing class discussions. Both the number and direction of student remarks can be charted to gain some idea of the quantity and focus of their verbal participation in class.

One of the easiest ways to do this is to prepare a seating chart on which a box is drawn for each student in the class being observed. A tally mark is then placed in the box of a particular student each time he or she makes a verbal comment. To indicate the direction of individual student comments, arrows can be drawn from the box of a student making a comment to the box of the student to whom the comment is directed. Figure 6.6 on page 98 illustrates what such a flow chart might look like. This chart suggests that Robert, Felix, and Mercedes dominated the discussion, with contributions from Al, Gail, Jack, and Sam. Joe and Nancy said nothing. Note that a subsequent discussion, or a different topic, however, might reveal quite a different pattern.

Performance Checklists. One of the most frequently used of all measuring instruments is the *checklist*. A performance checklist consists of a list of behaviors that make up a certain type of performance (using a microscope, typing a letter, solving a mathematics problem, and so on). It is used to determine whether or not an individual behaves in a certain (usually desired) way when asked to complete a particular task. If a particular behavior is present when an

FIGURE 6.5

Discussion Analysis Tally Sheet

Type of Remark		
1. Asks question calling for factual information	Related to lesson Not related to lesson	JHT I
2. Asks question calling for clarification	Related to lesson Not related to lesson	JHT II
3. Asks question calling for explanation	Related to lesson Not related to lesson	JHT III
4. Asks question calling for speculation	Related to lesson Not related to lesson	I
5. Asks question of another student	Related to lesson Not related to lesson	I II
6. Gives own opinion on issue	Related to lesson Not related to lesson	I III
7. Responds to another student	Related to lesson Not related to lesson	IIII
8. Summarizes remarks of another student	Related to lesson Not related to lesson	
9. Does not respond when addressed by teacher	Related to lesson Not related to lesson	II
10. Does not respond when addressed by another student	Related to lesson Not related to lesson	I

individual is observed, the researcher places a check opposite it on the list.

Figure 6.7 presents part of a performance checklist developed over fifty years ago to assess a student's skill in using a microscope. Note that the items on this checklist (as any well-constructed checklist should) ask the observer to indicate only *if* the desired behaviors take place. No subjective judgments are called for on the part of the observer as to how well the individual performs. Items that call for such judgments are best left to rating scales.

Anecdotal Records. Another way of recording the behavior of individuals is the anecdotal record. It is just what its name implies—a record of observed behaviors written down in the form of anecdotes. There is no set format; rather, observers are free to record any behavior they think is important and need not focus on the same behavior for all subjects. To be most useful, however, observers should try to be as specific and as factual as possible and to avoid evaluative, interpretive, or overly generalized remarks. The American Council on Education describes four types of anecdote, stating that the first three are to be avoided. Only the fourth is the type desired.

1. Anecdotes that evaluate or judge the behavior of the child as good or bad, desirable or undesirable, acceptable or unacceptable . . . *evaluative statements* (to be avoided).
2. Anecdotes that account for or explain the

FIGURE 6.6

Participation Flow Chart

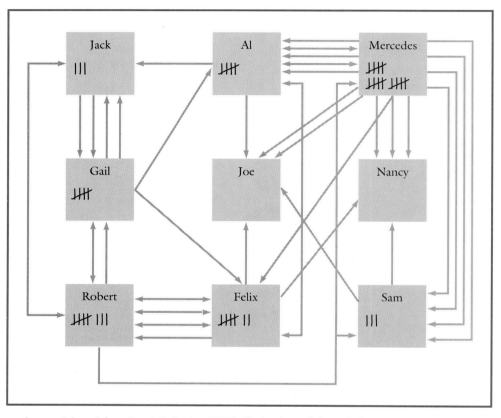

Source: Adapted from Enoch I. Sawin. (1969). *Evaluation and the work of the teacher.* Belmont, CA: Wadsworth, p. 179.

child's behavior, usually on the basis of a single fact or thesis . . . *interpretive statements* (to be avoided).

3. Anecdotes that describe certain behavior in general terms, as happening frequently, or as characterizing the child . . . *generalized statements* (to be avoided).

4. Anecdotes that tell exactly what the child did or said, that describe concretely the situation in which the action or comment occurred, and that tell clearly what other persons also did or said . . . *specific or concrete descriptive statements* (the type desired).[1]

An example of each of the four types is as follows.

Evaluative: Julius talked loud and much during poetry; wanted to do and say just what he wanted and didn't consider the right working out of things. Had to ask him to sit by me. Showed a bad attitude about it.

Interpretive: For the last week Sammy has been a perfect wiggle-tail. He is growing so fast he cannot be settled. . . . Of course the inward change that is taking place causes the restlessness.

Generalized: Sammy is awfully restless these days. He is whispering most of the time he is not kept busy. In the circle, during various discussions, even though he is interested, his arms are moving or he is punching the one sitting next to him. He smiles when I speak to him.

Specific (the type desired): The weather was so bitterly cold that we did not go on the playground today. The children played games in the room during the regular recess period. Andrew and Larry chose sides for a game which is known as stealing the bacon. I was talking to a group of children in the front of the room while the choosing was in process and in a moment I heard a loud altercation.

FIGURE 6.7

Performance Checklist Noting Student's Actions

1. Takes slide	____	31. Turns up coarse adjustment screw a great distance	____
2. Wipes slide with lens paper	____	32. With eye at eyepiece, turns down fine adjustment screw a great distance	____
3. Wipes slide with cloth	____		
4. Wipes slide with finger	____	33. With eye away from eyepiece, turns down fine adjustment screw a great distance	____
5. Moves bottle of culture along the table	____		
6. Places drop or two of culture on slide	____	34. Turns up fine adjustment screw a great distance.	____
7. Adds more culture	____	35. Turns fine adjustment screw a few turns	____
8. Adds few drops of water	____	36. Remove slide from stage	____
9. Hunts for cover glasses	____	37. Wipes objective with lens paper	____
10. Wipes cover glass with lens paper	____	38. Wipes objective with cloth	____
11. Wipes cover glass with cloth	____	39. Wipes objective with finger	____
12. Wipes cover with finger	____	40. Wipes eyepiece with lens paper	____
13. Adjusts cover with finger	____	41. Wipes eyepiece with cloth	____
14. Wipes off surplus fluid	____	42. Wipes eyepiece with finger	____
15. Places slide on stage	____	43. Makes another mount	____
16. Looks thru eyepiece with right eye	____	44. Takes another microscope	____
17. Looks thru eyepiece with left eye	____	45. Finds object	____
18. Turns to objective of lowest power	____	46. Pauses for an interval	____
19. Turns to low-power objective	____	47. Asks, "What do you want me to do?"	____
20. Turns to high-power objective	____	48. Asks whether to use high power	____
21. Holds one eye closed	____	49. Says, "I'm satisfied."	____
22. Looks for light	____	50. Says that the mount is all right for his or her eye	____
23. Adjusts concave mirror	____		
24. Adjusts plane mirror	____	51. Says, "I cannot do it."	____
25. Adjusts diaphragm	____	52. Told to start a new mount	____
26. Does not touch diaphragm	____	53. Directed to find object under low power	____
27. With eye at eyepiece, turns down coarse adjustment screw	____		
28. Breaks cover glass	____	54. Directed to find object under high power	____
29. Breaks slide	____		
30. With eye away from eyepiece, turns down coarse adjustment screw	____		

Source: Adapted from Ralph W. Tyler. (1930). A test of skill in using a microscope. *Educational Research Bulletin, 9 (11)*, 493–496.

Larry said that all the children wanted to be on Andrew's side rather than on his. Andrew remarked, "I can't help it if they all want to be on my side."[2]

Time and Motion Logs.   There are occasions when researchers want to make a very detailed observation of an individual or a group. This is often the case, for example, when trying to identify the reasons underlying a particular problem or difficulty that an individual or class is having (working very slowly, failing to complete assigned tasks, inattentiveness, and so on).

When a detailed observation is desired, a time-and-motion study can be performed. A time-and-motion study is the observation and detailed recording over a given period of time of the activities of one or more individuals (for example, during a fifteen-minute laboratory demonstration). Observers try to record as objectively as possible and at brief regular intervals (such as every three minutes, with a one-minute break interspersed between intervals) everything an individual does.

A colleague once cited an example of a fourth grade teacher who believed that her class's considerable slowness was due to the fact they were extremely meticulous in their work. To check this out, she decided to conduct a detailed time-and-motion study of one typical student. The results of her study indicated that this student, rather than being overly meticulous, actually was unable to focus her attention on a particular task for any concerted period of time. Figure 6.8 illustrates what she observed.

SUBJECT-COMPLETED INSTRUMENTS

Questionnaires.   The interview schedule shown in Figure 6.4 could be used as a questionnaire. In a questionnaire, the subjects respond to the questions by writing, or, more commonly, marking an answer sheet. Advantages of questionnaires are that they can be mailed or given to large numbers of people at the same time. The disadvantages are that unclear or seemingly ambiguous questions cannot be clarified and the respondent has no chance to expand on, or react verbally to, a question of particular interest or importance.

Selection-type items on questionnaires include multiple-choice, true-false, matching, or interpretive-exercise questions. Supply-type items include short-answer or essay questions. We'll give some examples of each of these types of items when we deal with achievement tests later in the chapter.

Self-Checklists.   A self-checklist is a list of several characteristics or activities presented to the individuals who are the subjects of a study. They are asked to study the list and then to place a mark opposite the characteristics they possess or the activities in which they have engaged for a particular length of time. Self-checklists are often used when researchers want students to diagnose or to appraise their own performance. One example of a self-checklist for use with elementary school students is shown in Figure 6.9.

Attitude Scales.   The basic assumption that underlies all attitude scales is that it is possible to discover attitudes by asking individuals to respond to a series of statements of preference. Thus if individuals agree with the statement "A course in philosophy should be required of all candidates for a teaching credential," researchers infer that these students have a positive attitude toward such a course (assuming students understand the meaning of the statement and are sincere in their responses). An attitude scale, therefore, consists of a set of statements to which an individual is asked to respond. The pattern of responses is then viewed as evidence of one or more underlying attitudes.

Attitude scales are identical to rating scales in form, with words and numbers placed on a continuum. Subjects are asked to circle the word or number that best represents how they feel about the topics included in the questions or statements in the scale. A commonly used attitude scale in educational research is the **Likert scale,** named after the man who designed it.[3] Figure 6.10 presents a few examples from a Likert scale. On some items, a 5 (strongly agree) will indicate a positive attitude, and be scored 5. On other items, a 1 (strongly disagree) will indicate a positive attitude and be scored 5 (thus the ends of scale are reversed when scoring), as shown in item 2 in Figure 6.10.

A unique sort of attitude scale that is es-pecially useful for classroom research is *the semantic differential*.[4] It allows a researcher to measure a subject's attitude toward a particular concept. Subjects are presented with a continuum of several pairs of adjectives ("good-bad," "cold-hot," "priceless-worthless," and so on) and asked to place a checkmark between each pair to indicate their attitudes. Figure 6.11 presents an example.

A suggestion that has particular value for

FIGURE 6.8

Time and Motion Log

Time	Activity	Time	Activity
11:32	Stacked paper		Watched L.
	Picked up pencil		Laughed at her
	Wrote name		Erased
	Moved paper closer		Hand up
	Continued with heading		Laughed. Watched D.
	Rubbed nose		Got help
	Looked at Art's paper	11:50	Looked at Lorrie
	Started to work . . .		Tapped fingers on desk
11:45	Worked and watched		Wrote
	Made funny faces		Slid down in desk
	Giggled. Looked at Lorrie and smiled		Hand to head, listened to D. helping Lorrie
	Borrowed Art's paper		Blew breath out hard
	Erased		Fidgeted with paper
	Stacked paper		Looked at other group
	Read		Held chin
	Slid paper around		Watched Charles
	Worked briefly		Read, hands holding head
	Picked up paper and read		Erased
	Thumb in mouth, watched Miss D		Watched other group, chin on hand
11:47	Worked and watched		Made faces—yawned—fidgeted
	Made funny face		Held head
	Giggled. Looked and smiled at Lorrie		Read, pointing to words
	Paper up—read		Wrote
	Picked eye		Put head on arm on desk
	Studied bulletin board		Held chin
	Paper down—read again		Read
	Fidgeted with paper		Rubbed eye
	Played with pencil and fingers	11:55	Wrote
	Watched me		

Source: Hilda Taba, "Problem Identification," in *Research for Curriculum Improvement*, 1957 Yearbook, pp. 60–61. Reprinted with permission of the Association for Supervision and Curriculum Development and Hilda Taba. Copyright © 1957 by the Association for Supervision and Curriculum Development. All rights reserved.

FIGURE 6.9

Example of a Self-Checklist

Date _____   Name _____

Instructions: Place a check (✔) in the space provided for those days, during the past week, when you have participated in the activity listed. Circle the activity if you feel you need to participate in it more frequently in the weeks to come.

	Mon	Tues	Wed	Thurs	Fri
1. I participated in class discussions.	✔	✔	✔		
2. I did not interrupt others while they were speaking.	✔	✔	✔	✔	✔
3. I encouraged others to offer their opinions.		✔			✔
4. I listened to what others had to say.	✔	✔	✔		✔
5. I helped others when asked.				✔	
6. I asked questions when I was unclear about what had been said.		✔		✔	
7. I looked up words in the dictionary that I did not know how to spell.					✔
8. I considered the suggestions of others.	✔	✔	✔		
9. I tried to be helpful in my remarks.	✔	✔		✔	
10. I praised others when I thought they did a good job.					✔

determining the attitudes of young children is to use simply drawn faces. When the subjects of an attitude study are primary-age children or younger, they can be asked to place an X under a face, such as the ones shown in Figure 6.12, to illustrate how they feel about a topic.

The subject of attitude scales is discussed rather extensively in the literature on evaluation and test development, and students interested in a more extended treatment should consult a standard textbook on these subjects.[5]

Personality (or Character) Inventories. Personality inventories are designed to measure certain traits of individuals or to assess their feelings about themselves. Examples of such inventories include the Minnesota Multiphasic Personality Inventory, the IPAT *Anxiety Scale,* the Piers-Harris Children's Self Concept Scale (How I Feel About Myself), and the Kuder Preference Record. Figure 6.13 presents an example of some typical items from this type of test. The specific items, of course, reflect the variable(s) the inventory addresses.

Achievement Tests.   **Achievement,** or ability, **tests** measure an individual's knowledge or skill in a given area or subject. They are mostly

FIGURE 6.10

Examples of Items from a Likert Scale Measuring Attitude toward Teacher Empowerment

Instructions: Circle the choice after each statement that indicates your opinion.

1. All university professors should be required to spend at least six months teaching at the elementary or secondary level every five years.

| Strongly agree (5) | Agree (4) | Undecided (3) | Disagree (2) | Strongly disagree (1) |

2. Teachers unions should be abolished.

| Strongly agree (5) | Agree (4) | Undecided (3) | Disagree (2) | Strongly disagree (1) |

3. All school administrators should be required by law to teach at least one class in a public school classroom every year.

| Strongly agree (5) | Agree (4) | Undecided (3) | Disagree (2) | Strongly disagree (1) |

FIGURE 6.11

Example of the Semantic Differential

Instructions: Listed below are several pairs of adjectives. Place a checkmark (✔) on the line between each pair to indicate how you feel. Example: Hockey:

exciting :____:____:____:____:____:____: dull

If you feel that hockey is very exciting, you would place a check in the first space next to the word "exciting." If you feel that hockey is very dull, you would place a checkmark in the space nearest to the word "dull." If you are sort of undecided, you would place a checkmark in the middle space between the two words. Now rate each of the activities that follow [*only one is listed*]:

Working with other students in small groups

friendly :____:____:____:____:____:____: unfriendly

happy :____:____:____:____:____:____: sad

easy :____:____:____:____:____:____: hard

fun :____:____:____:____:____:____: work

hot :____:____:____:____:____:____: cold

good :____:____:____:____:____:____: bad

laugh :____:____:____:____:____:____: cry

beautiful:____:____:____:____:____:____: ugly

FIGURE **6.12**

*Pictorial Attitude Scale
for Use with Young Children*

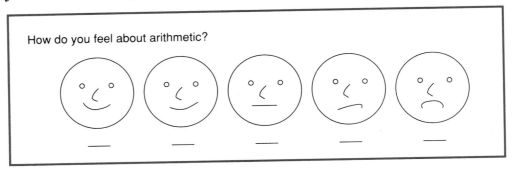

How do you feel about arithmetic?

used in schools to measure learning or the effectiveness of instruction. The California Achievement Test, for example, measures achievement in reading, language, and arithmetic. The Stanford Achievement Test measures a variety of areas, such as language usage, word meaning, spelling, arithmetic computation, social studies, and science. Other commonly used achievement tests include the Comprehensive Tests of Basic Skills, the Iowa Tests of Basic Skills, the Metropolitan Achievement Test, and the Sequential Tests of Educational Progress (STEP). In research that involves comparing instructional methods, achievement is frequently the dependent variable.

Achievement tests can be classified in several ways. General achievement tests are usually batteries of tests (such as the STEP tests) that measure such things as vocabulary, reading ability, language usage, math, and social studies. One of the most common general achievement tests is the Graduate Record Examination, which

FIGURE **6.13**

Sample Items from a Personality Test

		Quite Often	Sometimes	Almost Never
Instructions: Check the option that most correctly describes you.				
SELF-ESTEEM				
1. Do you think your friends are smarter than you?		——	——	——
2. Do you feel good about your appearance?		——	——	——
3. Do you avoid meeting new people?		——	——	——
		Usually	Sometimes	Almost Never
STRESS				
1. Do you have trouble sleeping?		——	——	——
2. Do you feel on top of things?		——	——	——
3. Do you feel you have too much to do?		——	——	——

FIGURE 6.14

Sample Items from an Achievement Test

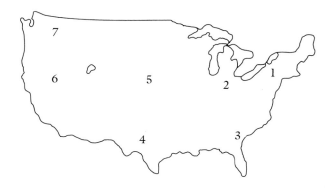

Instructions. Use this map to answer questions 1 and 2. Circle the correct answer.

1. Which number shows an area declining in population?

    A   1
    B   3
    C   5
    D   7

2. Which number shows an area that once belonged to Mexico?

    A   3
    B   5
    C   6
    D   None of the above

students must pass before they can be admitted to most graduate programs. Specific achievement tests, on the other hand, are tests that measure an individual's ability in a specific subject, such as English, world history, or biology. Figure 6.14 presents some examples of the kinds of items found on an achievement test.

Aptitude Tests. Another well-known type of ability test is the so-called general **aptitude** or intelligence **test,** which assesses intellectual abilities that are not in most cases specifically taught in school. Some measure of general ability is frequently used as either an independent or a dependent variable in research. In attempting to assess the effects of different instructional programs, for example, it is often necessary (and very important) to control this variable so that individuals exposed to the different programs are not markedly different in general ability.

Aptitude tests are intended to measure an individual's potential to achieve; in actuality, they measure present skills or abilities. They differ from ability tests in their purpose and often in content, usually including a wider variety of skills or knowledge. The same test may be either an aptitude or an achievement test, depending on the purpose for which it is used. A mathematics achievement test, for example, may also measure aptitude for additional mathematics. Although such tests are used primarily by counselors to help individuals identify areas in which they may have potential, they also can be used in research. In this regard, they are particularly useful for purposes of control. For example, to measure the effectiveness of an instructional program designed to increase problem-solving ability in mathematics, a researcher might decide to control for numerical aptitude and hence use an aptitude test. Figure 6.15 presents an example of the kinds of items found in an aptitude test.

Aptitude tests may be individually administered or group tests. Each method has both advantages and disadvantages. The big advantage of group tests is that they are more convenient to administer and hence save considerable time. Their disadvantages are that they require a great deal of reading, and students who are low in reading ability are thus at a disadvantage. Furthermore, it is difficult to have test instructions clarified or to have any interaction with the examiner (which sometimes can raise scores).

Lastly, the range of possible tasks on which to be examined is much less in a group-administered than in an individually administered test.

The California Test of Mental Maturity (CTMM) and the Otis-Lennon are examples of group tests. The best-known of the individual aptitude tests is the Stanford-Binet Intelligence Scale, although the Wechsler scales are being used more and more frequently. Whereas the Stanford-Binet gives only one IQ score, the Wechsler scales also yield a number of subscores. The two Wechsler scales are the Wechsler Intelligence Scale for Children (the WISC) for ages 5–15 and the Wechsler Adult Intelligence Scale (the WAIS) for older adolescents and adults.

Many intelligence tests provide reliable and valid evidence when used with certain kinds of individuals and for certain purposes (for example, predicting the college grades of middle-class Caucasians). On the other hand, they have increasingly come under attack when used with other persons or for other purposes (such as identifying members of certain minority groups to be placed in special classes). Furthermore, there is increasing recognition that most intelligence tests do not measure many important abilities, including the ability to identify or conceptualize unusual sorts of relationships. As a result, researchers must be especially careful in evaluating any such test before using it and must

FIGURE 6.15

Sample Item from an Aptitude Test

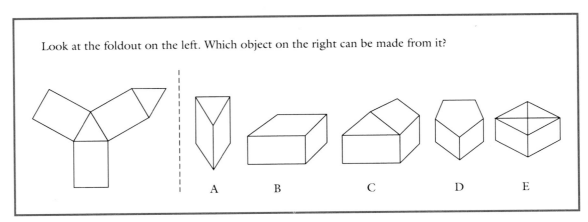

Look at the foldout on the left. Which object on the right can be made from it?

A   B   C   D   E

determine whether it is appropriate for the purpose of the study. (We discuss some ways to do this when we consider validity in Chapter Seven.) A good guide to locating tests is the *Mental Measurements Yearbook*.[6] Figure 6.16 presents examples of the kinds of items in an intelligence test.

Performance Tests. As we have mentioned, a performance test measures an individual's performance on a particular task. An example would be a typing test, in which individual scores are determined by how accurately and how rapidly people type.

As Sawin has suggested, it is not always easy to determine whether a particular instrument should be called a performance test, a performance checklist, or a performance rating scale.[7] A performance test is the most objective of the three. When a considerable amount of judgment is required to determine if the various aspects of a performance were done correctly, the device is likely to be classified as either a checklist or rating scale. Figure 6.17 presents an example of a performance test developed some forty years ago to measure sewing ability. In this test, the individual is requested to sew *on* the line in the A part of the test, and *between* the lines on the B part of the test.[8]

Projective Devices. A projective device is any sort of instrument with a vague stimulus that allows individuals to project their interests, preferences, anxieties, prejudices, needs, and so on through their responses to it. This kind of device has no "right" answers (or any clear-cut answers of any sort), and its format allows an individual to express something of his or her own personality. There is room for a wide variety of possible responses.

Perhaps the best-known example of a projective device is the Rorschach Ink Blot Test, in which individuals are presented with a series of ambiguously shaped ink blots and asked to describe what the blots look like. Another well-known projective test is the Thematic Apperception Test (TAT), in which pictures of events are presented and individuals are asked to make up a story about each picture. One application of

FIGURE 6.16

Sample Items from an Intelligence Test

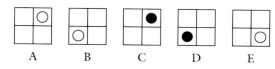

1. How are *frog* and *toy* alike and how are they different?

2. Here is a sequence of pictures.

A   B   C   D   E

Which of the following would come next in the sequence?

(F)   (G)   (H)

FIGURE 6.17

Example from the Blum Sewing Machine Test

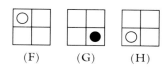

Directions: Sew on the line in part A and between the lines in part B.

NAME _____

A

NAME _____

B

Source: M. L. Blum. (1943). Selection of sewing machine operators. *Journal of Applied Psychology, 27*(2), p. 36.

FIGURE **6.18**

Sample Items from the Picture Situation Inventory

Source: N. T. Rowan. (1967). The relationship of teacher interaction in classroom situations to teacher personality variables. Unpublished doctoral dissertation, p. 68. Salt Lake City: University of Utah.

the projective approach to a classroom setting is the Picture Situation Inventory. This instrument consists of a series of cartoon-like drawings, each portraying a classroom situation in which a child is saying something. Students taking the test are to enter the response of the teacher, thereby presumably indicating something of their own tendencies in the situation. Two of the pictures in this test are reproduced in Figure 6.18.

Sociometric Devices. Sociometric devices ask individuals to rate their peers in some way. Two examples include the sociogram and the "group play." A *sociogram* is a visual representation, usually by means of arrows, of the choices people make about other individuals with whom

they interact. It is frequently used to assess the climate and structure of interpersonal relationships within a classroom, but it is by no means limited to such an environment. Each student is usually represented by a circle (if female) or a triangle (if male) and arrows are then drawn to indicate different student choices with regard to a particular question that has been asked. Students may be asked, for example, to list three students whom they think are leaders of the class; admire the most; find especially helpful; would like to have for a friend; would like to have as a partner in a research project; and so forth. The responses students give are then used to construct the sociogram. Figure 6.19 is an illustration of a sociogram.

FIGURE **6.19**

Example of a Sociogram

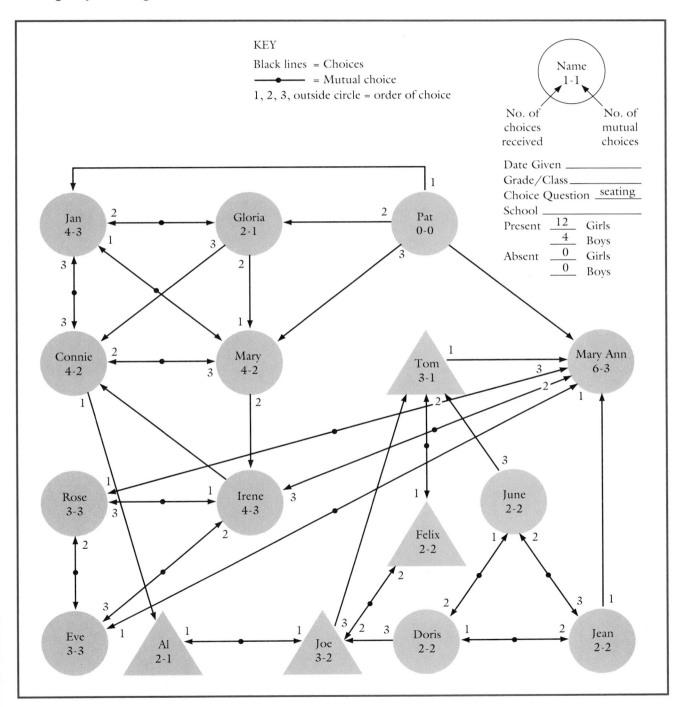

Another version of a sociometric device is the assigning of different individuals, on paper, to various parts in a *group play*. Students can be asked to cast different members of their group in various roles in a play to illustrate their interpersonal relationships. The roles are listed on a piece of paper, and then the members of the group are asked to write in the names of those students they think the role best describes. Almost any type of role can be suggested. The casting choices that individuals make often shed considerable light on how some individuals are viewed by others. Figure 6.20 presents an example of this device.

Item Formats.   Although the types of items or questions used in different instruments can take many forms, they all can be classified as either a selection-type or a supply-type item. A *selection-type* item presents a set of possible responses from which respondents are to select the most appropriate answer. A *supply-type* item, on the other hand, asks respondents to formulate and then supply their own answers. Here are some examples of each type.

SELECTION-TYPE ITEMS
True-False Items.   True-false items present either a true or a false statement, and the respondent has to mark either true (T) or false (F). Frequently used variations of the words "true" and "false" are "yes-no" or "right-wrong," which often are more useful when attempting to question or interview young children. Here is an example of a true-false item.

T   F   I get very nervous whenever I have to speak in public.

Multiple-Choice Items.   Multiple-choice items consist of two parts, the stem, which contains

FIGURE 6.20
Example of a Group Play

Directions: Imagine you are the casting director for a large play. Your job is to choose the individuals who will take the various parts (listed below) in the play. Since some of the parts are rather small, you may select the same individual to play more than one part. Choose individuals you think would be the most *natural* for the part, that is, those who are most like the role in real life.

1. The Parts

Part 1—someone who is well-liked by all members of the group _____

Part 2—someone who is disliked by many people _____

Part 3—someone who always gets angry about things of little consequence _____

Part 4—someone who has wit and a good sense of humor _____

Part 5—someone who is very quiet and rarely says anything _____

Part 6—someone who does not contribute much to the group _____

Part 7—someone who is angry a lot of the time _____

Part 8—etc. _____

2. Your Role

Which part do you think you could play best? _____

Which part would other members of the group ask you to play? _____

the question, and several (usually four) possible choices. Here is an example.

Which of the following expresses your opinion on abortion?
(a) It is immoral and should be prohibited.
(b) It should be discouraged but permitted under unusual circumstances.
(c) It should be available under a wide range of conditions.
(d) It is entirely a matter of individual choice.

Matching Items. Matching items are variations of the multiple-choice format. They consist of two groups or columns—the first, or leftmost, column containing the questions or items to be thought about, and the second, or rightmost column, containing the possible responses to the questions. The respondent is asked to pair the choice from the second column with the question or item in the first column to which it corresponds. Here is an example.

Instructions: For each item, in the left-hand column, select the item in the right-hand column that represents your first reaction. Place the appropriate letter in the blank. Each lettered item may be used more than once or not at all.

Column A	*Column B*
Special classes for the:	
_____ 1. severely retarded	a. should be increased
_____ 2. mildly retarded	b. should be maintained
_____ 3. hard of hearing	c. should be decreased
_____ 4. visually impaired	d. should be eliminated
_____ 5. learning handicapped	
_____ 6. emotionally disturbed	

INTERPRETIVE EXERCISES. One difficulty with using true-false, multiple-choice, and matching items to measure achievement is that these items often do not measure complex learning outcomes. One way to get at more complex learning outcomes is to use what is called an *interpretive exercise*. An interpretive exercise consists of a selection of introductory material (this may be a paragraph, map, diagram, picture, chart, and so on) followed by one or more selection-type items that ask a respondent to interpret this material. Two examples of interpretive exercises follow.

Example 1

Directions: Read the following comments a teacher made about testing. Then answer the question that follows the comments by circling the letter of the best answer.

"Students go to school to learn, not to take tests. In addition, tests cannot be used to indicate a student's absolute level of learning. All tests can do is rank students in order of achievement, and this relative ranking is influenced by guessing, bluffing, and the subjective opinions of the teacher doing the scoring. The teaching-learning process would benefit if we did away with tests and depended on student self-evaluation."

1. Which one of the following unstated assumptions is this teacher making?
   a. Students go to school to learn.
   b. Teachers use essay tests primarily.
   c. Tests make no contribution to learning.
   d. Tests do not indicate a student's absolute level of learning.

Example 2

Directions: Paragraph A contains a description of the testing practices of Mr. Smith, a high school teacher. Read the description and each of the statements that follow it. Mark each statement to indicate the type of *inference* that can be drawn about it from the material in the paragraph. Place the appropriate letter in front of each statement using the following *key:*

T – if the statement may be *inferred* as *true.*

F – if the statement may be *inferred* as *untrue.*

N – if *no inference* may be drawn about it from the paragraph.

Paragraph A

Approximately one week before a test is to be given, Mr. Smith carefully goes through the textbook and constructs multiple-choice items based on the material in the book. He always uses the exact wording of the textbook for the correct answer so that there will be no question concerning its correctness. He is careful to include some test items from each chapter. After the test is given, he lists the scores from high to low on the blackboard and tells each student his or her score. He does not return the test papers to the students, but he offers to answer any questions they might have about the test. He puts the items from each test into a test file, which he is building for future use.

Statements on Paragraph A

(T) 1. Mr. Smith's tests measure a limited range of learning outcomes.
(F) 2. Some of Mr. Smith's test items measure at the understanding level.
(N) 3. Mr. Smith's tests measure a balanced sample of subject matter.
(N) 4. Mr. Smith uses the type of test item that is best for his purpose.
(T) 5. Students can determine where they rank in the distribution of scores on Mr. Smith's tests.
(F) 6. Mr. Smith's testing practices are likely to motivate students to overcome their weaknesses.[9]

SUPPLY-TYPE ITEMS

Short-Answer Items. A short-answer item requires the respondent to supply a word, phrase, number, or symbol that is necessary to complete a statement or answer a question. Here is an example:

Directions: In the space provided, write the word that best completes the sentence.

When the number of items in a test is increased, the *(reliability)* of the scores on the test is likely to increase.

Short-answer items have one major disadvantage: It is usually difficult to write a short-answer item so only one word completes it correctly. In the question above, for example, many students might argue that the word "range" would also be correct.

Essay Questions. An essay question is one that respondents are asked to write about at length. As with short-answer questions, subjects must produce their own answers. Generally, however, they are free to determine how to answer the question, what facts to present, which to emphasize, what interpretations to make, and the like. For these reasons, the essay question is a particularly useful device for assessing an individual's ability to organize, integrate, analyze, and synthesize information. It is especially useful in measuring the so-called "higher" level learning outcomes, such as analysis, synthesis, and evaluation. Here are two examples of essay questions.

Example 1

Mr. Rogers, a ninth-grade science teacher, wants to measure his students' "ability to interpret scientific data" with a paper-and-pencil test.

1. Describe the steps that Mr. Rogers should follow.
2. Give reasons to justify each step.

Example 2

For a course that you are teaching or expect to teach, prepare a complete plan for evaluating student achievement. Be sure to include the procedures you would follow, the instruments you would use, and the reasons for your choices.[10]

UNOBTRUSIVE MEASURES

Many instruments require the cooperation of the respondent in one way or another and involve some kind of intrusion into on-going activities. On occasion, respondents will dislike or even resent being tested, observed, or interviewed. Furthermore, the reaction of respondents to the instrumentation process—that is, to being tested, observed, or interviewed—often will, to some degree, affect the nature of the information researchers obtain.

To eliminate this reactive effect, researchers at times attempt to use what are called **unobtrusive measures,**[11] which refer to data collection procedures that involve *no* intrusion into the naturally occurring course of events. In most instances, no instrument is required; only some form of recordkeeping. Here are some examples of such procedures.

- The degree of fear induced by a ghost-story-telling session can be measured by noting the shrinking diameter of a circle of seated children.
- Library withdrawals could be used to demonstrate the effect of the introduction of a new unit on Chinese history in a social studies curriculum.
- The interest of children in Christmas or other holidays might be demonstrated by the amount of distortion in the size of their drawings of Santa Claus or other holiday figures.
- Racial attitudes in two elementary schools might be compared by noting the degree of clustering of members of different ethnic groups in the lunchroom and on the playground.
- The values of different countries might be compared through analyzing different types of published materials, such as textbooks, plays, handbooks for youth organizations, magazine advertisements, newspaper headlines, and so on.
- Some idea of the attention paid to patients in a hospital might be determined by observing the frequency of notes, both informal and required, made by attending nurses to the patient's bedside record.
- Degree of stress of college students might be assessed by noting the frequency of sick-call visits to the college health center.
- Student attitudes toward, and interest in, various topics can be noted by observing the amount of graffiti about those topics written on school walls.

Many variables of interest can be assessed, at least to some degree, though the use of unobtrusive measures. The reliability and validity of inferences based on such measures will vary depending on the procedure used. Nevertheless, unobtrusive measures add an important and useful dimension to the array of possible data sources available to researchers. They are particularly valuable as supplements to the use of interviews and questionnaires, often providing a useful way to corroborate (or contradict) what these more traditional data sources reveal.[12]

Types of Scores

Quantitative data are usually reported in the form of scores. Scores can be reported in many ways, but an important distinction to understand is the difference between raw scores and derived scores.

RAW SCORES

Almost all measurement begins with what is called a **raw score,** which is the initial score obtained. It may be the total number of items an individual gets correct or answers in a certain way on a test, the number of times a certain behavior is tallied, the rating given by a teacher, and so forth. Examples include the number of questions answered correctly on a science test, the number of questions answered "positively" on an attitude scale, the number of times "aggressive" behavior is observed, a teacher's rating on a "self-esteem" measure, or the number of choices received on a sociogram.

Taken by itself, an individual raw score is difficult to interpret, since it has little meaning. What, for example, does it mean to say a student received a score of 62 on a test if that is all the information you have? Even if you know that there were 100 questions on the test, you don't know whether 62 is an extremely high (or extremely low) score since the test may be easy or difficult.

We often want to know how one individual's raw score compares to those of other individuals taking the same test, and (perhaps) how he or she has scored on similar tests taken at other times. This is true whenever we want to interpret an individual score. Because raw scores by themselves are difficult to interpret, they often are converted to what are called derived scores.

DERIVED SCORES

Derived scores are raw scores that have been translated into more useful scores on some type of standardized basis. They indicate where a particular individual's raw score falls in relation to all other raw scores in the same distribution. They enable a researcher to say how well the individual has performed compared to all others taking the same test. Examples of derived scores are (1) age and grade level equivalents; (2) percentile ranks; and (3) standard scores.

Age and Grade Level Equivalents. **Age equivalents** and **grade equivalents** tell us of what age or grade an individual score is typical. Suppose, for example, that the average score on a beginning-of-the-year arithmetic test for all eighth graders in a certain state is 62 out of a possible 100. Students who score 62 will have a grade equivalent of 8.0 on the test regardless of their actual grade placement—whether in sixth, seventh, eighth, ninth, or tenth grade, the student's performance is typical of beginning eighth graders. Similarly, a student who is ten years, six months old may have an age equivalent score of 12-2, meaning that his or her test performance is typical of students who are twelve years, two months old.

Percentile Ranks. A **percentile rank** refers to the percentage of individuals scoring at or below a given raw score. Percentile ranks are sometimes referred to as percentiles, although this term is not quite correct as a synonym.*

* A percentile is the *point* below which a certain percentage of scores fall. The 70th percentile, for example, is the *point* below which 70 percent of the scores in a distribution fall. The 99th percentile is the *point* below which 99 percent of the scores fall, and so forth. Thus, if 20 percent of the students in a sample score below 40 on a test, then the 20th percentile is a score of 40. A person who obtains a score of 40 has a percentile rank of 20.

Percentile ranks are easy to calculate. A simple formula for converting raw scores to percentile ranks (Pr) is as follows.

$$Pr = \frac{\begin{array}{c}\text{number of students} \\ \text{below score}\end{array} + \begin{array}{c}\text{all students} \\ \text{at score}\end{array}}{\text{total number in group}} \times 100$$

Suppose a total of 100 students took an examination, and eighteen of them received a raw score above 85, while two students received a score of 85. Eighty students, then, scored somewhere below 85. What is the percentile rank of the two students who received the score of 85? Using the formula:

$$Pr = \frac{80 + 2}{100} \times 100 = 82.$$

The percentile rank of these two students is 82.

Often percentile ranks are calculated for each of the scores in a group. Table 6.1 presents a group of scores with the percentile rank of each score indicated.

Standard Scores. Standard scores provide another means of indicating how an individual

TABLE 6.1

Hypothetical Example of Raw Scores and Accompanying Percentile Ranks

A Raw Score	B Frequency	C Cumulative Frequency	D Percentile Rank
95	1	25	100
93	1	24	96
88	2	23	92
85	3	21	84
79	1	18	72
75	4	17	68
70	6	13	52
65	2	7	28
62	1	5	20
58	1	4	16
54	2	3	12
50	1	1	4
	N = 25		

compares to other individuals in a group. **Standard scores** indicate how far a given raw score is from a reference point. They are particularly helpful in comparing an individual's relative achievement on different types of instruments (such as comparing a person's performance on a chemistry achievement test with ratings by an instructor in a laboratory). Many different systems of standard scores exist, but the two most commonly used and reported in educational research are *z* scores and *T* scores. Understanding them requires some knowledge of descriptive statistics, however, and hence we will postpone a discussion of them until Chapter Eight.

WHICH SCORES TO USE?

Given these various types of scores, how do researchers decide which to use? Recall that the usefulness of derived scores is primarily in making individual raw scores meaningful to students, parents, teachers, and others. Despite their value in this respect, some derived scores should *not* be used in research if the researcher is assuming an interval scale, as often is the case. Percentile ranks, for example, should never be used since they, almost certainly, do not constitute an interval scale. Age and grade equivalent scores likewise have serious limitations because of the way in which they are obtained. Usually the best scores to use are standard scores, which are sometimes provided in instrument manuals and, if not, can easily be calculated. (We discuss and show how to calculate standard scores in Chapter Eight.) If standard scores are not used, it is far more preferable to use raw scores—converting percentiles, for example, back to the original raw scores, if necessary—rather than use percentile ranks or age/grade equivalents.

Norm-Referenced Versus Criterion-Referenced Instruments

NORM-REFERENCED INSTRUMENTS

All derived scores give meaning to individual scores by comparing them to the scores of a group. This means that the nature of the group is extremely important. Whenever such scores are used, researchers must be sure that the reference group makes sense. Comparing a boy's score on a grammar test to a group of girls' scores on that test, for example, may be quite misleading since girls usually score higher in grammar. The group used in getting derived scores is called the *norm group,* and instruments that provide such scores are referred to as **norm-referenced instruments.**

CRITERION-REFERENCED INSTRUMENTS

An alternative to the use of customary achievement or performance instruments, most of which are norm-referenced, is to use a **criterion-referenced** instrument—usually a test. The intent of such tests is somewhat different from that of norm-referenced tests, in that criterion-referenced tests focus more directly on instruction. Rather than evaluating learner progress through gain in scores (for example, from 40 to 70 on an achievement test), a criterion-referenced test is based on a specific goal, or target (called a **criterion**), for each learner to achieve. This criterion for mastery or "pass" is usually stated as a fairly high percentage of questions (such as 80 or 90 percent) to be answered correctly. Examples of criterion-referenced and norm-referenced evaluation statements are as follows.

Criterion-Referenced: A student

- spelled every word in the weekly spelling list correctly;
- solved at least 75 percent of the assigned problems;
- achieved a score of at least 80 out of 100 on the final exam;
- did at least 25 pushups within a five-minute period;
- read a minimum of one nonfiction book a week.

Norm-Referenced: A student

- scored right at the 50th percentile in his group;

- scored above 90 percent of all the students in the class;
- received a higher grade point average in English literature than any other student in the school;
- ran faster than all but one other student on the team;
- and one other in the class were the only ones to receive a grade of A on the midterm.

The advantage of a criterion-referenced instrument is that it gives both teacher and students a clear-cut goal to work toward. As a result, it has considerable appeal as a means of improving instruction. In practice, however, several problems arise. First, teachers seldom set or reach the ideal of individualized student goals. Rather, class goals are more the rule, the idea being that all students will reach the criterion—though, of course, some may not and many will exceed it. The second problem is that it is difficult to establish even class criteria that are meaningful. What, precisely, should a class of fifth graders be able to do in mathematics? Solve story problems, many would say. We would agree, but of what complexity? and requiring which mathematics subskills? In the absence of independent criteria, we have little choice but to fall back on existing expectations, and this is typically (though not necessarily) done by examining existing texts and tests. As a result, the specific items in a criterion-referenced test often turn out to be indistinguishable from those in the usual norm-referenced test, with one important difference: The difference is that a criterion-referenced test at any grade level will almost certainly be easier than a norm-referenced test. It *must* be easier if most students are to get 80 or 90 percent of the items correct. In preparing such tests, researchers must try to write items that will be answered correctly by 80 percent of students—after all, they don't want 50 percent of their students to fail. The desired difficulty level for norm-referenced items, however, *is* 50 percent, in order to provide the maximum opportunity for the scores to distinguish the ability of one student from another.

While a criterion-referenced test *may* be more useful at times and in certain circumstances than the more customary norm-referenced test—this issue is still being debated—it is often inferior for research purposes. Why? Because, in general, a criterion-referenced test will provide much less variability of scores—since it is easier. Whereas the usual norm-referenced test will provide a range of scores somewhat less than the possible range (that is, from zero to the total number of items in the test), a criterion-referenced test, if it is true to its rationale, will have most of the students (surely at least half) getting a high score. Since, in research, we usually want maximum variability in order to have any hope of finding relationships with other variables, the use of criterion-referenced tests is often self-defeating.*

Measurement Scales

You will recall from Chapter Three that there are two basic types of variables—quantitative and categorical. Each uses a different type of analysis and measurement, requiring the use of different measurement scales. There are four types of measurement scales: nominal, ordinal, interval, and ratio (Figure 6.21).

NOMINAL SCALES

A **nominal scale** is the simplest, and also the lowest, form of measurement researchers can use. When using a nominal scale, researchers simply assign numbers to different categories in order to show differences. For example, a researcher might be concerned with the variable of gender and group data into two categories, male and female, and assign the number "1" to females and the number "2" to males. Another

---

* An exception is in program evaluation where some researchers advocate the use of criterion-referenced tests because they want to determine how many students reach a pre-determined standard (criterion).

FIGURE **6.21**

Four Types of Measurement Scales

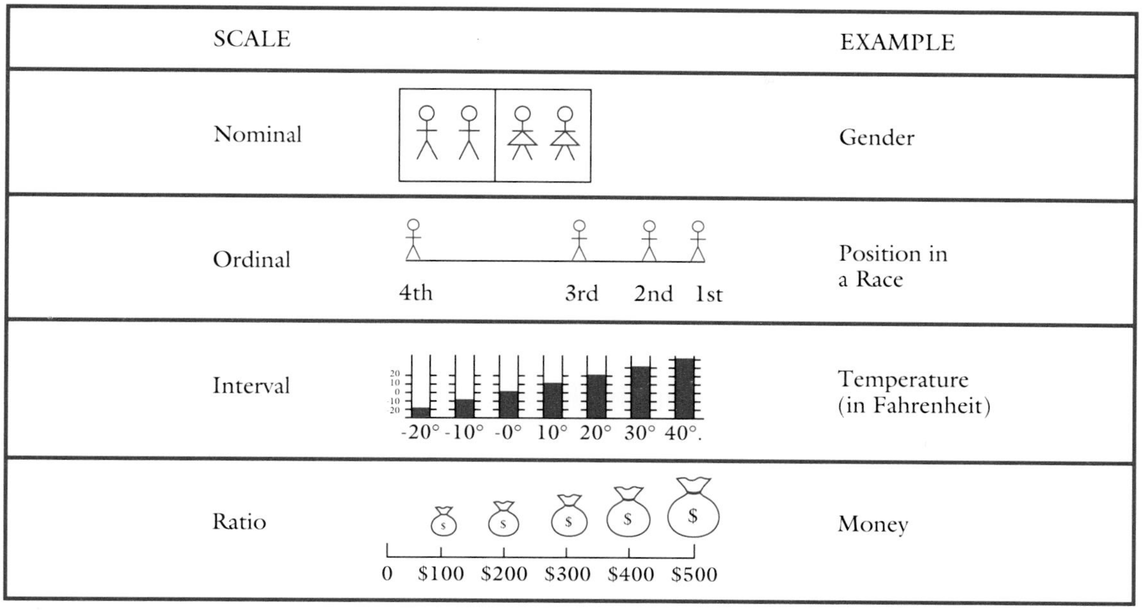

SCALE		EXAMPLE
Nominal		Gender
Ordinal	4th 3rd 2nd 1st	Position in a Race
Interval	-20° -10° -0° 10° 20° 30° 40°.	Temperature (in Fahrenheit)
Ratio	0 $100 $200 $300 $400 $500	Money

researcher, interested in studying methods of teaching reading, might assign the number "1" to the whole word method, the number "2" to the phonics method, and the number "3" to the "mixed" method. In most cases, the advantage to assigning numbers to the categories is to facilitate computer analysis. There is no implication that the phonics method (assigned number "2") is "more" of anything than the whole word method (assigned number "1").

ORDINAL SCALES

An **ordinal scale** is one in which data may be ordered in some way—high to low or least to most. For example, a researcher might rank-order student scores on a biology test from high to low. Notice, however, that the difference in scores or in actual ability between the first- and second-ranked students and between the fifth- and sixth-ranked students would not necessarily be the same. Ordinal scales indicate relative standing among individuals.

INTERVAL SCALES

An **interval scale** possesses all the characteristics of an ordinal scale with one additional feature: The distances between the points on the scale are equal. For example, the distances between scores on most commercially available mathematics achievement tests are usually considered equal. Thus, the distance between scores of 70 and 80 is considered to be the same as the distance between scores of 80 and 90. Notice that the zero point on an interval scale does not indicate a total absence of what is being measured, however. Thus, 0° (zero degrees) on the Farenheit scale, which measures temperature, does not indicate *no* temperature.

To illustrate further, consider the commonly used IQ score. Is the difference between an IQ of 90 and one of 100 (10 points) the same as the difference between an IQ of 40 and one of 50 (also 10 points)? Or between an IQ of 120 and one of 130? If we believe that the scores constitute an interval scale, we *must* assume that 10 points has the same meaning at different points on the scale. Do we know this? No, we do not, as we will explain below.

With respect to some measurements, we can demonstrate equal intervals. We do so by having an agreed upon standard unit. This is one reason why we have a Bureau of Standards, located in Washington, D.C. You could, if you wished to do so, go to the Bureau and actually "see" a standard "inch" ("foot," "ounce," etc.), which defines these units. While it might not be easy, you could conceivably check your carpenter's rule using the "standard inch" to see if an inch is an inch all along your rule. You literally could place the "standard inch" at various points along your rule.

There is no such standard unit for IQ or for virtually any variable commonly used in educational research. Over the years, sophisticated and clever techniques have been developed to create interval scales for use by researchers. The details are beyond the scope of this text, but you should know that they all are based on highly questionable assumptions.

In actual practice, most researchers prefer to "act as if" they had an interval scale because it permits the use of more sensitive data analysis procedures and because, over the years, the results of doing so make sense. Nevertheless, acting "as if" we had interval scales requires an assumption that (at least to date) cannot be proven.

RATIO SCALES

An interval scale that does possess an actual, or true, zero point is called a **ratio scale.** For example, a scale designed to measure height would be a ratio scale, because the zero point on the scale represents the absence of height (that is, *no* height). Similarly, the zero on a bathroom weight scale represents zero, or no, weight. Ratio scales are almost never encountered in educational research, since rarely do researchers engage in measurement involving a true zero point (even on those rare occasions when a student receives a zero on a test of some sort, this does not mean the student possesses a total absence of whatever is being measured). Some other variables that *do* have ratio scales are income, time on task, and age.

MEASUREMENT SCALES RECONSIDERED

At this point, you may be saying, "Well, okay, but so what? Why are these distinctions important?" There are two reasons why you should have at least a rudimentary understanding of the differences between these four types of scales. First, they convey different amounts of information. Ratio scales provide more information than do interval scales, interval more than ordinal, and ordinal more than nominal. Hence, if possible, researchers should use the type of measurement that will provide them with the maximum amount of information needed to answer the research question being investigated. Second, some types of statistical procedures are inappropriate for the different scales. The way in which the data in a research study are organized dictates the use of certain types of statistical analyses, but not others (we shall discuss this point in more detail in Chapter Nine). Table 6.2 presents a summary of the four types of measurement scales.

Often researchers have a choice to make. They must decide whether to consider data as ordinal or interval. For example, suppose a researcher uses a self-report questionnaire to measure "self-esteem." The questionnaire is scored for the number of items answered (yes or no) in the direction indicating high self-esteem. For a given sample of 60, the researcher finds that the scores range from 30 to 75.

The researcher may now decide to treat scores as interval data, in which case she assumes that equal distances (e.g., 30–34, 35–39, 40–44) in score represent equal differences in self-esteem.* If the researcher is uncomfortable with this assumption, she could use the scores to rank

---

* Notice that she cannot treat the scores as ratio data, since a score of zero cannot be assumed to represent zero (i.e., "no") self-esteem.

TABLE 6.2

Characteristics of the Four Types of Measurement Scales

Measurement Scale	Characteristics
Nominal	Groups and labels data only; reports frequencies or percentages
Ordinal	Ranks data; uses numbers only to indicate ranking
Interval	Assumes that differences between scores of equal magnitude really mean equal differences in the variable measured
Ratio	All of the above, plus true zero point

the individuals in her sample from highest (rank #1) to lowest (rank #60). If she were then to use only these rankings in subsequent analysis, she would now be assuming that her instrument provides only ordinal data.

Fortunately, researchers can avoid this choice. They have another option—to treat the data separately according to both assumptions. The important thing to realize is that a researcher must be prepared to defend the assumptions underlying her choice of a measurement scale used in the collection and organization of data.

Preparing Data for Analysis

Once the instrument(s) being used in a study have been administered, the researcher must score the data that has been collected and then organize them to facilitate analysis.

SCORING THE DATA

Collected data must be scored accurately and consistently. If they are not, any conclusions a researcher draws from the data may be erroneous or misleading. Each individual's test (questionnaire, essay, and so on) should be scored using the exact same procedures and criteria. When a commercially purchased instrument is used, the scoring procedures are made much easier. Usually a scoring manual will be provided by the instrument developer, listing the steps to follow in scoring the instrument, along with a scoring key. It is a good idea to doublecheck one's scoring to ensure that mistakes have not been made.

The scoring of a self-developed test can produce difficulties, and hence researchers have to take special care to ensure that scoring is accurate and consistent. Essay examinations, in particular, are often very difficult to score in a consistent manner. For this reason, it is usually advisable to have a second person also score the results. Researchers should carefully prepare their scoring plans, in writing, ahead of time and then try out their instrument by administering and scoring it with a group of individuals similar to the population they intend to sample in their study. Problems with administration and scoring can thus be identified early and corrected before it is too late.

TABULATING AND CODING THE DATA

When the data have been scored, the researcher must tally or tabulate them in some way. Usually this is done by transferring the data to some sort of summary data sheet or card. The important thing is to record one's data accurately and systematically. If categorical data are being recorded, the number of individuals scoring in each category are tallied. If quantitative data are being recorded the data are usually listed in one or more columns, depending on the number of groups involved in the study. For example, if the data analysis is to consist simply of a comparison of the scores of two groups on a post-test, the data would most likely be placed in two columns, one for each group, in descending order. Table 6.3, for example, presents some

TABLE **6.3**

Hypothetical Results of Study Involving a Comparison of Two Counseling Methods

Score for "Rapport"	Method A	Method B
96–100	0	0
91–95	0	2
86–90	0	3
81–85	2	3
76–80	2	4
71–75	5	3
66–70	6	4
61–65	9	4
56–60	4	5
51–55	5	3
46–50	2	2
41–45	0	1
36–40	0	1
	$N = 35$	35

hypothetical results of a study involving a comparison of two counseling methods on an instrument measuring "rapport." If pre- and post-test scores are to be compared, additional columns could be added. If subgroup scores will be looked at, these also could be indicated.

When a variety of different kinds of data are collected (e.g., scores on several different instruments), plus biographical information (gender, age, ethnicity, and so on), they are usually recorded on data cards, one card for each individual from whom data were collected. This facilitates easy comparison and grouping (and regrouping) of data for purposes of analysis. In addition, the data are coded. In other words, some type of code is used to protect the privacy of the individuals in the study. Thus, the names of males and females might be coded as "1" and "2." Coding of data is especially important when data are analyzed by computer, since any data not in numerical form must be coded in some systematic way before they can be entered into the computer. Thus categorical data, to be analyzed on a computer, are often coded numerically (e.g., pre-test scores = "A," and post-test scores = "B").

The first step in coding data is often to assign an ID number to every individual from whom data has been collected. If there were 100 individuals in a study, for example, the researcher would number them from 001 to 100. If the highest value for any variable being analyzed involves three digits (e.g., 100), then every individual code number must have three digits (e.g., the first individual to be numbered must be 001, not 1).

The next step would be to decide how any categorical data being analyzed are to be coded. Suppose a researcher wished to analyze certain demographic information obtained from 100 subjects who answered a questionnaire. If his study included juniors and seniors in a high school, he might code the juniors as "11" and the seniors as "12." Or, if respondents were asked to indicate which of four choices they preferred (as in certain multiple-choice questions), the researcher might code each of the choices (e.g., (a), etc.) as "1," "2," "3," or "4," respectively. The important thing to remember is to ensure that the coding is consistent—that is, once a decision is made how to code someone, all others must be coded the same way, and that this (and any other) coding rule must be communicated to everyone involved in coding the data.

Main Points of Chapter Six

- The term "data" refers to the kinds of information researchers obtain on the subjects of their research.
- The term "instrumentation" refers to the entire process of collecting data in a research investigation.

- An important consideration in the choice of an instrument to be used in a research investigation is validity: the extent to which it permits researchers to draw warranted conclusions about the characteristics of the individuals studied.
- A reliable instrument is one that gives consistent results.
- Whenever possible, researchers try to eliminate subjectivity from the judgments they make about the achievement, performance, or characteristics of subjects.
- An important consideration for any researcher in choosing or designing an instrument is how easy the instrument will actually be to use.
- Research instruments can be classified in many ways. Some of the more common are in terms of who provide the data, the method of data collection, who collects the data, and whether they require a written or a more general type of response by the subjects.
- Research data are data obtained by directly or indirectly assessing the subjects of a study.
- Self-report data are data provided by the subjects of a study themselves.
- Informant data are data provided by other people about the subjects of a study.
- Many types of researcher-completed instruments exist. Some of the more commonly used include rating scales, interview schedules, tally sheets, flow charts, performance checklists, anecdotal records, and time and motion logs.
- There are also many types of instruments that are completed by the subjects of a study rather than the researcher. Some of the more commonly used of this type include questionnaires, self-checklists, attitude scales, personality inventories, achievement, aptitude, and performance tests, projective devices, and sociometric devices.
- The types of items or questions used in subject-completed instruments can take many forms, but they all can be classified as either a selection-type or a supply-type item. Examples of selection-type items include true-false items, multiple-choice items, matching items, and interpretive exercises. Examples of supply-type items include short-answer items and essay questions.
- Unobtrusive measures require no intrusion into the normal course of affairs.
- Four types of measurement scales—nominal, ordinal, interval, and ratio scales—are used in educational research.
- A nominal scale involves the use of numbers to indicate membership in one or more categories.
- An ordinal scale involves the use of numbers to rank or order scores from high to low.
- An interval scale involves the use of numbers to represent equal intervals in different segments on a continuum.
- A ratio scale involves the use of numbers to represent equal distances from a known zero point.
- A raw score is the initial score obtained when using an instrument.
- Age/grade equivalents are scores that indicate the typical age or grade of an individual raw score.

- A percentile rank is the percentage of a specific group scoring at or below a given raw score.
- A standard score is a mathematically derived score having comparable meaning on different instruments.
- Collected data must be scored accurately and consistently.

For Discussion

1. What type of instrument do you think would be best suited to obtain data about each of the following?
   a. The free-throw shooting ability of a tenth-grade basketball team.
   b. How nurses feel about a new management policy recently instituted in their hospital.
   c. Parental reactions to a planned-for campaign to raise money for an addition to the school library.
   d. The "best-liked" boy and girl in the senior class.
   e. The "best" administrator in a particular school district.
   f. How well students in a food management class can prepare a balanced meal.
   g. Characteristics of all students who are biology majors at a midwestern university.
   h. How students at one school compare to students at another school in mathematics ability.
   i. The potential of various high school seniors for college work.
   j. What the members of a kindergarten class like and dislike about school.

2. Which of the following are examples of products and which are examples of procedures?
   a. A class discussion.
   b. An outline for a term report.
   c. A poem.
   d. Attentiveness.
   e. Running a mile in 4:12 minutes.
   f. A chemical solution.

3. Would the following be measured most appropriately by an achievement test or a personality test?
   a. Self-concept.
   b. Ability to compose a song.
   c. Ability to work with others on a research project.
   d. Ability to mix chemical solutions correctly.
   e. A student's feelings toward his or her classmates.
   f. Ability to use a dictionary.

4. Who would be best equipped to fill out each of the following instruments—a researcher or the subjects of a study?
   a. A checklist of the steps involved in tuning an automobile engine.
   b. A questionnaire asking for information about a person's previous work history.

    c. A rating scale evaluating performance in a basketball game.

    d. A tally sheet of questions asked by students in a biology class.

    e. An inventory of the supplies contained at a chemistry lab workstation.

    f. A record of monthly entries to and withdrawals from a payment book.

    g. A written description of an individual's behavior at a dance.

5. Of all the instruments presented in this chapter, which one(s) do you think would be the hardest to use? the easiest? Why? Which one(s) do you think would provide the most dependable information? Why?

6. What type of scale—nominal, ordinal, interval, or ratio—would a researcher be most likely to use to measure each of the following?
    a. Height of students in inches.
    b. Students ranked on aggressiveness of classroom behavior.
    c. Mechanical aptitude.
    d. Religious preference.
    e. Writing ability.
    f. Running speed.
    g. Weight gain or loss in pounds over a three-month period.

7. Match each score in Column A with the best choice from Column B

A	B
____1. standard score	a. poorest to use for research
____2. raw score	b. score expressed as 10-2
____3. age equivalent score	c. number of questions correct
____4. percentile rank	d. preferred for research purposes

8. "Any individual raw score, in and of itself, is meaningless." Would you agree? Explain.

9. "Derived scores give meaning to individual raw scores." Is this true? Explain.

10. It sometimes would not be fair to compare an individual's score on a test to the scores of other individuals taking the same test. Why?

Notes

1. American Council on Education. (1945). *Helping teachers understand children*. Washington, D.C.: American Council on Education. pp. 32–33.

2. *Ibid.*, p. 33

3. A Likert. (1932). A technique for the measurement of attitudes. *Archives de Psychologie*, 6(140).

4. Charles Osgood, G. Suci, and P. Tannenbaum. (1962). *The measurement of meaning*. Urbana: University of Illinois Press.

5. See, for example, W. James Popham. (1988). *Educational evaluation*, 2nd ed. Englewood Cliffs, N.J.: Prentice-Hall. pp. 150–173, and Bruce W. Tuckman. (1975). *Measuring educational outcomes: Fundamentals of testing*. New York: Harcourt Brace Jovanovich. pp. 138–167.

6. J. C. Conoley & J. J. Kramer (Eds.). (1989). *The tenth mental measurements yearbook*. Lincoln, NE: Buros Institute of Mental Measurements of the University of Nebraska.

7. Enoch I. Sawin. (1969). *Evaluation and the work of the teacher*. Belmont, CA: Wadsworth. p. 176.

8. M. L. Blum. (1943). Selection of sewing machine operators. *Journal of Applied Psychology*, 27(2), 35–40.

9. Norman E. Gronlund. (1988). *How to construct achievement tests,* 4th ed. Englewood Cliffs, N.J.: Prentice-Hall. pp. 66–67. Reprinted by permission of Prentice-Hall, Inc.

10. *Ibid.,* pp. 76–77. Reprinted by permission of Prentice-Hall, Inc.

11. E. J. Webb, D. T. Campbell, R. D. Schwartz, & L. Sechrest. (1966). *Unobtrusive measures: Nonreactive research in the social sciences.* Chicago: Rand McNally.

12. The use of unobtrusive measures is an art in itself. We can only scratch the surface of the topic here. For a more extended discussion, along with many, many interesting examples, the reader is referred to the book by Webb et al., *op. cit.*

Research Exercise Six:
Instrumentation

> Decide on the kind of instrument you will use to measure the dependent variable(s) in your study. Using Problem Sheet 6, name all the instruments you plan to use in your study. If you plan to use one or more already existing instruments, describe each. If you will need to develop an instrument, give two examples of the kind of questions you would ask (or tasks you would have students perform) as a part of each instrument. Indicate how you would describe and organize the data on each of the variables yielding numerical data.

1. The instrument I plan to use to measure my dependent variable is:

   _____

2. Other instruments I plan to use would be:

   _____

3. If I need to develop an instrument, here are two examples of the kind of questions I would ask (or tasks I would have students perform) as a part of my instrument:

   a. _____

   b. _____

4. These are the existing instruments I plan to use:

   _____

   _____

5. I would describe *each* variable yielding numerical data as follows:

   variable 1 _____   variable 2 _____   other _____

   quantitative
   or   _____   _____   _____
   categorical

   nominal
   or
   ordinal
   or   _____   _____   _____
   interval
   or
   ratio

6. For *each* variable yielding numerical data, I will treat it as follows (check one in each column):

raw score	_____	_____	_____
age/grade equivalents	_____	_____	_____
percentile	_____	_____	_____
standard score	_____	_____	_____

125

Chapter Seven

VALIDITY AND RELIABILITY

The quality of the instruments used in research is very important, for the conclusions researchers draw are based on the information they obtain using these instruments. In this chapter, we present several procedures used by researchers to ensure that the inferences they draw, based on the data they collect, are valid.

Validity refers to the appropriateness, meaningfulness, and usefulness of the inferences a researcher makes. Reliability refers to the consistency of scores or answers from one administration of an instrument to another, and from one set of items to another. We shall discuss both concepts in some detail.

Objectives

- *Explain* what is meant by the term "validity" as it applies to the use of instruments in educational research
- *Name* three types of evidence of validity that can be obtained, and *give an example* of each type
- *Explain* what is meant by the term "correlation coefficient" and *describe* briefly the difference between positive and negative correlation coefficients
- *Explain* what is meant by the terms "validity coefficient" and "reliability coefficient"
- *Explain* what is meant by the term "reliability" as it applies to the use of instruments in educational research
- *Explain* what is meant by the term "errors of measurement"
- *Describe* briefly three ways to estimate the reliability of the scores obtained using a particular instrument

---

Validity

Validity is the most important idea to consider when preparing or selecting an instrument for use. More than anything else, researchers want the information they obtain through the use of an instrument to serve their purposes. For example, to find out what teachers in a particular school district think about a recent policy passed by the school board, researchers need both an instrument to record the data and some sort of assurance that the information obtained will enable them *to draw correct conclusions* about teacher opinions. The drawing of correct conclusions based on the data obtained by use of an instrument is what validity is all about. While it is not essential, the comprehension and use of information is greatly simplified if some kind of score is obtained that summarizes the information for each person. While the ideas that follow are not limited to the use of scores, we discuss them in this context because the ideas are easier to understand, and most instruments provide such scores.

In recent years, **validity** has been defined as referring to the appropriateness, meaningfulness, and usefulness of the specific *inferences* researchers make based on the data they collect. *Validation* of an instrument is the process of collecting evidence to support such inferences. There are many ways to collect evidence, and we will discuss some of them shortly. The important point here is to realize that validity refers to the degree to which evidence supports any inferences a researcher makes based on the data he or she collects using a particular instrument. It is the inferences about the specific uses of an instrument that are validated, not the instrument itself.* These inferences should be appropriate, meaningful, and useful.

* This is somewhat of a change from past interpretations. It is based on the recent set of *Standards* prepared by a joint committee consisting of members of the American Educational Research Association, the American Psychological

An appropriate inference would be one that is relevant, that is, related, to the purposes of the study. If the purpose of a study was to determine what students know about African culture, for example, it would make no sense to make inferences about this from their scores on a test about the physical geography of Africa.

A meaningful inference is one that says something about the *meaning* of the information (such as test scores) obtained through the use of an instrument. What exactly does a high score on a particular test mean? What does such a score allow us to say about the individual who received it? In what way is an individual who receives a high score different from one who receives a low score? And so forth. It is one thing to collect information from people. We do this all the time—names, addresses, birthdates, shoe sizes, car license numbers, and so on. But unless we can make inferences that mean something from the information we obtain, it is of little use. The purpose of research is not merely to collect data, but to use such data to draw warranted conclusions about the people (and others like them) on whom the data were collected.

A useful inference is one that helps researchers make a decision related to what they were trying to find out. Researchers interested in the effects of inquiry-related teaching materials on student achievement, for example, need information that will enable them to infer if achievement is affected by such materials and, if so, how.

Validity, therefore, depends on the amount and type of evidence there is to support the interpretations researchers wish to make concerning data they have collected. The crucial question is: Does the instrument provide useful information about the topic or variable being measured?

What kinds of evidence might a researcher collect? Essentially, there are three main types.

Content-related evidence of validity: Refers to the nature of the content included within the instrument and the specifications the researcher used to formulate the content. How appropriate is the content? How comprehensive? Does it logically get at the intended variable? How adequately does the sample of items or questions represent the content to be assessed?

Criterion-related evidence of validity: Refers to the relationship between scores obtained using the instrument and scores obtained using one or more other instruments or measures (often called a criterion). How strong is this relationship? How well do such scores estimate present or predict future performance of a certain type?

Construct-related evidence of validity: Refers to the nature of the psychological construct or characteristic being measured by the instrument. How well does this construct explain differences in the behavior of individuals or their performance on certain tasks?

Ideally, a researcher would like to have evidence from all three of these categories. The important thing to remember, however, is that the more evidence a researcher has about the validity of the inferences made, the better.

CONTENT-RELATED EVIDENCE

Suppose a researcher is interested in the effects of a new math program on the mathematics ability of fifth graders. Upon completion of the program, the researcher expects students to be able to solve a number of different types of word problems correctly. To assess their mathematics ability, the researcher plans to give them a math test containing about fifteen such problems. The performance of the students on

Association, and The National Council on Measurement in Education. *See* American Psychological Association. (1985). *Standards for educational and psychological testing.* Washington, D.C.: APA. pp. 9–18 and 19–23.

One interpretation of this revision has been that test publishers no longer have a responsibility to provide evidence of validity. We do not agree; publishers have an obligation to state what an instrument is intended to measure and to provide evidence that it does. Nonetheless, researchers must still give attention to the way in which *they* intend to interpret the information.

this test is important only to the degree that it provides evidence of their ability to solve these kinds of problems. Hence, performance on the instrument in this case (the math test) would provide valid evidence of the mathematics ability of these students to the degree that the instrument provides an adequate sample of the types of word problems learned about in the program. If only easy problems are included in the test, or only very difficult or lengthy ones, or only problems involving subtraction, the test would be unrepresentative and hence not provide information from which valid inferences could be made.

One key element in content-related evidence, then, revolves around the adequacy of the sampling. Most instruments (and especially achievement tests) provide only a sample of the kinds of problems that might be solved or questions that might be asked. Content validation, therefore, is partly a matter of determining if the content that the instrument contains is an adequate sample of the domain of content it is supposed to represent.

The other aspect to content validation has to do with the format of the instrument. This includes such things as the clarity of printing, size of type, adequacy of work space (if needed), appropriateness of language, clarity of directions, and so on. Regardless of the adequacy of the questions in an instrument, if they are presented in an inappropriate format (such as giving a test in English to children whose English is minimal), valid results cannot be obtained.

How does one obtain content-related evidence of validity? A common way to do this is to have someone look at the content and format of the instrument and judge whether or not it is appropriate. The "someone," of course, should not be just anyone, but rather an individual who can be expected to render an intelligent judgment about the adequacy of the instrument—in other words, someone who knows enough about what is to be measured to be a competent judge.

The usual procedure is somewhat as follows. The researcher writes out the definition of what he or she want to measure on a separate sheet of paper and then gives this definition, along with the instrument, to one or more judges. The judges look at the definition, read over the items or questions in the instrument, and place a checkmark in front of each question or item that they feel does not measure one or more of the objectives. They also place a checkmark in front of each objective not assessed by any of the items. The researcher then rewrites any item or question so checked and resubmits it to the judges, and/or writes new items for objectives not adequately covered. This continues until the judges approve all the items or questions in the instrument and also indicate that they feel the total number of items is an adequate representation of the total domain of content covered by the variable being measured.

To illustrate how a researcher might go about trying to establish content-related validity, let us consider two examples.

Example 1. Suppose a researcher desires to measure students' ability to *use information that they have previously acquired*. When asked what she means by this phrase, she offers the following definition.

As evidence that students can use previously acquired information, they should be able to:

1. Draw a correct conclusion (verbally or in writing) that is based on information they are given.
2. Identify one or more logical implications that follow from a given point of view.
3. State (orally or in writing) whether two ideas are identical, similar, unrelated, or contradictory.

How might the researcher obtain such evidence? She decides to prepare a written test that will contain various questions for students to answer. Their answers will constitute the evidence she seeks. Here are three examples of the kinds of questions she has in mind, one designed to produce each of the three types of evidence listed above.

1. If A is greater than B, and B is greater than C, then:
   a. A must be greater than C.

b. C must be smaller than A.

c. B must be smaller than A.

d. All of the above are true.

2. Those who believe that increasing consumer expenditures would be the best way to stimulate the economy would advocate:

a. An increase in interest rates.

b. An increase in depletion allowances.

c. Tax reductions in the lower income brackets.

d. A reduction in government expenditures.

3. Compare the dollar amounts spent by the U.S. government during the past ten years for: a) Debt payments, b) Defense, c) Social Services.

Now, look at each of the questions and the corresponding objective they are supposed to measure. Do you think each question measures the objective it was designed for? If not, why not?*

Example 2. Here is what another researcher designed as an attempt to measure (at least in part) the ability of students to *explain why events occur.*

Read the directions that follow, and then answer the question.

Directions: Here are some facts.

Fact W: A camper started a fire to cook food on a windy day in a forest.

Fact X: A fire started in some dry grass near a campfire in a forest.

Here is another fact that happened later the same day in the same forest.

Fact Y: A house in the forest burned down.

You are to explain what might have caused the house to burn down (Fact Y). Would Fact W and X be useful as parts of your explanation?

a. Yes, both W and X and the possible cause-and-effect relationship between them would be useful.

b. Yes, both W and X would be useful, even though neither was likely a cause of the other.

c. No, because only one of Facts W and X was likely a cause of Y.

d. No, because neither W or X was likely a cause of Y.[1]

Once again, look at the question and the objective it was designed to measure. Does it measure this objective? If not, why not?*

Attempts like these to obtain evidence of some sort (in the above instances, the support of independent judges that the items measure what they are supposed to measure) typifies the process of obtaining content-related evidence of validity. As we mentioned previously, however, the qualifications of the judges are always an important consideration.

CRITERION-RELATED EVIDENCE

To obtain criterion-related evidence of validity, researchers usually compare performance on one instrument (the one being validated) with performance on some other, independent criterion. A **criterion** is a second test or other device by which something can be measured. For example, if an instrument has been designed to measure academic ability, student scores on the instrument might be compared with their grade-point averages (the external criterion). If the instrument does indeed measure academic ability, then students who score high on the test would also be expected to have high grade-point averages. Can you see why?

There are two forms of criterion-related validity—predictive and concurrent. To obtain evidence of **predictive validity**, researchers allow a time interval to elapse between administration of the instrument and obtaining the criterion scores. For example, a researcher might administer a science aptitude test to a group of high

---

* We would rate correct answers to questions 1 (choice d) and 2 (choice c) as valid evidence, although 1 could be considered questionable, since students might view it as somewhat tricky. We would not rate answers to 3 as valid, since students are not asked to contrast ideas, only facts.

* We would rate a correct answer to this question as valid evidence of student ability to explain why events occur.

school students to predict and later compare their scores on the test with their end-of-the-semester grades in science courses.

On the other hand, when instrument data and criterion data are gathered at nearly the same time, and the results compared, this is an attempt by researchers to obtain evidence of **concurrent validity**. An example is when a researcher administers a self-esteem inventory to a group of eighth graders and compares their scores on it with their teachers' ratings of student self-esteem obtained at about the same time.

A key index in both forms of criterion-related validity is the correlation coefficient.* A **correlation coefficient**, symbolized by the letter (r), indicates the degree of relationship that exists between the scores individuals obtain on two instruments. A positive relationship is indicated when a high score on one of the instruments is accompanied by a high score on the other or when a low score on one is accompanied by a low score on the other. A negative relationship is indicated when a high score on one instrument is accompanied by a low score on the other, and vice-versa. All correlation coefficients fall somewhere between $+1.00$ and -1.00. An r of .00 indicates that no relationship exists.

When a correlation coefficient is used to describe the relationship that exists between a set of scores obtained by the same group of individuals on a particular instrument and their scores on some criterion measure, it is called a **validity coefficient**. For example, a validity coefficient of $+1.00$ obtained by correlating a set of scores on a mathematics aptitude test (the predictor) and another set of scores, this time on a mathematics achievement test (the criterion), for the same individuals would indicate that each individual in the group had exactly the same relative standing on both measures. Such a correlation, if obtained, would allow the researcher to predict perfectly math achievement based on aptitude test scores. Although this correlation coefficient would be very unlikely, it

illustrates what such coefficients mean. The higher the validity coefficient obtained, the more accurate a researcher's predictions are likely to be.

Gronlund suggests the use of an expectancy table as another way to depict criterion-related evidence.[2] An *expectancy table* is nothing more than a two-way chart, with the scores on the instrument (the predictor) listed in categories down the lefthand side of the chart and the criterion scores listed horizontally along the top of the chart. For each category of scores on the predictor, the researcher then indicates the percentage of individuals who fall within each of the categories on the criterion.

Table 7.1 presents an example. As you can see from the table, 51 percent of the students who were classified outstanding by these judges received a course grade in orchestra of A, 35 percent received a B, and 14 percent received a C. Although this table refers only to this particular group, it could be used to predict the scores of other aspiring music students who are evaluated by these same judges. If a student obtains an evaluation of "outstanding," we might predict (approximately) that he or she would have a 51 percent chance of receiving an A, a 35 percent chance of receiving a B, and a 14 percent chance of receiving a C.

Expectancy tables are particularly useful devices for researchers to use with data collected

---

* The correlation coefficient explained in detail in Chapter Eight is an extremely useful statistic. This is one of its many applications or uses.

TABLE **7.1**

Example from an Expectancy Table

Judges' Classification of Music Aptitude	Course Grades in Orchestra (Percentage Receiving Each Grade)			
	A	*B*	*C*	*D*
Outstanding	51	35	14	0
Above average	20	43	37	0
Average	0	6	83	11
Below average	0	0	13	87

in schools. They are simple to construct, easily understood, and clearly show the relationship that exists between two measures.

It is important to realize that the nature of the criterion is the most important factor in gathering criterion-related evidence. High positive correlations do not mean much if the criterion measure does not make logical sense. For example, a high correlation between scores on an instrument designed to measure aptitude for science and scores on a physical fitness test would not be relevant criterion-related evidence for either instrument. Think back to the example we presented earlier of the questions designed to measure ability to explain. What sort of criterion could be used to establish criterion-referenced validity for those items?

CONSTRUCT-RELATED EVIDENCE

Construct-related evidence is the broadest of the three categories of evidence for validity that we are considering. There is no single piece of evidence that carries the day for construct-related validity. Rather, researchers attempt to collect a variety of *different* types of evidence—the more and varied the better—which will allow them to make warranted inferences: to assert, for example, that the scores obtained from administering a self-esteem inventory permit accurate inferences about the degree of self-esteem which people who receive those scores possess.

Usually, there are three steps involved in obtaining construct-related evidence of validity: (1) the variable being measured is clearly defined; (2) hypotheses, based on a theory underlying the variable, are formed about how people who possess a "lot" versus a "little" of the variable will behave in a particular situation; and (3) the hypotheses are tested both logically and empirically.

To make the process clearer, let us consider an example. Suppose a researcher interested in developing a pencil-and-paper test to measure "honesty" wants to use a construct-validity approach. First, he defines honesty. Next he formulates a theory about how "honest" people behave as compared to dishonest people. For example, he might theorize that honest individuals, if they find an object that does not belong to them, will make a reasonable effort to locate the individual to whom the object belongs. Based on this theory, the researcher might hypothesize that individuals who score highly on his "honesty test" will be more likely to attempt to locate the owner of an object they find than individuals who score low on the test. The researcher would then administer the honesty test, separate the names of those who score high and those who score low, and give all of them an opportunity to be honest. He might, for example, leave a wallet with $5.00 in it lying just outside the test-taking room so that the individuals taking the test can easily see it and pick it up. The wallet displays the name and phone number of the owner in plain view. If the researcher's hypothesis is substantiated, more of the high scorers than the low scorers on the honesty test would attempt to call the owner of the wallet. (This could be checked by having the number answered by a recording machine, asking the caller to leave his or her name and number.) This would be one piece of evidence that could be used to support inferences about the honesty of individuals, based on the scores they receive on this test.

We must stress, however, that a researcher must carry out a series of studies to obtain a variety of evidence that the scores from a particular instrument yield correct inferences about the variable that the instrument purports to measure. It is a broad array of evidence, rather than any one particular type of evidence, that is desired. Thus, some evidence that might be considered to support a test designed to measure mathematical reasoning ability might be as follows.

- Independent judges all indicate that all items in the test require mathematical reasoning.
- Independent judges all indicate that the features of the test itself (such as test format, directions, scoring, and reading level) would not in any way prevent students from engaging in mathematical reasoning.
- Independent judges all indicate that the

sample of tasks included in the test are relevant and representative of mathematical reasoning tasks.

- A high correlation exists between scores on the test and grades in mathematics.
- High scores have been made on the test by students who have had specific training in mathematical reasoning.
- Students actually engage in mathematical reasoning when they are asked to "think aloud" as they go about trying to solve the problems on the test.
- A high correlation exists between scores on the test and teacher ratings of competence in mathematical reasoning.
- Higher scores are obtained on the test by mathematics majors than by general science majors.

Other types of evidence might be listed for the above task (perhaps you can think of some), but we hope this is enough to make clear that it is not just one, but many types of evidence that a researcher seeks to obtain.

Determining whether the scores obtained through the use of a particular instrument measure a particular variable involves a study of how the test was developed, the theory underlying the test, how the test functions with a variety of people and in a variety of situations, and how scores on the test relate to scores on other appropriate instruments. Construct validation involves, then, a wide variety of procedures and many different types of evidence, including both content-related and criterion-related evidence. The more evidence researchers have from many different sources, the more confident they become about interpreting the scores obtained from a particular instrument.

Reliability

Reliability refers to the consistency of the scores obtained—how consistent they are for each individual from one administration of an instrument to another and from one set of items to another. Consider, for example, a test designed to measure typing ability. If the test is reliable,

we would expect a student who receives a high score the first time he takes the test to receive a high score the next time he takes the test. The scores would probably not be identical, but they should be close.

The scores obtained from an instrument can be quite reliable, but not valid. Suppose a researcher gave a group of eighth graders two forms of a test designed to measure their knowledge of the Constitution of the United States and found their scores to be consistent: Those who scored high on form A also scored high on form B; those who scored low on A scored low on B; and so on. We would say that the scores are reliable. But if the researcher then used these same test scores to predict the success of these students in their physical education classes, he would probably be looked at in amazement. Any inferences about success in physical education based on scores on a Constitution test would have no validity. Now, what about the reverse? Can an instrument that yields unreliable scores permit valid inferences? No! If scores are completely inconsistent for a person, they provide no useful information. We have no way of even knowing which score to use to infer an individual's ability, attitude, or other characteristic.

The distinction between reliability and validity is shown in Figure 7.1. Reliability and validity are always dependent on the context in which an instrument is used. Depending on the context, an instrument may or may not yield reliable (consistent) scores. If the data are unreliable, they cannot lead to valid (legitimate) inferences—as shown in target (a). As reliability improves, validity may improve, as shown in target (b), or it may not, as shown in target (c). An instrument may have good reliability but low validity, as shown in target (d). What is desired, of course, is both high reliability and high validity, as target (e) shows.

ERRORS OF MEASUREMENT

Whenever people take the same test twice, they will seldom perform exactly the same—that is, their scores or answers will not usually be identical. This may be due to a variety of factors (differences in motivation, energy, anxiety, a

FIGURE 7.1

Reliability and Validity

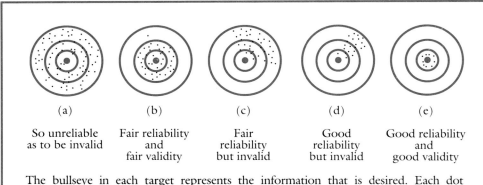

(a)	(b)	(c)	(d)	(e)
So unreliable as to be invalid	Fair reliability and fair validity	Fair reliability but invalid	Good reliability but invalid	Good reliability and good validity

The bullseye in each target represents the information that is desired. Each dot represents a separate score obtained with the instrument. A dot in the bullseye indicates that the information obtained (the score) is the information the researcher desires.

different testing situation, and so on), but it is inevitable. Such factors result in **errors of measurement.**

Since errors of measurement are always present to some degree, researchers expect some variation in test scores (in answers or ratings, for example) when an instrument is administered to the same group more than once, when two different forms of an instrument are used, or even from one part of an instrument to another. Reliability estimates provide researchers with an idea of how much variation to expect. Such estimates are usually expressed as another application of the correlation coefficient known as a **reliability coefficient.**

As we mentioned earlier, a validity coefficient expresses the relationship that exists between scores of the same individuals on two *different* instruments. A reliability coefficient also expresses a relationship, but this time it is between scores of the same individuals on the *same* instrument at two different times, or between two parts of the same instrument. The three best-known ways to obtain a reliability coefficient are the test-retest method; the equivalent-forms method; and the internal consistency methods. Unlike other uses of the correlation coefficient, reliability coefficients must range from 0.00 to 1.00.

TEST-RETEST METHOD

The **test-retest method** involves administering the same test twice to the *same* group after a certain time interval has elapsed. A reliability coefficient is then calculated to indicate the relationship between the two sets of scores obtained.

Reliability coefficients will be affected by the length of time that elapses between the two administrations of the test. The longer the time interval, the lower the reliability coefficient is likely to be, since there is a greater likelihood of changes in the individuals taking the test. In checking for evidence of test-retest validity, an appropriate time-interval should be selected. This interval should be that during which individuals would be assumed to retain their relative position in a meaningful group.

There is no point to studying, or even conceptualizing, a variable that has no permanence. When researchers assess someone as academically talented, for example, or skilled in typing or as having a poor self-concept, they assume that this characteristic will continue to differentiate individuals for some period of time. It is impossible to study a variable that is constantly changing.

Researchers do not expect all variables to be equally stable. Experience has shown that some abilities (such as writing) are more subject to change than others (such as abstract reasoning). Some personal characteristics (such as self-esteem) are considered to be more stable than others (such as teen-age vocational interests). "Mood" is a variable which, by definition, is considered to be stable for short periods of time—a matter of minutes or hours. But even here, unless the instrumentation used is reliable, meaningful relationships with other (perhaps causal) variables will not be found. For most educational research, stability of scores over a two to three month period is usually viewed as sufficient evidence of test-retest reliability. In reporting test-retest reliability coefficients, therefore, the time interval between the two testings should always be reported.

EQUIVALENT-FORMS METHOD

When the **equivalent-forms method** is used, two different but equivalent (also called alternate or parallel) forms of an instrument are administered to the *same* group of individuals during the same time period. Although the questions are different, they should sample the same content and they should be constructed separately from each other. A reliability coefficient is then calculated between the two sets of scores obtained. A high coefficient would indicate strong evidence of reliability—that the two forms are measuring the same thing.

It is possible to combine the test-retest and equivalent-forms methods by giving two different forms of the same test with a time interval between the two administrations. A high reliability coefficient would indicate not only that the two forms are measuring the same sort of performance but also what we might expect with regard to consistency over time.

INTERNAL CONSISTENCY METHODS

The methods mentioned so far all require two administration or testing sessions. There are several **internal consistency** methods of estimating reliabilty, however, that require only a single administration of an instrument.

Split-half Procedure. The **split-half procedure** involves scoring two halves (usually odd items versus even items) of a test separately for each person and then calculating a correlation coefficient for the two sets of scores. The coefficient indicates the degree to which the two halves of the test provide the same results, and hence describes the internal consistency of the test.

The reliability coefficient is calculated using what is known as the Spearman-Brown prophecy formula. A simplified version of this formula is as follows

$$\text{Reliability of scores on total test} = \frac{2 \times \text{reliability for } \frac{1}{2} \text{ test}}{1 + \text{reliability for } \frac{1}{2} \text{ test}}$$

Thus, if we obtained a correlation coefficient of .56 by comparing one-half of the test items to the other half, the reliability of scores for the total test would be:

$$\text{Reliability of scores on total test} = \frac{2 \times .56}{1 + .56} = \frac{1.12}{1.56} = .72$$

This illustrates an important characteristic of reliability. The reliability of a test (or any instrument) can generally be increased by increasing its length, if the items added are similar to the original ones.

Kuder-Richardson Approaches. Perhaps the most frequently employed method for determining internal consistency is the Kuder-Richardson approach, particularly formulas KR20 and KR21. These formulas require only three pieces of information—the number of items in the test, the mean, and the standard deviation. Note, however, that formula KR21 can be used only if it can be assumed that the items are of equal difficulty.* A frequently used version of the KR21 formula is the following:

$$\text{KR21 reliability coefficient} = \frac{K}{K-1}\left[1 - \frac{M(K-M)}{K(SD^2)}\right]$$

* Formula KR20 does not require the assumption that all items are of equal difficulty, although it is more difficult to calculate. Computer programs for doing so are commonly available, however, and should be used whenever a researcher cannot assume that all items are of equal difficulty.

where K = number of items in the test, M = mean of the set of test scores, and SD = standard deviation of the set of test scores.*

Although this formula may look somewhat intimidating, its use is actually quite simple. For example, if $K = 50$, $M = 40$, and $SD = 4$, the reliability coefficient would be calculated as shown below:

$$\text{Reliability} = \frac{50}{49}\left[1 - \frac{40(50 - 40)}{50(4^2)}\right]$$

$$= 1.02\left[1 - \frac{40(10)}{50(16)}\right]$$

$$= 1.02\left[1 - \frac{400}{800}\right]$$

$$= (1.02)(1 - .50)$$

$$= (1.02)(.50)$$

$$= .51$$

Thus, the reliability estimate for scores on this test is .51.

Is a reliability estimate of .51 good or bad, high or low? As with validity coefficients, there are two benchmarks we can use to evaluate reliability coefficients. First, we can compare a given coefficient with the extremes that are possible. As you will recall, a coefficient of .00 indicates a complete absence of a relationship; hence no reliability at all, whereas 1.00 is the maximum possible coefficient that can be obtained. Second, we can compare a given reliability coefficient with the sorts of coefficients that are usually obtained for measures of the same type. The reported reliability coefficients for many commercially available achievement tests, for example, are typically .90 or higher when Kuder-Richardson formulas are used. Many classroom tests report reliability coefficients of .70 and higher. Compared to these figures, our obtained coefficient must be judged rather low. For research purposes, a useful rule of thumb is that reliability should be at least .70 and preferably higher.

Alpha Coefficient. Another check on the internal consistency of an instrument is to cal-

culate an *alpha coefficient* (frequently called **Cronbach alpha** after the man who developed it). This coefficient (α) is a general form of the KR20 formula to be used in calculating the reliability of items that are not scored right versus wrong, as in some essay tests where more than one answer is possible.[3]

Following is a summary of the four methods of estimating the reliability of an instrument.

Method	Type of Information Provided
Test-retest	Stability of test scores over time.
Equivalent forms	Consistency of test scores over two different forms of an instrument.
Equivalent-forms plus test-retest	Consistency of scores over two different forms *and* a time interval.
Internal consistency	Consistency of test scores over different parts of an instrument.

An Example of Internal Consistency. To further illustrate the concept of reliability, let's take an actual test and calculate the internal consistency of the items included within it. Figure 7.2 on page 137 presents an example of a nontypical intelligence test that we have constructed. Follow the directions and take the test. Then we will calculate the split-half reliability.

Now look at the scoring key in the footnote at the bottom of this page.* Give yourself one point for each correct answer. Assume, for the moment, that a score on this test provides an indication of intelligence. If so, each item on the test should be a partial measure of intelligence. We could, therefore, divide the ten-item test into two five-item tests. One of these five-item tests can consist of all the odd-numbered items,

---

* See Chapter Eight for an explanation of standard deviation.

* Scoring key: 1. mother and son   2. Ulysses S. Grant 3. all of them   4. the match   5. one hour   6. white 7. nine   8. 70   9. two   10. none (It wasn't Moses, but Noah who took the animals on the Ark)

and the other five-item test can consist of all the even-numbered items. Now, record your score on the odd-numbered items, and also on the even-numbered items.

We now want to see if the odd-numbered items provide a measure of intelligence similar to that provided by the even-numbered items. If they do, your scores on the odd-numbered items and the even-numbered items should be pretty close. If they do not, then the two five-item tests do not give consistent results. If this is the case, then the total test (the ten items) probably does not give consistent results either, in which case the score could not be considered a reliable measure.

Ask some other people to take the test. Record their scores on the odd and even sets of items, using the worksheet shown in Figure 7.3. Take a look at the scores on each of the five-item sets for each of the five individuals, and compare them with your own. What would you conclude about the reliability of the scores? What would you say about any inferences about intelligence a researcher might make based on scores on this test? Could they be valid?*

Note that we have examined only one aspect of reliability (internal consistency) for results of this test. We still do not know how much a person's score might change if we gave the test at two different times (test-retest reliability). We could get a different indication of reliability if we gave one of the five-item tests at one time and the other five-item test at another time, to the same people (equivalent-forms reliability). You might try to do this with a few individuals, using a worksheet like the one shown in Figure 7.3.

The procedures in Figure 7.3 are the ones typically used by researchers in attempts to establish reliability. Normally, many more people are used, however (at least 100). You should also realize that most tests would have many more than ten items, since longer tests are usually more reliable than short ones, presumably be-

---

* You might want to assess the content validity of this test. How would you define intelligence? As you define the term, how would you evaluate this test as a measure of intelligence?

FIGURE **7.2**

The Q-E Intelligence Test

Directions: Read each of the following questions and write your answers on a separate sheet of paper. Suggested time to take the test is ten minutes.

1. There are two people in a room. The first person is the son of the second person, but the second person is not the first person's father. How are the two people related?

2. Who is buried in Grant's tomb?

3. Some months have thirty days, some have thirty-one. How many have twenty-eight days?

4. If you had only one match and entered a dark room in which there was an oil lamp, an oil heater, and some kindling wood, which would you light first?

5. If a physician gave you three pills and told you to take one every half hour, how long would they last?

6. A person builds a house with four sides to it, a rectangular structure, with each side having a southern exposure. A big bear comes wandering by. What color is the bear?

7. A farmer has seventeen sheep. All but nine died. How many did he have left?

8. Divide 30 by $\frac{1}{2}$. Add 10. What is the correct answer?

9. Take two apples from three apples. What do you have?

10. How many animals of each species did Moses take aboard the Ark?

FIGURE **7.3**

Reliability Worksheet

Person	Score on Five-Item Test 1 (#1, 3, 5, 7, 9)	Score on Five-Item Test 2 (#2, 4, 6, 8, 10)
You		
#1		
#2		
#3		
#4		
#5		

cause they provide a larger sampling of a person's behavior.

In sum, we hope it is clear that a major aspect of research design is the obtaining of reliable and valid information. Since both reliability and validity depend on the way in which instruments are used and on the inferences researchers wish to make from them, researchers can never simply assume that their instrumentation will provide satisfactory information. They can have more confidence if they use instruments on which there is previous evidence of reliability and validity, provided they use the instruments in the same way—that is, under the same conditions as existed previously. Even then, researchers cannot be sure; even when all else remains the same the mere passage of time may have impaired the instrument in some way.

What this means is that there is no substitute for checking reliability and validity as a part of the research procedure. There is seldom any excuse for failing to check internal consistency, since the necessary information is at hand and no additional data collection is required. Reliability over time does, in most cases, require an additional administration of an instrument, but this can usually be done. In considering this option, it should be noted that not all members of the sample need be retested, though this is desirable. It is better to retest a randomly selected subsample, or even a convenience subsample, than to have no evidence of reliability at all. Another option is to use a different, though very similar, sample to obtain retest evidence.

Obtaining evidence on validity is more difficult but seldom prohibitive. Content-related evidence can usually be obtained since it requires only a few knowledgeable and available judges. It is unreasonable to expect a great deal of construct-related evidence to be obtained but, in many studies, criterion-related evidence can be obtained. At a minimum, a second instrument should be administered. Locating or developing an additional means of instrumentation is sometimes difficult and occasionally impossible (for example, there is probably no way to validate a self report questionnaire on sexual behavior), but the results are well worth the time and energy involved. As with retest reliability, a subsample or different sample can be used.

Main Points of Chapter Seven

- The term "validity," as used in research, refers to the appropriateness, meaningfulness, and usefulness of any inferences a researcher draws based on data obtained through the use of an instrument.
- Content-related evidence of validity refers to judgments on the adequacy of an instrument.
- Criterion-related evidence of validity refers to the degree to which information provided by an instrument agrees with information obtained on other, independent instruments.
- A criterion is a standard for judging: with reference to validity, it is a second instrument against which scores on an instrument can be checked.
- Construct-related evidence of validity refers to the degree to which the totality of evidence obtained is consistent with theoretical expectations.
- A validity coefficient is a numerical index representing the degree of correspondence between scores on an instrument and a criterion measure.
- An expectancy table is a two-way chart used to evaluate criterion-related evidence of validity.
- The term "reliability," as used in research, refers to the consistency of scores or answers provided by an instrument.
- Errors of measurement refer to variations in scores obtained by the same individuals on the same instrument.

- The test-retest method of estimating reliability involves administering the same instrument twice to the same group of individuals after a certain time interval has elapsed.
- The equivalent-forms method of estimating reliability involves administering two different, but equivalent, forms of an instrument to the same group of individuals at the same time.
- The internal consistency method of estimating reliability involves comparing different sets of items that are part of an instrument.

For Discussion

1. We point out in the chapter that scores from an instrument may be reliable but not valid, yet not the reverse. Why would this be so?

2. What type of evidence—content-related, criterion-related, or construct-related—would each of the following represent?
   a. Ninety percent of the students who score high on a biology test receive A's as end-of-the-semester grades in biology.
   b. A professor of ancient history at a large university looks over a test to measure student knowledge of Greek and Roman civilizations and states that, in his opinion, the test measures such knowledge.
   c. A researcher discovers that students who score high on a teacher-made test of writing ability also receive high marks in writing courses. She finds that they are also rated high in writing ability by their teachers and that when they are asked to write a letter, they prepare one that two writing instructors independently judge to be clear and grammatically correct.
   d. A typing instructor receives a letter from the local office of a large corporation stating that several of his recently hired students are "excellent typists" on the job. In checking his records, the instructor finds that all but one of these students scored high on his end-of-the-year typing test.

3. If you calculated a correlation coefficient for two sets of scores and obtained a value of 3.7, you would have to say that:
   a. A very positive relationship existed between the two sets of scores.
   b. Students who had high scores on one of the instruments involved had poor scores on the other instrument.
   c. A negative relationship existed between the two sets of scores.
   d. Something is wrong with the calculation of the coefficient.

4. What sorts of evidence might a researcher obtain to check on the validity of results from each of the following types of instruments?
   a. A test designed to measure what ninth graders know about world geography.
   b. A performance test designed to measure an individual's ability to tune an automobile engine.
   c. A questionnaire designed to find out what people think will be the most pressing world problems in the next decade.
   d. A scale designed to measure the attitudes of people toward candidates running for political office in a given year.

    e. A participation flow chart designed to measure the amount of student participation in a class discussion.

    f. A performance checklist designed to measure how accurately and quickly soldiers can fieldstrip and clean a rifle.

    g. A scale designed to measure what students think about their classmates.

    h. An essay examination designed to measure student ability to draw warranted conclusions from a historical document.

    i. A projective device designed to assess an individual's feelings of hostility.

5. What might be some examples of errors of measurement that could affect an individual's score on a typing test?

6. Which do you think is harder to obtain, validity or reliability? Why?

7. Might reliability ever be more important than validity? Explain.

8. How would you assess the Q-E Intelligence Test in Figure 7.2 with respect to validity? Explain.

Notes

1. Norman E. Wallen, Mary C. Durkin, Jack R. Fraenkel, Anthony J. McNaughton, & Enoch I. Sawin. (1969). *The Taba Curriculum Development Project in Social Studies: Development of a comprehensive curriculum model for social studies for grades one through eight, inclusive of procedures for implementation and dissemination.* Menlo Park, CA: Addison-Wesley. p. 307.

2. Norman E. Gronlund, *How to construct achievement tests,* 4th Ed. (Englewood Cliffs, N.J.: Prentice-Hall, 1988), p. 140.

3. See Lee J. Cronbach. (1951). Coefficient alpha and the internal structure of tests, *Psychometrika, 16*: 297–334.

Research Exercise Seven:
Validity and Reliability

Use Problem Sheet 7 to describe how you plan to check on the validity and reliability of scores obtained with your instruments. If you plan to use an existing instrument, summarize what you have been able to learn about the validity and reliability of results obtained with it. If you plan to develop an instrument, explain how you will attempt to ensure validity and reliability. In either case, explain how you will obtain evidence to check validity and reliability.

1. I plan to use the following existing instruments:

_____

_____

In summary, I have learned the following about the validity and reliability of scores obtained with these instruments. _____

_____

_____

2. I plan to develop the following instruments:

_____

_____

I will try to ensure reliability and validity of results obtained with these instruments by: _____

_____

_____

3. For each instrument I plan to use:
   a. This is how I will collect evidence to check internal consistency:

   _____

   b. This is how I will collect evidence to check reliability over time (stability):

   _____

   c. This is how I will collect evidence to check validity:

   _____

Chapter Eight

DESCRIPTIVE STATISTICS

After instruments have been administered, and data have been scored and tabulated, the first step in data analysis is to describe it in a summary fashion using one or more descriptive statistics. Indeed, in some types of research, such as questionnaire studies, the entire process of analysis may consist of computing and then interpreting such statistics. In this chapter we discuss the use of descriptive statistics in detail.

Objectives

Reading this chapter should enable you to:

- *Differentiate* between categorical and quantitative data and *give an example* of each
- *Explain* the difference between a statistic and a parameter
- *Construct* a frequency polygon from data
- *Explain* what is meant by the terms "normal distribution" and "normal curve"
- *Calculate* the mean, median, and mode for a frequency distribution of data
- *Calculate* the range and standard deviation for a frequency distribution of data
- *Explain* how any particular score in a normal distribution can be interpreted in standard deviation units
- *Explain* what a "z score" is and *tell* why it is advantageous to be able to describe scores in z score terms
- *Explain* how to interpret a normal distribution
- *Construct* and *interpret* a scatterplot
- *Explain* more fully what a correlation coefficient is
- *Calculate* a Pearson correlation coefficient
- *Prepare* and *interpret* a frequency table, a bar graph, and a pie chart
- *Prepare* and *interpret* a crossbreak table

Two Fundamental Types of Numerical Data

In Chapter Six, we presented a number of instruments used in educational research. The researchers' intention in using these instruments is to collect information of some sort—abilities, attitudes, beliefs, reactions, and so forth—that will enable them to draw some conclusions about the sample of individuals they are studying.

As we have seen, such information can be collected in several ways, but it can be reported in only two ways: through either words or numbers. In certain types of research, such as interviews, ethnographic studies, or case studies, researchers often try to describe their findings through a narrative description of some sort. Their intent is not to reduce the information to numerical form but to present it in a descriptive form, and often as richly as possible. We give some examples of this method of reporting information in Chapters Sixteen and Seventeen.

In this chapter, however, we concentrate on numerical ways of reporting information.

Much of the information reported in educational research consists of numbers of some sort—test scores, percentages, grade-point averages, ratings, frequencies, and the like. The reason is an obvious one—numbers are a useful way to simplify information. Numerical information, usually referred to as *data*, can be classified in one of two basic ways: as either categorical or quantitative data.

Just as there are categorical and quantitative variables (see Chapter 3), there are two types of numerical data. Categorical data differ in *kind*, but not in degree or amount. Quantitative data, on the other hand, do differ in *degree* or *amount*.

QUANTITATIVE DATA

Quantitative data are obtained when the variable being studied is measured along a scale that indicates "how much" of the variable is

143

present. Quantitative data are reported in terms of scores. Higher scores indicate more of the variable (such as weight, academic ability, self-esteem, or interest in mathematics) is present than do lower scores. As you will recall from Chapter Six, there are many types of scores used in educational research. Some examples of quantitative data follow.

- The amount of money spent by various schools in a particular district in a semester on sports equipment (the variable is *amount of money spent on sports equipment*).
- SAT scores (the variable is *scholastic aptitude*).
- The temperatures recorded each day during the months of September through December in Omaha, Nebraska, during a given year (the variable is *temperature*).
- The anxiety scores of all first-year students enrolled at San Francisco State University in 1990 (the variable is *anxiety*).

CATEGORICAL DATA

When using a categorical variable, researchers determine how many instances fall into each category. These are reported either as frequencies (in each category) or as percentages of the total number of instances. A researcher who counts the various types of automobiles in a university parking lot, for example, is able to say how many autos there are of each type.

Categorical data, then, simply indicate the total number of objects, individuals, or events a researcher finds in a particular category. Thus, a researcher who reports the number of people for or against a particular government policy, or the number of students completing a program in successive years, is reporting categorical data. Notice that what the researcher is looking for is the frequency of certain characteristics, objects, individuals, or events. Many times it is useful, however, to convert these frequencies into percentages. Some examples of categorical data follow.

- The representation of each ethnic group in a school (the variable is *ethnicity*), e.g.: Caucasian, 1462 (40%); Black, 853 (24%); Hispanic, 760 (21%); Asian, 530 (15%).
- The number of male and female students in a chemistry class (the variable is *gender*).
- The number of teachers in a large school district who use (a) the lecture and (b) the discussion method (the variable is *teaching method*).
- The number of each type of tool found in a work room (the variable is *type of tool*).
- The number of each kind of merchandise found in a large department store (the variable is *type of merchandise*).

Statistics Versus Parameters

The major advantage of descriptive statistics is that they permit researchers to describe the information contained in many, many scores with just a few indices, such as the mean or median (more about these in a moment). When such indices are calculated for a sample drawn from a population, they are called **statistics;** when they are calculated from the entire population, they are called **parameters.** Since most educational research involves data from samples rather than from populations, we refer to statistics only in the remainder of this chapter.

Earlier, we pointed out that all data are either categorical or quantitative. This chapter presents the most commonly used techniques for summarizing such data. Some form of summary is essential to interpret data collected on any variable—a long list of scores or categorical representations is simply unmanageable.

Techniques for Summarizing Quantitative Data

Note that none of these techniques for summarizing quantitative data is appropriate to categorical data; they are for use only with quantitative data.

FREQUENCY POLYGONS

Before any statistics can be computed for quantitative data, the scores to be summarized must be listed in some fashion. A common way to list quantitative data is to prepare a **frequency distribution.** This is done by listing, in rank order from high to low, all the scores to be summarized, with tallies to indicate the number of subjects receiving each score (see Table 8.1). Often, the scores in a distribution are grouped into intervals. This results in a grouped frequency distribution, as shown in Table 8.2.

Although frequency distributions like the ones in Tables 8.1 and 8.2 can be quite informative, often the information they contain is hard to visualize. To further the understanding and interpretation of data, it is helpful to present it graphically—that is, to view the data from a graphical perspective. One such graphical display is known as a **frequency polygon.** Figure 8.1 presents a frequency polygon of the data in Table 8.2.

The steps involved in the construction of a frequency polygon are as follows.

1. List all scores, and tally how many students receive each score. Group scores, if necessary, into intervals.*
2. Place all of the possible scores (or groupings) on the horizontal axis, at equal intervals, starting with the lowest score on the left.
3. Place the frequencies of scores on the vertical axis, at equal intervals, starting with zero at the horizontal axis.
4. For each score (or grouping of scores), find the point where it intersects with its frequency of occurrence, and place a dot at that point. Remember that each score (or grouping of scores) with zero frequency must still be plotted (Figure 8.1).
5. Connect all the dots with a straight line.

* Grouping scores into intervals such as five or more is often necessary when there are a large number of scores in the distribution. Generally, twelve to fifteen points on the *X* axis is recommended.

TABLE 8.1

Example of a Frequency Distribution[a]

Raw Score	Frequency
64	2
63	1
61	2
59	2
56	2
52	1
51	2
38	4
36	3
34	5
31	5
29	5
27	5
25	1
24	2
21	2
17	2
15	1
6	2
3	1
	$n = 50$

[a] Technically, the table should include all scores, including those for which there are zero frequencies. We have eliminated those to simplify the presentation.

TABLE 8.2

Example of a Grouped Frequency Distribution

Raw Scores (Intervals of five)	Frequency
60–64	5
55–59	4
50–54	3
45–49	0
40–44	0
35–39	7
30–34	10
25–29	11
20–24	4
15–19	3
10–14	0
5– 9	2
0– 4	1
	$n = 50$

FIGURE 8.1

Example of a Frequency Polygon

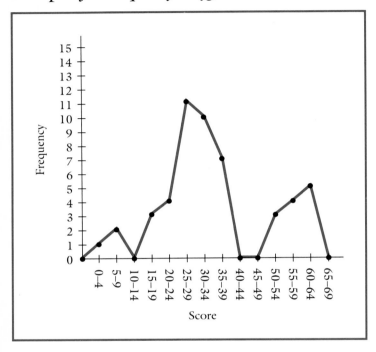

As you can see by looking at Figure 8.1, the fact that a large number of the students scored in the middle of this distribution is illustrated quite nicely.*

SKEWED POLYGONS

Data can be distributed in almost any shape. If a researcher obtains a set of data in which many individuals received low scores, for example, the shape of the distribution would look something like the frequency polygon shown in Figure 8.2. As you can see, in this particular distribution, only a few individuals received the higher scores. The frequency polygon in Figure 8.2 is said to be **positively skewed** because the tail of the distribution trails off to the right, in the direction of the higher (more *positive*) score

---

* A common mistake of students is to treat the vertical axis as if the numbers represented specific individuals. They do not. They represent *frequencies*. Each number on the vertical axis is used to plot the number of individuals at each score. In Figure 8.1, the dot above the interval 25–29 shows that eleven persons scored somewhere within the interval 25–29.

FIGURE 8.2

Example of a Positively Skewed Polygon

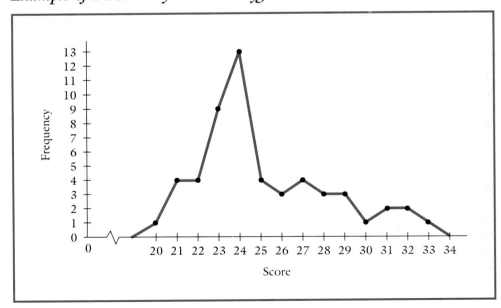

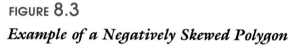

FIGURE 8.3

Example of a Negatively Skewed Polygon

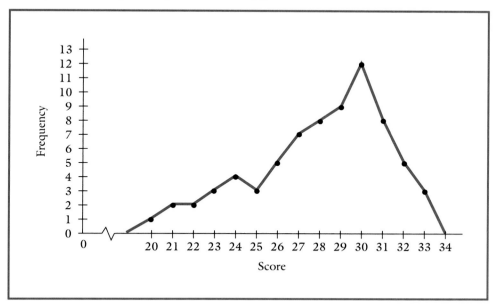

values. Suppose the reverse were true: Imagine that a researcher obtained a set of data in which few individuals received relatively low scores. Then the shape of the distribution would look like the frequency polygon in Figure 8.3. This polygon is said to be **negatively skewed**, since the tail of the distribution goes off to the left.

Frequency polygons are particularly useful in comparing two (or sometimes more) groups. In Chapter Six (see Table 6.2), we presented some hypothetical results of a study involving a comparison of two counseling methods. Figure 8.4 shows the polygons constructed using the data from Table 6.2.

This figure reveals several important findings. First, it is evident that method B resulted in higher scores, overall, than did method A. Second, it is clear that the scores for method B are more spread out. Third, it is clear that the reason for method B being higher overall is not that there are fewer scores at the low end of the scale (although this might have happened, it did not). In fact, the groups are almost identical in the number of scores below 61: A = 10, B =

12. The reason method B is higher overall is that there were fewer cases in the middle range of the scores (between 60 and 75), and more cases above 75. If this is not clear to you, study the shaded areas in the figure. Many times we want to know not only which group is higher overall but also where the differences are. In this example we see that method B results in more variability and that it results in a substantial number of scores higher than those in method A.

THE NORMAL CURVE

Often researchers draw a smooth curve instead of the series of straight lines in a frequency polygon. The smooth curve suggests that we are not just connecting a series of dots (that is, the actual frequencies of scores in a particular distribution), but rather showing a generalized distribution of scores that is not limited to one specific set of data. These smooth curves are known as **distribution curves.**

FIGURE **8.4**

Two Frequency Polygons Compared

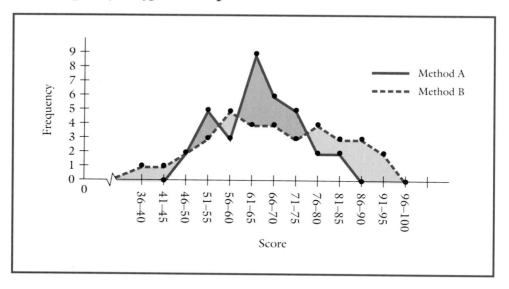

Many distributions of data tend to follow a certain specific shape of distribution curve called a **normal distribution.** When a distribution curve is normal, the large majority of the scores are concentrated in the middle of the distribution, and the scores decrease in frequency the further away from the middle they are, as shown in Figure 8.5.

The normal curve is based on a precise mathematical equation. As you can see, it is symmetrical and bell-shaped. The distribution of some human abilities, such as height and weight, approximate such a curve, while many others, such as spatial ability, manual dexterity, and creativity, are often assumed to do so. The normal curve is very useful to researchers. To fully understand its usefulness, however, you need to know something more about descriptive statistics, especially the standard deviation. We will postpone further discussion of the normal curve, therefore, until a bit later in this chapter.

FIGURE **8.5**

The Normal Curve

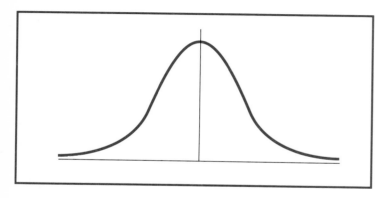

AVERAGES

Averages, or **measures of central tendency,** enable a researcher to summarize the data in a frequency distribution with a single number. The three most commonly used averages are the mode, the median, and the mean. Each represents a type of average or typical score attained by a group of individuals on some measure.

The Mode. The **mode** is the most frequent score in a distribution—that is, the score attained by more students than any other score. In the following distribution, what is the mode?

25, 20, 19, 17, 16, 16, 16,
  14, 14, 11, 10, 9, 9

Since it is the most frequent score, the mode is 16. What about this distribution?

25, 24, 24, 23, 22, 20, 19, 19, 18, 11, 10

This distribution (called a bimodal distribution) has two modes, 24 and 19. Since the mode really doesn't tell us very much about a distribution, however, it is not used very often in educational research.

The Median.   The **median** is the point below and above which 50 percent of the scores in a distribution fall. In short, it is the midpoint of the distribution (also the 50th percentile). In a distribution that contains an uneven number of scores, the median is the middlemost score (provided that the scores are listed in order). Thus, in the distribution 5, 4, 3, 2, 1, the median is 3. In a distribution that contains an even number of scores, the median is the point halfway between the two middlemost scores. Thus, in the distribution 70, 74, 82, 86, 88, 90, the median is 84. Hence, the median is not necessarily one of the actual scores in the distribution being summarized.

The median is only the midpoint and does not make use of all the information in each and every score in a distribution. It tends to ignore the actual numerical values of extreme scores, for example, except for determining which other scores it exceeds in size. Also, two very different distributions might have the same median. For example, look at the following two distributions.

Distribution 1: 98, 90, 84, 82, 76
Distribution 2: 90, 87, 84, 65, 41

In both distributions, the median is 84.

It may look like the median is fairly easy to determine. This is usually the case with un-grouped data. For grouped data, however, calculating the median requires somewhat more work. It can, however, be estimated by locating the score that has half of the area under the polygon above it and half below it.

The median is the most appropriate average to calculate when ordinal data are involved, although on occasion it should also be used when interval or ratio data result in very skewed distributions.

The Mean.   The **mean** is another average of all the scores in a distribution.* It is determined by adding up all of the scores and then dividing this sum by the total number of scores. Thus, the formula for computing the mean is as follows.

$$\text{Mean} = \frac{\text{Sum of all the scores in the distribution}}{\text{Total number of scores in the distribution}}$$

The mean of a distribution containing scores of 52, 68, 74, 86, 95, and 105 is 80. How did we determine this? We simply added up the total of all the scores in the distribution, which came to 480, and then divided this sum by six, the total number of scores. In symbolic form, the formula for computing the mean looks like this:

$$\overline{X} = \frac{\Sigma X}{n}$$

where Σ represents "sum of," X represents any raw score value, n represents the total number of scores, and $\overline{X}$ represents the mean. Thus, $480\% = 80$.

Table 8.3 presents a frequency distribution of scores on a test and each of the above measures of central tendency. As you can see, each of these indices tells us something a little different. The most frequent score was 62, but would we want to say that this was the most typical score? Probably not. The median of the scores was 64.5. The mean was 66.7. Perhaps this is the best description of the distribution of scores, but it, too, is not totally satisfactory because the distribution is skewed. Table 8.3 points up the

* Actually, there are several kinds of means (geometric, harmonic, etc.), but their use is specialized and infrequent. We refer here to the arithmetic average of several scores.

TABLE 8.3

Example of a Calculation of the Mode, Median, and Mean in a Distribution

Raw Score	Frequency
98	1
97	1
91	2
85	1
80	5
77	7
72	5
65	3
64	7
62	10
58	3
45	2
33	1
11	1
5	1
	$n = 50$

Mode = 62, Median = 64.5, Mean = 66.7

TABLE 8.4

Yearly Salaries of Workers in a Small Business

Mr. Davis	$ 6,500
Mr. Thompson	12,000
Ms. Angelo	12,500
Mr. Schmidt	13,000
Ms. Wills	15,500
Ms. Brown	18,500
Mr. Greene	20,000
Mr. Adams	25,000
Ms. Franklin	35,000
Mr. Payson (owner)	344,000

fact that these indexes are only *summaries* of all the scores in a distribution and hence cannot indicate the total variation that exists among the scores.

Which of the three averages (measures of central tendency), then, is best? It depends. The mean is the only one of the three that uses all the information in a distribution, since every score is used in calculating it, and it is generally preferred over the other two measures. However, it tends to be unduly influenced by extreme scores. (Can you see why?) On occasion, therefore, the median gives a more accurate indication of the average score in a distribution. Suppose, for example, that the yearly salaries earned by various workers in a small business were as shown in Table 8.4.

The mean of these salaries is $50,000. Would it be correct to say that this is the average yearly salary paid in this company? Obviously it would not. The extremely high salary paid to the owner of the company "inflates" the mean, so to speak. Using it as a summary figure to

indicate the average yearly salary would give an erroneous impression. In this instance, the median would be the more appropriate average to calculate, since it would not be as affected by the owner's salary. The median is $17,000, a far more accurate indication of the average salary for the year.

Figure 8.6 uses the frequency polygon presented in Figure 8.1 to illustrate how the three averages compare. Measures of central tendency can help researchers summarize their numerical findings. Furthermore, comparing averages—usually means—is the most common way to test hypotheses pertaining to different methods or treatments.*

SPREADS

While measures of central tendency are useful statistics for summarizing the scores in a distribution, they are not sufficient. Two distributions may have identical means and medians, for example, yet be quite different in other ways. For example, consider these two distributions:

Distribution A: 19, 20, 25, 32, 39
Distribution B: 2, 3, 25, 30, 75

---

* Use of the term "average" should be avoided in research reports. The specific average used should be indicated, e.g., mean or median.

FIGURE 8.6

The Three Averages (Measures of Central Tendency) Compared

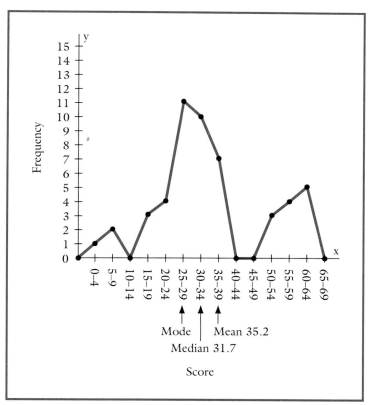

Score

The mean in both of these distributions is 27, and the median in both is 25. Yet you can see that the distributions differ considerably. In distribution A, the scores are rather close together, and tend to cluster around the mean. In distribution B, they are much more spread out. Hence the two distributions differ in what statisticians call **variability**. See Figure 8.7 for further examples.

There is a need, therefore, for measures researchers can use to describe the **spread,** or variability, that exists within a distribution. The two measures of variability that are most commonly employed in educational research are the range and the standard deviation. Range is by far the simpler of the two.

The Range. The **range** represents the distance between the highest and lowest scores in a distribution. It is very simple to compute. You simply determine the difference between the lowest score and the highest score. Thus, if the highest score in a distribution is 89 and the lowest is 11, the range would be 89 − 11, or 78. Since it involves only the two most extreme scores in a distribution, the range is but a crude indication of variability. Its main advantage is that it gives a quick (although rough) estimate of variability.

The Standard Deviation. The **standard deviation** is the most useful index of variability. Like the mean, every score in the distribution is

FIGURE 8.7

Different Distributions Compared with Respect to Averages and Spreads

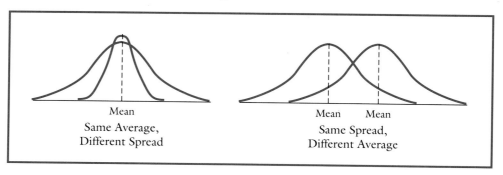

used to calculate it. The steps involved in calculating the standard deviation are straightforward.

1. Calculate the mean of the distribution.
2. Subtract the mean from each score. Each result is symbolized $X - \overline{X}$.
3. Square each of these scores $(X - \overline{X})^2$
4. Add up all the squares of these scores: $\sum (X - \overline{X})^2$
5. Divide the total by the number of scores. The result is called the **variance.**
6. Take the square root of the variance. This is the standard deviation.

The above steps can be summarized as follows:

$$SD = \sqrt{\frac{\Sigma(X - \overline{X})^2}{n}}$$

where SD is the symbol for standard deviation, Σ is the symbol for "sum of," X is the symbol for a raw score, $\overline{X}$ is the symbol for the mean, and n represents the number of scores in the distribution.

This procedure sounds more complicated than it is. It really is not difficult to calculate. Let us calculate the standard deviation of this distribution of ten scores: 80, 85, 60, 55, 25, 70, 40, 45, 50, 30. Follow along in Table 8.5.

TABLE 8.5

Calculation of the Standard Deviation of a Distribution

Raw Score	Mean	$X - \overline{X}$	$(X - \overline{X})^2$
85	54	31	961
80	54	26	676
70	54	16	256
60	54	6	36
55	54	1	1
50	54	−4	16
45	54	−9	81
40	54	−14	196
30	54	−24	576
25	54	−29	841
			$\Sigma = 3640$

$$\text{Variance } (SD^2) = \frac{\Sigma(X - \overline{X})^2}{n}$$

$$= \frac{3640}{10} = 364^a$$

$$\text{Standard Deviation } (SD) = \sqrt{\frac{\Sigma(X - \overline{X})^2}{n}}$$

$$= \sqrt{364} = 19.08^b$$

[a] The symbol for the variance of a sample sometimes is shown as s^2; the symbol for the variance of a population is σ^2.

[b] The symbol for the standard deviation of a sample sometimes is shown as s; the symbol for the standard deviation of a population is σ.

Step 1. Calculate the mean

$$\left(\overline{X} = \frac{\Sigma X}{n} = 54.\right)$$

Step 2. Subtract the mean from each raw score: $(X - \overline{X})$.

Step 3. Square each of these scores: $(X - \overline{X})^2$.

Step 4. Add up the squared scores and divide by the total number of such scores:

$$\Sigma \frac{(X - \overline{X})^2}{n}.$$ The total is 3640, which,

divided by 10, equals 364. This is the variance.

Step 5. Take the square root of the variance (use a calculator). It is 19.08. This is the standard deviation.

You will notice that the more spread out scores are, the greater the deviation scores will be and hence the larger the standard deviation. The closer the scores are to the mean, the less spread out they are and hence the smaller the standard deviation. Thus, if we were describing two sets of scores on the same test, and we stated that the standard deviation of the scores in set A was 2.7, while the standard deviation in set B was 8.3., we would know that there was much less variability in set A—that is, the scores were closer together.

When researchers know the mean and the standard deviation of a distribution, they can make useful interpretations and comparisons. Remember, however, that the most complete information about a distribution of scores is provided by a frequency polygon.

An interesting phenomenon about the standard deviation is that if a distribution is normal, then the mean plus or minus three standard deviations will encompass about 99 percent of all the scores in a distribution. For example, if the mean of a distribution is 72 and the standard deviation is 3, then just about 99

percent of the scores in the distribution would fall somewhere between scores of 63 and 81.

The Standard Deviation of a Normal Distribution. The total area under the normal curve represents all of the scores in a normal distribution. In such a curve, the mean, median, and mode are identical, so the mean falls at the exact center of the curve. It thus is also the most frequent score in the distribution. Since the curve is symmetrical, 50 percent of the scores must fall on each side of the mean.

We can illustrate graphically where the standard deviation is located on a normal curve in the following manner. Find the point on the curve at which it starts growing faster horizontally than it grows vertically. This is called the *point of inflection* of the curve. Draw a perpendicular line from this point to the base line, as shown in Figure 8.8. The distance between this point and the mean is the standard deviation.

It is a characteristic of the normal curve that other percentages can now be determined using the mean as a point of reference. For example, it can be shown mathematically that slightly more than 34 percent of the area under the curve falls between the mean and each of the vertical lines we drew in Figure 8.8. Hence, slightly more than 34 percent of the scores in a normal distribution are between the mean and one

FIGURE 8.8

The Normal Curve

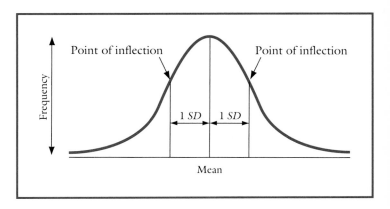

FIGURE 8.9

Percentages under the Normal Curve

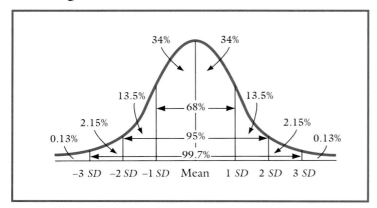

fall between 2 *SD* and 3 *SD*; some further arithmetic lets us determine that 99.7 percent of the scores lie between + 3 *SD* and − 3 *SD*. Hence we see that almost all of the scores in a normal distribution lie between the mean and plus or minus three standard deviations. Only .3 percent of all the scores fall above or below 3 *SD*.

If a set of scores is normally distributed, we can interpret any particular score if we know how far, in standard deviation units, it is from the mean. Suppose, for example, the mean of a normal distribution is 100 and the standard deviation is 15. A score that lies one standard deviation above the mean, therefore, would equal 115. A score that lies one standard deviation below the mean would equal 85. This distribution is shown in Figure 8.10. What would a score that lies 1.5 standard deviations about the mean equal?*

standard deviation (1 *SD*). This will be true for any set of scores that are normally distributed.

Since the curve is symmetrical, this holds true for both sides of the mean. Follow along in Figure 8.9 for these percentages. Approximately 68 percent of the scores fall between + 1 *SD* and − 1 *SD* (34 + 34 = 68). Furthermore, about 13.5 percent of the scores lie between 1 *SD* and 2 *SD*. By some simple arithmetic, then, we find that about 95 percent of the scores fall between + 2 *SD* and − 2 *SD* (68 + 13.5 + 13.5 = 95). Only about 2 percent of the scores

We also can determine how a particular individual's score compares with all the other scores in a normal distribution. For example, if a person's score lies exactly one standard deviation above the mean, then we know that slightly more than 84 percent of all the other scores in the distribution lie below his or her score.† If a distribution is normal, and we know the mean and the standard deviation of the distribution, we can determine the percentage of scores that lie above and below any given score. This is one of the most useful characteristics of the normal distribution.

FIGURE 8.10

A Normal Distribution of Scores

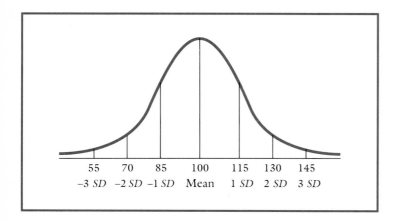

STANDARD SCORES AND THE NORMAL CURVE

Researchers often are interested in seeing how one person's score compares with another's. As we mentioned in Chapter Six, to determine this, researchers often convert raw scores to derived scores. We described two types of derived scores—age/grade equivalents and percentile

---

* 122.5
† 50% of the scores in the distribution must lie below the mean. 34% must lie between the mean and + 1 *SD*. Therefore 84% (50% + 34%) of the scores in the distribution must be below + 1 *SD*.

ranks—in that chapter, but mentioned another type—standard scores—only briefly. We discuss them now in somewhat more detail, since they are very useful.

Standard scores use a common scale to indicate how an individual compares to other individuals in a group. These scores are particularly helpful in comparing an individual's relative position on different instruments. The two standard scores that are most frequently used in educational research are z scores and T scores.

z Scores. z **scores** are the simplest form of standard score: They express how far a raw score is from the mean in standard deviation units. A raw score that is exactly on the mean corresponds to a z score of zero; a raw score that is exactly one standard deviation above the mean equals a z score of $+1$, while a raw score that is exactly one standard deviation below the mean equals a z score of -1. Similarly, a raw score that is exactly two standard deviations above the mean equals a z score of $+2$, while a raw score that is exactly two standard deviations below the mean equals a z score of -2, and so forth. One z, therefore, equals one standard deviation ($1\ z = 1\ SD$), $2\ z = 2\ SD$, $-0.5\ z = -0.5\ SD$, and so on (Figure 8.11). Thus, if the mean of a distribution was 50 and the standard deviation was 2, a raw score of 52 would equal a z score of $+1$, a raw score of 46 would equal a z score of -2, and so forth.

A big advantage of z scores is that they allow raw scores on different tests to be compared. For example, suppose a student received raw scores of 60 on a biology test and 80 on a chemistry test. A naive observer might be inclined to infer, at first glance, that the student was doing better in chemistry than in biology. But this might be unwise, for how "well" the student is doing comparatively cannot be determined until we know the mean and standard deviation for each distribution of scores. Let us further suppose that the mean on the biology test was 50, but on the chemistry test it was 90. Also assume the standard deviation on the biology test was 5, but on the chemistry test it was 10. What does this tell us? The student's

FIGURE 8.11

z Scores Associated with the Normal Curve

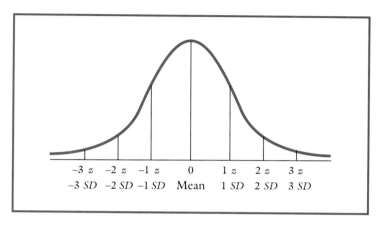

raw score in biology (60) is actually two standard deviations *above* the mean (a z score of $+2$), whereas his raw score in chemistry (80) is one standard deviation *below* the mean (a z score of -1). Rather than doing better in chemistry as the raw scores by themselves suggest, the student is actually doing better in biology. Table 8.6 compares both the raw scores, the z scores, and the percentile rank of the student on both tests.

Of course, z scores are not always exactly one or two standard deviations away from the mean. Usually, researchers apply the following formula to convert a raw score into a z score.

$$z\ \text{score} = \frac{\text{raw score} - \text{mean}}{\text{standard deviation}}$$

TABLE 8.6

Comparison of Raw Scores and z Scores on Two Tests

Test	Raw Score	Mean	SD	z Score	Percentile Rank
Biology	60	50	5	$+2$	98
Chemistry	80	90	10	-1	16

Thus for a raw score of 80, a mean of 65, and a standard deviation of 12 the z score will be

$$z = \left(\frac{80 - 65}{12}\right) = 1.25.$$

Probability and z Scores. Another important characteristic of the normal distribution is that the percentages associated with areas under the curve can be thought of as probabilities. A **probability** is a percentage stated in decimal form. For example, if there is a probability that an event will occur 25 percent of the time, this event can be said to have a probability of .25. Similarly, an event that will probably occur 90 percent of the time is said to have a probability of .90. All of the percentages associated with areas under a normal curve, therefore, can be expressed in decimal form and viewed as probability statements. Some of these probabilities are shown in Figure 8.12.

Considering the area under the normal curve in terms of probabilities is very helpful to a researcher. Let us consider an example. We have previously shown that approximately 34 percent of the scores in a normal distribution lie between the mean and 1 *SD*. Since 50 percent of the scores fall above the mean, roughly 16 percent of the scores must therefore lie above 1 *SD* (50 − 34 = 16). Now, if we express 16 percent in decimal form and interpret it as a probability,

we can say that the probability of randomly selecting an individual from the population who has a score of 1 *SD* or more above the mean is .16. Usually this is written as $p = .16$, with the p meaning probability. Similarly, we can determine the probability of randomly selecting an individual who has a score lying at or below −2 *SD* or lower, or between +1 *SD* and −1 *SD*, and so on. Figure 8.12 shows that the probability of selecting an individual who has a score lower than −2 *SD* is $p = .0228$, or roughly 2 in 100. The probability of randomly selecting an individual who has a score between −1 *SD* and +1 *SD* is $p = .6826$, and so forth.

Statistical tables exist (we include one in Appendix B) that give the percentage of scores associated with any z score in the normal distribution ($z = 1.05$; $z = 0.04$; $z = -2.35$; and so on). Hence a researcher can be very precise in describing the position of any particular score relative to other scores in a normal distribution. Figure 8.13 shows a portion of such a table (the full table is shown in Appendix B).

T Scores. Raw scores that are below the mean of a distribution convert to negative z scores. This is somewhat awkward. One way to eliminate negative z scores, therefore, is to convert them into T scores. **T scores** are simply z scores expressed in a different form. To change a z score to a T score, we simply multiply the z score by 10 and add 50. Thus, a z score of +1 equals a T score of 60 (1 × 10 = 10; 10 + 50 = 60). A z score of −2 equals a T score of 30 (−2 × 10 = −20; −20 + 50 = 30). A z score of zero (which is the equivalent of the mean of the raw scores) equals a T score of 50. You should see that a distribution of T scores has a mean of 50 and a standard deviation of 10. If you think about it, you should also see that a T score of 50 equals the 50th percentile.

When a researcher knows, or can assume, that a distribution of scores is normal, T and z scores can be interpreted in terms of percentile ranks because there is then a direct relationship between the two. Figure 8.14 illustrates this relationship. There are other systems similar to

FIGURE 8.12

Probabilities under the Normal Curve

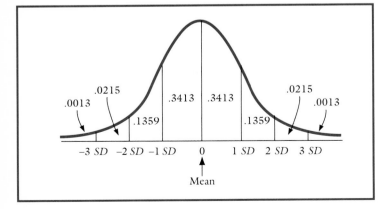

FIGURE **8.13**

*Table Showing Probability Areas
between the Mean and Different z Scores*

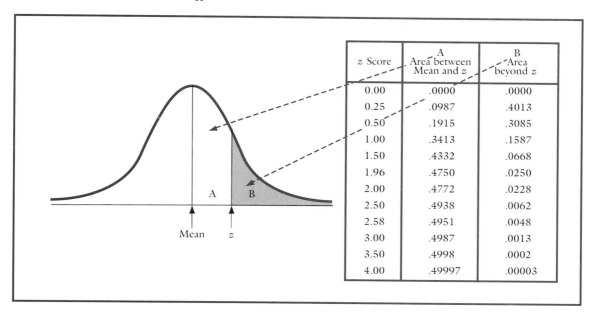

z Score	A Area between Mean and z	B Area beyond z
0.00	.0000	.0000
0.25	.0987	.4013
0.50	.1915	.3085
1.00	.3413	.1587
1.50	.4332	.0668
1.96	.4750	.0250
2.00	.4772	.0228
2.50	.4938	.0062
2.58	.4951	.0048
3.00	.4987	.0013
3.50	.4998	.0002
4.00	.49997	.00003

T scores, which differ only in the choice of values for the mean and standard deviation. Two of the most common, those used with the Graduate Record Examination ($\overline{X} = 500$, $SD = 100$) and the Wechsler Intelligence Scales ($\overline{X} = 100$, $SD = 15$), are also illustrated in Figure 8.14.

The Importance of the Normal Curve and z Scores.   You may have noticed that the preceding discussion of the use of *z* scores, percentages, and probabilities in relation to the normal curve was always qualified by the words *if* or *when* the distribution of scores is normal. You should recall that *z* scores can be calculated regardless of the shape of the distribution of original scores. But it is *only* when the distribution is normal that the conversion to percentages or probabilities as described above is legitimate. Fortunately, many distributions *do* approximate the normal curve. This is most likely when a sample is chosen randomly from a broadly defined population. (It would be very unlikely,

for example, with achievement scores in a sample that consisted only of gifted students.)

When actual data do not approximate the normal curve, they can be changed to do so. In other words, any distribution of scores can be "normalized." The procedure for doing so is not complicated, but it is too laborious to illustrate in this text. Most published tests which permit use of standard scores have normalized the score distributions in order to permit the translation of *z* scores to percentages. This relationship—between *z* scores and percentages of area under the normal curve—is also basic to many inferential statistics, which we shall discuss in Chapter Nine.

CORRELATION

In many places throughout this text we have stated that the most meaningful research is that which seeks to find, or verify, relationships among variables. Comparing the performance

FIGURE 8.14

Examples of Standard Scores

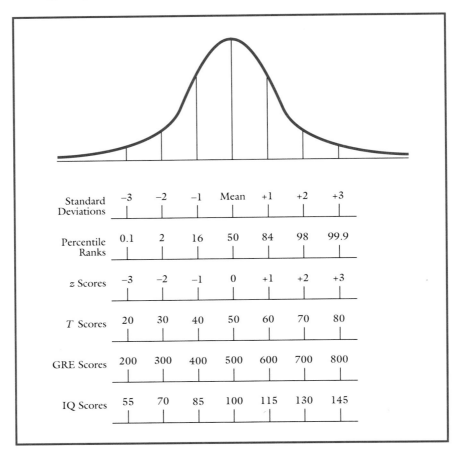

of different groups is, as you have seen, one way to study relationships. In such studies one variable is categorical—the variable that defines the groups (for example, method A versus method B). The other variable is most often quantitative and groups are typically compared using frequency polygons, averages, and spreads.

In correlational research, researchers seek to determine if a relationship exists between two (or more) quantitative variables, such as age and weight, reading and writing ability, etc. Sometimes, such relationships are useful in prediction, but most often the eventual goal is to say something about causation. Although causal relationships cannot be proven through correlational studies, researchers hope eventually to

make causal statements as an outgrowth of their work. The totality of studies showing a relationship between incidence of lung cancer and cigarette use is a current example. We will discuss correlational research in further detail in Chapter Thirteen.

Scatterplots. What is needed is a means to determine whether relationships exist in data. A useful technique for representing relationships with quantitative data is the scatterplot. A **scatterplot** is a pictorial representation of the relationship between two quantitative variables. Scatterplots are easy to construct, provided some common pitfalls are avoided: First, in order to be plotted, there must be a score on each variable

TABLE **8.7**

Data Used to Construct Scatterplot in Figure 8.15

FIGURE **8.15**

Scatterplot of Table 8.7

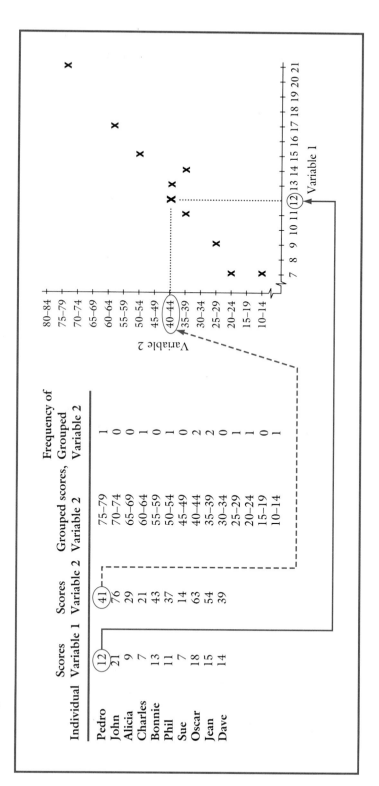

Individual	Scores Variable 1	Scores Variable 2	Grouped scores, Variable 2	Frequency of Grouped Variable 2
Pedro	12	41	75–79	1
John	21	76	70–74	0
Alicia	9	29	65–69	0
Charles	7	21	60–64	1
Bonnie	13	43	55–59	0
Phil	11	37	50–54	1
Sue	7	14	45–49	0
Oscar	18	63	40–44	2
Jean	15	54	35–39	2
Dave	14	39	30–34	0
			25–29	1
			20–24	1
			15–19	0
			10–14	1

for *each* individual; second, the intervals (if any) within each variable (axis) must be equal; third, each individual must be represented by one, and only one, point of intersection. We used the data in Table 8.7 to construct the scatterplot in Figure 8.15. The steps involved are the following.

1. Decide which variable will be represented on each axis. It makes no difference which variable is placed on which axis. We have used the horizontal (*x*) axis for variable one and the vertical (*y*) axis for variable two.
2. Divide each axis into about twelve to fifteen sections. Each point on the axis will represent a particular score or group of scores. Be sure all scores can be included.
3. Group scores if desirable. It was not necessary for us to group scores for variable one, since all of the scores fall within a fifteen-point range. For variable two, however, representing *each* score on the axis would result in a great many points on the vertical axis. Therefore, we grouped them within *equal sized* intervals of five points each.
4. Plot each person at the point where his or her scores on each variable intersect. For example, Pedro had a score of 12 on variable one, so we locate 12 on the horizontal axis. He had a score of 41 on variable two, so we locate that score (in the 40–44 grouping) on the vertical axis. We then draw imaginary lines from each of these points until they intersect, and mark an X or a dot at that point.
5. In the same way, plot the scores of all ten students on both variables. The completed result is a scatterplot.

Interpreting a Scatterplot. How do researchers interpret scatterplots? What are they intended to reveal? Researchers want to know not only *if* a relationship exists between variables, but also *to what degree*. The degree of relationship, if one exists, is what a scatterplot illustrates.

Consider Figure 8.15. What does it tell us about the relationship between variable one and

variable two? This question can be answered in several ways.

1. We might say that high scores on variable one go with high scores on variable two (as in John's case) and that low scores also tend to go together (as in Charles's case).
2. We might say that by knowing a student's score on one variable, we can estimate his or her score on the other variable fairly closely. Suppose, for example, a new student attains a score of 13 on variable one. What would you predict his or her score would be on variable two? You probably would *not* predict a score of 65 or one of 25 (we would predict a score somewhere from 35 to 45).
3. The customary answer for a scatterplot that looks like this would be that there is a strong or high degree of relationship between the two variables. If all the plotted points were on a straight line, we would speak of it as a "perfect linear relationship." Such relationships are very rare, however, and never attained in educational research.

Correlation Coefficients and Scatterplots. Figure 8.16 presents several other examples of scatterplots. Studying them will help you understand the notion of a relationship and also further your understanding of the correlation coefficient. As we mentioned in Chapter Seven, a correlation coefficient, designated by the symbol (*r*), expresses the degree of relationship that exists between two variables. A positive relationship is indicated when high scores on one variable are accompanied by high scores on the other, low scores on one are accompanied by low scores on the other, and so forth. A negative relationship is indicated when high scores on one variable are accompanied by low scores on the other, and vice versa.

You should recall that correlation coefficients are never more than +1.00, indicating a perfect positive relationship, or −1.00, indicating a perfect negative relationship. Perfect positive or negative correlations, however, are rarely, if ever, achieved. If the two variables are highly related, a coefficient somewhat close to +1.00

FIGURE 8.16

Further Examples of Scatterplots

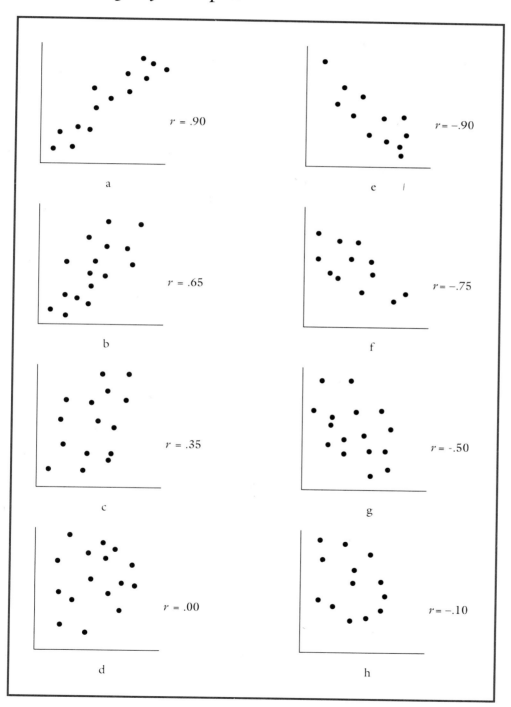

or -1.00 will be obtained (such as .85 or .93). The closer the coefficient is to either of these extremes, the greater the degree of the relationship. If there is no or hardly any relationship, a coefficient of .00 or close to it will be obtained. The coefficient is calculated directly from the same scores used to construct the scatterplot.

The scatterplots in Figure 8.16 illustrate different degrees of correlation. Both positive and negative correlations are shown. Scatterplots a, b, and c illustrate different degrees of positive correlation, while scatterplots e, f, g, and h illustrate different degrees of negative correlation. Scatterplot d indicates no relationship between the two variables involved.

THE PEARSON PRODUCT-MOMENT COEFFICIENT

Actually, there are many different correlation coefficients, each applying to a particular circumstance and each calculated by means of a different computational formula. The one we have been illustrating is the one most frequently used—the Pearson product-moment coefficient of correlation. It is symbolized by the lowercase letter r.

When the data for both variables are expressed in terms of quantitative scores, the Pearson r is the appropriate correlation coefficient to calculate. It is designed for use with interval or ratio data. The formula for calculating the Pearson r coefficient is:

$$r = \frac{n\Sigma XY - (\Sigma X)(\Sigma Y)}{\sqrt{[n\Sigma X^2 - (\Sigma X)^2][n\Sigma Y^2 - (\Sigma Y)^2]}}$$

The Pearson formula looks a lot more complicated than it really is. It does have a lot of steps to follow before we finally get to the end, but each step is easy to calculate. Let's take a look. As you will recall, we need two sets of scores to calculate any correlation coefficient, and the Pearson is no exception.

Let's imagine we have the following sets of scores for two variables, X and Y, for five students.

Student	Variable X	Variable Y
A	20	20
B	18	16
C	28	20
D	15	12
E	10	10

What we would like to know is whether these two variables are related, and if so, how—positively? negatively? To answer these questions, we apply the Pearson formula and calculate the correlation coefficient for the two sets of scores.

Student	X	Y	X^2	Y^2	XY
A	20	20	400	400	400
B	18	16	324	256	288
C	18	20	324	400	360
D	15	12	225	144	180
E	10	10	100	100	100
	81	78	1373	1300	1328
	$\uparrow$	$\uparrow$	$\uparrow$	$\uparrow$	$\uparrow$
	ΣX	ΣY	ΣX^2	ΣY^2	ΣXY

As you can see, ΣX equals the sum of the scores on the X variable. ΣY equals the sum of the scores on the Y variable. ΣX^2 equals the sum of the squares of each of the X scores. ΣY^2 equals the sum of the squares of each of the Y scores. ΣXY equals the sum of the products of the X and Y scores (i.e., the sum of each X score multiplied by its corresponding Y score). Now we simply substitute each of these sums into the formula as shown below.

$$r = \frac{5(1328) - (81)(78)}{\sqrt{[5(1373) - 81^2][5(1300) - 78^2]}}$$

The n in the formula simply refers to the number of *pairs* of scores there are (five in our example). To determine r, we now perform the following calculations.

1. First, multiply ΣXY by n. $1328(5) = 6640$
2. Multiply ΣX by ΣY. $81(78) = 6318$.
3. Subtract step 2 from step 1. $6640 - 6318 = 322$.

4. Multiply ΣX^2 by n. 1373(5) = 6865.
5. Square ΣX. (81)^2 = 6561.
6. Subtract step 5 from step 4. 6885 − 6561 = 304.
7. Multiply ΣY^2 by n. 1300(5) = 6500
8. Square ΣY. 78^2 = 6084.
9. Subtract step 8 from step 9. 6500 − 6084 = 416.
10. Multiply step 6 by step 9. 304(416) = 126464
11. Take the square root of step 10. $\sqrt{126464}$ = 355.61
12. Divide step 3 by step 11. $\dfrac{322}{355.61}$ = .90

ETA

Another index of correlation that you should become familiar with is called **eta** (symbolized as η). We shall not illustrate how to calculate eta (since it requires computational methods beyond the scope of this text), but you should know that it is used when a scatterplot shows that a straight line is not the best fit for the plotted points. In the examples shown in Figure 8.17, for example, you can see that a curved line provides a much better fit to the data than would a straight line.

Eta is interpreted in much the same way as the Pearson r, except that it ranges from .00 to 1.00, rather than from − 1.00 to + 1.00. Higher values, as with the other correlation coefficients, indicate higher degrees of relationship.

Techniques for Summarizing Categorical Data

THE FREQUENCY TABLE

Suppose a researcher, using a questionnaire, has been collecting data from a random sample of fifty teachers in a large, urban school district. The questionnaire covers many variables related to their activities and interests. One of the variables is "Learning activity I use most frequently in my classroom." The researcher arranges her data on this (and other) variables in

FIGURE 8.17

Examples of Nonlinear (Curvilinear) Relationships

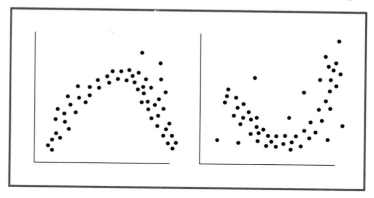

the form of a frequency table; which shows the frequency with which each type, or category, of learning activity is mentioned. The researcher simply places a tally mark for each individual in the sample alongside the activity mentioned. When she has tallied all fifty individuals, her results look like the following frequency listing.

Response	Tally	Frequency
Lecture	JHT JHT JHT	15
Class discussions	JHT JHT	10
Oral reports	||||	4
Library research	||	2
Seatwork	JHT	5
Demonstrations	JHT |||	8
Audiovisual presentations	JHT |	6
		$n = 50$

As you can see, the tally marks have been added up at the end of each row to show the total number of individuals who listed that activity. Often with categorical data researchers are interested in proportions, because they wish to estimate (if their sample is random) about the proportions in the total population from which the sample was selected. Thus, the total numbers in each category are often changed to percentages. This has been done in Table 8.8, with the categories arranged in descending order of frequency.

TABLE **8.8**

Frequency and Percentage of Total of Responses to Questionnaire

Response	Frequency	Percentage of Total (%)
Lecture	15	30
Class discussions	10	20
Demonstrations	8	16
Audiovisual presentations	6	12
Seatwork	5	10
Oral reports	4	8
Library research	2	4
Total	50	100

BAR GRAPHS AND PIE CHARTS

Two other ways are used to illustrate a difference in proportions. One is to use a **bar graph** or **histogram** as shown in Figure 8.18; another is to use a **pie chart**, as shown in Figure 8.19.

THE CROSSBREAK TABLE

When a relationship between two categorical variables is of interest, it is usually reported in the form of a **crossbreak table** (sometimes called a contingency table). The simplest crossbreak is a 2 by 2 table, as shown in Table 8.9. Each individual is tallied in one, and only one, cell that corresponds to the combination of

FIGURE **8.18**

Example of a Bar Graph

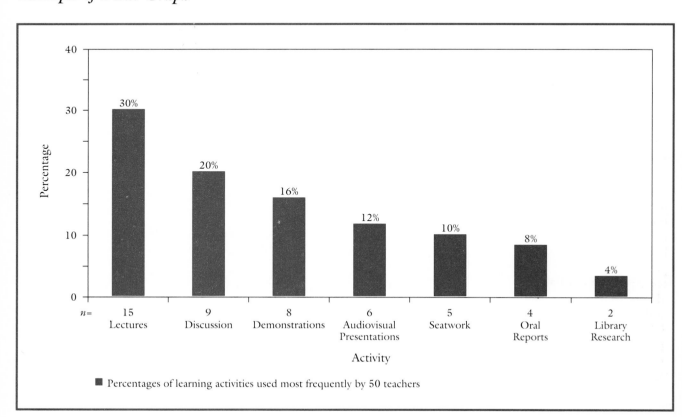

Percentages of learning activities used most frequently by 50 teachers

Example of a Pie Chart

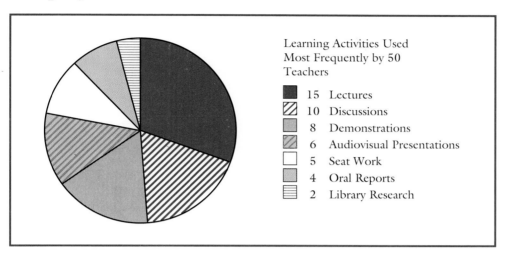

Learning Activities Used
Most Frequently by 50
Teachers

- 15 Lectures
- 10 Discussions
- 8 Demonstrations
- 6 Audiovisual Presentations
- 5 Seat Work
- 4 Oral Reports
- 2 Library Research

gender and grade level. You will notice that the numbers in each of the cells in Table 8.9 represent totals—the total number of individuals who fit the characteristics of the cell (for example, junior high males). Although percentages and proportions are sometimes calculated for cells, we do not recommend it, as this is often misleading.

It probably seems obvious that Table 8.9 reveals a relationship between teacher gender and grade level. A junior high school teacher is more likely to be female; a high school teacher is more likely to be male. Often, however, it is useful to calculate "expected" frequencies in order to see results more clearly. What do we mean by "expected"? If there is no relationship between variables, we would "expect" the proportion of cases within each cell of the table corresponding to a category of a variable to be identical to the proportion within that category in the entire group. Look, for example, at Table 8.10. Exactly one-half (50 percent) of the total group of teachers in this table are female. If gender is unrelated to grade level, we would "expect" that the same proportion (exactly one-half) of the junior high school teachers would be female. Similarly, we would "expect" that

TABLE **8.9**

Grade Level and Gender of Teachers (Hypothetical Data)

	Male	Female	Total
Junior High School Teachers	40	60	100
High School Teachers	60	40	100
Total	100	100	200

TABLE **8.10**

Repeat of Table 8.9 with Expected Frequencies (in parentheses)

	Male	Female	Total
Junior High School Teachers	40 (50)	60 (50)	100
High School Teachers	60 (50)	40 (50)	100
Total	100	100	200

TABLE **8.11**

Position, Gender, and Ethnicity of School Leaders (Hypothetical Data)

	Administrators		Teachers		Total
	White	*Non-White*	*White*	*Non-White*	
Male	50	20	150	80	300
Female	20	10	150	120	300
Total	70	30	300	280	600

one-half of the high school teachers would be female. The "expected" frequencies, in other words, would be fifty female junior high school teachers, and fifty female high school teachers, rather than the sixty female junior high school and forty female high school teachers that were actually obtained. These expected and actual, or "observed," frequencies are shown in each box (or "cell") in Table 8.10. The expected frequencies are shown in parentheses.

Comparing expected and actual frequencies makes the degree and direction of the relationship clearer. This is particularly helpful with more complex tables. Look, for example, at Table 8.11. This table contains not two, but three, variables.

The researcher who collected and summarized these data hypothesized that appointment to administrative (or other nonteaching) positions rather than teaching positions is related to (a) gender and (b) ethnicity. While it is possible to examine Table 8.11 in its entirety to evaluate these hypotheses, it is much easier to see the relationships by extracting components of the table. Let us look at the relationship of each variable in the table to the other two variables. By taking two variables at a time, we can compare (a) position and ethnicity, (b) position and gender, and (c) gender and ethnicity. Table 8.12 presents the data for position and ethnicity, Table 8.13 presents the data for position and gender, and Table 8.14 presents the data for gender and ethnicity.

Let us review the calculation of expected frequencies by referring to Table 8.12. This table shows the relationship between ethnicity and position. Since one-sixth of the total group (100/600) are administrators, we would expect 62

TABLE **8.12**

Position and Ethnicity of School Leaders with Expected Frequencies (Derived from Table 8.11)

	Administrators	Teachers	Total
White	70 (62)	300 (308)	370
Nonwhite	30 (38)	200 (192)	230
Total	100	500	600

TABLE **8.13**

Position and Gender of School Leaders with Expected Frequencies (Derived from Table 8.11)

	Administrators	Teachers	Total
Male	70 (50)	230 (250)	300
Female	30 (50)	270 (250)	300
Total	100	500	600

whites to be administrators ($\frac{1}{6}$ of 370). Likewise, we would expect 38 of the nonwhites to be administrators ($\frac{1}{6}$ of 230). Since five-sixths of the total group are teachers, we would expect 308 of the whites ($\frac{5}{6}$ of 370), and 192 of the non-whites ($\frac{5}{6}$ of 230), to be teachers. As you can see, however, the actual frequencies for administrators were 70 (rather than 62) whites, and 30 (rather than 38) nonwhites, and the actual frequencies for teachers were 300 (rather than 308) whites, and 200 (rather than 192) nonwhites. This tells us that there is a discrepancy between what we would expect (if there is no relationship) and what we actually obtained. A discrepancy between the frequency expected and that actually obtained can also be seen in Tables 8.13 and 8.14.

An index of the strength of the relationships can be obtained by summing the discrepancies in each table. In Table 8.12, the sum equals 32, in Table 8.13, it equals 80, and in Table 8.14 it equals 60. The calculation of these sums is shown in Table 8.15. The discrepancy between expected and observed frequencies is greatest in Table 8.13, position by gender; less in Table 8.14, gender by ethnicity; and least in Table 8.12, position by ethnicity. A numerical index showing degree of relationship—the contingency coefficient—will be discussed in Chapter Nine.

Thus, the data in the crossbreak tables reveal that there is a slight tendency for there to be more white administrators and more nonwhite teachers than would be expected (Table 8.12). There is a stronger tendency toward more white males and nonwhite females than would be expected (Table 8.14). The strongest relationship indicates more male administrators and more female teachers than would be expected (Table 8.13). In sum, the chances of having an administrative position appear to be considerably greater if one is male, and slightly enhanced if one is white.

In contrast to the preceding example, where each variable (ethnicity, gender, role) is clearly categorical, a researcher sometimes has a choice whether to treat data as quantitative or as categorical. Take the case of a researcher who measures self-esteem by a self-report questionnaire

TABLE 8.14

Gender and Ethnicity of School Leaders with Expected Frequencies (Derived from Table 8.11)

	White	Nonwhite	Total
Male	200 (185)	100 (115)	300
Female	170 (185)	130 (115)	300
Total	370	230	600

TABLE 8.15

Total of Discrepancies between Expected and Observed Frequencies in Tables 8.12 through 8.14

Table 8.12		Table 8.13		Table 8.14	
(70 vs. 62)	= 8	(70 vs. 50)	= 20	(200 vs. 185)	= 15
(30 vs. 38)	= 8	(30 vs. 50)	= 20	(170 vs. 185)	= 15
(300 vs. 308)	= 8	(230 vs. 250)	= 20	(100 vs. 115)	= 15
(200 vs. 192)	= 8	(270 vs. 250)	= 20	(130 vs. 115)	= 15
Total	32		80		60

scored for number of items answered (yes or no) in the direction indicating high self-esteem. The researcher might decide to use these scores to divide the sample ($n = 60$) into high, middle, and low thirds. She might use only this information for each individual and subsequently treat the data as categorical, as is shown, for example, in Table 8.16.

Most researchers would advise against treating the data this way, however, since it "wastes" so much information—for example, distinctions in scores within each category are ignored. A quantitative analysis, by way of contrast, would compare the mean self-esteem scores of males and females.

TABLE 8.16

Crossbreak Table Showing Relationship between Self-Esteem and Gender (Hypothetical Data)

Gender	Self-Esteem		
	Low	*Middle*	*High*
Male	10	15	5
Female	5	10	15

Main Points of Chapter Eight

- There are two fundamental types of numerical data a researcher can collect. Categorical data are data obtained by determining the frequency of occurrences in each of several categories. Quantitative data are data obtained by determining placement on a scale that indicates amount or degree.
- A statistic is a numerical or graphic way of summarizing data from a sample.
- A parameter is a numerical or graphic way of summarizing data from a population.
- A frequency distribution is a listing, from high to low, of all the scores in a distribution. A grouped frequency distribution is a distribution in which the scores have been grouped into equal intervals.
- A frequency polygon is a graphic display of a frequency distribution. It is a graphic way to summarize quantitative data for one variable.
- A graphic distribution of scores in which only a few individuals receive high scores is called a positively skewed polygon; one in which only a few individuals receive low scores is called a negatively skewed polygon.
- A theoretical distribution that is symmetrical, and in which a large majority of the scores are concentrated in the middle of the distribution, is called a normal distribution.
- A distribution curve is a smoothed out frequency polygon.
- The distribution curve of a normal distribution is called a normal curve. It is bell-shaped, and its mean, median, and mode are identical.
- There are several measures of central tendency (averages) that are used to summarize quantitative data. The two most common are the mean and the median.
- The mean of a distribution is determined by adding up all of the scores and dividing this sum by the total number of scores.
- The median of a distribution marks the point at and below which half of the scores in the distribution lie.
- The mode is the most frequent score in a distribution.
- The term "variability," as used in research, refers to the extent to which the scores on a quantitative variable in a distribution are spread out.

- The most common measure of variability used in educational research is the standard deviation.
- The range, another measure of variability, represents the difference between the highest and lowest scores in a distribution.
- Standard scores use a common scale to indicate how an individual compares to other individuals in a group. The simplest form of standard score is a z score. A z score expresses how far a raw score is from the mean in standard deviation units.
- The big advantage of z scores is that they allow raw scores on different tests to be compared.
- The term "probability," as used in research, refers to how often a particular event occurs. Probabilities are usually expressed in decimal form.
- A correlation coefficient is a numerical index expressing the degree of relationship that exists between two quantitative variables. The one most commonly used in educational research is the Pearson r.
- A scatterplot is a graphic way to report a relationship between two quantitative variables.
- There are a variety of graphic techniques researchers use to summarize categorical data, including frequency tables, bar graphs, and pie charts.
- A crossbreak table is a graphic way to report a relationship between two or more categorical variables.

For Discussion

1. What would be the most appropriate average to use to answer each of the following questions?
   a. What was the most frequent score in the class?
   b. Which score had half of the scores in the class below it?
   c. Which average uses all of the information available?

2. Would you expect the following correlations to be positive or negative? Why?
   a. Bowling scores and golf scores for professional athletes
   b. Reading scores and arithmetic scores for sixth graders
   c. Age and weight for a group of five year olds; for a group of fifty year olds
   d. Life expectancy at age 40 and frequency of smoking
   e. Size and strength for junior high students

3. Match each item in column A with the best choice from column B

A	B
____ 1. correlation coefficient	a. measure of central tendency
____ 2. standard score	b. measure of variability
____ 3. median	c. measure of relationship
____ 4. standard deviation	d. measure of relative position

4. Why do you think so many people mistrust statistics? How might such mistrust be alleviated?

5. Could the range of a distribution ever be smaller than the standard deviation of that distribution? Why or why not?

6. Would it be possible for two different distributions to have the same standard deviation but different means? What about the reverse? Explain.

7. "The larger the standard deviation of a distribution, the more heterogeneous the scores in that distribution." Is this true? Explain.

8. "The most complete information about a distribution of scores is provided by a frequency polygon." Explain.

9. Grouping scores in a frequency distribution has its advantages, but also its disadvantages. What might be some examples of each?

10. Any single raw score, in and of itself, tells us nothing. Would you agree? Explain.

11. Why can a correlation coefficient never be larger than plus or minus 1.00?

Research Exercise Eight:
Descriptive Statistics

Using Problem Sheet 8, state again the question or hypothesis of your study and list your variables. Then indicate how you would summarize the results for each variable in your study. Lastly, indicate how you would describe the relationship between variables one and two.

1. The question or hypothesis of my study is: _____
   _____

2. My variables are: (1) _____
   (2) _____ (others) _____

3. I consider variable 1 to be: quantitative _____ or categorical _____

4. I consider variable 2 to be: quantitative _____ or categorical _____

5. I would summarize the results for each variable as follows (indicate with a checkmark ✔):

variable 1 _____	variable 2 _____	other _____
a. frequency polygon		
b. mean		
c. median		
d. range		
e. standard deviation		
f. frequency table		
g. bar graph		
h. pie chart		

6. I will describe the relationship between variables 1 and 2 by (indicate with a checkmark ✔):

   a. comparison of frequency polygons _____

   b. comparison of averages _____

   c. crossbreak tables(s) _____

   d. correlation coefficient _____

   e. scatterplot _____

171

Chapter Nine

INFERENTIAL STATISTICS

Descriptive statistics are but one type of statistic that researchers use to analyze their data. Many times they also wish to make inferences about a population on the basis of data obtained from a sample. Various inferential statistics techniques allow them to do this. This chapter presents several such techniques and discusses when they are and are not warranted in educational research.

- *Explain* what is meant by the term "inferential statistics"
- *Explain* the concept of sampling error
- *Describe* briefly how to calculate a confidence interval
- *State* the difference between a research hypothesis and a null hypothesis
- *Describe* briefly the logic underlying hypothesis testing
- *State* what is meant by the terms "significance level" and "statistically significant"
- *Explain* the difference between a one- and a two-tailed test of significance
- *Explain* the difference between parametric and nonparametric tests of significance
- *Name* three examples of parametric tests used by educational researchers
- *Name* three examples of nonparametric tests used by educational researchers
- *Explain* the importance of random sampling

What Are Inferential Statistics?

Suppose a researcher administers a commercially available IQ test to a sample of sixty-five students selected from a particular elementary school district and finds their average score is 85. What does this tell her about the IQ scores of the entire population of students in the district? Does the average IQ score of students in the district also equal 85? Or is this sample of students different, on the average, from other students in the district? If these students are different, how are they different? Are their IQ scores higher—or lower?

What the researcher needs is some way to compare the IQ scores of her sample to the scores in the population to see if they differ, on the average, from them and if so, how. Inferential statistics provide such a way.

Inferential statistics refer to certain types of procedures that allow researchers to make

inferences about a population based on findings from a sample. In Chapter Five we discussed the concept of a random sample and pointed out that obtaining a random sample is desirable because it helps ensure that one's sample is representative of a larger population. When a sample is representative, all the characteristics of the population are assumed to be present in the sample in the same degree. No sampling procedure, not even random sampling, guarantees a totally representative sample, but the chance of obtaining one is greater with random sampling than with any other method. And the more a sample represents a population, the more researchers are entitled to assume that what they find out about the sample will also be true of that population. Making inferences about populations on the basis of random samples is what inferential statistics is all about.

As with descriptive statistics, the techniques of inferential statistics differ depending on which type of data—categorical or quantitative—a researcher wishes to analyze. This chapter begins with techniques applicable to quantitative data since they provide the best introduction to the logic behind inference techniques and because most educational research involves such data. Some techniques for the analysis of categorical data are presented at the end of the chapter.

Inference Techniques for Use with Quantitative Data

Suppose a researcher is interested in the difference between males and females with respect to interest in history. He hypothesizes that female students find history more interesting than do male students. To test the hypothesis, he decides to perform the following study. He obtains one random sample of 30 male history students from the population of 500 male tenth grade students taking history in a nearby school district and another random sample of 30 female history students from the female population of 550 tenth grade history students in the district. All students are given an attitude scale to complete. The researcher now has two sets of data: the attitude scores for the male group and the attitude scores for the female group. The design of the study is shown in Figure 9.1. The researcher wants to know whether or not the male population is different from the female population—that is, is the mean score of the male group any different from the mean score of the female group? But the researcher does not know the means of the two populations. All he has are the means of the two samples. He has to rely on the two samples to provide information about the populations.

Is it reasonable to assume that each sample will give a fairly accurate picture of its population? It certainly is possible. Each sample was randomly selected from its population, and therefore it should represent the total group of tenth grade history students. On the other hand, the students in each group in the sample are only a small portion of the whole population, and only rarely is a sample absolutely identical to its parent population on a given characteristic. Moreover, the data the researcher obtains from the two groups in the sample will depend on the individual students selected to be in the sample. If a different sample of students were randomly selected, the makeup of the two groups would be different, their means on the attitude scale would be somewhat different, and the researcher would end up with a different set of data. How can the researcher be sure that the particular sample he has selected is, indeed, a representative one? Maybe another sample would be better.

SAMPLING ERROR

This is the basic difficulty that confronts us when we work with samples: Samples are virtually never identical to their parent populations. This difference between a sample and its population is referred to as **sampling error.** Furthermore, no two samples will be the same in all their characteristics. Two different samples from the same population will not be identical: They will be composed of different individuals, they will have different scores on a test (or other measure), and they will have different sample means.

Consider the population of high school students in the United States. It would be possible to select literally thousands of different samples from this population. Suppose we took two samples of twenty-five students each from

FIGURE 9.1

Selection of Two Samples from Two Distinct Populations

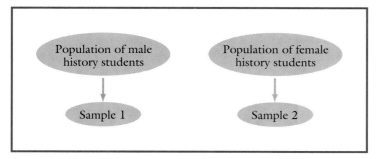

this population and measured their heights. What would you estimate our chances would be of finding exactly the same mean height in both samples? Very, very unlikely. In fact, we could probably take sample after sample after sample and seldom obtain two sets of people having exactly the same mean height.

DISTRIBUTION OF SAMPLE MEANS

All this might suggest that it is impossible to formulate any rules that researchers can use to determine similarities between samples and populations. Not so. Fortunately, large collections of random samples do pattern themselves in such a way that it is possible for researchers to predict accurately some characteristics of the population from which the sample was selected.

Were we able to select an infinite number of random samples (all of the same size) from a population, calculate the mean of each, and then arrange these means into a frequency polygon, we would find that they shape themselves into a particular pattern. The means of a large number of random samples tend to be normally distributed, unless the size of each of the samples is small (less than thirty), *and* the scores in the population are *not* normally distributed. Once sample size reaches thirty, however, the distribution of sample means is very nearly normal, even if the population is not normally distributed. (We realize that this is not immediately obvious; should you wish more explanation of why this happens to be a fact, consult any introductory statistics text.)

Like all normal distributions, a distribution of sample means (called a **sampling distribution**) has its own mean and standard deviation. The mean of a sampling distribution (the "mean of the means") is equal to the mean of the population. In an infinite number of samples, some will have means larger than the population mean and some will have means smaller than the population mean. These data tend to neutralize each other, resulting in an overall average that is equal to the mean of the population. Consider an example. Suppose you have a population of only three scores—1, 2, 3. The mean

of this population is 2. Now, take all of the possible types of samples of size two. How many would there be? Six—(1, 1); (1, 2); (1, 3); (2, 2); (2, 3); (3, 3). The means of these samples are 1, 1.5, 2, 2, 2.5, and 3, respectively. Add up all these means and divide by six (that is, 12 ÷ 6), and you see that the mean of these means equals 2, the same as the population mean.

STANDARD ERROR OF THE MEAN

The standard deviation of a sampling distribution of means is called the **standard error of the mean** (*SEM*). As in all normal distributions, therefore, approximately 68 percent of the sample means fall between plus and minus 1 *SEM*; approximately 95 percent fall between plus and minus 2 *SEM*, and 99+ percent fall between plus and minus 3 *SEM* (Figure 9.2).

Thus, if we know the mean and the standard deviation of the sampling distribution, we can determine whether it is likely or unlikely that a particular sample mean could be obtained from that population. Suppose the mean of a population is 100, for example, and the standard error of the mean is 10. A sample mean of 110 would fall at 1 *SEM*; a sample mean of 120 would fall

FIGURE 9.2

Sampling Distribution of the Mean

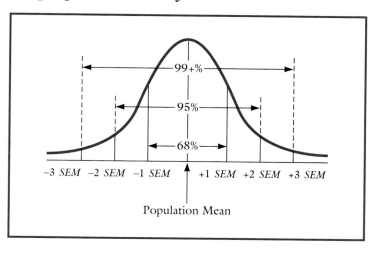

FIGURE **9.3**

Distribution of Sample Means[a]

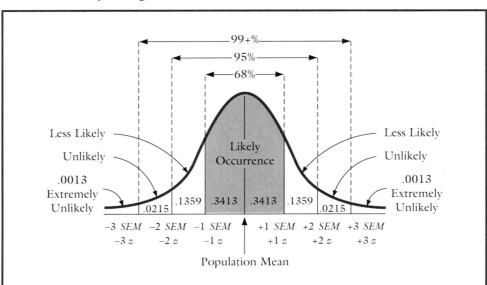

[a] Notice that these values are approximate.

at 2 *SEM*; a sample mean of 130 would fall at 3 *SEM*; and so forth (Figure 9.3).

It would be very unlikely to draw a sample from this population whose mean fell above 3 *SEM*. Why? Because, as in all normal distributions (and remember, the sampling distribution is a normal distribution—of means), only 0.0013 of all values (in this case, sample means) fall above +3 *SEM*. It would not be unusual to select a sample from this population and find that its mean is 105, but selecting a sample with a mean of 130 would be unlikely—very unlikely!

It is possible to use z scores to describe the position of any particular sample mean within a distribution of sample means. We discussed z scores in Chapter Eight. We now want to express means as z scores. Remember that a z score simply states how far a score (or mean) differs from the mean of scores (or means) in standard deviation units. The z score tells a researcher exactly where a particular sample mean is located relative to all other sample means that could have been obtained. For example, a z score of +2 would indicate that a particular sample mean is two standard errors above the population mean. Only about 2 percent of all sample means fall above a z score of +2. Hence, a sample with such a mean would be unusual.

ESTIMATING THE STANDARD ERROR OF THE MEAN

How do we obtain the standard error of the mean? Clearly, we cannot calculate it directly, since we would need, literally, to obtain a huge number of samples and their means.* Statisticians have shown, however, that the standard error can be calculated using a simple formula requiring the standard deviation of the population and the size of the sample. Although we seldom know the standard deviation of the

---

* If we did have these means, we would calculate the standard error just like any other standard deviation, treating each mean as a score.

population, fortunately it can be *estimated** using the standard deviation of the sample. To calculate the *SEM*, then, simply divide the standard deviation of the sample by the square root of the sample size minus one:

$$SEM = \frac{SD}{\sqrt{n-1}}$$

Let's review the basic ideas we have presented so far.

1. The sampling distribution of the mean (or any descriptive statistic) is the distribution of the means (or other statistic) obtained (theoretically) from an infinitely large number of samples of the same size.
2. The shape of the sampling distribution in many (but not all) cases is the shape of the normal distribution.
3. The *SEM* (the standard error of the mean), that is, the standard deviation of a sampling distribution of means, can be estimated by dividing the standard deviation of the sample by the square root of the sample size minus one.
4. The frequency with which a particular sample mean will occur can be determined by using z scores to indicate its position in the sampling distribution.

Confidence Intervals

We now can use the *SEM* to indicate boundaries, or limits, within which the population mean lies. Such boundaries are called **confidence intervals.** How are they determined?

Let us return to the example of the researcher who administered an IQ test to a sample of sixty-five elementary school students. You will recall that she obtained a sample mean of 85 and wanted to know how much the population mean might differ from this value. We are now in a position to give her some help in this regard.

* The fact that the standard error is based on an estimated value rather than a known value does introduce an unknown degree of imprecision into this process.

THE 95 AND 99 PERCENT CONFIDENCE INTERVALS

Let us assume that we have calculated the standard error of the mean for her sample and found it to equal 2.0. Applying this to a sampling distribution of means, we can say that 95 percent of the time the population mean will be between $85 \pm 1.96 (2) = 85 \pm 3.92 = 81.08$ to 88.92. Why plus or minus 1.96? Because the area between plus and minus 1.96 z equals 95 percent (.95) of the total area under the normal curve.* This is shown in Figure 9.4.†

Suppose this researcher then wished to establish an interval that would give her more confidence than $p = .95$ in making a statement about the population mean. This can be done by calculating the 99 percent confidence interval.

* By looking at the normal curve table in Appendix B, we see that the area between the mean and 1.96 $z = .4750$. Multiplied by two, this equals .95, or 95 percent, of the total area under the curve.
† Strictly speaking, it is not proper to consider a distribution of population means around the sample mean. In practice, we interpret confidence intervals in this way. The legitimacy of doing so requires a demonstration beyond the level of an introductory text.

FIGURE 9.4

The 95 Percent Confidence Interval

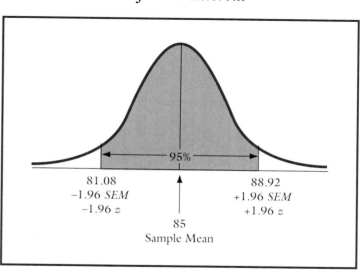

The 99 percent confidence interval is determined in a manner similar to that for determining the 95 percent confidence interval. Given the characteristics of a normal distribution, we know that 0.5 percent of the sample means will lie below -2.58 SEM and another 0.5 percent will lie above 2.58 SEM (see Figure 8.9 in Chapter Eight). Using the previous example in which the mean of the sample was 85 and the SEM was 2, we calculate the interval as follows: 85 ± 2.58 (SEM) $= 85 \pm 2.58$ (2.0) $= 85 \pm 5.16 = 79.84$ to 90.16. Thus the 99 percent confidence interval lies between 79.84 and 90.16 (Figure 9.5).

Our researcher can now answer her question about how much the population mean differs from the sample mean. While she cannot know exactly what the population mean is, she can indicate the "boundaries" or limits within which it is likely to fall. To repeat, these limits are called confidence intervals. The 95 percent confidence interval spans a segment on the horizontal axis that we are 95 percent certain contains the population mean. The 99 percent confidence interval spans a segment on the horizontal axis, within which we are even more certain (99

percent certain) that the population mean falls.* We could be mistaken, of course—the population mean could lie outside these intervals—but it is not very likely.†

CONFIDENCE INTERVALS AND PROBABILITY

Let us return to the concept of probability introduced in Chapter Eight. As we use the term here, probability is nothing more than relative occurrence, or relative frequency. When we say that something would occur 5 times in 100, we are expressing a probability. We could just as well say the probability is 5 in 100. In our earlier example, we can say, therefore, that the probability of the population mean being *outside* the 81.08–88.92 limits (the 95 percent confidence interval) is only 5 in 100. The probability of it being *outside* the 79.84–90.16 limits (the 99 percent confidence interval) is even less—only one in 100. Remember that it is customary to express probabilities in decimal form, e.g., $p = .05$ or $p = .01$. What would $p = .10$ signify?‡

Comparing More Than One Sample

Up to this point we have been explaining how to make inferences about the population

FIGURE **9.5**

The 99 Percent Confidence Interval

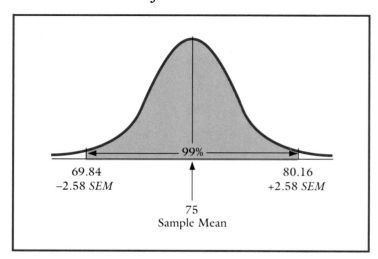

69.84	80.16
−2.58 *SEM*	+2.58 *SEM*

75
Sample Mean

99%

* Notice that it is *not* correct to say that the probability is 95 out of 100 that the population mean falls within the 95 percent confidence interval. The population mean is a fixed value, and it either does—or does not fall within this interval. The correct way to think of a confidence interval is to view it in terms of replicating the study. Suppose we were to replicate the study with another sample and calculate the 95 percent confidence interval for that sample. Suppose we were then to replicate the study once again with a third sample and calculate the 95 percent confidence interval for this third sample. We continue until we have drawn 100 samples, and calculated the 95 percent confidence interval for each of these 100 samples. We will find that the population mean lies within 95 percent of these intervals.
† The likelihood of the population mean being outside the 95 percent confidence interval is only 5 percent; of being outside the 99 percent confidence interval, only 1 percent. Analogous reasoning and procedures can be used with sample sizes less than thirty.
‡ A probability of 10 in 100.

mean using data from just one sample. More typically, however, researchers want to compare two or more samples. Thus, a researcher might want to determine if there is a difference in attitude between fourth grade boys and girls in mathematics; whether there is a difference in achievement between students taught by the discussion method as compared to the lecture method; and so forth.

Our previous logic also applies to a difference between means. For example, if a difference between means is found between the test scores of two samples in a study, a researcher wants to know if a difference exists in the population from which the two samples were selected (Figure 9.6). In essence, we ask the same question we asked about one mean, only this time we ask it about a difference *between* means. Hence we ask, "Is the difference we have found a likely or an unlikely occurrence?" It is possible that the difference can be attributed simply to sampling error—to the fact that certain samples, rather than others, were selected (the "luck of the draw," so to speak). Once again, inferential statistics help us out.

THE STANDARD ERROR OF THE DIFFERENCE BETWEEN SAMPLE MEANS

Fortunately, differences between sample means are also likely to be normally distributed. The distribution of differences between sample means also has its own mean and standard deviation. The mean of the sampling distribution of differences between sample means is equal to the difference between the means of the two populations. The standard deviation of this distribution is called the **standard error of the difference** (*SED*). The formula for computing the *SED* is:

$$SED = \sqrt{SEM_1^2 + SEM_2^2}$$

where $_1$ and $_2$ refer to the respective samples.

Since the distribution is normal, slightly more than 68 percent of the differences between sample means will fall between plus and minus 1 *SED* (again, remember that the standard error

FIGURE 9.6

Does a Sample Difference Reflect a Population Difference?[a]

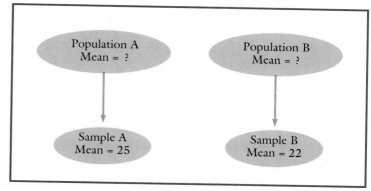

[a] Question: Does the difference between the means of sample A and sample B of three points reflect a difference between the means of population A and population B?

of the difference is a standard deviation); about 95 percent of the differences between sample means will fall between plus and minus 2 *SED*, and 99+ percent of these differences will fall between plus and minus 3 *SED* (Figure 9.7).

FIGURE 9.7

Distribution of the Difference between Sample Means

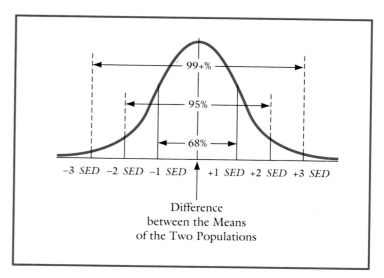

Now we can proceed similarly to the way we did with individual sample means. A researcher estimates the standard error of the difference between means, and then uses it, along with the difference between the two sample means and the normal curve, to estimate probable limits (confidence intervals) within which the difference between the means of the two populations is likely to fall.

Let us consider an example. Imagine that the difference between two sample means is 14 and the calculated *SED* is 3. Just as we did with one sample population mean, we can now indicate limits within which the difference between the means of the two populations is likely to fall. If we say that the difference between the means of the two populations is between 11 and 17 (plus or minus 1 *SED*), we have slightly more than a 68 percent chance of being right; we have somewhat more than a 95 percent chance of being right if we say the difference between the means of the two populations is between 8 and 20 (plus or minus 2 *SED*); and better than a 99 percent chance of being right if we say the difference between the means of the two populations is between 5 and 23 (plus or minus 3 *SED*). Figure 9.8 illustrates these confidence intervals.

Suppose the difference between two other sample means is 12. If we calculated the *SED* to be 2, would it be likely or unlikely for the difference between population means to fall between 10 and 14?*

Hypothesis Testing

How does all this apply to research questions and research hypotheses? You will recall that many hypotheses predict a relationship. In Chapter Eight, we presented techniques for examining data for the existence of relationships. We pointed out in previous chapters that virtually all relationships in data can be examined through one (or more) of three procedures: a comparison of means, a correlation, or a crossbreak table. In each instance, some degree of relationship may be found. If a relationship is found in the data, is there likely to be a similar relationship in the population, or is it simply due to sampling error—to the fact that a particular sample, rather than another, was selected for study? Once again, inferential statistics can be of help.

The logic discussed earlier applies to any particular form of a hypothesis and to all the techniques used to examine data. Thus, correlation coefficients and differences between them can be evaluated in essentially the same way as means and differences between means; we just need to obtain the standard error of the correlation coefficient(s). The procedure used with crossbreak tables differs in technique, but the logic is the same. We will discuss it later in the chapter.

When testing hypotheses, it is customary to proceed in a slightly different way. Instead of determining the boundaries within which the population mean (or other parameter) can be said to fall, a researcher determines the likelihood

FIGURE 9.8

Confidence Intervals

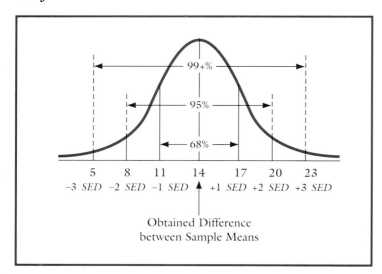

Obtained Difference
between Sample Means

---

* Likely, since 68 percent of the differences between population means fall between these values.

of obtaining a sample value (for example, a difference between two sample means) if there is *no* relationship (that is, no difference between the means of the two populations) in the populations from which the samples were drawn. The researcher formulates both a research hypothesis and a null hypothesis. To test the research hypothesis, the researcher must formulate a null hypothesis.

THE NULL HYPOTHESIS

As you will recall, the **research hypothesis** specifies the predicted outcome of a study. Many research hypotheses predict the nature of the relationship the researcher thinks exists in the population, for example: "The population mean of students using method A is greater than the population mean of students using method B."

The **null hypothesis** most commonly used specifies there is *no* relationship in the population, for example: "There is no difference between the population mean of students using method A and the population mean of students using method B." (This is the same thing as saying the difference between the means of the two populations is zero.)

The researcher then proceeds to test the null hypothesis. The same information is needed as before: both the knowledge that the sampling distribution is normal and the calculated standard error of the difference (*SED*). What is different in a hypothesis test is that instead of using the obtained sample value (e.g., the obtained difference between sample means) as the mean of the sampling distribution (as we did with confidence intervals), we use zero.*

We then can determine the probability of obtaining a particular sample value (such as an obtained difference between sample means) by seeing where such a value falls on the sampling distribution. If the probability is small, the null hypothesis is rejected, thereby providing support for the research hypothesis.

---

* Actually, any value could be used, but zero is used in virtually all educational research.

What counts as "small"? In other words, what constitutes an unlikely outcome? Probably you have guessed. It is customary in educational research to view as unlikely any outcome that has a probability of .05 ($p = .05$) or less. This is referred to as the .05 **level of significance.** When we reject a null hypothesis at the .05 level, we are saying that the probability of obtaining such an outcome is only 5 times (or less) in 100. Some researchers prefer to be even more stringent and choose a .01 level of significance. When a null hypothesis is rejected at the .01 level, it means that the likelihood of obtaining the outcome is only 1 time (or less) in 100.

HYPOTHESIS TESTING: A REVIEW

Let us review what we have said. The logical sequence for a researcher who wishes to engage in hypothesis testing is as follows.

1. State the research hypothesis—e.g., there is a difference between the population mean of students using method A and the population mean of students using method B.
2. State the null hypothesis—e.g., there is *no* difference between the population mean of students using method A and the population mean of students using method B (or, the difference between the two population means is zero).
3. Determine the sample statistics pertinent to the hypothesis (e.g., the mean of sample A and the mean of sample B).
4. Determine the probability of obtaining the sample results if the null hypothesis is true.
5. If the probability is small, reject the null hypothesis, thus affirming the research hypothesis.
6. If the probability is large, do not reject the null hypothesis, which means you cannot affirm the research hypothesis.

Let us use our previous example in which the difference between sample means was 14 points and the *SED* was 3 (Figure 9.8). In Figure 9.9 we see that the sample difference of 14 is way past +3 *SED*—in fact, it exceeds 4 *SED*. Thus the probability of obtaining such a sample

FIGURE 9.9

Illustration of When a Researcher Would Reject the Null Hypothesis

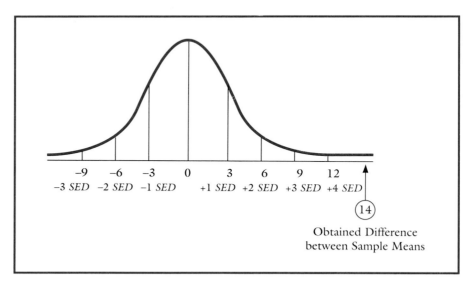

result is considerably less than .01, and as a result, the null hypothesis is rejected. If the difference in sample means had been 4 instead of 14, would the null hypothesis be rejected?*

ONE- AND TWO-TAILED TESTS

In Chapter Three, we made a distinction between directional and nondirectional hypotheses. There is sometimes an advantage to stating hypotheses in directional form that is related to significance testing. We refer again to a hypothetical example of a sampling distribution of differences between means in which the calculated *SED* equals 3. Previously, we interpreted the statistical significance of an obtained difference between sample means of 14 points. The statistical significance of this difference was quite clearcut, since it was so large. Suppose, however, that the obtained difference was not 14, but 5.5 points. To determine the probability associated with this outcome, we must know whether the

researcher's hypothesis was a directional or a nondirectional one. If the hypothesis was directional, the researcher specified ahead of time (before collecting any data) which group would have the higher mean (for example, the mean score of students using method A would be higher than the mean score of students using method B).

Should this have been the case, the researcher's hypothesis would be supported only if the mean of sample A is higher than the mean of sample B. The researcher must decide beforehand that he or she will subtract the mean of sample B from the mean of sample A. A large difference between sample means in the opposite direction would *not* support the research hypothesis. A difference between sample means of +2 is in the hypothesized direction, therefore, but a difference of −2 (should the mean of sample B be higher than the mean of sample A) is not. Since the researcher's hypothesis can only be supported if he or she obtains a positive difference between the sample means, the researcher is justified in using only the positive tail of the sampling distribution to locate the obtained difference.

---

* No. The probability of a difference of 4 is too high—much larger than .05.

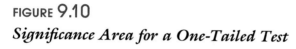

FIGURE 9.10

Significance Area for a One-Tailed Test

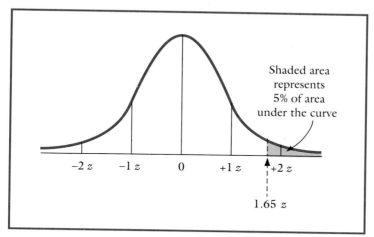

This is referred to as a **one-tailed test** of statistical significance (Figure 9.10).

At the 5 percent level of significance ($p = .05$), the null hypothesis may be rejected only if the obtained difference between sample means reaches or exceeds 1.65 SED* in the one tail. As shown in Figure 9.11, this requires a difference between sample means of 5 points or more.† Our previously obtained difference of 5.5 would be significant at this level, therefore, since it not only reaches, but exceeds, 1.65 SED.

What if the hypothesis were nondirectional? Should this have been the case, the researcher would not have specified beforehand which group would have the higher mean. In that case, the hypothesis would be supported by a suitable difference in *either* tail. This is called a **two-tailed test** of statistical significance. If the researcher uses the .05 level of significance, this requires that the 5 percent of the total area must include both tails—that is, there is 2.5 percent in each tail. As a result, a difference in sample

means of at least 6 points (either $+6$ or -6) is required to reject the null hypothesis (Figure 9.12), since 2.0 (3) = 6.0.

USE OF THE NULL HYPOTHESIS: AN EVALUATION

There appears to be much misunderstanding regarding the use of the null hypothesis. First, it often is stated in place of a research hypothesis. While it is easy to replace a research hypothesis (which predicts a relationship) with a null hypothesis (which predicts no relationship), there is no good reason for doing so. As we have seen, the null hypothesis is merely a useful methodological device.

Second, there is nothing sacred about the customary .05 and .01 significance levels—they are merely conventions. It is a little ridiculous, for example, to fail to reject the null hypothesis with a sample value that has a probability of .06. To do so might very well result in what is known as a **Type II error**—this error results when a researcher fails to reject a null hypothesis that is false. A **Type I error**, on the other hand, results when a researcher rejects a null hypothesis that is true. In our example in which there was a 14-point difference between sample means, for ex-

* By looking in the normal curve table in Appendix B, we see that the area beyond 1.65 z equals .05, or 5 percent of the area under the curve.

† Since an area of .05 in one tail equals a z of 1.65, and the SED is 3, we multiply 1.65 (3) to find the score value at this point. 1.65 (3) = 4.95, or 5 points.

FIGURE **9.11**

One-Tailed Test Using a Distribution of Differences between Sample Means

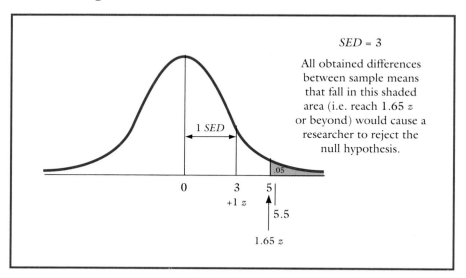

ample, we rejected the null hypothesis at the .05 level. In doing so, we realized that a 5 percent chance remained of being wrong—that is, a 5 percent chance that the null hypothesis was true.

Finally, there is also nothing sacrosanct about testing an obtained result against zero. In our previous example, for instance, why not test the obtained value of 14 (or 5.5, etc.) against a

FIGURE **9.12**

Two-Tailed Test Using Distribution of Differences between Sample Means

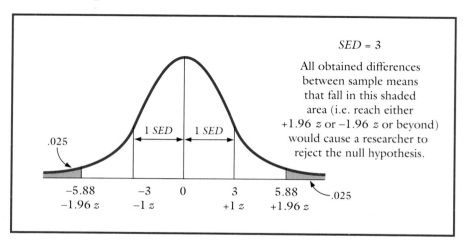

hypothetical population difference of 1 (or 3, etc.)? Testing only against zero can mislead one into exaggerating the importance of the obtained relationship. We believe the reporting of inferential statistics should rely more on confidence intervals and less on whether a particular level of significance has been attained.

Inference Techniques

It is beyond the scope of this text to treat in detail each of the many techniques that exist for answering inference questions about data. We shall, however, present a brief summary of the more commonly used tests of statistical significance that researchers employ and then illustrate how to do one such test.

TYPES OF DATA

In Chapter Eight, we made a distinction between quantitative and categorical data. We pointed out that the type of data a researcher collects often influences the type of statistical analysis required. A statistical technique appropriate for quantitative data, for example, will generally be inappropriate for categorical data.

PARAMETRIC VERSUS NONPARAMETRIC TECHNIQUES

There are two basic types of inference techniques that researchers use. **Parametric techniques** make various kinds of assumptions about the nature of the population from which the sample(s) involved in the research study are drawn. **Nonparametric techniques,** on the other hand, make few (if any) assumptions about the nature of the population from which the samples are taken. An advantage of parametric techniques is that they are generally more powerful than nonparametric techniques and hence much more likely to reveal a true difference or relationship if one really exists. Their disadvantage is that often a researcher cannot satisfy the assumptions they require (for example, that the population

is normally distributed on the characteristics of interest).

The advantage of nonparametric techniques is that they are safer to use when a researcher cannot satisfy the assumptions underlying the use of parametric techniques.

PARAMETRIC TECHNIQUES FOR ANALYZING QUANTITATIVE DATA*

The t Test for Means. The t test is a parametric statistical test used to see whether a difference between the means of two samples is significant. The test produces a value for t (called an obtained "t"), which the researcher then checks in a statistical table (similar to the ones shown in Appendix B) to determine the level of significance that has been reached. As we mentioned earlier, if the .05 level of significance is reached, the researcher customarily rejects the null hypothesis and concludes that a real difference does exist.

There are two forms of this t test, a t test for independent means and a t test for correlated means. The t test for independent means is used to compare the mean scores of two *different*, or independent, groups. For example, if two groups of eighth graders were exposed to two different methods of teaching for a semester and then given the same achievement test at the end of the semester, their achievement scores could be compared using a t test. The t test for correlated means is used to compare the mean scores of the *same* group before and after a treatment of some sort is given to see if any observed gain is significant, or when the research design involves two matched groups. It is also used when the *same* subjects receive two different treatments in a study.

---

* Many texts distinguish between techniques appropriate for nominal, ordinal, and interval scales of measurement (see Chapter Six). It turns out that parametric techniques are most appropriate for interval data, while nonparametric techniques are more appropriate for ordinal and nominal data. Researchers rarely know for certain whether their data justify the assumption that interval scales have actually been used. We do not consider this distinction, therefore, to be a particularly useful one.

Analysis of Variance (ANOVA). When researchers desire to find out if there are significant differences between the means of *more than* two groups, they commonly use a technique called **analysis of variance** (shortened to ANOVA), which is actually a more general form of the *t* test that is appropriate to use with three or more groups (it also can be used with two groups). In brief, variation both within and between each of the groups is analyzed statistically, yielding what is known as an *F* value. As in a *t* test, this *F* value is then checked in a statistical table to see if it is statistically significant. It is interpreted quite similarly to the *t* value, in that the larger the obtained value of *F*, the greater the likelihood that statistical significance exists. When only two groups are being compared, the *F*-test is sufficient to tell the researcher if significance has been achieved. When more than three groups are being compared, the *F*-test will not, by itself, tell us which pairs of means are significant. A further (but quite simple) procedure, called a *post hoc* analysis, is required to find this out.

Analysis of Covariance (ANCOVA). **Analysis of covariance** (ANCOVA) is a variation of ANOVA used when, for example, groups are given a pretest related in some way to the dependent variable and their mean scores on this pretest are found to differ. ANCOVA enables the researcher to adjust the posttest mean scores on the dependent variable for each group to compensate for the initial differences between the groups on the pretest. The pretest is called the *covariate*. How much the posttest mean scores must be adjusted depends on how large the difference between the pretest scores is and the degree of relationship between the covariate and the dependent variable. Several covariates can be used in an ANCOVA test, so in addition to (or instead of) adjusting for a pretest, the researcher can adjust for the effect of other variables. (We discuss this further in Chapter Twelve.) Like ANOVA, ANCOVA produces an *F* value, which is then looked up in a statistical table to determine if it is significant.

The t Test for r. This *t* test is used to see whether a correlation coefficient calculated on sample data is significant—that is, whether it represents a correlation in the population from which the sample was drawn. It is similar to the *t* test for means, except that here the statistic being dealt with is a correlation coefficient (*r*) rather than a difference between means. The test produces a value for *t* (again called an obtained "t"), which the researcher checks in a statistical probability table to see if it is statistically significant. As with the other parametric tests, the larger the obtained value for *t*, the greater the likelihood that significance has been achieved.

NONPARAMETRIC TECHNIQUES FOR ANALYZING QUANTITATIVE DATA

The Mann-Whitney U Test. **The Mann-Whitney *U* test** is a nonparametric alternative to the *t* test used when a researcher wishes to analyze ranked data. The researcher intermingles the scores of the two groups and then ranks them as if they were all from just one group. The test produces a value (*U*), whose probability of occurrence is then checked by the researcher in the appropriate statistical table. The logic of the test is as follows: If the two groups are essentially similar, then the sum of the pooled rankings for *each* group should be about the same. If the summed ranks are markedly different, on the other hand, then this difference is likely to be statistically significant.

The Kruskal-Wallis One-Way Analysis of Variance. The **Kruskal-Wallis one-way analysis of variance** is used when researchers have more than two independent groups to compare. The procedure is quite similar to the Mann-Whitney *U* test. The scores of the individuals in the several groups are pooled and then ranked as though they all came from one group. The sums of the ranks added together for each of the separate groups are then compared. This analysis produces a value (*H*), whose probability of occurrence is checked by the researcher in the appropriate statistical table.

The Sign Test. The **sign test** is used when a researcher wants to analyze two related (as opposed to independent) samples. Related samples are connected in some way. For example, often a researcher will try to equalize groups on IQ, gender, age, or some other variable. The groups are *matched*, so to speak, on these variables. Another example of a related sample is when the same group is both pre- and posttested (that is, tested twice). Each individual, in other words, is tested on two different occasions (as with the *t* test for correlated means).

This test is very easy to use. The researcher simply lines up the pairs of related subjects and then determines how many times the paired subjects in one group scored higher than those in the other group. If the groups do not differ significantly, the totals for the two groups should be about equal. If there is a marked difference in scoring (such as many more in one group scoring higher), the difference may be statistically significant. Again, the probability of this occurrence can be determined by consulting the appropriate statistical table.

The Friedman Two-Way Analysis of Variance. If more than two related groups are involved, then the **Friedman two-way analysis of variance** test can be used. For example, if a researcher employs four matched groups, this test would be appropriate.

NONPARAMETRIC TECHNIQUES FOR ANALYZING CATEGORICAL DATA*

The Chi-Square Test. The **chi-square test** is used to analyze data that are reported in categories. For example, a researcher might want to compare how many male and female teachers favor a new curriculum to be instituted in a

* There are no parametric techniques for analyzing categorical data.

particular school district. He asks a sample of 50 teachers if they favor or oppose the new curriculum. If they do not differ significantly in their responses, then we would expect that about the same proportion of males and females would be in favor of (or opposed to) instituting the curriculum.

The chi-square test is based on a comparison between expected frequencies and actual, obtained frequencies. If the obtained frequencies are similar to the expected frequencies, then researchers conclude that the groups do not differ (in our example just above, they do not differ in their attitude toward the new curriculum). If there are considerable differences between the expected and obtained frequencies, on the other hand, then researchers conclude that there is a significant difference in attitude between the two groups.

The chi-square test is not limited to comparing expected and obtained frequencies for only two variables. As with all of these inference techniques, the chi-square test yields a value (χ^2) whose probability of occurrence can be determined by checking the appropriate statistical table.

The calculation of chi-square is a necessary step in determining the *contingency coefficient*—a descriptive statistic referred to in Chapter Eight, but whose computation we deferred until now. We will use Table 8.14 in Chapter Eight for our illustration and reproduce it here as Table 9.1.

TABLE 9.1

Gender and Ethnicity of School Leaders with Expected Frequencies (Reproduction of Table 8.14)

	White	Nonwhite	Total
Male	200 (185)	100 (115)	300
Female	170 (185)	130 (115)	300
Total	370	230	600

Remember that the first numbers in each cell represent obtained frequencies while the numbers in parentheses represent expected frequencies. Let us use the letter O to represent obtained frequencies, and the letter E to represent expected frequencies. The calculation of chi-square then proceeds as follows.

A. Calculate as follows.
  1. For cell 1:
     (a) Subtract E from O:
         $O - E = 200 - 185 = 15$
     (b) Square the result:
         $(O - E)^2 = 15^2 = 225$
     (c) Divide the result by E:
         $\dfrac{(O - E)^2}{E} = \dfrac{225}{185} = 1.22$

B. Repeat this process for each cell (you can do this in any order, just be sure that all cells are calculated).
  2. For cell 2:
     (a) $170 - 185 = -15$
     (b) $(-15)^2 = 225$
     (c) $\dfrac{225}{185} = 1.22$

  3. For cell 3:
     (a) $100 - 115 = 15$
     (b) $(-15)^2 = 225$
     (c) $\dfrac{225}{115} = 1.96$

  4. For cell 4:
     (a) $130 - 115 = 15$
     (b) $(15)^2 = 225$
     (c) $\dfrac{225}{115} = 1.96$

C. Add the results of all cells.
   $1.22 + 1.22 + 1.96 + 1.96 = 6.36$

The formula that symbolizes these calculations is $\chi^2 = \Sigma \dfrac{(O - E)^2}{E}$.

After the value for χ^2 has been calculated, we want to determine how likely it is that such a result could occur if there were no relationship in the population—that is, whether the obtained frequencies do not exist in the population but occurred because of the particular sample that was selected. As with all inferential tests, we determine this by consulting a probability table (similar to the one shown in Appendix B).

You will notice that this table has a column headed "degrees of freedom." This concept is important in many inferential statistics. In essence, it refers to the number of scores in a frequency distribution that are "free to vary"—that is, that are not fixed. For example, suppose you had a distribution of only three scores, a, b, and c, which must add up to 10. It is apparent that a, b, and c can have a number of different values (such as 3, 5, and 2; 1, 6, and 3; 2, 2, and 6) and still add up to 10. But, once any two of these values are fixed—set—then the third is also set—it cannot vary. Thus, should a = 3 and b = 5, c *must* equal 2. Hence, we say that there are two degrees of freedom in this distribution—any two of the values are "free to vary," so to speak, but once they are set, the third is also fixed. **Degrees of freedom** are calculated in crossbreak tables as follows (using the same example as before).

Step 1: Subtract 1 from the number of rows: 2 − 1 = 1

Step 2: Subtract 1 from the number of columns: 2 − 1 = 1

Step 3: Multiply step 1 by step 2: (1)(1) = 1

Thus, in our example above, there is only one degree of freedom. If we look opposite one degree of freedom in the chi-square table in appendix C, we find under .05 (the .05 significance level) a value of 3.84. Since our obtained chi-square value is 6.36, which exceeds 3.84, we conclude that our obtained results are unlikely to have occurred (only a 5 percent probability) if there is no such relationship in the population.

Contingency Coefficient. The final step in the process is to calculate the contingency coefficient, symbolized by the letter C, to which we referred in Chapter Eight. This is done as follows.

Step 1: Add the obtained chi-square value to n (the number of cases): $6.36 + 600 = 606.36$

Step 2: Divide the chi-square value by step 1: $6.36/606.36 = .01$

Step 3: Take the square root of step 2: $\sqrt{.01} = .10$. This is the contingency coefficient (C).

These steps can be summarized by the formula:

$$C = \sqrt{\frac{\chi^2}{\chi^2 + n}}$$

The contingency coefficient cannot be interpreted in exactly the same way as the correlation coefficient. It must be interpreted by using Table 9.2. This table gives the upper limit for C, depending on the number of cells in the crossbreak table. Since Table 9.1 was a 2 by 2 table, C can be any value between .00 and .71. Our obtained C of .10, therefore, indicates a low degree of relationship.

SUMMARY OF TECHNIQUES
The above calculations of chi-square and the contingency coefficient should give you an idea of the steps involved in an inferential test of statistical significance. The names of the most commonly used inferential procedures and the data type appropriate to their use are summarized in Table 9.3.

This summary should be useful to you whenever you encounter these terms in your reading. While the details of both mathematical rationale and calculation differ greatly among these techniques, the most important things to remember are as follows.

1. The end product of all inference procedures is the same—a statement of probability relating the sample data to hypothesized population characteristics.
2. All inference techniques assume random sampling. Without random sampling, the resulting probabilities are in error—to an unknown degree.
3. Inference techniques are intended to answer only one question: "Given the sample data, what are probable population characteristics?" These techniques do *not* help decide whether the data show results that are meaningful or useful—only the extent to which they may be generalizable. (We discuss another, very specific, use of inferential techniques in Chapter Twelve.)

TABLE 9.2

Contingency Coefficient Values for Different-Sized Crossbreak Tables

Size of Table (no. of cells)	Upper limit[a] for C Calculated
2 by 2	.71
3 by 3	.82
4 by 4	.87
5 by 5	.90
6 by 6	.91

[a] The upper limits for unequal-sized tables (such as 2 by 3 or 3 by 4) are unknown but can be estimated from the values given. Thus, the upper limit for a 3 by 4 table would approximate .85.

TABLE 9.3

Commonly Used Inferential Techniques

	Parametric	Nonparametric
Quantitative	t test for independent means t test for correlated means Analysis of variance (ANOVA) Analysis of covariance (ANCOVA) t test for r	Mann-Whitney U test Kruskal-Wallis one-way analysis of variance Sign test Friedman two-way analysis of variance
Categorical	———	Chi-square

Main Points of Chapter Nine

- Inferential statistics refer to certain procedures that allow researchers to make inferences about a population based on data obtained from a sample

- The term "probability," as used in research, refers to the relative frequency with which a given event will occur.

- The term "sampling error" refers to the variations in sample statistics that occur as a result of repeated sampling from the same population.

- A distribution of sample means is a frequency distribution resulting from plotting the means of a very large number of samples from the same population.

- The standard error of the mean is the standard deviation of a sampling distribution of means. The standard error of the difference between means is the standard deviation of a sampling distribution of *differences* between sample means.

- A confidence interval is a region around a sample statistic (such as a sample mean) within which a population parameter (such as the population mean) may be said to fall with a specified probability of being wrong.

- Statistical hypothesis testing is a way of determining the probability that an obtained sample statistic will occur, given a hypothetical population parameter.

- A research hypothesis specifies the nature of the relationship the researcher thinks exists in the population.

- The null hypothesis typically specifies that there is no relationship in the population.

- The term "significance level" (or "level of significance"), as used in research, refers to the probability of a sample statistic occurring as a result of sampling error.

- The significance levels most commonly used in educational research are the .05 and .01 levels.

- A one-tailed test of significance involves the use of probabilities based on one-half of a sampling distribution because the research hypothesis is a directional hypothesis.

- A two-tailed test, on the other hand, involves the use of probabilities based on both sides of a sampling distribution because the research hypothesis is a nondirectional hypothesis.

- A parametric statistical test makes various kinds of assumptions about the nature of the population from which the samples involved in the research study were taken.

- Some of the commonly used parametric techniques for analyzing quantitative data include the t test for means, ANOVA, ANCOVA, and the t test for r.

- There are no parametric techniques for analyzing categorical data.

- A nonparametric statistical technique makes few, if any, assumptions about the nature of the population from which the samples in the study were taken.

- Some of the commonly used nonparametric techniques for analyzing quantitative data include the Mann-Whitney U test, the Kruskal-Wallis one-way analysis of variance, the sign test, and the Friedman two-way analysis of variance.

- The chi-square test is the nonparametric technique most commonly used to analyze categorical data.

- The contingency coefficient is a descriptive statistic indicating the degree of relationship that exists between two categorical variables.

For Discussion

1. If your hypothesis is that the mean score on a test of critical thinking will be higher for women than men and you get the following data:

   Mean for women = 91.8
   Mean for men = 86.3
   SEM = 3

   a. State the null hypothesis.
   b. Would you use a one-tailed or a two-tailed test of significance?
   c. At the .05 level of significance, would you reject or not reject the null hypothesis?
   d. Would you say the research hypothesis is affirmed?
   e. What is the 99 percent confidence interval for the difference between the populations (of men and women)?
   f. What assumption is necessary in order for the answers to a–e to be precise?

2. What is wrong with each of the following statements?
   a. Inferential statistics are used to summarize data.
   b. A researcher wants to be very confident that the population means falls within the 95 percent confidence interval, so she calculates (sample mean) (± 1 SEM).
   c. All inferential statistics require the assumption of interval scales.
   d. A researcher decides to make his research hypothesis and his null hypothesis identical.
   e. It is sometimes easier to reject the null hypothesis with a two-tailed than with a one-tailed test.
   f. Making inferences about samples is what inferential statistics is all about.

3. What would you say to a researcher who decides to use a .20 level of significance? Why?

4. "Hypotheses can never be proven, only supported." Is this true or not? Explain.

5. Is it possible for the results of a study to be of practical importance even though they are not statistically significant? Why or why not?

6. No two samples will be the same in all of their characteristics. Why won't they?

7. The standard error of the mean can never be larger than the standard deviation of the sample. Why?

8. How are z scores related to the standard error of the mean?

Research Exercise Nine:
Inferential Statistics

Using Problem Sheet 9, once again state the question or hypothesis of your study. Summarize the descriptive statistics you would use to describe the relationship you are hypothesizing. Indicate which inference technique(s) is appropriate. Tell whether you would or would not do a significance test and/or calculate a confidence interval, and if not, why. Lastly, describe the type of sample used in your study and explain any limitations that are placed on your using inferential statistics due to the nature of the sample.

1. The question or hypothesis of my study is: _____
_____

2. The descriptive statistic(s) I would use to describe the relationship I am hypothesizing would
be: _____
_____

3. The appropriate inference technique for my study would be: _____
_____

4. I would use a parametric _____ or a nonparametric _____ technique because:
_____

5. I would _____ or would not _____ do a significance test because: _____
_____

6. I would _____ or would not _____ calculate a confidence interval because:
_____

7. The type of sample used in my study is: _____

8. The type of sample used in my study places the following limitation(s) on my use of inferential
statistics: _____
_____
_____

Chapter Ten

STATISTICS
IN PERSPECTIVE

There are appropriate uses for both descriptive and inferential statistics in educational research. Sometimes, however, either or both types of statistics can be used inappropriately. This chapter, therefore, discusses appropriate use of the descriptive and inferential statistics described in the previous two chapters. We present some recommendations for comparing data obtained from two or more groups, or for relating variables within only one group, and discuss the use and implications of frequency polygons, scatterplots, and crossbreak tables. We stress the importance of distinguishing between statistical and practical significance and illustrate some ways to do so.

Objectives

Reading this chapter should enable you to:

- *Apply* several recommendations when comparing data obtained from two or more groups
- *Apply* several recommendations when relating variables within a single group
- *Explain* what is meant by the term "effect size"
- *Describe* briefly how to use frequency polygons, scatterplots, and crossbreak tables to interpret data
- *Differentiate* between statistically significant and practically significant research results

Approaches to Research

Now that you are somewhat familiar with both descriptive and inferential statistics, we want to relate them more specifically to practice. What are appropriate uses of these statistics? What are appropriate interpretations of them? What are the common errors or mistakes you should watch out for as either a participant in or consumer of research?

Much research in education is done in one of two ways: Either two or more groups are compared or variables within one group are related. Furthermore, as you have seen, the data in a study may be either quantitative or categorical. Thus four different combinations of research are possible as shown in Figure 10.1.

Remember that all groups are made up of individual units. In most cases, the unit is one person and the group is a group of people. Sometimes, however, the unit is itself a group (for example, a class). In such cases, the "group" would be a collection of classes. This is illustrated by the hypothesis: "Teacher friendliness is related to student learning." This hypothesis could be studied with a group of classes and a measuring

FIGURE 10.1

Combinations of Data and Approaches to Research

	Data	
	Quantitative	Categorical
Two or more groups are compared		
Variables within one group are related		

of both teacher "friendliness" and average student learning for each *class*.

Another complication arises in studies in which the same individuals receive two or more different treatments or methods. In comparing treatments, we are not then comparing different groups of people but different groups of scores obtained by the same group at different times. Nevertheless, the statistical analysis fits the comparison group model. We discuss this point further in Chapter Twelve.

Comparing Groups: Quantitative Data

TECHNIQUES

Whenever two or more groups are compared using quantitative data, the comparisons can be made in a variety of ways: through frequency polygons, calculation of one or more measures of central tendency (averages), and/or calculation of one or more measures of variability (spreads). Frequency polygons provide the most information, averages are useful summaries of each group's performance, and spreads provide information about the degree of variability in each group.

When analyzing data obtained from two groups, therefore, the first thing researchers should do is construct a frequency polygon of each group's scores. This will show all the information available about each group and also help researchers decide which of the shorter and more convenient indices to calculate. For example, examination of the frequency polygon of a group's scores can indicate whether the median or the mean is the most appropriate measure of central tendency to use. When comparing quantitative data from two groups, therefore, we recommend the following.

Recommendation 1: As a first step, prepare a frequency polygon of each group's scores.
Recommendation 2: Use these polygons to decide which measure of central tendency is appro-

priate to calculate. If any polygon shows extreme scores at one end, use medians for all groups rather than, or in addition to, means.

INTERPRETATION

Once the descriptive statistics have been calculated, they must be interpreted. At this point, the task is to describe, in words, what the polygons and averages tell researchers about the questions or hypothesis being investigated. A key question that arises is: "How large does a difference in means between two groups have to be in order to be important?" When will this difference *make a difference*? How does one decide?

Use Information about Known Groups. Unfortunately, in most educational research, this question is very difficult to answer. Sometimes, prior experience can be helpful. One of the advantages of IQ scores is that, over the years, many educators have had enough experience with them to make differences between them meaningful. Most experienced counselors, administrators, and teachers realize, for example, that a difference in means between two groups of less than five points has little useful meaning—no matter how statistically significant the difference may be. They also know that a difference between means of ten points is enough to have important implications. At other times, a researcher may have available a frame of reference, or standard, to use in interpreting the magnitude of a difference between means. One such standard consists of the mean scores of known groups. In a study of critical thinking in which one of the present authors participated, for example, the end-of-year mean score for a group of eleventh graders who received a special curriculum was shown to be higher than is typical of the mean scores of eleventh graders in general *and* close to the mean score of a group of college students, whereas a comparison group scored lower than both. Since the "special curriculum" group also demonstrated a Fall to Spring mean gain twice that of the comparison group, the total evidence obtained through comparing their performance with other groups indicated that the gains made by the special curriculum group were important.

Calculate the Effect Size.   Another technique for assessing the magnitude of a difference between the means of two groups is to calculate what is known as **effect size** (E.S.).* Effect size takes into account the *size* of the difference between means that is obtained, regardless of whether it is statistically significant. It is obtained by dividing the difference between the means of the two groups being compared by the standard deviation of the comparison group. Thus:

$$\text{E.S.} = \frac{\text{mean of experimental group} - \text{mean of comparison group}}{\text{standard deviation of comparison group}}$$

When pre- to post-gains in the mean scores of two groups are compared, the formula is modified as follows:

$$\text{E.S.} = \frac{\text{mean experimental gain} - \text{mean comparison gain}}{\text{standard deviation of gain of comparison group}}$$

The standard deviation of gain scores is obtained by first getting the gain (post − pre) score for each individual and then calculating the standard deviation as usual.†

While effect size is a useful tool for assessing the magnitude of a difference between the means of two groups, it does not, in and of itself, answer the question of how large an E.S. must be for researchers to consider an obtained difference important. As is the case with significance levels, this is essentially an arbitrary decision. Most researchers consider that any E.S. of .50 (that is, half a standard deviation of the com-

parison group's scores) or larger is an important finding. If the scores fit the normal distribution, such an E.S. indicates that the difference in means between the two groups is about one-twelfth the distance between the highest and lowest scores of the comparison group. When assessing the magnitude of a difference between the means of two groups, therefore, we recommend the following.

Recommendation 3: Compare obtained results with data on the means of known groups if possible.

Recommendation 4: Calculate an effect size. Interpret an E.S. of .50 or larger as important.

Use Inferential Statistics.   A third method for judging the importance of a difference between the means of two groups is by the use of inferential statistics. It is a commonplace to find, even before examining polygons or differences in means, that a researcher has applied an inference technique (a *t* test, an analysis of variance, and so on) and then used the results as the *only* criterion for evaluating the importance of the results. This practice has come under increasing attack because:

1. Unless the groups compared are random samples from specified populations (which is unusual), the results (probabilities, significance levels, and confidence intervals) are to an unknown degree in error and hence misleading.

2. The outcome is greatly affected by sample size. With 100 cases in each of two groups, a mean difference in IQ score of 4.2 points is statistically significant at the .05 level (assuming the standard deviation is 15, as is typical with most IQ tests). Such a difference is so small as to be meaningless in any practical sense.

3. The actual magnitude of difference is minimized or sometimes overlooked.

4. The purpose of inferential statistics is to

---

* Some authors use the term "effect size" to describe a group of statistical indexes, all of which have the common purpose of clarifying the magnitude of relationship. Our intent here is to clarify the idea by discussing the most common of such indexes.

† There are more effective ways to obtain gain scores, but we will delay a discussion until subsequent chapters.

provide information pertinent to generalizing sample results to populations—not to evaluate sample results.

With regard to the use of inferential statistics, therefore, we recommend the following.

Recommendation 5: Calculate inferential statistics only if you can make a convincing argument that a difference between means of the magnitude obtained is important.

Recommendation 6: Do not use tests of statistical significance to evaluate the magnitude of a difference between sample means. Use them only as they were intended—to judge the generalizability of results.

Recommendation 7: Unless random samples were used, interpret probabilities and/or significance levels as crude indices, not as precise values.

Recommendation 8: Report the results of inference techniques as confidence intervals rather than (or in addition to) significance levels.

AN EXAMPLE

Let us present an example in which we incorporate the preceding recommendations. Imagine we have two groups of eighth grade students, sixty in each group, who receive different methods of social studies instruction for one semester. The teacher of one group uses an inquiry method of instruction, while the teacher of the other group uses the lecture method. The researcher's hypothesis is that the inquiry method will result in greater improvement than the lecture method in explaining skills as measured by the "Test of Ability to Explain" (see p. 130 in Chapter Seven). Each student is tested at the beginning and at the end of the semester. The test consists of 40 items; the range of scores on the pretest is from 3 to 32, or 29 points. A gain score (posttest − pretest) is obtained. These scores are shown in the frequency distributions in Table 10.1 and the frequency polygons in Figure 10.2.

These polygons indicate that a comparison of means is appropriate. Why?* The mean of the inquiry group is 5.6 compared to the mean of 4.4 for the lecture group. The difference between means is 1.2. In this instance, a comparison with the means of known groups is not possible since such data are not available. A calculation of Effect Size results in an E.S. of .44, somewhat below the .50 that most researchers recommend for significance. Inspection of Figure 10.2, however, suggests that the difference between the means of the two groups should not be discounted. Table 10.1 and Figure 10.2 show that the number of students gaining seven or more points is twenty-five in the inquiry group and thirteen (or about half as many) in the lecture group. A gain of seven points on a forty-item test can be considered substantial, even more so when it is recalled that the range was 29 points (3–32) on the pretest. If a gain of eight points is used, the numbers are sixteen in the inquiry group and nine in the lecture group. If a gain of six points is used, the numbers become thirty-four and twenty. We would argue that these discrepancies are large enough, in context, to commend the inquiry method over the lecture method.

The use of an inference technique (a *t* test for independent means) indicates that $p < .05$ in one tail (Table 10.2).† This leads the researcher to conclude that the observed difference between means of 1.2 points probably is not due to the particular samples used. Whether this probability can be taken as exact depends primarily on whether the samples were randomly selected. The 90 percent confidence interval is shown in Figure 10.3.‡ Notice that a difference of zero between the population means is not within the confidence interval.

---

* There are no extreme scores.
† A directional hypothesis justifies use of a one-tailed test.
‡ 1.65 *SED* gives .05 in one tail of the normal curve. 1.65 (*SED*) = 1.65 (.49) = .81. 1.2 ± .81 equals .39 to 2.01. This is the 90 percent confidence interval, which is justified because the researcher is really only interested in a one tailed-test that includes differences smaller than the one obtained. The 95 percent or any other confidence interval could of course be determined.

TABLE 10.1

Gain Scores on Test of Ability to Explain:
Inquiry and Lecture Groups

Gain Scores[a]	Inquiry		Lecture	
	Frequency	*Cumulative Frequency*	*Frequency*	*Cumulative Frequency*
11	1	60	0	
10	3	59	2	60
9	5	56	3	58
8	7	51	4	55
7	9	44	4	51
6	9	35	7	47
5	6	26	9	40
4	6	20	8	31
3	5	14	7	23
2	4	9	6	16
1	2	5	4	10
0	3	3	5	6
−1	0	0	1	1

[a] A negative score indicates the pretest was higher than the posttest.

FIGURE 10.2

Frequency Polygons of Gain Scores on Test
of Ability to Explain: Inquiry and Lecture Groups

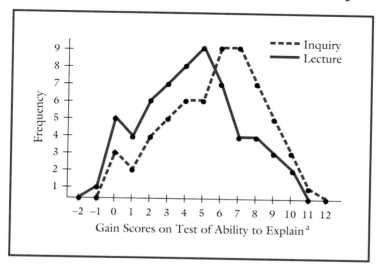

[a] A negative score indicates the pretest was higher than the posttest.

TABLE 10.2

Calculations from Table 10.1

		Inquiry Group						Lecture Group			
Gain Score	f^a	fX^b	$X - \bar{X}^c$	$(X - \bar{X})^{2\,d}$	$f(X - \bar{X})^{2\,e}$	Gain Score	f	fX	$X - \bar{X}$	$(X - \bar{X})^2$	$f(X - \bar{X})^2$
11	1	11	5.4	29.2	29.2	11	0	0	6.6	43.6	0.0
10	3	30	4.4	19.4	58.2	10	2	20	5.6	31.4	62.8
9	5	45	3.4	11.6	58.0	9	3	27	4.6	21.2	63.6
8	7	56	2.4	5.8	40.6	8	4	32	3.6	13.0	52.0
7	9	63	1.4	2.0	18.0	7	4	28	2.6	6.8	27.2
6	9	54	0.4	0.2	1.8	6	7	42	1.6	2.6	18.2
5	6	30	−0.6	0.4	2.4	5	9	45	0.6	0.4	3.6
4	6	24	−1.6	2.6	15.6	4	8	32	−0.4	0.2	1.6
3	5	15	−2.6	6.8	34.0	3	7	21	−1.4	2.0	14.0
2	4	8	−3.6	13.0	52.0	2	6	12	−2.4	5.8	34.8
1	2	2	−4.6	21.2	42.4	1	4	4	−3.4	11.6	46.4
0	3	0	−5.6	31.4	94.2	0	5	0	−4.4	19.4	97.0
−1	0	0	−6.6	43.6	0.0	−1	1	−1	−5.4	29.2	29.2
−2	0	0	−7.6	57.8	0.0	−2	0	0	−6.4	41.0	0.0
Totals				$\Sigma = 338$	$\Sigma = 446.4$					$\Sigma = 262$	$\Sigma = 450.4$

$$\bar{X}_1 = \frac{\Sigma fX}{n} = \frac{338}{60} = 5.6 \qquad\qquad \bar{X}_2 = \frac{\Sigma fX}{n} = \frac{262}{60} = 4.4$$

$$SD_1 = \sqrt{\frac{f(X - \bar{X})^2}{n}} = \sqrt{\frac{446.4}{60}} = \sqrt{7.4} = 2.7 \qquad SD_2 = \sqrt{\frac{f(X - \bar{X})^2}{n}} = \sqrt{\frac{450.4}{60}} = \sqrt{7.5} = 2.7$$

$$SEM_1 = \frac{SD}{\sqrt{n-1}} = \frac{2.7}{\sqrt{59}} = \frac{2.7}{7.7} = .35 \qquad SEM_2 = \frac{SD}{\sqrt{n-1}} = \frac{2.7}{\sqrt{59}} = \frac{2.7}{7.7} = .35$$

$$SED = \sqrt{SEM_1^2 + SEM_2^2} = \sqrt{.35^2 + .35^2} = \sqrt{.12 + .12} = \sqrt{.24} = .49$$

$$t = \frac{\bar{X}_1 - \bar{X}_2}{SED} = \frac{1.2}{.49} = 2.45; \qquad p < .05$$

$$\text{E.S.} = \frac{\bar{X}_1 - \bar{X}_2}{SD_2} = \frac{1.2}{2.4} = .44$$

[a] f = frequency
[b] f = frequency × score
[c] $X - \bar{X}$ = score − mean
[d] $(X - \bar{X})^2$ = (score − mean)²
[e] $f(X - \bar{X})^2$ = frequency × (score − mean)²

Relating Variables within a Group: Quantitative Data

TECHNIQUES

Whenever a relationship between quantitative variables within a single group is examined, the appropriate techniques are the scatterplot and the correlation coefficient. The scatterplot illustrates all the data visually, while the correlation coefficient provides a numerical summary of the data. When analyzing data obtained from a single group, therefore, researchers should begin by constructing a scatterplot. Not only will it provide all the information available, but it will help them judge which correlation coefficient to calculate (the choice usually will be

FIGURE 10.3

90 Percent Confidence Interval for a Difference between Sample Means of 1.2

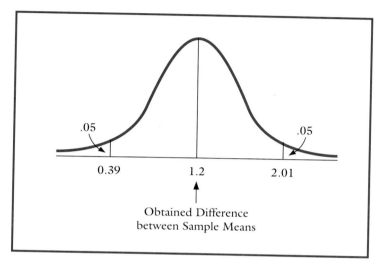

between the Pearson r, which assumes a straight line relationship, and eta, which describes a curved or curvilinear relationship).

Consider Figure 10.4. All of the five scatterplots shown represent a Pearson correlation of about .50. Only in a, however, does this coefficient (.50) completely convey the nature of the relationship. In b, the relationship is understated, since it is a curvilinear one, and eta would give a higher coefficient. In c, the nu-

merical index does not reflect the fan-shaped nature of the relationship. In d, the coefficient does not reveal that there are two distinct subgroups. In e the coefficient is greatly inflated by a few unusual cases. While these illustrations are a bit exaggerated, similar results are often found in real data.

When examining relationships within a single group, therefore, we recommend the following.

FIGURE 10.4

Scatterplots with a Pearson r of .50

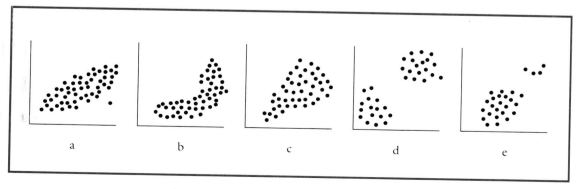

Recommendation 9: Begin by constructing a scatterplot.

Recommendation 10: Use the scatterplot to determine which correlation coefficient is appropriate to calculate.

Recommendation 11: Use *both* the scatterplot and the correlation coefficient to interpret results.

INTERPRETATION

Interpretation of scatterplots and correlations presents problems similar to those we discussed in relation to differences in means. How large must a correlation coefficient be to suggest an *important* relationship? What does an important relationship look like on a scatterplot?

As you are beginning to see, doing or evaluating research is not cut and dried; it is not a matter of following a set of rules but rather requires informed judgment. In judging correlation coefficients, one must first assess their appropriateness, as was done with those in Figure 10.4. If the Pearson correlation coefficient is an adequate summary (and we have shown in Figure 10.4 that this is not always the case), most researchers would agree to the interpreta-

TABLE 10.3

Interpretation of Correlation Coefficients when Testing Research Hypotheses

Magnitude of r	Interpretation
.00 to .40	Of little practical importance except in unusual circumstances;[a] perhaps of theoretical value
.41 to .60	Large enough to be of practical as well as theoretical use
.61 to .80	Very important, but rarely obtained in educational research
.81 or above	Probably an error in calculation; if not, a very sizable relationship

[a] When selecting a very few people from a large group, even correlations this small may have predictive value.

tions shown in Table 10.3 when testing a research hypothesis.

As with a comparison of means, the use of inferential statistics to judge the importance of the magnitude of a relationship is both common and misleading. With a sample of 100, a correlation of only .20 is statistically significant at the .05 level with a two-tailed test. Accordingly, we recommend the following.

Recommendation 12: When interpreting scatterplots, draw a line which best fits all points and note the extent of deviations from it. The smaller the deviations all along the line, the more useful the relationship.*

Recommendation 13: Calculate inferential statistics only if you can give a convincing argument for the importance of the relationship found in the sample.

Recommendation 14: Do not use tests of statistical significance to evaluate the magnitude of a relationship. Use them, as they were intended, to judge generalizability.

Recommendation 15: Unless a random sample was used, interpret probabilities and/or significance levels as crude indices, not as precise values.

Recommendation 16: Report the results of inference techniques as confidence intervals rather than as significance levels.

A SECOND EXAMPLE

Suppose a researcher wishes to test the hypothesis that, among counseling clients, improvement in marital satisfaction after six months of counseling is related to self-esteem at the beginning of counseling. In other words, people with higher self-esteem would be expected to show more improvement in marital satisfaction after undergoing therapy for a period of six months than people with lower self-esteem. The researcher obtains a group of thirty clients, each of whom takes a self-esteem inventory and a

* Try this with Figure 10.4.

marital satisfaction inventory prior to counseling. The marital satisfaction inventory is taken again at the end of six months of counseling. The data are shown in Table 10.4.

The researcher plots a scatterplot and finds that it reveals two things. First, there is a tendency for individuals with higher initial self-esteem scores to show greater improvement in marital satisfaction than those with lower initial self-esteem scores. Second, it also shows that the

TABLE 10.4

Self-Esteem Scores and Gains in Marital Satisfaction

Client	Self-Esteem Score before Counseling (X)	X^2	Gain in Marital Satisfaction after Counseling (Y)	Y^2	XY
1	20	400	-4	16	-80
2	21	441	-2	4	-42
3	22	484	-7	49	-154
4	24	576	1	1	24
5	24	576	4	16	96
6	25	625	5	25	125
7	26	676	-1	1	-26
8	27	729	8	64	216
9	29	841	2	4	58
10	28	784	5	25	140
11	30	900	5	25	150
12	30	900	14	196	420
13	32	1024	7	49	219
14	33	1089	15	225	495
15	35	1225	6	36	210
16	35	1225	16	256	560
17	36	1269	11	121	396
18	37	1396	14	196	518
19	36	1296	18	324	648
20	38	1444	9	81	342
21	39	1527	14	196	546
22	39	1527	15	225	585
23	40	1600	4	16	160
24	41	1681	8	64	328
25	42	1764	0	0	0
26	43	1849	3	9	129
27	43	1849	5	25	215
28	43	1849	8	64	344
29	44	1936	4	16	176
30	45	2025	5	25	225
Total	1007	35,507	192	2354	7023

$$r = \frac{n\,\Sigma XY - \Sigma X \Sigma Y}{\sqrt{[n\Sigma X^2 - (\Sigma X)^2][n\Sigma Y^2 - (\Sigma Y^2)]}} = \frac{30\,(7023) - (1007)(192)}{\sqrt{[30(35{,}507) - (1007)^2][30(2354) - (192)^2]}}$$

$$= \frac{210690 - 193344}{\sqrt{(1065210 - 1014049)(70620 - 36864)}} = \frac{17346}{\sqrt{(51161)(33753)}}$$

$$= \frac{17346}{\sqrt{1725837233}} = \frac{17346}{41543} = .42$$

relationship is more correctly described as cur-vilinear—that is, clients with low *or* high self esteem show less improvement than those with a moderate level of self-esteem (remember, these data are fictional). Pearson *r* equals .42. The valve of eta obtained for these same data is .82, indicating a substantial degree of relationship between the two variables. We have not shown the calculations for eta since they are somewhat more complicated than those for *r*. The relation-ship is illustrated by the smoothed curve shown in Figure 10.5.

The researcher calculates the appropriate inference statistic (a *t* test for *r*), as shown below, to determine whether *r* = .42 is significant.

$$\text{Standard error of } r = SE_r = \frac{1}{\sqrt{n-1}}$$

$$= \frac{1}{\sqrt{29}} = .185$$

$$t_r = \frac{r - .00}{SE_r} = \frac{.42 - .00}{.185} = 2.3; p < .01$$

As you can see, it results in an obtained value of 2.3 and a probability of *p* = <.01, using a one-tailed test (see Appendix C). A one-tailed test is appropriate for *r* if the direction of the relationship was predicted before examining the data. The probability associated with eta would (presumably) be obtained using a two-tailed test (unless the researcher predicted the shape of the curve from Figure 10.5 before examining the data). An eta of .82 is also significant at *p* = <.01, indicating that the relationship is unlikely to be due to the particular sample studied. Whether or not these probabilities are correct depends on whether or not the sample was randomly selected. The 95 percent confidence interval around the obtained value for *r* is shown in Figure 10.6.

FIGURE 10.5

Scatterplot Illustrating the Relationship between Initial Self-Esteem and Gain in Marital Satisfaction among Counseling Clients

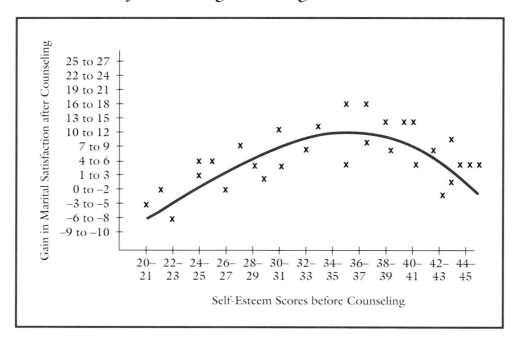

FIGURE 10.6

95 Percent Confidence Interval for r = .42

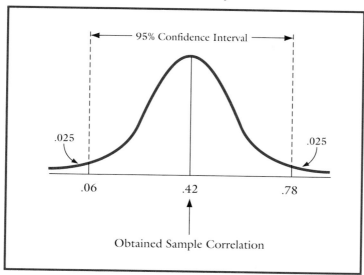

Comparing Groups: Categorical Data

TECHNIQUES

Groups may be compared when the data involved are categorical data by reporting either percentages (or proportions) or by frequencies in crossbreak tables. Table 10.5 gives a fictitious example.

INTERPRETATION

Once again, we must look at summary statistics—even percentages—carefully. Percentages can be misleading unless the number of cases is also given. At first glance, Table 10.5 may look impressive—until one discovers that the data in it represent sixty females and only ten males. In crossbreak form, Table 10.5 represents the following *numbers,* as opposed to percentages, of individuals.

	Male	Female
Democrat	2	30
Republican	7	27
Other	1	3

TABLE 10.5

Gender and Political Preference

	Percentage of Males	Percentage of Females
Democrat	20	50
Republican	70	45
Other	10	5
Total	100	100

Table 10.6 illustrates a fictitious relationship between teacher gender and grade level taught. As you can see, the largest number of male teachers is to be found in grade 7, and the largest number of female teachers is to be found in grade 4. Here, too, however, we must ask: How much difference must there be between these frequencies for us to consider them important? One of the limitations of categorical data is that such evaluations are even harder than they are with quantitative data. One possible approach is by examining prior experience or knowledge. Table 10.6 does suggest a trend toward an

TABLE 10.6

Teacher Gender and Grade Level Taught: Case 1

	Grade 4	Grade 5	Grade 6	Grade 7	Total
Male	10	20	20	30	80
Female	40	30	30	20	120
Total	50	50	50	50	200

increasingly larger proportion of male teachers in the higher grades—but, again, is the trend important?

The data in Table 10.7 show the same trend, but the pattern is much less striking. Perhaps prior experience or research shows (somehow) that gender differences become important whenever the within-grade difference is more than 10 percent (or a frequency of five in these data). Such knowledge is seldom available, however, which leads us to consider the summary statistic (similar to the correlation coefficient) known as the contingency coefficient (see Chapter Nine). In order to use it, however, remember that the data *must* be presented in crossbreak tables. Calculating the contingency coefficient is easily done by hand or by computer. You will recall that this statistic is not as straightforward in interpretation as the correlation coefficient, since its interpretation depends on the number of cells

TABLE 10.7

Teacher Gender and Grade Level Taught: Case 2

	Grade 4	Grade 5	Grade 6	Grade 7	Total
Male	22	22	25	28	97
Female	28	28	25	22	103
Total	50	50	50	50	200

in the crossbreak table. Nevertheless, we recommend its use.

Perhaps because of the difficulties mentioned above, most research reports using percentages or crossbreaks rely on inference techniques to evaluate the magnitude of relationships. In the absence of random sampling, their use suffers from the same liabilities as with quantitative data. When analyzing categorical data, therefore, we recommend the following.

Recommendation 17: Place all data into crossbreak tables.

Recommendation 18: To evaluate the importance of relationships, patterns, or trends, calculate a contingency coefficient.

Recommendation 19: Do not use tests of statistical significance to evaluate the magnitude of relationships. Use them, as intended, to judge generalizability.

Recommendation 20: Unless a random sample was used, interpret probabilities and/or significance levels as crude indices, not as precise values.

A THIRD EXAMPLE

Let us return to Tables 10.6 and 10.7 to illustrate the above recommendations for analyzing categorical data. We shall consider Table 10.6 first. Since there are 50 teachers, or 25 percent, of the total of 200 teachers at each grade level (4–7), we would expect that there would be 25 percent of the total number of male teachers and 25 percent of the total number of female teachers at *each* grade level as well. Out of the total of 200 teachers, 80 are male and 120 are female. Hence the expected frequency for male teachers at each of the grade levels would be 20 (25 percent of 80), and for female teachers 30 (25 percent of 120). These expected frequencies are shown in parentheses in Table 10.8. We then calculate the contingency coefficient, which equals .28.

By referring to Table 9.2 in Chapter Nine, we estimate that the upper limit for a 2 by 4 table (which we have here) is approximately .80. Accordingly, a contingency coefficient of .28 indicates only a slight degree of relationship. As a result, we would not recommend testing for significance. Were we to do so, however, we would find by looking in a chi-square probability table that three degrees of freedom requires a chi-square value of 7.82 to be considered significant at the .05 level. Our obtained value for chi-square was 16.66, indicating that the small relationship we have discovered probably does exist in the population from which the sample was drawn. This is a good example of the difference between statistical and practical significance. Our obtained correlation of .28 is statistically significant, but practically insignificant. A correlation of .28 would be considered by most researchers as having little practical importance.

If we carry out the same analysis for Table 10.7, the resulting contingency coefficient is .10. Such a correlation is, for all practical purposes, meaningless, but should we (for some reason) wish to see if it was statistically significant, we would find that it is not significant at the .05 level (the chi-square value = 1.98, far below the 7.82 needed for significance).

Relating Variables within a Group: Categorical Data

The preceding section also applies to hypotheses that examine relationships among categorical variables within a group. A moment's thought shows why. The procedures available to us are the same—percentages or crossbreak tables. Suppose our hypothesis is that, among college students, gender is related to political preference. To test this we must divide the data we obtain from this group by gender and political preference. This gives us the crossbreak in Table 10.5. Since all such hypotheses must be tested by dividing people into groups, the statistical analysis is the same whether seen as one group, subdivided, or as two or more different groups.

TABLE 10.8

Crossbreak Table Showing Teacher Gender and Grade Level with Calculations for Chi-Square and Contingency Coefficient Added (Data from Table 10.6)

	Grade 4	Grade 5	Grade 6	Grade 7	Total
Male	10 (20)	20 (20)	20 (20)	30 (20)	80
Female	40 (30)	30 (30)	30 (30)	20 (30)	120
Total	50	50	50	50	200

O	E	$O - E$	$(O - E)^2$	$\dfrac{(O - E)^2}{E}$
10	20	10	100	100/20 = 5.00
40	30	10	100	100/30 = 3.33
20	20	0	0	0
30	30	0	0	0
20	20	0	0	0
30	30	0	0	0
30	20	10	100	100/20 = 5.00
20	30	10	100	100/30 = 3.33

$$\text{Sum} = 16.66 = \text{chi-square}$$

$$\text{Contingency coefficient} = \sqrt{\frac{\text{chi-square}}{\text{chi-square} + n}} = \sqrt{\frac{16.66}{16.66 + 200}}$$

$$= \sqrt{\frac{16.66}{216.66}} = \sqrt{0.077} = .28$$

A Recap of Recommendations

You may have noticed that many of our recommendations are essentially the same, regardless of the method of statistical analysis involved. To stress their importance, we want to state them again here, all together, phrased more generally.

We recommend that researchers:

• use graphic techniques before calculating numerical summary indices;

- use both graphs and summary indices to interpret results of a study;
- make use of external criteria (such as prior experience or scores of known groups) to assess the magnitude of a relationship whenever such are available;
- use professional consensus when evaluating the magnitude of an effect size or a correlation;
- calculate inferential statistics only if you can make a convincing case for the importance of the relationship found in the sample;
- use tests of statistical significance only to evaluate generalizability, not to evaluate the magnitude of relationships;

- when random sampling has not occurred, treat probabilities as approximations or crude indices rather than as precise values;
- report confidence intervals rather than, or in addition to, significance levels whenever possible

We also want to make a final recommendation involving the distinction between parametric and nonparametric statistics. Since the calculation of statistics has now become rather easy and quick due to the availability of many computer programs, we suggest that researchers:

- use *both* parametric and nonparametric techniques to analyze data. When the

TABLE 10.9

Summary of Commonly Used Statistical Techniques

	Data	
	Quantitative	*Categorical*
Two or more groups are compared		
Descriptive Statistics	*Frequency polygons *Averages *Spreads *Effect size	*Percentages *Bar graphs *Pie charts *Crossbreak (contingency) tables
Inferential Statistics	*t test for means *ANOVA *ANCOVA *Confidence interval *Mann-Whitney U test *Kruskal-Wallis ANOVA *Sign test *Friedman ANOVA	*Chi-square
Relationships among variables are studied within one group		
Descriptive Statistics	*Scatterplot *Correlation coefficient (r) *eta	*Crossbreak (contingency) tables *Contingency coefficient
Inferential Statistics	*t test for r *confidence interval	*Chi-square

results are consistent, interpretation will thereby be strengthened. When the results are not consistent, discuss possible reasons.

A summary of the most commonly used statistical techniques, both descriptive and inferential, as used with quantitative and categorical data, is shown in Table 10.9.

Main Points of Chapter Ten

- The construction of frequency polygons, the use of data on the means of known groups, the calculation of effect sizes, and the reporting of confidence intervals are recommended when comparing quantitative data from two or more groups.
- The construction of scatterplots and the use of both scatterplots and correlation coefficients are recommended when relating variables involving quantitative data within a single group.
- The construction of crossbreak tables and the calculation of contingency coefficients are recommended when comparing categorical data involving two or more groups or when examining relationships among categorical data within one group.
- When tests of statistical significance could be applied, it is recommended that they be used to evaluate generalizability only, not to evaluate the magnitude of relationships. Whenever possible, confidence intervals should be reported in addition to significance levels.
- Both parametric and nonparametric techniques should be used to analyze data rather than either one alone.

For Discussion

1. Give some examples of how the results of a study might be significant statistically, yet unimportant educationally. Could the reverse be true?

2. How would you interpret the following hypothetical results of a comparison of computer-based vs. no-computer mathematics classes on a final examination?

	Computer Group	No-Computer Group
n	82	82
mean	63	60
range	30–85	26–90
SD	8.5	10.4

A t test for independent means results in $p < .05$ (one-tailed test)

3. How would you interpret the following hypothetical results of a study correlating anxiety with task performance? What additional information would you want to have?

$$r = .20 \text{ (not significant at the .05 level)}$$

$$\text{eta} = .50 \text{ (significant at the .05 level)}$$

4. How would you interpret the following hypothetical data from a study relating gender and handedness? What additional information would you want to have?

	Male	Female	Total
Righthanded	100 (120)	170 (150)	270
Lefthanded	60 (40)	30 (50)	90
Total	160	200	360

Research Exercise Ten:
Statistics in Perspective

Using Problem Sheet 10, once again state the question or hypothesis of your study. Summarize the descriptive and inferential statistics you would use to describe the relationship you are hypothesizing. Then tell how you would evaluate the magnitude of any relationship you might find. Finally, describe the changes in techniques to be used from those you described in Problem Sheets 8 and 9, if any.

PROBLEM SHEET 10
Statistics in Perspective

1. The question or hypothesis of my study is: _____
_____

2. My expected relationship(s) would be described using the following descriptive statistics: _____
_____
_____

3. The inferential statistics I would use are: _____
_____
_____
_____

4. I would evaluate the magnitude of the relationship(s) I find by: _____
_____
_____
_____

5. The changes in my use of descriptive or inferential statistics from those I described in Problem
Sheets 8 and 9 are as follows: _____
_____
_____
_____

Chapter Eleven

INTERNAL VALIDITY

There are usually many possible ways to explain the outcomes of a study. The possibility of such alternative explanations, usually referred to as "threats to internal validity," exists in almost all research endeavors. In this chapter, we discuss several of these threats, as well as ways to prevent their effects.

- *Explain* what is meant by the term "internal validity"
- *Explain* what is meant by a "subject characteristics" threat to internal validity and *give an example* of such a threat
- *Explain* what is meant by a "location" threat to internal validity and *give an example* of such a threat
- *Explain* what is meant by an "instrumentation" threat to internal validity and *give an example* of such a threat
- *Explain* what is meant by a "testing" threat to internal validity and *give an example* of such a threat
- *Explain* what is meant by a "history" threat to internal validity and *give an example* of such a threat
- *Explain* what is meant by a "maturation" threat to internal validity and *give an example* of such a threat
- *Explain* what is meant by a "subject attitude" threat to internal validity and *give an example* of such a threat
- *Explain* what is meant by a "regression" threat to internal validity and *give an example* of such a threat
- *Explain* what is meant by an "implementation" threat to internal validity and *give an example* of such a threat
- *Identify* various threats to internal validity in published research articles
- *Suggest* possible remedies for specific examples of the various threats to internal validity

---

What Is Internal Validity?

Imagine the results of a study show that high school students taught by the "inquiry method" score higher on a test of critical thinking, on the average, than do students taught by the "lecture method." Is this difference in scores due to the difference in methods—to the fact that the two groups have been taught differently? Certainly, the researcher who is conducting the study would like to conclude this. Your first inclination may be to think the same. This may not be a legitimate interpretation, however.

What if the students who were taught the inquiry method were better critical thinkers to begin with? What if some of the students in the inquiry group were also taking a related course during this time at a nearby university? What if the teachers of the inquiry group were simply better teachers? Any of these (or other) factors might explain why the inquiry group scored

higher on the critical thinking test. Should this be the case, the researcher may be mistaken in concluding that there is a difference in effectiveness between the two methods, for the obtained difference in results may be due *not* to the difference in methods, but to something else.

In any study that either describes or tests relationships, there is always the possibility that the relationship shown in the data is, in fact, due to or explained by, something else. If so, then the relationship observed is not at all what it seems and it may lose whatever meaning it appears to have. Many alternative hypotheses may exist, in other words, to explain the outcomes of a study. These alternative explanations are often referred to as "threats to internal validity," and they are what this chapter is about.

Perhaps unfortunately, the term "validity" is used in three different ways by researchers. In addition to internal validity, which we discuss in this chapter, you will see reference to instrument (or measurement) validity, as discussed in Chapter Seven, and external (or generalization) validity, as discussed in Chapter Five.

When a study has **internal validity**, it means that any relationship observed between two or more variables should be meaningful in its own right, rather than being due to "something else." The "something else" may, as we suggested above, be any one (or more) of a number of factors, such as the age or ability of the subjects, the conditions under which the study is conducted, the type of materials used, and the like. If these factors are not in some way or another controlled or accounted for, the researcher can never be sure that they are not the reason for any observed results. Stated differently, internal validity means that observed differences on the dependent variable are directly related to the independent variable, and not due to some other unintended variable.

Consider another example. Suppose a researcher finds a correlation of .80 between height and mathematics test scores for a group of elementary school students (grades 1–5), that is, the taller boys have higher math scores. Such a result is quite misleading. Why? Because it is clearly a by-product of age. Fifth graders are taller and better in math than first graders simply because they are older and more developed. To explore this relationship further is pointless; to let it affect school practice would be absurd.

Or consider a study in which the researcher hypothesizes that, in classes for educationally handicapped students, teacher expectation of failure is related to amount of disruptive behavior. Suppose the researcher finds a high correlation between these two variables. Should he or she conclude that this is a meaningful relationship? Perhaps. But the correlation might also be explained by another variable, such as the ability level of the class (classes low in ability might be expected to have more disruptive behavior *and* higher teacher expectation of failure).*

---

* Can you suggest any other variables that would explain a high correlation (should it be found) between a teacher's expectation of failure and the amount of disruptive behavior that occurs in class?

In our experience, a systematic consideration of possible threats to internal validity receives the least attention of all the aspects of planning a study. Often, the possibility of such threats is not discussed at all. Probably this is due to the fact that their consideration is not seen as an essential step in carrying out a study. Researchers cannot avoid deciding on what variables to study, or how the sample will be obtained, or how the data will be collected and analyzed. They can, however, ignore or simply not think about possible alternative explanations for the outcomes of a study until after the study is completed—at which point it is almost always too late to do anything about them. Identifying possible threats during the planning stage of a study, on the other hand, can often lead researchers to design ways of eliminating or at least minimizing these threats.

In recent years many useful categories within which to consider possible threats to internal validity have been identified. Although most of these categories were originally designed for application to experimental studies, some apply to other types of methodologies as well. We discuss the most important of these possible threats in this chapter.

Various ways of controlling for these threats have also been identified. Some of these are discussed in the remainder of this chapter; others are discussed in subsequent chapters.

Threats to Internal Validity

SUBJECT CHARACTERISTICS

The selection of people for a study may result in the individuals (or groups) differing from one another in unintended ways that are related to the variables to be studied. This is sometimes referred to as "selection bias," or a **subject characteristics threat.** In our example of teacher expectation and class disruptive behavior, the ability level of the class fits this category. In studies that compare groups, subjects in the groups to be compared may differ on such variables as age, gender, ability, socioeconomic background, and the like. If not controlled, these variables may "explain away" whatever differences between groups are found. The list of such subject characteristics is virtually unlimited. Some examples of subject characteristics that might affect the results of a study include the following.

- age
- strength
- maturity
- gender
- ethnicity
- coordination
- speed
- intelligence
- vocabulary
- attitude
- reading ability
- fluency
- manual dexterity
- socioeconomic status
- religious beliefs
- political beliefs

In a particular study, the researcher must decide, based on previous research or experience, which variables are most likely to create problems, and do his or her best to prevent or minimize their effects. In studies comparing groups, there are several methods of equating groups, which we discuss in Chapters Twelve and Fourteen. In correlational studies, there are certain statistical techniques that can be used to control such variables, provided information on each variable is obtained. We discuss these techniques in Chapter Thirteen.

LOSS OF SUBJECTS (MORTALITY)

No matter how carefully the subjects of a study are selected, it is common to "lose" some as the study progresses. This is known as a **mortality threat.** For one reason or another (for example, illness, family relocation, or the requirements of other activities), some individuals may drop out of the study. This is especially true in most intervention studies, since they take place over time.

Subjects may be absent during the collection of data or fail to complete tests, questionnaires, or other instruments. Failure to complete instruments is especially a problem in questionnaire studies. In such studies, it is not uncommon to find that 20 percent or more of the subjects involved do not return their forms. Remember, the actual sample in a study is not the total of those selected, but only those from whom data are obtained.

Loss of subjects, of course, not only limits generalizability, but also can introduce bias—*if* those subjects who are lost would have responded differently from those from whom data were obtained. Many times this is quite likely since those who do not respond or who are absent probably act this way for a reason. In the example we presented earlier in which the researcher was studying the possible relationship between amount of disruptive behavior by students in class and teacher expectations of failure, it is likely that those teachers who failed to describe their expectations to the researcher (and who would therefore be "lost" for the purposes of the study) would differ from those who did provide this information in ways affecting disruptive behavior.

In studies comparing groups, loss of subjects probably will not be a problem if the loss is about the same in all groups. But if there are sizeable differences between groups in terms of the numbers who drop out, this is certainly a conceivable alternative explanation for whatever findings appear. In comparing students taught by different methods (lecture vs. discussion, for example), one might expect the poorer students in each group to be more likely to drop out. If more of the poorer students drop out of either group, the other method may appear more effective than it actually is.

Mortality is perhaps the most difficult of all the threats to internal validity to control. A common misconception is that the threat is eliminated simply by replacing the lost subjects. No matter how this is done—even if they are replaced by new subjects selected randomly—researchers can never be sure that the replacement subjects respond as those who dropped out would have. It is more likely, in fact, that they would *not*. Can you see why?*

It is sometimes possible for a researcher to argue that the loss of subjects in a study is not a problem. This is done by exploring the reasons

---

* Since those who drop out have done so for a reason, their replacements would be different at least in this respect; thus, they may see things differently or feel differently, and their responses may accordingly be different.

for such loss, and then offering an argument as to why these reasons are not relevant to the particular study at hand. Absence from class on the day of testing, for example, probably would not in most cases favor a particular group, since it would be incidental rather than intentional—unless the day and time of the testing was announced beforehand.

Another attempt to eliminate the problem of mortality is to provide evidence that the subjects lost were similar to those remaining on pertinent characteristics such as demographics (such as age, gender, and ethnicity), pretest scores, or other variables that presumably might be related to the study outcomes. While desirable, such evidence can never demonstrate conclusively that those subjects who were lost would not have responded differently from those who remained. When all is said and done, the best solution to the problem of mortality is to do one's best to prevent or minimize the loss of subjects.

Some examples of a mortality threat include the following.

- A third grade teacher divides his class into two equal ability groups to compare the effectiveness of two methods of teaching spelling. The teacher has group one simply repeat out loud the new spelling words he introduces on Friday of each week. With group two, he uses each new word in a sentence as he introduces it, also on Friday. Some of the students in group one are in a special music program, however, and they are often excused from class on Fridays to attend this program. If they, as a group, are better students than the rest of their group, their loss will lower the spelling performance of group one.
- A researcher wishes to study the effects of a new diet on building endurance in long-distance runners. She receives a grant to study, over a two-year period, a group of such runners who are on the track team at several nearby high schools in a large urban high school district. The study is designed to compare runners who are

given the new diet with similar runners in the district who are not given the diet. About 5 percent of the runners who receive the diet and about 20 percent of those who do not receive the diet, however, are seniors, and they graduate at the end of the first year of the study. Since seniors are probably better runners, this loss will cause the remaining "no diet" group to appear "weaker" than the "diet" group.

LOCATION

The particular locations in which data are collected, or in which an intervention is carried out, may create alternative explanations for results. This is called a **location threat**. For example, classrooms in which students are taught by, say, the inquiry method may have more resources (texts and other supplies, equipment, parent support, and so on) available to them than classrooms in which students are taught by the lecture method. The classrooms themselves may be larger, have better lighting, or contain more fully equipped workstations. Such variables may account for higher performance by students. In our disruptive behavior versus teacher expectations example, the availability of support (resources, aides, and parent assistance) might explain the correlation between the major variables of interest. Classes with fewer resources might be expected to have more disruptive behavior and higher teacher expectations of failure.

The location in which tests, interviews, or other instruments are administered may affect responses. Parent assessments of their children may be different when done at home than at school. Student performance on tests may be lower if tests are given in noisy or poorly lighted rooms. Observations of student interaction may be affected by the physical arrangement in certain classrooms. Such differences might provide defensible alternative explanations for the results in a particular study.

The best method of control for a location threat is to hold location constant—that is, keep it the same for all participants. When this is not feasible, the researcher should try to ensure that different locations do not systematically favor the hypothesis. This may require the collection of additional descriptions of the various locations.

Here are some examples of a location threat.

- A researcher designs a study to compare the effects of team versus individual teaching of United States history on student attitudes toward history. The classrooms in which students are taught by a single teacher are markedly smaller than the ones in which students are taught by a team of three teachers.
- A researcher decides to interview counseling and special education students to compare their attitudes toward their respective master's degree programs. Over a three-week period, she manages to interview all of the students enrolled in the two programs. Although she is able to interview most of the students in one of the university classrooms, scheduling conflicts prevent this classroom being available for her to interview the remainder. As a result, she interviews twenty of the counseling students in the coffee shop of the student union.

INSTRUMENTATION

The way in which instruments are used may also constitute a threat to the internal validity of a study. As discussed in Chapter Six, the instruments used in a study can lack evidence of validity. Lack of validity, however, does not necessarily present a threat to *internal* validity—but it may.*

Instrument Decay.   Instrumentation can create problems if the nature of the instrument (including the scoring procedure) is *changed* in some way or another. This is usually referred to as instrument "decay." This is often the case when the instrument is of a type that permits different interpretations of results (as in essay tests), or is especially long or difficult to score, thereby resulting in fatigue of the scorer. Fatigue often happens when a researcher scores a number of tests one after the other; he or she becomes tired and scores the tests differently (more rigorously at first, more generously later) at different times. The principal way to control instrument decay is to schedule data collection and/or scoring so as to minimize changes in any of the instruments or scoring procedures.

Data Collector Characteristics.   The characteristics of the data gatherers—an inevitable part of most instrumentation—can also affect results. Gender, age, ethnicity, language patterns, or other characteristics of the individuals who collect the data in a study may have an effect on the nature of the data they obtain. If these characteristics are related to the variables being investigated, they may offer an alternative explanation for whatever findings appear. Suppose both male and female data gatherers were used in the example we presented of a researcher wishing to study the relationship between disruptive behavior and teacher expectations. It might be that the female data collectors would elicit more confessions of an expectation of failure on the part of teachers, and generate more incidents of disruptive behavior on the part of students during classroom observations, than would the males. If so, any correlation between teacher expectations of failure and the amount of disruptive behavior by students might be explained (at least partly) as an artifact of who collected the data.

The primary ways by which this threat is controlled are by using the same data collector(s) throughout; by analyzing data separately for each collector; or (in comparison-group studies) by ensuring that each collector is used equally in all groups.

Data Collector Bias.   There is also the possibility that the data collector(s) and/or scorer(s) may unconsciously distort the data in such a way as to make certain outcomes (such as support for the hypothesis) more likely. Ex-

---

* In general, we expect lack of validity to make it *less* likely that any relationships will be found. There are times, however, when "poor" instrumentation can *increase* the chances of "phony" or "spurious" relationships emerging.

amples include (1) some classes being allowed more time on tests than other classes, (2) interviewers asking "leading" questions of some interviewees, (3) observer knowledge of teacher expectations affecting quantity and type of observed behaviors of a class, and (4) judges of student essays favoring (unconsciously) one instructional method over another.

The two principal techniques for handling this problem are to standardize all procedures, which usually requires some sort of training of the data collectors, and planned ignorance—that is, ensuring that the data collectors lack the information they would need to distort results. They should be either unaware of the hypothesis or unable to identify the particular characteristics of the individuals or groups from whom the data are being collected. Data collectors do not need to be told which method group they are observing or testing, nor how the individuals they are testing performed on other tests.

Some examples of an instrumentation effect are as follows.

- A professor grades 100 essay-type final examinations in a five-hour period without taking a break. Each essay encompasses between ten and twelve pages. He grades the papers of each class in turn and then compares the results.
- The administration of a large school district changes its method of reporting absences. Only students who are considered truant (absence is unexcused) are reported as absent; students who have a written excuse (from parents or school officials) are not reported. The district reports a 55 percent decrease in absences since the new reporting system has been instituted.
- An interviewer unconsciously suggests possible answers to certain questions during an interview.
- An observer with a preference for inquiry methods observes more "attending behavior" in inquiry compared to non-inquiry-oriented classes.
- A researcher is aware, when scoring the end-of-study examinations, which students were exposed to which treatment in an intervention study.

TESTING

In intervention studies, where data are collected over a period of time, it is common to test subjects at the beginning of the intervention(s). By testing, we mean the use of any form of instrumentation, not just "tests." If substantial improvement is found in posttest (compared to pretest) scores, the researcher may conclude that this improvement is due to the intervention. An alternative explanation, however, may be that the improvement is due to the use of the pretest. Why is this? Let's look at the reasons.

Suppose the intervention in a particular study involves the use of a new textbook. The researcher wants to see if students score higher on an achievement test if they are taught the subject using this new text than did students who have used the regular text in the past. The researcher pretests the students before the new textbook is introduced and then posttests them at the end of a six-week period. The students may be "alerted" to what is being studied by the questions in the pretest, however, and accordingly make a greater effort to learn the material. This increased effort on the part of the students (rather than the new textbook) could account for the pre-to-post improvement. It may also be that "practice" on the pretest by itself is responsible for the improvement. This is known as a **testing threat.**

Consider another example. Suppose a counselor in a large high school is interested in finding out whether student attitudes toward mental health are affected by a special unit on the subject. He decides to administer an attitude questionnaire to the students before the unit is introduced and then administer it again after the unit is completed. Any change in attitude scores may be due to the students thinking about and discussing their opinions as a result of the pretest rather than as a result of the intervention.

Notice that it is not always the administration of a pretest *per se* that creates a possible testing effect, but rather the "interaction" that occurs between taking the test and the intervention. A pretest sometimes can make students more "alert" to or "aware" of what may be going to take place, making them more sensitive to and responsive toward the treatment that subsequently occurs. In some studies, the possible effects of pretesting are considered so serious that such testing is eliminated.

A similar problem is created if the instrumentation process permits subjects to figure out the nature of the study. This is most likely to happen in single-group (correlational) studies of attitudes, opinions, or other variables other than ability. Students might be asked their opinions, for example, about teachers and also about different subjects to test the hypothesis that student attitude toward teachers is related to student attitude toward the subjects taught. They may see a connection between the two sets of questions, especially if they are both included on the same form, and answer accordingly.

Some examples of a testing effect are as follows.

- A researcher uses the exact same set of problems to measure change over time in student ability to solve mathematics word problems. The first administration of the test is given at the beginning of a unit of instruction; the second administration is given at the end of the unit of instruction, three weeks later. If improvement in scores occurs, it may be due to sensitization to the problems produced by the first test and the practice effect rather than to any increase in problem-solving ability.
- A researcher incorporates items designed to measure "self-esteem" and "achievement" in the same questionnaire.
- A researcher uses pre- and posttests of "anxiety level" to compare students given relaxation training with students in a control group. Lower scores for the "relaxation" group on the posttest may be due to the training. But they also may be due to sensitivity (created by the pretest) to the training.

HISTORY

On occasion, one or more unanticipated, and unplanned for, events may occur during the course of a study, which can affect the responses of subjects. Such events are referred to in educational research as a **history effect.** In the study we suggested of students being taught by the inquiry versus the lecture method, for example, a boring visitor who "dropped in" on, and spoke to, the lecture class just before an upcoming examination would be an example. Should the visitor's remarks in some way discourage or "turn off" students in the lecture class, they might do less well on the examination than if the visitor had not appeared. Another example involves a personal experience of one of the authors of this text. He remembers clearly the day that President John F. Kennedy died since he had scheduled an examination for that very day. The author's students at that time, stunned into shock by the announcement of the President's death, were unable to take the examination. Any comparison of examination results taken on this day with the examination results of other classes taken on other days would have been meaningless.

Researchers can never be certain that one group has not had experiences that differ from those of other groups. As a result, they should continually be alert to any such influences that may occur (in schools, for example) during the course of a study. As you will see in Chapter Twelve, some research "designs" handle this threat better than do others.

An example of a history threat is as follows.

- A researcher designs a study to investigate the effects of simulation games on ethnocentrism. She plans to select two high schools to participate in an experiment. Students in both schools will be given a pretest designed to measure their attitudes toward minority groups. School A will then be given the simulation games during their social studies classes over a three-day period while school B sees travel films. Both schools will then be given the same test to see if their attitude toward minority groups has changed. The researcher conducts the study as planned, but a special documentary on racial prejudice is shown in school A between the pretest and the posttest.

MATURATION

Often change during an intervention may be due to factors associated with the passing of time rather than to the intervention itself. This is known as a **maturation threat.** Over the course of a semester, for example, very young students in particular will change in many ways due simply to aging and experience. Suppose, for example, that a researcher is interested in studying the effect of special "grasping exercises" on the ability of 2-year-olds to manipulate various objects. She finds that such exercises are associated with marked increases in the manipulative ability of the children over a six-month period. Two-year olds mature very rapidly, however, and the increase in their manipulative ability may be due simply to this fact rather than as a result of the grasping exercises. Maturation is a serious threat in studies using only pre-post data for the intervention group, or in studies that span a number of years. The best way to control for maturation is to include a well-selected comparison group in the study.

Examples of a maturation threat are shown below.

- A researcher reports that students in liberal arts colleges become less accepting of authority between their freshman and senior years and attributes this to the many "liberating" experiences they have undergone in college. This may be the reason, but it also may be due to the fact that they simply have grown older.
- A researcher tests a group of students enrolled in a special class for "students with artistic potential" every year for six years, beginning when they are aged five. She finds that their drawing ability improves markedly over the years.

ATTITUDE OF SUBJECTS

The way in which subjects view a study and their participation in it can create a threat to internal validity. One example is the well-known "Hawthorne effect" first observed in the Hawthorne plant of the Western Electric Company some years ago.[1] It was accidentally discovered that productivity improved not only when improvements were made in physical working conditions (such as an increase in the number of coffee breaks and better lighting), but also when such conditions were unintentionally made *worse* (for instance, the number of coffee breaks was reduced and the lighting was dimmed). The usual explanation for this is that the special attention and recognition received by the workers were responsible; they felt someone cared about them and was trying to help them. This increased attention and recognition of subjects has subsequently been referred to as the **Hawthorne effect.**

An opposite effect can occur whenever, in intervention studies, the members of the control group receive no treatment at all. As a result, they may become demoralized or resentful and hence perform more poorly than the treatment group. It may thus appear that the experimental group is performing better as a result of the treatment when this is not the case.

It has also been suggested that recipients of an experimental treatment may perform better due to the novelty of the treatment rather than because of the specific nature of the treatment.

It might be expected, then, that subjects who know they are part of a study may show improvement as a result of a feeling that they are receiving some sort of special treatment—no matter what this treatment may be. While this possibility should not be overlooked, it does not seem to us to be prevalent in education. If it were, we should expect new, innovative interventions to show much more dramatic, and consistent, effects than has usually been the case. Perhaps, unlike the Hawthorne workers, students and teachers do not see interventions as attempts to improve their conditions.

One remedy for these threats is to provide the control or comparison group(s) with special treatment and/or novelty comparable to that received by the experimental group. While simple in theory, this is not easy to do in most educational settings. Another possibility, in some cases, is to make it easy for students to believe that the treatment is just a regular part of instruction—that is, not part of an experiment. For example, it is sometimes unnecessary to announce that an experiment is being conducted.

Here is an example of a subject attitude threat:

- A researcher decides to investigate the possible reduction in test anxiety by playing classical music during examinations. She randomly selects ten freshman algebra classes from all such classes in the five high schools in a large urban school district. In five of these classes, she plays classical music softly in the background during the administration of examinations. In the other five (the control group), she plays no music. The students in the control group, however, learn that music is being played in the other classes and express some resentment when their teachers tell them that the music cannot be played in their class. This resentment may actually cause them to be more anxious during exams or to inflate their anxiety scores.

REGRESSION

This threat may be present whenever change is studied in a group that is extremely low or high in its pre-intervention performance. Studies in special education are particularly vulnerable to this threat, since the students in such studies are frequently selected on the basis of previous low performance. The regression phenomenon can be explained statistically, but for our purposes it simply describes the fact that a group selected because of unusually low (or high) performance will, on the average, score closer to the mean on subsequent testing, regardless of what transpires in the meantime. Thus a class of students of markedly low ability may be expected to score higher on posttests regardless of the effect of any intervention to which they are exposed. Like maturation, the use of an equivalent control or comparison group handles this threat—and this seems to be understood as reflected in published research.

Some examples of a possible **regression threat** are as follows.

- An Olympic track coach selects the members of her team from those who have the fastest times during the final trials for various events. She finds that their average time decreases the next time they run, however, which she attributes to differences in track conditions.
- Those students who score in the lowest 20 percent on a math test are given special help. Two weeks later their average score on a test involving similar problems has improved.

IMPLEMENTATION

The treatment or method in any experimental study must be administered by someone—the researcher, the teachers involved in the study, a counselor, or some other person. This fact raises the possibility that the experimental group may be treated in ways that are unintended and not a necessary part of the method, yet which give them an advantage of one sort or another. This is known as an **implementer threat.** It can happen in either of two ways.

The first way an implementer effect can occur is when different individuals are assigned to implement different methods, and these individuals differ in ways related to the outcome. Consider our previous example in which two groups of students are taught by either an inquiry or a lecture method. The inquiry teachers may simply be better teachers than the lecture teachers.

There are a number of ways to control for this possibility. The researcher can attempt to evaluate the individuals who implement each method on pertinent characteristics (such as teaching ability) and then, hopefully, equate the treatment groups on these dimensions (for example, by assigning teachers of equivalent ability to each group). Clearly, this is a difficult and time-consuming task. Another control is to require that each method be taught by all teachers in the study. Where feasible, this is a preferable solution, though it also is vulnerable to the possibility that some teachers may have different abilities to implement the different methods. Still another control is to use *several* different individuals to implement each method, thereby reducing the chances of an advantage to either method.

The second way an implementer effect can occur is when some individuals have a personal bias in favor of one method over the other. Their preference for the method, rather than the method itself, may account for the superior performance of students taught by this method. This is a good reason why a researcher should, if at all possible, *not* be one of the individuals who implement a method in an intervention study. It is sometimes possible to keep individuals who are implementers ignorant of the nature of a study, but it is generally very difficult—in part because teachers or others involved in a study will usually need to be given a rationale for their participation. One solution for this is to allow individuals to choose the method they wish to implement, but this creates the possibility of differences in characteristics discussed above. An alternative is to have all methods used by all implementers, but with their preferences known beforehand. Note that preference for a method as a *result* of using it does not constitute a threat—it is simply one of the by-products of the method itself. Finally, the researcher can observe in an attempt to see that the methods are administered as intended.

An example of an implementer threat is as follows.

- A researcher is interested in studying the effects of a new diet on young children. After obtaining the permission of the parents of the children to be involved, all of whom are first graders, he randomly assigns the children to an experimental group and a control group. The experimental group is to try the new diet for a period of three months, and the control group is to stay with its regular diet. The researcher overlooks the fact, however, that the teacher of the experimental group is an accomplished instructor of some five years experience, while the instructor of the control group is a first year teacher, newly appointed.

FACTORS THAT REDUCE THE LIKELIHOOD OF FINDING A RELATIONSHIP

In many studies, the various factors we have discussed could also serve to *reduce,* or even prevent, the chances of a relationship being found. For example, if the method(s) (the treatment) in a study are not adequately implemented, that is, adequately tried, the effect of actual differences between them on outcomes may be obscured. Similarly, if the members of a control or comparison group become "aware" of the experimental treatment, they may increase their efforts due to a feeling of being "left out," thereby reducing real differences in achievement between treatment groups that otherwise would be seen. Sometimes, teachers of a control group may unwittingly give some sort of "compensation" to the members of their group, thereby lessening the impact of the experimental treatment. Finally, the use of instruments that produce unreliable scores and small samples may result in a reduced likelihood of a relationship or relationships being observed.

How Can a Researcher Minimize These Threats to Internal Validity?

As we have discussed the various threats to internal validity, we have suggested a number of techniques or procedures that researchers can employ to control or minimize the possible effect of these threats. Essentially, they boil down to four alternatives. A researcher can try to do any or all of the following.

1. Standardize the conditions under which the study occurs—such as the way(s) in which the treatment is implemented (in intervention studies), the way(s) in which the data are collected, and so on. This helps control for location, instrumentation, attitude, and implementer threats.

2. Obtain more information on the subjects of the study—that is, on relevant characteristics of the subjects. This helps control for a subject characteristics threat and (possibly) a mortality threat.
3. Obtain more information on the details of the study—that is, where and when it takes place, extraneous events that occur, and so on. This helps control for location, instrumentation, history, subject attitude, and implementer threats.

TABLE 11.1

General Techniques for Controlling Threats to Internal Validity

| | *Technique* | | | |
Threat	Standardize Conditions	Obtain More Information on Subjects	Obtain More Information on Details	Choose Appropriate Design
Subject Characteristics		×		×
Mortality		×		×
Location	×		×	×
Instrumentation	×		×	
Testing				×
History			×	×
Maturation				×
Subject Attitude	×		×	×
Regression				×
Implementer	×		×	

4. Choose an appropriate design. The proper design can do much to control all but an implementer and instrumentation threat.

Since control by design applies primarily to experimental studies, we shall discuss it in detail in Chapter Twelve. The four alternatives are summarized in Table 11-1.

We want to end this chapter by emphasizing two things. The first is that the likelihood of any of these various threats to internal validity occurring can be greatly reduced by preplanning; the second is that such preplanning often requires the collection of additional information before a study begins (or while it is taking place). It is often too late to consider how to control these threats once the data in a study have been collected.

Main Points of Chapter Eleven

- When a study lacks internal validity, one or more alternative hypotheses exist to explain the outcomes of the study. These alternative hypotheses are referred to by educational researchers as "threats to internal validity."
- When a study has internal validity, it means that any relationship observed between two or more variables is meaningful in its own right, rather than being due to something else.
- Some of the more common threats to internal validity include differences in subject characteristics, mortality, location, instrumentation, testing, history, maturation, attitude of subjects, regression, and implementation.
- The selection of people for a study may result in the individuals or groups differing (i.e., the characteristics of the subjects may differ) from one another in unintended ways that are related to the variables to be studied.
- No matter how carefully the subjects of a study (the sample) are selected, it is common to lose some of them as the study progresses. This is known as "mortality." Such a loss of subjects may affect the outcomes of a study.
- The particular locations in which data are collected, or in which an intervention is carried out, may create alternative explanations for any results that are obtained.
- The way in which instruments are used may also constitute a threat to the internal validity of a study. Possible instrumentation threats include changes in the instrument, characteristics of the data collector(s), and/or bias on the part of the data collectors.
- The use of a pretest in intervention studies sometimes may create a "practice effect" that can affect the results of a study. A pretest can also sometimes affect the way subjects respond to an intervention.
- On occasion, one or more unanticipated, and unplanned for, events may occur during the course of a study that can affect the responses of subjects. This is known as a history threat.
- Sometimes change during an intervention study may be due to factors associated with the passing of time than to the intervention itself. This is known as a maturation threat.
- The attitude of subjects toward a study (and their participation in it) can create a threat to internal validity.
- When subjects are given increased attention and recognition because they are participating in a study, their responses may be affected. This is known as the "Hawthorne effect."

- Whenever a group is selected because of unusually high or low performance on a pretest, it will, on the average, score closer to the mean on subsequent testing, regardless of what transpires in the meantime. This is called a regression threat.
- Whenever an experimental group is treated in ways that are unintended and not a necessary part of the method being studied, an implementer threat can occur.
- There are a number of techniques or procedures that researchers can use to control or minimize threats to internal validity. Essentially they boil down to four alternatives: (1) standardizing the conditions under which the study occurs, (2) obtaining more information on the subjects of the study, (3) obtaining more information on the details of the study, and (4) choosing an appropriate design.

For Discussion

1. Can a researcher prove conclusively that a study has internal validity? Explain.

2. In Chapter Five, we discussed the concept of "external validity." In what ways, if any, are internal and external validity related? Can a study have internal validity, but not external validity? If so, how? What about the reverse?

3. Students often confuse the concept of "internal" validity with the idea of "instrument" validity. How would you explain the difference between the two?

4. What threat (or threats) to internal validity might exist in each of the following:
   a. A researcher decides to try out a new mathematics curriculum in a nearby elementary school and to compare student achievement in math with that of students in another elementary school using the regular curriculum. The researcher is not aware, however, that each of the students in the "new curriculum" school have computers to use in their classrooms.
   b. A researcher wishes to compare two different kinds of textbooks in two high school chemistry classes over a semester. She finds that 20 percent of one group and 10 percent of the other group are absent during the administration of unit tests.
   c. In a study investigating the possible relationship between marital status and perceived changes during the last five years in the women's liberation movement, men and women interviewers get different reactions from female respondents to the same questions.
   d. Teachers of an experimental English curriculum as well as teachers of the regular curriculum administer both pre- and posttests to their own students.
   e. Eighth grade students who volunteer to tutor third graders in reading show greater improvement in their own reading scores than a comparison group that does not participate in tutoring.

f. A researcher compares the effects of weekly individual and group counseling on the improvement of study habits. Each week the students counseled as a group fill out questionnaires on their progress at the end of their meetings. The students counseled individually, however, fill out the questionnaires at home.

g. Those students who score in the bottom 10 percent academically in a school in an economically depressed area are selected for a special program of enrichment. The program includes special games, extra materials, special "snacks," specially colored materials to use, and new books. The students score substantially higher on achievement tests six months after the program is instituted.

h. A group of elderly people are asked to fill out a questionnaire designed to investigate the possible relationship between "activity level" and "sense of life satisfaction."

5. How could you determine whether the threats you identified in each of the situations in #4 actually exist?

6. Which threats discussed in this chapter do you think are the most important for a researcher to consider? Why? Which do you think would be the most difficult to control? Explain.

Note

1. F. J. Roethlisberger and W. J. Dickson. (1939). *Management and the worker*. Cambridge, MA: Harvard University Press.

Research Exercise Eleven: Internal Validity

State the question or hypothesis of your study at the top of Problem Sheet 11. In the spaces indicated, place an X after each of the threats to internal validity that apply to your study, explain why they are threats, and describe how you intend to control for those most likely to occur (i.e., prevent their having an effect on the outcome of your study).

PROBLEM SHEET 11
Internal Validity

1. My question or hypothesis is: _____

_____

2. I have placed an X in the blank in front of four of the threats listed below that apply to my study. I explain why I think each one is a problem and then explain how I would attempt to control for the threat.

Threats: _____ Subject Characteristics _____ Mortality _____ Location _____ Instrumentation

_____ Testing _____ History _____ Maturation _____ Subject Attitude _____ Regression

_____ Implementation _____ Other

Threat 1: _____ Why? _____

_____

I will control by _____

_____

Threat 2: _____ Why? _____

_____

I will control by _____

_____

Threat 3: _____ Why? _____

_____

I will control by _____

_____

Threat 4: _____ Why? _____

_____

I will control by _____

_____

Part Three

RESEARCH
METHODOLOGIES

Chapter Twelve

EXPERIMENTAL RESEARCH

Experimental research is one of the most powerful research methodologies researchers can use. Of the many types of research, it has the best capability to establish cause-and-effect relationships between variables. Yet experiments are not always easy to conduct. This chapter discusses the power and problems involved in conducting experiments and presents several commonly used experimental designs.

Objectives

Reading this chapter should enable you to:

- *Describe* briefly the purpose of experimental research
- *Name* the basic steps involved in conducting an experiment
- *Describe* two ways in which experimental research differs from other forms of educational research
- *Explain* the difference between random assignment and random selection, and the importance of each
- *Explain* what is meant by the phrase "manipulation of variables" and *describe* three ways in which such manipulation can occur
- *Distinguish* between examples of weak and strong experimental designs and *draw diagrams* of such designs
- *Identify* various threats to internal validity associated with different experimental designs
- *Explain* three ways in which various threats to internal validity in experimental research can be controlled
- *Explain* how matching can be used to equate groups in experimental studies
- *Describe* briefly the purpose of factorial and counterbalanced designs and *draw diagrams* of such designs
- *Describe* briefly the purpose of a time-series design and *draw a diagram* of this design
- *Describe* briefly the purpose of single-subject designs and *draw diagrams* of two such designs
- *Explain* briefly why it is important to replicate single-subject designs
- *Describe* briefly how to assess probable threats to internal validity in an experimental study
- *Recognize* an experimental study when you see one in the literature

The Uniqueness of Experimental Research

Of all the research methodologies described in this book, **experimental research** is unique in two very important respects: It is the only type of research that directly attempts to influence a particular variable, and it is the only type that can really test hypotheses about cause-and-effect relationships. In an experimental study, researchers look at the effect(s) of at least one independent variable on one or more dependent variables. The **independent variable** in experimental research is also frequently referred to as the *experimental* or *treatment* variable. The **dependent variable,** also known as the *criterion* or *outcome* variable, refers to the results or outcomes of the study.

The major characteristic of experimental research, which distinguishes it from all other types of research, is that researchers *manipulate* the independent variable. They decide the nature of the treatment (that is, what is going to happen to the subjects of the study), to whom it is to be applied, and to what extent. Independent variables frequently manipulated in educational research include methods of instruction, types of assignment, learning materials, rewards given to students, and types of questions asked by teachers. Dependent variables that are frequently studied include achievement, interest in a subject, attention span, motivation, and attitudes toward school.

After the treatment has been administered for an appropriate length of time, researchers observe or measure the groups receiving different treatments (by means of a posttest of some sort) to see if they differ. Another way of saying this is that researchers want to see if the treatment made a difference. If the average scores of the two groups on the posttest do differ, and researchers cannot find any sensible alternative explanations for this difference, they can conclude that the treatment did have an effect and is likely the cause of the difference.

Experimental research, therefore, enables

231

researchers to go beyond description and prediction, beyond the identification of relationships, to at least a partial determination of what causes them. Correlational studies may demonstrate a strong relationship between socioeconomic level and academic achievement, for instance, but they cannot demonstrate that improving socioeconomic level will necessarily improve achievement. Only experimental research has this capability. Some actual examples of the kinds of experimental studies that have been conducted by educational researchers are as follows.

- Quality of learning with an active versus passive motivational set[1]
- Comparison of computer-assisted cooperative, competitive, and individualistic learning[2]
- An intensive group counseling dropout prevention intervention: . . . isolating at-risk adolescents within high schools[3]
- The effects of student questions and teacher questions on concept acquisition[4]
- Changing teaching practices in mainstream classrooms to improve bonding and behavior of low achievers[5]
- Mnemonic versus nonmnemonic vocabulary-learning strategies for children[6]

Essential Characteristics of Experimental Research

The word **"experiment"** has a long and illustrious history in the annals of research. It has often been hailed as the most powerful method of investigating relationships that exists. Its origins go back to the very beginnings of history when, for example, primeval humans first experimented with ways to produce fire. One can imagine countless trial-and-error attempts on their part before success was achieved by sparking rocks or by spinning wooden spindles in dry leaves. Much of the success of modern science is due to carefully designed and meticulously implemented experiments.

The basic idea underlying all experimental research is really quite simple—try something and systematically observe what happens. Formal experiments consist of two basic conditions. First, at least two (but often more) conditions or methods are *compared* to assess the effect(s) of particular conditions or "treatments" (the independent variable). Second, the independent variable is directly *manipulated* by the researcher. Change is planned for and deliberately manipulated in order to study its effect(s) on one or more outcomes (the dependent variable). Let us discuss each of these characteristics in a bit more detail.

COMPARISON OF GROUPS

An experiment usually involves two groups of subjects, an experimental group and a control or a comparison group, although it is possible to conduct an experiment with only one group (by providing all treatments to the same subjects) or with three or more groups. The **experimental group** receives a treatment of some sort (such as a new textbook or a different method of teaching), while the **control group** receives no treatment (or the **comparison group** receives a different treatment). The control or the comparison group is crucially important in all experimental research, for it serves the purpose of determining whether the treatment has had an effect or whether one treatment is more effective than another.

Historically, a pure control group is one that receives no treatment at all. While this is often the case in medical or psychological research, it is rarely true in educational research. The control group almost always receives a different treatment of some sort. Some educational researchers, therefore, refer to comparison groups rather than to control groups.

Consider an example. Suppose a researcher wished to study the effectiveness of a new method of teaching science. He or she would have the students in the experimental group taught by the new method, but the students in the comparison group would continue to be taught by their teacher's usual method. The researcher would not administer the new method to the experimental group and have a control group *do nothing*. Any method of instruction would likely be more effective than no method at all!

MANIPULATION OF THE INDEPENDENT VARIABLE

The second essential characteristic of all experiments is that the researcher actively manipulates the independent variable. What does this mean? Simply put, it means that the researcher deliberately and directly determines what forms the independent variable will take and then which group will get which form. For example, if the independent variable in a study is the amount of enthusiasm an instructor displays, a researcher might train two teachers to display different amounts of enthusiasm as they teach their classes.

Although many independent variables in education can be manipulated, many others cannot. Examples of independent variables that can be manipulated include teaching method, type of counseling, learning activities, assignments given, and materials used; examples of independent variables that cannot be manipulated include gender, ethnicity, age, and religious preference. Researchers can manipulate the kinds of learning activities to which students are exposed in a classroom, but they cannot manipulate, say, religious preference—that is, students cannot be "made into" Protestants, Catholics, Jews, or Muslims, for example, to serve the purposes of a study. To manipulate a variable, researchers must decide who is to get something and when, where, and how they will get it.

The independent variable in an experimental study may be established in several ways—either (a) one form of the variable versus another, (b) presence versus absence of a particular form, or (c) varying degrees of the same form. An example of (a) would be a study comparing the inquiry method (form 1) with the lecture method (form 2) of instruction in teaching chemistry. An example of (b) would be a study comparing the use of transparencies versus no transparencies in teaching statistics. An example of (c) would be

a study comparing the effects of different specified amounts of teacher enthusiasm on student attitudes toward mathematics. In both (a) and (b), the variable (method) is clearly categorical. In (c), a variable that in actuality is quantitative (*degree* of enthusiasm) is treated as categorical (the effects of only specified *amounts* of enthusiasm will be studied), in order for the researcher to manipulate (that is, to control for) the amount of enthusiasm.

Randomization

An important aspect of many experiments is the random assignment of subjects to groups. Although there are certain kinds of experiments in which random assignment is not possible, researchers try to use randomization whenever feasible. It is a crucial ingredient in the best kinds of experiments. Random assignment is similar, but not identical, to the concept of random selection we discussed in Chapter Five. **Random assignment** means that every individual who is participating in the experiment has an equal chance of being assigned to any of the experimental or control conditions being compared. **Random selection,** on the other hand, means that every member of a population has an equal chance of being selected to be a member of the sample. Under random assignment, each member of the sample is given a number (arbitrarily), and a table of random numbers (see Chapter Five) is then used to select the members of the experimental and control groups.

Three things should be noted about the random assignment of subjects to groups. First, it takes place before the experiment begins. Second, it is a *process* of assigning or distributing students to groups, not a result of such distribution. This means that you cannot look at two groups that have already been formed and be able to tell, just by looking, whether or not they were formed randomly. Third, the use of random assignment allows the researcher to form groups that, right at the beginning of the study, are *equivalent*—that is, they differ only by chance in any variables of interest. In other words, random assignment is intended to eliminate the threat of additional, or extraneous, variables—not only those of which researchers are aware, but also those of which they are not aware—that might affect the outcome of the study. This is the beauty and the power of random assignment. Its use is one of the fundamental reasons why experiments are stronger than all the other kinds of research.

This last statement is tempered, of course, by the realization that groups formed through random assignment may still differ somewhat. Random assignment ensures only that groups are equivalent (or at least as equivalent as human beings can make them) at the beginning of an experiment.

Furthermore, random assignment is no guarantee of equivalent groups unless both groups are sufficiently large. No one would count on random assignment having much of an effect if there were only five subjects to be assigned to each group, for example. There are no rules for determining how large groups must be, but most researchers are uncomfortable relying on random assignment if there are less than forty subjects in each group.

Control of Extraneous Variables

Researchers in an experimental study have an opportunity to exercise far more control than in most other forms of research. They determine the treatment (or treatments), select the sample, decide which group will get the treatment, try to control other factors besides the treatment that might influence the outcome of the study, and then (finally) observe or measure the effect of the treatment on the groups when the treatment is completed.

In Chapter Eleven, we introduced the idea of internal validity and pointed out that several threats to internal validity exist. It is very important for researchers conducting an experimental study to do their best to *control* for—that

is, to eliminate or to minimize the possible effect of—these threats. If researchers are unsure whether another variable might be the cause of a result observed in a study, they cannot be sure what the cause really is. For example, if a researcher attempted to compare the effects of two different methods of instruction on student attitudes toward history, but did not make sure that the groups involved were equivalent in ability, then ability might be a possible alternative explanation (to the difference in methods) for any differences in attitudes of the groups found on a posttest.

In particular, researchers who conduct experimental studies try their best to ensure that any and all subject characteristics that might affect the outcome of the study are controlled. This is done by ensuring that the two groups are as equivalent as possible on all variables other than the one being studied (that is, the independent variable).

How do researchers minimize or eliminate threats due to subject characteristics? Many ways exist. Here are some of the most common.

> *Randomization:* As we mention above, if enough subjects can be randomly assigned to the various groups involved in an experimental study, researchers can assume that the groups are equivalent. This is the best way to ensure that the effects of one or more possible extraneous variables have been controlled.
>
> *Hold certain variables constant:* The idea here is to eliminate the possible effects of a variable by removing it from the study. For example, if a researcher suspects that gender might influence the outcomes of a study, she could control for it by restricting the subjects of the study to females and by excluding all males. The variable of gender, in other words, has been held constant. There is a cost involved (as there almost always is) for this control, however, as the generalizability of the results of the study are correspondingly reduced.
>
> *Build the variable into the design:* This solution involves building the variable(s)

into the study to assess their effects. It is the exact opposite of the previous idea. Using the preceding example, a researcher would include *both* females and males (as distinct groups) in the design of the study and then analyze the effects of *both* gender and method on outcomes.

Matching: Often pairs of subjects can be matched on certain variables of interest. If a researcher felt that age, for example, might affect the outcome of a study, he might endeavor to match students according to their ages, and then assign one member of each pair (randomly if possible) to each of the comparison groups.

Use subjects as their own controls: When subjects are used as their own controls, their performance under both (or all) treatments is compared. Thus the same students might be taught algebra units both by an inquiry and a lecture method. Another example is the assessment of an individual's behavior during a period of time before a treatment is begun to see if possible changes in behavior occur after treatment.

Analysis of covariance: As mentioned in Chapter Nine, analysis of covariance can be used to equate groups statistically on the basis of a pretest or other variables. The posttest scores of the subjects in each group are then adjusted accordingly.

We will shortly show you a number of research designs that illustrate how several of the above controls can be implemented in an experimental study.

Group Designs in Experimental Research

The design of an experiment can take a variety of forms. Some of the designs we present in this section are better than others, however. Why "better"? Because of the various threats to internal validity identified in Chapter Eleven:

Good designs control many of these threats, while poor designs control only a few. The quality of an experiment depends on how well the various threats to internal validity are controlled.

WEAK EXPERIMENTAL DESIGNS

These designs are referred to as "weak" because they do not have built-in controls for threats to internal validity. In addition to the independent variable, there are a number of other plausible explanations for any outcomes that occur. As a result, any researcher who uses one of these designs has difficulty assessing the effectiveness of the independent variable.

The One-Shot Case Study. In the **one-shot case study design** a single group is exposed to a treatment or event, and a dependent variable is subsequently observed (measured) in order to assess the effect of the treatment. A diagram of this design is as follows.

The One-Shot Case Study Design

X	O
Treatment	Observation (Dependent variable)

The symbol X represents exposure of the group to the treatment of interest, while O refers to observation (measurement) of the dependent variable. The placement of the symbols from left to right indicates the order in time of X and O. As you can see, the treatment, X, comes before observation of the dependent variable, O.

Suppose a researcher wishes to see if a new textbook increases student interest in history. He uses the textbook (X) for a semester and then measures (O) student interest with an attitude scale. A diagram of this example is shown in Figure 12.1.

The most obvious weakness of this design is its absence of any control. The researcher has no way of knowing if the results obtained at O

FIGURE 12.1

Example of a One-Shot Case Study Design

X	O
New textbook	Attitude scale to measure interest
	(Dependent variable)

(as measured by the attitude scale) are due to the treatment X (the textbook). The design does not provide for any comparison, so the researcher cannot compare the treatment results (as measured by the attitude scale) with the same group before using the new textbook, or with those of another group using a different textbook. Since the group has not been pretested in any way, the researcher knows nothing about what the group was like before using the text. Thus he does not know whether the treatment had *any* effect at all. It is quite possible that the students who use the new textbook *will* indicate very favorable attitudes toward history. But the question remains—were these attitudes produced by the new textbook? Unfortunately, the one-shot case study does not help us answer this question. To remedy this design, a comparison could be made with another group of students who had the same course content presented in the regular textbook. (We shall show you just such a design shortly.) Fortunately, the flaws in the one-shot

FIGURE 12.2

Example of a One-Group Pretest-Posttest Design

O	X	O
Pretest Twenty-item attitude scale completed by students	Treatment	Posttest Twenty-item attitude scale completed by students
(Dependent variable)	Ten weeks of counseling	(Dependent variable)

design are so well-known that it is seldom used in educational research.

The One-Group Pretest-Posttest Design. In the **one-group pretest-posttest design,** a single group is measured or observed not only after being exposed to a treatment of some sort, but also *before.* A diagram of this design is as follows.

The One-Group Pretest-Posttest Design

O	X	O
Pretest	Treatment	Posttest

Consider an example of this design. A principal wants to assess the effects of weekly counseling sessions on the attitudes of certain "hard-to-reach" students in her school. She asks the counselors in the program to meet once a week with these students for a period of ten weeks, during which sessions the students are encouraged to express their feelings and concerns. She uses a twenty-item scale to measure student attitudes toward school both immediately before and after the ten-week period. Figure 12.2 presents a diagram of the design of the study.

This design is better than the one-shot case study (the researcher at least knows whether any change occurred), but it is still weak. Nine uncontrolled-for threats to internal validity exist that might also explain the results on the posttest. They are history, maturation, instrument decay, data collector characteristics, data collector bias, testing, statistical regression, attitude of subjects, and implementer. Any or all of these may influence the outcome of the study. The researcher would not know if any differences between the pretest and the posttest are due to the treatment or to one or more of these threats. To remedy this, a comparison group, which does not get the treatment, could be added. Then if a change in attitude occurs between the pretest and the posttest, the researcher has reason to believe that it was caused by the treatment (symbolized by X).

The Static-Group Comparison Design. In the **static-group comparison design,** two already existing, or *intact,* groups are used. These are sometimes referred to as *static* groups, hence the name for the design. Comparisons are made between groups receiving different treatments. A diagram of this design is as follows.

The Static-Group Comparison Design

$$X_1 \qquad O$$
$$\overline{}$$
$$X_2 \qquad O$$

The dashed line indicates that the two groups being compared are already formed— that is, the subjects are not randomly assigned to the two groups. X_1 and X_2 symbolize the two different treatments. The two O's are placed exactly vertical to each other, indicating that the observation or measurement of the two groups occurs at the same time.

Consider again the example used to illustrate the one-shot case study design. We could apply the static-group comparison design to this example. The researcher would (a) find two intact groups (two classes), (b) assign the new textbook (X_1) to one of the classes but have the other class use the regular textbook (X_2), and then (c) measure the degree of interest of all students in both classes at the same time (for example, at the end of the semester). Figure 12.3 presents a diagram of this example.

Although this design provides better control over history, maturation, testing, and regression threats,* it is more vulnerable not only to mortality and location,† but also, more importantly, to the possibility of differential subject characteristics.

TRUE EXPERIMENTAL DESIGNS

The essential ingredient of a true experimental design is that subjects are randomly

---

* History and maturation remain possible threats because the researcher cannot be sure that the two groups have been exposed to the same extraneous events or have the same maturational processes.
† Because the groups may differ in the number of subjects lost and/or in the kinds of resources provided.

FIGURE 12.3

Example of a Static-Group Comparison Design

X_1	O
New textbook	Attitude scale to measure interest
X_2	O
Regular text	Attitude scale to measure interest

assigned to treatment groups. As discussed earlier, random assignment is a powerful technique for controlling the subject characteristics threat to internal validity, a major consideration in educational research.

The Randomized Posttest-Only Control Group Design. The **posttest-only control group design** involves two groups, both of which are formed by random assignment. One group receives the experimental treatment while the other does not, and then both groups are posttested on the dependent variable. A diagram of this design is as follows.

The Randomized Posttest-Only Control Group Design

Treatment group	R	X_1	O
Control group	R	X_2	O

In this design, the control of certain threats is excellent. Through the use of random assignment, the threats of subject characteristics, maturation, and statistical regression are well controlled for. Since none of the subjects in the study are measured twice, testing is not a possible threat. This is perhaps the best of all designs to use in an experimental study, provided there are at least forty subjects in each group.

There are, unfortunately, some threats to internal validity that are not controlled for by this design. The first is mortality. Since the two groups are similar, we might expect an equal dropout rate from each group. However, exposure to the treatment may cause more individuals in the experimental group to drop out (or stay in) than in the control group. This may result in the two groups becoming dissimilar in terms of their characteristics, which in turn may affect the results on the posttest. For this reason researchers should always report how many subjects drop out of each group during an experiment. An attitudinal threat (Hawthorne effect) is possible. In addition, implementer, instrumentation, and history threats may exist. These threats cannot be controlled by any design, since they are independent of the design itself.

As an example of this design, consider a hypothetical study in which a researcher investigates the effects of a series of sensitivity training workshops on faculty morale in a large high school district. The researcher randomly selects a sample of 100 teachers from all the teachers in the district.* The researcher then (1) randomly assigns the teachers in the district to two groups, (2) exposes one group, but not the other, to the training, and then (3) measures the morale of each group using a questionnaire. Figure 12.4 presents a diagram of this hypothetical experiment.

The Randomized Pretest-Posttest Control Group Design.

The **pretest-posttest control group design** differs from the posttest-only control group design solely in the use of a pretest. Two groups of subjects are used, with both groups being measured or observed twice. The first measurement serves as the pretest, the second as the posttest. Random assignment is used to form the groups. The measurements or observations are collected at the same time for both groups. A diagram of this design is as follows.

---

* Again we stress that it is important to keep clear the distinction between random selection and random assignment. Both involve the process of randomization, but for a different purpose. Random selection, you will recall, is intended to provide a representative sample. But it may or may not be accompanied by the random assignment of subjects to groups. Random assignment is intended to equate groups. Random assignment oftentimes is not accompanied by random selection.

The Randomized Pretest-Posttest Control Group Design

Treatment group	R	O	X_1	O
Control group	R	O	X_2	O

The use of the pretest raises the possibility of an interaction of testing and treatment threat, since it may "alert" the members of the experimental group, thereby causing them to do better (or more poorly) than the members of the control group. A trade-off is that it provides the researcher with a means of checking whether or not the two groups are really similar—that is, whether random assignment actually succeeded in making the groups equivalent. This is particularly desirable if the number in each group is small (less than thirty). If the pretest shows that they are not equivalent, the researcher can seek to make them so by using one of the matching techniques discussed below. A pretest is also necessary if the amount of change over time is to be assessed.

Let us use our previous example involving the use of sensitivity workshops to illustrate this design. Figure 12.5 presents a diagram of how this design would be used.

The Randomized Solomon Four-Group Design.

The **Solomon four-group design** is an attempt to eliminate the possible effect of a pretest. It involves random assignment of subjects to four groups, with two of the groups being pretested and two not. One of the pretested groups and one of the unpretested groups is exposed to the experimental treatment. All four groups are then posttested. A diagram of this design is as follows.

The Randomized Solomon Four-Group Design

Treatment group	R	O	X_1	O
Control group	R	O	X_2	O
Treatment group	R		X_1	O
Control group	R		X_2	O

FIGURE 12.4

*Example of a Randomized Posttest-Only
Control Group Design*

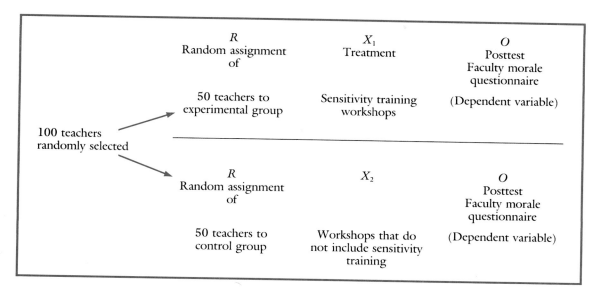

FIGURE 12.5

*Example of a Randomized Pretest-Posttest
Control Group Design*

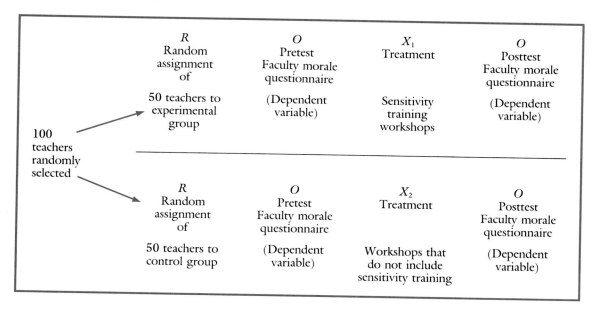

The Solomon four-group design combines the pretest-posttest control group and posttest-only control group designs. The first two groups represent the pretest-posttest control group design, while the last two groups represent the posttest-only control group design. Figure 12.6 presents an example of the Solomon four-group design.

The Solomon four-group design provides the best control of the threats to internal validity that we have discussed. A weakness, however, is that it requires a large sample, in that subjects must be assigned to four groups. Furthermore, conducting a study involving four groups at the same time requires a considerable amount of energy and effort on the part of the researcher.

FIGURE 12.6

Example of a Randomized Solomon Four-Group Design

	R Random assignment of	O Pretest Faculty morale questionnaire	X_1 Treatment	O Posttest Faculty morale questionnaire
	25 teachers to experimental group (Group I)	(Dependent variable)	Sensitivity training workshops	(Dependent variable)
	R Random assignment of	O Pretest Faculty morale questionnaire	X_2 Treatment	O Posttest Faculty morale questionnaire
100 teachers randomly selected, then divided into four groups	25 teachers to control group (Group II)	(Dependent variable)	Workshops that do not include sensitivity training	(Dependent variable)
	R Random assignment of		X_1 Treatment	O Posttest Faculty morale questionnaire
	25 teachers to experimental group (Group III)		Sensitivity training workshops	(Dependent variable)
	R Random assignment of		X_2 Treatment	O Posttest Faculty morale questionnaire
	25 teachers to control group (Group IV)		Workshops that do not include sensitivity training	(Dependent variable)

Random Assignment with Matching. In an attempt to increase the likelihood that the groups of subjects in an experiment will be equivalent, pairs of individuals may be *matched* on certain variables to ensure group equivalence on these variables. The choice of variables on which to match is based on previous research, theory, and/or the experience of the researcher. The members of each matched pair are then assigned to the experimental and control groups at random. This adaptation can be made of both the posttest-only control group design, and the pretest-posttest control group design, although the latter is more common. A diagram of these designs is as follows.

The Randomized Posttest-Only Control Group Design, Using Matched Subjects

Treatment Group	M_r	X_1	O
Control group	M_r	X_2	O

The Randomized Pretest-Posttest Control Group Design, Using Matched Subjects

Treatment group	O	M_r	X_1	O
Control group	O	M_r	X_2	O

The symbol M_r refers to the fact that the members of each matched pair are randomly assigned to the experimental and control groups.

Although a pretest of the dependent variable is commonly used to provide scores on which to match, a measurement of any variable that shows a substantial relationship to the dependent variable is appropriate. Matching may be done in either or both of two ways: mechanically or statistically. Both require a score for each subject on *each* variable on which subjects are to be matched.

Mechanical matching is a process of pairing two persons whose scores on a particular variable are similar. Two girls, for example, whose mathematics aptitude scores and test anxiety scores are similar might be matched on those variables. After the matching is completed for the entire sample, a check should be made (through the use of frequency polygons) to ensure that the two groups are indeed equivalent on each matching variable. Unfortunately, two problems limit the usefulness of mechanical matching. First, it is very difficult to match on more than two or three variables—people just don't pair up on more than a few characteristics, making it necessary to have a very large initial sample to draw from. Second, in order to match, it is almost inevitable that some subjects must be eliminated from the study, since no "matchee" for them can be found. Samples then are no longer random even though they may have been before matching occurred.

Statistical matching,[*] on the other hand, does not necessitate a loss of subjects, nor does it limit the number of matching variables. Each subject is given a "predicted" score on the dependent variable, based on the correlation between the dependent variable and the variable on which the subjects are being matched. The difference between the predicted and actual scores for each individual is then used to compare experimental and control groups.

When a pretest is used as the matching variable, the difference between the predicted and actual score is called a "regressed gain score." This score is preferable to the more straightforward gain scores (posttest minus pretest score for each individual) primarily because it is more reliable. We discuss a similar procedure under partial correlation in Chapter Thirteen.

If mechanical matching is used, one member of each matched pair is randomly assigned to the experimental group, the other to the control group. If statistical matching is used, the sample is divided randomly at the outset, and the statistical adjustments are made after all data have been collected. Although some researchers advocate the use of statistical over mechanical matching, statistical matching is not infallible. Its major weakness is that it assumes the relationship between the dependent variable and each predictor variable can be properly described by a straight line rather than being curvilinear.

---

[*] Statistical "equating" of groups is a more common term that is synonymous with statistical matching. We believe the meaning for the beginning student is better conveyed by the term "matching."

Whichever procedure is used, the researcher must (in this design) rely on random assignment to equate groups on all other variables related to the dependent variable.

As an example of a matching design with random assignment, suppose a researcher is interested in the effects of academic coaching on the grade-point averages (GPA) of low-achieving students in science classes. The researcher randomly selects a sample of 60 students from a population of 125 such students in a local elementary school, and matches them by pairs on GPA, finding that she can match 40 of the 60. She then randomly assigns each subject in the resulting 20 pairs to either the experimental or the control group. Figure 12.7 presents a diagram of this example.

QUASI-EXPERIMENTAL DESIGNS

Quasi-experimental designs do not include the use of random assignment. Researchers who employ these designs rely instead on other techniques to control (or at least reduce) threats to internal validity. We shall describe some of these techniques as we discuss several of these quasi-experimental designs.

The Matching Only Design. This design differs from random assignment with matching only in that random assignment is *not* used. The researcher still matches the subjects in the experimental and control groups on certain variables, but he or she has no assurance that they are equivalent on others. Why? Because even though matched, subjects are not then randomly assigned to groups. This is a serious limitation, but often is unavoidable when random assignment is impossible—that is, when intact groups must be used. When several (say, ten or more) groups are available for a method study, and the *groups* can be randomly assigned to different treatments, this design offers an alternative to random assignment of *subjects*. After the groups have been randomly assigned to the different treatments, the individuals receiving one treat-

FIGURE **12.7**

Example of a Randomized Posttest-Only Control Group Design, Using Matched Subjects

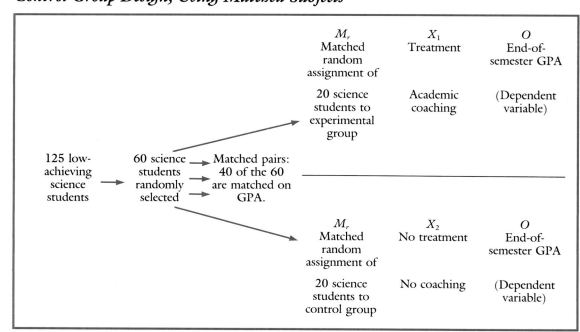

ment are matched with individuals receiving the other treatments. The design shown in Figure 12.7 is still preferred, however.

It should be emphasized that matching (whether mechanical or statistical) is never a substitute for random assignment. Furthermore, the correlation between the matching variable(s) and the dependent variable should be fairly substantial. (We suggest at least .40.) Realize also that, unless it is used in conjunction with random assignment, matching only controls for the variable(s) being matched. A diagram of the matching only designs is as follows.

The Matching Only Posttest-Only Control Group Design

Treatment Group	M	X_1	O
Control group	M	X_2	O

The Matching Only Pretest-Posttest Control Group Design

Treatment group	O	M	X_1	O
Control group	O	M	X_2	O

The M in this design refers to the fact that the subjects in each group have been matched (on certain variables), but not randomly assigned to the groups.

COUNTERBALANCED DESIGNS

Counterbalanced designs represent another technique for equating experimental and control groups. In this design, each group is exposed to *all* treatments, however many there are, but in a different order. Any number of treatments may be involved. An example of a diagram for a counterbalanced design involving three treatments is as follows.

A Three-Treatment Counterbalanced Design

Group one	X_1	O	X_2	O	X_3	O
Group two	X_2	O	X_3	O	X_1	O
Group three	X_3	O	X_1	O	X_2	O

This arrangement involves three groups. Group one receives treatment 1 and is posttested,

then receives treatment 2 and is posttested, and last receives treatment 3 and is posttested. Group two receives treatment 2 first, then treatment 3, and then treatment 1, being posttested after each treatment. Group three receives treatment 3 first, then treatment 1, followed by treatment 2, also being posttested after each treatment. The order in which the groups receive the treatments should be determined randomly.

How do researchers determine the effectiveness of the various treatments? Simply by comparing the average scores for all groups on the posttest for each treatment. In other words, the averaged posttest score for all groups for treatment 1 can be compared with the averaged posttest score for all groups for treatment 2, and so on, for however many treatments there are.

This design controls well for the subject characteristics threat to internal validity but is particularly vulnerable to multiple-treatment interference—that is, performance during a particular treatment may be affected by one or more of the previous treatments. Consequently, the results of any study in which the researcher has used a counterbalanced design must be examined carefully. Consider the two sets of hypothetical data shown in Figure 12.8.

The interpretation in A is clear: Method X is superior for both groups regardless of sequence and to the same degree. The interpretation in B, however, is much more complex. Overall, method X appears superior, and by the same amount as in A. In both A and B, the overall mean for X is 12, while for Y it is 8. In B, however, it appears that the difference between X and Y depends upon previous exposure to the other method. Group one performed much worse on method Y when it was exposed to it following X, and group two performed much better on X when it was exposed to it after method Y. When either X or Y was given first in the sequence, there is no difference in performance. It is not clear that method X is superior in all conditions in B, whereas this was quite clear in A.

TIME-SERIES DESIGNS

The typical pre- and posttest designs examined up to now involve observations or meas-

FIGURE 12.8

Results (Means) from a Study Using a Counterbalanced Design

	(A)		(B)	
	Weeks 1–4	Weeks 5–8	Weeks 1–4	Weeks 5–8
Group One	Method X = 12	Method Y = 8	Method X = 10	Method Y = 6
Group Two	Method Y = 8	Method X = 12	Method Y = 10	Method X = 14
Overall Means:	Method X = 12; Method Y = 8		Method X = 12; Method Y = 8	

urements taken immediately before and after treatment. A **time-series design,** however, involves *repeated* measurements or observations over a period of time both before and after treatment. It is really an elaboration of the one-group pretest posttest design presented in Figure 12.2. An extensive amount of data is collected on a single group. If the group scores essentially the same on the pretests and then considerably

improves on the posttests, the researcher has more confidence that the treatment is causing the improvement than if just one pretest and one posttest is given. An example might be when a teacher gives a weekly test to his or her class for several weeks before giving them a new textbook to use, and then sees how they score on a number of weekly tests after they have used the text. A diagram of the basic time-series design is as follows.

A Basic Time-Series Design

$$O_1 \quad O_2 \quad O_3 \quad O_4 \quad O_5 \quad X \quad O_6 \quad O_7 \quad O_8 \quad O_9 \quad O_{10}$$

The threats to internal validity that endanger use of this design include history (something could happen between the last pretest and the first posttest), instrumentation (if, for some reason, the test being used is changed at any time during the study), and testing (due to a practice effect). The possibility of a pretest-treatment interaction is also increased with the use of several pretests.

The effectiveness of the treatment in a time-series design is basically determined by analyzing the pattern of test scores that result from the several tests. Figure 12.9 illustrates several possible outcome patterns that might result from the introduction of an experimental variable (X).

The vertical line indicates the point at which the experimental treatment is introduced. In this figure, the change between time periods five and six gives the same data that would be obtained

FIGURE 12.9

Possible Outcome Patterns in a Time Series Design

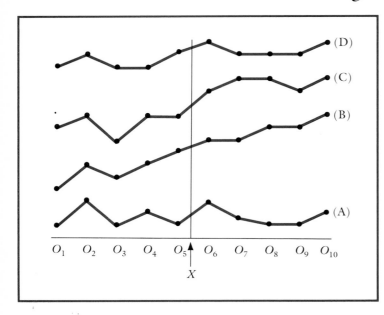

using a one group pretest-posttest design. The collection of additional data before and after the introduction of the treatment, however, shows how misleading a one group pretest-posttest design can be. In (A), the improvement is shown to be no more than occurs from one data collection period to another—regardless of method. You will notice that performance does improve from time to time, but no trend or overall increase is apparent. In (B), the gain from period five to six appears to be part of a trend already apparent before the treatment was begun (quite possibly an example of maturation). In (D) the higher score in period six is only temporary, as performance soon reverts back to what it was before the treatment was introduced (suggesting an extraneous event of transient impact). Only in (C) do we have evidence of a consistent effect of the treatment.

The time-series design is a strong design, although it is vulnerable to history (an extraneous event could occur between periods five and six) and instrumentation (due to the several test administrations at different points in time). The extensive amount of data collection required, in fact, is a likely reason why this design is infrequently used in educational research. In many studies, especially in schools, it simply is not feasible to give the same instrument eight to ten times. Even when it is possible, serious questions are raised concerning the validity of instrument interpretation with so many administrations. An exception to this is the use of observational devices that can be used over many occasions since interpretations based on them should remain valid.

FACTORIAL DESIGNS

Factorial designs extend the number of relationships that may be examined in an experimental study. They are essentially modifications of either the posttest-only control group or pretest-posttest control group designs (with or without random assignment), which permit the investigation of additional independent variables. Another value of a **factorial design** is that it allows a researcher to study the **interaction** of an independent variable with one or more

other variables, sometimes called moderator variables. **Moderator variables** may be either treatment variables or subject characteristic variables. A diagram of a factorial design is as follows.

Factorial Design

Treatment	R	O	X_1	Y_1	O
Control	R	O	X_2	Y_1	O
Treatment	R	O	X_1	Y_2	O
Control	R	O	X_2	Y_2	O

This design is a modification of the pretest-posttest control group design. It involves one treatment variable having two levels (X_1 and X_2), and one moderator variable, also having two levels (Y_1 and Y_2). In this example, two groups would receive the treatment (X_1) and two would not (X_2). Both groups receiving the treatment would differ on Y, however, as would the two groups not receiving the treatment. Since each variable, or factor, has two levels, the above design is called a 2 by 2 factorial design. This design can also be illustrated as follows.

Alternate Illustration of a 2 by 2 Factorial Design

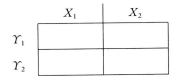

Consider the example we have used before of a researcher comparing the effectiveness of inquiry and lecture methods of instruction on achievement in history. The independent variable in this case (method of instruction) has two levels—inquiry (X_1) and lecture (X_2). Now imagine the researcher wants to see whether achievement is also influenced by class size. In that case, Y_1 might represent small classes and Y_2 might represent large classes.

As we suggest above, it is possible using a factorial design to assess not only the separate effect of each independent variable but also their joint effect. In other words, the researcher is

FIGURE 12.10

Using a Factorial Design to Study Effects of Method and Class Size on Achievement

Class Size	Method	
	Inquiry (X_1)	Lecture (X_2)
Small (Y_1)		
Large (Y_2)		

able to see how one of the variables might moderate the other (hence, the reason for these variables being called "moderator" variables). Let us return to the example of the researcher who wished to investigate the effects of method of instruction and class size on achievement in history. Figure 12.10 illustrates how various combinations of these variables could be studied in a factorial design.

Factorial designs, therefore, are an efficient way to study several relationships with one set of data. Let us emphasize again, however, that their greatest virtue lies in the fact that they enable a researcher to study interactions between variables. Figure 12.11, for example, illustrates two possible outcomes for the 2 by 2 factorial design shown in Figure 12.10. The scores for each group on the posttest (a fifty-item quiz on United States history) are shown in the boxes (usually called *cells*) corresponding to each combination of method and class size.

In (a) in Figure 12.11, the inquiry method was shown to be superior in both small and large classes, and small classes were superior to large classes for both methods. Hence no interaction effect is present. In (b), students did better in small than in large classes with both methods; however, students in small classes did better when they were taught by the inquiry method, but students in large classes did better when they were taught by the lecture method. Thus, even though students did better in small than in large classes in general, how well they

did depended on what method they were taught by. As a result, the researcher cannot say that either method was always better; it depends on the size of the class in which students were taught. There is an interaction, in other words, between class size and method, and this in turn affects achievement.

Suppose a factorial design was *not* used to study these variables. If the researcher simply compared the effect of the two methods, without taking class size into account, he or she would conclude that there was no difference in their effect on achievement (notice that the means of both groups = 40). The use of a factorial design enables us to see that the effectiveness of the method, in this case, depends on the size of the class in which it is used. It appears that an interaction exists between method and class size.

A factorial design involving four levels of the independent variable, and using a modification of the posttest-only control group design is presented by Tuckman.[7] The independent variable is type of instruction, and the moderator is amount of motivation. It is a 4 by 2 factorial design (see Figure 12.12). Many additional variations are also possible, such as 3 by 3, 4 by 3, and 3 by 2 by 3 designs. Factorial designs can be used to investigate more than two variables, although rarely are more than three variables studied in one design.

Single-Subject Designs in Experimental Research

All the designs presented heretofore involve the study of groups. At times, however, group designs are not appropriate for a researcher to use, particularly when the usual instruments are not pertinent and observation must be the method of data collection. Sometimes there just are not enough subjects available to make the use of a group design practical. Researchers who wish to study children who suffer from multiple handicaps (who are both blind and deaf, for example) may have only a very small number of such children at their disposal, say ten or less. It would make little sense to form two groups of five each

FIGURE 12.11

**Illustration of Interaction and No Interaction
in a 2 by 2 Factorial Design**

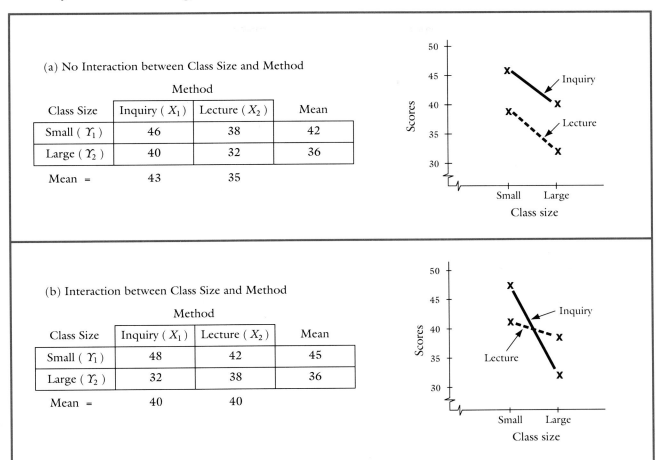

(a) No Interaction between Class Size and Method

Method

Class Size	Inquiry (X_1)	Lecture (X_2)	Mean
Small (Y_1)	46	38	42
Large (Y_2)	40	32	36
Mean =	43	35	

(b) Interaction between Class Size and Method

Method

Class Size	Inquiry (X_1)	Lecture (X_2)	Mean
Small (Y_1)	48	42	45
Large (Y_2)	32	38	36
Mean =	40	40	

FIGURE 12.12

Example of a 4 by 2 Factorial Design

Treatments (X)

R X_1 Y_1 O X_1 Computer-assisted instruction
R X_2 Y_1 O X_2 Programmed text
R X_3 Y_1 O X_3 Televised lecture
R X_4 Y_1 O X_4 Lecture-discussion

R X_1 Y_2 O   Moderator (Y)
R X_2 Y_2 O
R X_3 Y_2 O Y_1 High motivation
R X_4 Y_2 O Y_2 Low motivation

Treatments

	X_1	X_2	X_3	X_4
Y_1				
Y_2				

247

in such an instance. The use of a single-subject design would make more sense.

Single-subject designs are adaptations of the basic time-series design shown in Figure 12.9. The difference is that data are collected and analyzed for only one subject at a time. They are most commonly used to study the changes in behavior an individual exhibits after exposure to an intervention or treatment of some sort. Developed primarily in special education where most of the usual instrumentation is inappropriate, researchers using single-subject designs have been able to demonstrate that Down Syndrome children, for example, are capable of far more complex learning than was previously believed.

A-B-A DESIGNS

The basic approach of researchers using a single-subject design is to expose the same subject, operating as his or her own control, to two conditions or phases. The first condition or period is the pretreatment condition, typically called the **baseline** period, and identified as A.

During the baseline period, the subject is observed for several sessions until it appears that his or her typical behavior has been reliably determined. Then a treatment of some sort, typically identified as B, is introduced. During or following each administration of the treatment, the individual is again observed until the researcher can determine the effects of the treatment.

Typically, though not necessarily, a highly specific behavior is taught during the intervention condition, with the instructor also serving as the data collector—usually by recording the number of correct responses (e.g., comments) or behaviors (e.g., looking at the teacher) given by the subject during a fixed number of trials. The diagram below illustrates some of the most common single-subject designs.

In design (a), the baseline measurements or observations are made repeatedly until the researcher feels stability has been established. The treatment is then introduced, and a series of measurements or observations are made during or after each administration of the treatment. If the behavior of the subject improves during the

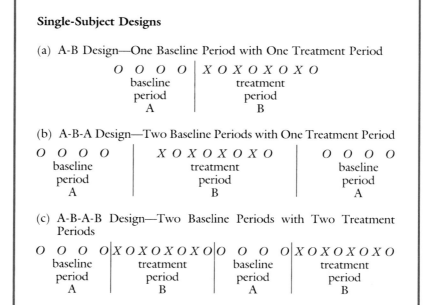

Single-Subject Designs

(a) A-B Design—One Baseline Period with One Treatment Period

$$O \quad O \quad O \quad O \mid X O X O X O X O$$

baseline period — A   treatment period — B

(b) A-B-A Design—Two Baseline Periods with One Treatment Period

$$O \quad O \quad O \quad O \mid X O X O X O X O \mid O \quad O \quad O \quad O$$

baseline period A   treatment period B   baseline period A

(c) A-B-A-B Design—Two Baseline Periods with Two Treatment Periods

$$O \quad O \quad O \quad O \mid X O X O X O X O O \mid O \quad O \quad O \quad O \mid X O X O X O X O$$

baseline period A   treatment period B   baseline period A   treatment period B

treatment period, the effectiveness of the treatment is presumed. As an example of the A-B design, consider a researcher interested in the effects of verbal praise on a particularly inattentive junior high school music student during orchestra rehearsals. The researcher could observe the student's behavior for, say, five days during the orchestra's daily practice sessions, then praise him verbally for five sessions, and observe his behavior immediately after the praise. The problem with this design, as with the one-shot case study that it resembles, is that the researcher does not know if any behavior change occurs *because* of the treatment. It is possible that some other variable (other than praise) actually caused the change, or even that the change would have occurred naturally, without any treatment at all.

In design (b), we simply add another baseline period. This improves the design considerably. If the behavior is different during the treatment period than during either baseline period, we have even stronger evidence for its effectiveness. In our previous example, the researcher could, after having praised the student for five days, eliminate the praise and observe the student's behavior for five days when no praise is forthcoming.*

* You will sometimes see A-B-A designs referred to in the literature as reversal designs.

In design (c), we have two baseline periods and two treatment periods. This further strengthens any conclusions about the effectiveness of the treatment, because it permits the effectiveness of the treatment to be demonstrated twice. In fact, the second treatment period can be extended indefinitely if a researcher desires. If the behavior of the subject is essentially the same during both treatment phases, and better (or worse) than both baseline periods, the likelihood of another variable being the cause of the change is decreased markedly.

To implement an **A-B-A-B design** in the previous example, the researcher would reinstate the experimental treatment, B (praise), for five days after the second baseline period and observe the subject's behavior. As with the A-B-A design, the researcher hopes to demonstrate that the dependent variable (attentiveness) changes whenever the independent variable (praise) is applied. If the subject's behavior changes from the first baseline to the first treatment period, from the first treatment period to the second baseline, and so on, the researcher has evidence that praise is indeed the cause of the change.

Figure 12.13 illustrates the results of a hypothetical study involving a single subject. Notice that a clear baseline is established, followed by improvement during treatment, followed by a decline in performance when treatment is stopped, followed by improvement once

FIGURE 12.13

Illustration of Results of Study Involving an A-B-A-B Design

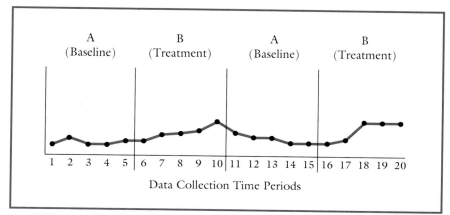

treatment is instituted again. This provides fairly strong evidence that it is the treatment, rather than history, maturation, or something else that is responsible for the improvement.

Although evidence such as that shown in Figure 12.13 would be considered a strong argument for causation, you should be aware that the A-B-A designs suffer from two limitations: the likelihood of data collector bias (the individual who is giving the treatment also usually collects the data), and the possibility of an instrumentation effect (the need for an extensive number of data collection periods can lead to changes in the administration conditions). It is also suspect on ethical grounds, in that the second baseline condition is introduced during an attempt to change behavior considered to be important. To some extent, the welfare of the subject is placed second to obtaining clear research results.

MULTIPLE BASELINE DESIGNS

An alternative to A-B-A designs is the multiple baseline design. **Multiple baseline designs** are used when it is not possible or ethical to withdraw a treatment and return to baseline. When a multiple-baseline design is used, researchers do more than collect data on one behavior for one subject in one setting; they collect data on several behaviors for one subject, obtaining a baseline for each during the *same* period of time. The researcher than systematically applies the treatment at different times for each behavior until all of them are undergoing the treatment. If behavior changes in each case only after the treatment has been applied, the treatment is judged to be the cause of the change.

It is important that the behaviors being treated, however, remain independent of each other. If behavior two, for example, is affected by the introduction of the treatment to behavior one, then the effectiveness of the treatment cannot be assessed. A diagram of a multiple-baseline design involving three behaviors is shown below.

In this design, treatment is applied first to change behavior one, then two, and then three until all three behaviors are undergoing the treatment. For example, a researcher might investigate the effects of "time out" (removing the student from class activities for a period of time) on decreasing various undesirable classroom behaviors of a particular student. Suppose the behaviors are (1) talking out of turn; (2) chewing gum; and (3) making derogatory remarks toward another student. The researcher would begin by applying the treatment first to behavior (1), then to behavior (2), and then to behavior (3). At that point, the treatment will have been applied to all three behaviors. The more behaviors that are eliminated or reduced, the more effective the treatment can be judged to be. How many times the researcher must apply the treatment is a matter of judgment and depends on the subjects, setting, and behaviors involved.

An illustration of the effects of a treatment in a hypothetical study using a multiple-baseline design is shown in Figure 12.14. Notice that each of the behaviors involved changed only when the treatment was introduced.

In practice, results of studies like this hypothetical one rarely fit the ideal model in that the data points often show more fluctuation, making trends less clear-cut. This feature makes

---

A Multiple-Baseline Design

Behavior one	O O O O X O X O X O X O X O X O X O X O X O
Behavior two	O O O O O O O X O X O X O X O X O X O X O
Behavior three	O O O O O O O O O O X O X O X O X O X O

data collector bias even more of a problem, particularly when the behavior in question is more complex than just a simple response such as picking up an object. Data collector bias in multiple-baseline studies remains a serious concern, as do the threats of implementation and instrumentation.

THE IMPORTANCE OF REPLICATING SINGLE-SUBJECT RESEARCH STUDIES

Single-subject designs are weak in generalizability—one would hardly advocate use of a treatment shown to be effective with only one subject. As a result, studies involving single-subject designs that show a particular treatment to be effective in changing behaviors must rely on replication—across individuals rather than groups—if such results are to be found worthy of generalization.

DATA ANALYSIS

The data collected in single-subject studies are usually analyzed visually (as opposed to statistically) by inspecting a graphic presentation (similar to Figure 12.14) of the results. Two questions are asked: (a) Were there enough collection points—i.e., was the subject observed or measured enough times? (b) How great was the change in behavior between baseline and treatment periods? Essentially, this is a matter of judgment on the part of the researcher.

Control of Threats to Internal Validity: A Summary

Table 12.1 presents our evaluation of the effectiveness of each of the preceding designs in controlling the threats to internal validity that we discussed in Chapter Eleven. You should remember that these assessments reflect our judgment; not all researchers would necessarily agree. We have assigned two pluses (+ +) to indicate a *strong* control (the threat is *unlikely* to

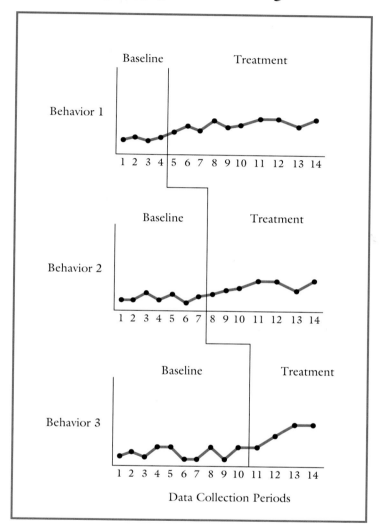

FIGURE 12.14

Illustration of Multiple Baseline Design

occur); one plus (+) to indicate *some* control (the threat *might* occur); a minus (−) to indicate a *weak* control (the threat *is* likely to occur); and a question mark (?) to those threats whose likelihood, due to the nature of the study, we cannot determine.

You will notice that these designs are most effective in controlling the threats of subject characteristics, mortality, history, maturation,

TABLE 12.1

Effectiveness of Experimental Designs in Controlling Threats to Internal Validity

Design	Subject Characteristics	Mortality	Location	Instrument Decay	Data Collector Characteristics	Data Collector Bias	Testing	History	Maturation	Attitudinal	Regression	Implementer
One-Shot Case Study	−	−	−	(N/A)	−	−	(NA)	−	−	−	−	−
One Group Pre-Posttest	−	+	−	−	−	−	−	−	−	−	−	−
Static-Group Comparison	−	−	−	+	−	−	+	+	+	−	−	−
Randomized Posttest-Only Control Group	+ +	+	−	+	−	−	+	+	+ +	−	+ +	
Randomized Pre-Posttest Control Group	+ +	+	−	+	−	−	−	+	+ +	−	+ +	
Solomon Four-Group	+ +	+ +	−	+	−	−	+ +	+	+ +	−	+ +	
Randomized Posttest-Only Control Group with Matched Subjects	+ +	+	−	+	−	−	+	+	+ +	−	+ +	
Matching only Pre-Posttest Control Group	+	+	−	+	−	−	+	+	+	−	+	
Counterbalanced	+ +	+ +	−	+	−	−	−	+ +	+ +	+	+ +	
Time-Series	+ +	−	+	−	+	−	+	+	+	−	+ +	
Factorial with Randomization	+ +	+ +	−	+ +	−	−	+	+	+ +	−	+ +	
Factorial without Randomization	?	?	−	+ +	−	−	+	+	+	−	?	
A-B-A-B	+ +	+ +	+	−	+	−	+ +	+ +	+	−	+	
Multiple Baseline	+ +	+ +	+	−	+	−	+ +	+ +	+	−	+	

Key: (+ +) = strong control, threat unlikely to occur; (+) = some control, threat may possibly occur; (−) = weak control, threat likely to occur; (?) = can't determine; (NA) = threat does not apply.

and regression. Note that mortality is controlled in several designs because any subject lost is lost to both the experimental and control groups, thus introducing no advantage to either. A location threat is a minor problem in the time-series and multiple-baseline designs because the location where the treatment is administered is usually constant throughout the study; the same is true for data collector characteristics, although such characteristics may be a problem in other designs if different collectors are used for differ-

ent methods. This is usually easy to control, however. Unfortunately, both of these designs do suffer from a strong likelihood of instrument decay and data collector bias, since data (by means of observations) must be collected over many trials, and the data collector can hardly be kept in the dark as to the intent of the study.

Data collector characteristics may be a problem in all but single-subject designs (if different data collectors are used for different treatments), but this can usually be easily controlled.

Unconscious bias on the part of data collectors is not controlled by any of these designs nor is an implementer or attitudinal effect. Either implementers or data collectors can, unintentionally, distort the results of a study. The data collector should be kept ignorant as to who received which treatment, if this is feasible. It should be verified that the treatment is administered and the data collected as the researcher intended. Such bias is a particular problem in many single-subject designs where the same person is both implementer (e.g., acting as teacher) and data collector. A second observer, recording independently, reduces this threat, but increases the amount of staff time needed to complete the study.

As you can see in Table 12.1, a testing threat may be present in all but the static-group, randomized subject (including factorial designs), and single-subject designs, although its magnitude depends on the nature and frequency of the instrumentation involved. It can occur only when subjects respond to an instrument on more than one occasion. It is usually not a threat in single-subject designs because the subject presumably cannot affect observational data.

The attitudinal (or demoralization) effect is best controlled by the counterbalanced design since each subject receives both (or all) special treatments. In the remaining designs, it can be controlled by providing another "special" experience during the alternative treatment. Regression is not likely to be a problem except in the single-group pre-post test design, since it should occur equally in experimental and control conditions if it occurs at all. It could, however, possibly occur in a nonequivalent (no random assignment) pretest-posttest control group design, if there are large initial differences between the two groups.

Evaluating the Likelihood of a Threat to Internal Validity in Experimental Studies

An important consideration in planning an experimental study or in evaluating the results of a reported study is the likelihood of possible threats to internal validity. As we have shown, there are a number of possible threats to internal validity that may exist. The question that a researcher must ask is: "How likely is it that any *particular* threat exists in *this* study?"

To aid in assessing this likelihood, we suggest the following procedures.

Step one: Ask: What specific factors either are known to affect the dependent variable or may logically be expected to affect this variable? (Note that researchers need *not* be concerned with factors unrelated to what they are studying.)

Step two: Ask: What is the likelihood of the comparison groups differing on each of these factors? (A difference between groups cannot be explained away by a factor that is the same for all groups.)

Step three: Evaluate the threats on the basis of how likely they are to have an effect and plan to control for them. If a given threat cannot be controlled, this should be acknowledged.

Let us consider an example to illustrate how these different steps might be employed. Suppose a researcher wishes to investigate the effects of two different teaching methods (for example, lecture versus inquiry instruction) on critical thinking ability of students (as measured by scores on a critical thinking test). The researcher plans to compare two groups of eleventh graders, one group being taught by an instructor who uses the lecture method, the other group being taught by an instructor who uses the inquiry method. Several of the threats to internal validity discussed in Chapter Eleven are considered and evaluated using the steps just presented. We would argue that this is the kind of thinking researchers should engage in when planning a research project.

Subject Characteristics. Although there are many possible subject characteristics that might affect critical thinking ability, we identify only two here—initial critical thinking ability and gender.

1. **Variable a.** *Step one:* Post-treatment critical thinking ability of students in the two groups is almost certainly related to initial critical thinking ability. *Step two:* Groups may well differ unless randomly assigned or matched. *Step three:* Likelihood of having an effect unless controlled: High.

2. **Variable b.** *Step One:* Post-treatment critical ability may be related to gender. *Step two:* If groups differ significantly in proportions of each gender, threat exists. Although possible, this probably is unlikely. *Step three:* Likelihood of having an effect unless controlled: Low.

Mortality.   *Step one:* Likely to affect post-treatment scores on any measure of critical thinking since those subjects who drop out or are otherwise lost would likely have lower scores. *Step two:* Groups probably would not differ in numbers lost, but this should be verified. *Step three:* Likelihood of having an effect unless controlled: Moderate.

Location.   *Step one:* If location of implementation of treatment and/or of data collection differs for the two groups, this could affect post-treatment scores on critical thinking test. Post-treatment scores would be expected to be affected by such resources as class size, availability of reading materials, films, and so forth. *Step two:* May differ for groups unless controlled for by standardizing locations for implementation and data collection. The classrooms using each method may differ systematically unless steps are taken to ensure resources are comparable. *Step three:* Likelihood of having an effect unless controlled: Moderate to High.

Instrumentation

1. **Instrument Decay.** *Step one:* May affect any outcome. *Step two:* Could differ for groups. This should not be a major problem, providing all instruments used are carefully examined and any alterations found are corrected. *Step three:* Likelihood of having an effect unless controlled: Low.

2. **Data Collector Characteristics.** *Step one:* Might affect scores on critical thinking test.

Step two: Might differ for groups unless controlled by using the same data collector(s) for all groups. *Step three:* Likelihood of having an effect unless controlled: Moderate.

3. **Data Collector Bias.** *Step one:* Could certainly affect scores on critical thinking test. *Step two:* Might differ for groups unless controlled by training them in administration of the instrument and/or keeping them ignorant as to which treatment group is being tested. *Step three:* Likelihood of having an effect unless controlled: High.

Testing.   *Step one:* Pretesting might well affect posttest scores on critical thinking test. *Step two:* Presumably the pretest would affect both groups equally, however, and would not be likely to interact with method, since instructors using each method are teaching critical thinking skills. *Step three:* Likelihood of having an effect unless controlled: Low.

History.   *Step one:* Extraneous events that might affect critical thinking skills are difficult to conjecture, but they might include such things as a special TV series on thinking, attendance at a district workshop on critical thinking by some students, or participation in certain extracurricular activities (e.g., debates) that occur during the course of the study. *Step two:* In most cases, these events would likely affect both groups equally and hence are not likely to constitute a threat. Such events should be noted and their impact on each group assessed to the degree possible. *Step three:* Likelihood of having an effect unless controlled: Low.

Maturation.   *Step one:* Could affect outcome scores since critical thinking is presumably related to individual growth. *Step two:* Presuming that the instructors teach each method over the same time period, maturation should not be a threat. *Step three:* Likelihood of having an effect unless controlled: Low.

Attitudinal Effect.   *Step one:* Could affect posttest scores. *Step two:* If the members of either group perceive that they are receiving any sort of "special attention," this could be a threat. The extent to which either treatment is "novel" should be evaluated. *Step three:* Likelihood of having an effect unless controlled: Low to Moderate.

Regression. *Step one:* Unlikely to affect posttest scores unless subjects selected on the basis of extreme scores. *Step two:* Unlikely, though possible, to affect groups differently. *Step three:* Likelihood of having an effect unless controlled: Low.

Implementation. *Step one:* Instructor ability is likely to affect post-treatment scores. *Step two:* Since different instructors teach the methods, they may well differ in how adequately each method is implemented. Could be controlled by having several instructors of each method or by monitoring instruction. *Step three:* Likelihood of having an effect unless controlled: High.

The trick, then, to identifying threats to internal validity is, first, to think of different variables (conditions, subject characteristics, and so on) that might affect the outcome variable of the study and, second, to decide, based on evidence and/or experience, whether these things would affect the comparison groups differently. If so, this may provide an alternative explanation for the results. If this seems likely, a threat to internal validity of the study may indeed be present and needs to be minimized or eliminated.

Control of Experimental Treatments

The designs discussed in this chapter are all intended to improve the internal validity of an experimental study. As you have seen, each has its advantages and disadvantages and each provides a way of handling some threats but not others.

Another issue, however, cuts across all designs. While it has been touched upon in earlier sections, particularly in connection with location and implementer threats, it deserves more attention than it customarily receives. The issue is that of researcher control over the experimental

treatment(s). Of course, an essential requirement of a well-conducted experiment is that researchers have control over the treatment—that is, they control the what, who, when, and how of it. A clear example of researcher control is the testing of a new drug; clearly, the drug is the treatment and the researcher can control who administers it, under what conditions, when it is given, to whom, and how much. Unfortunately, researchers seldom have this degree of control in educational research.

In the ideal situation, a researcher can specify precisely the ingredients of the treatment; in actual practice, many treatments or methods are too complex to describe precisely. Consider the example we have previously given of a study comparing the effectiveness of inquiry and lecture methods of instruction. What, exactly, is the individual who implements each method to do? Researchers may differ greatly in their answers to this question. Ambiguity in specifying exactly what the person who is to conduct the treatment is to do leads to major problems in implementation. How are researchers to train teachers to implement the methods involved in a study if they can't specify the essential characteristics of those methods? Even supposing that adequate specification can be achieved and training methods developed, how can researchers be sure the methods are implemented *correctly*? These problems must be faced by any researcher using any of the designs we have discussed.

A consideration of this issue frequently leads to consideration (and assessment) of possible trade-offs. The greatest control is likely to occur when the researcher is the one implementing the treatment; this, however, also provides the greatest opportunity for an implementer threat to occur. The more the researcher diffuses implementation by adding other implementers in the interest of reducing threats, however, the more he or she risks distortion or dilution of the treatment. The extreme case is presented by the use of existing treatment groups, that is, groups located by the researcher which already are receiving certain treatments. Most authors refer to these as causal-comparative or *ex post facto studies,* and do not consider them to fall under the category of experimental research (see Chapter

Fourteen). In such studies, the researcher must locate groups receiving the specified treatment(s) and then use a matching-only design or, if sufficient lead time exists before implementation of the treatment, a time-series design. We are not persuaded that such studies, if treatments are carefully identified, are necessarily inferior with respect to cause-effect conclusions than treatments assigned to teachers (or others) by the researcher. Both are equally open to most of the threats we have discussed. The existing groups are more susceptible to subject characteristic and location threats than true experiments, but not necessarily more so than quasi-experiments. One would expect fewer problems with an attitudinal effect, since existing practice is not altered. The major difference has to do with implementation: It would be expected that implementers of a method that they have selected would be predisposed toward it. On the other hand, teachers who agree to attempt a new method (to them) may be equally predisposed. Conversely, teachers who participate reluctantly are unlikely to give the method a fair trial. We conclude that both types of study are needed and are equally defensible.

An Example of Experimental Research

In the remainder of the chapter, we present a published example of experimental research. Along with a reprint of the actual study itself, we critique the study, identify its strengths, and discuss areas we think could be improved. We do this at the end of Chapters Thirteen through Seventeen as well, in each case analyzing the type of study discussed in the chapter. In selecting the studies for review, we used the following criteria:

- the study had to exemplify good, but not outstanding, methodology and permit constructive criticism;
- the study had to have enough interest value to hold the attention of students, even though specific professional interests may not be directly addressed;
- the study had to be concisely reported.

In total, the studies we present represent the diversity of special interests that exist in the field of education.

In critiquing each of these studies, we used a series of categories and questions that should, by now, be familiar to you. They are:

Purpose/Justification: Is it logical? Is it convincing? Is it sufficient? Do the authors show how the results of the study would have important implications for theory, practice, or both?

Definitions: Are major terms clearly defined? If not, are they clear in context?

Prior research: Has previous work on the topic been covered adequately? Is it clearly connected to the present study?

Hypotheses: Are they stated? Implied? Appropriate for the study?

Sampling: What type of sample is used? Is it a random sample? If not, is it adequately described? Do the authors recommend or imply generalizing to a population? If so, is the target population clearly indicated? Are possible limits to generalizing discussed?

Instrumentation: Is it adequately described? Is evidence of adequate reliability presented? Is evidence of validity provided? How persuasive is the evidence or the argument for validity of inferences made from the instruments?

Internal validity: What threats are evident? Were they controlled? If not, were they discussed?

Data analysis: Are data summarized and reported appropriately? Are descriptive and inferential statistics (if any) used appropriately? Are the statistics interpreted correctly? Are limitations discussed?

Results: Are they clearly presented? Is the written summary consistent with the data reported?

Interpretations/Discussion: Do the authors place the study in a broader context? Do they recognize limitations of the study, especially with regard to population and ecological generalizing of results?

From: Journal of Educational Research, 80 (6), 338–342, 1987. Reprinted with permission of the Helen Dwight Reid Educational Foundation. Published by Heldref Publications, 4000 Albemarle St., N.W., Washington, D.C. 20016. Copyright © 1987.

The Effects of Word Processing on Written Composition

David W. Dalton
Indiana University

Michael J. Hannafin
The Pennsylvania State University

Abstract

In the present study, the effects of a year-long word processing program on holistic writing skills were examined. Learners in the treatment group used a word processor three times per week to complete writing assignments. Students in the control group used conventional pen-and-paper writing techniques to complete their writing assignments. An analysis of writing samples taken upon completion of this study suggested that word processing alone was of little consequence for able learners, but proportionately most effective for low-achieving students. These effects were found despite logistical problems encountered during the study that probably precluded more dramatic results.

Computer-assisted instruction (CAI) has been effective in improving learning across a wide variety of instructional settings and subjects (Kulik, 1983). Indeed, some contemporary visionaries have suggested that the computer possesses educational potential that has scarcely been exploited (Bork, 1981; Papert, 1980). Much of the focus of this potential has been on tutoring in subject areas and providing drills to strengthen learning.

One of the greatest instructional benefits of computers may be found in open-ended computer activities such as word processing, where the computer is used more as a learning tool than as an electronic tutor or tutee (Dudley-Marling, 1985; O'Brien, 1984; Piper, 1984; Shostak, 1984; cf. Taylor, 1980). In this capacity, the computer provides not only a conventional resource for recording and printing student compositions, but a vehicle through which writing can be easily analyzed, reviewed, edited, and improved (Bean, 1983; Bradley, 1982; Burns, 1984; Schrantz, 1983; Wresch, 1984).

Though considerable interest has been expressed in the use of word processing for the teaching of composition, differences of opinion exist as to the effectiveness, and even the desirability, of such approaches (Daiute, 1985). While many language and communication authorities have applauded the potential of word processing for teaching composition skills, others have expressed concern. (See, for example, Bertram, Michaels, & Watson-Gegea, 1985; Gula, 1983; Hale, 1984; Jarchow, 1984; Moran, 1983; Vacc, 1984; Wheeler, 1985.)

Perhaps some of the disagreement concerning the teaching of writing skills via computerized word processing can be traced to fundamental differences in teaching philosophy. Traditionally, writing skills have been taught through either of two distinct methods: the reductive approach or the holistic approach (Hartwell, 1985). In the reductive approach, writing is taught by focusing on discrete, often isolated mechanical skills, including punctuation, syntactical rules, and so forth.

The holistic approach concentrates attention on the process of writing as opposed to specific mechanics. The basic assumption of this method is that as learners concentrate on meaning and on composition as a whole, mechanical skills develop naturally. Learners are taught that writing consists of three distinct steps: pre-writing or planning, writing, and most importantly, revision. This approach to composition instruction is now widely accepted and implemented (Moffet, 1968).

There is considerable evidence to support the efficacy of the holistic approach to writing instruction. In a study comparing the two approaches, no significant differences were found in the technical writing quality between treatment groups. This leads to the conclusion that the reductive approach, while improving the mechanical skills, does little to improve overall writing quality (Meckel, 1963). In addition, the holistic approach can be especially effective in improving the writing skills of low-achieving learners, because these students tend to become preoccupied with the form, rather than the substance, of their writing (Rose, 1983).

The results of skill-based approaches to the teaching of writing, such as grammar drills and punctuation tutorials, have been less promising. The findings of the RSVP project revealed that while computer instruction improved mechanical writing skills, no discernable impact on the overall quality of student composition was found. Results of such projects have contraindicated the reductive approach for the teaching of composition skills (Blum & Furlong, 1983).

In fact, a recent review of the literature comparing the two approaches to writing instruction suggested that mechanistic approaches often had negative effects on the overall quality of students' writing. Because concentration on basic grammatical skills often caused learners and their instructors to neglect the important steps in the writing process, including pre-planning and revision, the overall writing process was hampered (Hartwell, 1985).

The potential of computerized word processing to assist learners in writing, especially in the writing and revising processes, seems self-evident to many. Though endorsements of word processing methods for the teaching of composition have been widespread (see, for example, Hennings, 1981, 1983; Palmer, Dowd, & James, 1984; Schwartz, 1984; Sharples, 1983; Smith, 1985), few empirical studies have been reported to date. One recent study conducted with elementary students reported that the inclusion of word processors in the writing program produced significant improvements in the attitudes of the learners (Willer, 1984). Learners reported favorable attitudes toward revision when accomplished via microcomputer, and as a result spent additional time revising their writing. Similar favorable results have been reported for word processing approaches with primary grade learners (Phenix & Hannan, 1985).

Although the potential of word processing in aiding the writing process seems formidable, many questions remain. The purpose of this study was to examine the effects of a year-long holistic writing program featuring word processing on the composition skills of junior high school students.

METHODS

Subjects

The subjects were 80 seventh-grade students, drawn from four remedial language arts courses. Learners were placed in the remedial programs based on below-average scores on the Comprehensive Test of Basic Skills (CTBS) and through the recommendations of sixth-grade classroom teachers. Although below-average in language skills, many subjects possessed average to above-average skills in related content areas, such as mathematics and science.

Materials

Two treatments were employed: a computer-based word processing treatment and a conventional pen-and-paper writing treatment.

Word processing treatment.   During the academic year, students in the word processing group completed all of their writing assignments on an Apple IIe microcomputer equipped with *FreeWriter*. *FreeWriter* is a moderately powerful public domain word processing program. The program includes editing features such as the ability to find and replace text, to move blocks of text within a document, and to format documents on screen. Neither spelling checking nor inherent grammar checking features were available through *FreeWriter*. In effect, the word processing provided only the electronic capability to organize and manipulate text, with no embedded diagnostic or corrective writing features. Each student was furnished with word processing softward and data diskettes and was provided approximately three instructional periods per week to compose via the computer.

The students were also given two weekly writing exercises to complete on the word processor. These exercises included developing fictional short stories, writing letters, and preparing expository prose. The exercises each typically required the learner to produce approximately one page of text. In addition to the writing exercises, the students completed four major papers on the word processor. The students were given a general topic and asked to produce a final printed document of between three and five pages.

In all cases, learners were encouraged to complete pre-planning activities, including the development of an outline and a skeletal rough draft by hand before using the word processing system. Once at the computer terminal, they then entered their first draft and completed two additional revisions before the document was evaluated by the instructor.

Conventional writing program.   Students in the conventional writing program used pen-and-paper methods to complete the same writing activities. The same basic process-oriented sequence of teaching activities and required projects was employed, including preplanning, writing, and revision processes, but all writing was completed in handwritten form.

Writing sample.   A standardized writing sample was collected during the last month of the school year, and served as the dependent performance measure. Learners were asked to produce a one-to-two page expository essay on a common topic. These writing samples were then evaluated by three expert "blind" examiners who judged each essay according to its structure and organization, correct usage of the parts of speech, punctuation, capitalization, and spelling. Scoring of the writing sample was accomplished by each evaluator independently subtracting points from the maximum score of 100. In order to account for potential differences across evaluators, the evaluations were averaged to compute the final score. All writing samples, including those for the students in the word processing treatment, were handwritten.

Procedure

Prior to the beginning of the study, the learners were designated as relatively high or low in prior writing ability based on scores from sixth-grade Comprehensive Test of Basic Skills (CTBS) total language subscales. The learners were then assigned to their respective treatment groups where they completed all writing assignments throughout the academic year as described abvove. At the conclusion of the study, the learners were given the writing sample posttest previously described.

TABLE 1.

Mean Scores and Standard Deviations for Writing Sample

Prior achievement		Instructional treatment		
		Word processing	Control	Totals
High	M	77.13	78.00	77.56
	SD	10.10	8.85	9.35
Low	M	74.25	67.88	71.06
	SD	7.86	7.71	8.32
Totals	M	75.69	72.94	74.31
	SD	9.02	9.65	9.37

Note: n's per cell = 16; total n = 64.

Experimental Design and Data Analysis

The design of this study was a 2×2 completely crossed treatment-by-achievement factorial design, featuring two levels of writing (word processing, conventional), and two levels of prior writing ability (high and low) based on CTBS scores. Posttest writing sample scores were analyzed via ANOVA procedures.

RESULTS

The posttest cell means for the writing sample are contained in Table 1. Overall, the mean of the relatively high achieving learners (77.56) was significantly greater than the mean of the relatively low achieving learners (71.06), $F(1, 60) = 8.96, p < .005$.

The differences for the writing treatments were not significant, $F(1, 60) = 1.60, p > .05$. The mean for the word processing group was marginally higher (75.69) than the mean for the conventional writing group (72.94). However, a marginal Achievement-by-Writing Technique interaction was detected, $F(1, 60) = 2.79, p < .07$. This interaction is illustrated in Figure 1. The writing treatments resulted in similar performance for high achievers (77.13 vs. 78.00), but word processing was superior to conventional instruction for low achievers (74.25 vs. 67.88).

DISCUSSION

There are a number of results from this study that warrant further discussion. First, there was a significant achievement by writing treatment interaction. This interaction indicated that the relatively low achievers

FIGURE 1.

Achievement-by-Treatment Interaction for the Writing Sample

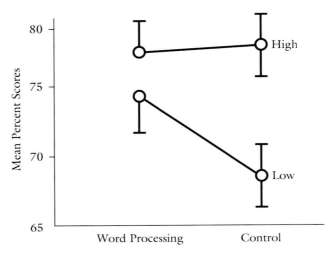

benefited more from composition taught via word processing than conventional instructional methods. This result supports the limited previous research indicating that low ability learners and other special populations can benefit by word processing even though other types of "special" interventions have had little effect (cf. Fischer, 1983; Rodrigues, 1985; Rose, 1983).

In addition, the results of this study, paired with the informal observations made during the study, support the notion that word processing can improve the revision process and consequently make writing less tedious for low ability learners (Bean, 1983; Bradley, 1982; Hummel, 1985; Wresch, 1984). For many low ability learners, the revision process is perceived as difficult, tedious, and burdensome. Consequently, low achievers are often disinclined to edit and revise their writing. The ease of revision resulting from word processing, however, seems to increase the likelihood of revision by low ability learners.

Although no formal data were collected to corroborate the claims, the teachers involved in this study noted that learners using the word processor required less encouragement to revise drafts of their writing assignments and generally spent more time revising their writing than their counterparts using conventional methods. Student interviews conducted following the study were consistent with the findings of Willer (1984), suggesting that the word processor made the writing process more tolerable because error correction was simplified, and the computer minimized much of the reticence with which many learners have associated paper-and-pencil writing.

Although the predicted pattern was evident, the absence of a main effect for writing treatments was probably due to several factors. First, the writing samples were all constructed using pen-and-paper despite the presumed facility of students in the word processing group to manipulate writing electronically. This was done in order to examine writing transfer to nonelectronic form because this is more typically associated with expected written expression in school settings. However, in doing so, the word processing students were not provided access to the system around which their writing skills were cultivated. It seems reasonable that many students had acquired effective writing skills via word processing and resisted the process writing task when the computer support was removed. If so, concern for the transfer of writing techniques to non-computer environments must be expressed.

Next, some students experienced initial difficulty with typing. Learners at this age level had received little or no formal typing instruction, and only cursory attention was paid to formal typing fluency during the present study. As a result, students spent inordinate amounts of time "hunting and pecking" about the keyboard for even simple typed entries. Many learners stated that they found typing time-consuming and distracting when compared with pencil-and-paper writing. Some noted that typing problems also interrupted their concentration while attempting to write.

Another problem observed for the word processing treatment was the complicated, and often untimely, process of gaining access to the computers. In the school environment used in this study, all computers were grouped into two laboratories. Although ready access was obtained during the teaching period designated for the study, each trip to the computer lab was time-consuming. Each trip required the distribution of necessary software, further reducing the amount of time available for instruction and practice. Several students stated that they preferred remaining in class rather then the disruption and "hassle" of relocating in the computer lab. In addition, other students said that they often intentionally wasted time during the required transitional periods, suggesting that only a portion of the word processing students contributed to the observed effect. Though these complications can be avoided fairly readily through effective planning once such a program has been institutionalized, problems were noted due to the experimental nature of the present study.

Finally, some students in the word processing group reported that they occasionally neglected the careful planning ordinarily completed prior to composing. They attributed this neglect to their impression that the word processor simplified editing to the extent that planning was no longer as important as for conventional paper and pencil writing. This observation is consistent with the comments of several authors who have cautioned that word processing per se does not teach students how or what to write; it only simplifies a method for recording composition (Burns, 1984; Daiute, 1983; Woodruff, 1984). These cautions appear well advised based on the reports of participants in the present study.

Although this study demonstrated some of the considerable potential of word processing to improve composition skills, several important questions remain. First, the question of interference resulting from inadequate key-boarding skills must be resolved. The absence or presence of effective keyboarding skills will be a powerful variable affecting the utility of word processing for any learner. The effects of word processing writing methods on near transfer learning, that is on writing composed on the computer versus that transferred to hand-written form, must be established conclusively. To the extent that word processing aids the writing process, the need for transfer to hand-written form versus the extension of the computer as a basic writing tool must be explored.

Future studies are also needed to determine ways in which the pre-writing, re-writing, and editing processes appropriate to word processing can be emphasized. Indeed, systems that integrate outlining and other preplanning activities, as well as spelling- and grammar-checking utilities, have already been developed and tested successfully for adults. While a number of promising recommendations have been published to support the processes of teaching composing via word processing (Burns, 1984; Collins, Bruce, & Rubin, 1984; Wresch, 1984), little evidence exists to either support or refute such procedures. Additional research is needed to identify methods most likely to improve writing skills using word processing.

The results of this study suggest that word processing offers significant potential for the development of writing skills. However, several logistical and methodological barriers must be overcome before this potential can be realized. Future research, with an emphasis on both the computer as tool *and* the teaching methods needed to support the writing process, should provide informed insights into the preparation of educated writers.

References

Bean, H. C. (1983). Computerized word processing as an aid to revision. *College Composition and Communication, 34,* 146–148.

Bertram, B., Michaels, S., & Watson-Gegea, K. (1985). How computers can change the writing process. *Language Arts, 2,* 143–149.

Blum, I., & Furlong, M. (1983). The "Writing to Read" Project. *Momentum, 14(3),* 4–6.

Bork, A. (1981). *Learning with computers.* Bedford, MA: Digital Equipment Corp.

Bradley, V. (1982). Improving student's writing with microcomputers. *Language Arts, 59,* 732–743.

Burns, H. (1984). Computer-assisted prewriting activities: Harmonics for invention. In R. Shostak (Ed.), *Computers in composition instruction.* Eugene, OR: ICCE Publications.

Collins, A., Bruce, B., & Rubin, A. (1984). Microcomputer-based writing activities for the upper elementary grades. *Proceedings of the Fourth International Congress and Exposition of the Society for Applied Learning and Technology.* Orlando, FL: SALT.

Dauite, C. (1983). Word processing: Can it make good writers even better? *Electronic Learning, 1(1),* 29–33.

Daiute, C. (1985). Issues in using computers to socialize the writing process. *Educational Communication and Technology Journal, 33,* 41–50.

Dudley-Marling, C. (1985). Microcomputers, reading, and writing: Alternatives to drill and practice. *Reading Teacher, 38(4),* 388–91.

Fischer, G., (1983). Word processing: Will it make all kids love to write? *Instructor, 92(6),* 87–88.

Green, J. (1984). Computers, kids, and writing: An interview with Donald Graves. *Classroom Computer Learning,* March, 44–46.

Gula, R. (1983). Beyond the typewriter: An English teacher looks at word processing. *Independent School,* February, 44–46.

Hale, D. (1984). Word processing: Panacea or problem? *The English Record, 35(3).*

Hartwell, P. (1985). Grammar, grammars, and the teaching of grammar. *College English, 47(2),* 105–27.

Hennings, D. (1981). Input: Enter the word processing computer. *Language Arts, 58,* 18–22.

Hennings, D. (1983). Words processed here: Write with your computer. *Phi Delta Kappan, 65,* 122–123.

Hummel, J. (1985). Word processing and word processing related software for the learning disabled. *Journal of Learning Disabilities, 18.*

Jarchow, E. (1984). Computers and composing: The pros and cons. *Electronic Education, 3(8),* p. 38.

Kulik, J. (1983). A synthesis of the research on computer-based education. *Educational Leadership, 41,* 19–21.

Meckel, H. (1963). Research on teaching composition and literature. In N. L. Gage (ed.). *Handbook of research on teaching.* Chicago: Rand McNally and Company.

Moffet, J. (1968). *A student centered language arts curriculum: Grades K–13,* Boston, MA: Houghton Mifflin.

Moran, C. (1983). Word processing and the teaching of writing. *English Journal, 72(2).*

O'Brien, P. (1984). Using microcomputers in the writing class. *The Computing Teacher, 11(9),* 20–21.

Palmer, A., Dowd, T., & James, K. (1984). Changing teacher and student attitudes through word processing. *The Computing Teacher, 11(9),* 45–47.

Papert, S. (1980). *Mindstorms.* New York: Basic Books.

Phenix, J., & Hannan, E. (1984). Word processing in the grade one classroom. *Language Arts, 61(8),* 804–812.

Piper, K. (1984). The electronic writing machine: Using word processors with students. *The Computing Teacher, 11(10),* 82–83.

Rodrigues, D. (1985). Computers and basic writers. *College Composition and Computers, 36,* 336–339.

Rose, M. (1983). Remedial writing courses: A critique and a proposal. *College English, 45(2)*.

Schrantz, L. (1983). The computer as tutor, tool, and tutee in composition. *The Computing Teacher*, October, 60–62.

Schwartz, H. (1984). Computers and the teaching of writing. *Educational Technology*, November, 27–29.

Sharples, M. (1983). The use of computers to aid the teaching of writing. *AEDS Journal, 16*, 79–91.

Shostak, R. (1984). Computer-assisted composition instruction: The state of the art. In R. Shostak (Ed.), *Computers in composition instruction*. Eugene, OR: ICCE Publications.

Smith, N. J. (1985). The word processing approach to language experience. *Reading Teacher, 38*, 556–559.

Taylor, R. (1980). *The computer in the schools: Tutor, tool, tutee*. New York: Columbia University Press.

Vacc, N. N. (1984). Computers in language arts: Potential benefits and problems. *Journal of Educational Technology Systems, 13*, 15–21.

Wheeler, F. (1985). Can word processing help the writing process? *Learning*, March, 54–62.

Willer, A. (1984). Creative writing with computers: What do elementary students have to say? *Computers, Reading and Language Arts, 2(1)*, 39–42.

Woodruff, E. (1984). Computers and the composing process: An examination of computer-writer interaction. In R. Shostak (Ed.). *Computers in composition instruction*. Eugene, OR: ICCE Publications.

Wresch, W. (1984). Writers' helper: A system approach to computer-assisted writing. In R. Shostak (Ed.), *Computers in composition instruction*. Eugene, OR: ICCE Publications.

Analysis of the Study

PURPOSE/JUSTIFICATION

The purpose of this study is made clear in the title—to study the effects on written composition of using a word processor. Justification rests on the assertion that despite the many advocates of this method, few studies have been done to evaluate outcomes. The authors might have strengthened their justification by reviewing the widespread concern over the poor quality of writing evidenced by high school graduates—thus the need for more effective instruction.

PRIOR RESEARCH

The authors cite several references to support their contention that word processing has potential for improving writing skills. They re-view the controversy over wholistic versus reductive teaching methods and conclude that the wholistic method—of which word processing is one aspect—is generally superior. They state that few studies of outcomes using word processing have been done and these (apparently) have been limited to attitudinal outcomes, which are summarized. Our only uneasiness is that the authors have not specifically discussed the concerns about the use of word processing that are referenced. They imply that these concerns have to do with the reductive versus wholistic approaches, but this is not made clear. We are left wondering what other "concerns" have been voiced.

DEFINITIONS

Specific definitions, as such, are not provided, although we believe they should be. Key terms are, however, made relatively clear in context. Both the word processing method and the comparison method (the "conventional writing program") are described in sufficient detail. We believe that the essential distinction between the two methods has been made clear.

What is meant by "writing skills" or "composition skills" is clarified as part of an operational definition—that is, three expert judges graded each essay according to five criteria: structure and organization and correct usage of the parts of speech, punctuation, capitalization, and spelling. All but the first of these are straightforward; it is not clear to us what is meant by the term "structure and organization." Does this mean only that proper sentences are adequately sequenced into paragraphs, or does it also include, for example, such features as overall coherence and consistency of argument? This matter is particularly important since at least some wholistic scoring systems stress such qualities more than grammar.

HYPOTHESES

Although not specifically stated, the clearly implied hypothesis is that a difference would be found between methods. It also seems likely from previous studies and the method of data analysis used that a difference was anticipated between initial writing levels (high or low) and (less clearly) that an interaction between method and initial writing level was expected. If so, we think these hypotheses should be stated directly.

SAMPLE

As is customary (unfortunately), a convenience sample was used. The only information we are given about the sample is that the students were all seventh graders in remedial language arts courses and that many had "average to above average skills in related content areas, such as mathematics and science." This is, clearly, too little information to permit any sort of generalization. Further, it is stated that the students were "drawn from" four classes, implying some basis for selection, but we are not told what the

basis was. Finally, the sample size is not 80, as is stated, but rather 64. The sample is the group on whom data are collected and for whom comparisons are made.

INSTRUMENTATION

A one- to two-page essay on a common topic was obtained for each student and independently scored by three "experts." The three scores were averaged to obtain the final score. We are not told whether each essay was scored separately for each of the five criteria, or whether one overall score was given by each scorer, although the latter is implied. Nor are we informed as to how the scorers qualified as experts. With such scoring methods it is usually necessary for the scorers to receive some kind of training.

We also are not given any information as to scoring agreement, an important aspect of reliability. No evidence is provided on either equivalent-forms reliability or stability; the former would require obtaining a second essay for all (or at least some) of the students; the latter would require a time interval between essays. Both of these seem feasible possibilities to us. While it is true that the finding of differences between groups is indicative of some degree of reliability (since completely unreliable instruments would not be expected to show systematic group differences), the study would be greatly strengthened by evidence that "writing skills," as measured, showed consistency over time and over essays. In the absence of such evidence, it is quite possible that a different essay topic could result in very different findings.

The authors appear to take the validity of their essay scores at face value. Credibility would have been strengthened by a clearer definition of writing skills; by information on the selection and/or training of scorers; by a clearer description of scoring procedures; and by demonstration of good scoring agreement between the scorers. With the information provided, it is possible to argue that the essay scores primarily measure grammatical correctness—a definition of writing skill that many would find unacceptable. There is a considerable literature pertaining to these issues, but the authors make no reference to it.

PROCEDURES/INTERNAL VALIDITY

The design of the study, as described by the authors, is clear-cut. The students were divided into two groups according to their CTBS language scores and half of each of these groups were then assigned to either the word processing or the conventional method. Although not specifically stated, we assume the assignment to method was done randomly; if not, the study is highly suspect. What is not clear is how the methods were made to fit into daily classroom activities. The eighty original students were drawn from four remedial classes. Presumably each class had approximately equal numbers receiving each method. Did the word processing group go to the two laboratories from their regular classes, as is implied? More details on such matters would greatly strengthen this report.

With regard to threats to internal validity, subject characteristics were presumably controlled through random assignment to methods, though less confidence can be placed in this method when interactions are examined (since the number of students participating in each method was reduced to sixteen). Loss of subjects did occur when the original sample of eighty was reduced to sixty-four for data analysis. Since it is unlikely that exactly four were lost per cell (see Table 1 in the report), readers should be told how many were lost and how many were deleted (presumably randomly). A location threat should not exist, provided that word processor use was the only resource provided in the computer lab—as seems likely (although the distraction of noise level could have been a location factor). The authors were evidently aware of a possible data scoring threat—hence their reference to "blind" scoring, which we take to mean that the scorers could not identify the group from which an essay came. While this might not hold for ability groups (since handwriting might identify the poorer students), comparison of ability groups was not crucial to this study.

No information is given pertinent to a data collection or data collector threat. If essays were administered by one of the researchers or by classroom teachers to total classes containing all experimental groups, the occurrence of this threat seems unlikely. Instrument decay is not a threat with a one-time only instrument. Testing was not a threat in this study since there was no pre-post comparison and because the periodic ("pre") essay writing was (a) common to both method groups and (b) an intrinsic part of both methods. An implementer effect seems unlikely since each teacher taught both methods groups two days a week and the word processing presumably had little, if anything, to do with an implementer. We assume that supervision was limited to the mechanics of computer use.

Maturation should not have influenced results since it was presumably the same for both groups. Similarly, it seems unlikely that history (extraneous events) would have constituted a threat since it is unlikely that one method group would systematically have received more "help" in learning such specific skills. An attitudinal (Hawthorne effect) threat does seem quite likely, however, since all students must have been aware of the special treatment afforded to half of each class for an entire school year. This threat seems particularly troublesome given the interests in computer usage shown by many students at this age. Although the students were all in remedial classes, regression should not have affected this study since students were not selected on the basis of a pretest of writing ability.

DATA ANALYSIS

A comparison of means of the four treatment groups is probably the appropriate method of examining differences, although some assurance that extreme cases were not present is desirable. Standard deviations were also reported, thereby permitting calculation of effect sizes, which we would recommend. The calculation of significance tests (ANOVA) is perhaps appropriate as a way of determining whether differences were attributable to method or to the initial inequality of groups, but they are not justifiable as indices of generalizability since random samples were not used.

RESULTS

We agree with the results presented. The difference in means for the low group (based on prior CTBS scores) is substantial. It yields an effect size of nearly 1.00 (74.3 − 67.9 ÷ 7.7 = .83) in favor of the word processing method. The difference in means for the high group is minimal, yielding an effect size of .10. The overall difference in means yields an effect size of approximately .30, but this is less informative than the results previously mentioned for the low group.

DISCUSSION

The beginning discussion follows clearly from the results; use of the word processor appeared to have value for students having the most difficulty in writing. It should be noted, however, that the low ability group was defined by scores on the CTBS language subtests—a debatable measure of writing ability since the tests do not require writing as such. The conclusion that word processing improves the revision process seems appropriate since that is primarily how the word processor was used. The conclusion that the revision process is made easier and more tolerable for poorer students seems sensible, but it is supported *not* by the data, but by logic and by previously unmentioned teacher reports and student interviews. Such data must be viewed with considerable caution.

The authors give several possible explanations for the lack of impact of word processing on the more able students.* These include lack of typing skill, insufficient access to the computer, and neglect of preplanning. We do not find these explanations persuasive, since there is no evidence that they impacted the better students more than the poorer; just the reverse would be expected, in fact. These problems do illustrate the difficulties faced by researchers when trying to control the nature of experimental treatments. We agree that the nature of the outcome measure, requiring handwritten essays, may have penalized the word processing group, but this is a matter of desired outcome. If the outcome desired is the ability to produce handwritten material, then the measure is appropriate; if the outcome desired is an essay produced in any fashion, then the word processing group should have been allowed to prepare their essay using the computer. In any case, we do not see why this disadvantage should be greater for the more able group.

Finally, we are concerned to find no recognition of the severe limitations on generalization imposed by the use of a convenience sample. Although the authors do not specifically recommend such overgeneralization, neither do they warn against it. The nature of their recommendations, in fact, suggests that effectiveness has been demonstrated.

* The term "more able" must be considered in the context that *all* of the subjects in this study were identified as needing remedial help in language.

Main Points of Chapter Twelve

- Experimental research is unique in that it is the only type of research that directly attempts to influence a particular variable, and it is the only type that can really test hypotheses about cause-and-effect relationships. Experimental designs are some of the strongest available for educational researchers to use in determining cause and effect.
- Experiments differ from other types of research in two basic ways—comparison of treatments and the direct manipulation of one or more independent variables by the researcher.
- Random assignment is an important ingredient in the best kinds of experiments. It means that every individual who is participating in the experiment has an equal chance of being assigned to any of the experimental or control conditions that are being compared.
- The researcher in an experimental study has an opportunity to exercise far more control than in most other forms of research.

- Some of the most common ways to control for the possibility of differential subject characteristics (in the various groups being compared) include randomization, holding certain variables constant, building the variable into the design, matching, using subjects as their own controls, and the statistical technique of ANCOVA.
- Three weak designs that are occasionally used in experimental research are the one-shot case study design, the one-group pretest-posttest design, and the static-group design. They are considered weak because they do not have built-in controls for threats to internal validity.
- In a one-shot case study, a single group is exposed to a treatment or event, and its effects assessed.
- In the one-group pretest-posttest design, a single group is measured or observed both before and after exposure to a treatment.
- In the static-group comparison design, two intact groups receive different treatments.
- Several stronger designs that are more commonly used include true experimental designs, matching designs, counterbalanced designs, time-series designs, and factorial designs. These designs do have at least some controls built into the design to control for threats to internal validity.
- The randomized posttest-only control group design involves two groups formed by random assignment and receiving different treatments.
- The randomized pretest-posttest control group design differs from the posttest-only control group only in the use of a pretest.
- The randomized Solomon four-group design involves random assignment of subjects to four groups, with two being pretested and two not.
- To increase the likelihood that groups of subjects will be equivalent, pairs of subjects may be matched on certain variables. The members of the matched groups are then assigned to the experimental and control groups.
- In a counterbalanced design, all groups are exposed to all treatments, but in a different order.
- A time-series design involves repeated measurements or observations over time, both before and after treatment.
- Factorial designs extend the number of relationships that may be examined in an experimental study.
- Single-subject designs involve extensive collection of data on one subject at a time.
- Two commonly used single-subject designs include the A-B-A-B and multiple-baseline designs
- It is very important to replicate single-subject designs.

For Discussion

1. An occasional criticism of experimental research is that it is very difficult to conduct in schools. Would you agree? Why or why not?

2. Are there any cause-and-effect statements you can make that you believe would be true in most schools? Would you say, for example, that a

sympathetic teacher "causes" elementary school students to like school more?

3. Are there any advantages to having more than one independent variable in an experimental design? If so, what are they? What about more than one dependent variable?

4. What designs could be used in each of the following studies? (Note: More than one design is possible in each instance.)
   a. A comparison of two different ways of teaching spelling to first graders.
   b. The effectiveness of weekly tutoring sessions on the reading ability of third graders.
   c. A comparison of a third period high school English class taught by the discussion method with a third period (same high school) English class taught by the lecture method.
   d. The effectiveness of reinforcement on decreasing stuttering in a student with this speech defect.
   e. The effects of a year long weight-training program on a group of high school athletes.
   f. The possible effects of age, gender, and method on student liking for history.

5. What flaw can you find in each of the following studies?
   a. A teacher tries out a new mathematics textbook with her class for a semester. At the end of the semester, she reports that the interest of the class in mathematics is markedly higher than she has ever seen it in the past with other classes using another text.
   b. A teacher divides his class into two subgroups, with each subgroup being taught spelling by a different method. Each group listens to the teacher instruct the other group while they wait their turn.
   c. A researcher calls for eighth grade students to volunteer to tutor third grade students who are having difficulty in reading. She gives those who volunteer a pretest designed to measure their "willingness to be a tutor." She compares their effectiveness as tutors with a control group not given the pretest. They have a much higher mean effectiveness score.
   d. A teacher decides to try out a new textbook in one of her social studies classes. She uses it for four weeks and then compares the scores on a unit test of this class with the scores of her previous classes. All classes are studying the same material. During the unit test, however, a fire drill occurs, and the class loses about ten minutes of the time allotted for the test.
   e. Two groups of third graders are compared with regard to running ability, subsequent to different training schedules. One group is tested during physical education class in the school gymnasium, while the other is tested after school on the football field.
   f. A researcher compares a third-period English class with a fifth-period chemistry class in terms of student interest in the subject taught. The English class is taught by the discussion method, while the chemistry class is taught by the lecture method.

Notes

1. Carl A. Benware and Edward L. Deci. (1984). *American Educational Research Journal,* 21(4):755–766.

2. Roger T. Johnson, David W. Johnson, & Mary Beth Stanne. (1986). *American Educational Research Journal,* 23(3):382–392.

3. James S. Catteralll. (1987). *American Educational Research Journal,* 24(4):521–540.

4. Alison G. Gilmore & C. Warren McKinney. (1986). *Theory and Research in Social Education,* 14(3):225–244.

5. J. David Hawkins, Howard J. Doueck, & Denise M. Lishner. (1988). *American Educational Research Journal,* 25(1):31–50.

6. Joel R. Levin, Christine B. McCormick, Gloria E. Miller, Jill K. Berry & Michael Pressley. (1982). *American Educational Research Journal,* 19(1):121–136.

7. Bruce W. Tuckman. (1988). *Conducting educational research* (3rd ed.) New York: Harcourt Brace Jovanovich. p. 146.

Research Exercise Twelve: Experimental Research

You should complete Problem Sheet 12 only if you are planning an experimental study. If your intended study involves a different methodology, you will find a similar problem sheet at the end of the chapter that deals with that methodology. You might wish to consider, however, whether your research question could be investigated by means of an experiment.

Using Problem Sheet 12, once again state the question or hypothesis of your study. Then describe, briefly but thoroughly, the procedures of your study, including analysis of results—that is, *what* you intend to do, *when, where,* and *how.* Lastly, indicate any unresolved problems you see at this point in your planning.

PROBLEM SHEET **12**
Experimental Research

1. The question or hypothesis of my study is: _____

_____

_____

2. A brief summary of *what* I intend to do, *when, where,* and *how* is as follows:

_____

_____

_____

_____

_____

_____

_____

_____

_____

3. The experimental design I intend to use is the: _____

_____

_____

_____

4. The major problems I foresee at this point include the following: _____

_____

_____

_____

_____

_____

_____

273

Chapter Thirteen

CORRELATIONAL RESEARCH

Correlational research attempts to investigate possible relationships among variables without trying to influence those variables. Although correlational studies cannot determine the causes of relationships, they can suggest them. These suggestions often provide the impetus for future experimental studies. In this chapter, we discuss the nature of correlational research, provide several examples of correlational studies, and describe some of the problems involved in conducting such research.

Objectives

Reading this chapter should enable you to:

- *Describe* briefly what is meant by associational research
- *State* the two major purposes of correlational studies
- *Distinguish* between predictor and criterion variables
- *Explain* the role of correlational studies in exploring causation
- *Explain* how a scatterplot can be used to predict an outcome
- *Describe* what is meant by a prediction equation
- *Explain* briefly the ideas underlying multiple correlation, factor analysis, and path analysis
- *Identify* and *describe* briefly the steps involved in conducting a correlational study
- *Interpret* correlation coefficients of different magnitude
- *Explain* the rationale underlying partial correlation
- *Describe* some of the threats to internal validity that exist in correlation studies and *explain* how to identify them
- *Discuss* how to control for these threats
- *Recognize* a correlation study when you come across one in the educational research literature

---

The Nature of Correlational Research

Correlational research, like causal-comparative research (which we discuss in Chapter Fourteen), is an example of what is sometimes called *associational research*. In associational research, the relationships among two or more variables are studied without any attempt to influence them. In their simplest form, correlational studies investigate the possibility of relationships between only two variables, although investigations of more than two variables are common. In contrast to experimental research, however, there is no manipulation of variables in correlational research.

Correlational research is also sometimes referred to as a form of descriptive research because it describes an existing relationship between variables. The way it describes this relationship, however, is quite different from the descriptions found in other types of studies. A correlational study describes the degree to which two or more quantitative variables are related, and it does so by use of a correlation coefficient.*

When a correlation is found to exist between two variables, it means that scores within a certain range on the one variable are associated with scores within a certain range on the other variable. You will recall that a positive correlation means high scores on the one variable tend to be associated with high scores on the other variable, while low scores on the one are associated with low scores on the other. A negative correlation, on the other hand, means high scores on the one variable are associated with low scores on the other variable, and low scores on the one are associated with high scores on the other (Table 13.1). As we also have indicated before, relationships like those shown in Table 13.1 can be illustrated graphically through the use of

---

* Although associations among two or more categorical variables can also be studied; such studies are not usually referred to as correlational. They are similar with respect to overall design and threats to internal validity, however, and we discuss them further in Chapter Fourteen.

TABLE 13.1

Three Sets of Data Showing Different Directions and Degrees of Correation

(A)r = +1.00		(B)r = −1.00		(C)r = 0	
X	Y	X	Y	X	Y
5	5	5	1	2	1
4	4	4	2	5	2
3	3	3	3	3	3
2	2	2	4	1	4
1	1	1	5	4	5

scatterplots. Figure 13.1, for example, illustrates the relationship shown in (A) of Table 13.1.

Purposes of Correlational Research

Correlational research is carried out for one of two basic purposes—either to help explain important human behaviors or to predict likely outcomes.

FIGURE 13.1

Scatterplot Illustrating a Correlation of +1.00

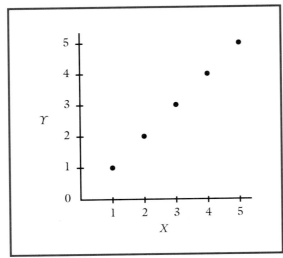

EXPLANATORY STUDIES

A major purpose of correlational research is to clarify our understanding of important phenomena through the identification of relationships among variables. Particularly in developmental psychology where experimental studies are especially difficult to design, much has been learned by analyzing relationships among several variables. For example, correlations found between variables such as complexity of parent speech and rate of language acquisition have taught researchers much about how language is acquired. Similarly, the discovery that, among variables related to reading skill, auditory memory shows a substantial correlation has expanded our understanding of the complex phenomenon of reading. The current belief that smoking causes lung cancer, although based in part on experimental studies of animals, rests heavily on correlational evidence of the relationship between amount of smoking and the incidence of lung cancer.

Researchers who conduct explanatory studies often investigate a number of variables they believe are related to a more complex variable, such as motivation or learning. Variables found not to be related or only slightly related (i.e., when correlations below .20 are obtained) are then dropped from further consideration, while those found to be more highly related (i.e., when correlations beyond +.40 or −.40 are obtained) often serve as the focus of additional research, using an experimental design, to see if the relationships are causal.

Let us say a bit more here about causation. Although the discovery of a correlational relationship does not establish a causal connection, most researchers who engage in correlational research are probably trying to gain some idea about cause and effect. A researcher who carried out the fictitious study whose results are illustrated in Figure 13.2, for example, would probably be inclined to hypothesize that a teacher's expectation of failure is a partial (or at least a contributing) cause of the amount of disruptive behavior his or her students display in class.

It must be stressed, however, that correlational studies *do not*, in and of themselves, establish cause and effect. In the previous example, one could just as well argue that the amount of disruptive behavior in a class would cause a teacher's expectation of failure, or that *both* teacher expectation and disruptive behavior were caused by some third factor—such as the ability level of the class.

The possibility of causation is strengthened, however, if a time lapse occurs between measurement of the variables being studied. If the teachers' expectation of failure was measured before assigning students to classes, for example, it would seem unreasonable to assume that class behavior (or, likewise, the ability level of the class) would cause their failure expectations. The reverse, in fact, would make more sense. Certain other causal explanations, however, remain persuasive, such as the socioeconomic level of the classes involved. Teachers might have higher expectations of failure for economically poor students. Such students also might exhibit a greater amount of disruptive behavior in class regardless of their teacher's expectations. The search for cause and effect in correlational studies, therefore, is fraught with difficulty. Nonetheless, it can be a fruitful source of causal hypotheses to be tested experimentally.

PREDICTION STUDIES

A second purpose of correlational research is that of **prediction:** If a relationship of sufficient magnitude exists between two variables, it becomes possible to predict a score on either variable if a score on the other variable is known. Researchers have found, for example, that high school grades are highly related to college grades. Hence, high school grades can be used to predict college grades. We would predict that a person who has a high GPA in high school would be likely to have a high GPA in college. The variable that is used to make the prediction is called the **predictor variable**; the variable about which the prediction is made is called the **criterion variable.** Hence, in the above example, high school grades would be the predictor variable, and college grades would be the criterion variable. As we mentioned in Chapter Seven, prediction

TABLE **13.2**

Teacher Expectation of Failure and Amount of Disruptive Behavior Scores for a Sample of Twelve Classes

Class	Teacher Expectation of Failure (Ratings)	Amount of Disruptive Behavior (Ratings)
1	10	11
2	4	3
3	2	2
4	4	6
5	12	10
6	9	6
7	8	9
8	8	6
9	6	8
10	5	5
11	5	9
12	7	4

studies are also used to determine the predictive validity of measuring instruments.

Using Scatterplots to Predict a Score.   Prediction can be illustrated through the use of scatterplots. Suppose, for example, that we obtain the data shown in Table 13.2 from a sample of twelve classes. Using these data, we find a correlation of .71 between the variables "teacher expectation of failure" and "amount of disruptive behavior."

Plotting the data in Table 13.2 produces the scatterplot shown in Figure 13.2. Once a scatterplot such as this has been constructed, a straight line, known as a "regression" line, can be calculated mathematically. The calculation of this line is beyond the scope of this text, but a general understanding of its use can be obtained by looking at Figure 13.2. The regression line comes the closest to all of the scores depicted on the scatterplot of any straight line that could be drawn. A researcher can then use the line as a basis for prediction. Thus, as you can see, a teacher with an "expectation of failure" score of 10 would be predicted to have a class with an

FIGURE 13.2

Prediction Using a Scatterplot

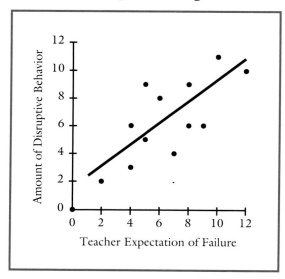

"amount of disruptive behavior" score of 8, and a teacher with an expectation score of 6 would be predicted to have a class with a "disruptive behavior" score of 6. Similarly, a second regression line can be drawn to predict a "teacher expectation of failure" score if we know his or her class's "amount of disruptive behavior" score.

Being able to predict a score for an individual (or group) on one variable from knowing the individual's (or group's) score on another variable is extremely useful. A school administrator, for example, could use Figure 13.2 (if it were based on real data) to (a) identify and select teachers who are likely to have less disruptive classes, (b) provide training to those teachers who are predicted to have a large amount of disruptive behavior in their classes, or (c) plan for additional assistance for such teachers. Both the teachers and students involved should benefit accordingly.

A Simple Prediction Equation. Although the drawing of scatterplots is a fairly easy device to use in making predictions, it is inefficient when pairs of scores from a large number of

individuals have been collected. Fortunately, the regression line we described above can be expressed in the form of a *prediction equation*, which has the following form:

$$Y_i' = a + bX_i$$

where Y_i' = the predicted score on Y (the criterion variable) for individual i, X_i = individual i's score on X (the predictor variable), and a, b = values calculated mathematically from the original scores. For any given set of data, a and b are constants.

We mentioned earlier that high school GPA has been found to be highly related to college GPA. In this example, therefore, the symbol Y' stands for the predicted first semester college GPA (the criterion variable), and X stands for the individual's high school GPA (the predictor variable). Let us assume that $a = .18$ and $b = .73$. By substituting in the equation, we can predict a student's first semester college GPA. Thus, if an individual's high school GPA is 3.5, we would predict that his or her first semester college GPA would be 2.735 (that is, .18 + .73 × 3.5 = 2.735). We later can compare the student's actual first semester college GPA to the predicted GPA. If there is a close similarity between the two, we gain confidence in using the prediction equation to make future predictions.

This predicted score will not be exact, however, and hence researchers also calculate an index of prediction error, known as the *standard error of estimate*. This index gives an estimate of the degree to which the predicted score is likely to be incorrect. The smaller the standard error of estimate, the more accurate the prediction. This index of error, as you would expect, is much larger for small values of r than for large r's.*

Furthermore, if we have more information on the individuals about whom we wish to predict, we should be able to decrease our errors of prediction. This is what a technique known

---

* If the reason for this is unclear to you, refer again to the scatterplots in Figure 8.16.

as multiple regression (or multiple correlation) is designed to do.

MORE COMPLEX CORRELATIONAL TECHNIQUES

Multiple Regression   **Multiple regression** is a technique that enables researchers to determine a correlation between a criterion variable and the best combination of *two or more* predictor variables. Let us return to our previous example involving the high positive correlation that has been found to exist between high school GPA and first semester college GPA. Suppose it is also found that a high positive correlation ($r = +.68$) exists between first semester college GPA and the verbal scores on the Scholastic Aptitude Test (SAT) of the College Entrance Examination, and a moderately high positive correlation ($r = +.51$) exists between the mathematics scores on the SAT and first semester college GPA. It is possible, using a multiple regression prediction formula, to use *all three* of these variables to predict what a student's GPA will be during his or her first semester in college. The formula is similar to the simple prediction equation, except that it now includes more than one predictor variable and more than two constants. It takes the following form:

$$Y' = a + b_1X_1 + b_2X_2 + b_3X_3 \ldots$$

where Y' once again stands for the predicted first semester college GPA, a and b are constants, X_1 = the high school GPA, X_2 = the verbal SAT score, and X_3 = the mathematics SAT score. Let us imagine that $a = .18$, $b_1 = .73$, $b_2 = .0005$, and $b_3 = .0002$. We know that the student's high school GPA is 3.5. Suppose his or her SAT verbal and mathematics scores are 580 and 600, respectively. Substituting in the formula, we would predict that the student's first semester GPA would be 3.15.

$$Y' = .18 + .73(3.5) + .0005(580)$$
$$+ .0002(600)$$
$$= .18 + 2.56 + .29 + .12 = 3.15$$

Again, we could later compare the actual first semester college GPA obtained by this student with the predicted score to determine how accurate our prediction was.

The Coefficient of Multiple Correlation. The coefficient of multiple correlation, symbolized by R, indicates the strength of the correlation between the combination of the predictor variables and the criterion variable. It can be thought of as a simple Pearson correlation between the actual scores on the criterion variable and the predicted scores on that variable. In the previous example, we used a combination of high school GPA, SAT verbal score, and SAT mathematics score to predict that a particular student's first semester college GPA would be 3.15. We then could obtain that same student's *actual* first semester college GPA (it might be 2.95, for example). If we did this for 100 students, we could then calculate the correlation (R) between predicted and actual GPA. If R turned out to be $+1.00$, for example, it would mean that the predicted scores correlate perfectly with the actual scores on the criterion variable. An R of $+1.00$, of course, would be very unlikely to obtain. In actual practice, Rs of .70 or .80 are considered quite high. The higher R is, of course, the more reliable a prediction will be.

The Coefficient of Determination. The square of the correlation between one predictor variable and a criterion variable is known as the *coefficient of determination*, symbolized by r^2. If the correlation between high school GPA and college GPA, for example, equals .70, then the coefficient of determination would equal .49. What does this mean? In short, the coefficient of determination indicates the percentage of the variability among the criterion scores that can be attributed to differences in the scores on the predictor variable. Thus, if the correlation between high school GPA and college GPA for a group of students is .70, 49 percent ($.70^2$) of the differences in the college GPA's of those students can be attributed to differences in their high school GPAs.

The interpretation of R^2 (for multiple regression) is similar to that of r^2 (for simple regression). Suppose in our example that used three predictor variables, the multiple correlation coefficient is equal to .78. The coefficient of determination, then, is equal to $(.78)^2$, or .61. Thus, it would be appropriate to say that 61 percent of the variability in the criterion variable is predictable on the basis of the three predictor variables. Another way of saying this is that high school GPA, verbal SAT scores, and mathematics SAT scores (the three predictor variables), taken together, account for about 61 percent of the variability in college GPA (the criterion variable).

The value of a prediction equation depends on whether it can be used with a *new* group of individuals. Researchers can never be sure the prediction equation they developed will work successfully when it is used to predict criterion scores for a new group of persons. In fact, it is quite likely that it will be less accurate when so used, since the new group is not identical to the one used to develop the prediction equation. The success of a particular prediction equation with a new group, therefore, usually depends on the group's similarity to the group used to develop the prediction equation originally.

Discriminant Function Analysis.   In most prediction studies, the criterion variable is quantitative—that is, it involves scores that can fall anywhere along a continuum from low to high. Our previous example of college GPA is a quantitative variable, for scores on the variable can fall anywhere at or between 0.00 and 4.00. Sometimes, however, the criterion variable may be a categorical variable, that is, it involves membership in a group (or category) rather than scores along a continuum. For example, a researcher might be interested in predicting whether an individual is more like engineering majors or business majors. In this instance, the criterion variable is dichotomous—an individual is either in one group or the other. Of course, a categorical variable can have more than just two categories (for example, engineering majors, business majors, education majors, science majors, and so on). The technique of multiple regression cannot be used when the criterion variable is categorical; instead, a technique known as **discriminant function analysis** is used. The purpose of the analysis and the form of the prediction equation, however, is similar to multiple regression.

Factor Analysis.   When a number of variables are investigated in a single study, analysis and interpretation of data can become rather cumbersome. It is often desirable, therefore, to reduce the number of variables by grouping those which are moderately or highly correlated with one another into factors.

Factor analysis is a technique that allows a researcher to determine if many variables can be described by a few factors. The mathematical calculations involved are beyond the scope of this book, but the technique essentially involves a search for "clusters" of variables, all of which are correlated with each other. Each cluster represents a factor. Studies of group IQ tests, for example, have suggested that the many specific scores used could be explained as a result of a relatively small number of factors. While controversial, these results did provide one means of comprehending the mental abilities required to perform well on such tests. They also led to new tests designed to test these identified abilities more effectively.

Path Analysis.   **Path analysis** is used to test the possibility of a causal connection among three or more variables. Some of the other techniques we have described can be used to explore theories about causality, but path analysis is far more powerful than the rest. Although a detailed explanation of this technique is too technical for inclusion here, the essential idea behind path analysis is to formulate a theory about the possible causes of a particular phenomenon (such as student alienation)—that is, to identify causal variables that could explain why the phenomenon occurs—and then to determine whether correlations among all the variables are consistent with the theory.

Suppose a researcher theorizes as follows: (1) certain students are more alienated in school than others because they do not find school enjoyable and because they have few friends; (2) they do not find school enjoyable partly because they have few friends and partly because they do not perceive their courses as being in any way related to their needs; and (3) perceived relevance of courses is related slightly to number of friends. The researcher would then measure each of these variables ("degree of alienation," "personal relevance of courses," "enjoyment in school," and "number of friends") for a number of students. Correlations between pairs of each of the variables would then be calculated. Let us imagine that the researcher obtains the correlations shown in the correlation matrix in Table 13.3.

What does this table reveal about possible causes of student alienation? Two of the variables (relevance of courses at $-.48$ and school enjoyment at $-.53$) shown in the table are sizable predictors of such alienation. Nevertheless, to remind you again, just because these variables predict student alienation does not mean that they cause it. Furthermore, something of a problem exists in the fact that the two predictor variables correlate with *each other*. As you can see, school enjoyment and perceived relevance of courses not only predict student alienation, but they also correlate highly with each other ($r = .65$). Now, does perceived relevance of courses affect student alienation independently of school enjoyment? Does school enjoyment affect student alienation independently of perception of course relevance? Path analysis can help the researcher determine the answers to these questions.

Path analysis, then, involves four basic steps. First, a theory that links several variables is formulated to explain a particular phenomenon of interest. In our example, the researcher theorized the following causal connections: "When students perceive their courses as being unrelated to their needs, they will not enjoy school. Secondly, if they have few friends in school, this will contribute to their lack of enjoyment. And the more a student dislikes school, and the fewer friends he or she has, the more alienated he or she will be." Second, the variables specified by

TABLE 13.3
Correlation Matrix for Variables in Student Alienation Study

	School Enjoyment	Number of Friends	Alienation
Relevance of Courses	.65	.24	$-.48$
School Enjoyment		.58	$-.53$
Number of Friends			$-.27$

the theory are then measured in some way.* Third, correlation coefficients are computed to indicate the strength of the relationship between each of the pairs of variables postulated in the theory. And, fourth, relationships among the correlation coefficients are analyzed in relation to the theory.

Path analysis variables are typically shown in the type of diagram in Figure 13.3.† Each variable in the theory is shown in the figure. Each arrow indicates a hypothesized causal relationship in the direction of the arrow. Thus, liking for school is hypothesized to influence alienation; number of friends influences school enjoyment, and so on. Notice that all of the arrows point in one direction only. This means that the first variable is hypothesized to influence the second variable, but not vice-versa. Numbers similar (but not identical) to correlation coefficients are calculated for each pair of variables. If the results were as shown in Figure 13.3, the causal theory of the researcher would be supported. Do you see why?‡

* Note that this step is very important. The measures must be valid representations of the variables. The results of the path analysis will be invalid if this is not the case.
† The process of path analysis and the diagrams drawn are, in practice, often more complex than the one shown here.
‡ Because alienation is "caused" primarily by lack of enjoyment ($-.55$) and number of friends ($-.60$). The perceived lack of relevance of courses does contribute to degree of alienation, but primarily because relevance "causes" enjoyment. Enjoyment is partly caused by number of friends. Perceived relevance of courses is only slightly caused by number of friends.

FIGURE 13.3

Path Analysis Diagram

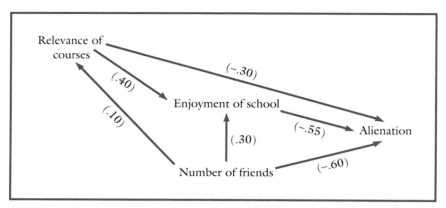

Basic Steps in Correlational Research

PROBLEM SELECTION

The variables to be included in a correlational study should be chosen based on a sound rationale growing out of experience or theory. The researcher should have some reason for thinking certain variables may be related. As always, clarity in defining variables will avoid many problems later on. In general, three major types of problems are the focus of correlational studies:

Is variable X related to variable Y?

How well does variable P predict variable C?

What are the relationships among a larger number of variables and what predictions can be made that are based on them?

Almost all correlational studies will revolve around one of these types of questions. Some examples of published correlational studies are as follows.

- The accuracy of principals' judgments of teacher performance[1]
- Teacher clarity and its relationship to student achievement and satisfaction[2]

- Factors associated with the drug use of fifth through eighth grade students[3]
- Moral development and empathy in counseling[4]
- The relationship among health beliefs, health values, and health promotion activity[5]
- The relationship of student ability and small-group interaction to student achievement[6]
- Predicting students' outcomes from their perceptions of classroom psychosocial environment[7]

SAMPLE

The sample for a correlational study, as in any type of study, should be selected carefully and, if possible, randomly. The first step in selecting a sample, of course, is to identify an appropriate population, one that is meaningful and from which data on *each* of the variables of interest can be collected. The minimum acceptable sample size for a correlational study is considered by most researchers to be no less than thirty. Data obtained from a sample smaller than thirty may give an inaccurate estimate of the degree of relationship that exists. Samples larger than thirty are much more likely to provide meaningful results.

INSTRUMENTS

The instruments used to measure the two (or more) variables involved in a correlational study may take any one of a number of forms (see Chapter Six), but they must yield quantitative data. Although data sometimes can be collected from records of one sort or another (grade transcripts, for example), most correlational studies involve the administration of some type of instrument (tests, questionnaires, and so on) and sometimes observation. As with any study, whatever instruments are used must yield reliable scores. In an explanatory study, the instruments must also show evidence of validity. If they do not truly measure the intended variables, then any correlation that is obtained will not be an indication of the intended relationship. In a prediction study, it is not essential that we know what variable is actually being measured—if it works as a predictor, it is useful. However, prediction studies are most likely to be successful, and certainly more satisfying, if we know what we are measuring!

DESIGN AND PROCEDURES

The basic design used in a correlational study is quite straightforward. Using the symbols introduced in our discussion of experimental designs in Chapter Twelve, this design can be diagrammed as shown below:

Design for a Correlational Study

Subjects	Observations	
	O_1	O_2
A	—	—
B	—	—
C	—	—
D	—	—
E	—	—
F	—	—
G	—	—
etc.		

As you can see, two (or more) scores are obtained from *each* individual in the sample, one score for each variable of interest. The pairs of scores are then correlated, and the resulting correlation coefficient indicates the degree of relationship between the variables.

Notice, again, that we cannot say that the variable being measured by the first instrument (O_1) is the cause of any differences in scores we may find in the variables being measured by the second instrument (O_2). As we have mentioned before, three possibilities exist:

1. The variable being measured by O_1 may cause the variable being measured by O_2.
2. The variable being measured by O_2 may cause the variable being measured by O_1.
3. Some third, perhaps unidentified and unmeasured, variable may cause *either* or *both* of the other variables.

Different numbers of variables can be investigated in correlational studies, and sometimes quite complex statistical procedures are used. The basic research design for all correlational studies, however, is similar to the one shown above. An example of data obtained from a correlational design is shown in Table 13.4.

DATA COLLECTION

In a relationship study, all the data on both variables will usually be collected within a fairly short time. Often, the instruments used are

TABLE 13.4

Example of Results from a Correlational Design

Student	(O_1) Self-Esteem	(O_2) Mathematics Achievement
José	25	95
Felix	23	88
Rosita	25	96
Phil	18	81
Jenny	12	65
Natty	23	73
Lina	22	92
Jill	15	71
Jack	24	93
James	17	78

administered in a single session, or in two sessions immediately after each other. Thus, if a researcher were interested in measuring the relationship between verbal aptitude and memory, a test of verbal aptitude and another of memory would be administered closely together in time to the same group of subjects. In a prediction study, the measurement of the criterion variables often takes place sometime after the measurement of the predictor variables. If a researcher were interested in studying the predictive value of a mathematics aptitude test, the aptitude test might be administered just prior to the beginning of a course in mathematics. Success in the course (the criterion variable, as indicated by course grades) would then be measured at the end of the course.

DATA ANALYSIS AND INTERPRETATION

As we have mentioned previously, when variables are correlated, a correlation coefficient is produced. This coefficient will be a decimal, somewhere between 0.00 and − 1.00 or + 1.00. The closer the coefficient is to + 1.00 or − 1.00, the stronger the relationship is. If the sign is positive, the relationship is positive, indicating that high scores on the one variable tend to go with high scores on the other variable. If the sign is negative, the relationship is negative, indicating that high scores on the one variable tend to go with low scores on the other variable. Coefficients that are at or near .00 indicate no relationship exists between the variables involved.

What Do Correlation Coefficients Tell Us?

It is important to be able to interpret correlation coefficients sensibly since they appear so frequently in articles about education and educational research. Unfortunately, they are seldom accompanied by scatterplots, which usually help interpretation and understanding.

The meaning of a given correlation coefficient depends on how it is applied. Correlation coefficients below .35 show only a slight rela-

tionship between variables. Such relationships have almost no value in any predictive sense. (It may, of course, be important to know that certain variables are *not* related. Thus we would *expect* to find a very *low* correlation, for instance, between years of teaching experience and number of students failed.) Correlations between .40 and .60 are often found in educational research and may have theoretical or practical value, depending on the context. A correlation of at least .50 must be obtained before any crude predictions can be made about individuals. Even then such predictions are likely to be frequently in error. Only when a correlation of .65 or higher is obtained can individual predictions that are reasonably accurate for most purposes be made. Correlations over .85 indicate a close relationship between the variables correlated and are useful in predicting individual performance, but correlations this high are rarely obtained in educational research, except when indicating instrument reliability.

As we illustrated in Chapter Seven, correlation coefficients are also used to check the reliability and validity of scores obtained from tests and other instruments used in research; when so used, they are called reliability and validity coefficients. When used to check reliability of scores, the coefficient should be at least .70, hopefully higher; many tests achieve reliability coefficients of .90. The correlation between two different scorers, working independently, should be at least .90. When used to check validity of scores, the coefficient should be at least .50, and preferably higher.

Threats to Internal Validity in Correlational Research

Recall from Chapter Eleven that a major concern to researchers is that extraneous variables may "explain" any results that are obtained.* A

* It can be argued that this threat is irrelevant to the predictive use of correlational research. The argument is that one can predict even if the relationship is an artifact of other variables. Thus predictions of college achievement can be made from high school grades even if both are highly related to socioeconomic status. While we agree with the practical utility of such predictions we believe that research should seek to illuminate *meaningful* relationships.

somewhat similar concern applies to correlational studies.

A researcher who conducts a correlational study should always be alert to alternative explanations for relationships found in the data. What might account for any correlations that are reported as existing between two or more variables?

Some of the threats we discussed in Chapter Eleven do not usually apply to correlational studies. Implementer, history, maturation, attitude of subjects, and regression threats are not applicable since no intervention occurs. There are some threats, however, which do apply.

SUBJECT CHARACTERISTICS

Whenever two or more characteristics of individuals are correlated, there may be a possibility that yet *other* characteristics of these individuals may explain any relationships that are found. The other characteristics of subjects can be controlled through a statistical technique known as **partial correlation.** Let us illustrate the logic involved by using the example of the relationship between teachers' expectations of failure and the amount of disruptive behavior by students in their classes. This relationship is shown in scatterplot A (repeated from Figure 13.2) in Figure 13.4.

The researcher desires to control, or "get rid of," the variable of "ability level" for the classes involved, since it is logical to assume that it might be a cause of variation in the other two variables. In order to control for this variable, the researcher needs to measure the ability level of each class. She can then construct scatterplots B and C, as shown in Figure 13.4. Scatterplot B shows the correlation between amount of disruptive behavior and class ability level; scatterplot C shows the correlation between teacher expectation of failure and class ability level.

The researcher can now use scatterplot B to predict the "disruptive behavior" score for class 1, based on the ability score for class 1. In doing so, the researcher would be assuming that the regression line shown in scatterplot B correctly represents the relationship between these variables (class ability level and amount of dis-

ruptive behavior) in the data. Next, the researcher subtracts the *predicted* disruptive behavior score from the *actual* disruptive behavior score. The result is called the adjusted disruptive behavior score—that is, the score has been "adjusted" by taking out the influence of ability level. For class 1, the predicted disruptive behavior score is 7 (based on a class ability score of 5). In actuality this class scored 11 (higher than expected), so the adjusted score for amount of disruptive behavior is $+4$ ($11 - 7$).

The same procedure is then followed to adjust teacher expectation scores for class ability level, as shown in scatterplot C ($10 - 7 = 3$). After repeating this process for the entire sample of classes, the researcher is now in a position to determine the correlation between the *adjusted* disruptive behavior scores and the *adjusted* teacher expectation scores. The result is the correlation between the two major variables with the effect of class ability eliminated, and thus controlled. Methods of calculation are available that greatly simplify this procedure.[8]

LOCATION

A location threat is possible whenever all instruments are administered to each subject at a specified location, but the location is different for different subjects. It is not uncommon for researchers to encounter differences in testing conditions, particularly when individual tests are required. In one school, a comfortable, well-lit, and ventilated room may be available. In another, a custodian's closet may have to do. Such conditions can increase (or decrease) subject scores. If both measures are not administered to all subjects under the same conditions, the conditions rather than the variables being studied may account for the relationship. If only part of a group, for example, respond to instruments in an uncomfortable, poorly lit room, they might score lower on an achievement test and respond more negatively to a rating scale measuring student "liking for school," thus producing a misleading correlation coefficient.

Similarly, conditions in different schools may account for observed relationships. A high negative correlation between amount of disrup-

FIGURE 13.4

Scatterplots for Combinations of Variables

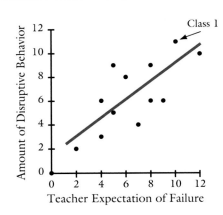

(A)
Amount of Disruptive Behavior in Class as Related to Teacher Expectation of Failure

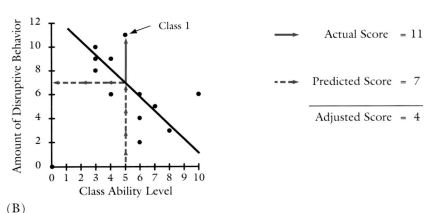

(B)
Amount of Disruptive Behavior as Related to Ability Level of Class

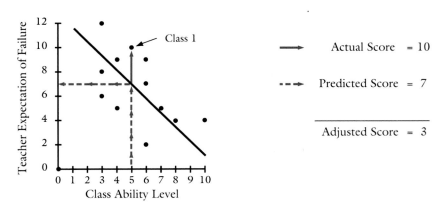

(C)
Teacher Expectation of Failure as Related to Ability Level of Class

tive behavior in class and achievement may be simply a reflection of differing resources. Students in schools with few science materials can be expected to do poorly in science and also to be disruptive due to boredom or hostility. The only solutions to location problems such as these are either to measure the extraneous variables (such as resource level) and use partial correlation or to determine correlations separately for each location, provided the number of students at each location is sufficiently large (a minimum *n* of thirty).

INSTRUMENTATION

Instrument Decay. In any study using a particular instrument many times, thought must be given to the possibility of instrument decay. This is most likely in observational studies since most other correlational studies do not use instruments many times (with the same subjects at least). When both variables are measured by an observational device at the same time, care must be taken to ensure that observers don't become tired, bored, or inattentive (this may require using additional observers). In a study in which observers are asked to record (during the same time period) both the number of "thought questions" asked by the teacher and the attentiveness of students, for example, a tired (or bored) observer might miss instances of each, resulting in low scores for the class on both variables, and thus distortion in the correlation.

Data Collector Characteristics. Characteristics of data collectors can create a threat if different persons administer both instruments. Gender, age, or ethnicity, for example, may affect specific responses, particularly with opinion or attitudinal instruments, as well as the seriousness with which respondents answer certain questions. One might expect an Air Force colonel in uniform, for example, to engender different scores on instruments measuring attitudes toward the military and the aerospace industry than a civilian data collector would. If each data collector gives both instruments to several groups, the correlation between these scores will be

higher as a result of the impact of the data collector. Fortunately, this threat is easily avoided by having each instrument administered by a different individual.

Data Collector Bias. Another instrumentation threat can result from unconscious bias on the part of the data gatherers whenever both instruments are given or scored by the same person. It is not uncommon, particularly with individually administered performance tests, for the same person to administer both tests to the same student, and even during the same time period. It is likely that the observed or scored performance on the first test will affect the way in which the second test is administered and/or scored. It is almost impossible to avoid expectations based on the first test, and these may well affect the examiner's behavior on the second testing. A high score on the first test, for example, may lead to examiner expectation of a high score on the second, resulting in students being given additional time or encouragement on the second test. While precise instructions for administering instruments are helpful, a better solution is to have different administrators for each test.

TESTING

The experience of responding to the first instrument that is administered in a correlational study may influence subject responses to the second instrument. Students asked to respond first to a "liking for teacher" scale, and then shortly thereafter to a "liking for social studies" scale are likely to see a connection. You can imagine them saying, perhaps, something like "Oh, I see, if I don't like the teacher, I'm not supposed to like the subject." To the extent that this happens, the results obtained can be misleading. The solution is to administer instruments, if possible, at different times and in different contexts.

MORTALITY

Mortality, strictly speaking, is not a problem of internal validity in correlational studies since anyone "lost" must be excluded from the study—correlations cannot be obtained unless a researcher has a score for each person on *both* of the variables being measured.

There are times, however, when loss of subjects may make a relationship more likely in the remaining data, thus creating a threat to *external validity*. Why external validity? Because the sample actually studied is often not the sample initially selected, due to mortality. Let us refer again to the study hypothesizing that teacher expectation of failure would be positively correlated with amount of disruptive student behavior. It might be that those teachers who refused to participate in the study were those who had a low expectation of failure—who, in fact, expected their students to achieve at un-realistically high levels. It also seems likely that the classes of those same teachers would exhibit a lot of disruptive behavior as a result of such unrealistic pressure from these teachers. Their loss would serve to *increase* the correlation ob-tained. Since there is no way to know whether this possibility is correct, the only thing the researcher can do is to try to avoid losing subjects.

Evaluating Threats to Internal Validity in Correlational Studies

The evaluation of specific threats to internal validity in correlational studies follows a proce-dure similar to that for experimental studies.

Step one: Ask: What are the specific factors that are known to affect one of the variables being correlated or which logi-cally could affect it? It does not matter which variable is selected.

Step two: Ask: What is the likelihood of each of these factors also affecting the *other* variable being correlated with the first? We need not be concerned with any factor unrelated to either variable. A factor must be related to *both* variables in order to be a threat.*

* This rule must be modified with respect to data collector and testing threats, where knowledge about the first instru-ment (or scores on it) may influence performance or assess-ment on the second instrument.

Step three: Evaluate the various threats in terms of their likelihood and plan to control them. If a given threat cannot be controlled, this should be acknowledged and discussed.

As we did in Chapter Twelve, let us con-sider an example to show how these steps might be applied. Suppose a researcher wishes to study the relationship between social skills (as observed) and job success (as rated by super-visors) of a group of severely disabled young adults in a career education program. Listed below again are several threats to internal validity discussed in Chapter Eleven and our evaluation of each.

Subject Characteristics. We consider here only four of many possible characteristics.

1. Severity of handicap. *Step one:* Rated job success can be expected to be related to severity of handicap. *Step two:* Severity of handicap can also be expected to be related to social skills. Therefore, severity should be assessed and con-trolled (using partial correlation). *Step three:* Likelihood of having an effect unless controlled: High.

2. Socioeconomic level of parents. *Step one:* Likely to be related to social skills. *Step two:* Parental socioeconomic status not likely to be related to job success for this group. While it is desirable to obtain socioeconomic data (to find out more about the sample), it is not of high priority. *Step three:* Likelihood of having an effect unless controlled: Low.

3. Physical strength and coordination. *Step one:* May be related to job success. *Step two:* Strength and coordination not likely to be related to social skills. While desirable to obtain such information, it is not of high priority. *Step three:* Likelihood of having an effect unless controlled: Low.

4. Physical appearance. *Step one:* Likely to be related to social skills. *Step two:* Also likely to be related to rated job success. Therefore, this variable *should* be assessed and controlled (again by using partial correlation). *Step three:* Likeli-hood of having an effect unless controlled: High.

Mortality. *Step one:* Subjects "lost" are likely to have poorer job performance. *Step two:* Lost subjects are also more likely to have poorer social skills. Thus, loss of subjects can be expected to reduce magnitude of correlation. *Step three:* Likelihood of having an effect unless controlled: Moderate to High.

Location. *Step one:* Since the subjects of the study would (inevitably) be working at different job sites and under different conditions, location may well be related to rated job success. *Step two:* If observation of social skills is done on site, it may be related to the specific site conditions. While it is possible that this threat could be controlled by independently assessing the job site environments, a better solution would be to assess social skills at a common site such as that used for group training. *Step three:* Likelihood of having an effect unless controlled: High.

Instrumentation

1. **Instrument Decay.** *Step one:* Instrument decay, if it has occurred, is likely to be related to how accurately social skills are measured. Observations should be scheduled, therefore, to preclude this possibility. *Step two:* Instrument decay would be unlikely to affect job ratings. Therefore, its occurrence would not be expected to account for any relationship found between the major variables. *Step three:* Likelihood of having an effect unless controlled: Low.

2. **Data Collector Characteristics.** *Step one:* Might well be related to job ratings since interaction of data collectors and supervisors is a necessary part of this study. *Step two:* Characteristics of data collectors presumably would not be related to their observation of social skills; nevertheless, to be on the safe side, this possibility should be controlled by having the same data collectors observe all subjects. *Step three:* Likelihood of having an effect unless controlled: Moderate.

3. **Data Collector Bias.** *Step one:* Ratings of job success should not be subject to data collector bias, since different supervisors will rate each subject. *Step two:* Observations of social skills may be related to preconceptions of ob-

servers about the subjects especially if they have prior knowledge of job success ratings. Therefore, observers should have no knowledge of job ratings. *Step three:* Likelihood of having an effect unless controlled: High.

4. **Testing.** *Step one:* Performance on the first instrument administered cannot, of course, be affected by performance on the second. *Step two:* In this study, scores on the second instrument cannot be affected by performance on the first, since the subjects are unaware of their performance on the first instrument. *Step three:* Likelihood of having an effect unless controlled: Zero.

Rationale for the Process of Evaluating Threats in Correlational Studies. We will try to demonstrate the logic behind the principle that a factor must be related to *both* correlated variables in order to explain a correlation between them. Consider the three scatterplots shown in Figure 13.5, which represent the scores of a group of individuals on three variables: A, B, and C. Scatterplot 1 shows a substantial correlation between A and B; scatterplot 2 shows a substantial correlation between A and C; scatterplot 3 shows a zero correlation between B and C.

Suppose the researcher is interested in determining whether the correlation between variables A and B can be "explained" by variable C. A and B, in other words, represent the variables being studied, while C represents a third variable being evaluated as a potential threat to internal validity. If the researcher tries to explain the correlation between A and B as due to C, he or she cannot. Here's why.

Suppose we say that person 1, shown in scatterplot 1, is high on A and B *because* he or she is high on C. Sure enough, being high on C *would* predict being high on A. You can see this in scatterplot 2. However, being high on C does *not* predict being high on B because although some individuals who scored high on C did score high on B, others who scored high on C scored in the middle or low on B. You can see this in scatterplot 3.

Another way of portraying this logic is with circle diagrams, as shown in Figure 13.6.

FIGURE **13.5**

Scatterplots Illustrating How a Factor (C)
May Not Be a Threat to Internal Validity

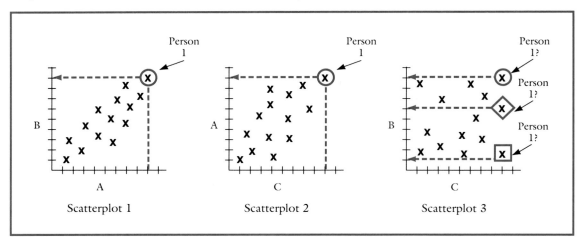

FIGURE **13.6**

Circle Diagrams Illustrating Relationships among Variables

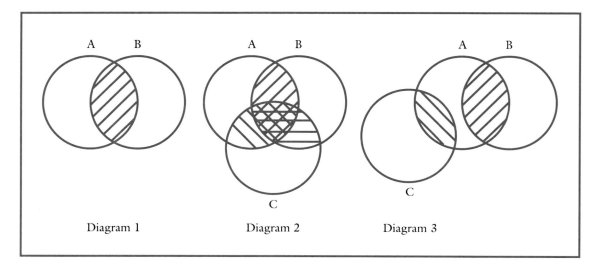

Diagram 1 in Figure 13.6 illustrates a correlation between A and B. This is shown by the overlap in circles; the greater the overlap, the greater the correlation. Diagram 2 shows a third circle (C), which represents the additional variable that is being considered as a possible threat to internal validity. Since it is correlated with *both* A and B, it may be considered a possible explanation for at least part of the correlation between them. This is shown by the fact that circle C overlaps *both* A and B. By way of contrast, diagram 3 shows that whereas C is correlated with A, it is *not* correlated with B (there is no overlap). Since C overlaps only with A (i.e., it does not overlap with *both* variables), it *cannot* be considered a possible alternative explanation for the correlation between A and B. Diagram 3, in other words, shows what the three scatterplots in Figure 13.5 do, namely, that A is correlated with B, and that A is correlated with C, but that B is *not* correlated with C.

An Example of Correlational Research

In the remainder of this chapter, we present a published example of correlational research, followed by a critique of its strengths and weaknesses. As we did in our critique of the experimental study analyzed in Chapter Twelve, we use several of the concepts introduced in earlier parts of the book in our analysis.

From *Counselor Education and Supervision,*
June 1987, 293–298. Reprinted by permission of
American Association for Counseling and Development.

Moral Development and Empathy in Counseling

James T. Bowman

T. Glen Reeves

Of interest to counselor educators are variables associated with helper empathy. The authors investigated the relationship between empathy and moral development. Students enrolled in a facilitative skills development course completed a measure of moral development before making their first counseling audiotape. After approximately 12 weeks of skills training, they were subsequently rated for their demonstration of empathic understanding to client statements on an analog videotape and on a counseling audiotape made for their course evaluation. Empathy ratings of their responses to the analog videotape correlated .61 ($p<.001$) with moral development scores and .35 ($p<.05$) with supervisory empathy ratings of their final audiotape and moral development scores. Implications for counselor education are discussed.

For counselor educators and others concerned with improving the effectiveness of counselor training programs, variables associated with trainee empathy are of interest. According to Gladstein (1983), there are two definitions of the empathy construct apparent in the literature. One, termed *emotional empathy,* emphasizes the counselor's ability to be affected by a client's emotional experience, and the other, *role-taking empathy,* emphasizes the counselor's ability to understand the client's frame of reference or point of view. Of the two, Gladstein concluded that role-taking empathy seemed to be more important in establishing rapport and developing a counseling relationship.

Kohlberg's (1969) moral development model offers an approach to the study of role-taking empathy. According to Kohlberg, the capacity for role taking—the ability to take and share the perspectives of others—is central to and a precondition for the process of moral development. In this cognitive-developmental theory, three major levels in the evolution of moral judgment are described, and each level is composed of two stages, forming a sequence of six stages of moral development. Each higher stage provides a more coherent and rational means of resolving moral conflicts than do the preceding stages. Kohlberg and Mayer (1972) theorized that the level of moral development cannot exceed, but may lag behind, the cognitive-developmental level. The progression of moralization is characterized by movement from egocentric solutions to moral conflicts (Preconventional Level I, Stages 1 and 2) to solutions concerned with maintaining social order and conformity to cultural images (Conventional Level II, Stages 3 and 4) to solutions offering relativistic values and ethical principles (Postconventional Level III, Stages 5 and 6). Beginning in Stage 2, with an acknowledgment that points of view other than one's own exist, role-taking capacity gains in complexity through Stage 6.

Hoffman (1976) delineated a view of moral development that highlights the role of empathic development. This view stresses the naturally evolving course of empathy in human development as well as the cognitive phenomena associated with it. On one level, Hoffman stated that an "altruistic motive system . . . may exist within the individual" (p. 125), and he cited evidence that empathy is a natural response evident even in young children. The further development of empathy depends on cognitive development, however, because empathy is essentially a response to cues about another person's affective state. If, as Hoffman theorized, cognitive processes help determine how empathic emotion is expressed, these processes must further mediate the development of altruistic or moral motives. Eisenberg-Berg and Mussen (1978) linked empathy and moral reasoning by concluding that empathy is a "critical predisposing" factor (p. 186) for moral or prosocial reasoning in adolescents.

Relative to the relationship between empathy and the helping process, Erle, Diaz-Loving, and Archer (1982) investigated the role of empathy and values in college students and found that moral values serve to facilitate helping responses that are aroused by empathic emotion. Welfel and Lipsitz (1983) raised the possibility that specific aspects of counselor training experiences influence or are influenced by the student's moral development level. With this line of reasoning, it is conceivable that a counselor who possesses high level moral reasoning capacities is likely to respond empathically to the client.

In a pilot study in which they investigated the possible difference in the demonstration of empathy between students with high and low moral development, Bowman and Allen (in press) found a significant difference in empathy ratings between the two groups. After 15 weeks of empathy training, the high moral development group produced significantly higher empathy ratings on counseling audiotapes than did the low group. As a follow-up on the results of Bowman and Allen's study, this study was designed to determine whether there is a relationship between moral judgment scores and empathy ratings using participants trained in empathic listening and responding who exhibit a wide range of moral development scores rather than using groups with high and low moral development.

METHOD

Participants

Participants were beginning master's-level students in counselor education, educational psychology, and psychology. Of the 44 students enrolled in three sections of a counseling practicum in facilitative skills development, 35 completed the study (29 women with an average age of 29.3 years and 6 men with an average age of 30.8 years).

Instruments

Two instruments were used: the Defining Issues Test (DIT), developed by Rest, Cooper, Coder, Masanza, and Anderson (1974), and the Empathic Understanding Scale (Carkhuff, 1983). The DIT measures the degree that principled moral reasoning is used in resolving moral dilemmas. It employs a multiple-choice format that requires the individual to choose and rank the most important considerations used in making decisions on six moral dilemmas. Those responses that represent principled moral thinking (Stages 5 and 6) are added together, yielding a numerical measure (P score) of moral judgment level. Test-retest reliability coefficients range from the high .70s to the .80s (Rest, 1979).

The Empathic Understanding Scale (EU) is a 5-point scale, ranging from *least facilitative response* (1) to *most facilitative response* (5), on which the facilitative level of a counseling response is defined. This scale permits judges to rate the facilitative level of counselors' responses. The EU scale was used as the dependent measure in this study because it is widely used in both research and training as a measure of the communication of empathy (Carkhuff, 1983).

Procedure

Before making their first counseling audiotape in the facilitative skills development class, all students were administered the DIT during a class session. Beginning on the day of the administration of the DIT, the students participated in 12 weeks of facilitative skills training based on the model proposed by Egan (1985). This three-stage model involves exploration, understanding and goal setting, and facilitative action. Training included explanation, demonstration, in-class practice and feedback, and audiotape and videotape recording with feedback of counseling sessions. Trainees were required to provide three practice tapes and a final tape for course evaluation.

Two empathy measures were obtained at the conclusion of this training. On one of these measures, participants responded in writing to client statements recorded during a videotaped counseling interview. We edited this videotape to delete the counselor's responses to the client's statements and also to select client statements that were audible and substantial enough in terms of potential response content. These written responses were rated by the experimenters, who had no knowledge of participants' DIT scores, using the EU scale. Interrater reliabilities for these two raters have ranged from .88 to .91 in previous studies (Bowman & Allen, in press; Prasertwong, 1984; Wahome, 1984). The final counseling tapes were rated for empathic understanding by the faculty member who taught all three sections of facilitative skills (and who had no knowledge of participants' DIT scores). These ratings were used as a basis for course evaluation. Pearson product-moment correlation coefficients were computed for the data.

RESULTS

Statistical analysis revealed significant relationships between DIT scores and the two empathy ratings: the supervisor's ratings of final audiotapes and DIT, $r(34) = .36$, $p<.05$, and the judges' rating of the written responses to the videotape and DIT, $r(34) = .61, p<.001$. These two empathy ratings were significantly related to each other, $r(34) = .40$, $p<.05$. These data suggest that the moral development level of the counselor trainee is related to the trainee's ability to empathize.

DISCUSSION

The results indicate significant correlation between moral development and two measures of empathy. The greater relationship between the trainees' written responses and the DIT scores than between DIT scores and supervisors' ratings of counseling may have resulted from the nature of the two tasks. Basically, the videotape analog seems to be a less complex task for several reasons. First, client statements on the videotape were preselected on the basis of what the experimenters believed would be possible to respond to with both content and feeling. No such control is possible when counseling an actual client. Second, responding to a videotape in written form is a different task than face-to-face counseling. Consequently, possible anxiety associated with the demand of having to respond to an actual client should be reduced in the videotape situation.

Although the constructs of empathy and moral development seem to be closely related, the implications for counselor education and related fields have yet to be fully explored. The results are consistent with the theory that role-taking ability is central to the development of successively higher levels of moral reasoning and the ability to empathize. But role-taking ability may not be the only variable that accounts for the relationship between moral development and empathy. As stated by Kohlberg and Mayer (1972), cognitive development is a requisite for moral development. It may be that there is an interaction or interdependence between people's cognitive development and their role-taking ability that contributes to their ability to empathize.

If moral development level is a predictor of counselor empathy, then questions will be raised regarding the potential for success of students who are low on this dimension. Specifically, should these students be encouraged to pursue graduate work in counseling, or is it possible or realistic to attempt to improve the moral reasoning levels of graduate students? Although the improvement of moral reasonong was not investigated in this study, it is conceivable that such a change occurs as an indirect result of counselor trainees' educational experiences, as Welfel and Lipsitz (1983) suggested. If moral judgment is viewed as a developmental phenomenon, it is feasible that this capacity may be expanded as the individual encounters the perspectives of a diversity of clients, interaction with students and faculty members, and assimilation of the theoretical orientation of the counseling program. The nature and content of these experiences may be such that the counseling student, who is learning to interact in an accepting, empathic, and otherwise facilitative manner with other people, will experience a state of cognitive disequilibrium. According to many cognitive development theorists, the result of such a cognitive "shake-up" will be movement toward higher level functioning as the student uses more principled and complex moral reasoning to resolve the internal dissonance. It is likely that the counseling student's personal growth and moral development follows this developmental pattern as novel encounters are experienced.

These data indicate a direct relationship between level of moral development and counselor empathy. Further research is needed to clarify the nature of the relationship. Specifically, there is a need for studies aimed at determining whether high moral development leads to inherently more empathic behavior, whether high moral development predisposes the trainee to benefit from empathy training, whether empathy training enhances principled moral development, and whether cognitive development interacts with moral development in leading to empathic behavior.

References

Bowman, J., & Allen, B. (in press). Moral development and counselor trainee empathy. *Counseling and Values.*

Carkhuff, R.R. (1983). *The art of helping* (5th ed.). Amherst, MA: Human Resources Development Press.

Earle, W.B., Diaz-Loving, R., & Archer, R.L. (1982). *Antecedents of helping: Assessing the role of empathy and values* (Report No. CG 016 462). Austin, TX: University of Texas at Austin, Department of Psychology. (ERIC Document Reproduction Service No. ED 226 269)

Egan, G. (1985). *The skilled helper: Model, skills, and methods for effective helping* (3rd ed.). Monterey, CA: Brooks/Cole.

Eisenberg-Berg, N., & Mussen, P. (1978). Empathy and moral development in adolescence. *Developmental Psychology, 14,* 185–186.

Gladstein, G. (1983). Understanding empathy: Integrating counseling, developmental, and social psychology perspectives. *Journal of Counseling Psychology, 30,* 467–482.

Hoffman, M. (1976). Empathy, role-taking, guilt, and development of altruistic motives. In T. Lickona (Ed.), *Moral development and behavior* (pp. 124–143). New York: Holt, Rinehart and Winston.

Kohlberg, L. (1969). *Stages in the development of moral thought and action.* New York: Holt, Rinehart and Winston.

Kohlberg, L., & Mayer, R. (1972). Development as the aim of education. *Harvard Educational Review, 42,* 449–496.

Prasertwong, P. (1984). The effects of self-as-a-model and peer-as-a-model on counselor trainee attending behavior (Doctoral dissertation, Mississippi State University, 1984). *Dissertation Abstracts International, 46,* 898A.

Rest, J.R. (1979). *Revised manual for the Defining Issues Test: An objective test of moral judgment development.* Minneapolis: University of Minnesota Press.

Rest, J.R., Cooper, D., Coder, R., Masanza, J., & Anderson, D. (1974). Judging the important issues in moral dilemmas: An objective measure of development. *Developmental Psychology, 10,* 491–501.

Wahome, L. (1984). A comparison of the effects of self-as-model and other-as-model on counselor trainee verbal responses (Doctoral dissertation, Mississippi State University, 1984). *Dissertation Abstracts International, 45,* 1043A.

Welfel, E.R., & Lipsitz, N.E. (1983). Moral reasoning of counselors: Its relationship to level of training and counseling experience. *Counseling and Values, 27,* 194–203.

Analysis of the Study

PURPOSE/JUSTIFICATION

The primary rationale for this study, as presented in the introduction, is theoretical. The authors cite several well-known authorities who theorize that moral development and role-taking empathy are related. The position taken is that role-taking empathy is a prerequisite to the higher stages of moral development.

Unfortunately, it is not clear that all these authorities are discussing role-taking empathy as distinct from "emotional empathy." Further, the rationale is somewhat confused by reference to the Erle, Diaz-Loving, and Archer (1982) study, which concluded that moral development facilitates helping responses that are aroused by empathic emotion. Does this mean that the sequence is: empathic feelings lead to moral judgment which in turn leads to empathic role-taking? Finally, the authors suggest that level of moral development is predictive of empathic response (by which they presumably mean role-taking empathy).

The authors have indicated several lines of thought and research that imply the relationship they wish to study, but, although they discuss causation, it is unclear when or how moral development is presumed to "cause" role-taking empathy or when or how the reverse would be presumed (role-taking empathy causing moral development). We conclude, therefore, that the authors' rationale lacks clarity and internal consistency.

The authors' rationale for studying role-taking empathy as an important variable rests on a citation of one writer who asserts that role-taking empathy seemed to be more important than emotional empathy in establishing rapport and developing a counseling relationship. A much stronger justification could, and should, be made.

DEFINITIONS

The key variables to be defined are "role-taking empathy" and "moral development." Although neither is explicitly defined, the reader can infer the following:

- Role-taking empathy—an ability to understand a client's frame of reference or point of view.
- Moral development—the extent to which an individual has changed from using a purely self-centered solution to moral conflicts to using a conformity stage to using solutions reflecting relativist values and ethical principles.

While both of these definitions contain considerable ambiguity (what is meant by "understand," for example?), the reader can arrive at a fair degree of clarity about the meaning of role-taking empathy. We suspect a reader unfa-miliar with Lawrence Kohlberg's work, however, would not be clear as to the meaning of "moral development."

Finally, the authors should be more consistent in their use of terms. They often use the term "empathy" when they presumably intend "role-taking empathy," as we noted earlier. They use the term "moral development" interchangeably with the term "moral reasoning" when the latter would be more accurate throughout.

PRIOR RESEARCH

Other than the Erle, Diaz-Loving, and Archer (1982) study mentioned previously, the only other research cited is a previous study by one of the authors in which students with high moral development scores were found to be higher in "empathy ratings on counseling audiotapes" (role-taking empathy) than students with low moral development scores. While this study is clearly relevant, it is not clear how the present study is different except in the treatment of data (i.e., using correlation rather than a comparison of groups). Are the subjects different? Are the instruments different? We do not know.

HYPOTHESES

No hypotheses are explicitly stated, but one is clearly implied: "There is a positive correlation between level of moral development (reasoning) and role-taking empathy among counselor trainees."

SAMPLE

The sample is a convenience sample, consisting of thirty-five master's degree students in three sections of a counseling practicum at one university. No population is indicated. Descriptive information is minimal, consisting only of subjects' gender and age.

INSTRUMENTATION

The instruments used to measure each of the variables are described. The content of the

DIT (a test of moral reasoning ability) appears valid to us, based on the brief description that is given. No evidence is provided regarding either content or criterion-related validity.

Reported reliability coefficients are adequate for the study, but both the time interval and the subjects on which the coefficients are based should be reported. Test-retest reliabilities are the most appropriate to report, since stability of the characteristic over a time period of at least several months is assumed in such a study. The study would be strengthened by a built-in check on reliability using the subjects of this study. As always, use of a second instrument to check validity would help to strengthen reader confidence in the validity of the instrumentation process.

Use of the empathic understanding scale is poorly defended. The fact that it is widely used is a weak recommendation; many poor instruments are widely used. If it has been used often in other research, there should be evidence available. If so, it should be reported. Furthermore, the scale is used in two quite different ways, thereby providing, in effect, two different instruments: (1) the written response to recorded client statements and (2) faculty judgment of the final counseling tapes (see Procedures section). These are different instruments since format, response mode, and scorer requirements all differ—only the scoring categories are the same. Scoring agreement appears adequate for instrument one, but should be reported for the *current* study. A second scorer could (presumably) have been used with instrument two, but this was not done. Reliability over time would be difficult, but not impossible, to check. Internal consistency (i.e., split-half reliability) should be reported for both instruments.

The use of two instruments to measure role-taking empathy does provide a check on validity, although it is not discussed as such. The correlation of .40 (see Results section) provides some (but not strong) support for the validity of scores obtained from each of these instruments. Additional information on reliability would make it possible to determine the degree to which this correlation is limited by unreliability.

PROCEDURES/INTERNAL VALIDITY

The authors do not explain why the measures of role-taking empathy were administered twelve weeks after the administration of the moral reasoning instrument, during which time the subjects completed a course in facilitation skills. Presumably the course enrollees provided not only a convenient sample, but a feasible means of access to each student's behavior in the role of counselor. It may also be that the training was expected to increase the range of "empathy" scores, although this is not stated.

Of the possible threats to internal validity, there are three that cause us concern. The first is with respect to the objectivity of scoring the instruments, an instrumentation threat. The authors correctly ensured that the instructor/scorer of the counseling tapes had no knowledge of the moral reasoning scores. Presumably this was also the case with the scorers of the written instrument, although this is not stated. Since it appears that the authors scored both of these paper-and-pencil instruments, the possibility of a recall of the "moral reasoning" scores influencing the scoring of the "empathy" responses should have been eliminated by the researcher by deleting names (or other means of identification) of students during scoring.

The second concern is related to the nature of the paper-and-pencil instruments. Both require an intellectual analysis of a given situation, followed by a response to the situation (evaluation of choices or reaction to client statements). Both are susceptible to "psyching out"—that is, to a respondent determining the socially or professionally desirable response. An astute respondent may well be able to provide the "best" answers without behaving accordingly. If so, a correlation simply reflects this phenomenon (a testing threat) rather than a real relationship between the intended variables. This possibility would be reduced by evidence that scores on the instruments represent valid measures of behavior, but such evidence is either lacking or, at best, modest.

Finally, no attempt was made to control for the cognitive ability of the subjects (subjects characteristics), despite frequent reference by the authors in their introduction as to its importance. Perhaps a positive correlation between moral reasoning and role-taking empathy is trivial, with both being highly related to cognitive ability. Some attempt at controlling for this variable (for example, by partial correlation) would greatly strengthen the study.

DATA ANALYSIS

The reported correlations are the appropriate method of data analysis, provided the relationships are appropriately described by a straight line. Either scatterplots or a verbal statement to this effect should be provided. The authors commit the commonplace error of reporting the results of a significance test (in terms of probabilities) without qualification. Lack of random sampling makes such indicators of questionable value.

RESULTS

While it is true that the obtained correlations of .34 and .61 suggest that level of moral development is related to ability to empathize, the several alternative explanations mentioned in the section on internal validity should be discussed.

DISCUSSION

The authors make too much of the *statistical significance* of the correlations they obtained. The *magnitude* of these correlations is far more important, particularly when the use of moral

reasoning as a predictor of counselor behavior is suggested. A correlation of .36 (with taped behavior) is much too low for predictive use.

The authors discuss the possibility that training affects both moral reasoning and role-taking empathy as one of the issues for further research, certainly a legitimate issue raised by their data, as are their other suggested extensions.

It seems to us that this interesting study and the more general topic it explores could be stated in a more straightforward manner. We would suggest the following points to consider.

1. Further justification of the importance of role-taking empathy in successful counseling.
2. Further development and defense of the videotape rating method of assessing role-taking empathy. This would include adequate agreement among different scorers and evidence of stability over a meaningful time period (say, three weeks). Evidence of validity could be a combination of logical analysis of the scoring system by authorities in the field, and correlation with other indices (e.g., client ratings or judgments by colleagues and/or instructors based on long-term association). The .40 correlation with the written instrument does not provide much support for validity, although it may be affected by inadequate reliability of either or both measures.
3. Further discussion of relationships with other variables, including those suggested by the authors. In doing so, the authors should pay more attention to defining terms and then using them consistently throughout.

Main Points of Chapter Thirteen

- The major characteristic of correlational research is to seek out associations among variables.
- Correlational studies are carried out either to help explain important human behaviors or to predict likely outcomes.
- If a relationship of sufficient magnitude exists between two variables, it becomes possible to predict a score on either variable if a score on the other variable is known.
- The variable that is used to make the prediction is called the predictor variable.

- The variable about which the prediction is made is called the criterion variable.
- Both scatterplots and regression lines are used in correlational studies to predict a score on a criterion variable.
- A predicted score is never exact. As a result, researchers calculate an index of prediction error, which is known as the "standard error of estimate."
- Multiple regression is a technique that enables a researcher to determine a correlation between a criterion variable and the best combination of two or more predictor variables.
- The coefficient of multiple correlation (R) indicates the strength of the correlation between the combination of the predictor variables and the criterion variable.
- The value of a prediction equation depends on whether it predicts successfully with a new group of individuals.
- When the criterion variable is categorical rather than quantitative, discriminant function analysis (rather than multiple regression) must be used.
- Factor analysis is a technique that allows a researcher to determine whether many variables can be described by a few factors.
- Path analysis is a technique used to test a theory about the causal connections among three or more variables.
- The meaning of a given correlation coefficient depends on how it is applied.
- Correlation coefficients below .35 show only a slight relationship between variables.
- Correlations between .40 and .60 may have theoretical and/or practical value depending on the context.
- Only when a correlation of .65 or higher is obtained can reasonably accurate individual predictions be made.
- Correlations over .85 indicate a very strong relationship between the variables correlated.
- Threats to the internal validity of correlational studies include characteristics of the subjects involved, location, instrumentation, data collection, and testing.
- The results of correlational studies must always be interpreted with caution, since they may suggest, but they cannot establish, causation.

For Discussion

1. A researcher finds a correlation of .43 between the scores on a test of writing ability and a test of speaking ability for a group of high school sophomores. On the basis of this correlation, which of the following conclusions, if any, would be justified?
   a. Students who write well also speak well.
   b. Students who speak poorly also write poorly.
   c. No relationship exists between writing and speaking ability.

2. What is wrong with the following statements?
   a. If each of two variables are correlated with a third variable, then they will also be correlated with each other.
   b. A correlation of $+.51$ is better than a correlation of $-.51$.

c. On the whole, a researcher would generally be more pleased if the results of a study revealed a strongly positive correlation between two variables than if they revealed a strongly negative one.

3. What is the difference between an effect and a relationship?

4. Suppose a researcher finds that a particular student's high school GPA is 2.75. Use the prediction equation on page 278 to predict the student's GPA (assume that $a = .23$ and $b = .69$).

5. Why are samples smaller than thirty likely to give an inaccurate estimate of the degree of relationship that exists between two variables?

6. What is the difference, if any, between the *sign* of a correlation and the *strength* of a correlation?

7. Which correlation is more indicative of a strong relationship: $r = -.78$ or $r = +53$?

8. Are there any types of instruments that could *not* be used in a correlational study? If so, why?

9. Would it be possible for a correlation to be statistically significant, yet educationally insignificant? If so, give an example.

10. Why do you suppose people often interpret correlational results as proving causation?

Notes

1. Donald M. Medley & Homer Coker. (1987). *Journal of Educational Research*, 80 (4):242–247.

2. Constance V. Hines, Donald R. Cruickshank, & John J. Kennedy. (1985). *American Educational Research Journal*, 22(1):87–100.

3. L. Douglas Ried, O. B. Martinson, & L. C. Weaver. (1987). *Journal of Drug Education*, 17(2):149–161.

4. James T. Bowman & T. Glen Reeves. (1987). *Counselor Education and Supervision*, 6:293–297.

5. N. Brown, A. Muhlenkamp, L. Fox, & M. Osborn. (1983). *Western Journal of Nursing Research*, 5(2):155–163.

6. Susan R. Swing & Penelope L. Peterson. (1982). *American Educational Research Journal*, 19(2):259–274.

7. Barry J. Fraser & Darrell L. Fisher. (1982). *American Educational Research Journal*, 19(4):498–518.

8. Dennis E. Hinkle, William Wiersma, & Stephen G. Jurs. (1981). *Applied Statistics for the Behavioral Sciences* (Chicago: Rand McNally).

Research Exercise Thirteen: Correlational Research

You should complete Problem Sheet 13 only if you are planning a correlational study. If your intended study involves a different methodology, you will find a similar problem sheet at the end of the chapter that deals with that methodology. You might wish to consider, however, whether your research question could be investigated by means of a correlational study.

> Using Problem Sheet 13, once again state the question or hypothesis of your study. Then describe, briefly but thoroughly, the procedures of your study, including the analysis of results—that is, *what* you intend to do, *when, where,* and *how*. Lastly, indicate any unresolved problems you see at this point in your planning.

PROBLEM SHEET 13
Correlational Research

1. The question or hypothesis of my study is: _____
_____
_____

2. A brief summary of **what** I intend to do, **when, where,** and **how** is as follows: _____
_____
_____
_____
_____
_____
_____
_____
_____

3. The major problems I foresee at this point are as follows: _____
_____
_____
_____

Chapter Fourteen

CAUSAL-COMPARATIVE RESEARCH

Causal-comparative research allows researchers to investigate the possibility of a causal relationship among variables that cannot, as in experimental research, be manipulated. In a causal-comparative study, two groups that are different on a particular variable are compared on another variable. In this chapter, we discuss the steps involved in causal-comparative research.

- *Explain* what is meant by the term causal-comparative research
- *Describe* briefly how causal-comparative research is both similar to, yet different from, both correlational and experimental research
- *Identify* and *describe* briefly the steps involved in conducting a causal-comparative study
- *Draw* a *diagram* of a design for a causal-comparative study
- *Describe* how data are collected in causal-comparative research
- *Describe* some of the threats to internal validity that exist in causal-comparative studies
- *Discuss* how to control for these threats
- *Recognize* a causal-comparative study when you come across one in the educational research literature

What Is Causal-Comparative Research?

Causal-comparative research attempts to determine the cause *or* consequences of differences that *already exist* between or among groups of individuals. As a result, it is sometimes viewed, along with correlational research, as a form of associational research, since both describe conditions that already exist. A researcher might observe, for example, that two groups of individuals differ on some variable (such as teaching style) and then attempt to determine the *reason* for, or the *results* of, this difference. The difference between the groups, however, has *already occurred*. Since both the effect(s) and the alleged cause(s) have already occurred, and hence are studied in retrospect, causal-comparative research is also referred to sometimes as *ex post facto* (from the Latin for "after the fact") research. This is in contrast to an experimental study, where a researcher *creates* a difference between or among groups, and then compares their performance (on one or more dependent variables) to determine the effects of the created difference.

The group difference variable in a causal-comparative study is either a variable that cannot be manipulated (such as ethnicity) or one that might have been manipulated but for one reason or another has not been (such as teaching style). Sometimes, ethical constraints prevent a variable from being manipulated, thus preventing the effects of variations in the variable from being examined by means of an experimental study. A researcher might be interested, for example, in the effects of a new diet on very young children. Ethical considerations, however, might prevent the researcher from deliberately varying the diet to which the children are exposed. Causal-comparative research, however, would allow the researcher to study the effects of the diet if he or she could find a group of children who have *already been exposed* to the diet. The researcher could then compare them with a similar group of children who had not been exposed to the

305

diet. Much of the research on smoking and lung cancer is causal-comparative in nature.

Another example is the comparison of scientists and engineers in terms of their originality. As in correlational research, explanations or predictions can be made from either variable to the other: Originality could be predicted from group membership, or group membership could be predicted from originality. However, most such studies attempt to explore causation rather than to foster prediction. Are "original" individuals more likely to become scientists? Do scientists become more original as they become immersed in their work? And so forth. Notice that if it were possible, a correlational study would be conducted, but that it is not appropriate when one of the variables (in this case, the nature of the groups) is a categorical variable.

Following are some examples of different types of causal-comparative research.

> *Type 1:* Exploration of *effects* (dependent variable) caused by membership in a given group.
> *Question:* What differences in abilities are caused by gender?
> *Research hypothesis:* Females have a greater amount of linguistic ability than males.
> *Type 2:* Exploration of *causes* (independent variable) of group membership.
> *Question:* What causes individuals to join a gang?
> *Research hypothesis:* Individuals who are members of gangs have more aggressive personalities than individuals who are not members of gangs.
> *Type 3:* Exploration of the *consequences* (dependent variable) of an intervention.
> *Question:* How do students taught by the inquiry method react to propaganda?
> *Research hypothesis:* Students who were taught by the inquiry method are more critical of propaganda than are those who were taught by the lecture method.

Causal-comparative studies have been used frequently to study the differences between males and females. They have demonstrated the su-periority of girls in language and of boys in math at certain age levels. The attributing of these differences to gender—as cause—must be tentative. One could hardly view "gender" as being caused by ability, but there are many other probable links in the causal chain, including societal expectations of males and females.

The basic causal-comparative approach, therefore, is to begin with a noted difference between two groups—and to look for possible causes for, or consequences of, this difference. A researcher might be interested, for example, in the reason(s) why some individuals become addicted to alcohol while others develop a dependence on pills. How can this be explained? Descriptions of the two groups (alcoholics and pill-poppers) might be compared to see if their characteristics differ in ways that might account for the difference in choice of drug.

Sometimes, causal-comparative studies are conducted solely as an alternative to experiments. Suppose, for example, that the curriculum director in a large urban high school district is considering implementing a new English curriculum. The director might try the curriculum out experimentally, selecting a few classes at random throughout the district, and compare student performance in these classes with comparison groups who continue to experience the regular curriculum. This might take a considerable amount of time, however, and be quite costly in terms of materials, teacher preparation workshops, and so on. As an alternative, the director might consider a causal-comparative study and compare the achievement of students in school districts that are currently using this curriculum with the achievement of students in similar districts that do not use the new curriculum. If the results show that students in districts (similar to his) with the new curriculum are achieving higher scores in English, the director would have a basis for going ahead and implementing the new curriculum in his district. Like correlational studies, causal-comparative investigations often identify relationships that later are studied experimentally.

Despite their advantages, however, causal-comparative studies do have serious limitations.

The most serious lie in the lack of control over threats to internal validity. Since the manipulation of the independent variable has already occurred, many of the controls we discussed in Chapter Twelve cannot be applied. Thus considerable caution must be expressed in interpreting the outcomes of a causal-comparative study. As with correlational studies, relationships can be identified, but causation cannot be established. As we have pointed out before, the alleged cause may really be an effect, the effect may be a cause, or there may be a third variable that caused both the alleged cause and effect.

SIMILARITIES AND DIFFERENCES BETWEEN CAUSAL-COMPARATIVE AND CORRELATIONAL RESEARCH

Causal-comparative research is sometimes confused with correlational research. Although similarities do exist, there are notable differences as well.

Similarities. Both causal-comparative and correlational studies are examples of associational research, that is, researchers who conduct them seek to explore relationships among variables. Both attempt to explain phenomena of interest. Both seek to identify variables that are worthy of later exploration through experimental research, and both often provide guidance for subsequent experimental studies. Neither permits the manipulation of variables by the researcher, however.

Differences. Causal-comparative studies typically compare two or more groups of subjects, while correlational studies require two (or more) scores on each variable for *each* subject. Correlational studies investigate two (or more) quantitative variables, whereas causal-comparative studies involve at least one categorical variable (group membership). Correlational studies analyze data using scatterplots and/or correlation coefficients, while causal-comparative studies compare averages or use crossbreak tables.

SIMILARITIES AND DIFFERENCES BETWEEN CAUSAL-COMPARATIVE AND EXPERIMENTAL RESEARCH

Similarities. Both causal-comparative and experimental studies typically require at least one categorical variable (group membership). Both compare group performances (average scores) to determine relationships. Both typically compare separate groups of subjects.*

Differences. In experimental research, the independent variable is manipulated; in causal-comparative research, no manipulation takes place. Causal-comparative studies provide much weaker evidence for causation than do experimental studies. In experimental research, the researcher can sometimes assign subjects to treatment groups; in causal-comparative research, the groups are already formed—the researcher must locate them. In experimental studies, the researcher has much greater flexibility in formulating the structure of the design.

Steps Involved in Causal-Comparative Research

PROBLEM FORMULATION

The first step in formulating a problem in causal-comparative research is usually to identify and define the particular phenomena of interest and then to consider possible causes for, or consequences of, these phenomena. Suppose, for example, that a researcher is interested in student creativity. What causes creativity? Why are a few students highly creative while most are not? Why do some students who initially appear to be creative seem to lose this characteristic? Why do others who at one time are not creative later become so? And so forth.

The researcher speculates, for example, that high-level creativity might be caused by a combination of social failure, on the one hand, and personal recognition for artistic or scientific

*Except in counterbalanced or time-series experimental designs (see Chapter Twelve).

achievement, on the other. The researcher also identifies a number of alternative hypotheses that might account for a difference between highly creative and noncreative students. Both the quantity and quality of a student's interests, for example, might account for differences in creativity. Highly creative students might tend to have many diverse interests. Parental encouragement to explore ideas might also account partly for creativity, as might some types of intellectual skills.

Once the researcher has identified possible causes of the phenomena, they are (usually) incorporated into a more precise statement of the research problem he or she wishes to investigate. In this instance, the researcher might state the objective of his research as "to examine possible differences between students of high and low creativity." Note that differences in a number of variables can be investigated in a causal-comparative study in order to determine which variable (or combination of variables) seems most likely to cause the phenomena (creativity in this case) being studied. This testing of several alternative hypotheses is a basic characteristic of good causal-comparative research, and whenever possible should be the basis for identifying the variables on which the comparison groups are to be contrasted. This provides a rational basis for selection of the variables to be investigated, rather than relying on what is often called the "shotgun" approach, in which a large number of measures are administered simply because they seem interesting or are available. They also serve to remind the researcher that the findings of a causal-comparative study are open to a variety of causal explanations.

SAMPLE

Once the researcher has formulated the problem statement, the next step is to select the sample of individuals to be studied. The important thing here is to define carefully the characteristic to be studied and then to select groups that differ in this characteristic. In the above example, this means defining as clearly as possible the term "creativity." If possible, operational definitions should be employed. A highly creative student might be defined, for example, as one who "has produced an award-winning scientific or artistic product."

The researcher also needs to think about whether the group obtained using the operational definition is likely to be reasonably homogeneous in terms of factors causing creativity. For example, are students who are creative in science similar to students who are creative in art with respect to causation? This is a very important question to ask. If creativity has different "causes" in different fields, the search for causation is only confused by combining students from such fields. Do ethnic, age, or gender differences produce differences in creativity? The success of a causal-comparative study depends in large degree on how carefully the comparison groups are defined.

It is very important to select groups that are homogeneous with regard to at least some important variables. For example, if the researcher assumes that the same causes are operating for all creative students, regardless of gender, ethnicity, or age, he or she may find no differences between comparison groups simply because too many other variables are involved. If all creative students are treated as a homogeneous group, no differences may be found between highly creative and noncreative students, whereas if only creative and noncreative female art students were compared, differences might be found.

Once the defined groups have been selected, they can be matched on one or more variables. This process of matching controls certain variables, thereby eliminating any group differences on these variables. This is desirable in Type 1 and Type 3 studies (see page 306) since the researcher wants the groups as similar as possible in order to explain differences on the dependent variable(s) as being due to group membership. Matching is not appropriate in Type 2 studies because the researcher presumably knows little about the extraneous variables that might be related to group differences and as a result cannot match on them.

INSTRUMENTATION

There are no limits on the types of instruments that may be used in causal-comparative studies. Achievement tests, questionnaires, interview schedules, attitudinal measures, observational devices—any of the devices discussed in Chapter Six can be used.

DESIGN

The basic causal-comparative design involves selecting two or more groups that differ on a particular variable of interest and comparing them on another variable or variables. No manipulation is involved. The groups differ in one of two ways: One group either possesses a characteristic (often called a criterion) that the other does not, or the groups differ on known characteristics. These two variations of the same basic design (sometimes called a criterion-group design) are as follows.

The Basic Causal-Comparative Designs

(a)	Group	Independent variable	Dependent variable
	I	C (Group possesses characteristic)	O (Measurement)
	II	−C (Group does not possess characteristic)	O (Measurement)

(b)	Group	Independent variable	Dependent variable
	I	C_1 (Group possesses characteristic one)	O (Measurement)
	II	C_2 (Group possesses characteristic two)	O (Measurement)

The letter C is used in this design to represent the presence of the characteristic. The dashed line is used to show that intact groups are being compared. Examples of these causal-comparative designs are presented in Figure 14.1.

FIGURE **14.1**

Example of the Basic Causal-Comparative Designs

(a)	Group	Independent variable	Dependent variable
	I	C Dropouts	O Level of self-esteem
	II	(−C) Nondropouts	O Level of self-esteem

(b)	Group	Independent variable	Dependent variable
	I	C_1 Counselors	O Amount of job satisfaction
	II	C_2 Teachers	O Amount of job satisfaction

Threats to Internal Validity in Causal-Comparative Research

Two weaknesses in causal-comparative research are lack of randomization and inability to manipulate an independent variable. As we have mentioned, random assignment of subjects to groups is not possible in causal-comparative research since the groups are already formed. Manipulation of the independent variable is not possible because the groups have already been exposed to the independent variable.

SUBJECT CHARACTERISTICS

The major threat to the internal validity of a causal-comparative study is the possibility of a subject characteristics threat. Since the researcher has had no say in either the selection or formation of the comparison groups, there is always the likelihood that the groups are not equivalent on one or more important variables other than the identified group membership variable. A group of girls, for example, might be older than a comparison group of boys.

There are a number of procedures that a researcher can use to reduce the chance of a subject characteristics threat in a causal-comparative study. Many of these are also used in experimental research (see Chapter Twelve).

Matching of Subjects. One way to control for an extraneous variable is to match subjects from the comparison groups on that variable. In other words, pairs of subjects, one from each group, are found that are similar on that variable. Students might be matched on GPA, for example, in an achievement study. Individuals with similar GPA's would be matched. If a match cannot be found for a particular subject, he or she is then eliminated from the study. As you have probably realized, the problem with matching is often that just this happens—matches cannot be found for many subjects, and hence the size of the sample involved is accordingly reduced. Matching becomes even more difficult when the researcher tries to match on two or more variables.

Finding or Creating Homogeneous Subgroups. Another way to control for an extraneous variable is either to find, or restrict one's comparison to, groups that are homogeneous on that variable. Thus, in matching students on GPA, the researcher could either seek to find two groups that have similar GPA's (say, all 3.5 GPA or above) or form subgroups that represent various levels of the extraneous variable (divide the groups into high, middle, and low GPA subgroups, for example), and then compare the comparable subgroups (low IQ subgroup with the other low IQ subgroup, and so on).

Statistical Matching. The third way to control for an important extraneous variable is to match the groups on that variable, using the technique of statistical matching. As described in Chapter Twelve, statistical matching adjusts scores on a posttest for initial differences on some other variable that is assumed to be related to performance on the dependent variable.

OTHER THREATS

The likelihood of the remaining threats to internal validity depends on the type of study being considered. In nonintervention studies, the main concerns are loss of subjects, location, and instrumentation. If the persons who are lost to data collection are different from those who remain (as is often probable), *and* if more are lost from one group than the other(s), internal validity is threatened. If unequal numbers are lost, an effort should be made to determine the probable reasons.

A *location* threat is possible if the data are collected under different conditions for different groups. Similarly, if different data collectors are used with different groups, an *instrumentation* threat is introduced. Fortunately, it is usually relatively easy to ensure that variations in location and data collectors do not exist.

The possibility of a *data collector bias* can usually be controlled, as in experimental studies, by ensuring that whoever collects the data lacks any information that might bias results. *Instrument decay* is likely only in observational studies and can be controlled as in experimental studies.

In intervention-type studies, in addition to the threats discussed above, all of the remaining threats that we discussed in Chapter Twelve may be present. Unfortunately, most are less easy to control in causal-comparative research than in experimental studies. The fact that the researcher does not directly manipulate the treatment variable makes it more likely that an *implementer* and/or a *history* threat may exist. It may also mean that the length of the treatment time may have varied, thus creating a possible *maturation* threat. Either *Hawthorne* or demoralization threats may or may not exist, but the researcher has no control over them. *Regression* may be a threat if one of the groups was initially selected on the basis of extreme scores. Finally, a *pretest/treatment interaction* effect, as in experimental studies, may exist if a pretest was used in the study.

Evaluating Threats to Internal Validity in Causal-Comparative Studies

The evaluation of specific threats to internal validity in causal-comparative studies involves a set of steps similar to those presented in Chapter Twelve for experimental studies.

Step one: Ask: What specific factors either are known to affect the variable on which groups are being compared, or may logically be expected to affect this variable? Note that this is the dependent variable for studies of Type 1 and Type 3, but the independent variable for studies of Type 2. As we mentioned with regard to experimental studies, the researcher need not be concerned with factors unrelated to what is being studied.

Step two: Ask: What is the likelihood of the comparison groups differing on each of these factors? (Remember that a difference between groups *cannot* be explained away by a factor that is the same for all groups.)

Step three: Evaluate the threats on the basis of how likely they are to have an effect and plan to control for them. If a given threat cannot be controlled, this should be acknowledged.

Again, let us consider an example to illustrate how these steps might be employed. Suppose a researcher wishes to explore possible causes of students "dropping out" in inner-city high schools. He or she hypothesizes three possible causes: (1) family instability, (2) low student self-esteem, and (3) lack of a support system related to school and its requirements. The researcher compiles a list of recent dropouts and randomly selects a comparison group of students still in school. He or she then interviews students in both groups to obtain data on each of her three possible causal variables.

As we did in Chapters Twelve and Thirteen, we list below a number of the threats to internal validity discussed in Chapter Eleven, followed by our evaluation of each as they might apply to this study.

Subject Characteristics. Although there are many possible subject characteristics that might be considered, we deal with only four here—socioeconomic level of the family, gender, ethnicity, and marketable job skills.

1. Socioeconomic level of the family. *Step one:* Socioeconomic level can be expected to be related to dropping out versus staying in school. *Step two:* Socioeconomic level may be related to all three of the hypothesized causal variables. It should therefore be controlled by some form of matching. *Step three:* Likelihood of having an effect unless controlled: High.

2. Gender. *Step one:* May well be related to dropping out. *Step two:* Gender may also be related to each of the three hypothesized causal variables. Accordingly, the researcher should either restrict this study only to males or females or ensure that the comparison group has the same gender proportions as the dropout group.* *Step three:* Likelihood of having an effect unless controlled: High.

3. Ethnicity. *Step one:* May be related to dropping out. *Step two:* Ethnicity may also be related to all three of the hypothesized causal variables; therefore, the two groups should be matched with respect to ethnicity. *Step three:* Likelihood of having an effect unless controlled: Moderate to High.

4. Marketable job skills. *Step one:* Likely to be related to dropping out, since students often drop out if they are able to make money working. *Step two:* Job skills may be related to each of the hypothesized three causal variables. It would be desirable, therefore, to assess this and then control by some form of matching. *Step three:* Likelihood of having an effect unless controlled: Moderate to High.

Mortality. *Step one:* It is probable that more students in the dropout group will refuse to be interviewed (since they are working, it may be harder to arrange time for an interview)

* This is an example of stratifying a sample—in this case, the comparison group.

than students in the comparison group. *Step two:* It is also probable that refusing to be interviewed is related to each of the three hypothesized causal variables. The only solution would be to make every effort to get cooperation for the interviews from all subjects in both groups. *Step three:* Likelihood of having an effect unless controlled: High.

Location. *Step one:* It is quite likely that location (that is, the specific high schools involved in the study) is related to dropping out. (Dropout rates typically differ in different schools.) *Step two:* While it seems less likely that the causal variables would differ for different schools, this might be the case. The best solution is to analyze the data separately for each school. *Step three:* Likelihood of having an effect unless controlled: Moderate.

Instrumentation

1. **Instrument Decay.** *Step one:* Instrument decay in this study means interviewer fatigue. This certainly could affect the information obtained from students in both groups. *Step two:* The fatigue factor could be different for the two groups, depending on how interviews are scheduled; the solution is to try to schedule interviews to prevent fatigue from occurring. *Step three:* Likelihood of having an effect unless controlled: Moderate.

2. **Data Collector Characteristics.** *Step one:* Can be expected to influence the information obtained on the three hypothesized causal variables; for this reason, training of interviewers to standardize the interview process is very important. *Step two:* Despite such training, different interviewers might elicit different information. Therefore interviewers should be balanced across the two groups, i.e., each interviewer should be scheduled to do the same number of interviews with each group. *Step three:* Likelihood of having an effect unless controlled: Moderate.

3. **Data Collector Bias.** *Step one:* Bias might well be related to information obtained on the three hypothesized causal variables. *Step two:* Might differ for the two groups, e.g., interviewer might behave differently when interviewing

dropouts. The solution is to keep interviewers ignorant as to which group subjects belong. To do this, care has to be taken both with questions to be asked and in training interviewers. *Step three:* Likelihood of having an effect unless controlled: High.

Other Threats. Testing, implementer, history, maturation, attitudinal, and regression do not affect this kind (Type 2) of causal-comparative study.

The trick to identifying threats to internal validity in causal-comparative studies, as in experimental studies, is, first, to think of various things (conditions, other variables, and so on) that might affect the outcome variable of the study and then, second, to decide, based on evidence or experience, whether these things would be likely to affect the comparison groups differently. If so, this may provide an alternative explanation for the results. If this seems likely, a threat to internal validity of the study may indeed be present and needs to be controlled.

Data Analysis

The first step in an analysis of a causal-comparative study is to calculate the mean and standard deviation of each group if the variables are quantitative. These descriptive statistics are then assessed for magnitude (see Chapter Ten). A statistical inference test may or may not be appropriate, depending on whether random samples were used from identified populations (such as creative versus noncreative high school seniors). The most commonly used test in causal-comparative studies is a t test for differences between means. When more than two groups are used, then either an analysis of variance or an analysis of covariance is the appropriate test. Analysis of covariance is particularly helpful in causal-comparative research because a researcher cannot always match the comparison groups on all relevant variables other than the ones of primary interest. As mentioned in Chapter Nine, analysis of covariance provides a way to match groups "after the fact" on such variables as age, socioeconomic status, aptitude, and so on. Before analysis of covariance can be used, however, the data involved need to satisfy certain assumptions.[1]

The results of a causal-comparative study must be interpreted with caution. As with correlational studies, causal-comparative studies are good at identifying relationships between variables, but they do not prove cause and effect.

There are two ways to strengthen the interpretability of causal-comparative studies. First, as we mentioned earlier, alternative hypotheses should be formulated and investigated whenever possible. Second, if the dependent variables involved are categorical, the relationships among all of the variables in the study should be examined using the technique of discriminant function analysis, which we briefly described in Chapter Thirteen.

The most powerful way to check on the possible causes identified in a causal-comparative study, of course, is to perform an experiment. The presumed cause (or causes) identified could be manipulated. Should differences between experimental and control groups now be found, the researcher then has a reason for inferring causation.

Associations between Categorical Variables

Up to this point our discussion of associational methods has considered only the situations in which (a) one variable is categorical and the other(s) are quantitative; and (b) both variables are quantitative. It is also possible to investigate associations between categorical variables. Both crossbreak tables (see Chapter Eight) and contingency coefficients are used. An example of a relationship between categorical variables is shown in Table 14.1.

As was true with correlation, such data can be used for purposes of prediction and, with caution, in the search for cause and effect. Knowing that a person is a teacher, and male,

TABLE **14.1**

Teacher Gender and Grade Level

	Male	Female	Total
Elementary	40	60	100
Junior High	60	40	100
High School	70	30	100
Total	170	130	300

for example, we can predict, with some degree of confidence (on the basis of the date in Table 14.1), that he teaches either junior or senior high school, since 70 percent of males who are teachers do so. We can also estimate how much in error our prediction is likely to be. Based on the data in Table 14.1, the probability of our prediction being in error is 40/170, or .24. In this example, the possibility that gender is a major *cause* of teaching level seems quite remote—there are other variables, such as historical patterns of teacher preparation and hiring, that make more sense when one tries to explain the relationship.

There are no techniques analogous to partial correlation (see Chapter Thirteen) or the other techniques that have evolved from correlational research that can be used with categorical variables. Further, prediction from crossbreak tables is much less precise than from scatterplots. Fortunately, there are relatively few questions of interest in education that involve two categorical variables. It is common, however, to find a researcher treating variables that are conceptually quantitative (and measured accordingly) as if they were categorical. This is done when a researcher arbitrarily divides a set of quantitative scores into high, middle, and low groups. Nothing is gained by this procedure and it suffers from two serious defects: the loss of the precision that is acquired through the use of correlational techniques, and the essential arbitrariness of the division into groups. How does one decide which score separates "high" scores from "middle" scores, for example? In general, therefore, such arbitrary division should be avoided.*

* There are times when a quantitative variable is justifiably treated as a categorical variable. For example, creatively is generally considered to be a quantitative variable. One might, however, establish criteria for dividing this continuum into only two categories—"highly creative" and "typically creative"—as a way of studying relationships with other variables more efficiently as was done in our earlier example.

An Example of Causal-Comparative Research

In the remainder of this chapter, we present a published example of causal-comparative research, followed by a critique of its strengths and weaknesses. As we did in our critiques of the different types of research studies we analyzed in other chapters, we use several of the concepts introduced in earlier parts of the book in our analysis.

From *Journal of Educational Research, 80,* 343–347, 1987.
Reprinted by permission of Mark Dewalt and Donald W. Ball.

Some Effects of Training on the Competence of Beginning Teachers

Mark Dewalt
Susquehanna University

Donald W. Ball
University of Virginia

Abstract

This study investigated the relationship between training and 12 dimensions of teacher competence. Measures of these competencies were obtained from actual classroom observation utilizing a low-inference instrument. The sample of subjects was composed of 230 beginning teachers who were employed in 108 of Virginia's 139 school divisions and taught in grades 7–12. Teachers were observed three separate times by three different trained observers in the fall of 1985. The teachers who had had teacher training scored significantly higher on two competencies, affective climate and individual differences; teachers who had had no teacher training scored significantly higher on two other competencies, accountability and questioning skill. There were no significant differences between the two groups on the other eight competencies.

Recent reforms in education at the state level have served to alter the evaluation of beginning teachers. States such as Florida, Alabama, and Virginia have instituted programs to assess the competence of beginning teachers by recording classroom behavior using low-inference instruments. The data from these programs provide a rich source of information about the competence of beginning teachers. The data used in this study were obtained from the Virginia Beginning Teacher Assistance Program (Virginia State Department of Education, 1985).

Critics of teacher education argue that education majors spend too much time taking methodology courses and not enough time in subject matter courses. Keisling (1984) asserted that professional education courses were not intellectually demanding and reported that teachers invariably say that the education courses they took were useless. Sugg (1986) found it ludicrous that a retired physician, chemist, or accountant would not be able to teach in many states until he/she took the required education courses. He argued that those who know their subject matter will figure out a way to get this information across to those who want to learn. Others, including Berliner (1984), disagreed. Berliner stated that it was not the time to abolish teacher education courses because there was a scientific basis of research on classroom instruction. Many of these findings, which have occurred in the last 10 years, showed significant relationships between teacher behavior and student learning. Berliner argued that if preservice teachers can learn how to use this knowledge in their teaching then both teacher competence and student achievement will improve.

Studies investigating the relationship between number of education courses and principal's ratings have usually found higher ratings for teachers who had taken more education courses. However, the validity of rating scales has been questioned. Medley and Mitzel (1958), for example, found that a teacher receiving a low rating is likely to be just as competent as a teacher receiving a high rating. Brandt (1981) discussed several problems with rating scales. The first is the ambiguity of the trait being measured. For example, what one rater considers generosity, another does not. The second concerns the bias of the rater or the halo effect. If a rater is generally favorable toward a person, he/she will rate the individual high on all positive attributes. If, on the other hand, an evaluator is generally unfavorable toward a person, he/she will give the individual lower ratings. Another source of rater bias is the tendency of some people to be consistently too severe or too lenient in their judgments.

The present study sought to avoid these problems by using the low-inference observation system developed for and employed in the Virginia Beginning Teacher Assistance Program.

The Virginia Beginning Teacher Assistance Program (BTAP) began in 1982. In February of that year, the Board of Education adopted a resolution concerning the certification of Virginia's teachers.

Beginning July 1, 1985, first-time applicants for initial certification were granted a 2-year nonrenewable teaching certificate. To gain the Collegiate Professional Certificate, a 5-year renewable certificate, the teacher must demonstrate functional knowledge of 14 competencies through satisfactory performance in the classroom. Assistance is provided to teachers who fail to demonstrate knowledge on their first attempt and they are given additional opportunities to do so. Both the assessment and the assistance components of the program are based upon the research in effective teacher behavior.

This study focused on 12 of the competencies in the BTAP program.

(Two of the competencies, consistent rules and awareness, were not used for this study because there was some question whether these two were more a measure of student behavior than teacher behavior). The 12 competencies were (1) Academic Learning Time, (2) Accountability, (3) Clarity of Structure, (4) Individual Differences, (5) Evaluation, (6) Affective Climate, (7) Learner Self-concept, (8) Meaningfulness, (9) Planning, (10) Questioning Skill, (11) Reinforcement, and (12) Close Supervision. The definitions are in the Appendix.

Measures of the competencies were obtained from two instruments: a planning classroom performance record (CPR) and a planning record (PR).

The Classroom Performance Record is a sign system, that is, a list of more than 100 specific classroom behaviors or events called signs; the observer indicates which of the signs he or she observes during a 3-minute period, but not how often. The CPR is a low-inference measure of teacher observation; observers do not judge a behavior to be appropriate or inappropriate, but simply record its occurrence. Because of this the CPR is free from many problems associated with rating scales and other high-inference measures of teacher competence.

A different observer (trained by the State Department of Education) coded the behaviors displayed by a teacher in seven 3-minute segments during each of three class periods. Thus, a total of 21 CPRs were completed for each teacher.

In addition, each observer completed one planning record, using data obtained from a lesson plan description completed by the teacher before the observation. The lesson plan description asks teachers to respond to nine questions such as: What are the objectives of this lesson? Demographic information on the beginning teachers was collected on a form filled out by the teacher at the first beginning teacher orientation session held in September 1985.

METHOD

Sample

The sample of teachers selected for this study consisted of 230 beginning secondary school teachers who were observed in the fall of 1985 as part of the certification process. These teachers began teaching at the start of the 1985–86 school year in 108 of Virginia's 139 school divisions, in grades 7–12. All academic subject areas taught in the secondary schools in Virginia were represented. Fifty-six percent of the teachers were women and 44% were men. Minority teachers comprised 11% of the sample.

Data Analysis

Each teacher's scores on the 12 competencies were computed using combinations of items from the classroom performance record and the planning form used by the State Department of Education. Scores on each item were standardized, using the means and standard deviations of the 230 teachers in this study, to insure that each item had an equal weight in the final competency score. These standardized item scores were combined to provide a competency score. Finally, each of the competency scores was restandardized, so that each would have a mean of zero and a standard deviation of one in the sample of 230 teachers.

The Virginia State Department of Education has not authorized and will not authorize in the foreseeable future the publication of the scoring keys used to compute each competency because these competencies are currently used in the evaluation of beginning teachers as part of the certification process. A hypothetical competency would be scored in the following way:

> Competency score = $11 + 17 + 18 - 143 - 116$ ... where 11 = standardized item score for the first item on the observation instrument.

BTAP scores are based on frequencies of events that reflect one or another of the indicators in terms of which of the 14 competencies are defined. An event occurs when a teacher behavior (makes eye contact with off-task learner, re-orients learner after change of activity) is recorded in a specified situation (way of organizing a class).

Records were made in 662 classes of all grades and subjects on temporary forms of the two instruments. Provisional keys were scored on half of these records and the correlation between each event on a key and the total score on that key were examined. Keys were revised in an iterative process designed to maximize the internal consistency of each key. The revised keys were then used to score the other half of the records and the internal consistency (alpha) coefficient of each competency was estimated. Alpha coefficients for the 12 competencies used in this study ranged from .27 to .82 with a median value of .50.

Records of behaviors obtained with the BTAP instruments are not assumed to be representative of the behavior of the teachers observed. Teachers are asked not to demonstrate their best teaching behavior but to demonstrate the 14 BTAP competencies, regardless of whether they use them in their actual teaching or not. And because it is difficult to demonstrate all 14 competencies during one visit, they are advised to demonstrate some of them on one visit and some on another, so that scores on any one competency based on different visits to the same teacher cannot be regarded as equivalent.

TABLE 1.

**Demographic Data on Secondary Teachers With
and Without Full Preparation to Teach**

	Group 1 (not prepared)		Group 2 (prepared)	
	n	Percentage	*n*	Percentage
Sex				
Men	21	37	82	47
Women	36	63	91	53
Race				
Minority	9	16	10	6
White	48	84	163	94

For these reasons, it was not possible to estimate either the stability or the reliability of scores from these data. The alpha coefficients listed above are therefore the only information available about the reliability of BTAP scores.

The principal question this study sought to answer was, Do fully prepared teachers display more of the twelve competencies than teachers not fully prepared? To address this question, two groups of teachers were selected from the sample. Group 1 ($n = 57$) was comprised of secondary teachers who had had no professional education courses and no student teaching experience. Group 2 ($n = 173$) was comprised of secondary school teachers who had had 12 or more hours of education courses and student teaching. Some demographic characteristics of these groups are presented in Table 1.

RESULTS

The two groups were compared simultaneously on all twelve competencies by a multivariate analysis of variance procedure, and univariate *F*-tests were used to test differences between the two groups on each competency. Means, standard deviations, and differences on each competency are presented in Table 2. The multivariate analysis of variance resulted in a Wilks Lambda of .862 that was significant at the .001 level. The results of each of the univariate *F*-tests are shown in Table 2.

"Prepared" teachers (Group 2) scored higher on two competencies, Affective Climate and Individual Differences. "Unprepared" teachers (Group 1) scored higher on two other competencies, Accountability and Questioning Skill. No differences were found on the other eight competencies. A repeated measures analysis of variance of the 12 competency scores in each group indicated that the mean competency scores in the unprepared group (Group 1) had greater variability that those in the "prepared" group (Group 2).

TABLE 2.

Means and Standard Deviations for Groups 1 and 2 on Each of the 12 Teacher Competencies

Competency	Group 1 ($n = 57$) (Unprepared)		Group 2 ($n = 173$) (Prepared)		
	M	SD	M	SD	Difference
Academic learning time	−.070	1.140	.023	.951	−.093
Accountability	.318	1.133	−.105	.932	.423*
Clarity of structure	−.071	.857	.023	1.044	−.094
Individual differences	−.278	.661	.092	1.075	−.370*
Evaluation	.196	.942	−.063	1.013	.259
Affective climate	−.270	1.018	.089	.981	−.359*
Learner self-concept	−.107	.654	.035	1.090	−.142
Meaningfulness	−.116	1.021	.038	.993	−.154
Reinforcement	−.016	.876	.005	1.040	−.021
Questioning skill	.363	1.126	−.120	.927	.483*
Close supervision	.089	.988	−.029	1.005	.118
Planning	.007	1.026	−.002	.994	.009
Ms	.045	—	−.014	—	+0.59

*$p < .05$

DISCUSSION

The results indicate at best a mixed relationship between teacher training and the competence of beginning teachers as measured in this study. Unprepared teachers (ones who had had no education courses or student teaching) scored lower than prepared teachers (teachers who had had 12 or more hours of education courses plus student teaching) on two competencies, Affective Climate and Individual Differences. These findings are consistent with those of LuPone (1961) and Copley (1974). LuPone found that provisionally certified teachers scored lower than did regularly certified teachers in the area of pupil relations, and Copley found that arts and sciences graduates scored lower than education graduates in the area of consideration of pupils.

Unprepared teachers scored higher than prepared teachers on two competencies, Accountability and Questioning Skill. This result seems to be similar to Hoffman and Roper's (1985) finding that beginning teachers perceived themselves as deficient in the ability to keep students on task. No other differences were found between the two groups.

These results do not support the notion that teacher training increases the competence of beginning secondary teachers as measured in this study. Since the competencies reflect knowledge of recent research in teacher effectiveness, these results do not indicate that preservice teachers learn anything about this research in their professional education courses. If preservice teacher education students were taught about this research, there should have been differences in some competencies that favored the prepared group; and prepared teachers should have scored higher on the average than unprepared teachers. The differences that exist may of course reflect the effects of self-selection or interests of students who do or do not decide to take education courses; the lack of difference in mean scores seems explainable only in terms of a lack of training in these areas.

The fact that unprepared teachers' mean scores on the 12 competencies varied more than those of prepared teachers may indicate that education courses tend to standardize the competence of beginning teachers. That is, it may increase the competence of those who had little competence before taking the education courses and perhaps even impair some of the competence of those with oustanding ability. The fact that all 12 means are so close to the means across both groups does not lend much support to this conclusion, however.

The findings of this study also recall an assertion by Lasley and Applegate (1982) that the education of secondary teachers presently operates under three false assumptions: (a) secondary teachers must be content specialists; (b) secondary teachers teach best by telling; and (c) all students are the same. They also recall findings reported by von Eschenbach and Ley (1984) that elementary teachers are more likely than secondary teachers to accept and implement individual instruction and student-centered activities.

There is some research that indicates that teachers who implement findings of research in teacher effectiveness in their classroom are more effective (see, for example, Anderson, Evertson and Brophy, 1979). The findings of this study indicate that graduates of teacher education programs for secondary school teachers are largely ignorant of these findings. If graduates of these programs are to be more effective than teachers who have not benefited from them, research findings must be included in the professional education curriculum.

APPENDIX

Definitions of the Competencies of the Virginia Beginning Teacher Assistance Program (McNergney, Caldwell, Medley, & McLaughlin, 1985)

1. *Academic Learning Time.* The competent teacher knows that learning is directly related to the amount of time learners are actively engaged in planned learning activities.

2. *Accountability.* The competent teacher knows the importance of holding learners responsible for completing assigned tasks.

3. *Clarity of Structure.* The competent teacher knows that learning is facilitated if the lesson is presented in a clear systematic sequence consistent with the objectives of instruction.

4. *Individual Differences.* The competent teacher knows that learners progress at different speeds, learn in different ways, and respond to different kinds of motivation.

5. *Evaluation.* The competent teacher knows that learner progress is facilitated by instructional objectives which are known to the learners and which coincide with the objectives of evaluation.

6. *Affective Climate.* The competent teacher knows that learning occurs more readily in a classroom environment which is nonpunitive and accepting.

7. *Learner Self-Concept.* The competent teacher knows that a learner's achievement may be enhanced by improving his self-concept, and that his self-concept is enhanced if the teacher's expectations are high and if the teacher shows appreciation of the learner's personal worth.

8. *Meaningfulness.* The competent teacher knows that learning is facilitated when content is related to learners' interests, common experiences, or to information with which they are familiar.

9. *Planning.* The competent teacher knows the importance of deliberate and varied planning activities.

10. *Questioning Skill.* The competent teacher knows how to phrase convergent, divergent and probing questions and to use them to develop learners' academic knowledge.

11. *Reinforcement.* The competent teacher denotes awareness that the skillful use of reinforcement is an effective means of encouraging and discouraging particular behaviors.

12. *Close supervision.* The competent teacher knows that more is learned during individual, small and whole group activities if the learners are monitored.

References

Anderson, L., Evertson, C., & Brophy, J. (1979). An experimental study of effective teaching in first grade reading groups. *Elementary School Journal, 79,* 193–223.

Berliner, D. (1984). Making the right changes in preservice teacher education. *Phi Delta Kappan, 66,* 94–96.

Brandt, R. M. (1981). *Studying behavior in natural settings.* New York: Holt.

Copley, P. (1974). *A study of the effects of professional education courses in beginning teachers.* Springfield: Southwest Missouri State University. (ERIC Document Reproduction Service No. ED 098 147.)

Hoffman, D. E., & Roper, S. R. (1985, April). *How valuable is teacher training to beginning teachers? An analysis of graduate feedback from a rural teacher training program.* Paper presented at the annual meeting of the American Educational

Research Association, Chicago, Illinois. (ERIC Document Reproduction Service No. ED 258 967.)

Keisling, P. (1984). How not to teach teachers. *Principal, 64*, 18–20.

Lasley, T. J., & Applegate, J. H. (1982). The education of secondary teachers: Rhetoric or reform. *Journal of Teacher Education, 33*, 1–2.

LuPone, O. J. (1961). A comparison of provisionally certified and permanently certified elementary school teachers and their cooperating teachers (Doctoral dissertation, Stanford University). *Dissertation Abstracts International, 28*, 144A.

McNergney, R., Caldwell, M., Medley, D., & McLaughlin, R. (1985). *Assisting the beginning teacher*. Richmond, VA: Department of Education.

Medley, D. M., & Mitzel, H. (1958). A technique for measuring classroom behavior. *Journal of Educational Psychology, 49*, 86–92.

Sugg, H. (1986, January 13). The liberal arts for school teachers. *Roanoke Times and World News*. p. 4.

Virginia State Department of Education. (1985). *Beginning teacher assistance program*. Richmond, VA: Author.

von Eschenbach, J., & Ley, T. (1984). Differences between elementary and secondary teachers' perceptions of instructional practices. *The High School Journal, 68*, 31–36.

Analysis of the Study

PURPOSE/JUSTIFICATION

The purpose of this study is clear at the outset—to see if teacher training affects teacher competence—and the justification is persuasive. The authors cite recent attempts to assess beginning teacher competence and use the results in certification decisions. The rationale for such usage is given. They also document the controversy as to the value of teacher training. Finally, the use of an observation method rather than ratings of competence is well defended.

DEFINITIONS

One of the major variables in the study, training versus no training, is clearly identified: the former means twelve or more hours of education courses plus student teaching; the latter means no such experience. The second major variable, teacher competence, is defined as comprising twelve dimensions of behavior, which are then listed. Definitions of each dimension are included in an appendix. Although

these definitions are sufficiently clear, they raise a question that confuses the study throughout—each competency is defined as something the teacher "knows." We shall return to this point later when we discuss instrumentation.

PRIOR RESEARCH

Only one previous study (to support the authors' criticism of ratings) is mentioned in the introductory section. They do, however, cite a secondary source (Berliner) who summarized the results of research on teacher behavior and student learning. In their discussion, the authors cite studies that are consistent with their results, a practice which is defensible, but leaves the reader with the impression that pertinent research has been reviewed and included selectively—when it agreed with the results. It is not clear that prior research on the topic was comprehensively reviewed.

HYPOTHESES

No hypotheses are stated explicitly. It is clearly implied, however, that a directional hypothesis was tested for each competency—that is, that the trained teacher would demonstrate more competence than the untrained.

SAMPLE

The sample of each group (trained and untrained teachers) was large: 173 and 57, respectively. Seventy-seven percent of all school districts in Virginia were represented. All subject areas in grades 7–12 were included; all were observed during the fall semester as part of the certification process. It is not clear, however, whether they included all first-year secondary school teachers. If not, how and why were teachers selected? While it may be the case that the sample is representative of all beginning secondary school teachers in Virginia, the authors have not made this clear. Whether the results are generalizable outside of Virginia rests on the reader's assessment of similarities between Virginia and other states or areas. The authors make no recommendations nor indicate any limitations on generalizing.

INSTRUMENTATION

Description of instruments is good as far as it goes. The authors make it clear that the observation procedure requires the recording of specific behaviors when they occur during seven three-minute teaching segments. Observations were made during three different twenty-one-minute periods by different observers. Specific items were combined to derive a standard score on each competency. It appears (from the examples given) that the items (behaviors) are indeed low-inference—they require a minimum of observer inferences. It is not clear how the lesson plan description was used to assess competencies, however; evidently responses were somehow combined with observation scores.

The scoring of observations is somewhat unclear. Use of half the records to refine the scoring key for each competency is legitimate, but it is not clear how the key was revised. Since the raw data consist of frequencies of behaviors for each of the items observed, revision presum-

ably means changing the weight given each item. More importantly, alpha coefficients based (correctly) on the other half of the records indicate that the indicators (the behaviors) for some competencies are good ($\alpha = .82$), whereas they are very poor for others ($\alpha = .27$). The median alpha (.50) is of no consequence since groups are compared on each competency. For reasons given, it was not possible in this study to assess stability or observer agreement.

Finally, we question the content validity of the indicators (the items). Definitions of the competencies indicate that the teacher is competent, not if he or she teaches effectively, but if he or she "knows," for example, that learning is related to time on task. Example items do not appear to assess knowledge, however, but rather behavior: "makes eye contact with off-task learner," "re-orients learner after change of activity," and so on. Surely these behaviors can occur with or without such "knowledge." Since the authors stress that representative teacher behavior was *not* necessarily assessed, but rather that teachers were asked to demonstrate the competencies, our conclusion is that they were really measuring the extent to which the teachers could comprehend the competencies and figure out what behaviors the observers might have been looking for. The validity of the criterion measures used, therefore, seems open to serious question.

DATA ANALYSIS

The procedures used are appropriate—multivariate analysis of variance, followed by univariate analysis of variance for evaluating mean differences on each competency. As usual, qualifications due to the (probable) lack of randomness should be stated. In fact, if the sample was, indeed, all first year teachers—the target population—no inference techniques are needed. Although means are informative, frequency polygons would provide more information.

RESULTS

Means and standard deviations are appropriately provided. They permit the calculation of effect sizes (using the standard deviation of the untrained group) that range from .37 to .48 on the four competencies reported as significant. While not all at the recommended .50 level, they do provide support for the authors' conclusion that there are differences on these competencies.

DISCUSSION

We question the authors' interpretation of their results as demonstrating lack of teaching about research on teacher effectiveness in preservice programs. Their interpretation would be justified if they were measuring (observing) "knowledge" as described in competency definitions. We do not find persuasive evidence, however, that this is the case. As stated earlier, their observed behaviors appear to us actually to measure teacher ability to "psyche out" the observational system in terms of competency description. It does seem to us that trained teachers should have been expected to demonstrate more behaviors designed to "keep students on task," "provide close supervision," "present clear lessons," "plan for a variety of activities," and so on, since these behaviors are presumably learned and practiced in training; perhaps they would have if typical behavior rather than "show time" had been observed. It may also be the case that many of these "no difference" results are due to the poor reliability of the scales; it would be helpful to have such reliability data. The finding that trained teachers showed more "competence" on "affective climate" and "individual differences" would have been expected. The unexpected result is that trained teachers performed less well on "accountability" and "questioning skill."

INTERNAL VALIDITY

In this study, alternative explanations must be considered with respect to the pattern of results that emerged. The authors point out that the differences that exist may "reflect the effects of self-selection or interests of students who do or do not decide to take education courses. . . ." This is, as you know, one of the limitations of causal-comparative studies.

The question is: Why would the group of trained teachers exhibit more "concern for students" but less ability to "hold students responsible for tasks" or "use questions to develop learner's knowledge"? One possible answer is that there is good reason to suggest some teachers are more "student-oriented," while others are more "content-oriented." We would expect the former to be more likely to take education courses. There are instruments that assess this variable, but they were not used in this study. Another possibility is suggested by Table 1 in the report, which shows that the untrained group of teachers contained more women and more minorities—hence, by implication, more minority women. Perhaps they were more traditionally academic in orientation and less concerned with climate and individual differences. In the absence of any evidence, however, this explanation is also conjecture.

The other category of threat that concerns us is the possibility of observer bias. Apparently the data were collected before any intention of using them for the purposes of this study. This should be made clear since observations could have been affected by knowledge on the part of even some observers as to which teachers were trained and which were not. Although there was loss of data—a total of 662 classes were observed rather than the 690 (230 $\times$ 3) intended, it seems unlikely that this would favor one of the groups over the other.

The final conclusion of the authors, that graduates of secondary teacher education programs are largely ignorant of the research on teaching effectiveness, seems to us unjustified for the reasons explained above. Studies of this kind are often done to validate instruments. Had that been the purpose of this study, the conclusion would have been that scores on the instrument lacked validity, in part because of poor reliability. The validity of scores obtained even from low-inference instruments cannot be assumed, it must be demonstrated.

Main Points of Chapter Fourteen

- Causal-comparative research, like correlational research, seeks to identify associations among variables.
- Causal-comparative research attempts to determine the cause or consequences of differences that already exist between or among groups of individuals.
- The basic causal-comparative approach is to begin with a noted difference between two groups and then to look for possible causes for, or consequences of, this difference.
- There are three types of causal-comparative research, which differ in their purposes and structure.
- When an experiment would take a considerable length of time and be quite costly to conduct, a causal-comparative study is sometimes used as an alternative.
- As in correlational studies, relationships can be identified in a causal-comparative study, but causation cannot be established.
- The basic similarity between causal-comparative and correlational studies is that both seek to explore relationships among variables. When relationships are identified through causal-comparative research (or in correlational research), they often are studied at a later time by means of experimental research.
- In experimental research, the group membership variable is manipulated; in causal-comparative research the group differences already exist.
- The first step in formulating a problem in causal-comparative research is usually to identify and define the particular phenomena of interest, and then to consider possible causes for, or consequences of, these phenomona.
- The important thing in selecting a sample for a causal-comparative study is to define carefully the characteristic to be studied and then to select groups that differ in this characteristic.
- There are no limits to the kinds of instruments that can be used in a causal-comparative study.
- The basic causal-comparative design involves selecting two groups that differ on a particular variable of interest and then comparing them on another variable or variables.
- Two weaknesses in causal-comparative research are lack of randomization and inability to manipulate an independent variable.
- The major threat to the internal validity of causal-comparative study is the possiblity of a subject selection bias. The chief procedures that a researcher can use to reduce this threat include matching subjects on a variable related to performance on the dependent variable, finding or creating homogeneous subgroups, and the technique of statistical matching.
- Other threats to internal validity in causal-comparative studies include location, instrumentation, and loss of subjects. In addition, type 3 studies are subject to implementer, history, maturation, attitude of subjects, regression, and testing threats.
- The results of causal-comparative studies should always be interpreted with caution, since they do not prove cause and effect.
- Both crossbreak tables and contingency coefficients can be used to investigate

possible associations between categorical variables, although predictions from crossbreak tables are not precise. Fortunately, there are relatively few questions of interest in education that involve two categorical variables.

For Discussion

1. Suppose a researcher was interested in finding out what factors cause delinquent behavior in teenagers. What might be a suitable comparison group for the researcher to use in investigating this question?

2. Could observation be used in a causal-comparative study? If so, how?

3. Can you suggest any other threats to internal validity besides those we mention in this chapter that might endanger a causal-comparative study?

4. When, if ever, might a researcher prefer to conduct a causal-comparative study rather than an experimental study? Suggest an example.

5. What sorts of questions might lend themselves better to causal-comparative research than to experimental research? Why?

6. Which do you think would be easier to do, causal-comparative or experimental research? Why?

7. Is random assignment possible in causal-comparative research? What about random selection? Explain.

8. Suppose a researcher was interested in the effects of team teaching on student attitudes toward history. Could such a topic be studied by means of causal-comparative research? If so, how?

9. What sorts of variables might it be wise for a researcher to think about controlling for in a causal-comparative study? What sorts of variables, if any, might be irrelevant?

10. Might a researcher ever study the exact same variables in an experimental study that he or she studied in a causal-comparative study? If so, why?

11. We state in the text that in general quantitative variables should not be collapsed into categorical variables because (a) the decision to do so is almost always an arbitrary one, and (b) too much information is lost by doing so. Can you suggest any quantitative variables that, for these reasons, should not be collapsed into categorical variables? Can you suggest some quantitative variables that could justifiably be treated as categorical variables?

12. Suppose a researcher reports a higher incidence of childhood sexual abuse in adult women who have eating disorders than in a comparison group of women without eating disorders. Which variable is more likely to be the cause of the other? What other variables could be alternative or contributing causes?

13. Are there any research questions that cannot be studied by the causal-comparative method?

14. A professor at a private women's college wishes to assess the degree of alienation present in undergraduates as compared to graduate students at her institution, using an instrument that she has developed. (a) Which method, causal-comparative or experimental, would you recommend she use in her inquiry? Why? (b) Would the fact that the researcher plans to use an instrument that she herself developed make any difference in your recommendation?

Note

1. The interested reader is referred to Janet D. Elashoff. (1969). Analysis of covariance: A delicate instrument. *American Educational Research Journal* 6:383–399.

Research Exercise Fourteen: Causal-Comparative Research

You should complete Problem Sheet 14 only if you are planning a causal-comparative study. If your intended study involves a different methodology, you will find a similar problem sheet at the end of the chapter that deals with that methodology. You might wish to consider, however, whether your research question could be investigated by means of a causal-comparative study.

Using Problem Sheet 14, once again state the question of hypothesis of your study. Then describe, briefly but thoroughly, the procedures of your study, including analysis of results—that is, *what* you intend to do, *when, where,* and *how*. Lastly, indicate any unresolved problems you see at this point in your planning.

PROBLEM SHEET 14
Causal-Comparative Research

1. The question or hypothesis of my study is: _____
   _____
   _____

2. A brief summary of **what** I intend to do, **when, where,** and **how** is as follows: _____
   _____
   _____
   _____
   _____
   _____
   _____
   _____
   _____
   _____
   _____

3. The major problems I foresee at this point are as follows: _____
   _____
   _____

Chapter Fifteen

SURVEY RESEARCH

Survey research is one of the most common forms of research engaged in by educational researchers. It involves researchers asking a large group of people questions about a particular topic or issue. This asking of questions, all related to the issue of interest, is called a survey, and it can be done in a number of ways—face-to-face with individuals or groups, by mail, or by telephone. Each method has its advantages and disadvantages, but obtaining answers from a large group of people to a set of carefully designed and administered questions lies at the heart of survey research.

Objectives

Reading this chapter should enable you to:

- *Explain* what a survey is
- *Name* three types of surveys conducted in educational research
- *Explain* the purpose of surveys
- *Explain* the difference between a cross-sectional and a longitudinal survey
- *Describe* how survey research differs from other types of research
- *Describe* briefly how a survey is conducted
- *Describe* briefly how mail surveys, telephone surveys, and face-to-face interviews differ and *state* two advantages and disadvantages of each type
- *Describe* the most common pitfalls in developing survey questions
- *Explain* the difference between a closed-ended and an open-ended question, *give* an example of each, and *state* two advantages and disadvantages of each type
- *Explain* why nonresponse is a problem in survey research and *name* two ways to improve the rate of response in surveys
- *Name* two threats to validity that can affect the results of a survey and *explain* how such threats can be controlled
- *Recognize* an example of survey research when you come across it in the educational literature

What Is a Survey?

Researchers are often interested in the opinions of a large group of people about a particular topic or issue. They ask a number of questions, all related to the issue, to find answers. For example, imagine that the chairperson of the counseling department at a large university is interested in determining how students who are seeking a master's degree feel about the program. She decides to conduct a survey to find out. She selects a sample of fifty students from among those currently enrolled in the master's degree program and constructs questions designed to elicit their attitudes toward the program. She administers the questions to each of the fifty students in the sample in face-to-face interviews over a two-week period. The responses given by each student in the sample are coded into standardized categories for purposes of analysis, and these standardized records are then analyzed to provide descriptions of the students in the sample. The chairperson draws some conclusions about the opinions of the sample, which she then generalizes to the population from which the sample was selected, in this case, all of the graduate students seeking a master's degree in counseling from this university.

The above example illustrates the three major characteristics that all surveys possess.

1. Information is collected from a group of people in order to *describe* some aspects or characteristics (such as abilities, opinions, attitudes, beliefs, and/or knowledge) of the population of which that group is a part.
2. The main way in which the information is collected is through *asking questions;* the answers to these questions by the members of the group constitute the data of the study.
3. Information is collected from a *sample* rather than from every member of the population.

Why Are Surveys Conducted?

The major purpose of surveys is to describe the characteristics of a population. In essence, what researchers want to find out is how the members of a population distribute themselves on one or more variables (for example, age, ethnicity, religious preference, and attitudes toward school). As in other types of research, of course, the population as a whole is rarely studied. Instead, a carefully selected sample of respondents is surveyed and a description of the population is inferred from what is found out about the sample.

Researchers might be interested in describing how certain characteristics (age, gender, ethnicity, political involvement, and so on) of teachers in inner-city high schools are distributed within the group. The researcher would select a sample of teachers from inner-city high schools to survey. Generally in a descriptive survey such as this, researchers are not so much concerned with why the observed distribution exists as with what the distribution *is*.

Types of Surveys

There are two major types of surveys that can be conducted—a cross-sectional survey and a longitudinal survey.

CROSS-SECTIONAL SURVEYS

A **cross-sectional survey** collects information from a sample that has been drawn from a predetermined population. Furthermore, the information is collected at just one point in time, although the time it takes to collect all of the data desired may take anywhere from a day to a few weeks or more. Thus, a professor of mathematics might collect data from a sample of all the high school mathematics teachers in a particular state about their interest in earning a master's degree in mathematics from his university, or another researcher might take a survey of the kinds of personal problems experienced by students at ten, thirteen, and sixteen years of age. All these groups could be surveyed at approximately the same point in time.

When an entire population is surveyed, it is called a **census**. The prime example is the census conducted by the U.S. Bureau of the Census every ten years, which attempts to collect data about everyone in the United States.

LONGITUDINAL SURVEYS

A **longitudinal survey,** on the other hand, collects information at different points in time in order to study changes over time. Three longitudinal designs are commonly employed in survey research: trend studies, cohort studies, and panel studies.

In a **trend study,** different samples from the same population are surveyed at different points in time. For example, a researcher might be interested in the attitudes of high school principals toward the use of flexible scheduling. He would select a sample each year from a current listing of high school principals throughout the state. Although the population would change somewhat and the same individuals would not be sampled each year, if random selection was used to obtain the samples, the responses obtained each year could be considered representative of the population of high school principals. The researcher would then examine and compare responses from year to year to see if any trends are apparent.

In a **cohort study,** a *specific* population is followed over a period of time. Whereas a trend study samples a population whose members change over time, a cohort study samples a particular population whose members do not change over the course of the survey. Thus, a researcher might want to study growth in teaching effectiveness of all the first year teachers who had graduated the past year from San Francisco State University. The names of all of these teachers would be listed and then a different sample would be selected from this listing at different times.

In a **panel study,** on the other hand, the researcher selects a sample right at the beginning of her study. She then surveys the *same* individuals at different times during the course of the survey. Since the researcher is studying the same individuals, she can note changes in their characteristics or behavior and explore the reasons for these changes. Thus, the researcher in our previous example might select a sample of last year's graduates from San Francisco State University who are first year teachers and survey the same individuals several times during the teaching year. Loss of individuals is a frequent problem in panel studies, however, particularly if the study extends over a fairly long period of time.

Following are the titles of some published reports of surveys that have been conducted by educational researchers.

- The status of state history instruction[1]
- Dimensions of effective school leadership: The teacher's perspective[2]
- Teacher perceptions of discipline problems in a central Virginia middle school[3]
- Two thousand teachers view their profession[4]
- Grading problems: A matter of communication[5]
- Peers or parents: Who has the most influence on *cannabis* use?[6]
- A career ladder's effect on teacher career and work attitudes[7]
- Ethical practices of licensed professional counselors: A survey of state licensing boards[8]

Survey Research and Correlational Research

It is not uncommon to find researchers examining the relationship of responses to one question in a survey to another, or of a score based on one set of survey questions to a score based on another set. In such instances, the techniques of correlational research described in Chapter Fourteen are frequently appropriate.

Suppose a researcher is interested in studying the relationship between attitude toward school of high school students and their outside-of-school interests. A questionnaire containing items dealing with these two variables could be prepared and administered to a sample of high school students, and then relationships could be determined by calculating correlation coefficients or by preparing contingency tables. The researcher may find that students who have a positive attitude toward school also have a lot of outside interests, while those who have a negative attitude toward school have very few outside interests.

Steps in Survey Research

PROBLEM DEFINITION

The problem to be investigated by means of a survey should be sufficiently interesting and important enough to motivate the individuals surveyed to respond. Trivial questions usually get what they deserve—tossed into the nearest wastebasket. We would not be surprised to learn that you have done this yourself to a survey questionnaire you considered unimportant or found boring.

Researchers need to define clearly their objectives in conducting a survey. Each question to be asked should relate to one or more of the survey's objectives. One strategy for defining survey questions is to use a hierarchical approach, beginning with the broadest, most general questions, and ending with the most specific. Richard Jaeger gives a detailed example of such a survey on the question of why many public school teachers "burn out" and leave the profession within a few years. He suggests three general factors—economics, working conditions, and perceived social status—around which to structure possible questions for the survey. Here are the questions he developed with regard to economic factors.

I. Do economic factors cause teachers to leave the profession early?
   A. Do teachers leave the profession early because of inadequate yearly income?
      1. Do teachers leave the profession early

because their monthly income during the school year is too small?

2. Do teachers leave the profession early because they are not paid during the summer months?

3. Do teachers leave the profession early because their salary forces them to hold a second job during the school year?

4. Do teachers leave the profession early because their lack of income forces them to hold a different job during the summer months?

B. Do teachers leave the profession early because of the structure of their pay scale?

1. Do teachers leave the profession early because the upper limit on their pay scale is too low?

2. Do teachers leave the profession early because their rate of progress on the pay scale is too slow?

C. Do teachers leave the profession early because of inadequate fringe benefits?

1. Do teachers leave the profession early because their health insurance benefits are inadequate?

2. Do teachers leave the profession early because their life insurance benefits are inadequate?

3. Do teachers leave the profession early because their retirement benefits are inadequate?[9]

A hierarchical set of research questions like this can help researchers identify large categories of issues, suggest more specific issues within each category, and conceive of possible questions. By determining whether a proposed question fits the purposes of the intended survey, researchers can eliminate those that do not. This is important since the length of a survey's questionnaire or interview schedule is a crucial factor in determining the survey's success.

IDENTIFICATION OF THE TARGET POPULATION

Almost anything can be described by means of a survey. That which is studied in a survey is called the **unit of analysis.** Although typically people, units of analysis can also be objects, clubs, companies, classrooms, schools, government agencies, and others. For example, in a survey of faculty opinion about a new discipline policy recently instituted in a particular school district, each faculty member sampled and surveyed would be the unit of analysis. In a survey of urban school districts, the school district would be the unit of analysis.

Survey data are collected from a number of individual units of analysis to describe those units; these descriptions are then summarized to describe the population that the units of analysis represent. In the example given above, data collected from a sample of faculty members (the unit of analysis) would be summarized to describe the population that this sample represents (all of the faculty members in that particular school district).

As in other types of research, the group of persons (objects, institutions, and so on) that is the focus of the study is called the target population. To make trustworthy statements about the target population, it must be very well defined. In fact, it must be so well defined that it is possible to state with certainty whether or not a particular unit of analysis is a member of this population. Suppose, for example, that the target population is defined as "all of the faculty members in a particular school district." Is this definition sufficiently clear so that one can state with certainty who is or is not a member of this population? At first glance, you may be tempted to say yes. But what about administrators who also teach? What about substitute teachers, or those who teach only part-time? What about student teachers? What about counselors? Unless the target population is defined in sufficient detail so that it is unequivocally clear as to who is, or is not, a member of it, any statements made about this population, based on a survey of a sample of it, may be misleading or incorrect.

MODE OF DATA COLLECTION

There are four basic ways to collect data in a survey—by administering the survey instrument "live" to a group; by mail; by telephone; or through face-to-face interviews. Each has its advantages and disadvantages.

Direct Administration to a Group.
This method is used whenever a researcher has access to all (or most) of the members of a particular group in one place. The instrument is administered to all members of the group at the same time and usually in the same place. Examples would include students being given a questionnaire to complete in their classrooms or workers at their job settings. The chief advantage of this approach is the high rate of response—often close to 100 percent (usually in a single setting). Other advantages include a generally low cost factor, plus the fact that the researcher has an opportunity to explain the study and answer any questions that the respondents may have before they complete the questionnaire. The chief disadvantage is that there are not too many types of surveys that can use samples of individuals that are collected together as a group.

Mail Surveys.
When the data in a survey are collected by mail, the questionnaire is sent to each individual in the sample by mail, with a request that it be completed and then returned by a given date. The advantages of this approach are that it is relatively inexpensive and it can be accomplished by the researcher alone (or with only a few assistants). It also allows the researcher to have access to samples that might be hard to reach in person or by telephone (such as the disabled), and it permits the respondents to take sufficient time to give thoughtful answers to the questions asked.

The disadvantages of mail surveys are that there is less opportunity to encourage the co-operation of the respondents (through building rapport, for example) or to provide assistance (through answering their questions, clarifying instructions, and so on). As a result, mail surveys have a tendency to produce low response rates. Mail surveys also do not lend themselves well to obtaining information from certain types of samples (such as individuals who are illiterate).

Telephone Surveys.
In a telephone survey, of course, the researcher (or his or her assistants) asks questions of the respondents over the telephone. The advantages of telephone surveys are they are cheaper than personal interviews, can be conducted fairly quickly, and lend themselves easily to standardized questioning procedures. They also allow the researcher to assist the respondent (by clarifying questions, asking follow-up questions, encouraging hesitant respondents, and so on), permit a greater amount of follow-up (through several callbacks), and provide better coverage in certain areas where personal interviewers often are reluctant to go.*

The disadvantages of telephone surveys are that access to some samples (obviously, those without telephones and those whose phones are unlisted) is not possible. Telephone interviews also prevent visual observation of respondents and are somewhat less effective in obtaining information about sensitive issues or personal questions. Generally, telephone surveys are reported to result in a five percent lower response rate than that obtained by personal interviews.[10]

Personal Interviews.
In a personal interview, the researcher (or trained assistants) conducts a face-to-face interview with the respondent. As a result, this method has many advantages. It is probably the most effective way there is to enlist the cooperation of the respondents in a survey. Rapport can be established, questions can be clarified, unclear or incomplete answers can be followed up, and so on. Face-to-face interviewing also places less of a burden on the reading and writing skills of the respondents and, when necessary, permits spending more time with respondents.

---

* Computers are being used more and more in telephone surveys. Typically, an interviewer sits in front of a computer screen. A central computer randomly selects a telephone number and dials it. The interviewer, wearing a headset, hears the respondent answer the phone. On the computer screen appears a typed introduction, such as "Hello, my name is ———", for the interviewer to read, followed by the first question for him or her to ask. The interviewer then types the respondent's answer into the computer. The answer is immediately stored inside the central computer. The next question to be asked then appears on the screen, and the interviewer continues the questioning.

TABLE **15.1**

Advantages and Disadvantages
of Survey Data Collection Methods

	Direct Administration	Telephone	Mail	Interview
Comparative cost	lowest	about the same		high
Facilities needed?	yes	no	no	yes
Require training of questioner?	yes	yes	no	yes
Data collection time	shortest	short	longer	longest
Response rate	very high	good	poorest	very high
Group administration possible?	yes	no	no	yes
Allow for random sampling?	possibly	yes	yes	yes
Require literate sample?	yes	no	yes	no
Permit follow-up questions?	no	yes	no	yes
Encourage response to sensitive topics?	somewhat	somewhat	best	weak
Standardization of responses	easy	somewhat	easy	hardest

The biggest disadvantage of face-to-face interviews is that they are more costly than either mail or telephone surveys. They also require a trained staff of interviewers, with all that implies in terms of training costs and time. The total data collection time required is also likely to be quite a bit longer than in either of the other two methods. It is possible, too, that the lack of anonymity (the respondent is obviously known to the interviewer, at least temporarily) may result in less valid responses to personally sensitive questions. Last, some types of samples (individuals in high crime areas, workers in large corporations, students, and so on) are often difficult to contact in sufficient numbers. Table 15.1 presents a summary of the advantages and disadvantages of each of the four survey methods with regard to a number of factors.

SELECTION OF THE SAMPLE

The subjects to be surveyed should be selected (randomly, if possible) from the population of interest. Researchers must ensure, how-ever, that the subjects they intend to question possess the information the researcher wants to obtain and that they will be willing to answer these questions. Individuals who possess the necessary information but who are uninterested in the topic of the survey (or who do not see it as important) are unlikely to respond. Accordingly, it is often a good idea for researchers to conduct a preliminary inquiry among potential respondents to assess their receptivity. Frequently, in school-based surveys, a higher response rate can be obtained if a questionnaire is sent to persons in authority to administer to the potential respondents rather than to the respondents themselves. For example, a researcher might ask classroom teachers to administer a questionnaire to their students rather than asking the students directly.

Some examples of samples that have been surveyed by educational researchers are as follows.

- A sample of all students attending an urban university concerning their views on the adequacy of the general education program at the university.

- A sample of all faculty members in an inner-city high school district as to the changes needed to help "at-risk" students learn more effectively.
- A sample of all such students in the same district concerning their views on the same topic.
- A sample of all women school superintendents in a particular state concerning their views as to the problems they encounter in their administrations.
- A sample of all the counselors in a particular high school district concerning their perceptions as to the adequacy of the school counseling program.

PREPARATION OF THE INSTRUMENT

The most common types of instruments used in survey research are the questionnaire and the interview schedule (see Chapter Six).* They are virtually identical, except that the questionnaire is usually self-administered by the respondent, while the interview schedule is administered verbally by the researcher (or trained assistants). In the case of a mailed or self-administered questionnaire, the appearance of the instrument is very important to the overall success of the study. It should be attractive and not too long† and the questions should be as easy to answer as possible. The questions in a survey, and the way they are asked, are of crucial importance. Floyd Fowler points out that there are four practical standards that all survey questions should meet:

1. Is this a question that can be asked exactly the way it is written?
2. Is this a question that will mean the same thing to everyone?
3. Is this a question that people can answer?

4. Is this a question that people will be willing to answer, given the data collection procedures?[11]

The answers to each of the above questions for every question in a survey should be "yes." Any survey question that violates one or more of these standards should be rewritten.

In the case of a personal interview or a telephone survey, the manner of the questioner becomes of paramount importance. He or she must ask the questions in such a way as to encourage the subjects of the study to want to respond.

In either case, the audience to whom the questions are to be directed should be clearly identified. Specialized or unusual words should be avoided if possible, or if they must be used, defined clearly in the instructions written on the instrument. The most important thing for researchers to keep in mind, however, is that whatever type of instrument is used, the *same* questions must be asked of all respondents in the sample. Furthermore, the conditions under which the questionnaire is administered or the interview is conducted should be as similar as possible for all respondents.

Types of Questions. The nature of the questions, and the way they are asked, are extremely important in survey research. Poorly worded questions can doom a survey to failure. Hence they must be clearly written in a manner that is easily understandable by the respondents.[12]

Most surveys rely on multiple-choice or other forms of what are called closed-ended questions. Multiple-choice questions allow a respondent to select his or her answer from a number of options. They may be used to measure opinions, attitudes, or knowledge.

Some examples of closed-ended questions are the following.

1. Which subject do you like *least*?
   a. Social studies
   b. English
   c. Science
   d. Mathematics
   e. Other (specify) _____

---

* Tests of various types can also be used in survey research, as when a researcher uses them to describe the reading proficiency of students in a school district. We restrict our discussion here, however, to the description of preferences, opinions, and beliefs.

† This is very important. Long questionnaires discourage people from completing and returning them.

2. Please rate each of the following parts of your master's degree program by circling the number under the phrase that describes how you feel.

		very dissatisfied	dissatisfied	satisfied	very satisfied
a.	Coursework	1	2	3	4
b.	Professors	1	2	3	4
c.	Advising	1	2	3	4
d.	Requirements	1	2	3	4
e.	Cost	1	2	3	4
f.	Other (specify)				
	_____	1	2	3	4

Closed-ended questions are easy to use, score, and code for analysis on a computer. Since all subjects respond to the same options, standardized data are provided. They are somewhat more difficult to write than open-ended questions, however. They also pose the possibility that an individual's true response is not present among the options given. For this reason, the researcher usually should provide an "other" choice for each item, where the subject can write in a response that the researcher may not have anticipated.

Open-ended questions allow for more individualized responses, but they are sometimes difficult to interpret. They are also often hard to score, since so many different kinds of responses are received. Furthermore, respondents sometimes do not like them. Some examples of open-ended questions are as follows.

1. What characteristics of a person would lead you to rate her or him as a good administrator?
2. What do you consider to be the most important problem facing classroom teachers in high schools today?
3. What were the three things about this class you found most useful during the past semester?

Generally, therefore, closed-ended or short-answer questions are preferable, although some-times researchers find it useful to combine both formats in a single question, as shown in the following example of a question using both open and closed-ended formats.

1. Please rate and comment on each of the following aspects of this course:

		very dissatisfied	dissatisfied	satisfied	very satisfied
a.	Coursework	1	2	3	4
	Comment				
b.	Professor	1	2	3	4
	Comment				

Table 15.2 presents a brief comparison of the advantages and disadvantages of closed-ended and open-ended questions.

Some Suggestions for Improving Closed-Ended Questions. There are a number of relatively simple tips that researchers have found to be of value in writing good survey questions. A few of the most frequently mentioned ones are as follows.[13]

1. Be sure the question is *unambiguous*.
   Poor: Do you spend a lot of time studying?
   Better: How much time do you spend each day studying?
      a. More than two hours.
      b. One to two hours.
      c. Thirty minutes to one hour.
      d. Less than thirty minutes.
      e. Other (specify).
2. Keep the focus as simple as possible.
   Poor: Who do you think are more satisfied with teaching in elementary and secondary schools, men or women?

a. Men are more satisfied.
b. Women are more satisfied.
c. Men and women are about equally satisfied.
d. Don't know.

Better: Who do you think are more satisfied with teaching in elementary schools, men or women?
a. Men are more satisfied.
b. Women are more satisfied.
c. Men and women are about equally satisfied.
d. Don't know.

3. Keep the questions short.

Poor: What part of the district's English curriculum, in your opinion, is of the most importance in terms of the overall development of the students in the program?

Better: What part of the district's English curriculum is the most important?

4. Use common language.

Poor: What do you think is the principal reason schools are experiencing increased student absenteeism today?
a. Problems at home.
b. Lack of interest in school.
c. Illness.
d. Don't know.

Better: What do you think is the main reason students are absent more today?
a. Problems at home.
b. Lack of interest in school.
c. Illness.
d. Don't know.

5. Avoid the use of terms that might "bias" responses.

Poor: Do you support the superintendent's "no smoking" policy on campus grounds while school is in session?
a. I support the policy.
b. I am opposed to the policy.
c. I don't care one way or the other about the policy.
d. I am undecided about the policy.

Better: Do you support a policy of "no smoking" on campus grounds while school is in session?

TABLE 15.2

Advantages and Disadvantages of Closed-ended versus Open-ended Questions

Closed-ended	Open-ended
Advantages	
• Enhances consistency of response across respondents	• Allows more freedom of response
• Easier and faster to tabulate	• Easier to construct
• More popular with respondents	• Permits follow-up by interviewer
Disadvantages	
• May limit breadth of responses	• Responses tend to be inconsistent in length and content across respondents
• Takes more time to construct	• Both questions and responses subject to misinterpretation
• Requires more questions to cover the research topic	• Harder to tabulate and synthesize

a. I support the policy.
b. I am opposed to the policy.
c. I don't care one way or the other about the policy.
d. I am undecided about the policy.

6. Avoid leading questions.

Poor: Why do you favor standards in your classes?

Better: Circle each of the following that describes a standard you set in your classes.
a. All homework must be turned in on the date due.
b. Students are not to interrupt other students during class discussions.
c. Late homework is not accepted.
d. Students are counted tardy if they are more than five minutes late to class.
e. Other (specify) _____

7. Avoid double negatives.

Poor: Would you not be opposed to supervising students outside of your classroom?
a. Yes.
b. No.
c. Undecided.

Better: Would you be willing to supervise students outside of your classroom?
 a. Yes.
 b. No.
 c. Undecided.

Pretesting the Questionnaire. Once the questions to be included in the questionnaire or the interview schedule have been written, the researcher is well-advised to try them out with a small sample similar to the potential respondents. A "pretest" of the questionnaire or interview schedule can reveal ambiguities, poorly worded questions, questions that are not understood, and unclear choices and can also indicate whether the instructions to the respondents are clear.

Overall Format. The format of a questionnaire—how the questions look to the respondents—is very important in encouraging them to respond. Perhaps the most important rule to follow is to ensure that the questions are spread out, that is, uncluttered. No more than one question should be presented on a single line. When respondents have to spend a lot of time reading a question, they quickly become discouraged from continuing.

There are a variety of ways to present the response categories from which respondents are asked to choose. Earl Babbie suggests that boxes, as shown in the question below, are the best.[14]

Have you ever taught an advanced placement class?

 [   ] Yes
 [   ] No

Sometimes, certain questions will apply to only a portion of the subjects in the sample. When this is the case, follow-up questions can be included in the questionnaire. For example, a researcher might ask respondents if they are familiar with a particular activity, and then ask those who say "yes" to give their opinion of the activity. The follow-up question is called a **contingency question**—it is contingent upon how a respondent answers the first question. If prop-

erly used, contingency questions are a valuable tool to use in surveys, in that they can make it easier for a respondent to answer a given question and also improve the quality of the data a researcher receives. Although there are a variety of contingency formats that might be used, the easiest to prepare is simply to set off the contingency question by indenting it, enclosing it in a box, and connecting it to the base question by means of an arrow to the appropriate response, as follows.

Have you ever taught an advanced placement class?

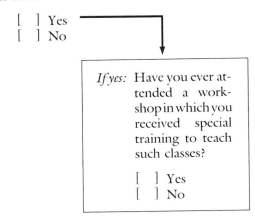

A clear and well-organized presentation of contingency questions is particularly important in interview schedules. An individual who receives a questionnaire in the mail can reread a question if it is unclear the first time through. If an interviewer becomes confused, however, or reads a question poorly or in an unclear manner, the whole interview may become jeopardized. Figure 15.1 illustrates a portion of an interview schedule designed to determine certain characteristics of substitute teachers that includes several contingency questions.

PREPARATION OF THE COVER LETTER

Mailed surveys require something that telephone surveys and face-to-face personal interviews do not—a cover letter explaining the purpose of the questionnaire. Ideally, the cover letter also motivates the members of the sample to respond.

FIGURE 15.1

Example of Several Contingency Questions in an Interview Schedule

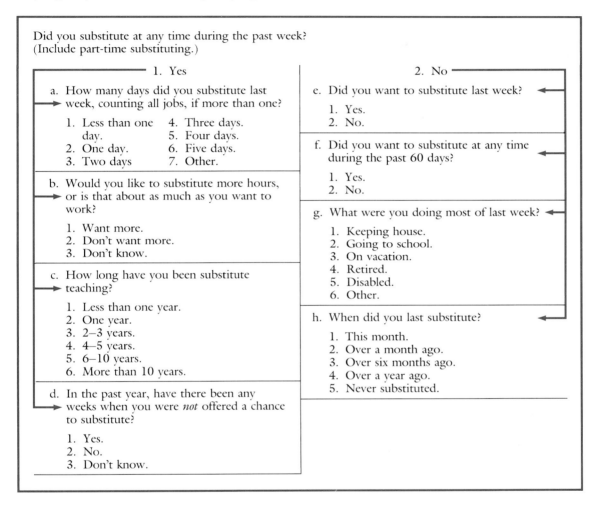

Adapted from Earl S. Babbie. (1973). *Survey research methods.* Belmont, CA: Wadsworth. p. 149.

The cover letter should be brief and addressed specifically to the individual being asked to respond. It should explain the purpose of the survey, emphasize the importance of the topic of the research, and (hopefully) engage the respondent's cooperation. If possible, it should indicate a willingness on the part of the researcher to share the results of the study once it is completed. Confidentiality and anonymity of the respondents should be assured.* It also helps if the researcher obtains the sponsorship of an institution of some importance that is known to the respondent. The specific deadline date by which the completed questionnaire is to be

* If done under a university (or other agency) sponsorship, the letter should indicate that the study has been approved by the "Research with Human Subjects" review committee.

returned should be indicated, and the letter should be individually signed by the researcher. Every effort should be made to avoid the appearance of a form letter. Finally, the return should be made as easy as possible; hence enclosing a stamped, self-addressed envelope is always a good idea. Figure 15.2 presents an example of a cover letter.

TRAINING OF INTERVIEWERS

Both telephone and face-to-face interviewers need to be trained beforehand. Many suggestions have been made in this regard, and we have space to mention only a few of them here.[15] Telephone interviewers need to be shown how to engage their interviewees so that they do not hang up on them before the interview has even begun. They need to know how to explain quickly the purpose of their call, and why it is important to obtain information from the respondent. They need to learn how to ask questions in a way so as to encourage those they call to respond honestly.

Face-to-face interviewers need all of the above and more. They need to learn how to establish rapport with their interviewees and to put them at ease. If a respondent seems to be threatened by a particular line of questioning, the interviewer needs to know how to move on to a new set of questions and return to the previous questions later. The interviewer needs to know when and how to "follow-up" on an unusual answer or one that is ambiguous or unclear. Interviewers also need training in gestures, manner, facial expression, and dress. A frown at the wrong time can discourage a respondent from even attempting to answer a question! In sum, the general topics to be covered in training interviewers should always include at least the following.

1. Procedures for contacting respondents and introducing the study. All interviewers should have a common understanding of the purposes of the study.
2. The conventions that are used in the design of the questionnaire with respect to wording and instructions for skipping questions (if necessary) so that interviewers can ask the questions in a consistent and standardized way.
3. Procedures for probing inadequate answers in a nondirective way. *Probing* refers to following up incomplete answers in ways that do not favor one particular answer over another. Certain kinds of standard probes, such as asking "Anything else?" "Tell me more," or "How do you mean that?" usually will handle most situations.
4. Procedures for recording answers to open-ended and closed-ended questions. This is especially important with regard to answers to open-ended questions, which interviewers are expected to record verbatim.
5. Rules and guidelines for handling the interpersonal aspects of the interview in a non-biasing way. Of particular importance here is for interviewers to focus on the task at hand and to avoid expressing their views or opinions (verbally or with body language) on any of the questions being asked.[16]

USING AN INTERVIEW TO MEASURE ABILITY

Although the interview has been used primarily to obtain information on variables other than cognitive ability, an important exception can be found in the field of developmental and cognitive psychology. Interviews have been used extensively in this field to study both the content and processes of cognition. The best known example of such use is to be found in the work of Jean Piaget and his colleagues. They used a semi-structured sequence of contingency questions to determine a child's cognitive level of development.

Other psychologists have used interviewing procedures to study thought processes and sequences employed in problem solving. While not used very extensively, to date, in educational research, an illustrative study is that of Peter Freyberg and Roger Osborne who studied student understanding of basic science concepts. They found frequent and important misconcep-

FIGURE 15.2

Example of a Cover Letter for Use in a Survey

SCHOOL OF EDUCATION

San Francisco State University

October 1, 19--

Mr. Robert R. Johnson
Social Studies Department
Oceana High School
Pacifica, California 96321

Dear Mr. Johnson,

The Department of Secondary Education at San Francisco University prepares over 100 student teachers every year to teach in the public and private schools of California. It is our goal to help our graduates become as well prepared as possible to teach in today's schools. The enclosed questionnaire is designed to obtain your views on what we can do to improve the quality of our training program. Your suggestions will be considered in planning for revisions in the program in the coming academic year. We will also provide you with a copy of the results of our study.

We will greatly appreciate it if you will complete the questionnaire and return it in the enclosed stamped, self-addressed envelope by October 15th. We realize your schedule is a busy one and that your time is valuable, but we are sure that you want to improve the quality of teacher training as much as we do. Your responses will be kept completely confidential; we ask for no identifying information on the questionnaire form. The study has been approved by the University's Research with Human Subjects review committee.

We want to thank you in advance for your cooperation.

William P. Jones
Chair of the Department

tions of which teachers were often unaware. Teachers often assumed that students used such terms as "gravity," "condensation," "conservation of energy," and "wasteland community" in the same way as they did themselves. Many 10-year-olds and even some older children, for example, believed that condensation on the outside of a water glass was caused by water getting through the glass. One 15-year-old displayed ingenious (although incorrect) thinking as shown in the following excerpt:

> (Jenny, aged 15): Through the glass—the particles of water have gone through the glass, like diffusion through air—well, it hasn't got there any other way. (Researcher: A lot of younger people I have talked to have been worried about this water . . . it troubles them.) (Jenny): Yes, because they haven't studied things like we have studied. (Researcher: What have you studied which helps?) (Jenny): Things that pass through air, and concentrations and how things diffuse . . . .[17]

Freyberg and Osborne make the argument that teachers and curriculum developers must have such information on student conceptions if they are to teach effectively. They have also shown how such research can improve the content of achievement tests by including items specifically directed at common misconceptions.

Nonresponse

In almost all surveys, some members of the sample will not respond. This is referred to as *nonresponse*. It may be due to a number of reasons (lack of interest in the topic being surveyed, forgetfulness, unwillingness to be surveyed, and so on), but it is a major problem that seems to be increasing in recent years as more and more people seem (for whatever reason) to be unwilling to participate in surveys.

Why is nonresponse a problem? The chief reason is that those who do not respond will very likely differ from the respondents with regard to answers to the survey questions. Should this be the case, any conclusions drawn on the basis of the respondents' replies will be misleading and not a true indication of the views of the population from which the sample was drawn.

Nonresponse can be divided into two categories: *total nonresponse* (when no information at all is collected from one or more individuals) and *item nonresponse* (when some, but not all information is collected from one or more individuals).

TOTAL NONRESPONSE

Graham Kalton points out that total nonresponse can occur in interview surveys for any of the following reasons: intended respondents can refuse to be interviewed, not be at home when the interviewer calls, be unable to take part in the interview for various reasons (such as illness, deafness, unable to speak the language), or sometimes not even be located.[18] Of these, refusals and not-at-homes are the most common.

In mail surveys, a few questionnaires may not be deliverable, and occasionally a few respondents will return their questionnaires unanswered as an indication of their refusal to participate. Generally, however, all that is known about most mail survey nonresponse is that the questionnaire has not been returned. The reason for the lack of return may be any of the ones we have already mentioned.

A variety of techniques are employed by survey researchers to reduce nonresponse. In interview surveys, the interviewers are carefully trained to be courteous, to ask questions pleasantly and sensitively, to dress conservatively, or to return to conduct an interview at a more appropriate time if the situation warrants. Assurances of anonymity and confidentiality are made (this is done in mailed surveys as well). Questionnaires are usually organized to start with fairly simple and nonthreatening questions. Not-at-homes are treated by callbacks (a second, third, or even a fourth visit), on different days and at different times during the day. Sometimes appointments are set up at a convenient time for the respondent. Mailed questionnaires can be followed up with a reminder letter and often a second or sometimes even a third mailing. A frequently overlooked technique is the offering of a tangible reward as an inducement to respond. There is nothing inappropriate about paying (in some manner) respondents for providing information.

Nonresponse is a serious problem in many surveys. Some observers have stated that response rates for uncomplicated face-to-face surveys by nongovernment survey organizations are about 70–75 percent. Refusals make up the majority of nonrespondents in face-to-face interviews, with not-at-homes constituting most of the remainder. Telephone surveys generally have somewhat lower response rates than face-to-face surveys (respondents simply hang up). Response rates in mail surveys are quite varied, ranging from as low as 10 percent to as high as 90 percent.[19] Furthermore, nonresponse is not evenly spread out among various subgroups within the United States. Nonresponse rates in face-to-face interview surveys, for example, are much higher in inner cities.

ITEM NONRESPONSE

Partial gaps in the information provided by respondents can also occur for a variety of reasons: The respondent may not know the answer to a particular question; he or she may find certain questions embarrassing or perhaps irrelevant; the respondent may be pressed for time, and the interviewer may decide to skip over part of the questions; the interviewer may fail to record an answer. Sometimes during the data analysis phase of a survey, the answers to certain questions are thrown out because they are inconsistent with other answers. Some answers may be unclear or illegible.

Item nonresponse is rarely as high as total nonresponse. Generally it varies according to the nature of the question asked, and the mode of data collection. Very simple demographic questions usually have almost no nonresponse. Kalton estimates that items of income and expenditures may experience item nonresponse rates of 10 percent or more, while extremely sensitive or difficult questions may produce nonresponse rates that are much higher.[20]

Listed below is a summary of some of the more common suggestions made to increase the response rate in surveys.

Administration of the Questionnaire or Interview Schedule

- Make conditions under which the interview is conducted, or the questionnaire administered, as similar as possible for each individual in the sample.
- Be sure that the group to be surveyed knows something about the information you want to obtain.
- Train face-to-face or telephone interviewers how to ask questions.
- Train face-to-face interviewers in how to dress.

Format of the Questionnaire or Interview Schedule

- Be sure that sufficient space is provided for respondents (or the interviewer) to fill in the necessary biographical data that is needed (age, gender, grade level taught, and so on).
- Specify in precise terms the objectives the questionnaire or interview schedule is intended to achieve—exactly what kind of information is wanted from the respondents?
- Be sure each item in the questionnaire or interview schedule is related to one of the objectives of the study—that is, it will help obtain information about the objective.
- Use closed-ended (e.g., multiple-choice) rather than or in addition to open-ended (e.g., free response) questions alone.
- Ensure that no psychologically threatening questions are included.
- Eliminate any leading questions.
- Check for ambiguity of items with a panel of judges. Revise as needed.
- Pretest the questionnaire or interview schedule with a small group similar to the sample to be surveyed.

Problems in the Instrumentation Process in Survey Research

Several threats to the validity of the instrumentation process in surveys can cause individuals to respond differently than they might otherwise. Suppose, for example, that a group of individuals are brought together to be interviewed all in one place, and an extraneous event (say, a fire drill) occurs during the interview process. The event might upset or otherwise affect various individuals, causing them to respond to the interview questions differently than they would had the event not occurred.

Whenever researchers do not take care in preparing their questionnaires it may cause individuals to respond differently—if questions are leading or insensitive, for example. If the conditions under which individuals are questioned in interview studies are somewhat unusual (during the dinner hour; in poorly lit rooms; and so on), they may react in certain ways unrelated to the nature of the questions themselves.

Finally, the characteristics of a data collector (such as garish dress, insensitivity, rudeness, and use of offensive language) can affect how individuals respond, causing them to react in part to the data collector rather than to the questions. There is also the possibility of an unconscious bias on the part of the data collector, as when he or she asks "leading" questions of some individuals but not others.

Data Analysis in Survey Research

After the answers to the survey questions have been recorded, there remains the final task of summarizing the responses in order to draw some conclusions from the results. The total size of the sample should be reported, along with the overall percentage of returns. The percentage of the total sample responding for each item should then be reported. Finally, the percentage of respondents who chose each alternative for each question should be given. For example, a typical reported result might be as follows: "For item 26, regarding the approval of a no-smoking policy while school is in session, 80 percent indicated they were in favor of such a policy, 15 percent indicated they were not in favor, and 5 percent said they were neutral."

An Example of Survey Research

In the remainder of this chapter, we present a published example of survey research, followed by a critique of its strengths and weaknesses. As we did in our critiques of the different types of research studies we analyzed in other chapters, we use several of the concepts introduced in earlier parts of the book in our analysis.

From: Journal of Educational Research, 80, (6), 352–358, 1987. Reprinted with permission of the Helen Dwight Reid Educational Foundation. Published by Heldred Publications, 4000 Albemarle St., N.W., Washington, D.C. 20016. Copyright © 1987.

Essay Versus Multiple-Choice Type Classroom Exams: The Student's Perspective

Moshe Zeidner
Haifa University, Israel

Abstract

The major aim of the present research was to compare students' attitudes and dispositions toward teacher-made essay versus multiple-choice type exams. The primary study was conducted on a sample of 174 junior high school students, who were administered a test attitude inventory specifically designed to assess students' attitudes towards essay versus multiple-choice type formats on a variety of critical dimensions. The study was partially replicated on a sample of 101 seventh- and eighth-grade students who were administered a modified version of the test attitude inventory that was used in the first study. Overall, the data from both studies were remarkably consistent, pointing to more favorable student attitudes towards multiple-choice compared to essay type formats on most dimensions assessed. The practical significance of the results for classroom test construction are discussed and some suggestions are made about potential future applications of test attitude inventories in the classroom setting.

Planning and developing a classroom test typically entails, among other things, the specification of the particular format the test exercises are to take. As classroom testing experts (e.g., Gronlund, 1976; Thorndike & Hagen, 1969) have pointed out, the choice of a particular item format should normally be determined by theoretical as well as practical considerations, such as: the relative ease with which various test objectives are measured; the degree of difficulty in constructing or scoring items; freedom from irrelevent sources of variation in test results; degree of precision required in reporting results; and so on.

The item formats most often used in the construction of classroom tests may be conveniently classified into two broad categories (Gronlund, 1976): the more objective and structured selection type formats (e.g., multiple-choice, true/false, matching, etc.), requiring the examinee to select the correct answer among a number of given alternatives, and the more subjective construction type format (e.g., essay, short answer), permitting the examinee to organize, construct, and present the answer in written form. Over the past three decades or so, the multiple-choice and essay type formats have become two of the most popular formats employed in the construction of classroom achievement tests (cf. Thorndike, 1982).

The diverse considerations delineated and discussed in the measurement literature for choosing one item format over another in planning a classroom test generally revolve around three major factors of concern in the test enterprise: (a) the subject matter domain assessed (e.g., adequacy and ease of measuring specific course objectives); (b) the test constructor or user (e.g., ease of test preparation, ease of scoring test, etc.); and (c) various extraneous factors (e.g., guessing, copying, bluffing) possibly affecting the psychometric properties of test scores. However, one major factor which has been generally ignored by educational measurement specialists, and probably should be given serious attention and due consideration when planning a classroom test, is the perspective of the student examinee taking the test.

Unfortunately, aside from a sprinkling of studies (e.g., Zeidner, 1985; Zeidner, 1987) focusing on students' perceptions of various facets of the standardized psychometric ability test situation, very little is presently known about student attitudes, dispositions, and preferences with respect to varying tests (e.g., achievement, personality, etc.) in general or test formats (e.g., essay vs. multiple-choice) in particular. Which particular format do students perceive to be more convenient, interesting, motivating, anxiety evoking, eliciting greater success expectancies, and so on? These and other questions have not been sufficiently addressed in school-based evaluation research, with classroom testing experts generally paying little attention to the examinees' perspective—one of the most potentially useful sources of information about the subjective qualities of a test or its constituent components.

Given the assumption that examinees, who experience the test first hand, are one of the best sources of information about the subjective qualities of a test (or its constituent components), and that examinees' test attitudes and dispositions should be taken into consideration by test constructors and users when deciding upon test construction and administration policy (Nevo, 1985, 1986; Zeidner, 1985, 1986, 1987), it is truly surprising that so little research has been devoted towards assessing examinees' attitudes towards varying facets of classroom testing. Furthermore, very little work has been devoted towards the development and implementation of specific feedback systems designed to study examinees' reactions towards various facets of the classroom test.

In view of the gaps in the classroom testing and evaluation literature, the major aim of the present study is twofold: (a) to systematically compare and contrast the preferences, attitudes, and perceptions of student examinees with respect to two of the most popular test formats currently in use for constructing teacher-made tests, namely, essay versus multiple-choice type formats; and (b) to delineate the construction, characteristics, potential use, and application of a test attitude inventory, specifically designed to gather data on examinees' attitudes towards varying item formats. The research is based on two independent field studies conducted among junior high school student groups, with the second study designed to serve as a partial replication of the first.

STUDY 1

Method

Subjects. The sample consisted of 174 junior-high school students drawn from two middle-class neighborhood schools situated in northern Israel. The entire sample was distributed about equally by sex (boys, 49%; girls, 51%), but unevenly by grade levels (7th grade, 33%; 8th grade, 51%; 9th grade, 16%).

Instruments and procedure. A test attitude inventory was specifically constructed and pretested for the purpose of gathering data on students' perceptions and attitudes towards varying test formats (i.e., multiple-choice vs. essay). Students were provided with several examples of essay and multiple-choice type items on the blackboard before responding to the attitude inventory. The inventory consists of two main instruments, briefly described below:

1. Likert-type rating scale, composed of 10 Likert-type items, on a five-point continuum. Examinees were asked to rate each stimuli, "Multiple-Choice Type Classroom Test" and "Essay Type Classroom Test," separately along the following 10 different dimensions: (a) perceived facility (5 = very easy, 1 = very difficult); (b) perceived complexity (5 = not complex at all, 1 = very complex); (c) perceived clarity (5 = very clear, 1 = very unclear); (d) perceived interest (5 = very interesting, 1 = not at all interesting); (e) judged trickiness (5 = not tricky at all, 1 = very tricky); (f) perceived fairness (5 = very fair, 1 = not at all fair); (g) perceived value (5 = very valuable, 1 = not at all valuable); (h) success expectancy (5 = very high, 1 = very low); (i) degree of anxiety evoked (5 = minimal degree of anxiety evoked, 1 = high degree of anxiety evoked); and (j) feeling at ease with format (5 = feeling very much at ease, 1 = feeling very ill at ease). The stimuli appeared on the inventory in counterbalanced order.

The alpha reliability estimates, calculated separately for scale ratings of essay and multiple-choice exams, were about .85 in each case, which is considered to be quite satisfactory for group comparison purposes. Individual scales were linearly combined and averaged, using equal weights, to form a composite attitude scale, with higher scores indicating more favorable dispositions towards the test format under consideration.

2. Relative rating scales. The second part of the inventory consisted of a series of relative rating scales, asking students to directly compare essay and multiple-choice exams along the following relevant dimensions, indicating their preference in each case: (a) relative ease of preparing for exam; (b) reflection of students' actual knowledge; (c) technical ease or convenience of usage; (d) perceived expectancy of success; (e) perceived degree of fairness; (f) degree of anxiety evoked by particular test format; and (g) overall preference for format. Also, students were asked to explain their choice in each case. The reasons given by students for their choices on each dimension were categorized into predetermined categories by two independent coders, who reached an agreement level of about 88%.

Students were told that school authorities were directing efforts at improving classroom testing and were therefore interested in students' reactions towards various aspects of the classroom test, including item formats. The inventory was administered with no set time limit and responded to anonymously by students.

Results

Likert-type rating scales.   Table 1 shows the sample means and standard deviations for the composite score and individual ratings of essay versus multiple-choice exams. On the whole, multiple-choice type exams ($M = 3.48$) were rated significantly higher, on average, than essay ($M = 3.02$) type exams, $t(172) = 6.53, p < .001$. Furthermore, multiple-choice exams were judged more favorably than essay exams by both boys ($3.54 > 3.42$), $t(87) = 4.14, p < .0001$, and girls ($3.42 > 2.97$), $t(83) = 5.16, p < .001$.

Consistently higher mean ratings were observed for the multiple-choice type exam on 9 out of the 10 individual scales appearing on the inventory. Specifically, the multiple-choice type format was viewed as being significantly easier than the essay type ($3.37 > 2.63$), with about half (51%) of the students judging multiple-choice exams to be very easy or easy in contrast to only about 12% similarly perceiving the essay exam. Furthermore, the multiple-choice exam was judged to be less complex ($2.97 > 2.39$) and clearer ($3.92 > 3.47$) than the essay-type exam.

Furthermore, students tended to view the multiple-choice exam, in

TABLE 1.

Attitude Scale Ratings of Essay versus Multiple-Choice Type Exams for Study 1: *M*s and *SD*s

Scale	Essay		Multiple-choice		
	M	*SD*	*M*	*SD*	*t* values[a]
Difficulty	2.63	.85	3.37	1.02	7.09***
Complexity	2.39	1.00	2.97	1.19	5.03***
Clarity	3.47	.86	3.92	.85	5.27***
Interest	3.20	.99	3.62	.95	3.84***
Trickiness	3.07	.88	3.32	1.02	2.37*
Fairness	3.44	.95	3.87	.80	4.47***
Value	3.81	.90	3.62	.95	−2.20*
Success	2.86	.84	3.47	.98	5.93***
Anxiety	2.83	1.04	3.39	1.00	5.11***
At ease	2.30	.96	3.23	1.14	7.67***
Composite scale	3.02	.60	3.48	.65	6.53***

Note. All the above scales range from 1 to 5 and were scored so that higher scores are indicative of more favorable test attitudes than lower scores.
[a] The *t* tests for correlated measures were conducted with 172 degrees of freedom.
* $p < .05$.   ** $p < .01$.   *** $p < .001$.

comparison to the essay exam, as relatively more interesting (3.62 > 3.20), less tricky (3.32 > 3.07), and fairer (3.87 > 3.44). Inspection of the category response distribution for the foregoing scales shows that about 60% of the sample perceived multiple-choice exams to be interesting or very interesting, in comparison to only about 39% similarly perceiving the essay exam. In addition, whereas about 47% of the sample judged the multiple-choice type exam as being not tricky or not at all tricky, only about 28% felt similarly about essay items. Furthermore, multiple-choice and essay exams were viewed as fair or very fair by about 73% and 53% of the sample, respectively.

With respect to the motivational variables assessed, the multiple-choice exam, in comparison to the essay exam, was viewed as eliciting higher success expectancies (3.47 > 2.86), was perceived to be less anxiety evoking (3.39 > 2.83), and made respondents feel more at ease while taking the exam (3.23 > 2.30). The scale response distributions show that about 53% of the sample expected to receive high or very high scores on multiple-choice type exams, compared to only about 19% on essay exams. A meaningfully higher percentage of the sample (51%) reported that essay exams are anxiety evoking (or very anxiety evoking), relative to only about 18% who felt similarly about multiple-choice exams. Similarly, about twice the percentage of students (about 56%) reported feeling ill at ease with essay formats compared to multiple-choice type formats (about 25%).

Relative rating scales. As mentioned, students were also asked to directly compare and state their preference for one of the two item types with respect to a selected number of criteria, and provide reasons for their choice in each case. Following are some of the salient results, organized according to the major criteria for comparison among the formats.

1. Ease of preparation. The majority of the sample (67%) found it easier to prepare for multiple-choice than for essay exams, because preparing for multiple-choice type exams normally requires less rote memorization of factual material than preparing for essay exams ($f = 45$) and multiple-choice exams also typically require somewhat less time and effort for adequate preparation ($f = 36$). The minority of students who found it easier to prepare for essay exams believe that the latter require a more superficial and less profound mastery of the subject matter material relative to multiple-choice exams ($f = 18$), that the key topics appearing on the essay exam are more easily identifiable ($f = 5$), and that it is, as a last resort, easier to bluff one's way through an essay exam ($f = 5$).

2. Reflection of students' knowledge. About 70% of the students in the sample believed that grades on essay exams are more reflective indicators of the students' knowledge of the exam material compared to grades on multiple-choice type exams. The major reason offered is that essay exams provide students the opportunity of accurately and optimally expressing their knowledge and ideas in writing ($f = 105$). The remainder of the students believed that multiple-choice exam scores are a more sensitive index of students' knowledge, mainly because the latter normally cover a broader range of topics and sample a greater range of facts, concepts, and principles than typically is the case on essay exams ($f = 18$).

3. Convenience of format usage. The majority (81%) of the students in the sample felt that the multiple-choice format is more convenient than the essay format, because there is no need to express answers in written form ($f = 75$); it is possible to guess the correct answer with some probability of success ($f = 26$); and a minimal amount of preparation is required for success ($f = 12$). On the other hand, students who found the essay format more convenient attribute this primarily to the possibility of freely and accurately expressing ideas in writing ($f = 7$).

4. Success expectancy. About three quarters of the students in the sample believed that students actually have a better chance of succeeding on multiple-choice relative to essay exams, for the following reasons: multiple-choice exams, as a rule, are relatively easier than essay exams ($f = 79$); the

availability of options on multiple-choice type exams provides examinees with a sense of security and increased confidence while taking the test ($f = 26$); examinees can guess (or copy) the correct answer ($f = 13$); multiple-choice exams preclude the possibility that examinees' scores will be unfairly lowered by grader on account of students' spelling mistakes or poor writing ability ($f = 6$); and multiple-choice exams require less preparation and effort in order to succeed ($f = 3$). The remainder of the students, who believed that they have a higher probability of succeeding on essay exams, attributed their expectancies mainly to the fact that essay exams allow students, in principle, to give expression to their maximum degree of knowledge on the topic ($f = 26$), They further believed the tendency for teachers' subjective grading of essay papers works to the advantage of students, thus increasing their grades and probability of success on the exam ($f = 8$).

5. Perceived fairness. To about half (51%) of the sample, essay exams were perceived to be more fair than multiple-choice exams, for two main reasons: the nil probability of guessing the correct answer assures that examinees' scores reflect actual knowledge rather than luck or error ($f = 25$) and students are offered the possibility of accurately expressing and elaborating on ideas, thereby maximizing their chances for success ($f = 17$). The remainder of the sample believed that multiple-choice type exams are fairer than essay exams mainly because of the partial information provided students by the availability of options ($f = 36$), and the freedom from having to construct and present the answer in written form ($f = 12$).

6. Degree of anxiety evoked. The vast majority (89%) of the students reported that taking an essay exam is more anxiety evoking than taking a multiple choice type exam, because additional effort is expended and emotional energy is demanded of students having to select, organize, and express ideas in essay form ($f = 52$). Further there is a total absence of information or clues leading to the correct answer ($f = 33$) as well as a marked degree of overlearning required to succeed on essay exams ($f = 27$); relatively greater length and complexity of responses are required in construction type items ($f = 26$). The minority of the students who reported that multiple-choice type exams are relatively more anxiety evoking attribute this mainly to the difficulty and stress involved in choosing among given options ($f = 10$), the relatively large number of items students normally have to respond to on multiple-choice exams ($f = 6$), and the increased probability of error ($f = 4$).

7. Overall preference. About three quarters of the sample (77%) clearly reported an overall preference for multiple-choice over essay exams, for four

main reasons: (a) the availability of options to choose from ($f = 66$), (b) the convenient item format ($f = 62$), (c) the freedom from having to organize and write the answer ($f = 12$), and (d) the possibility of guessing or copying the correct answer ($f = 7$). The minority (23%) of the students reported a preference for essay over multiple-choice type exams, attributing their choice mainly to (a) the possibility of accurately communicating ideas in written form ($f = 19$), (b) simplicity of the item format ($f = 10$), and (c) the possibility of obtaining some credit for a partially correct response ($f = 2$).

In sum, the data presented in Study 1 point to a more positive attitudinal disposition of students towards multiple-choice relative to essay type exams with respect to the majority of dimensions assessed.

STUDY 2

Method

Sample. The present study, designed as a partial replication of Study 1, was conducted on a sample of 101 seventh- and eighth-grade students studying in two neighborhood schools (i.e., middle-class, $n = 62$; lower-class, $n = 39$) in northern Israel. The sample was about evenly divided by sex (boys, 47%; girls, 53%) and grade level (7th grade, 54%; 8th grade, 46%).

Instruments and Procedure

Semantic differential rating scale. First, students were asked to evaluate multiple-choice versus essay type classroom exams along essentially the same 10 dimensions used in Study 1 (see Methods section, Study 1). However, for convergent validity purposes, the items in the present study were presented in the format of a seven-step semantic differential scale continuum (Osgood & Tannenbaum, 1957), anchored by the following adjective pairs: difficult/easy, complicated/simple, unclear/clear, boring/interesting, tricky/straightforward, unfair/fair, worthless/valuable, low expectancy of success/high expectancy of success, maximally anxiety evoking/minimally anxiety arousing, feeling uncomfortable with exam/feeling at ease with exam.

Comparative rating scale. Furthermore, as in Study 1, students were asked to compare and choose between essay and multiple-choice exam types with respect to the following seven criteria: (a) ease of exam preparation, (b) accuracy in reflecting students' knowledge, (c) convenience of usage, (d) success expectancies, (e) perceived fairness, (f) degree of anxiety evoked, and (g) overall preference. In contrast to Study 1, students were not required to explain their choices.

In addition, students filled out a personal data inventory and rated themselves with respect to scholastic achievement along a five-point scale (5 = very much above average, 1 = very much below average).

Results

Semantic differential scale ratings. Table 2 presents the means and standard deviations for the semantic differential scale ratings of essay versus multiple-choice type exams. Overall, the mean composite attitude score (average linear combination of semantic differential scale ratings) was significantly higher for multiple-choice than for essay type exams (5.44 > 4.11), $t(99) = 8.55$, $p < .001$. With respect to specific scales, as shown in Table 2, multiple-choice exams, relative to essay type exams, were viewed as significantly easier (5.70 > 3.30), less complicated (4.48 > 2.91), clearer (6.01 > 4.94), more interesting (6.01 > 5.01), less tricky (4.82 > 4.00), fairer (5.79 > 5.40), eliciting higher success expectancies (5.23 > 3.35), less anxiety evoking (5.25 > 2.78), and making students feel more at ease (5.28 > 3.65) during the exam. Thus, with the exception of perceived value, multiple-choice exam formats were evaluated more favorably than essay type exams on 8 out of 10 scales included on the inventory.

TABLE 2.

Attitude Scale Ratings of Essay versus Multiple-Choice Type Exams for Study 2: *M*s and *SD*s

Scale	Essay		Multiple-choice		t values[a]
	M	*SD*	*M*	*SD*	
Difficulty	3.30	1.60	5.70	1.77	9.27***
Complexity	2.91	1.84	4.48	2.22	5.05***
Clarity	4.94	1.98	6.01	1.51	3.75***
Interest	5.01	1.95	6.01	1.76	3.90***
Trickiness	4.00	1.85	4.82	2.06	2.62*
Fairness	5.40	1.97	5.79	1.71	1.59
Value	5.73	1.79	5.82	1.70	.27
Success	3.35	1.74	5.23	1.70	8.36***
Anxiety	2.78	1.71	5.25	1.99	9.14***
At ease	3.65	2.19	5.28	1.93	5.45***
Composite scale	4.11	.96	5.44	1.07	8.55***

Note. All the above scales range from 1 to 7 and were scored so that higher scores are indicative of more favorable test attitudes than lower scores.
[a] The *t* tests for correlated measures were conducted with 99 degrees of freedom.
* $p < .05$.　　** $p < .01$.　　*** $p < .001$.

An ANOVA for the effects of sex, social background (disadvantaged vs. advantaged—as assessed by official criteria used by the Ministry of Education in classifying school populations) and the Sex × Social background interaction effect all provided to be nonsignificant. Thus, both disadvantaged (5.64 > 3.94), $t(38) = 6.94$, $p < .001$, and middle-class (5.32 > 4.21), $t(60) = 5.49$, $p < .0001$, students favored the multiple-choice over essay type exams. By the same token, both boys (5.31 > 4.15), $t(44) = 6.10$, $p < .001$) and girls (5.53 > 4.13), $t(51) = 5.81$, $p < .001$, preferred the multiple-choice to the essay type exam. In addition, the ratings of students perceiving themselves to be above average and those perceiving themselves to be below average were virtually identical. Thus, students' attitudes towards varying test formats were not correlated with gender, social background, and perceived classroom achievement.

Direct comparison of multiple-choice and essay exams. Multiple-choice type exams were judged by 80% of the respondents to be easier than essay type exams and were also believed to elicit higher success expectancies by about three quarters of the sample as well. In addition, 83% of the students in the sample reported that multiple-choice type exams evoke less anxiety than essay type exams. About 83% of the respondents reported an overall preference for the multiple-choice type exam. However, the essay type exam was judged to be a more valid and suitable measure of subject matter content by the majority (66%), with a slight majority (56%) also viewing the essay type test as a slightly fairer measure as well.

In sum, the data of this study attest to more favorable student attitudes towards the multiple-choice relative to essay type exams by most criteria under consideration, with the exception of perceived value, fairness, and validity in assessing students' knowledge.

GENERAL DISCUSSION

Overall, the data presented for the two independent field studies constituting this research were highly consistent, with the various lines of evidence indicating that multiple-choice type exams are generally perceived more favorably than essay type items along most dimensions assessed. The observed preference for multiple-choice type exams is observed to hold true for students of varying gender and social background. In both studies, multiple-choice and essay formats were perceived to be most differentiated, in favor of the multiple-choice test, along the dimensions of perceived difficulty, anxiety, success expectancy, complexity, and feeling at ease with the format. Also, in both studies, the smallest differences between the formats were evidenced on the dimensions of trickiness, perceived interest, and perceived value. Furthermore, students perceive essay exams to be somewhat more appropriate than multiple-choice exams for the purpose of reflecting one's knowledge in the subject matter tested.

From a methodological point of view, it should be held in mind that the student samples were not drawn at random, and that the research was conducted among junior high school students only. It may very well be that different results would have been obtained for other age groups or students in different educational or cultural settings. Therefore, future research is needed in order to extend the validity of the findings beyond the specific age groups studied and the specific educational and cultural settings in which this study is imbedded.

Bearing the methodological caveats in mind, the data clearly indicate that students perceive multiple-choice items more favorably than essay type items. Curiously, over the past few years, multiple-choice type tests have been the target of severe public and professional attack on various grounds (e.g., failure to measure higher cognitive or psychological processes, penalizing the creative examinee, placing too much emphasis on speed and rote memory, etc.; cf. Allen & Yen, 1979). Indeed, the attitude and semantic profile of multiple-choice exams emerging from the examinee's perspective is largely at variance with the unfavorable and negative profile of multiple-choice exams often emerging from some of the anti-test literature.

Educational measurement specialists would appear to agree that examinees' attitudes, perceptions, and motivational dispositions with respect to classroom testing should be given due consideration and weight in the course of assessing a test's face validity or in determining classroom testing policy and procedure (Nevo, 1985). It is assumed that direct examinee feedback bearing on various facets of the classroom test, or its constituent components, is a potentially valuable source of information about the test for both the teacher and test specialist. It is plausible that students' attitudes and perceptions about the test form are important factors in affecting students' test preparation behavior; students' cooperation and test motivation during the exam; and possibly influencing the level of students' test performance and attainment on the exam. If examinees actually perceive a particular test form in a favorable light, the likelihood of examinee cooperation, teacher-student rapport, and optimal test motivation would be enhanced, whereas aversive emotional reactions and debilitating motivational dispositions would be diminished. Indeed, the strong preference of student examinees for multiple-choice over essay type formats evidenced in this research deserves to be given due weight and careful consideration by teachers during the initial stages of planning a classroom test, particularly when deciding upon the appropriate item format for the planned test.

Furthermore, students' attitudes and perceptions with respect to test forms are important pieces of information for the teacher and measurement specialist alike, since they serve as indicators of a test's face validity from the point of view of those most affected by the test results, namely, the student examinee. As pointed out in the literature, the concept of face validity implies that a test should not only be valid from a content, construct, or predictive validity point of view, but also appear to be valid to a variety of judges—including test takers (Nevo, 1985). A test which takes the examinees' point of view into consideration, all other things being equal, would also be expected to evidence superior face validity as well. Thus, it would seem important for teachers to routinely assess the face validity of their instruments, from the examinees' judgmental perspective.

More generally, teachers may profit from the routine administration of test attitude inventories designed to gauge students' attitudes and dispositions towards varying facets of the classroom test (e.g., format, time limits, instruction, wording, etc.).

The use of test attitude inventories on a large-scale and routine basis in the classroom may serve to fill the needed gap for a judgmental approach to the face validity of classroom tests and their constituent components, providing teachers and educational researchers with useful information about key dimensions in the test situation—from the examinee's point of view. Furthermore, information elicited via test attitude inventories might help teachers identify specific problem areas of classroom testing and use this information for modifying or remedying certain testing conditions perceived to be problematic from the examinee's point of view. In sum, then, examinee feedback appears to be one of the most valuable yet neglected sources of information about the subjective qualities of a classroom test or its components.

References

Allen, M. J., & Yen, W. M. (1979). *An introduction to measurement theory.* Monterey, CA: Brooks/Cole.

Gronlund, N. E. (1976). *Measurement and evaluation in teaching* (3rd ed.). New York: Macmillan.

Nevo, B. (1985). Face validity revisited. *Journal of Educational Measurement 22,* 287–293.

Nevo, B. (1986, July). *The practical value of examinee's feedback questionnaires.* Paper presented at the 21st Congress of the International Association of Applied Psychology, Jerusalem, Israel.

Osgood, C. S., & Tannenbaum, P. (1957). *The measurement of meaning.* Urbana, IL: University of Illinois Press.

Thorndike, R. L. (1982). *Applied psychometrics.* Boston: Houghton-Mifflin.

Thorndike, R. L., & Hagen, E. (1969). *Measurement and evaluation in psychology and education* (3rd ed.). New York: Wiley.

Zeidner, M. (1985, February). *Psychological testing: The examinee's perspective.* Symposium conducted at the annual meeting of the Israeli Psychological Association, Ramat-Gan, Israel.

Zeidner, M. (1986). Situational bias—The examinee's perspective. In B. Nevo & R. S. Jäger (Eds.), *Psychological testing: The examinee perspective* (pp. 93–120). Göttingen: Hogrefe Intl.

Zeidner, M. (1987). Sociocultural differences in test attitudes and motivations. In R. Schwarzer, H. M. Van der Ploeg, & C. D. Spielberger (Eds.), *Advances in test anxiety research* (pp. 241–250). Lisse/Berwyn, PA: Swets & Zeitlinger.

Analysis of the Study

PURPOSE/JUSTIFICATION

The purpose of this study is clearly stated: to determine which question format—essay or multiple choice—junior high students prefer on examinations (and to develop an instrument for future use in assessing such preferences). The author, in our judgment, adequately defends the importance of such information, although he might have gone into greater detail as to why authorities believe student attitude toward examinations is important, presumably because their attitude can affect their responses. In fact, this argument is actually made later, in the discussion section of the report.

DEFINITIONS

No formal definitions, as such, are provided. The author does describe, however, both examination formats in what seems to us to be sufficient detail. But student "attitudes" and "dispositions" should be defined. Are they different? In actuality, students were asked to judge several dimensions of two different formats as they perceived them. The dimensions were ease, complexity, clarity, interest, trickiness, fairness, value, success expectancy, anxiety evoked, ease of format, reflection of knowledge, convenience, and overall liking. These dimensions might have been provided to the reader at the outset.

PRIOR RESEARCH

The author states that the only directly related prior research is a "sprinkling of studies" and then cites two of his own publications. The reader has a right to expect that these studies be at least reviewed briefly and their results summarized.

HYPOTHESES

Although we are less concerned about hypotheses in a descriptive study, the author might have indicated that he expected a difference in preference for the examination types and even (perhaps) which one he expected to be favored.

SAMPLE

Both of the study samples are convenience samples; the second study is a partial replication of the first. This is certainly a desirable feature of the study. Both samples, however, are predominantly middle-class, a limitation on generalizability which should be emphasized more than it is.

INSTRUMENTATION

Study One. The content of both instruments appears to us to be valid, although it is not clear why some dimensions appear on both and some on only one. The internal consistency of the Likert-type scales is adequate, but no evidence is provided on the "relative" rating scales. Scorer agreement is adequate for the open-ended "reasons" section. No description of prior try-out of these scales is provided. No evidence of validity is given, perhaps because what is measured are student "perceptions." Nonetheless, perceptions can, and should be, validated. At the least, the two scales (Likert and relative) should have been compared (using the difference between multiple-choice and essay scores as indicated on the Likert scales).

Study Two. In the replication, students again filled out the "relative" rating scale, but a semantic differential format was substituted for the Likert format. While the author's rationale for "convergent validity" has some merit in that results might be replicated with different students and a different format, no direct comparison with the instrument of known adequate reliability (the Likert scale) is possible, since it was not used. Further, no reliability data on the semantic differential instrument is provided. Once again, the correlations between this scale and the relative rating scale would provide direct evidence of validity. Why was this scale used rather than the Likert, particularly since, this time, student reasons for their preferences were not obtained?

We must presume that the administrators did not attempt to influence responses in any way—which seems probable unless the classroom teachers, whose preferences would likely be known by students, administered the scales.

DATA ANALYSIS

Comparison of means for each dimension, as well as the composite score, on the Likert scales (Study One) and the semantic differential (Study Two) is appropriate. As usual when random sampling does not occur, the use of inferential statistics is highly questionable, yet it is reported here with no qualifications. Of more value in judging magnitude of differences is effect size, which should have been reported. The effect size for the composite score on the Likert scale is $.46/.63 = .76$, and on the semantic differential $1.33/1.00 = 1.33$. There is good reason, therefore, to take the difference in favor of multiple-choice examinations seriously. Effect sizes on the subscales are generally in agreement

with the author's interpretations. The finding that preferences were *not* related to socioeconomic level, gender, or perceived ability level lends additional clarity to the study and enhances somewhat the generalizability of the results.

Apparently, no scores were derived, for either study, on the relative rating scale. We find this hard to understand. Why then, was it given—particularly in the second study? The author's discussion of student reasons for their preferences (Study One only), and their actual preferences (Study Two only) generally supports the results on the other instruments. For example, the success expectancy dimension on the Likert scale favors the multiple choice format (3.47 versus 2.86), and three quarters of the group are reported to have chosen this format on the relative scale. This suggests that total (composite) score correlations would have supported the validity of these scales. The author correctly points out that the overall preference for multiple-choice examinations does *not* include "reflection of student knowledge" wherein 70 percent of Group One and 66 percent of Group Two favored the essay format.

DISCUSSION

The author, to his credit, points out the limitations on his sampling. We find fault only with his discussion of the current criticism of multiple-choice examinations. He states that critics allege that this format is guilty of "failure to measure higher cognitive or psychological processes, penalizing the creative examinee, placing too much emphasis on speed and rote memory, etc." He then interprets his results as "largely at variance with the unfavorable and negative profile of multiple-choice examinations often emerging from some of the anti-test literature." But the index that is logically most related to the critics' charges is that of "reflecting students knowledge," on which the students agree with the critics!

One serious omission in the author's interpretation of results is failure to recognize the importance of the quality and other characteristics of the multiple-choice and essay items to which the students were exposed. For example, if the essay items were poorly written and hence ambiguous, the students would surely think they were "hard." If the multiple-choice items tended to be easy, and of a superficial nature, students would likely say they were easier than essay items, and measured less important concepts. It is impossible for readers of the article to comprehend fully the implications of the findings without seeing at least a representative sample of the kinds of items that the students were referring to when they responded to the instruments. If the items of both types were generally of high quality and measured learning outcomes at appropriately high levels of intellectual skills, the results of the survey are important. If they were of generally low or uneven quality and measured superficial or irrelevant information, the findings in the article are nearly useless.

The author gave insufficient attention to the general belief that validity of assessments is more important than student preferences regarding item format. The fact that students prefer the multiple-choice format is not a sufficient reason to use that format if the outcome in question (for example, ability to express ideas in own words) cannot be measured with items in that format. Priority must be given to using the format that is most suitable for assessing the student characteristics that one wishes to measure.

Main Points of Chapter Fifteen

- All surveys possess three basic characteristics: (a) the collection of information (b) from a sample (c) by asking questions, in order to describe some aspects of the population of which the group is a part.
- The major purpose of all surveys is to describe the characteristics of a population.
- There are two major types of surveys that can be conducted: cross-sectional surveys and longitudinal surveys.
- Three longitudinal designs commonly employed in survey research include trend studies, cohort studies, and panel studies.
- In a trend study, different samples from the same general population are surveyed at different points in time.
- In a cohort study, a particular subpopulation is sampled over the course of the survey.
- In a panel study, the same individuals are surveyed at different times over the course of the survey.
- Surveys are not suitable for all research topics, especially those that require observation of subjects or the manipulation of variables.
- Whatever is studied in a survey is called the unit of analysis.
- As in other types of research, the group of persons that is the focus of the study is called the target population.
- There are four basic ways to collect data in a survey—by direct administration of the survey instrument to a group, by mail, by telephone, or by personal interview. Each has both advantages and disadvantages.
- The sample to be surveyed should be selected randomly if possible.
- The most common types of instruments used in survey research are the questionnaire and the interview schedule.

- The nature of the questions, and the way they are asked, are extremely important in survey research.
- Most surveys use some form of close-ended question.
- The survey instrument should be pretested with a small sample similar to the potential respondents.
- A contingency question is a question whose answer is contingent upon how a respondent answers a prior question to which the contingency question is related. Well-organized and sequenced contingency questions are particularly important in interview schedules.
- A cover letter is a letter sent to potential respondents in a mail survey explaining the purpose of the survey questionnaire.
- Both telephone and face-to-face interviewers need to be trained before they administer the survey instrument.
- Both total and item nonresponse are major problems in survey research that seem to be increasing in recent years. This is a problem because those who do not respond are very likely to differ from the respondents in terms of how they answer the survey questions.
- Threats to the validity of the instrumentation process in survey research include location, history, and instrumentation.
- The percentage of the total sample responding for each item on a survey questionnaire should be reported, as well as the percentage of the total sample who chose each alternative for each question.

For Discussion

1. For what kinds of topics might a personal interview be superior to a mail or telephone survey? Give an example.

2. When, if ever, might a telephone survey be preferable to a mail survey? to a personal interview?

3. Give an example of a question a researcher might use to assess each of the following characteristics of members of a teachers group:
   a. Their income.
   b. Their teaching style.
   c. Their biggest worry.
   d. Their knowledge of teaching methods.
   e. Their opinions about homogeneous grouping of students.

4. Suppose a researcher is interested in finding out how elementary school administrators feel about elementary school counseling. Write a series of three contingency questions that could be used in a personal interview and be prepared to discuss them.

5. Which mode of data collection—mail, telephone, or personal interview—would be best for each of the following surveys?
   a. The reasons why some students drop out of college before they graduate.

    b. The feelings of high school teachers about special classes for the gifted.

    c. The attitudes of people about raising taxes to pay for the construction of new schools.

    d. The duties of secondary school superintendents in a midwestern state.

    e. The reasons why individuals of differing ethnicity did or did not decide to enter the teaching profession.

    f. The opinions of teachers toward the idea of minimum competency testing before permanent tenure would be granted.

    g. The opinions of parents of students in a private school toward the elimination of certain subjects from the curriculum.

6. Listed below are some definitions of target populations from which a sample is to be selected and surveyed. See if you can improve (make more precise) the definitions of each:

    a. "All of the counselors in the school."

    b. "All of the parents of the students in our school."

    c. "All of the administrators in the school district."

    d. "All chemistry students."

    e. "All of the teachers of the gifted."

7. Look at each of the open-ended questions in the example on pp. 337–338. See if you can restate them in a closed-ended form.

8. Try to restate one of the close-ended questions in the same example in a contingency format.

9. What suggestions can you offer, beyond those given in this chapter, for improving the rate of response in surveys?

Notes

1. Blaga, Jeffrey L. & Lynn E. Nielsen. (1983). *Journal of Social Studies Research, 7*(1): 45–57.

2. Blase, Joseph J. (1987). *American Educational Research Journal, 24*(4):589–610.

3. Tlou, Josiah & Clifford Bennett. (1983). *Journal of Social Studies Research, 7*(2):37–59.

4. Chase, Clinton I. (1985). *Journal of Educational Research, 79*(1):12–18.

5. Raths, James, Madonna Wojtaszek-Healy, & Connie Kubo Della-Plana. (1987). *Journal of Educational Research, 80*(3):133–137.

6. Sheppard, Margaret A., Michael S. Goodstadt, & Margaret M. Willett. (1987). *Journal of Drug Education, 17*(2):123–128.

7. Hart, Ann Weaver. (1987). *American Educational Research Journal, 24*(4):479–504.

8. Herlihy, Barbara, Madelyn Healy, Ellen Piel Cook, & Pat Hudson. (1987). *Counselor Education and Supervision*, September, 69–76.

9. Jaeger, Richard M. (1988). Survey research methods in education. In Richard M. Jaeger, (Ed.), *Complementary methods for research in education.* Washington, D.C.: American Educational Research Association. pp. 308–310.

10. Grovers, R. M., & R. L. Kahn. (1979). *Surveys by telephone: A national comparison with personal interviews.* New York: Academic Press.

11. Fowler, Floyd J. Jr. (1984). *Survey research methods.* Beverly Hills, CA.: Sage Publications. p. 101.

12. The development of survey questions is an art in itself. We can only begin to deal with the topic here. For a more detailed discussion, see Converse, Jean M. & Stanley Presser. (1986). *Survey questions: Handcrafting the standardized questionnaire.* Beverly Hills, CA.: Sage.

13. For further suggestions, see Gronlund, Norman E. (1988). *How to construct achievement tests*. Englewood Cliffs, N.J.: Prentice-Hall.

14. Babbie, Earl S. (1973). *Survey research methods*. Belmont, CA.: Wadsworth. p. 145.

15. For a more detailed discussion, see Fowler, *op. cit.*, Chapter 7.

16. *Ibid.*, pp. 109–110.

17. Freyberg, Peter, and Rober Osborne. (1981). Who structures the curriculum: Teacher or learner? *Research Information for Teachers, Number Two*. SET, Hamilton, New Zealand.

18. Kalton, Graham. (1983). *Introduction to survey sampling*. Beverly Hills, CA.: Sage. p. 64.

19. *Ibid.*, p. 66.

20. *Ibid.*, p. 67.

Research Exercise Fifteen: Survey Research

You should complete Problem Sheet 15 only if you are planning a survey. If your intended study involves a different methodology, you will find a similar problem sheet at the end of the chapter that deals with that methodology. You might wish to consider, however, whether your research question could be investigated by means of a survey.

Using Problem Sheet 15, once again state the question or hypothesis of your study. Then describe, briefly but thoroughly, the procedures of your study—that is, *what* you intend to do, *when, where,* and *how.* Lastly, indicate any unresolved problems you see at this point in your planning.

1. The question or hypothesis of my study is: _____
   _____
   _____

2. A brief summary of **what** I intend to do, **when, where,** and **how** is as follows:
   _____
   _____
   _____
   _____
   _____
   _____
   _____
   _____

3. The major problems I foresee at this point are as follows: _____
   _____
   _____

Chapter Sixteen

QUALITATIVE RESEARCH

Sometimes a researcher wants to obtain an in-depth look at a particular individual, situation, or set of materials. Instead of asking such questions as "*What* do people think about this?" (as in survey research), or "*What* might happen if I do this?" (as in experimental research), the researcher asks "*How* do these people act?" or "*How* are things done?" or "*How* are people portrayed?" To answer questions such as these, researchers use a number of methodologies that bear the label "qualitative research." In this chapter, we discuss some examples of this type of research.

Objectives

Reading this chapter should enable you to:

- *Explain* what is meant by the term "qualitative research"
- *Describe* four general characteristics that most qualitative studies have in common
- *Name* three types of qualitative research conducted in education
- *Explain* what is meant by the term "participant observation"
- *Explain* what is meant by the term "nonparticipant observation" and *describe* three different forms of nonparticipant observation studies that are conducted in education
- *Describe* briefly four roles that an observer can take in a qualitative study
- *Explain* what is meant by the terms "observer effect" and "observer bias" and *give an example* of each that might occur in educational research
- *Explain* what is meant by the term "ethnographic research" and *give an example* of a research question that might be investigated in an ethnographic study
- *Name* one advantage and disadvantage of ethnographic research
- *Describe* briefly three techniques ethnographic researchers use to check on the validity and reliability of their perceptions
- *Explain* what is meant by the term "field notes" and how they differ from field jottings, a field diary, and a field log
- *Differentiate* between descriptive and reflective field notes
- *Recognize* an example of a qualitative study when you come across one in the educational research literature

---

What Is Qualitative Research?

The questions being asked by researchers who use the methodologies discussed in previous chapters all involve the extent to which various learnings, attitudes, or ideas exist, or how well or how accurately they are being developed. Thus, possible avenues of research included comparisons between alternative methods of teaching (as in experimental research); comparing groups of individuals in terms of existing differences on certain variables (as in causal-comparative research); or interviewing different groups of educational professionals, such as teachers, administrators, and counselors (as in survey research).

As we mentioned in Chapter One, however, researchers might wish to obtain a more wholistic impression of teaching and learning than answers to the above questions can provide. A researcher might wish to know more than just "to what extent" or "how well" something is done. He or she might wish to obtain a more complete picture, for example, of what goes on in a particular classroom or school.

Consider the teaching of history in secondary schools. Just how do history teachers teach their subject? What kinds of things do they do as they go about their daily routine? What sorts of things do students do? In what kinds of activities do they engage? What are the explicit and implicit "rules of the game" in history classes that seem to help or hinder the process of learning?

To gain some insight into these concerns, a researcher might try to document or portray the everyday experiences of students (and teachers) in history classrooms. The focus would be on only one classroom (or a small number of them at most). The researcher would observe the classroom on as regular a basis as possible and attempt to describe, as fully and as richly as possible, what he or she sees.

The above example points to the fact that many researchers are more interested in the *quality* of a particular activity than in how often

367

it occurs, or how it should otherwise be evaluated. Research studies that investigate the quality of relationships, activities, situations, or materials are frequently referred to as **qualitative research.** This type of research differs from the methodologies discussed in earlier chapters in that there is a greater emphasis on wholistic description—that is, on describing in detail all of what goes on in a particular activity or situation rather than on comparing the effects of a particular treatment (as in experimental research), say, or on describing the attitudes or behaviors of people (as in survey research).

General Characteristics of Qualitative Research

Many different types of qualitative methodologies exist, but there are certain general features that characterize most qualitative research studies. Not all qualitative studies will necessarily display all of these characteristics with equal strength. Nevertheless, taken together, they give a good overall picture of what is involved in this type of research. Robert Bogdan and Sari Knopp Biklen describe five such features.[1]

1. *The natural setting is the direct source of data and the researcher is the key instrument in qualitative research.* Qualitative researchers go directly to the particular setting in which they are interested to observe and collect their data. They spend a considerable amount of time actually being in a school, sitting in on faculty meetings, attending parent-teacher association meetings, observing teachers in their classrooms and in other locales, and in general directly observing and interviewing individuals as they go about their daily routines.

Sometimes they come equipped only with a pad and a pencil to take notes, but often they use sophisticated audio- and videotaping equipment. Even when such equipment is used, however, the data are collected right at the scene and supplemented by the researcher's observations and insights about what occurred. As Bogdan and Biklen point out, qualitative researchers go

to the particular setting of interest because they are concerned with *context*—they feel that activities can best be understood in the actual settings in which they occur. They also feel that human behavior is vastly influenced by the setting in which such behavior takes place, and, hence, whenever possible they visit such settings.

2. *Qualitative data are collected in the form of words or pictures rather than numbers.* The kinds of data collected in qualitative research include interview transcripts, field notes, photographs, audio recordings, videotapes, diaries, personal comments, memos, official records, textbook passages, and anything else that can convey the actual words or actions of people. In their search for understanding, qualitative researchers do not usually attempt to reduce their data to numerical symbols,[2] but rather seek to portray what they have observed and recorded in all of its richness. Hence they do their best to ignore virtually nothing that might lend insight to a situation. Gestures, jokes, conversational gambits, artwork or other decorations in a room—all are noted by qualitative researchers. To a qualitative researcher, no data are trivial or unworthy of notice.

3. *Qualitative researchers are concerned with process as well as product.* Qualitative researchers are especially interested in *how* things occur. Hence they are likely to observe how people interact with each other; how certain kinds of questions are answered; the meanings that people give to certain words and actions; how people's attitudes are translated into actions; how students seem to be affected by a teacher's manner, or gestures, or comments; and the like.

4. *Qualitative researchers tend to analyze their data inductively.* Qualitative researchers do not, usually, formulate a hypothesis beforehand and then seek to test it out. Rather, they tend to "play it as it goes." They spend a considerable amount of time collecting their data (again, primarily through observing and interviewing) before they decide what are the important questions to consider. As Bogdan and Biklen suggest, qualitative researchers are not putting together a puzzle whose picture they already know. They are *constructing* a picture that takes shape as they collect and examine the parts.[3]

5. *How people make sense out of their lives is a major concern to qualitative researchers.* A special interest of qualitative researchers lies in the perspectives of the subjects of a study. Qualitative researchers want to know what the participants in a study are thinking, and why they think what they do. Assumptions, motives, reasons, goals and values—all are of interest and likely to be the focus of the researcher's questions. It also is not uncommon for a researcher to show a completed videotape or the contents of his or her notes to a participant to check on the accuracy of the researcher's interpretations. In other words, the researcher does his or her best to capture the thinking of the participants from the *participants'* perspective (as opposed to the researcher merely reporting what he or she thinks) as accurately as possible.

Qualitative research takes many forms, but perhaps the three most commonly employed by educational researchers are participant observation, nonparticipant observation, and ethnographic research.

Participant Observation

Certain kinds of research questions can best be answered by *observing* how people act or how things look. For example researchers could interview teachers about how their students behave during class discussions of sensitive issues, but a more accurate indication of their activities would probably be obtained by actually observing such discussions while they take place.

In **participant observation** studies, researchers actually participate in the situation or setting they are observing. Participant observation can be *overt*, in that the researcher is easily identified and the subjects know that they are being observed, or *covert*, in which case the researcher disguises his or her identity and acts just like any of the other participants. For example, a researcher might ask a ninth grade geography teacher to allow him or her to observe one of that teacher's classes over the course of a semester. Both teacher and students would know the researcher's identity. This would be an exam-

ple of overt observation. Overt participant observation is a key ingredient in ethnographic research, which we will discuss in more detail later in this chapter.

On the other hand, another researcher might take the trouble to become certified as an elementary school teacher and then spend a period of time actually teaching in an elementary school while he or she at the same time observes what is going on. No one would know the researcher's identity (with the possible exception of the district administration from whom permission would have been obtained beforehand). This would be an example of covert observation. Covert participant observation, although likely to produce more valid observations of what really happens, is often criticized on ethical grounds. Observing people without their knowledge (and/or recording their comments without their permission) seems at best a highly questionable practice.

Nonparticipant Observation

In a **nonparticipant observation** study, researchers do not participate in the activity being observed but rather "sit on the sidelines" and watch; they are not directly involved in the situation they are observing. There are several types of nonparticipant observation that researchers use, but the most common are naturalistic observation, simulations, case studies, and content analysis.

NATURALISTIC OBSERVATION

Naturalistic observation involves observing individuals in their natural settings. The researcher makes no effort whatsoever to manipulate variables or to control the activities of individuals, but simply observes and records what happens as things naturally occur. The activities of students at an athletic event, the interactions between students and teachers on the playground, or the activities of very young children in a nursery, for example, are probably best understood through naturalistic observation.

Much of the work of the famous child psychologist Jean Piaget involved naturalistic observation. Many of his conclusions on the cognitive development of children grew out of watching his own children as they developed, and they have stimulated other researchers to do further research in this area. Insights obtained as a result of naturalistic observation, in fact, often serve as the basis for more formal experiments.

SIMULATIONS

To investigate certain variables, researchers sometimes will *create* a situation and ask subjects to act out, or *simulate,* certain roles. In **simulations,** the researcher, in effect, actually tells the subjects what to do (but not how to do it). This permits a researcher to observe what happens in certain kinds of situations, including those that occur fairly infrequently in schools or other educational settings. For example, individuals might be asked to portray a counselor interacting with a distraught parent, a teacher disciplining a student, or two administrators discussing their views on enhancing teacher morale.

There are two main types of role-playing simulations used by researchers in education—individual role-playing and team role-playing. In individual role-playing, a person is asked to role-play how he or she thinks a particular individual might act in a given situation. The researcher then observes and records what happens. Here is an example:

> You are an elementary school counselor. You have an appointment with a student who is frequently abusive toward his teachers. The student has just arrived for his 9:00 a.m. appointment with you and is sitting before you in your office. What do you say to this student?

In team role-playing, a group of individuals is asked to act out a particular situation, with the researcher again observing and recording what goes on. Particular attention is paid to how the members of the group interact. Here is an example:

> You and five of your faculty colleagues have been appointed as a special committee to discuss and come up with solutions to the problem of student cutting of classes, which has been increasing this semester. Many of the faculty support a "get tough" policy and have openly advocated suspending students who are frequent cutters. Your assignment is to come up with other alternatives that the faculty will accept. What do you propose?

The main disadvantage to simulations, as you might have recognized, is their artificiality. Situations are being acted out, and there is no guarantee that what the researcher sees is what would normally occur in a real-life situation. The results of a simulation often serve, however, as hypotheses in other kinds of research investigations.

CASE STUDIES

Sometimes much can be learned from studying just one individual, one classroom, one school, or one school district. This is called a **case study.** For example, there are some students who learn a second language rather easily. In hopes of gaining insight into why this is the case, one such student could be observed on a regular basis to see if there are any noticeable patterns or regularities in the student's behavior. The student, as well as his or her teacher, counselors, parents, and friends, might also be interviewed in depth. A similar series of observations (and interviews) might be conducted with a student who finds learning another language very difficult. As much information as possible (study style, attitudes toward the language, approach to the subject, behavior in class, and so on) would be collected. The hope here is that through the study of a somewhat unique individual, insights can be gained that will suggest ways to help other language students in the future.

Similarly, a detailed study might be made of a single school. There might be a particular elementary school in a given school district, for example, that is noteworthy for its success with "at-risk" students. A researcher might visit the school on a regular basis, observing what goes on in classrooms, during recess periods, in the hallways and lunchroom, during faculty meetings, and so on. Faculty members, administrators, support staff, and counselors could be interviewed. Again, as much information as possible (such as teaching strategies, administrative style, school activities, parental involvement, attitudes of faculty and staff toward students, classroom and other activites) would be collected. Here too, the hope would be that through the study of a single rather unique case (only in this instance not an individual but a school) valuable insights would be gained.

CONTENT ANALYSIS

Content analysis is just what its name implies—the analysis of the written or visual contents of a document. Textbooks, essays, newspapers, novels, magazine articles, cookbooks, political speeches, advertisements, pictures—in fact, the contents of virtually any type of written or visual communication can be analyzed in various ways. A person's or group's conscious and unconscious beliefs, attitudes, values, and ideas are often revealed in the documents they produce.

Suppose a researcher is interested, for example, in the accuracy of the images or concepts presented in high school English texts. She wonders if the written or visual content in these books is biased in any way and, if it is, how. She decides to do a content analysis to obtain some answers to these questions. The researcher must first plan how to select and order the contents that are available for analysis—in this case, the textbooks. Pertinent categories must be developed that will allow her to identify what she thinks is important and then compare the presence of these categories among the various textbooks she is analyzing.

This is the nub of content analysis—defining as precisely as possible those aspects of a document's contents that the researcher wants to investigate and then formulating relevant categories that are so explicit that another researcher who uses them to examine the same material would find essentially the same proportion of topics emphasized or ignored.

Let us imagine that the researcher decides to look, in particular, at how women are presented in these texts. She would first select the sample of textbooks to be analyzed—i.e., which texts she will read (in this case, perhaps, all of the textbooks used at a certain grade level in a particular school district). Categories could then be formulated. How are women described? What traits do they possess? What are their physical, emotional, and social characteristics? These questions suggest categories for analysis, which in turn can be broken down into even smaller coding units such as the following:

Physical	Emotional	Social
clothing	warm	race
size	aloof	religion
age	hostile	occupation
etc.	etc.	etc.

A coding sheet would then be prepared to tally the data in each of the categories as they are identified in each unit selected for analysis in the document. Comparisons can then readily be made. The units can be entities such as words, sentences, paragraphs, chapters, themes, examples, exercises, and test questions. If the analysis is to be based on only a sample of the units, the sample should be selected randomly so it will be representative.

A major advantage of content analysis is that it is unobtrusive. A researcher can "observe" without being observed, since the "contents" being analyzed are not influenced by the researcher's presence. Information that might be difficult or even impossible to obtain through direct observation or other means can be gained through analysis of textbooks and other available communication materials without the author or publisher being aware that it is being examined. Furthermore, replication of a content analysis by another researcher is relatively easy.

The Roles of an Observer: A Summary

DEGREE OF PARTICIPATION

It should be evident (we hope) that the degree of observer participation in what he or she is observing can vary considerably. Raymond Gold (1969) identified four different roles that a researcher can take (Figure 16.1), ranging on a continuum from complete participant to complete observer.[4]

When a researcher takes on the role of a *complete participant* in a group, his identity is not known to any of the individuals being observed. The researcher interacts with members of the group as naturally as possible and, for all intents and purposes (so far as they are concerned) is one of them. Thus, a researcher might arrange to serve for a year as an actual teacher in an inner-city classroom and carry out all of the duties and responsibilities that are a part of that role, but not reveal that he is also a researcher. As we mentioned above, such covert observation is suspect on ethical grounds.

When a researcher chooses the role of *participant-as-observer,* he participates fully in the activities in the group being studied, but also makes it clear that he is doing research. As an example, the researcher described above might tell the faculty that he is a researcher and intends to describe as thoroughly and accurately as he can what goes on in the school over the course of a year's time.

When a researcher chooses the role of *observer-as-participant,* she identifies herself straight off as a researcher, but makes no pretense of actually being a member of the group she is observing. An example here might be a university professor who is interested in what goes on in an inner-city school. The researcher might conduct a series of interviews with teachers in the school, visit classes, attend faculty meetings and collective bargaining negotiations, talk with principals and the superintendent, and talk with students, but she would not attempt to participate in the activities of the group other than superficially. She remains essentially (and does not hide the fact that she is) an interested observer who is doing research.

Finally, the role of *complete observer* is just that—a role at the opposite extreme from the role of complete participant. The researcher observes the activities of a group without in any way becoming a participant in those activities. The subjects of the researcher's observations may, or may not, realize they are being observed. An example would be a researcher who observes the activities that go on daily in a school lunchroom.

Each of the above roles has both advantages and disadvantages. The complete participant is probably most likely to get the truest picture of a group's activities, and the others less so, but the ethical question involving covert observation remains. The complete observer is probably least likely to affect the actions of the group being studied, the others more so. The participant-as-observer, since he or she is an actual member of the group being studied, will have some (and often an important) effect on what the group does. The participant-as-observer and the observer-as-participant are both likely, in varying degrees, to focus the attention of the group on the activities of the researcher and away from their normal routine, thereby making their activities no longer typical.*

OBSERVER EFFECT

Observer effect refers to both the fact that the presence of an observer can have a considerable effect on the behavior of the subjects and

---

* This is similar to what is called the Hawthorne or attitudinal effect. See Chapter Twelve.

FIGURE 16.1

Roles of an Observer in Qualitative Research

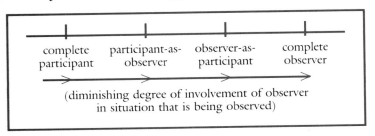

complete participant — participant-as-observer — observer-as-participant — complete observer

(diminishing degree of involvement of observer in situation that is being observed)

hence on the outcomes of a study and the fact that the data reported (that which the observer records) reflect more the biases and viewpoints of the observer than of those being observed. Let us consider each of these facts a bit further.

What effect does the observer's presence have on the observed? Unless a researcher is concealed, it is quite likely that he or she will have some effect on the behavior of those individuals who are being observed. Two things can happen, particularly if an observer is unexpected. First, he or she is likely to arouse curiosity and result in a lack of attention to the task at hand, thus producing other-than-normal behavior. An inexperienced researcher who records such behavior might easily be misled. It is for this reason that researchers who observe in classrooms, for example, usually alert the teacher beforehand and ask to be introduced. They then may spend four to five days in the classroom before starting to record observations (to enable the students to become accustomed to their presence and to go about their usual activities).

The second thing that can happen is that the behavior of those who are being observed might be influenced by the researcher's purpose. For example, suppose a researcher was interested in observing whether social studies teachers ask "high-level questions" during class discussions of controversial issues. If the teachers are aware of what the researcher is looking for, they may tend to ask more questions than normal, thus giving a distorted impression of what really goes on during a typical class discussion. The data obtained by the researcher's observation would not be representative of how the teachers normally behave. It is for this reason that many researchers argue that the participants in a study should not be informed of the study's purposes until after the data have been collected. Instead the researchers should meet with the participants before the study begins and tell them that they cannot be informed of the purpose of the study since it might affect the study's outcomes. As soon as the data have been collected, however, the researcher should promise to reveal the findings to those who are interested.

What about observer bias? **Observer bias** refers to the possibility that certain characteristics or ideas of observers may bias what they "see." It is probably true that no matter how hard observers try to be impartial, their observations will possess some degree of bias. No one can be totally objective, as we all are influenced to some degree by our past experiences, which in turn affect how we see the world and the people within it. Nevertheless, all researchers should do their best to become aware of, and try to control, their biases.

A related concern here is *observer expectations*. If researchers know they are to observe subjects who have certain characteristics (such as a certain IQ range, ethnicity, or religion), they may "expect" a certain type of behavior, which may not be how the subjects normally behave. It is in this regard that audiotapings and videotapings are so valuable, as they allow researchers to check their observations against the impressions of others.

Using Audiotapes and Videotapes. A major difficulty in both participant and nonparticipant observation is the fact that much that goes on may be missed by the observer. This is especially true when several behaviors of interest are occurring rapidly in an educational setting. Furthermore, sometimes a researcher wants to have someone else (such as an expert on the topic of interest) offer his or her insights about what is happening. A researcher who observes a number of children's play sessions in a nursery school setting, for example, might want to obtain the ideas of a qualified child psychologist or an experienced teacher of preschool children about what is happening.

To overcome these obstacles, many researchers use audiotapes or videotapes to record their observations. These have several advantages. The tapes may be replayed several times for continued study and analysis. Experts or interested others can also hear and/or see what the researcher observed and offer their insights accordingly. And a permanent record of certain kinds of behaviors is obtained for comparison with later or different samples.

There are a few disadvantages to such tapings, however, which also should be noted. Videotapings are not always the easiest to obtain and usually require trained technicians to do the taping unless the researcher has had some training and experience in this area. Often several microphones must be set up, which can distort the behavior of those being observed. Prolonged taping can be expensive. Audiotapings are somewhat easier to do, but they of course only record verbal behavior. Furthermore, sometimes it is difficult to distinguish among different speakers when one hears only their recorded voices. Noise is difficult to control and often seriously interferes with the understanding of content. Nevertheless, if these difficulties can be overcome, the use of audio- and videotapings offers considerable promise to researchers as a way to collect, store, and analyze data.

Sampling in Observational Studies

No researcher can observe every move and hear every utterance made by every individual in the group being observed. No matter how hard he or she tries, only a portion of what might be observed in a given situation will actually be observed. To that extent, what the researcher actually observes is a sample of all that might be observed. Similarly, the faculty meetings that a researcher attends over the course of a year represent a sample of all such faculty meetings. The ninth grade geography class that another researcher observes represents a sample of all such classes.

Generally speaking, researchers who engage in some form of observational study are likely to select a *purposive sample* (see Chapter Five)—that is, researchers select a sample of observations they feel will yield the best understanding of whatever they wish to study. Earl Babbie (1986) suggests two stages of sampling that researchers should keep in mind. First, to what extent are the situations *available* to the researcher representative of all such situations? Are those chemistry classes that are available for observation, for example, representative of all chemistry classes? Second, are the *actual* observations the researcher makes representative of all the possible observations that could be made? In other words, has a representative sample of all students in the chemistry classes been observed? Has a representative sample of the interactions that take place within such classes been observed?[5] These are important questions to ask, not so much because researchers wish to generalize beyond their data to a larger population (although often this is true), but to ensure that they are not getting a distorted picture of what normally happens in the situation that they are observing.

Ethnographic Research

Ethnographic research combines participant observation and many of the characteristics of nonparticipant observation studies in an attempt to obtain as wholistic a picture as possible of a particular society, group, institution, setting, or situation. The emphasis in ethnographic research is on documenting or portraying the everyday experiences of individuals by observing and interviewing them and relevant others. The key tools, in fact, in all ethnographic studies are in-depth interviewing and continual, ongoing participant observation of a situation. Researchers try to capture as much of what is going on as they can—the "whole picture," so to speak. H. R. Bernard described the process briefly, but well:

It involves establishing rapport in a new community; learning to act so that people go about their business as usual when you show up; and removing yourself every day from cultural immersion so you can intellectualize what you've learned, put it into perspective, and write about it convincingly. If you are a successful participant observer you will know when to laugh at what your informants think is funny; and when informants laugh at what you say, it will be because you *meant* it to be a joke.[6]

Ethnographic researchers seldom initiate their research with precise hypotheses that they have formulated ahead of time. Rather, they attempt to understand an ongoing situation or set of activities that cannot be predicted in advance. They observe for a period of time, formulate some initial conclusions that suggest to them additional kinds of observations that may lead them to revise their initial conclusions, and so on. Ethnographic research, perhaps more so than any other kind of research, relies on both observation and interviewing that is continual and sustained over time since it attempts to capture the processes as well as identify the products of education.

An example of a question that might be investigated through ethnographic research would be the following: "What is life like in an inner-city high school?" The researcher's goal would be to document or portray the daily, ongoing experiences of the teachers, students, administrators, and staff in such a school. The school would be regularly visited over a considerable length of time (a year would not be uncommon). Classrooms would be observed on a regular basis, and an attempt made to describe, as fully and as richly as possible, what exists and what happens in those classrooms. Several of the teachers, the students, the administrators and the support staffs would be interviewed in depth.

Descriptions (a better word might be "portrayals") might depict the social atmosphere of the school; the intellectual and emotional experiences of students; the manner in which administrators and teachers (and staff and students) act toward and react to others of different ethnic groups, sexes, or abilities; how the "rules" of the school (and the classroom) are learned, modified, and enforced; the kinds of concerns teachers (and students) have; the views students have of the school, and how these compare with the views of the administration and the faculty; and so forth.

The data to be collected might include detailed prose descriptions written out on writing tablets by the researcher/observer; audiotapes of pupil-student, administrator-student, and administrator-faculty conferences; videotapes of classroom discussions and faculty meetings; examples of teacher lesson plans and student work; sociograms depicting "power" relationships that exist in a classroom; flowcharts illustrating the direction and frequency of certain types of comments (for example, the kinds of questions asked by teacher and students to one another, and the responses that different kinds produce); and anything else the researcher thinks would provide insights into what goes on in this school.

In short, then, the goal of researchers engaging in ethnographic research is to "paint a portrait" of a school or a classroom (or any other educational setting) in as thorough, accurate, and vivid a manner as possible so that others can also truly "see" that school or that classroom and its participants and what they do. Indeed, ethnographic research seems a particularly viable approach for use in classrooms. As some observers have remarked, "the ethnographic approach to research affords a richness of description that has great potential fruitfulness for understanding . . . education."[7]

ADVANTAGES AND DISADVANTAGES OF ETHNOGRAPHIC RESEARCH

Ethnographic research has a number of unique strengths, but also several weaknesses. A key strength is that it provides the researcher with a much more comprehensive perspective than do other forms of educational research. By observing the actual behavior of individuals in their natural settings, a much deeper and richer understanding of such behavior is possible. Ethnographic research also lends itself well to research topics that are not easily quantified. The thoughts of teachers and students, ideas, and other nuances of behavior that might escape researchers using other methodologies can often be detected by ethnographic researchers.

Furthermore, ethnographic research is particularly appropriate to behaviors that are best understood by observing them within their natural settings. Experimental studies and surveys often can measure attitudes and behaviors well in somewhat artificial settings, but they frequently do not lend themselves well to naturalistic settings. The "dynamics" of a faculty meeting, or the "interaction" between students and teacher in a classroom, for example, can best be studied through ethnographic investigation. Finally, ethnographic research is especially suited to studying group behavior over time. Thus, to understand as fully as possible the "life" of an inner-city school over a year-long period, an ethnographic approach may well be the most appropriate methodology for a researcher to use.

Ethnographic research, like all research, however, is not without its limitations. It is highly dependent on the particular researcher's observations, and since numerical data are rarely provided, there is usually no way to check the validity of the researcher's conclusions. As a result, observer bias is almost impossible to eliminate. Since usually only a single situation (such as one classroom or one school) is observed, generalizability is almost nonexistent. Since the researcher usually begins his or her observations without a specific hypothesis to confirm or deny, terms may not be defined, and hence the specific variables or relationships being investigated (if any) may remain unclear.

Because of the inevitable ambiguity that accompanies this method, preplanning and review are much less useful than in quantitative studies. While it is true that no study is ever carried out precisely as planned, potential pitfalls are more easily identified and corrected in other methodologies. For this reason, we believe ethnographic research to be a very difficult type of research to do well. It follows that beginning researchers using this method should receive close supervision.

THE UNIQUE VALUE OF ETHNOGRAPHIC RESEARCH

Nevertheless, ethnographic research has a particular strength that makes it particularly appealing to many researchers. It can reveal nuances and subtleties that other methodologies miss. An excellent example is offered by Babbie.

If you were walking through a public park and you threw down a bunch of trash,

you'd discover that your action was unacceptable to those around you. People would glare at you, grumble to each other, and perhaps someone would say something to you about it. Whatever the form, you'd be subjected to definite, negative sanctions for littering. Now here's the irony. If you were walking through that same park, came across a bunch of trash that someone else had dropped, and cleaned it up, it's likely that your action would also be unacceptable to those around you. You'd probably be subject to definite, negative sanctions for cleaning it up.

Most [of my students] felt (that this notion) was absurd. . . . Although we would be negatively sanctioned for littering, . . . people would be pleased with us for [cleaning up a public place]. Certainly, all my students said *they* would be pleased if someone cleaned up a public place.

To settle the issue, I suggested that my students start fixing the public problems they came across in the course of their everyday activities. . . .

My students picked up litter, fixed street signs, put knocked-over traffic cones back in place, cleaned and decorated communal lounges in their dorms, trimmed trees that blocked visibility at intersections, repaired public playground equipment, cleaned public restrooms, and took care of a hundred other public problems that weren't "their responsibility."

Most reported feeling very uncomfortable doing whatever they did. They felt foolish, goody-goody, conspicuous. . . . In almost every case, their personal feelings of discomfort were increased by the reactions of those around them. One student was removing a damaged and long-unused newspaper box from the bus stop where it had been a problem for months when the police arrived, having been summoned by a neighbor. Another student decided to clean out a clogged storm drain on his street and found himself being yelled at by a neighbor who insisted that the mess should be left for the street cleaners. Everyone who picked up litter was sneered at, laughed at, and generally put down. One young man was picking up litter scattered around a trash can when a passerby sneered, "Clumsy!"[8]

The point of the above example, we hope, is obvious. What people think and say happens (or is likely to happen) often is not really the case. By going out into the world and observing things as they occur we are (usually) better able to obtain a more accurate picture. This is what ethnographers try to do—study people in their natural habitat in order to "see" things that otherwise might not even be anticipated. This is a major advantage of the ethnographic approach.

ROGER HARKER AND HIS FIFTH GRADE CLASSROOM

Let us look, then, at an example of ethnographic research. What follows is a short description, by the researcher, of an ethnographic study of a fifth grade classroom.

I [*the researcher*] worked in depth with Roger Harker for six months. I did an ethnography of his classroom and the interaction between him and his pupils. This young man had taught for three years in the elementary school. He volunteered for the study in order, he said, "to improve my professional competence."

My collection of data fell into the following categories: (1) personal, autobiographical, and psychological data on the teacher; (2) ratings of him by his principal and other superiors in the superintendent's office; (3) his own self-estimates on the same points; (4) observations of his classroom, emphasizing interaction with children; (5) interviews with each child and the elicitation of ratings of the teacher in many different dimensions, both formally and informally; (6) his ratings and estimates for each child in his classroom, including estimates of popularity with peers, academic performance and capacity, personal adjustment, home background, and liking for him; (7) sociometric data from the children about each other; and (8) interviews with each person (superintendent, principal, supervisors, children) who supplied ratings of him.

I also participated in the life of the school to the extent possible, accompanying the teacher where I could and "melting" into the classroom as much as feasible. I was always there, but I had no authority and assumed none. I became a friend and confidant to the children.

This teacher was regarded by his superiors as most promising—"clear and well-organized," "sensitive to children's needs," "fair and just to all of the children," "knowing his subject areas well." I was not able to elicit either with rating scales or in interviews any criticisms or negative evaluations. There were very few suggestions for change— and these were all in the area of subject matter and curriculum.

Roger Harker described himself as "fair and just to all my pupils," as making "fair decisions," and as "playing no favorites." This was a particular point of pride with him.

His classroom was made up of children from a broad social stratum—upper-middle, middle, and lower classes—and the children represented Mexican-American, Anglo-European, and Japanese-American ethnic groups. I was particularly attentive to the relationships between the teacher and children from these various groups.

One could go into much detail, but a few items will suffice since they all point in the same direction, and that direction challenges both his perceptions of his own behavior and those of his superiors. He ranked highest on all dimensions, including personal and academic factors, those children who were most like himself—Anglo, middle to upper-middle social class, and, like him, ambitious (achievement-oriented). He also estimated that these children were the most popular with their peers and were the leaders of the classroom group. His knowledge about the individual children, elicited without recourse to files or notes, was distributed in the same way. He knew significantly more about the children culturally like himself (on items concerned with home background as well as academic performance) and least about those culturally most different.

The children had quite different views of the situation. Some children described him as not always so "fair and just," as "having special pets," as not being easy to go to with their problems. On sociometric "maps" of the classroom showing which children wanted to spend time with other specific children, or work with them, sit near them, invite them to a party or a show, etc., the most popular children were not at all those the teacher rated highest. And his negative ratings proved to be equally inaccurate. Children he rated as isolated or badly adjusted socially, most of whom were non-Anglo and non-middle-class, more often than not turned out to be "stars of attraction" from the point of view of the children.

Observations of his classroom behavior supported the data collected by other means. He most frequently called on, touched, helped, and looked directly at the children culturally like himself. He was never mean or cruel to the other children. It was almost as though they weren't there. His interaction with the children of Anglo-European ethnicity and middle and upper-middle social class background was more frequent than with the other children, and the quality of the interaction appeared to be differentiated in the same way.

This young man, with the best of intentions, was confirming the negative hypotheses and predictions (as well as the positive ones) already made within the social system. He was informing Anglo middle-class children that they were capable, had bright futures, were socially acceptable, and were worth a lot of trouble. He was also informing non-Anglo children that they were less capable, less socially acceptable, less worth the trouble. He was defeating his own declared educational goals.

This young teacher did not know that he was discriminating. He was rated very positively by his superiors on all counts, including being "fair and just to all the children." Apparently they were as blind to his discrimination as he was. The school system supported him and his classroom behavior without questioning or criticizing him. And the dominant social structure of the community supported the school.[9]

Notice several things about this description.

- The study took place in a naturalistic setting—in the classroom and school of Roger Harker.

- The researcher did not try to manipulate the situation in any way.
- There was no comparison of methods or treatments (as is often the case in experimental or causal-comparative research).
- The study involved only a single classroom (an n of one).
- The researcher was a participant observer, participating "in the life of the school to the extent possible."
- The researcher used several different kinds of instruments to collect his data.
- The researcher tried to present a wholistic description of this teacher's fifth grade classroom.
- The study revealed much that would have been missed by researchers using other methodologies.
- No attempt was made to generalize the researcher's findings to other settings or situations. The "external validity" of the study, in other words, was very limited.
- There is no way, unfortunately, to check the validity of the data or the researcher's interpretations.

TOPICS THAT LEND THEMSELVES WELL TO ETHNOGRAPHIC RESEARCH

As the example above suggests, researchers who undertake an ethnographic study want to obtain as wholistic a picture of an educational setting as possible. Indeed, one of the key strengths of ethnographic research is the comprehensiveness of perspective it provides. Since the researcher goes directly to the situation or setting that he or she wishes to study, deeper and more complete understanding becomes possible. As a result, ethnographic research is particularly suitable for topics such as the following.

- Those that by their very nature defy simple quantification (for example, the interaction of students and teachers in classroom discussions).
- Those that can best be understood in a natural (as opposed to an artificial) setting (for example, the behavior of students at a school event).

- Those that involve the study of individual or group activities over time (such as the changes that occur in the attitudes of "at-risk" students as they participate in a specially designed, year-long, reading program.
- Those involving the study of the roles that educators play, and the behaviors associated with those roles (the behavior of classroom teachers, students, counselors, administrators, coaches, staff, and other school personnel as they fulfill their various roles and how such behavior changes over time).
- Those that involve the study of the activities and behavior of groups as a unit (classes, athletic teams, subject matter departments, administrative units, work teams, etc.).
- Those involving the study of formal organizations in their totality (schools, school districts, and so forth).

Some examples of the kinds of studies that ethnographers have conducted in education are as follows.

- Small town teacher[10]
- Questioning at home and at school: A comparative study[11]
- Cultural organization of participation structures in two classrooms of Indian students[12]
- The ethnography of children's spontaneous play[13]
- Hempies and squeaks, truckers and cruisers: a participant observer study in a city high school[14]
- Elementary school teachers' planning for social studies and other subjects[15]

SAMPLING IN ETHNOGRAPHIC RESEARCH

Since ethnographers attempt to observe everything within the setting or situation they are observing, in a sense they do not sample at all. But as we have mentioned before, no researcher can observe everything. To the extent that what is observed is only a portion of what might be observed, what a researcher observes is, therefore, a de facto sample of all the possible observations that might be made.

Nevertheless, the samples studied by ethnographers are typically small (often only a few individuals, or a single class) and do not permit generalization to a larger population. Many ethnographers, in fact, state right at the outset of a study that they have no intention of generalizing the results of their study. What they are after, they point out, is a more complete understanding of a particular situation. The applicability of their findings can best be determined by replication of their work in other settings or situations by other researchers.

VALIDITY AND RELIABILITY IN ETHNOGRAPHIC RESEARCH

In Chapter Seven, we introduced the concepts of validity and reliability as they apply to the use of instruments in educational research. These two concepts are also very important in ethnographic research, only here they apply to the observations researchers make and to the responses they receive to the interview questions asked. A fundamental concern in ethnographic research, in fact, revolves around the degree of confidence researchers can place in what they have seen or heard. In other words, how can researchers be sure that they are not being misled?

You will recall that validity refers to the appropriateness, meaningfulness, and usefulness of the inferences researchers make based on the data they collect, while reliability refers to the consistency of these inferences over time.

In an ethnographic study, much depends on the perspective of the researcher. As we discussed earlier under observer bias, all researchers (like the rest of us) have certain biases. Accordingly, different researchers see some things more clearly than others. Ethnographers use a number of techniques, therefore, to check their perceptions in order to ensure that they are not being misinformed—that they are, in effect, seeing (and hearing) what they think they are seeing. These procedures for checking on or enhancing validity and reliability include the following.

- Using a variety of instruments to collect their data. When a conclusion is supported by data collected from a number of different instruments, its validity is thereby enhanced. This kind of checking is often referred to as **triangulation.**
- Checking one informant's descriptions of something (a way of doing things or a reason for doing something) against another informant's descriptions of that same thing. Discrepancies in descriptions *may* mean the data are invalid.*
- Learning to understand and, where appropriate, speak the vocabulary of the group being studied. If researchers do not understand what informants mean when they use certain terms (especially slang) or if they take such terms to mean something that they do not, the recording of invalid data will surely result.
- Writing down the questions they ask (in addition to the answers they receive to these questions). This helps researchers make sense at a later date out of answers recorded earlier.
- Recording their own thoughts as they go about their observations and interviews. Responses that seem unusual or incorrect can be noted and checked later against other remarks or observations.
- Documenting the sources of remarks whenever possible and appropriate. This helps researchers make sense out of comments that otherwise might seem misplaced.
- Documenting the bases for inferences they make.
- Describing the context in which questions are asked and situations are observed.
- Using audiotapes and videotapes when possible and appropriate.
- Drawing conclusions based on one's un-

derstanding of the situation being observed and then acting on these conclusions. If these conclusions are invalid, the researcher will soon find out after acting on them.
- Interviewing individuals more than once. Inconsistencies over time in what the same individual reports may suggest that he or she is an unreliable informant.
- Observing the setting or situation of interest over a period of time. The length of an observation is extremely important in ethnographic research. Consistency over time with regard to what researchers are seeing or hearing is a strong indication of reliability. Furthermore, there is much about a group that does not even begin to emerge until some time has passed, and the members of the group become familiar with, and willing to trust, the researcher.

Field Notes

A major check on the validity and reliability of an ethnographer's observations lies in the quality of his or her *field notes*. To place an ethnographic report in perspective, interested readers need to know as much as possible about the ideas and views of the researcher. That is why the researcher's field notes are so important. Unfortunately, this remains a major problem in the reporting of much ethnographic research, in that the readers of ethnographic reports seldom, if ever, have access to the researcher's field notes. Rarely do ethnographers tell us how their information was collected, and hence it often is difficult to determine the reliability of the researcher's observations.

Field notes are just what their name implies—the notes researchers take in the field. In educational research, this usually means the detailed notes researchers take in the educational setting (classroom or school) as they observe what is going on or as they interview their informants. They are the researchers' written

* Not necessarily, of course. It may simply mean a difference in viewpoint or perception.

account of what they hear, see, experience, and think in the course of collecting and reflecting on their data.[16]

Bernard (1988) suggests that field notes be distinguished, however, from three other types of writing: field jottings, a field diary, and a field log.[17]

Field jottings refer to quick notes about something the researcher wants to write more about later. They provide the stimulus to help researchers recall a lot of details they do not have time to write down during an observation or an interview.

A field diary is, in effect, a personal statement of the researcher's feelings, opinions, and perceptions about others with whom the researcher comes in contact during the course of his or her work. It provides a place where researchers can "let their hair down," so to speak—an outlet for writing things down that the researcher does not want to become part of the public record. Here is an example of part of a page from such a diary of one of the authors of this book, written during a semester-long observation of a social studies class in a suburban high school.

Monday, 11/5. Cold, very rainy day. Makes me feel sort of depressed. Phil, Felix, Alicia, Robert, & Susan came into classroom early today to discuss yesterday's assignment. Susan is looking more disheveled than usual today—seems preoccupied while others are discussing ways to prepare the group report. She doesn't speak to me, although all others say hello. I regret my failure to support her idea during yesterday's discussion when she asked me to. Hope that it will not result in her refusing to be interviewed.

Tuesday, 11/13. Susan and other members of committee supposed to meet me in library before school today for help with their report. Nobody showed. Feel that I've done something to turn these kids off, especially Susan. Makes me angry toward her, as this will now be the third time that she has missed a meeting with me. Only first time for the others. Perhaps she has more influence on them than I thought? I don't feel I am getting anywhere in understanding her, or why she has such influence on so many of the other kids.

Thursday, 11/29. Wow! Mrs. R (teacher) had extremely good discussion today. Seems like entire class participated (note: check discussion tally sheet to corroborate). I think secret is to start off with something that they perceive as interesting. Why is it that sometimes they are so—so good! so involved in ideas and thinking and other times so apathetic? I can't figure it out. . . .

Field work is often an intense, emotionally draining experience, and a diary can serve as a way for the researcher to let out his or her feelings, yet still keep them private.

A field log is a sort of running account of how researchers plan to spend their time compared to how they actually spend it. It is, in effect, the researcher's plan for collecting his or her data systematically. A field log consists of books of blank, lined paper. Each day in the field is represented by two pages of the log. On the left page, the researcher lists what he or she plans to do that day—where to go, who to interview, what to observe, and so on. On the right side, the researcher lists what he or she *actually* did that day. As the study progresses, and things come to mind that the researcher wants to know, the log provides a place for them to be scheduled. Bernard gives an example of how such a log is used.

Suppose you're studying a local educational system. It's April 5 and you are talking with an informant called MJR. She tells you that since the military government took over, children have to study politics for two hours every day, and she doesn't like it. Write a note to yourself in your log to ask other mothers about this issue, and to interview the school principal.

Later on, when you are writing up your notes, you may decide not to interview the principal until after you have accumulated more data about how mothers in the community feel about the new curriculum. On the left-hand page for April 23 you note:

"target date for interview with school principal." On the left-hand page of April 10 you note "make appointment for interview on 23rd with school principal." For April 6 you note "need more interviews with mothers about new curriculum."[18]

The value of maintaining a log is that it forces the researcher to think hard about the questions he or she truly wants answered, the procedures to be followed, and the data really needed.

THE CONTENT OF FIELD NOTES

The taking of field notes is an art in itself. We can only give a brief introduction here, but the points presented below should give you some idea of the importance and complexity of the task.

Bogdan and Biklen (1982) state that field notes consist of two kinds of materials—descriptive and reflective. *Descriptive field notes* attempt to describe the setting, the people and what they do according to what the researcher observes. They include the following.

- Portraits of the subjects—their physical appearance, mannerisms, gestures, how they act, talk, and so on.
- Reconstruction of dialogue—conversations between subjects, as well as what they say to the researcher. Unique or particularly revealing statements should be quoted.
- Description of the physical setting—a quick sketch of the room arrangements, placement of materials, and so on.
- Accounts of particular events—who was involved, when, where, and how.
- Depiction of activities—a detailed description of what happened, along with the order in which it happened.
- The observer's behavior—the researcher's actions, dress, conversations with participants, reactions, and so on.

Reflective field notes present more of what the researcher himself or herself is thinking *about* as he or she observes. These include the following.

- Reflections on analysis—the researcher's speculations about what he or she is learning, ideas that are developing, patterns or connections seen, and so on.
- Reflections on method—procedures and materials the researcher is using in the study, comments about the design of the study, problems that are arising, and so on.
- Reflections on ethical dilemmas and conflicts—such as any concerns that arise over responsibilities to subjects or value conflicts.
- Reflections on the observer's frame of mind—such as on what the researcher is thinking as the study progresses—his or her attitudes, opinions, and beliefs—and how these might be affecting the study.
- Points of clarification—notes to the researcher about things that need to be clarified, checked later, etc.[19]

In no other form of research is the actual doing of the study—the process itself—considered as consciously and deliberately as it is in ethnographic research. The reflective aspect of field notes is the researcher's way of attempting to control for the danger of observer effect that we mentioned earlier, and to remind us that research, to be done well, requires ongoing evaluation and judgment.

An Example of Qualitative Research

In the remainder of this chapter, we present a published example of an ethnographic study, followed by a critique of its strengths and weaknesses. As we did in our critiques of the different types of research studies we analyzed in other chapters, we use several of the concepts introduced in earlier parts of the book in our analysis.

From: *Theory and Research in Social Education*
Summer, 1985. Volume XIII Number 2, pp. 1–20
© by the College and University Faculty Assembly
of the National Council for the Social Studies

Becoming an Elementary Social Studies Teacher: A Study of Perspectives

Jesse Goodman
Indiana University

Susan Adler
Rockhurst College

Abstract

Student teachers' perspectives toward social studies education are analyzed in this paper. Sixteen elementary-level student teachers were selected at two university teacher education programs. One year's observations and interviews with the student teachers and their colleagues provided the data. The 16 participants held one or more of six perspectives. They viewed social studies as a nonsubject, as human relations, as citizenship indoctrination, as school knowledge, as the integrative core of the elementary curriculum, and as education for social action. A case study of a representative student illustrated the complexity of how perspectives develop. These findings suggested that official conceptions of social studies have little to do with student teachers' beliefs and actions in the classroom and that methods courses should address this discrepancy.

Throughout the 20th century, educators have sought to create an overarching statement of the definition and purposes of social studies education. Such statements, abstracted from classroom practice, comprise the conceptions of social studies held by scholars. Despite differences among educators in their views of what social studies is or ought to be, several conceptions persist. The most dominant is social studies as citizenship education. The 1916 report of the Committee on Social Studies of the Commission on Secondary Education of the National Education Association described social studies as the subject that develops in young people the skills and attitudes necessary to good citizenship (Clements, Fielder, &

Tabachnick, 1966, p. 6). Citizenship meant active participation in community and national decision making. This conception of social studies has remained important. In the 1981 statement on the Essentials of the Social Studies, the National Council for the Social Studies affirmed:

> Citizenship participation in public life is essential to the health of our democratic system. Effective social studies programs help prepare young people who can identify, understand, and work to solve the problems that face our increasingly diverse nation and interdependent world. (p. 2)

Other conceptions of social studies are often portrayed as supporting this overall goal. An example of such a conception is social studies as reflective inquiry or decision making (e.g., Clements et al., 1966; Engle, 1960; Hennings, Hennings, & Banich, 1980; Massialas & Cox, 1966; Pagano, 1978). Here the emphasis is on the process of inquiry to formulate and solve social problems. Another conception is social studies as social science. Emphasis is placed on having students learn the facts, concepts, and processes of the social science disciplines (Barr, Barth, & Shermis, 1977, p. 62). Pupils would, for example, learn the structure of anthropology by participating in anthropological inquiry to discover anthropological concepts. Still another conception places emphasis "on how most people participate in . . . society" (Superka & Hawke, 1980, p. 574): Social studies content should deal with the major roles people play in their lives and with learning to understand, value, and function creatively in these roles.

But how are these conceptions of social studies played out — or not played out — in classroom practice? Although teachers may use the terminology found in the literature, evidence indicates that these conceptions have little bearing on practice (e.g., Shaver, Davis, & Helburn, 1979). How then do practitioners, rather than scholars, give meaning and purpose to social studies? Meanings, in the context of classroom teaching, are not abstract conceptions removed from the act of teaching. Rather, meaning is what Beard (1934) referred to as the frame of reference on which thought and action are consciously or unconsciously based. The concept of teacher perspectives is useful for capturing this notion of meaning.

TEACHER PERSPECTIVES

The concept of teacher perspectives captures the ideas, behaviors, and contexts of particular teaching acts (Becker, Geer, Hughes, & Strauss, 1961; Cornbleth, 1982; Grace, 1978; Hammersley, 1977; Janesick, 1978; Sharp & Green, 1975). Unlike more abstract constructs, perspectives are set in the concrete world of actual situations and refer to particular actions. Teacher perspectives take into account how the situation of the school and classroom is experienced; how this situation is interpreted given the teacher's background of experiences, beliefs, and assumptions; and how this interpretation is manifested in behaviors.

Several studies (e.g., Becker et al., 1961; Lortie, 1975) found that perspectives are formed early in a career. It follows, then, that a crucial period for examining the development of teachers' perspectives is during their preservice education. In general, literature relating field experiences to social studies has not been very illuminating. We have learned little about how students[1] incorporate, or fail to incorporate, their thinking about social studies into actual practice.

An exception to this generalization is a study by Adler (1984) in which she examined the perspectives of four students. In this study, the work of Berlak and Berlak (1981) was used to provide a linguistic framework for an analysis of perspectives. They suggested conceptualizing teachers' acts as ongoing resolutions to a set of competing demands or dilemmas. The use of dilemma language provides a way to capture the complexity, connections, and contradictions of teachers' behaviors and ideas. It allows the researcher to move beyond the assumption that perspectives can be adequately captured by static dichotomies such as traditional vs. progressive, conservative vs. liberal, or reproductive vs. transformation. Using Berlak and Berlak's framework, Adler described the students' patterns of dilemma resolution toward social studies and teaching. As suggested in Adler's article, these descriptions only began to explore the perspectives that students might hold or develop.

As Glaser and Strauss (1967) noted, one of the values of ethnographic data is that their depth provides researchers with the opportunity to reanalyze data and reevaluate conclusions. Analysis is not a static product. Instead, it is "an ever-developing entity" (p. 32). Analysis is open to modification by the originator as well as other scholars. Indeed, verification of such reports is a continuous process, and one important — but all too often neglected — aspect of verification is the reviewing of data with colleagues to establish intersubjective consensus, as well as the extending of studies to include more informants and richer data.

In addressing the preceding point, this article reports the findings of a reanalysis and extension of the original Adler (1984) study. Through this examination of new data and reexamination of original data, Adler's report has been refined in several ways.

First, as is discussed subsequently, an additional sample of 12 students was investigated. Unlike Adler's (1984) group, which was carefully screened, this new group was randomly chosen. This extended data base was useful in cross-referencing and developing new analytical categories.

The second distinction lies in the level of analysis. The emphasis of Adler's article is to describe the components of perspectives held by four focal students. In increasing the sample from these four to sixteen, six patterns of perspectives emerged from this new analysis. From what began as a description of individuals, we built conceptual categories. In this way, our insights into the relationship between people's beliefs and actions have crystallized.

Third, rather than using a predetermined linguistic framework as the basis of analysis, we formulated the perspectives reported in this paper more directly from the informants themselves. In this sense, the analysis has become more grounded in social reality (Glaser & Strauss, 1967). Although this new analytical framework does not contradict the dilemma language originally used, it more accurately describes the range of perspectives found in our sample groups.

Finally, the development of this grounded framework required richer and more detailed reporting of field notes than in the previous work. As a result, the lived quality of these perspectives has been enhanced.

This reanalysis and extension of Adler's (1984) original report is important for two reasons. First, as it stands alone, this article contributes to a growing body of literature that is helping us gain an understanding of what it means to become a teacher. Second, in relation to Adler's original article, it exemplifies the process of extended analysis for those researchers interested in ethnographic methodology.

In addressing these points, the paper is divided into four sections. After a discussion of the methodology used, we describe the perspectives that emerged from our analysis of the field data. This section does not quantify the numbers or percentages of students who held each perspective. Rather it provides a base for understanding the kinds of perspectives students developed. Furthermore, each of our informants showed evidence of holding a perspective other than a dominant one. Hence, the next section is a portrayal of one individual. Through this portrayal, the complexity of students' perspectives is illuminated. The paper concludes with a discussion of the implications of this research for educators.

METHODOLOGY

The rationale for choosing one methodology over another is connected to the nature of the subject studied and the underlying goals of the research. Weber's (1977) notion of verstehen was particularly helpful in outlining our purpose. Through empathic understanding and direct experience of the social world, we gain insight into a given social phenomenon. Because this study explored the complex interconnection between people's beliefs and actions and the effect of this connection on the social studies education found in classrooms, we felt it was necessary to use a methodology that incorporated the existential experience of the participants themselves — their actions, thoughts, feelings, and perceptions — as a major focus for investigation and interpretation. Therefore, the methods used were those associated with ethnographic field studies (e.g., Bruyn, 1966; Glaser & Strauss, 1967). As Blumer (1969) emphasized, this methodology permits the researcher to meet all of the basic requirements of an empirical science: to confront the social world being studied; to raise abstract questions about this world; to discover relations between categories of data; to formulate propositions about these relations; to organize these propositions into an analytical scheme that others can understand; and to test the questions, data, relations, propositions, and analysis through renewed examination of the social world.

Methods and Sample Selection

As already noted, this paper extends Adler's (1984) study through a reanalysis based on additional data. Hence this study is somewhat unusual in that it contains two disparate samples. Although the methods used to collect data were similar, they were not identical. In both cases, observations and interviews — formal and informal — were the main methods of data collection. Other data sources such as questionnaires, student logs, completed assignments, course syllabi, and official program literature were used as part of our final analysis. Data were recorded in field notes during two university quarters for Sample A and one semester for Sample B.[2]

Sample A was located in an elementary teacher education program at a large, southeastern state university. Approximately 75 students were enrolled in this program while the fieldwork was conducted. Twelve randomly chosen students were observed as they participated in university courses, seminar meetings, and practicum experiences. Ten students were placed in early field experiences while they attended university classes, and two were student teaching full time. Field placements ranged from first through sixth grades. All of these students attended the same weekly seminar meetings. They were observed in their practicum sites one to four times, and each observation lasted between two hours and the entire school day. Approximately 40% of their university class sessions were observed during the fall and spring quarters, and each of the sample group's seminar meetings were observed during this time.

Sample B was located in a large midwestern state university. During the semester before the fieldwork began, the researcher informally observed the university social studies methods courses. From the 64 individuals in these classes, 4 representative students were chosen as the focus of study. The selection of these 4 students was based on (a) their student-teaching placement in upper elementary grades, (b) their scores on the Conceptions of Social Studies Inventory given to all students prior to their student teaching, and (c) recommendations by their social studies methods profes-sors.[3] Each student was extensively observed at least five times during the student-teaching semester.

The purpose of these observations was to discover what actually happened in the field placements, university courses, and seminar meetings. Rather than predetermining items to look for, we used a number of general questions to initially guide these observations: How is each setting organized? What kind of interpersonal dynamics exist? How do the students, cooperating teachers, faculty members, and pupils act? What activities occur in each setting? What topics are discussed, and what information, opinions, and beliefs are exchanged among the participants? More specific observation questions, particularly about the teaching of social studies, were developed from reviewing notes as the fieldwork continued. These observations not only illuminated what happened in each setting, but they also were used as the focus for in-depth interviews about the nature and meaning of the participants' actions.

Scheduled interviews were conducted weekly or biweekly with each student from both samples. Each social studies methods faculty member and each cooperating teacher were also interviewed. In addition, other students not in the sample groups were informally interviewed. Students were interviewed before and after each field placement observation, and students and faculty members were often interviewed immediately following a given class session.

Much of this interviewing was conducted using Glaser and Strauss's (1967) theoretical sampling and constant comparative method of analysis. Interviews were not organized into predetermined questions. Instead, they were structured around areas of concern: the purpose of teaching a given lesson; perceptions of what happened in a given situation; individual responses to the organization, people, activities, and topics addressed in a given situation; and perceptions of the relationship between beliefs and actions. After reviewing field notes, more specific questions emerged and were then asked during interviews to gain deeper insight into situations and to clarify misconceptions and ambiguities. Responses from students within the sample groups were cross-checked with other students enrolled in these programs. The purpose of interviewing was not only to listen to the words, but also to derive meanings, motivations, and conflicts — often hidden by surface conversation — that lay behind behavior. Interviews were designed to discover how individuals interpreted the social world around them and how these interpretations were used as the basis for their actions.

Analysis

As a result of these observations and interviews, the analysis examined the students' perspectives of social studies education. Throughout the fieldwork, interview and observation notes were reviewed daily. Incidents and bits of information were at first coded into tentative conceptual categories. As these categories emerged, questions arose that were used to guide further investigation into the field. The findings from these investigations were then compared to the initial categories. Early analysis by Adler (1984) was modified when data from both sample groups were pooled. Special attention was given to data that seemed to challenge original conceptualizations. Through this constant comparison of data, theoretical categories crystallized. For example, initially it seemed that there were five major perspectives that students had toward social studies education. However, further investigation clarified that some data did not easily fit into these existing categories. Although data to support the development of an additional category were sparse, we felt that they were significant, and thus a sixth category emerged. This return to the data source, followed by modification or generation of ideas, continued until the findings could be presented in some detail. Finally, the participants were given an opportunity to respond to the initial analysis before a final draft of the study was written.

As suggested by Glaser and Strauss (1967), the analysis presented in this paper takes a narrative form, using examples from the data to clarify concepts and to demonstrate the interrelationship between analysis and social reality. The data presented in this paper are not designed to prove the infallibility of the study's results. Rather, the goal is to illuminate concepts and thus provide a basis for further discussion and debate. Presenting the analysis in narrative form reflects its ever-developing nature.

PERSPECTIVES OF SOCIAL STUDIES EDUCATION

As described previously, this study examined student perspectives toward social studies education. Six major perspectives were expressed through these students' beliefs and actions. These perspectives were neither static nor mutually exclusive. Although individual students held a dominant perspective, careful observation revealed that students also expressed qualities of other perspectives as they taught. In addition, a number of individuals altered their perspectives during their field experiences. In describing these six perspectives, we have temporarily frozen life, and the dynamic character of people's beliefs and actions is muffled.

Social Studies as a Nonsubject

Unlike the other perspectives described in this paper, social studies as a nonsubject was limited to the students within Sample A.[4] Many of these students did not consider social studies a major subject within the curriculum. Social studies content was rarely observed being taught in Sample A's practicum sites. Reading and math dominated the curriculum in most classrooms. Students often said that they had taught nothing but these two subjects in their early field experiences. In grades 1–3, social studies even lacked an official time slot during the day. Fourth-grade teachers taught social studies for half the year and science the other half. However, these lessons were often taught only if there was enough time at the end of a day. Little continuity, organization, or thought were put into these lessons. Debra, who was placed in a fourth-grade classroom, summarized the experience of a number of students.

> Well, in the afternoon, if we have some time to kill, we might show a filmstrip or movie on some social studies topic. We're supposed to teach it more often, but there are too many other things to do. (interview with Debra)

Many students said that their cooperating teachers were under pressure to raise the nationally standardized reading scores of their pupils, and as a result, little time could be devoted to other educational goals. For many of these students, social studies did not exist as part of the curriculum. Although social studies was taught in the middle level grades, compared to other subjects such as reading, it was not considered important.

What is most surprising is that students and many faculty members in Sample A seemed to take for granted the dominance of reading over other elementary subjects. This crucial issue was never discussed in any of the university classes observed. Whatever their answers when asked if they felt this dominance was educationally sound, students all said it was the first time anyone had asked them that question.

Social Studies as Human Relations

Other students also failed to view social studies as a field of knowledge; they saw it as teaching children techniques of human relations. Rather than using history, anthropology, sociology, political science, or some other social science to explore the nature or human beings and the world around them, these students emphasized teaching children about themselves and how to cooperate with the other children in their class.

> I think social studies should help children become more aware of themselves and how to get along with others. [She was asked how these goals should be accomplished.] I think the best way is to have them do things that make them more aware of their feelings and values. We use *T.A.* [Transactional Analysis] *for Kids* a lot. It's a great book for improving children's self-image and helping them communicate better. (interview with Jean)

Students with this perspective did not plan and implement units of study around a given body of knowledge, but instead taught interpersonal communication, problem solving, or self-concept lessons.

Jill had her third-grade class make *Me Mobiles.* Each pupil had to paint faces that reflected feelings they often felt. After the period was over, Jill and her cooperating teacher collected the plates and later made mobiles out of them and hung them up around the room. When asked to explain the meanings of this activity, Jill responded, "We have them do this kind of stuff every Tuesday and Thursday. Each time we pick out a different activity from one of these books [She pointed to three books on teaching children about human relationships.] that helps them get in touch with themselves or other kids in the class. Personally, I think this stuff is a lot more meaningful than the traditional social studies I had as a kid." (observation of and interview with Jill)

The predominant characteristic of this perspective is that all these activities were conducted under the general heading of human relations. No real content was explored, nor was there a context into which these activities were placed. For example, the preceding activity was not part of a unit on what it means to be a human being or even a unit on human emotions, but was simply one of many activities that the children participated in twice each week. Like social studies as a nonsubject, this perspective portrayed social studies as devoid of any substantive content.

Social Studies as Citizenship

This perspective saw social studies as the means to teach children the value of being a good citizen. Unlike the conception of social studies described in the introduction of this paper, the term *good* to these students did not imply thoughtful, involved, and socially active individuals. Instead, it meant an uncritical loyalty to the economic and political institutions and customs of our society. For example, Barb taught her first-grade class to memorize the Pledge of Allegiance as one of her social studies activities. In these lessons there was no attempt to help the pupils understand what it means to pledge allegiance or what the flag might symbolize to different individuals (observation of and interview with Barb).

A few students expressed the view that setting up classroom rules was social studies in that it helped pupils become better citizens.

Sooner or later kids have to learn that they can't do everything they want. Learning to obey rules and how to get along in society is just part of growing up, and it's important for teachers to teach these things to kids. So in this way I teach some social studies indirectly. (interview with Tom)

In teaching subject matter, students encouraged children to emulate individuals who exemplified this unquestioning loyalty.

Pupils were giving their oral reports on famous Americans in history. While there were numerous reports on presidents, military heros, and sports figures, there were virtually no reports on controversial individuals or outspoken critics of American society. The only social activist mentioned was Martin Luther King, and the emphasis of this report was on Dr. King's peaceful, nonviolent intentions and his loyalty to America. The fact that individuals in the civil rights movement openly defied state and federal laws, spoke against the injustices within our society, and often spent time in jail was never really explored in this report. Neither Andy nor his cooperating teacher raised these points at any time during or after the pupils' presentations. (observation of Andy)

When Andy, who was placed in a sixth-grade classroom, was asked why there were few social critics among the reports, he responded:

This is a pretty conservative community, and that kind of stuff I don't think would go over real big here. [He was asked if he agreed with this point of view.] Yes, I guess so. There's no better place to live in the world today, and I think we should teach these kids how lucky they are instead of always focusing on the negative. (interview with Andy)

This perspective also promoted the notion that to be an American citizen was intrinsically best. When compared to other cultures, for example, there was often a subtle but consistent message that our governmental institutions, production of consumer goods, written laws, wealth, city size, or scientific discoveries meant that our society was more advanced than other nations of the world. These messages were often evident in lessons of history, political science, sociology, as well as anthropology.

Social Studies as School Knowledge

In this perspective, social studies was seen as textbook knowledge; a major concern of students who held this perspective was the need to cover the material. These students depended on textbooks and such textbook-like materials as mimeographed handouts in their teaching. Learning was defined as the passive acquisition of information, with little time given to questioning, challenging, or critically analyzing this school knowledge. Whether the information was the names of state capitals, the causes of the Civil War, or the effects of the Industrial Revolution, pupils were expected to memorize specific information for a specified time period. Proof of learning was limited to successful scores on tests of recall and comprehension.

Students with this perspective often became dependent on the textbooks and rarely questioned the information found in them.

> Ann was verbally quizzing the children in preparation for their test on chapter six in their textbook, which compared democracy to communism. She asked various questions about the characteristics of each system, and if a child missed the question, the pupil had to look up the answer in the text. (observation of Ann)

Ann was later asked if she thought the comparison between communism and democracy was an accurate approach to take because one reflects a political system and the other an economic system. Her response was typical of students with this perspective.

> Maybe that kind of questioning is appropriate for college, but I don't think these kids [sixth-graders] can handle it. Besides, if I spend a lot of time discussing every little point, we won't finish the chapter in time. (interview with Ann)

When asked why they were teaching what they were teaching, students who held this perspective commonly gave one or more of the following answers: (a) the cooperating teacher told me what to teach; (b) the lesson was next in line in the textbook; (c) this curriculum was required by the principal, the school board, or the state; or (d) this is what the teachers in the next grade would expect pupils to know. These students had a deferential attitude toward curriculum experts, textbook authors, and professors; they know what to teach and it is the job of teachers to follow the plan accordingly. Social studies was limited to the official knowledge found in professionally developed curriculum materials.

The effects of covering the material were dramatic. Instead of instruction being an activity in which teachers and pupils explore and share knowledge, stimulate interest, and work together toward a commonly arrived at intellectual goal, teaching became an activity or a problem of management.

> When I look back at my field experiences, the thing that strikes me most is just how little actual teaching went on. [She was asked for clarification.] You know, where you sit down with the kids and teach them something [content]. Mostly, you just organized the day — made sure everyone was doing what they were supposed to do, passed out worksheets, and graded tests. No one seemed to teach much; we just set things up for kids to work. (observation of Susan's final conference with her university supervisor)

The most important managerial concern for these students was discipline. Students were observed experimenting with various techniques such as turning lights on and off, counting down from ten, and putting names on the blackboard. These techniques were used to keep the pupils on task, maintain order, and "ensure that work is being done and that learning is taking place" (interview with David).

Social Studies as the Great Connection

Social studies as the great connection or core of the curriculum was the dominant theme in the perspectives of a few of our informants. Students who held this perspective emphasized the integration of knowledge; they taught as if there were no hard boundaries between school subjects. An observer in the classroom might be unsure what subject was scheduled for a particular time. For example, during observations of Peter's teaching, a math lesson on measurement included measuring map distances to various national parks and was tied to a social studies unit on John Muir.

Students who held this perspective were independent of textbooks. Not only did they see knowledge as integrated, but they also viewed knowledge as coming from many different sources, both inside and outside the school.

> The most interesting thing I did was plan a unit on ecology. I did a lot of my own research on the topic. . . . Instead of having the kids read only textbooks and fill out worksheets, I had them make an art display illustrating the balance between all things; they saw a movie about the habitats of wild animals and how they are being destroyed; I brought in a guest speaker from a local environmental group and from the local utility company; and I had the kids read newspaper articles and children's books that dealt with endangered species and man's relationship to the earth. I ended the unit by having the students . . . write poems about this topic. It was neat deciding what to teach and how to teach it. (interview with Judy)

These students were more than managers of predetermined curriculum. In interviews they expressed the importance of teachers developing curriculum based on their own and their pupils' interests. They believed that they could best promote inquiry and reflection among their pupils if they could exercise more control over the curriculum in their classrooms. They suggested that by integrating subjects, they got their students more involved in learning.

Social Studies as Social Action

This last perspective is similar to the preceding one. Like the great connectors, the two students who held this perspective developed their own curriculum and promoted reflective inquiry among their pupils. However, this perspective emphasized a more critical stance toward textbooks, the role of the teacher, knowledge, and the sociopolitical contexts within which schools exist. As part of their case histories, both Kate and Peter mentioned being influenced by the civil rights and antiwar movements of the 1960s and 1970s. They saw the relationship between the dominant political, social, and economic forces within the United States and the role schools play in perpetuating the existing order. Each expressed a desire to, in some small way, help change our society through their teaching. They wanted their pupils to become more critical and to question many of our social norms.

> What I'd like to be doing in social studies does definitely reflect what I think people, as thinking members of society, need to be able to do — that is, question things they read and the prevailing tides [sociopolitical ideologies] of the country. (interview with Peter)

As a result of these beliefs, Peter and Kate chose topics of study that would increase their pupils' sociopolitical awareness and would stimulate them to become more socially active citizens.

> The textbook covered the aging process, and generally, it did a pretty good job of pointing out some of the problems old people face in our country. However, we [Kate and her cooperating teachers] felt that it [the textbook] lacked a sense of real life. So we had the kids visit a nursing home down the block from the school. The kids got really involved. They started to adopt grandparents from the home, and we took numerous field trips there. When they [the grandparents] died, the kids wrote letters to their relatives and in some cases even went to the funerals. So we started talking about death with the kids. But then we realized that we were focusing only on the problems of the elderly. So we started talking about how some elderly people regain their childhood in their last years. Some travel and develop hobbies; some learn how to really enjoy life. This is something the textbook totally ignored. We discovered that a big factor in enjoying one's later years was health and having enough money. So we ended the unit by writing to the President, local Congress people, and Representative Pepper to find out what the government does or does not do to ensure proper care for the elderly. (interview with Kate)

From this perspective, social studies was a means to increase pupils' sense of social responsibility and, as a result, promote a more humane society. Although this perspective was dominant in only two students, its effect in the classrooms observed was clearly noticeable.

PORTRAYAL OF SALLY

The six perspectives capture and freeze the beliefs and actions of two groups of student teachers. But these perspectives were not as static or clear cut as the preceding descriptions imply. Each student observed was involved in the dynamic life of the classroom; each was faced with processing, consciously or unconsciously, classroom activities, events, and people; each had to confront a role as a teacher. Although each student manifested a consistent pattern of social studies teaching captured by one of the six perspectives, each occasionally taught in inconsistent or contradictory ways. Each occasionally displayed some characteristic of holding, or being attracted toward, other perspectives. In some cases, we observed students move from one dominant perspective to another. Thus, the following portrayal is intended to capture some of this dynamic quality by describing the evolving perspectives of one student teacher, Sally.

Sally was, in some ways, typical. She began her student teaching feeling nervous about taking charge of a class, worried about how she would manage fifth-grade students, and unsure of her role as a teacher. Social studies was, however, an interest of hers and something she looked forward to teaching. Her academic focus in history and her involvement in community politics may help explain why she showed little attraction toward the first three perspectives. She was even critical of the first perspective, social studies as nonsubject. Not enough time, she said, was being spent on social studies, and she was indignant that it was the subject dropped when room was needed in the school day for extra activities.

Sally's dominant perspective, during the first part of the semester, was social studies as school knowledge. She expressed concern about having enough time to cover all the material and confided that she was reluctant to be too innovative in her teaching lest the pupils become disorderly and waste time. She taught from the textbook and seemed to depend on expert knowledge as the basis of her social studies curriculum. But even while she worried about covering the material, she began to express doubt about the meaningfulness of textbook learning.

> To memorize facts is too easily forgotten. When you do things, you tend to remember them more. Especially if it's some exciting sort of activities that the kids can be proud of and that they can learn from. . . . I want them to start thinking about and to start doing their own thing. (interview with Sally)

Furthermore, her conceptions of social studies even at the beginning of the semester expressed, albeit vaguely, a view of social studies as something more than covering the material. When asked to define social studies, Sally said:

> To me there is no set definition because it involves so many things and covers such a wide area. Practically any topic in the classroom can fit under the heading social studies. Basically, I see social studies as learning about ourselves and the world, very broad. (interview with Sally)

An observer, watching Sally early in the semester teaching textbook lessons and listening to her contradictory talk about the importance of having pupils start thinking and getting actively involved, might have concluded that her talk was mere empty rhetoric, a rhetoric she acquired in a methods class but was unwilling to put into practice. Her early perspective, characterized by a concern for order and covering the material, might also have been a reflection of her overriding concerns about classroom management rather than a conception of social studies as the knowledge of experts passed on to the younger generation.

As her practicum experience continued, Sally found her solution to keeping order in the classroom to be less than satisfactory. She talked about wanting her students to enjoy social studies, about the importance of getting them actively involved, about wanting them to develop empathy for other people. Her cooperating teacher encouraged her to take chances — to try new activities and approaches.

> I think I've given Sally the security to go ahead and try what she wants. . . . She didn't have to worry about what my reaction was going to be because she knew I was supporting her. (interview with Sally's cooperating teacher)

As the semester progressed, Sally began to incorporate a variety of activities into her social studies lessons that reflected movement toward the last two perspectives described in this paper. She got her pupils involved in small group research projects and began to help them analyze and evaluate the information they were finding. "Check more than one book," she told one group, "they don't always give you the same information." (observation of Sally)

> I've learned that we never trust the textbook alone to do a good job of teaching. . . . I like to provide kids with a lot of different sources, to get them in the habit of looking at more than one thing and not just going by their books. (interview with Sally)

Sally began to apply her belief that providing structure to a lesson did not necessarily mean all pupils had to do the same things and that ways could be found to give pupils choices. To Sally, structure came to mean that the teacher should create an orderly learning environment, providing experiences which would stimulate and encourage pupil learning. Her concern for establishing and maintaining order was balanced by a concern for stimulating the children's interest in social studies.

By the end of the semester, Sally had moved away from social studies as school knowledge and toward a view of social studies as the great connection. Her lessons began to tap her pupils' personal experiences, to encourage their creativity, to help children see connections between past and present. She began to talk about how social studies should be "more a part of the whole classroom" and wanted to try "integrating it with other courses." Finally, Sally began to talk about social studies as social action.

> I adamantly believe that too many of us don't care about what's going on and because of that we [our society] are in a mess. I think [sociopolitical] awareness is a really big thing and learning that there are ways to act on that [is important]. (interview with Sally)

It cannot be said that Sally's perspectives toward social studies at the end of the semester were characterized by social action. Although she was abstractly committed to helping students learn to think critically and then act on the stands they take, she was unsure how to go about teaching the skills necessary to do so. It had not occurred to her that there were social action skills involved in social studies until one of us raised the point in question. However, slowly and unsystematically she was beginning to offer her pupils opportunities for critical inquiry as she encouraged them to seek out new sources, evaluate the data they uncovered, and draw their own conclusions based on that data.

By the end of the semester, Sally had gained more confidence in herself as a teacher, and in the process her perspectives toward social studies had evolved away from a concern with school knowledge and strict order. Not surprisingly her teaching was still marked by some uncertainty, and her perspective remained open and fluid.

CONCLUSION AND IMPLICATIONS FOR PRACTICE

The findings reported in this paper built on Adler's (1984) article as we sought to extend our knowledge of teachers' perspectives toward social studies education. These findings raise concerns that deserve consideration among social studies educators. As discussed in the introduction of this paper, similar conceptions of social studies education are held by many educators. Social studies should promote inquiry, active participation in society, and an understanding of social science. Given these goals, two concerns emerge from the findings of this study.

First, the findings suggest that official conceptions of social studies have little to do with students' beliefs and actions in the classroom. Even when students' conceptions of social studies are similar to our idealistic notions, as is the case with Sample B, their perspectives provide a more accurate portrayal of the work these students do and the meaning they give to this work. Rather than focusing on our own conceptions of what social studies education should be, we need to put more effort into understanding the perspectives toward social studies education that students develop during their professional preparation. It does little good to expose students to innovative ideas if they view social studies as a nonsubject.

If the preceding implication is correct, we need more research that illuminates the perspectives students generate during their professional education. Traditional analysis and categorization of students' beliefs and actions into predetermined continuums such as conservative-liberal tell us little about how the informants themselves give meaning to and act on the professional world they are about to enter. This study, then, reaffirms the value of ethnographic methods of descriptive analysis in helping us gain insights into the complex process of becoming a social studies teacher. Are these perspectives common in other programs? If so, why; if not, why not? Just as additional data prompted the reanalysis of Adler's (1984) study, additional research may uncover more subtle perspectives missed in this study. If we are to improve the professional education of social studies teachers, then we need research that helps us understand students' perspectives toward this activity.

In addition to discovering what perspectives students have, we need research that investigates how their perspectives have developed. As the description of Sally demonstrates, students' perspectives are complex, interacting in unique ways under specific circumstances. This study suggests that a number of factors contribute to the development of student perspectives: conceptions of social studies education growing from childhood experiences; significant individuals such as family members, cooperating teachers, and university faculty members; institutional expectations found in the practicum sites; and social forces outside the classroom such as the accountability movement and social demands for higher reading scores.

In examining these forces, we also need to ask why some perspectives seem to dominate over others. For example, in our samples the first four perspectives were much more common than the last two. A number of educators have argued that schools are a major force in perpetuating a technocratic, utilitarian, and object-oriented national ideology (e.g., Apple, 1982; Giroux, 1983). They argue that this ideology lacks concern for human inquiry, values, and needs. These individuals might suggest that the dominance of the first four perspectives in our study reflects the influence that this ideology has on those individuals going into the teaching profession as well as the reproductive force they play in our schools on entering the profession. These educators recognize, however, that individuals are not merely shaped into a uniform mold by this ideology. The presence of our last two perspectives supports this notion. To various degrees, students chose which beliefs and actions they thought were worthwhile. Some students acted on their practicum environment as well as conformed to it. However, these findings and theoretical notions are inconclusive. More research into the external forces that influence students' perspectives and the students' responses to these forces would give educators insights into the professional socialization of future teachers.

The second concern that emerges from this study addresses recommendations for social studies education courses. Although it is important to have clear conceptions of and goals for social studies education, it is also necessary to focus on how these goals and ideals can be manifested. The juxtaposition of the perspectives, social studies as human relations and school knowledge against social studies as the great connection and social action, suggests that students need to learn more than just how to teach from the textbook or even how to supplement it. The work of such students as Peter, Kate, and Judy suggests that preparation courses should focus on the skills of curriculum development and implementation. Students need to learn how to develop curriculum based on their own and their pupils' intellectual interests. Preparation courses should teach students to choose worthwhile topics of study; develop the themes, concepts, or areas of content that make up this topic; research these themes to increase their own level of knowledge on this topic; discover resources that children can use to explore these themes; develop activities that illuminate the themes of this topic and promote creativity and thoughtfulness among pupils; and organize these themes, resources, and activities into a coherent unit of study.

Developing curriculum is similar to writing a documentary or an article. It requires interest in the subject matter, motivation and skill to research relevant information, energy to discover new sources, and the ability to organize the findings of this work into a form that other people can understand and enjoy. Although most students want to teach because they like children (e.g., Buchmann, 1982; Goodman, 1983; Tabachnick, Popkewitz, & Zeichner, 1979–80), this study suggests that preparation courses must attempt to stimulate students' curiosity toward the world of knowledge and the dynamics of learning.

It is not enough, however, to teach students only how to develop their own curriculum. Perspectives such as social studies as a nonsubject, as human relations, and as citizenship suggest that preparation courses need to examine underlying purposes and principles of social studies education. As part of these courses, we need to examine the relationship between our students' beliefs and actions, explore the perspectives that students have and what forces influence them, and discuss the relative merits of these various perspectives. Integrated into these courses should be questions such as: What role should social studies play in the elementary and middle schools? Who should decide what content is taught? What criteria should be used to determine worthwhile social studies content and activities? What kind of learning should be emphasized during the teaching of social studies? What is the relationship between social studies content found in the classroom and the sociopolitical forces found within the broader society? As Beyer and Zeichner (1982) suggest, underlying questions of practice do not have to be limited to foundation courses. To the contrary, this study suggests that this level of analysis should be central to preparation courses.

Finally, as Stake and Easley (1978) emphasized, it takes more than good intentions and the existence of viable alternatives to change school practice. The institutional demands found within the practicum sites seem to have a strong influence on students' perspectives. As a result, preparation courses need to ask students to consider the importance of becoming change agents in the schools. As Kohl (1976) said, students should be exposed to the politics of teaching. Preparation courses should have students consider the problems of initiating substantive change without needlessly alienating administrators, other staff, and parents. Planning for short-term and long-term change, creating freedom within constraints, developing a support system within the school and the community, writing proposals for curriculum change, and presenting ideas for curriculum design and implementation at local and stage conferences are some of the strategies than can be examined within preparation courses.

Becoming an elementary social studies teacher is a complex human endeavor. It often involves subtle, and at times, contradictory beliefs and actions. In our attempts to best educate these future teachers, it is mandatory that we begin to penetrate this complexity of human life. Developing innovative conceptions of social studies education is important — after all, if we don't dream, we will stagnate. It is equally important to examine how our ideals can be concretely manifested. Preparation courses are not a panacea for the problems that face social studies education; however, based on careful research, useful and substantive strategies for these future teachers can be developed.

Endnotes

1. To enhance the reading of this paper, the following word guide is provided: *Educator*—one who teaches in a university teacher preparation program or conducts research into social studies education; *Student*—one who is enrolled in a college-level teacher education program; *Pupil*—a child enrolled in an elementary or middle school.

2. For a complete discussion of the rationale, theoretical principles, and methods used to collect and analyze the data, see Goodman (1983) and Adler (1982).

3. This selection procedure was used to find students who appeared to hold conceptions of social studies education deemed desirable in the social studies literature: the importance of teaching social studies, orientation toward critical thinking, integrated curriculum, social interaction, and involvement. For a more detailed discussion of the selection criteria and process, see Adler (1982, 1984).

4. Because of the selection process, each student in Sample B believed social studies was an important subject to be taught, and they were given more opportunities to teach it. Because students made special efforts to teach them, we observed more social studies lessons being taught.

References

Adler, S. A. (1984). A field study of selected student teacher perspectives toward social studies. *Theory and Research in Social Education, 12*(1), 13–30.

Adler, S. A. (1982). Elementary school social studies: Student teacher perspectives (Doctoral dissertation, University of Wisconsin, Madison, 1982). *Dissertation Abstracts International, 43,* 3199A.

Apple, M. (1982). *Education and power.* London: Routledge & Kegan Paul.

Barr, R. D., Barth, J. L., & Shermis, S. S. (1977). *Defining the social studies.* Washington, DC: National Council for the Social Studies.

Beard, C. A. (1934). *The nature of the social sciences.* New York: Charles Scribner's Sons.

Becker, H.S., Geer, B., Hughes, E. C., & Strauss, A. L. (1961). *Boys in white: Student culture in medical school.* Chicago: University of Chicago Press.

Berlak, A., & Berlak, H. (1981). *The dilemmas of schooling: Teaching and social change.* New York: Methuen.

Beyer, L., & Zeichner, K. (1982). Teacher training and educational foundations: A plea for discontent. *Journal of Teacher Education, 33*(3), 18–23.

Blumer, H. (1969). *Symbolic interactionism: Perspective and method.* Englewood Cliffs, NJ: Prentice-Hall.

Bruyn, S. (1966). *The human perspective in sociology: The methodology of participant observation.* Englewood Cliffs, NJ: Prentice-Hall.

Buchmann, M. (1982). The flight away from content in teacher education and teaching. *Journal of Curriculum Studies, 14,* 61–68.

Clements, H. M., Fielder, W. R., & Tabachnick, B. R. (1966). *Social study: Inquiry in elementary classrooms.* Indianapolis: Bobbs-Merrill.

Cornbleth, C. (1982, March). *On the social study of social studies.* Paper presented at the meeting of the American Educational Research Association, New York.

Engle, S. H. (1960). Decision making: The heart of social studies instruction. *Social Education, 24,* 301–304, 306.

Giroux, H. (1983). Theories of reproduction and resistance in the new sociology of education: A critical analysis. *Harvard Educational Review, 53,* 257–293.

Glaser, B., & Strauss, A. (1967). *The discovery of grounded theory: Strategies for qualitative research.* Chicago: Aldine.

Goodman, J. (1983). Learning to teach: A study of a humanistic approach (Doctoral dissertation, University of Wisconsin, Madison, 1982). *Dissertation Abstracts International, 43,* 3295A.

Grace, G. (1978). *Teachers, ideology, and control: A study in urban education.* London: Routledge & Kegan Paul.

Hammersley, M. (1977). *Teacher Perspectives.* Milton Keynes, Great Britain: The Open University Press.

Hennings, D. G., Hennings, G., & Banich, S. F. (1980). *Today's elementary social studies.* Chicago: Rand McNally.

Janesick, V. J. (1978). *An ethnographic study of a teacher's classroom perspective: Implications for curriculum.* East Lansing, MI: Institute for Research on Teaching.

Kohl, H. (1976). *On teaching.* New York: Schocken.

Lortie, D. (1975). *Schoolteacher: A sociological study.* Chicago: University of Chicago Press.

Massialas, B., & Cox, C. B. (1966). *Inquiry in social studies.* New York: McGraw-Hill.

National Council for the Social Studies. (1981). *Essentials of the social studies*. Washington, DC: Author.

Pagano, A. L. (Ed.). (1978). *Social studies in early childhood: An interactionist point of view*. Washington, DC: National Council for the Social Studies.

Sharp, R., & Green, A. (1975). *Education and social control: A study in progressive primary education*. London: Routledge & Kegan Paul.

Shaver, J. P., Davis, O. L., & Helburn, S. W. (1979). The status of social studies education: Impressions from three NSF studies. *Social Education, 43*, 150–153.

Stake, R., & Easley, J. (1978). *Case studies in science education*. Urbana, IL: Center for Instructional Research and Curriculum Evaluation.

Superka, D. P., & Hawke, S. (1980). Social roles: A focus for the social studies in the 1980s. *Social Education, 44*, 577–586.

Tabachnick, B. R., Popkewitz, T., & Zeichner, K. (1979–80). Teacher education and the professional perspectives of student teachers. *Interchange, 10*(4), 12–29.

Weber, M. (1977). Basic sociological terms. In F. Dallmayr & T. McCarthy (Eds.), *Understanding and social inquiry* (pp. 38–55). Notre Dame, IN: University of Notre Dame Press.

Analysis of the Study

PURPOSE/JUSTIFICATION

The purpose of this study, to elucidate frames of reference, or "perspectives," actually used by social studies teachers and compare them with those commonly presumed by writers and teacher educators, is clearly stated at the outset. The justification rests on the presumed relationship between teaching behavior and such perspectives. Those persons involved in the preparation of teachers, it is argued, should know how teachers view their subjects.

While we agree with this position, we think it could have been more thoroughly justified. What, for example, are the implications if actual teacher perspectives are quite different from those presumed by teacher educators? (The authors do discuss some such implications in the conclusions section of the article.)

We think the authors present a good justification for use of the ethnographic method in a study such as this.

DEFINITIONS

The authors might have provided a clear definition of the term "perspectives," since it is central to their study. Although the meaning is probably clear in context to most readers, a definition such as the following would be helpful: "The term 'perspectives' is defined as the teachers' concept of the overall purpose of the social studies curriculum, which is reflected in teacher practices."

The authors allow the specific perspectives and their definitions to emerge from their data, as would be expected in an ethnographic study. Again, we think the meaning of each perspective becomes clear in context, but the report would benefit from explicit statements for each, as in the examples that follow.

- The "nonsubject" perspective has no articulated goals for social studies; rather, social studies is viewed as nonessential to the curriculum.
- The "human relations" perspective has as its goal teaching children about them-

selves and their relationships with others through direct experience.

- The "citizenship" perspective has as its goal inculcating students into the traditional economic and political systems of our society.
- The "textbook knowledge" perspective has as its goal teaching whatever material is required by the official curriculum.
- The "great connection" perspective has as its goal promoting inquiry and reflection on themes that integrate different subject areas.
- The "social action" perspective has as its goal fostering more socially active citizens.

PRIOR RESEARCH

The authors cite several references in support of their contention that teachers in practice do not hold the same views of social studies as do teacher educators. They claim that only one study has previously examined teacher perspectives; that study is briefly reviewed. The results of that study are not included, however, and would provide additional background for the present study.

SAMPLE

The study used a sample comprised of two groups selected differently. The first group consisted of twelve students randomly chosen from seventy-five enrollees in an elementary education program at a large, southeastern university. All were directly involved in classrooms as student teachers or in practicum placements. The second group consisted of four students at a large midwestern university. This was a purposive sample, specifically selected to include students with views similar to the views of teacher educators. In total, the sample of sixteen cannot be said to be representative of any meaningful population. While this would be a serious limitation in a study designed to examine relationships (for example, between type of perspective and childhood experiences), it is not a major

limitation in a study attempting to identify and clarify important characteristics—in this case, teacher perspectives. No generalizations to a larger population were intended.

INSTRUMENTATION AND DATA ANALYSIS

As is usual in ethnographic studies, observation and interviews were the primary methods of collecting data. These were supplemented by questionnaires, student logs, and other materials. No data on reliability or validity are provided; the reader must assume that the interpretations made by the researchers are valid ones. Commendable efforts to enhance validity include the use of follow-up questions to verify initial interpretations; the reviewing of data with colleagues to "establish intersubjective consensus"; and "paying attention to data that seemed to challenge original conceptualizations." Unfortunately, the reader must assume on faith that the process was free of the biases so easily created by the wording of questions and the persuasive power of some individuals to affect group consensus. While it is (probably) impossible to document completely the ongoing process of data collection and interpretation in a study like this, a few examples would enhance credibility.

In ethnographic research, data collection and data analysis are intertwined. As is often the case, the researchers did a content analysis to organize the information they collected into categories and then revised these until the final organization into six perspectives emerged. The provision of asking teacher participants to verify the resulting categories is a good one, but unclear. What is meant by "initial analysis"; what did the participants disagree with (if anything); and what use was made of these discrepancies?

While elaborate statistics are unnecessary in a study like this, some organization of information in tabular form would be useful. It might be possible, for example, to identify the major subcategories under each perspective (such as "taught only math and reading in beginning field experience; supervising teacher under pressure to raise reading scores") and then report the frequency with which each appeared for each perspective. It should also be possible to indicate which of such specifics were identified by more than one data source (e.g., observation and interview) as evidence of validity.

The authors rely heavily on examples both to clarify the different perspectives and to justify them. While such examples are useful, they do not suffice to document results.

INTERNAL VALIDITY

Since the authors' main thrust is not to study a relationship among variables, internal validity is, strictly speaking, irrelevant. As mentioned previously, ethnographic studies provide no clear controls over researcher bias as it affects both data collection and data interpretation. In a study of an exploratory nature such as this, such considerations are much less serious than in a study seeking to find relationships or describe group characteristics. In their conclusions, however, the researchers do state a relationship that is not supported by any discussion of results: "the institutional demands found within the practicum sites seem to have a strong influence on student perspectives." Such a relationship may well be subject to certain threats to internal validity, namely subject characteristics, location, extraneous events (college supervisor interaction, for example), and instrumentation.

EXTERNAL VALIDITY

For the most part, the authors do not attempt to generalize beyond this particular study, limiting themselves to the potential value of the perspectives they have identified. Their statement that "some perspectives seem to dominate over others" would, at first glance, seem a gross overgeneralization, in that their sample can hardly be considered representative. However, since one-fourth of the sample was specifically selected to reflect the perspectives of teacher educators, thus biasing the sample in favor of the "great connection" and "social action" perspectives, the fact that (apparently) very few of their random sample fit these categories lends support to their contention. The statement that "the findings suggest that official conceptions of social studies have little to do with student beliefs and actions in the classroom" should be tempered by a reminder of the small and unrepresentative nature of the sample.

RESULTS AND CONCLUSIONS

The result of this study is the identification of a potentially useful typology for thinking about and studying teacher behavior. It would be helpful to know how many subjects were categorized under each perspective since more confidence can be placed in the usefulness of perspectives that are based on data from more than one subject. The authors recommend future studies exploring variables that may be related to the development of perspectives, an appropriate suggestion. The recommendation that students should receive more training in curriculum development and in the goals of social studies are consistent with their results, but also assume particular value judgments (e.g., that the "nonsubject" perspective is an undesirable one to hold).

The final recommendation, that teacher preparation programs should "ask students to consider the importance of becoming change agents," reflects a second value position of the authors. While we happen to agree with their position and applaud them for including it, we think they should make it clear that these recommendations are their opinions and do not follow only from the results of their study. Further, the indication of personal bias raises the question of possible intrusion of such values into the data collection and analysis. While we believe all researchers have some biases (indeed, they could not avoid having them), the major disadvantage of ethnographic research is that the controls that are available to quantitative researchers are much less applicable here.

Main Points of Chapter Sixteen

- The term "qualitative research" refers to research investigations that investigate the quality of relationships, activities, situations or materials.
- The natural setting is a direct source of data and the researcher is a key part of the instrumentation process in qualitative research.
- Qualitative data are collected mainly in the form or words or pictures and seldom involve numbers.
- Qualitative researchers are especially interested in how things occur and particularly in the perspectives of the subjects of a study.
- Qualitative researchers do not, usually, formulate a hypothesis beforehand and then seek to test it. Rather, they allow hypotheses to emerge as a study develops.
- The three most commonly employed forms of qualitative research in education are participant observation, nonparticipant observation, and ethnographic research.
- In participant observation studies, the researcher actually participates as an active member of the group in the situation or setting he or she is observing.
- In nonparticipant observation studies, the researcher does not participate in an activity or situation, but observes "from the sidelines."
- The most common forms of nonparticipant observation studies include naturalistic observation, simulations, case studies, and content analysis.
- A simulation is an artificially created situation in which subjects are asked to act out certain roles.
- A case study is a detailed study of one or (at most) a few individuals or other social units, such as a classroom, a school, or a neighborhood.
- Content analysis involves an analysis of the written or visual contents of a document.
- There are four roles that an observer can play in a qualitative research study, ranging from complete participant to participant-as-observer, to observer-as-participant, to complete observer. The degree of involvement of the observer in the observed situation diminishes accordingly for each of these roles.
- The term "observer effect" refers to either the fact that the presence of an observer can have an effect on the behavior of the subjects or the fact that the data reported reflects the biases of the observer. The use of audio- and videotapings is especially helpful in guarding against this effect.
- Researchers who engage in a qualitative study of some type usually select a purposive sample.
- Ethnographic research is particularly appropriate for behaviors that are best understood by observing them within their natural settings.
- The key techniques in all ethnographic studies are in-depth interviewing and highly detailed, almost continual, ongoing participant observation of a situation.
- A key strength of ethnographic research is that it provides the researcher with a much more comprehensive perspective than do other forms of educational research.
- The data obtained from ethnographic research samples rarely, if ever, permit generalization to a population.
- Researchers use a variety of instruments in ethnographic studies to collect data and to check validity. This is frequently referred to as triangulation.

- A major check on the validity and reliability of the researcher's interpretations in ethnographic research is to compare one informant's description of something with another informant's description of that same thing.
- Field notes are the notes a researcher in an ethnographic study takes in the field. They include both descriptive field notes (what he or she sees and hears) and reflective field notes (what he or she thinks about what has been observed)
- Field jottings refer to quick notes about something the researcher wants to write more about later.
- A field diary is a personal statement of the researcher's feelings and opinions about the people and situations he or she is observing.
- A field log is a sort of running account of how the researcher plans to spend his or her time compared to how he or she actually spends it.

For Discussion

1. What do you see as the greatest strength of qualitative research? the biggest weakness?

2. Are there any topics or questions that could *not* be studied using an ethnographic approach? If so, give an example. Is there any type of information that ethnographic research cannot provide? If so, what might it be?

3. A major criticism of ethnographic research is that there is no way for the researcher to be totally objective about what he or she observes. Would you agree? What might an ethnographer say to rebut this charge?

4. Supporters of ethnographic research say that it can do something that no other type of research can do. If true, what might this be?

5. Are there any kinds of information that other types of research can provide *better* than ethnographic research? If so, what might they be?

6. How would you compare qualitative research to the other types of research we have discussed in this book in terms of difficulty? Explain your reasoning.

7. "Observing people without their knowledge and/or recording their comments without their permission is unethical." Would you agree? Explain your reasoning.

Notes

1. Bogdan, Robert C. & Sari Knopp Biklen. (1982). *Qualitative research for education: An introduction to theory and methods*. Boston: Allyn & Bacon.

2. Recently, however, some qualitative researchers have begun to use statistical procedures to clarify their data. See, for example, Miles, Matthew B. and A. Michael Huberman. (1984). *Qualitative data analysis*. Beverly Hills, CA.: Sage.

3. Bogdan and Biklen, *op cit.*, p. 29.

4. Gold, Raymond L. (1969). Roles in sociological field observation. In George J. McCall & J. L. Simmons (Eds.). *Issues in participant observation*. Reading, MA: Addison-Wesley. pp. 30–39.

5. Babbie, Earl (1986). *The practice of social research*. Belmont, CA: Wadsworth. p. 247.

6. Bernard, H. R. (1988). *Research methods in cultural anthropology*. Beverly Hills, CA.: Sage.

7. Shaver, James P., O. L. Davis, Jr., and Suzanne W. Helburn. (1979). The status of social studies education: Impressions from three NSF studies. *Social Education, 43*(2): 150–153.

8. Babbie, *op cit.*, pp. 241–242.

9. "From the Familiar to the Strange and Back Again" from *Doing the Ethnography of Schooling: Educational Anthropology in Action* by George Spindler. Copyright © 1982 by Holt, Rinehart, and Winston, Inc. Reprinted by permission of the publisher.

10. McPherson, G. (1972). Cambridge, MA: Harvard University.

11. Heath, S. B. (1982). In G. Spindler, *op. cit.*, pp. 102–131.

12. Erickson, F. & G. Mohatt. (1982). In *Ibid.*, pp. 132–175.

13. Finnan, C. R. (1982). In *Ibid*, pp. 356–380.

14. Palonsky, S. B. (1975). *Educational Administration Quarterly, 11*(2): 86–103.

15. McCutcheon, G. (1981). *Theory and Research in Social Education, 9*(1). 45–66.

16. For a good discussion of field notes, see Chapter Three in Bogdan and Biklen, *op. cit.*, pp. 74–97.

17. Bernard, *op. cit.*, pp. 181–182.

18. Bernard, *op. cit.*, pp. 186–187.

19. Bogdan & Biklen, *op. cit.*, pp. 84–89.

Research Exercise Sixteen: Qualitative Research

You should complete Problem Sheet 16 only if you are planning a qualitative study. If your intended study involves a different methodology, you will find a similar problem sheet at the end of the chapter that deals with that methodology. You might wish to consider, however, whether your research question could be investigated by means of a qualitative study.

> Using Problem Sheet 16, state the question or hypothesis for your study. Then describe, briefly but thoroughly, the procedures of your study—that is, *what* you intend to do, *when, where,* and *how*. Lastly, indicate any unresolved problems you see at this point in your planning.

---

1. The question or hypothesis of my study is: _____
_____
_____

2. A brief summary of **what** I intend to do, **when, where,** and **how** is as follows:

_____
_____
_____
_____
_____
_____
_____
_____
_____
_____

3. The major problems I foresee at this point are as follows: _____
_____
_____

Chapter Seventeen

HISTORICAL RESEARCH

Historical research is different from all of the other research methodologies we have discussed in that it focuses exclusively on past occurrences and events. As a result, historical researchers in some ways operate differently from other educational researchers. In this chapter, we discuss the nature of historical research, the kinds of topics that are investigated in such research, and the problems historical researchers face.

- *Describe* briefly what historical research involves
- *State* three purposes of historical research
- *Give some examples* of the kinds of questions investigated in historical research
- *Name* and *describe* briefly the major steps involved in historical research
- *Give some examples* of historical sources
- *Distinguish* between primary and secondary sources
- *Distinguish* between external and internal criticism
- *Discuss* when generalization in historical research is appropriate
- *Locate* examples of published historical studies and *critique* some of the strengths and weaknesses of these studies
- *Recognize* an example of a historical study when you come across it in the literature

What Is Historical Research?

Like ethnographic research, historical research takes a somewhat different tack than much of the other research we have described in other chapters. There is, of course, no manipulation or control of variables as there is in experimental research, but more particularly, it is unique in that it focuses strictly on the *past*. As we mentioned in Chapter One, some aspect of the past is studied, by perusing documents of the period, by examining relics, or by interviewing individuals who lived during the time. An attempt is then made to reconstruct what happened during that time as completely and as accurately as possible, and (usually) to explain why it happened—although this can never be fully accomplished, since information from and about the past is always incomplete. Historical research, then, is the systematic collection and evaluation of data to describe, explain, and thereby understand actions or events that occurred sometime in the past.

THE PURPOSES OF HISTORICAL RESEARCH

Educational researchers undertake historical studies for a variety of reasons:

1. To make people aware of what has happened in the past so they may learn from past failures and successes. A researcher might be interested, for example, in investigating why a particular curriculum modification (such as a new "inquiry-oriented" English curriculum) succeeded in some school districts but not in others.
2. To learn how things were done in the past to see if they might be applicable to present-day problems and concerns. Rather than "reinventing the wheel" all over again, for example, it often may be wiser to look to the past to see if a proposed innovation has not been tried before. Sometimes an idea proposed as "a radical innovation" is not all that new. Along this line, the "review of literature" that we discussed in detail in Chapter Four,

411

and that is done as a part of many other kinds of studies, is a kind of historical research. Often a review of the literature will show that what we think is new has been done before (and surprisingly many times!).

3. To assist in prediction. If a particular idea or approach has been tried before, even under somewhat different circumstances, past results may offer policymakers some ideas about how present plans may turn out. Thus, if "language laboratories" have been found effective (or the reverse) in certain school districts in the past, a district contemplating their use would have evidence upon which to base its own decisions in this regard.

4. To test hypotheses concerning relationships or trends. Many inexperienced researchers tend to think of historical research as purely descriptive in nature. When well-designed and carefully executed, however, historical research can lead to the confirmation or rejection of relational hypotheses as well. Here are some examples of hypotheses which would lend themselves to historical research:

   a. In the early 1900s, most female teachers came from the upper middle class, but most male teachers did not.

   b. Curriculum changes that did not involve extensive planning and participation by the teachers involved usually failed.

   c. Nineteenth century social studies textbooks show increasing reference to the contributions of women to the culture of the United States from 1800 to 1900.

   d. Secondary school teachers have enjoyed greater prestige than elementary school teachers since 1940.

   Many other hypotheses are possible, of course; the ones above are intended to illustrate only that historical research can lend itself to hypothesis-testing studies.

5. To understand present educational practices and policies more fully. Many current practices in education are by no means new. Inquiry teaching, character education, open classrooms, an emphasis on "basics," Socratic teaching, the use of case studies, individualized instruction, team teaching, and teaching

"laboratories" are but a few of many ideas that reappear from time to time as "the" salvation for education.

WHAT KINDS OF QUESTIONS ARE PURSUED THROUGH HISTORICAL RESEARCH?

Although historical research focuses on the past, the types of questions that lend themselves to historical research are quite varied. Here are some examples:

- How were students educated in the South during the Civil War?
- How many bills dealing with education were passed during the presidency of Lyndon B. Johnson, and what was the major intent of those bills?
- What was instruction like in a typical fourth grade classroom 100 years ago?
- How have working conditions for teachers changed since 1900?
- What were the major discipline problems in schools in 1940 as compared to today?
- What educational issues has the general public perceived to be most important during the last twenty years?
- How have the ideas of John Dewey influenced present-day educational practices?
- How have women contributed to education?
- How have minorities (or the disabled) been treated in our public schools during the twentieth century?
- How were the policies and practices of school administrators in the early years of this century different from those today?
- What has been the role of the federal government in education?

Steps Involved in Historical Research

There are four essential steps involved in doing a historical study in education. These include defining the problem or question to be investigated (including the formulation of hypotheses if appropriate); locating relevant sources of historical information; summarizing and evaluating the information obtained from these sources; and presenting and interpreting this information as it relates to the problem or question that originated the study.

DEFINING THE PROBLEM

In the simplest sense, the purpose of a historical study in education is to describe clearly and accurately some aspect of the past as it related to education and/or schooling. As we mentioned above, however, historical researchers aim to do more than just describe; they want to go beyond description to clarify and explain, and sometimes to correct (as when a researcher finds previous accounts of an action or event to be in error).

Historical research problems, therefore, are identified in much the same way as are problems studied through other types of research. Like any research problem, they should be clearly and concisely stated, be manageable, have a defensible rationale, and (if possible) investigate a hypothesized relationship among variables. A concern somewhat unique to historical research is that a problem may be selected for study for which insufficient data are available. Often important data of interest (certain kinds of documents, such as diaries or maps, from a particular period) simply cannot be located in historical research. This is particularly true the further back in the past an investigator looks. As a result, it is better to study a well-defined problem in depth that is perhaps more narrow than one would like than to pursue a more broadly stated problem that cannot be sharply defined, or fully resolved. As with all research, the nature of the problem or hypothesis guides the study; if it is well-defined, the investigator is off to a good start.

Some examples of historical studies that have been published are as follows.

- The schooling process in first grade: Two samples a decade apart[1]
- Teacher survival rates in St. Louis, 1969–1982[2]
- Women teachers on the frontier[3]
- Origins of the modern social studies: 1900–1916[4]
- Missing the mark: Intelligence testing in Los Angeles public schools, 1922–1932[5]
- The responses of American Indian children to Presbyterian schooling in the nineteenth century: An analysis through missionary sources[6]
- The 1960s and the transformation of campus cultures[7]
- Emma Willard: Pioneer in social studies education[8]
- Inquiry into educational administration: The last twenty-five years and the next[9]
- Bertrand Russell and education in world citizenship[10]
- The decline in age at leaving home, 1920–1979[11]

LOCATING RELEVANT SOURCES

Categories of Sources. Once a researcher has decided on the problem or question he or she wishes to investigate, the search for sources begins. Just about everything that has been written down in some form or other, and virtually every object imaginable, is a potential source for historical research. In general, however, historical source material can be grouped into four basic categories: documents, numerical records, oral statements and records, and relics.

1. *Documents.* *Documents* are written or printed materials that have been produced in some form or another—annual reports, artwork, bills, books, cartoons, circulars, court records, diaries, diplomas, legal records, newspapers, magazines, notebooks, school yearbooks, memos, tests, and so on. They may be handwritten, printed, typewritten, drawn, or sketched; they may be published or unpublished; they may be intended for private or public consumption; they may be original works or copies. In short, documents refer to any kind of information that exists in some type of written or printed form.

2. *Numerical Records.* Numerical, or *quantitative,* records can be considered either as a separate type of source in and of themselves or as a subcategory of documents. Such records include any type of numerical data in printed form: test scores, attendance figures, census reports, school budgets, and the like. In recent years, historical researchers are making increasing use of computers to analyze the vast amounts of numerical data that are available to them.

3. *Oral Statements.* Another valuable source of information for the historical researcher lies in the statements people make orally. Stories, myths, tales, legends, chants, songs and other forms of oral expression have been used by people down through the ages to leave a record for future generations. But historians can also conduct *oral interviews* with people who were a part of or witnessed past events. This is a special form of historical research, called *oral history,* which is currently undergoing somewhat of a renaissance.

4. *Relics.* The fourth type of historical source is the relic. A *relic* is any object whose physical or visual characteristics can provide some information about the past. Examples include furniture, artwork, clothing, buildings, monuments, or equipment.

Following are different examples of historical sources.

- a primer used in a 17th century schoolroom
- a diary kept by a woman teacher on the Ohio frontier in the 1800s
- the written arguments for and against a new school bond issue as published in a newspaper at a particular time
- a 1958 junior high school yearbook
- samples of clothing worn by students in the early nineteenth century in rural Georgia
- high school graduation diplomas from the 1920s
- a written memo from a school superintendent to his faculty
- attendance records from two different school districts over a forty-year period

- essays written by elementary school children during the Civil War
- test scores attained by students in various states at different times
- the architectural plans for a school to be organized around flexible scheduling
- a taped oral interview with the secretary of education in the administration of three different presidents of the United States

Primary versus Secondary Sources. As in all research, it is important to distinguish between primary and secondary sources. A **primary source** is one prepared by an individual who was a participant in or a direct witness to the event being described. An eyewitness account of the opening of a new school would be an example, as would the reporting of the results of an experiment carried out directly by a researcher. Other examples of primary source material are as follows.

- a nineteenth-century teacher's account of what it was like to live with a frontier family
- a transcript of an oral interview with the superintendent of a large urban high school district concerning the problems his district faces
- essays written by students to the question: "What I like most and least about school"
- songs composed by members of a high school glee club
- minutes of a school board meeting taken by the secretary of the board
- a written evaluation by a paid consultant of a new French curriculum recently adopted in a particular school district
- a photograph of an eighth grade graduating class in 1930
- letters written between an American student and a Japanese student describing their school experiences

A **secondary source,** on the other hand, is a document prepared by an individual who was not a direct witness to an event, but who obtained his or her description of the event from someone else. They are "one step removed," so to speak, from the event. A newspaper editorial commenting on a recent teacher's strike would be an example. Other examples of secondary source material are as follows.

- an encyclopedia describing various types of educational research conducted over a ten-year period
- a magazine article summarizing Aristotle's views on education
- a newspaper account of a school board meeting based on oral interviews with members of the board
- a book describing schooling in the New England colonies during the 1700s
- a parent's description of a conversation (at which she was not present) between her son and his teacher
- a student's report to her counselor of why her teacher said she was being suspended from school
- a textbook (including this one) on educational research

Whenever possible, historians (like other researchers) want to use primary rather than secondary sources. Can you see why?* Unfortunately, primary sources are admittedly more difficult to acquire, especially the further back in time a researcher searches. Secondary sources are of necessity, therefore, used quite extensively in historical research. If it is at all possible, however, the use of primary sources if to be preferred.

SUMMARIZING INFORMATION OBTAINED FROM HISTORICAL SOURCES

The process of reviewing and extracting data from historical sources is essentially the one described in Chapter Four—determining the relevancy of the particular material to the question or problem being investigated; recording the full bibliographic data of the source; organizing the data one collects under categories related to the problem being studied (for a study investigating the daily activities that occurred in

nineteenth century elementary schoolrooms, a researcher might organize his or her facts under such categories as "subjects taught," "learning activities," "play activities," and "class rules"); and summarizing pertinent information (important facts, quotations, and questions) on note cards.

The reading and summarization of historical data is rarely, if ever, a neat, orderly sequence of steps to be followed, however. Often reading and writing are interspersed. Edward H. Carr, a noted historian, provides the following description of how historians engage in research:

> [A common] assumption [among laymen] appears to be that the historian divides his [or her] work into two sharply distinguishable phases or periods. First, [s]he spends a long preliminary period reading his [or her] sources and filling his [or her] notebooks with facts; then, when this is over he [or she] puts away his [or her] sources, takes out his [or her] notebooks, and writes his [or her] book from beginning to end. This is to me an unconvincing and unplausible picture. For myself, as soon as I have got going on a few of what I take to be the capital sources, the itch becomes too strong and I begin to write—not necessarily at the beginning, but somewhere, anywhere. Thereafter, reading and writing go on simultaneously. The writing is added to, subtracted from, re-shaped, and cancelled, as I go on reading. The reading is guided and directed and made fruitful by the writing; the more I write, the more I know what I am looking for, the better I understand the significance and relevance of what I find.[12]

THE EVALUATION OF HISTORICAL SOURCES

Perhaps more so than in any other form of research, the historical researcher must adopt a critical attitude toward any and all sources he or she reviews. A researcher can never be sure about the genuineness and accuracy of historical sources. A memo may have been written by someone other than the person whose signature one finds on it. A letter may refer to events that did not

---

* When a researcher must rely on secondary data sources, he or she increases the chance of the data being less detailed and/or less accurate. The accuracy of what is being reported also becomes more difficult to check.

occur, or that occurred at a different time or in a different place. A document may have been forged or information deliberately falsified. Key questions for any historical researcher are:

- Was this document really written by the supposed author (i.e., is it *genuine*)?
- Is the information contained in this document true (i.e., is it *accurate*)?

The first question refers to what is known as *external criticism;* the second to what is known as *internal criticism.*

External Criticism. **External criticism** refers to the genuineness of any and all documents the researcher uses. Researchers engaged in historical research want to know whether or not the documents they find were really prepared by the (supposed) author(s) of the document. Obviously, falsified documents can (and sometimes do) lead to erroneous conclusions. Several questions come to mind in evaluating the genuineness of a historical source.

- *Who* wrote this document? Was the author living at that time? Some historical documents have been shown to be *forgeries.* An article supposedly written by, say, Martin Luther King, Jr., might actually have been prepared by someone who is alive wishing to tarnish his reputation.
- *For what purpose* was the document written? For whom was it intended? And why? (Toward whom was a memo from a school superintendent directed? What was the intent of the memo?)
- *When* was the document written? Is the date on the document accurate? Could the details described have actually happened during this time? (Sometimes people write the date of the previous year on correspondence in the first days of a new year.)
- *Where* was the document written? Could the details described have occurred in this location? (A description of an inner-city school supposedly written by a teacher in Fremont, Nebraska, might well be viewed with caution.)

- *Under what conditions* was the document written? Is there any possibility that what was written might have been directly or subtly coerced? (A description of a particular school's curriculum and administration prepared by a committee of nontenured teachers might give quite a different view than one written by those who have tenure.)
- Do *different forms or versions* of the document exist? (Sometimes two versions of a letter are found with nearly identical wording and only very slight differences in handwriting, suggesting that one may be a forgery.)

The important thing to remember with regard to external criticism is that researchers should do their best to ensure that the documents they are using are genuine. The above questions (and others like them) are directed toward this end.

Internal Criticism. Once researchers have satisfied themselves that a source document is genuine, they need to determine if the *contents* of the document are *accurate.* This involves what is known as **internal criticism.** Both the accuracy of the information contained in a document and the truthfulness of the author need to be evaluated. Whereas external criticism has to do with the nature or authenticity of the document itself, internal criticism has to do with what the document says. Is it likely that what the author says happened really did happen? Would people at that time have behaved as they are portrayed? Could events have occurred this way? Are the data presented (attendance records, budget figures, test scores, and so on) reasonable? Note, however, that researchers should not dismiss a statement as inaccurate just because it is unlikely—unlikely events do occur. What researchers must determine is whether a particular event *might* have occurred, even if it is unlikely. As with external criticism, several questions need to be asked in attempting to evaluate the accuracy of a document and the truthfulness of its author.

With regard to the author of the document:

- Was the author *present* at the event he or

she is describing? In other words, is the document a primary or a secondary source? As we have mentioned before, primary sources are to be preferred over secondary sources because they usually (though not always) are considered to be more accurate.

- Was the author a *participant* in *or* an *observer* of the event? In general, we might expect an observer to present a more detached and comprehensive view of an event than a participant. Eyewitnesses do differ in their accounts of the same event, however, and hence the statements of an observer are not necessarily more accurate than those of a participant.
- Was the author *competent* to describe the event? This refers to the qualifications of the author. Was he or she an expert on whatever is being described or discussed? An interested observer? A "passer-by?"
- Was the author *emotionally involved* in the event? The wife of a fired teacher, for example, might well give a distorted view of the teacher's contributions to the profession.
- Did the author have any *vested interest* in the outcomes of the event? Might he or she have an ax of some sort to grind, for example, or possibly be biased in some way? A student who continually was in disagreement with his teacher, for example, might tend to describe the teacher more negatively than would the teacher's colleagues.

With regard to the contents of the document:

- Do the contents make *sense* (i.e., given the nature of the events described, does it seem reasonable that they could have happened as portrayed)?
- Could the event described have occured *at that time?* For example, a researcher might justifiably be suspicious of a document describing a World War II battle that took place in 1946.
- Would people have behaved as described? A major danger here is what is known as *presentism*—ascribing present-day beliefs, values, and ideas to people who lived at another time. A somewhat related problem is that of *historical hindsight.* Just because we know how an event came out does not mean that people who lived before or during the occurrence of an event believed an outcome would turn out the way it did.

- Does the language of the document suggest a *bias* of any sort? Is it emotionally charged, intemperate, or otherwise slanted in a particular way? Might the ethnicity, gender, religion, political party, socioeconomic status, or position of the author suggest a particular orientation? For example, a teacher's account of a school board meeting in which a pay raise was voted down might differ from one of the board member's accounts.
- Do *other versions* of the event exist? Do they present a different description or interpretation of what happened? But note that just because the majority of observers of an event agree about what happened, this does not mean they are necessarily always right. On more than one occasion, a minority view has proven to be correct.

Generalization in Historical Research

Can researchers engaged in historical research generalize from their findings? It depends. As perhaps is obvious to you, historical researchers are rarely, if ever, able to study an entire population of individuals or events. They usually have little choice but to study a sample of the phenomena of interest. And the sample studied is determined by the historical sources that remain from the past. This is a particular problem for the historian, since almost always certain documents, relics, and others are missing, have been lost, or otherwise cannot be found. Those sources that are available perhaps are not representative of all the possible sources that did exist.

Suppose, for example, that a researcher is interested in understanding how social studies was taught in high schools in the late 1800s.

She is limited to studying whatever sources remain from that time. The researcher may locate several textbooks of the period, plus assignment books, lesson plans, tests, letters and other correspondence written by teachers, and their diaries, all from this period. On the basis of a careful review of this source material, the researcher draws some conclusions about the nature of social studies teaching at that time. The researcher needs to take care to remember, however, that all of these are written sources—and they may reflect quite a different view from that held by people who were not inclined to write down their thoughts, ideas, or assignments. What might the researcher do? As with all research, the validity of any generalizations that are drawn can be strengthened by increasing the size and diversity of the sample of data on which the generalizations are based. For those historical studies that involve the study of quantitative records, the computer has made it possible, in many instances, for a researcher to draw a representative sample of data from large groups of students, teachers, and others who are represented in school records, test scores, census reports, and other documents.

Advantages and Disadvantages of Historical Research

The principal advantage of historical research is that it permits investigation of topics and questions that can be studied in no other way. It is the only research method that can study evidence from the past in relation to questions such as those presented earlier in the chapter. In addition, historical research makes use of more different kinds of evidence than does any other method (with the possible exception of ethnographic research). It thus provides an alternative and perhaps richer source of information on certain topics that *can* also be studied with other methodologies. A researcher might, for example, wish to investigate the hypothesis that "curriculum changes that did not involve extensive planning and participation by the teachers involved usually fail(ed)" by collecting interview or observational data on groups of teachers who (a) have and (b) have not participated in developing curricular changes (a causal-comparative study), or by arranging for variations in teacher participation (an experimental study). The question might also be studied, however, by examining documents prepared over the past fifty years by disseminators of new curricula (their reports); by teachers (their diaries); and so forth.

The disadvantage of historical research is that the controls used in other methods to control for threats to internal validity are simply not possible in a historical study. Limitations imposed by the nature of the sample of documents and the instrumentation process (document analysis) are likely to be severe. Researchers cannot ensure representativeness of the sample, nor can they (usually) check the reliability and validity of the inferences made from the data available. Depending on the question studied, all or many of the threats to internal validity we discussed in Chapter Eleven are likely to exist. The possibility of bias due to researcher characteristics (in data collection and analysis) is always present. The possibility that any observed relationships are due to a subject characteristic (the individuals who prepared the documents), implementation, history, maturation, attitude, or location threat also is always present. Although any particular threat depends on the nature of a particular study, methods for their control are unfortunately unavailable to the researcher. Because so much depends on the skill and integrity of the researcher—since methodological controls are unavailable—we believe that historical research is among the most difficult of all types of research to conduct.

An Example of Historical Research

In the remainder of this chapter, we present a published example of historical research, followed by a critique of its strengths and weaknesses. As we did in our critiques of the different types of research studies we analyzed in other chapters, we use several of the concepts introduced in earlier parts of the book in our analysis.

From: Theory and Research in Social Education
Summer, 1986. Volume XIV Number 3, pp. 187–200
© by The College and University Faculty Assembly
of the National Council for the Social Studies

The Social Studies Component of the Southern Literacy Campaign: 1915–1930

James E. Akenson and Harvey G. Neufeldt
Tennessee Technological University

Abstract

Social studies aspects of the southern literacy campaign of 1915–1930 are examined. Special adult schools dedicated to instruction in reading and writing frequently attempted to meet simple goals of civic education. Relevant topics included the assumed link between literacy and crime, patriotic goals related to support of our role in World War I, support for public works such as road construction, personal values such as thrift and cleanliness, and general knowledge of history and geography. Texts and instructional methods which now seem quaint nevertheless have some striking similarities to current practice.

This paper identifies the extent of southern illiteracy in the twentieth century and examines social studies components grafted onto the literacy campaign's primary mission of teaching adults to read and write. The southern literacy campaign provides historical evidence of the ease with which social studies content mixes with conceptions of citizenship. Pursued with the greatest vigor from 1915–1930, this campaign sought to impart knowledge, attitudes, and skills designed to help black and white adult illiterates function successfully in a modernized southern culture. Overtly geared to the teaching of reading and writing skills, the southern literacy campaign incorporated a haphazard social studies component which blended content with a view of citizenship surprisingly consistent with some contemporary thought. The manner in which the social studies component meshed with the goals of this campaign provides sobering evidence for those persons wishing to alter fundamental orientations within the social studies profession. The experience of the southern literacy campaign may imply that conceptions of citizenship education based upon alternative models, higher order thinking skills, and more sophisticated value commitments may prove harder to achieve then [sic] one might wish (Shaver, 1977; Branson & Torney-Purta, 1982).

SOUTHERN ILLITERACY: THE EARLY TWENTIETH CENTURY

Ten years into the twentieth century southern states exhibited a substantial, if not staggering, illiteracy rate among blacks and whites. Based on county averages, total illiteracy rates in 1910 ranged from 12.6% in Arkansas to 34.3% in Louisiana for persons over 10 years of age. White illiteracy ranged from 4.5% in Mississippi to 14.1% in Louisiana. Black illiteracy ranged from 21.5% in Arkansas to 51.4% in Louisiana. Most significantly, illiteracy distributed itself unequally according to age. The older the person, the higher the illiteracy rate. Thus, blacks over 65 years of age had an 81% illiteracy rate and 20% of whites over 65 years of age were illiterate (Bureau of the Census, 1913a, 1913b).

The solution to the problem of adult illiteracy in southern states came in the form of an evangelistic crusade designed to raise public awareness and support for special adult schools devoted to teaching basic reading and writing skills. Most frequently called Opportunity Schools or Moonlight Schools, the majority of adult literacy schools took place in the evening or during July and August after crops had been laid-by. During the lay-by season Opportunity Schools met four hours each day during the six-week period. Teachers provided basic instruction in literacy skills as well as a variety of enrichment lessons for literate adults who attended due to lack of recreational alternatives (E. Alford & G. Alford, personal communication, December 16, 1982). The primary thrust, however, sought to develop reading, writing, and arithmetic skills. Other components received much less instructional time.

The southern literacy campaign caught fire in Kentucky and spread to other southern states after 1915. Never the truly systematic, comprehensive effort desired by its advocates, the campaign consisted of scattered efforts of varying scope, quality, and effectiveness. Alabama, Kentucky, and South Carolina developed the most consistent literacy campaigns and institution-alized them within the bureaucratic framework of their respective Departments of Education. The scope, mechanics, impact, and detailed structure of the southern literacy campaign merit separate attention and have been analyzed in other discussions (Akenson & Neufeldt, 1984, 1985).

ILLITERACY AND CITIZENSHIP

Conceived in patriotic fervor, citizenship represented a major concern of the southern literacy campaign from its inception. The proclamation of

Alabama Governor Charles Henderson linked the need to eliminate illiteracy and promote modernization as "the people of Alabama look forward with pride upon her remarkable record and are moved with a passionate desire to promote her industrial, intellectual, and moral efficiency . . ." (Alabama Illiteracy Commission, 1915, p. 1). Duties of citizenship required "every literate man, woman, and child of every station, community, or creed to consecrate himself to this stupendous, though surmountable work." By making the illiterate adult literate a better Alabama citizen might emerge.

> If in addition to learning to read and write, and perform operations in arithmetic, a person gains the power to read a newspaper, a farm journal, and the Bible, and has developed in him health and civic consciousness, he is well on the way toward a normal life. (Alabama Department of Education, 1919, p. 111)

Not only was it claimed that illiterates lacked the ability to function as citizens in a modern commercial, industrial South, but that illiterates engaged in crime. The Illiteracy Commission of South Carolina (no date a) linked crime and illiteracy in a causal relationship, asserting that:

> Sentences of the 92 women prisoners in the State Penitentiary
> equal. . . . . .627 Years
> For maintenance of these prisoners the state must spend $121,000
> 41% of these are illiterate.
> All 92 could have been educated through high school at cost of . . . $10,000
> Therefore: Probably for the lack of education the State will lose . . $111,000

Cora Wilson Stewart, founder of the Kentucky literacy crusade, made the following argument in a report to the National Education Association:

> In the most illiterate sections of the United States conditions approach the barbaric. Marriage has no sanctity whatever, and commerce is carried on through trade and barter, as when America was roamed over by savage Indians. In these densely illiterate communities the currency of the county is an unknown medium of exchange, neither silver, gold nor paper money being used anywhere is [sic] the locality. It is needless to add that in a section where even the currency of the country does not circulate, none of its progressive or helpful ideas can flow or will be adopted. (Stewart, 1923, p. 266)

Illiteracy thus became viewed as antithetical to good citizenship and to the needs of a modernized South. The southern literacy campaign included a social studies component designed to focus directly upon the knowledge, attitudes, and skills of good citizenship. Specific teaching materials, curriculum outlines, and experiences helped address the citizenship question.

PATRIOTISM

Early in the southern literacy campaign the entry of the United States into World War I resulted in specific efforts to instill positive attitudes toward the war effort. Illiterate draftees constituted a danger due to their inability to read safety instructions and sanitary regulations. More importantly, literacy training could instill a patriotic attitude toward America's war goals. The Alabama Illiteracy Commission reported that the illiterate draftee was:

> . . . .a dangerous man in camp because of his low spirits, his poor morale. Cut off from any effective communication with home and friends, understanding little of the great events of the day and less of the purposes of the great nation at war; and with slight chance of promotion in the military profession, he was not likely to be a cheerful soldier. (Alabama Department of Education, 1918, p. 1)

Although illiterates willingly marched off to combat throughout the course of history, illiterates in 1917 posed a threat because of inefficiency and an inability to absorb the motivation need to engage in national defense. In a letter circulated throughout South Carolina, the Illiteracy Commission pleaded:

> Our illiterate men are being drafted by the thousands and valuable time is taken from drilling and preparing for a war which is to save civilization and Christianity, to teach these men to read and write.
>
> Russia's fall was caused by German propaganda among the ignorant classes. There is a fertile field for German propaganda in our state and as you know it is going on all around us. A great effort must be made to mobilize our illiterates and near illiterates into the night schools where they will be taught not only reading and writing but farming, industry, and patriotism. Will you do your part so that your country will keep pace with the rest? (Illiteracy Commission of South Carolina, no date b).

Development of curriculum materials and special literacy classes for draftees quickly found their way into the campaign.

At Camp Sheridan, Professor W. C. Blasingame of Alabama Polytechnic Institute directed a literacy program for native born and foreign born whites. Teachers for the draftees included some of the most cultured women of the state as well as female teachers from Montgomery who were transported by the Women's Motor Corps Division. Cora Wilson Stewart of Kentucky aided the war effort by producing a variety of materials including *Soldier's First Book*. Reading exercises reflected the patriotic theme as the young recruit read:

See the flag.
It is our flag.
Our flag never knew defeat!
Why did our flag never know defeat?
Because our flag has always stood for the right.

If the recruit needed a reason for defending his country, there existed appropriate passages supplying the needed rationale.

Why are we at war?
To keep our country free.
To keep other peoples free.
To make the world safe to live in.
To stop the rule of kings.
To put an end to war. (Stewart, 1918, pp. 6, 14)

Devotion to country meshed neatly with the remainder of perceived needs of the adult illiterates.

Following World War I, Cora Wilson Stewart made certain that specific social studies content focused upon the effects of the war effort upon the peace which followed. The *Moonlight School Course of Study, 1919* included geography drills and history drills. Geography drill No. 3 titled Development included the following:

(Q) What changes have taken place in the relative standing of various nations?
(A) Germany and her associates in the war have become discredited nations; Russia is at present in a disorganized, weakened condition; America has risen to a position of commanding importance as an arbiter of world affairs. (Stewart, 1919, p. 25)

The reason for America's commanding role in world affairs could be identified in history drill No. 3, How America Helped Save The World. Initial questions of the drill deal with when the war began, when America entered the war, and when the war ended. More important points also received attention:

(Q) Why did Germany quit?
(A) Because she began to see and feel the mightiness of America.
(Q) How did the power of America begin to show itself?
(A) We were making more field artillery, more shoulder rifles, more powder and more poisonous gas (and of a much more poisonous nature) than England and France together were making.
(Q) How did Germany know these things?
(A) She had 100,000 German spies in the United States, some of whom were sending information directly to Germany.

(Q) What is the task of America concerning these spies?
(A) To educate all of them we can into good citizens and drive the others from our shores.
(Q) Why did the Allies and America win?
(A) Because they were fighting a just cause against an unjust one. General Foch prayed to Jesus Christ and God while the Kaiser prayed to Woden and Thor. The Allies prayed for justice while the Germans prayed for plunder. (Stewart, 1919, p. 30)

Other drills stressed that America had given "the world complete toleration," "equal political privileges to all," and "civil privileges to all." If victory in World War I left any doubt as to the mission of America, history drill No. 4 indicated that tasks included "making good citizens of all who are not so now," providing the "right kind of education for all," and carrying "democracy and liberty that we enjoy to the rest of the world." Social studies thus helped motivate soldiers as well as explain the history and consequences of World War I. In addition, America had a national and international agenda, built around good citizenship, which shared the benefits of a democratic society.

COMPONENTS OF GOOD CITIZENSHIP

Social studies in the southern literacy campaign thus took on a mission geared to developing good citizens. Most significantly, citizenship fit within the perceived needs of southern states to develop commerce, agriculture, and industry to compete in the twentieth century. A basic set of attributes linked good citizenship to cleanliness, good manners, modern agriculture, literacy and arithmetic skills, Godliness, and increased governmental services. The cover of Kentucky Illiteracy Commission teaching materials (Stewart, 1918) depicted a Moonlight School to which the paths of thrift, better homes, good roads, health, and education converged. One assignment for Alabama Opportunity School teachers required students to:

> Show how cooperation makes road buildings, health protection, good schools, church buildings possible. What does the Bible mean by 'No man liveth unto himself?' (Alabama Department of Education, 1930, p. 15)

Not surprisingly, the efforts of adult school teachers, the official course outlines, and specially produced supplementary materials manifested such dimensions of citizenship in the teaching of basic reading, writing, and computational skills. Alabama, Kentucky, and South Carolina included materials which stressed belief in the Bible as a component of citizenship.

Wil Lou Gray, director of the Division of Adult Education for the South Carolina State Department of Education, provides insight into the social studies component of the southern literacy campaign. As part of her masters degree at Teachers College, Columbia University, Gray wrote a supplementary civics text, *Elementary Studies in Civics,* a blend of attributes believed to constitute good citizenship: Good Manners, Health, Education, Budgeting, How to Invest Money, Our Government, How Our Country Works for Us, What Our State Does for Us, and What Our National Government Does for Us (Gray, 1927, p. xi). Such chapter headings suggest that she saw good citizenship as including a variety of appropriate behaviors beyond mere knowledge of, and participation in, governmental processes.

Good manners for Gray started with the assertion that it is "thinking about the other fellow. It is obeying the Golden Rule." A series of examples provided adult students with an opportunity for discussion:

> A girl had just finished a course in table manners. She had learned that she must never put her knife into her mouth. She had a guest for dinner. The guest ate with her knife and the girl laughed. Do you think that girl had good manners? Why not? (Gray, 1927, p. 1)

Throughout the text adults learned about coughing in handkerchiefs, germs, vaccinations, the need for education, budgeting skills, the budgets of Mr. Tightwad, Mr. Spendthrift, and Mr. Thrifty, and methods of investing. The first 27 pages focused directly upon the various aspects of local, state, and national government.

This section, Our Government—What It Is and What It Does for Us, introduced adult South Carolinians to the need for government. Gray began by dealing with the concept of dependence (interdependence in contemporary social studies language). A listing of food, clothing, road, lights, and other items to a series of questions followed by a series of points regarding dependence.

> . . . It may be that you are depending on the labors of someone in another state or even in some far off land across the ocean. Have you ever thought how many people aid in giving you your cup of coffee? (Gray, 1927, p. 29)

The laborers in the foreign country, the wholesale company, government regulation, salespeople, bankers and store clerks all receive mention to make the point of dependence. Subsequently, the text pointed out difficulties if each individual attempted to make one's own laws, build roads, coin money, and punish criminals. According to Gray it would be a "case of everybody for himself and the devil take the hindmost." Government provided for the common good. Throughout the remainder of the text specific topics deal with local, state, and national government.

Elementary Studies in Civics (1927) received praise from businessmen and professionals throughout the United States. One review by the Florida State College for Women librarian stated:

> Miss Wil Lou Gray in her *Elementary Studies in Civics* has given education and citizenship in South Carolina an outline which, if followed, will go far toward making progress in our state an easy matter. Her straightforward questions are veritable searchlights turned on every voter, prospective and real and on every office holder in South Carolina. For example, take the questions . . . "Have you every [sic] known an officer, sworn to obey the laws of the land, arrest one man for having a pint of whiskey and yet take a drink with another man? Do you call that law abiding? Did you help elect these men?"
>
> Make these questions personal ones and see just how far so-called "good" citizens are to blame for regrettable conditions about which we complain. These and scores of other especially pertinent questions are certainly thought provoking and if men and women who form the citizenship of South Carolina can be helped and inspired to think, happier homes, better schools and a noble state are realities of the near future. (Richardson, 1927)

Gray could hardly be considered an extreme liberal by contemporary standards or those of her own time. However, the following example and questions evince a concern for evenhanded justice set within the parameters of racial segregation.

> Have you ever known an officer to arrest a group of Negroes for shooting craps and failed to see some of his friends playing poker? Is that right? (Gray, 1927, p. 48)

Used in the special black and white Opportunity Schools held during the summer and in the adult night school program throughout the year, Gray's civics text helped provide adults with social studies lessons with a particular notion of citizenship. The frequency of use, however, cannot be determined given available data. Given the literacy campaign's primary emphasis on basic literacy and a wide variation between individual county and city adult programs, the use of *Elementary Studies in Civics* was inconsistent.

Within *Elementary Studies in Civics* and within Cora Wilson Stewart's *Country Life Readers* (1915, 1917) stood lessons to alter student attitudes toward the role of government and the need for taxation to improve the quality of life. In Stewart's *Country Life Reader, First Book* (1915, p. 10), the adult read a passage beneath a drawing of a two-lane highway flanked by well maintained shoulders and power lines running on either side.

> This is a road.
> It is a good road.

It will save my team.
It will save my wagon.
The good road is my friend.
I will work for the good road.

In contrast, the following page pictured a muddy, shoulderless road, over which a team of horses labored to pull a buggy. The passage stated:

See this bad road!
It will waste my time.
It will hurt my team.
It will hurt my wagon.
The bad road is my foe.
I will get rid of the bad road.

By the time an adult made it to Stewart's *Country Life Reader, Third Book (1917),* a more sophisticated article reprinted from *American Highways* dealt with aesthetic conditions of roads. Gray also stressed a multitude of government services such as roads, streets, education, health, and mail.

Maintaining desirable governmental services required a willingness to pay for them. Cora Wilson Stewart dealt with taxes in a straight-forward manner in the *Country Life Reader.*

I shall pay my taxes.
I pay a tax on my home.
I pay a tax on my land.
I pay a tax on my cattle.
I pay a tax on my money.
I pay tax on many other things.
Where does the money go?
It goes to keep up the schools.
It goes to keep up the roads.
It goes to keep down crime.
It goes to keep down disease.
I am glad that I have a home to pay taxes on.
(Stewart, 1915, p. 22)

Writing and recitation of such statements helped reinforce their social message. Likewise, Gray (1927) made certain that taxes and tax reform came to the attention of adults. In the chapter on state-services, Gray made clear that South Carolinians should not complain about state taxation.

Most of the money for state activities come from taxation of property. The people pay taxes and together buy common benefits and common services at the lowest prices. The number of benefits and services depends largely on the amount of taxes paid. A man cannot eat his candy and keep it too.

"No taxes, no state service, Low taxes, low state service."

Let us be honest. When we applaud the cry low taxes, it may mean:

Cheap government.
Higher sick rate.
Higher death rate.
Rougher roads.
Poorer schools.
Suppose we look at our tax system. We may find we need a new system and not lower taxes. (Gray, 1927, p. 61)

Numerous other examples dealt with county and state tax rates, the low ($5.12 per capita) South Carolina tax rate, and the many benefits of state services. Good citizens not only were polite and clean, but voted to support the many governmental services needed to make South Carolina a progressive state. Of course, both Gray and Stewart advocated voting as a way to help citizens achieve the services for a progressive state.

OTHER ASPECTS OF CITIZENSHIP EDUCATION

Social studies and good citizenship found development in other ways and through other experiences. Alabama adults encountered an incidental mixture of history, government, and geography supplementing the basic instruction in reading and writing. At the 1927 Mountain Adult School in Clay County, Alabama teachers M. G. Satterfield and J. M. Teal dealt with specific Alabama historical events such as the battle of Horseshoe Bend where "Andrew Jackson whupped the Indians" (G. Alford & J. Alford, personal communication, March 18, 1984). Social studies for black teacher Marie Coles of Chambers County, Alabama included geography material such as the shape of the earth, water comprising three-fourths of the earth's surface, the discovery of America, and map work dealing with Alabama, Mississippi, and Georgia. She also used history to teach about the United States flag, George Washington Carver, and Booker T. Washington (M. Coles, personal communication, March 17, 1984). Grover Hill, not yet out of high school, taught black Chambers County, Alabama illiterates about the United States and foreign countries such as Holland and England. Hill's adult students read assignments which stressed the crops of varied regions and countries as well as planting dates, cultivation, and the harvesting process (G. Hill, personal communication, March 17, 1984).

More ambitious social studies experiences took place under Wil Lou Gray's leadership in South Carolina. Trips to Columbia and Charleston, SC as well as to Washington, DC taught adults a variety of important lessons. In 1928 Gray orchestrated a special trip to Charleston, with the following objectives:

1. To create in pupils desire to see and appreciate the beauties of Charleston and get South Carolina history first hand.
2. To provide for pupils a motive for saving.
3. To create in pupils an understanding of civic and social values. (Department of Adult Education, 1928)

The Charleston trip guidelines suggested that teachers break down the preparations into the following activities (a) getting ready for trip (budget, manners, clothes, travel), (b) the city beautiful by the sea (pictures of Charleston and environs), (c) beauty spots (gardens, trees, iron gates, and such), (d) a study in contrasts: Charleston 1778–1928 (dress, customs, improvements brought about by taxes, transportation, schools), (e) noted seacoast people, and (f) what Charleston does for South Carolina. A project outline helped teachers deal with creation of a transportation committee, hotel committee, sightseeing committee, and history committee. Lessons VII to XIX dealth with the "Report of History Committees" whose tasks were the "assembling of a library and other materials, references, . . ." Through the history committees, adults could learn the use of the index and the table of contents as well as learn about important South Carolinians such as John C. Calhoun, Francis Marion, and Thomas Sumter. In addition, students could make reports on outstanding sights of Charleston such as the Tea Gardens, The Battery, Fort Sumter, and the Old Powder Magazine (Department of Adult Education, 1928, pp. 1–5). Carefully organized and well publicized, the trip to Charleston provided adults with an experience far beyond their usual domains and combined the multiplicity of objectives common to the southern literacy campaign. Money management, politeness, appreciation for and understanding of South Carolina government and history all meshed conveniently in such travel experiences.

Virtually every year created a travel opportunity with objectives similar to the Charleston trip. Annual pilgrimages to Columbia, SC provided thousands of blacks and whites with intensive experiences designed to broaden their backgrounds and learn important lessons about the functioning of state government and state history. The exhaustive logistical and educational planning by Gray and her secretary resulted in exposure to a variety of places. A letter dated 6 April 1932 informed adult teachers of the itinerary:

We will spend the morning seeing the State House and grounds under expert guides. After assembling in the House of Representatives and hearing about five or six state relics, we will go to Washington Street Methodist Church where there will be a short religious service, an Opportunity School reunion, and lunch. After lunch will begin the ride over the city to the State Hospital, the Home for the Blind, the Confederate Home, the Governor's Mansion, the Penitentiary, the University, Woodrow Wilson's Boyhood Home, the new Auditorium, Ann Pamela Cunningham's grave in the Presbyterian Churchyard, the graves of Timrod, Hampton, and the late Governor Manning. After memorial exercises at the grave of Governor Manning, we will attend a short vesper service in Trinity Church. (Letter to Teachers or Opportunity School Chairman, 1932)

Likewise a 1930 trip to Washington, DC allowed adults to enjoy "two glorious days of sightseeing, fellowship, and jollity!" (All Aboard, 1930). For $25.00 adults traveled by train to Washington, DC and learned United States history and government through a nonstop tour of Mount Vernon, the White House, the Capital, the Tomb of the Unknown Soldier, the Library of Congress, as well as museums and residential areas. Courtesy, cleanliness, and wise money management received reinforcement throughout the trip.

IMPLICATIONS

Two major observations emerge from the data on the southern literacy campaign. First, the social studies content of the campaign appears consistent with some social studies curriculum content in the late twentieth century. On the surface, answers in Cora Wilson Stewart's history drills sound strident and their verbatim memorization seems inappropriate. However, it is our experience that present-day classroom conduct of social studies comes closer to duplicating such procedures than current high-sounding rhetoric might wish one to believe. Contemporary sophistication aside, the authors suspect that a majority of present-day laypersons, classroom teachers, and administrators would feel comfortable with the literacy campaign's mixture of United States history and government, reinforcement of voting behavior, understanding and loyalty to existing democratic institutions, and measures designed to provide basic services such that the economic system can function effectively.

Patrons of the literacy campaign such as state departments of education, civic groups such as Rotary and the Federation of Women's Clubs, and cotton mill owners hardly represented the constituency likely to spawn revolutionary zeal. In 1918 the South Carolina Sunday School Association passed resolutions supporting the eradication of illiteracy (Illiteracy Commission of South Carolina, 1918), and in 1926 Ku Klux Klan members from Gaffney, SC made contributions (Illiteracy Commission of South

Carolina, 1926). The social studies component did not aim at the development of analytical skills designed to question the emerging progressive South or other social and economic structures dominating the distribution of power, wealth, or privilege. Neither did the poor whites and poor blacks learn political and economic strategies which could be utilized to change existing institutional structures. The limited social studies component, however, is still recognizable as social studies. Field trips to the state capital retain the same identity and purpose in the 1980s as they had in the 1920s. Despite overt dissimilarities, the contemporary mainstream perception of social studies apparently still has much in common with the perceptions of social studies which were supported by the southern literacy campaign.

A second observation relates to the continued status of social studies as the runt of the litter in public education. The role of social studies instruction within the southern literacy campaign proved secondary to primary objectives related to reading, writing, computation, and a modernized South. Good citizenship, be it cleanliness or knowledge of government, played second fiddle to the overall purpose of bringing adults into the twentieth century. Indeed, good citizenship via cleanliness and related virtues was emphasized regardless of whether history, government, or geography was actually taught to adults. There is some evidence that those who attended the adult classes failed to be motivated by opportunities to learn social studies and citizenship. Grady and Edna Alford attended the 1927 Opportunity School in Clay County, Alabama "to play games and mess around." (E. Alford & G. Alford, personal communication, December 16, 1982); J. B. Fuller attended to better estimate the board feet content of timber logs (J. Fuller, personal communication, March 18, 1984); George James, John Waldrip, and Will Parish attended to learn to read, write their names, and sign a check (A. Kennedy, personal communication, December 17, 1982). L. J. Tanner attended Covington County (Alabama) Opportunity Schools to improve his skills for leisure time reading (L. Tanner, personal communication, March 19, 1984). A few even earned a better living from their Opportunity School efforts. Evelyn L. Berry reported how her father attended Opportunity Schools in Dadeville, Alabama in the late 1920s and 1930s.

> . . . My father, Johnny Smith attended. I was about eleven years old. He worked so hard. I can remember him doing his homework at night, while we children did ours. He worked for the textile plant in Dadeville many years. At the time he was going to school he was an oil and band man in the Spinning Room. He was promoted to Fixer later and held this job until his retirement in 1965. Later years he studied and did radio repair as an extra job. Later TV. He had his own shop. Worked the textile plant, his shop morning hours.
>
> The schooling helped him to be able to learn these jobs. (E. Berry, personal communication, March 18, 1984)

The proverbial bottom line motivated Johnny Smith, not the opportunity to learn about history, geography, or government. Social studies placed a distant, second, third, or fourth place in the motives of those attending adult schools. We expect that similar concerns continue to affect the status of social studies in the modern public schools.

References

Akenson, J., & Neufeldt, H. (1984). Southern illiteracy and adult education in the early twentieth century. *The Educator, 4*(1), 15–19.

Akenson, J., & Neufeldt, H. (1985). Alabama's illiteracy campaign for black adults. *Journal of Negro Education, 54,* 189–195.

Alabama Department of Education. (1918). Special drive against illiteracy among men of draft age. Montgomery, AL: Brown Printing Co.

Alabama Department of Education. (1919). *Annual report*. Montgomery, AL: Brown Printing Co.

Alabama Department of Education. (1930). *Opportunity schools for white adults: Course of study and suggestions to teachers* (2nd ed.). Birmingham, AL: Birmingham Printing Co.

Alabama Illiteracy Commission. (1915). *Illiteracy day in Alabama: The problem, the plan, the proclamation of the governor*. Montgomery, AL: Brown Printing Co.

All aboard: Advance information on the Washington trip. Columbia, SC: Box 1, Folder 35, Wil Lou Gray Papers, South Carolina collection, University of South Carolina.

Branson, M., & Torney-Purta, J. (Eds.). (1982). *International human rights, society, and the schools* (Bul. 68). Washington, DC: National Council for the Social Studies.

Bureau of the Census. (1913a). *Thirteenth census of the United States. Population. Alabama-Montana* (Vol. 1). Washington, DC: Government Printing Office.

Bureau of the Census. (1913b). *Thirteenth census of the United States. Population. Nebraska-Wyoming, Hawaii, Alaska, and Puerto Rico* (Vol. 2). Washington, DC: Government Printing Office.

Department of Adult Education. (1928). Project in travel for the stressing of the appreciation of beauty and history. Columbia, SC: Box 2, Wil Lou Gray papers, South Carolina collection, University of South Carolina.

Gray, W. (1927). *Elementary studies in civics* (rev. ed.). Columbia, SC: The State Co.

Illiteracy Commission of South Carolina. (no date a). High cost of illiteracy. Columbia, SC: Wil Lou Gray papers, South Carolina collection, University of South Carolina.

Illiteracy Commission of South Carolina. (no date b). Appeal letter. Columbia, SC: Box 1, Folder 26, Wil Lou Gray papers, South Carolina collection, University of South Carolina.

Illiteracy Commission of South Carolina. (1918). South Carolina Sunday school association resolution. Columbia, SC: Box 1, Folder 6, South Carolina collection, University of South Carolina.

Illiteracy Commission of South Carolina. (1926). County lay-by schools: Ku Klux Klan helps in adult work. Columbia, SC: Box 1, *1919–1935,* South Carolina collection, University of South Carolina.

Letter to teachers or opportunity school chairman. (1932). Columbia, SC: Box 2, Wil Lou Gray Papers, South Carolina collection, University of South Carolina.

Richardson, L. (1927). *Review of elementary studies in civics*. Columbia, SC: Box 1, Folder 63, Wil Lou Gray papers, South Carolina collection, University of South Carolina.

Shaver, J. P. (Ed.). (1977). *Building rationales for citizenship education* (Bul. 52). Washington, DC: National Council for Social Studies.

Stewart, C. (1915). *Country life readers: First book*. Richmond, VA: B. F. Johnson Publishing Co.

Stewart, C. (1917). *Country life readers: Third book*. Richmond, VA: B. F. Johnson Publishing Co.

Stewart, C. (1918). *Soldier's first book. Part 1*. New York: Association Press.

Stewart, C. (1918). *Moonlight school course of study*. Frankfort, KY: Kentucky Illiteracy Commission.

Stewart, C. (1919). *Moonlight school course of study, 1919*. Frankfort, KY: Kentucky Illiteracy Commission.

Stewart, C. (1923). Report of illiteracy commission. Frankfort, KY: Kentucky Illiteracy Commission.

Analysis of the Study

PURPOSE/JUSTIFICATION

The purpose of this study is clear: to examine the role of social studies instruction in the Southern literacy campaign of 1915–1930. The justification of the study, however, is less clear. Why is it important to clarify the connections between social studies and the primary goal of the movement, which was to improve literacy? The authors believe that the results of their analysis have implications for present attempts to change the social studies profession, but they do not directly justify their study on these (or other) grounds.

DEFINITIONS

No definitions, as such, are given. The authors do, however, describe the literacy campaign in considerable detail. Other major terms, including "social studies," "citizenship," and "patriotism," are not defined except by implication in context.

PRIOR RESEARCH

None is cited; presumably there is none specifically directed to the topic of this study.

As is customary in historical research, the references serve as information sources, not previous research on this topic.

HYPOTHESES

None are stated or clearly implied. It seems to us that the authors did have expectations as to what their data would show and, if so, could have improved their study by stating them. For example: "The curriculum materials developed as a part of the Southern literacy campaign demonstrate a deliberate attempt to teach that the United States, in war and peace, has acted from high moral principles."

SAMPLE

The sampling issue is quite a different matter in historical research than in other kinds of studies. There is no population of persons to be sampled. It could be argued that a population of relevant documents (or other information sources) exists and could, therefore, be randomly sampled. There is seldom, if ever, any compelling reason for not using *all* such documents, however. The historical researcher's task is to locate such documents, analyze them for authenticity, and, if necessary, judge their relative merits. We must assume that this was done in this study.

INSTRUMENTATION

Once again, there is no instrumentation in the sense discussed in this text. The "instrument" here is the researcher's talent for locating, evaluating, and analyzing pertinent sources. The concept of reliability has little relevance to historical data since each item of data is not meaningfully considered a sample across either content or time. The issue of validity, on the other hand, is paramount. It is addressed by evaluation of sources and by comparison of sources regarding the same specifics (events, objects, and so on). In this study, the authors have not defended their sources—we must assume their credibility. Neither have they presented direct evidence that different sources agree with respect to specifics. They have cited several sources of curriculum materials to support their conclusion that patriotism was embedded in the literary materials. The citations, however, are all taken from the work of one author (Cora Wilson Stewart), with no demonstration that her work was either typical or dominant in instructional use. With respect to "citizenship," two authors are cited, but not in support of the same specifics, that is, Gray is cited as emphasizing equal application of justice to all, while Stewart is cited as promoting government services.

PROCEDURES/VALIDITY

This report is weak in its attention to systematic planning. No discussion is provided of plans as to the kinds of sources to be pursued, criteria as to which were to be analyzed in detail, or how the analysis would be conducted. After the introduction, the authors moved immediately into giving quotations without providing a rationale as to how or why these quotations were selected. A section on *method* seems needed.

Overall, the procedures that were followed are clear-cut. They involved essentially the locating and subsequent analysis of pertinent information sources. Replication of the study requires only that the same (or perhaps alternative) documents be obtained and analyzed. The nature of this study makes most of the threats to internal validity we have discussed in other studies in-applicable here, since no relationships among variables were reported. The exceptions are data collector bias and data collector characteristics. Since historical research relies entirely on the interpretations and supportive documentation provided by the researcher, one can never be certain that an individual study, such as this one, is not a product of the researcher's personal bias or characteristics.

DATA ANALYSIS

Data analysis procedures, as we have discussed them, are not used in this study, nor is it clear how they could be. Some tabulations of the frequency of occurrence of specific topics might have strengthened the authors' interpretations.

RESULTS AND DISCUSSION

While we think that, in general, the results of a study should be kept separate from a discussion of those results, such separation is very difficult to maintain in historical research. The question to be asked here is whether the data provided justify the authors' conclusions. Their contention that the social studies content of the Southern Literacy Campaign fits current societal expectations is undocumented, requiring that the reader make his or her own comparisons in this regard. Their statement that analytical, critical skills were not emphasized is consistent with the examples given, but is not specifically documented.

The authors' conclusion that social studies was secondary to other objectives in the campaign seems a given since the primary emphasis, as they state at the outset, was on reading and writing. Nor is it surprising that social studies objectives were secondary to economic goals in the motivation of planners of the campaign. While we agree that these patterns exist today, we do not see that the authors have documented that this is the case.

Finally, it is not clear to us how this study justifies the conclusion, stated in the introduction, that changing social studies may prove very difficult. Evidence is offered that recent concepts were not reflected in these literacy materials (which is to be expected), but there is no evidence, that we can see, that attempts through the social studies to promote citizenship and patriotism were unsuccessful. Where, then, are the parallels to today?

Main Points of Chapter Seventeen

- The unique characteristic of historical research is that it focuses exclusively on the past.
- Educational researchers conduct historical studies for a variety of reasons, but perhaps the most frequently cited is to help people learn from past failures and successes.
- When well-designed and carefully executed, historical research can lead to the confirmation or rejection of relational hypotheses.
- There are four essential steps involved in doing a historical study. These include defining the problem or hypothesis to be investigated; searching for relevant source material; summarizing and evaluating the sources the researcher is able to locate; interpreting the evidence obtained and then drawing some conclusions about the problem or hypothesis being investigated.
- Most historical source material can be grouped into four basic categories: documents, numerical records, oral statements, and relics.
- Documents are written or printed materials that have been produced in one form or another sometime in the past.
- Numerical records include any type of numerical data in printed form.
- Oral statements include any form of statement made orally by someone.
- Relics are any objects whose physical or visual characteristics can provide some information about the past.
- A primary source is one prepared by an individual who was a participant in, or a direct witness to, the event that is being described.
- A secondary source is a document prepared by an individual who was not a direct witness to an event, but who obtained his or her description of the event from someone else.
- External criticism refers to the genuineness of the documents a researcher uses in a historical study.
- Internal criticism refers to the accuracy of the contents of a document. Whereas external criticism has to do with the authenticity of a document, internal criticism has to do with what the document says.
- As in all research, researchers who conduct historical studies should exercise caution in generalizing from small or nonrepresentative samples.

For Discussion

1. A researcher wishes to investigate changes in graduation requirements since 1900. Pose a possible hypothesis the researcher might investigate. What sources might he or she consult?

2. Which of the following would constitute examples of a primary historical source? (Assume they are genuine.)

    a. An article on intelligence testing written by a school psychologist.
    b. The *Encyclopedia of Educational Research*.
    c. A final examination booklet.
    d. A spelling primer used in a midwestern school in 1840.
    e. A bulletin from a school principal.
    f. An eighteenth century school desk.
    g. A 1969 newspaper announcing the landing of men on the moon.
    h. A menu from a school cafeteria.

3. Why might a researcher be cautious or suspicious about each of the following sources?
    a. A typewriter imprinted with the name "Christopher Columbus."
    b. A letter from Franklin D. Roosevelt endorsing John F. Kennedy for the Presidency of the United States.
    c. A "Letter to the Editor" from an eighth grade student complaining about the adequacy of the school's advanced mathematics program.
    d. A typed report of an oral interview with a recently fired teacher describing the teacher's complaints against the school district.
    e. A 1920 high school diploma indicating a student had graduated from the tenth grade.
    f. A high school teacher's attendance book indicating no absences by any member of her class during the entire year of 1942.
    g. A photograph of an elementary school classroom in 1800.

Notes

1. Entwisele, Doris R. et. al. (1986). *American Educational Research Journal, 23*(4):587–613.
2. Mark, Jonathan H. and Barry D. Anderson. (1985). *American Educational Research Journal, 22*(2):413–422.
3. Kaufman, Polly Welts. (1985). New Haven, CT: Yale University Press.
4. Lybarger, Michael. (1983). *History of Education Quarterly, 23*(4):445–468.
5. Rafferty, Judith R. (1988). *History of Education Quarterly, 28*(1):73–93.
6. Coleman, Michael C. (1987). *History of Education Quarterly, 27*(4):473–498.
7. Horowitz, Helen Lefkowitz. (1986). *History of Education Quarterly, 26*(1):1–38.
8. Nelson, Murry R. (1987). *Theory and Research in Social Education, 15*(4):245–256.
9. Willower, Donald J. (1987). *The Journal of Educational Administration, 15*(1):12–28.
10. Jespersen, Shirley D. (1987). *The Journal of Social Studies Research, 11*(1):1–6.
11. Goldscheider, Frances Kobrin & Celine LeBourdars. (1986). *Sociology and Social Research: An International Journal, 70*(2):143–145
12. Carr, Edward J. (1967). *What is history?* New York: Random House. pp. 32–33.

Research Exercise Seventeen: Historical Research

You should complete Problem Sheet 17 only if you are planning an historical study. If you intended study involves a different methodology, you will find a similar problem sheet at the end of the chapter that deals with that methodology. You might wish to consider, however, whether your research question could be investigated by means of an historical study.

> Using Problem Sheet 17, once again state the question or hypothesis of your study. Then describe, briefly but thoroughly, the procedures of your study—that is, *what* you intend to do, *when, where,* and *how.* Last, indicate any unresolved problems you see at this point in your planning.

PROBLEM SHEET 17
Historical Research

1. The question or hypothesis of my study is: _____
_____
_____

2. A brief summary of **what** I intend to do, **when, where,** and **how** is as follows:
_____
_____
_____
_____
_____
_____
_____
_____
_____
_____

3. The major problems I foresee at this point are as follows: _____
_____
_____

Part Four

PREPARING RESEARCH PROPOSALS AND REPORTS

Chapter Eighteen

WRITING RESEARCH PROPOSALS AND REPORTS

By now we hope you have learned many of the concepts and procedures involved in educational research. You may, in fact, have done considerable thinking about a research study of your own. To help you further, we discuss in this chapter the major components involved in proposal and report writing. A research proposal is nothing more than a written plan for conducting a research study. It is a generally accepted and commonly required prerequisite for carrying out a research investigation.

Objectives

Reading this chapter should enable you to:

- *Describe* briefly the main sections of a research proposal and a research report
- *Describe* the major difference between a research proposal and a research report
- *Write* a research proposal
- *Understand* and *critique* a typical research report

What Is the Purpose of a Research Proposal?

A **research proposal** communicates the intentions of the researcher—the purpose of his or her intended study and its importance, together with a step-by-step plan for conducting the study. Problems are identified, questions or hypotheses are stated, variables are identified, and terms are defined. The subjects to be included in the sample, the instrument(s) to be used, the research design, the procedures to be followed, how the data will be analyzed—all are spelled out in some detail, and at least a partial review of previous related research is included. Such a written plan is highly desirable, since it allows interested others to evaluate the worth of a proposed study and to make suggestions for improvement.

A research proposal, then, is a written plan for a study. It spells out in detail what the researcher intends to do. It permits others to learn about the intended research and to offer suggestions for improving the study. It helps the researcher clarify what needs to be done and avoid unintentional pitfalls or unknown problems. A **research report** follows much the same format as a proposal, with two main differences: (1) it states what *was* done rather than what *will be* done (some alterations are almost inevitable), and (2) it includes the actual results of the study, along with a discussion of them.

This chapter describes what is expected in each category of a research proposal or report. It also discusses what is appropriate in the results and discussion sections of a research report. We highlight what we have found to be the most common mistakes made by beginning researchers in preparing research proposals. Finally, we present an example of a research proposal prepared by one of our students and comment on its strengths and weaknesses.

The Major Sections of a Research Proposal or Report

PROBLEM TO BE INVESTIGATED

There are usually four topics addressed in this section: (1) the purpose of the study, (2) the justification for the study, (3) the research question and/or hypotheses (including the variables to be investigated, and (4) the definition of terms.

Purpose of the Study. Usually the first section in the proposal or report, the purpose states succinctly what the researcher proposes to investigate. The purpose should be a concise statement, providing a framework to which details are added later. Generally speaking, any study should seek to clarify some aspect of the field of interest that is considered important, thereby contributing both to overall knowledge and to current practice. Here are some examples of the purpose in research reports taken from the literature.

- The purpose of this study was to identify and describe the bedtime routines and self-reported nocturnal sleep patterns of women over age 65 and to determine the differences and relationships between these routines and patterns according to whether or not the subject was institutionalized.[1]
- The purpose of this study was to explore how young adolescents portray the ideal person in drawing and in response to a survey.[2]
- This study attempts to identify some of the processes mediating self-fulfilling prophesies in the classroom.[3]

Justification for the Study. In the justification, researchers must make clear why this particular study is important to investigate. They must present an argument for the "worth" of the study, so to speak. For example, if a researcher intends to study a particular method for modifying student attitudes toward government, he or she must make the case that such a study is important—that people are, or should be, concerned about it. The researcher must also make clear why he or she chooses to investigate the particular method. In many such proposals, there is the implication that current methods are not good enough; this should be made explicit, however.

A good justification should also include any specific implications that follow if relationships are identified. In an intervention study, for example, if the method being studied appears to be successful, changes in pre-service or in-service training for teachers may be necessary; money may need to be spent in different ways; materials and other resources may need to be used differently, and so on. In survey studies, strong opinions on certain issues (such as peer opinions about drug use) may have implications for teachers, counselors, parents, and others. Relationships found in correlational or causal-comparative studies may justify predictive uses. Also, results of correlational or ethnographic studies may suggest possibilities for subsequent experimental studies. These should be discussed.

Here is an example of a justification. It taken from a report of a study investigating the relationship between narrative and historical understanding in a literature-based sixth grade history program.

Recent research on the development of historical understanding has focused on secondary students. For several decades research has rested on the premise that historical understanding is demonstrated in the ability to analyze and interpret passages of history—or at least passages containing historical names, dates, and events. The results have indicated that if historical understanding develops at all, it does not appear until late adolescence (Hallam, 1970, 1979; Peel, 1967). From the perspective of those who work with younger children, however, this approach reflects an incomplete view of historical understanding.

The inference often drawn from the research is that young children cannot understand history; therefore history should not be part of their curriculum. Certainly, surveys have shown that young children do not indicate much interest in history as a school subject. Yet teachers and parents know that children evince interest in the old days, in historical events or characters, and in descriptions of everyday life in historic times, such as Laura Ingalls Wilder's *Little House* books (e.g., 1953). Children respond to history long before they are capable of handling current tests of historical understanding. The research, however, has not taken historical response into account in the development of mature understanding.

The research on children's response to literature provides some guidelines for examining historical response. Research by Applebee (1978), Favat (1977), and Schlager (1975) suggests that aspects of response are developmental. Other scholars (Britton, 1978; Egan, 1983; Rosenblatt, 1938) extend that suggestion to historical understanding, arguing that early, personal responses to history—especially history embedded in narrative—are precursors to more mature and objective historical understanding.

Little has been done to study the form of such early historical response. Kennedy's (1983) study examined the relationship between information-processing capacity and historical understanding, but concentrated on adolescents. Reviews of research on historical understanding also fail to uncover studies of early response. There is nothing describing how children respond to historical material in a regular classroom setting. How do children respond on their own, or in contact with peers? What forms of history elicit the strongest responses? How do children express interest in historical material? Does the classroom context influence responses? What teacher behaviors inhibit or encourage response?

These are important questions for the elementary teacher faced with a social studies curriculum that continues to emphasize history, as well as for the theorist interested in the development of historical understanding. Yet these questions cannot easily be answered by traditional empirical models. Research needs to be extended to include focus on the range of evidence available through naturalistic inquiry.

Using Naturalistic Inquiry to Study Historical Response

Classroom observation suggests that narrative is a potent spur to historical interest. Teachers note the interest exhibited by students in such historical stories as *The Diary of Anne Frank* (Frank, 1952) and *Little House on the Prairie* (Wilder, 1953) and in the oral tradition of family history (Huck, 1981). Research in discourse analysis and schema theory suggests that narrative may help children make sense of history. White and Gagne (1976), for instance, found that connected discourse leads to better memory for meaning. Such discourse provides a framework that improves recall and helps children recognize important features in a text (Kintsch, Kozminsky, Streby, McKoon & Keenan, 1975). DeVilliers (1974) and Levin (1970) found that readers processed words in connected discourse more deeply than when the same words appeared in sentences or lists. Cullinan, Harwood, and Galda (1983) suggest that readers may be better able to remember things in narratives where the "connected discourse allows the reader to organize and interrelate elements in the text" (p. 31).

One way to help children understand history, then, may be to use the connected discourse of literature. Such an approach also allows the researcher to focus on response as the ongoing construction of meaning as children encounter history in literature. The following study investigated children's responses to a literature-based approach to history.[4]

Key questions to ask yourself at this point:
1. Have I identified the specific research problem I wish to investigate?
2. Have I indicated what I intend to do about this problem?
3. Have I put forth an argument as to why this problem is worthy of investigation?

Research Questions or Hypothesis. The particular question to be investigated should be stated next. This is usually, but not always, a more specific form of the problem in question form. As you will recall, we, along with many other researchers, favor hypotheses for reasons of clarity and as a research strategy. If a researcher has a hypothesis in mind, it should be stated as clearly and as concisely as possible. It is unnecessarily frustrating for a reader to have to infer what a researcher's hypothesis or hypotheses might be. (See Chapter Two for several examples of typical research questions and hypotheses in education.)

Key questions to ask yourself at this point:
4. Have I asked the specific research question I wish to pursue?
5. Do I have a hypothesis in mind? If so, have I expressed it?
6. Do I intend to investigate a relationship? If so, have I indicated the variables I think may be related?

Definitions.   All key terms should be defined. In a hypothesis-testing study, these are primarily the terms that describe the variables of the study. The researcher's task is to make his or her definitions as clear as possible. If previous definitions found in the literature are clear to all concerned, well and good. Often, however, they need to be modified to fit the present study. It is often helpful to formulate operational definitions as a way of clarifying terms or phrases. While it is probably impossible to eliminate all ambiguity from definitions, the clearer the terms used in a study are—to both the researcher and others—the fewer difficulties will be encountered in subsequent planning and conducting of the study. (See Chapter Two for examples of different ways to define key terms in a research investigation.)

Key questions to ask yourself at this point:
7. Have I defined all key terms clearly (and, if possible, operationally)?

BACKGROUND AND REVIEW OF RELATED LITERATURE

In a research report, this may be a lengthy section, especially in a master's thesis or a doctoral dissertation. In a research proposal, it is a partial summary of previous work related to the hypothesis or focus of the study. The researcher is trying to show here that he or she is familiar with the major trends in previous research and opinion on the topic and understands their relevance to the study being planned. In our experience, the major weakness of many literature reviews is that they cite references (often many references) without indicating their relevance or implications for the planned study. (See Chapter Four for details on literature review. For examples of literature reviews, see the published studies presented in Chapters Twelve through Seventeen.)

Key questions to ask yourself at this point:
8. Have I surveyed and described relevant studies related to the problem?
9. Have I surveyed existing expert opinion on the problem?
10. Have I summarized the existing state of opinion and research on the problem?

PROCEDURES

The procedures section includes: 1) research design, 2) sample, 3) instrumentation, 4) procedural detail, 5) internal validity, and 6) data analysis.

Research Design.   In experimental or correlational studies, the research design should be described using the symbols presented in Chapters Twelve or Thirteen. In causal-comparative studies, the research design should be described using the symbols presented in Chapter Fourteen. The particular research design to be used in the study should be identified, as well as how it applies to the present study. In most studies, the basic design is fairly clear-cut and fits one of the models we presented in Chapters Twelve through Fourteen.

Sample.   In a proposal, a researcher should indicate in considerable detail how he or she will obtain the subjects—the sample—to be used in the study. If at all possible, a *random sample* should be used. If a **convenience sample** must be used, relevant **demographics** (gender, ethnicity, occupation, IQ, and so on) of the sample should be described. Lastly, the legitimate population to which the results of the study may be generalized should be indicated. (See Chapter 5 for details on sampling.)

Here is an example of a description of a sample. It was taken from the report of a study designed to investigate the effects of behavior modification on the classroom behavior of first and third graders.

> Thirty grade 1 (mean age = 7 years, 1 month) and 25 grade 3 children (mean age = 9 years, 3 months) were identified by their classroom teachers as exhibiting inappropriate classroom behavior, receiving no special services, and having intelligence quotients between 85 and 115. These children represented 23% of the grade 1 children in a large elementary school in the southeastern United States and 21% of the grade 3 children in the same school. All participants were from regular classrooms; none were receiving special educational services. Fifteen grade 1 subjects were assigned randomly to the experimental treatment and 15 to the control condition; 25 grade 3 subjects were assigned randomly to each of the two conditions, with the experimental treatment receiving 13 and control, 12. The experimental group included 22 boys, 6 girls; 11 black children, 17 white children; 14 of low socioeconomic status, 14 of middle to high socioeconomic status. The control group was composed of 15 boys, 12 girls; 15 black children, 12 white children; 7 of low socioeconomic status, 20 of middle to high socioeconomic status. No attrition occurred during this study.[5]

Key questions to ask yourself at this point:

11. Have I described my sampling plan?
12. Have I described the relevant characteristics of my sample in detail?
13. Have I identified the population to which the results of the study may legitimately be generalized?

Instrumentation.   Whenever possible, existing instruments should be used in a study, since construction of even the most straightforward test or questionnaire is often a very time-consuming and difficult task. The use of an existing instrument, however, is not justified unless sufficiently reliable and valid results can be obtained with it for the researcher's purpose. Too many studies are done with instruments that are merely convenient or well known. Usage is a poor criterion of quality, as shown by the continuing popularity of some widely used achievement tests despite years of scathing professional criticism. (See Chapter Six for examples of the many types of instruments that educational researchers can use.)

In the event that appropriate instruments are not available, the procedures to be followed in developing the instruments to be used in the study should be described with attention to how validity and reliability will (presumably) be enhanced. At least some sample items from the instrument should be included in the proposal.

Even with instruments for which reliability and validity of scores are supported by impressive evidence, there is no guarantee that these instruments will function in the same way in the study itself. Differences in subjects and conditions may make previous estimates of validity and reliability inapplicable to the current context. Further, validity always depends on the intent and interpretation of the researcher. For all these reasons, the reliability and validity of the scores obtained from all instruments should be checked as a part of every study, preferably before the study begins.

It is almost always feasible to check internal consistency reliability since no additional data are required. Checking reliability of scores over time (**stability**) is more difficult since an additional administration of the instrument is required. Even when feasible, repetition of exactly the same instrument may be questionable since individuals may alter their responses* as a result of taking the instrument the first time. Asking respondents to reply to a questionnaire or an interview a second time is often difficult since it seems rather foolish to them. Nonetheless, in-

---

* For example, knowledge of content.

genuity and the effort required to develop a parallel form of the instrument(s) can often overcome these obstacles.*

The most straightforward way to check validity is to use a second instrument to measure the same variable. Often, this is not as difficult as it may seem, given the variety of types of instruments that are available (see Chapter Six). Frequently, the judgment of knowledgeable persons (teachers, counselors, parents, and friends, for instance), expressed as ratings or as a ranking of the members of a group, can serve as the second instrument. Sometimes a useful means of validating the responses to attitude, opinion, or personality (such as self-esteem) scales filled out by subjects is to have a person who knows each subject well fill out the same scale (as it applies to the subject), and then check to see how well the ratings correspond. A final point is that reliability and validity data need not be obtained for the entire sample, although this is preferable. It is better to obtain such data for only a portion of the sample (or even for a separate although comparable sample) than to obtain no data at all. (For a more detailed discussion of reliability and validity, see Chapter Seven.)

Key questions to ask yourself at this point:
14. Have I described the instrument(s) to be used?
15. Have I indicated their relevance to the present study?
16. Have I stated how I will check the reliability of scores obtained from all instrument(s)?
17. Have I stated how I will check the validity of scores obtained from all instrument(s)?

Procedural Details. Next, the procedures to be followed in the study—what will be done, as well as when, where, and how—should be described in detail. In intervention studies in particular, additional details are usually needed on the nature of the intervention and on the means of introducing the method or treatment.

* A compromise is to divide the existing instrument into two halves (as in the split-half procedure) and administer each half with a time interval between administrations.

Keep in mind that the goal here is that of making replication of the study possible; another researcher should, on the basis of the information provided in this section, be able to repeat the study in exactly the same way as the original researcher. Certain procedures may change as the study is carried out, it is true, but a proposal should nonetheless have this level of clarity as its goal.

The researcher should also make clear how the information collected will be used to answer the original question or to test the original hypothesis.

Key question to ask yourself at this point:
18. Have I fully described the procedures to be followed in the study—what will be done, where, when, and how?

Internal Validity. At this point, the essential planning for a study should be nearly completed. It is now necessary for the researcher to examine the proposed methodology for the presence of any feasible alternative explanations for the results should the study's hypothesis be supported (or should nonhypothesized relationships be identified). We suggest that each of the threats to internal validity discussed in Chapter Eleven be reviewed to see if any apply to the proposed study. Should any troublesome areas be found, they should be mentioned and their likelihood discussed. The researcher should describe what he or she would do to eliminate or minimize them. Such an analysis often results in substantial changes in, or additions to, the methodology of the study; if this occurs, realize that it is better to become aware of the need for such changes at this stage than after the study is completed.

Key questions to ask yourself at this point:
19. Have I discussed any feasible alternative explanations that might exist for the results of the study?
20. Have I discussed how I will control for these alternative explanations?

Data Analysis. The researcher then should indicate how the data to be collected will be organized (see Chapter Six), and analyzed (see Chapters Eight, Nine, and Ten).

Key questions to ask yourself at this point:
21. Have I described how I will organize the data I will collect?
22. Have I described how I will analyze the data, including statistical procedures that will be used, and why these procedures are appropriate?

BUDGET

Research proposals are often submitted to government or private funding institutions in hopes of obtaining financial support. Such institutions almost always require submission of a tentative budget along with the proposal. Need-less to say, the amount of money involved in a research proposal can have a considerable impact on whether or not it is funded. Thus, great care should be given to preparation of the budget. Budgets usually include such items as salaries, materials, equipment costs, secretarial and other assistance, expenses (such as travel and postage), and overhead (Figure 18.1) presents an example of a typical budget sheet.

GENERAL COMMENTS

One other comment may seem unnecessary, but in our experience it is not. Remember that all sections of a proposal must be consistent. It is not uncommon to read a proposal in which each section by itself is quite acceptable but some sections contradict others. The terms used in a

FIGURE 18.1

Example of a Budget Sheet for a Research Proposal

BUDGET

Year 1 2 3 (circle one)

(Use Same Format for Each Continuing Year)

BUDGET ITEM

A. Direct Costs

    1. Salaries & Wages (Professional and Clerical) $_____

    2. Employee Benefits   _____

    3. Travel   _____

    4. Equipment (Purchase)   _____

    5. Materials & Supplies   _____

    6. Consultants or Contracts   _____

    7. Other (Equipment Rental, Printing, etc.)   _____

B. Indirect Costs

    TOTAL Requested $_____

C. Institutional Support (Project Costs Paid for by Home Institution) $_____

study, for example, must be used throughout as originally defined. The hypotheses must be consistent with the research question. Instrumentation must be consistent with, or appropriate for, the research question, the hypotheses, and the procedures for data collection. The method of obtaining the sample must be appropriate for the instruments that will be used and with the means of dealing with alternative explanations for the results, and so forth.

Sections Unique to Research Reports

FINDINGS

As discussed previously, the results of a study can only be presented in a research report; there are no results in a proposal. A report of the results, usually called the findings, is included near the end of the report. The findings of the study constitute the results of the researcher's analysis of his or her data—that is, what the collected data reveal. In comparison-group studies, the means and standard deviation for each group on the posttest measure(s) usually are reported. In correlational studies, correlation coefficients and scatterplots are reported. In survey studies, percentages of responses to the questions asked, crossbreak tables, contingency coefficients, etc. are given. (For examples of findings, see the published research reports presented in Chapters Twelve through Seventeen.)

SUMMARY AND CONCLUSIONS

In the summary, the researcher usually repeats the research question and summarizes what was done to investigate it. The conclusions section of a report presents a discussion by the researcher of what he or she thinks the findings imply. This usually includes a statement, in hypothesis-testing studies, of the extent to which the hypothesis was supported.

In nonhypothesis-testing studies, the implications of the study's results for overall knowledge and current practice are discussed. (For examples of summaries and conclusions, see any of the published research studies presented in Chapters Twelve through Seventeen.)

Suggestions for Further Research. Normally, this is the final section of a report. Based on the findings of the present study, the researcher suggests some related and follow-up studies that might be conducted in the future to advance knowledge in the field.

AN OUTLINE OF A RESEARCH REPORT

Figure 18.2 shows an outline of a research report. Although the topics listed are generally agreed to within the research community, the particular sequence may vary in different studies. This is partly because of different preferences among researchers and partly because the headings and organization of the outline will be somewhat different for different research methodologies. This outline may also be used for a research proposal, in which case sections D and E of Part II would be omitted (and the future tense used throughout). Also, a budget might be added.

A Sample Research Proposal

The research proposal that follows was prepared by a student in one of our classes. It is a good example of student work and will give you an idea of what a completed proposal looks like. We comment on both its strengths and weaknesses in the margins.*

---

* This proposal does not follow the organization recommended in Figure 18.2 exactly. It does, however, contain all of the major components previously discussed. It also includes a report of a pilot study. A **pilot study** is a small-scale trial of the proposed procedures. Its purpose is to detect any problems so that they can be remedied before the study proper is carried out.

FIGURE 18.2

Organization of a Research Report

I.   Introductory Section

    A. Title page
    B. Table of Contents
    C. List of Figures
    D. List of Tables

II. Main Body

    A. Problem to be investigated
       1. Purpose of the study
       2. Justification of the study
       3. Research question and hypotheses
       4. Definition of terms

    B. Background and review of related literature

    C. Procedures
       1. Description of the research design
       2. Description of the sample
       3. Description of the instrument(s) used
       4. Explanation of the procedures followed (the what, when, where, and how of the study)
       5. Discussion of internal validity
       6. Description and justification of the statistical techniques used

    D. Findings
       1. Description of findings pertinent to each of the research hypotheses or questions

    E. Summary and Conclusions
       1. Brief summary of the research question being investigated, the procedures employed, and the results obtained
       2. Discussion of the implications of the findings—their meaning and significance
       3. Suggestions for further research

III. References (Bibliography)

IV. Appendices

THE EFFECTS OF INDIVIDUALIZED READING
UPON STUDENT MOTIVATION IN GRADE FOUR

Nadine DeLuca*

Purpose

The general purpose of this research is to add to the existing knowledge about reading methods. Many educators have become dissatisfied with general reading programs in which teacher-directed group instruction means boredom and delay for quick students and embarrassment and lack of motivation for others. *[Requires documentation]* *[Demonstrates importance of study]* Although there has been a great deal of writing in favor of an individualized reading approach which is supposedly a highly-motivating method of teaching reading, sufficient data has not been presented to make the argument for or against individualized reading programs decisive. With the data supplied by this study (and future ones), soon schools will be free *(better able)* to make the choice between implementing an individualized reading program or retaining a basal reading method. *[Indicates implications if hypothesis is supported]*

Definitions

[Could be more specific to this study. An operational definition would help here]

Motivation: Motivation is inciting and sustaining action in an organism. The motivation to learn could be thought of as being derived from a combination of several more basic needs such as the need to achieve, to explore, to satisfy curiosity. *['Motivation to read' is really the variable]*

Individualization: [Individualization is characteristic of an individualized reading program.] *[Delete]* Individualized reading has as its basis the concepts of seeking, self-selection, and pacing. An individualized reading program has the following characteristics:

1) Literature books for children predominate.
2) Each child makes personal choices with regard to his reading materials.
3) Each child reads at his own rate and sets his own pace of accomplishment. *[good–clear and specific]*
4) Each child confers with the teacher about what he has read and the progress he has made.
5) Each child carries his reading into some form of summarizing activity.

* Used by permission of the author.

6) Some kind of record is kept by the teacher and/or the student.

7) Children work in groups for an immediate learning purpose and leave group when the purpose is accomplished.

8) Word recognition and related skills are taught and vocabulary is accumulated in a natural way at the point of each child's need.

Prior Research

Abbott, J. L., "Fifteen Reasons Why Personalized Reading Instruction Doesn't Work." Elementary English (January, 1972), 44:33-36.

This article refutes many of the usual arguments against individualized reading instruction. It lists those customary arguments then proceeds to explain why the objections are not valid ones. *ok*

It explains how such a program can be implemented by an ordinary classroom teacher in order to show the fallacy in the complaint that individualizing is impractical. Another fallacy involves the argument that unless a traditional basal reading program is used, children do not gain all the necessary reading skills.

Barbe, Walter B., Educator's Guide to Personalized Reading Instruction. Englewood Cliffs, New Jersey: Prentice-Hall, Inc., 1961.

Mr. Barbe outlines a complete individualized reading program. He explains the necessity of keeping records of children's reading. *ok* The book includes samples of book-summarizing activities as well as many checklists to ensure proper and complete skill development for reading.

Hunt, Lyman C., Jr., "Effect of Self-selection, Interest, and Motivation upon Independent, Instructional and Frustrational Levels." Reading Teacher (November, 1970), 24:146-151.

Dr. Hunt explains how self-selection, interest, and motivation *A good beginning* (some of the basic principles behind individualized reading), when *Additional material* used in a reading program, result in greater reading achievement. *should be added*

Miel, Alice, Ed., Individualizing Reading Practices. New York: Bureau of Publications, Teachers College, Columbia University, 1959.

Veatch, Jeanette, Reading in the Elementary School. New York: The Roland Press Co., 1966.

West, Roland, Individualized Reading Instruction. Port Washington, New York: Kennikat Press, 1964.

Good–shows relevance to present study

The three books listed above all provide examples of various individualized reading programs actually being used by different teachers. (The definitions and items on the rating scale were derived from these three books.)

Hypothesis

Variables are clear. Hypothesis is directional

The greater the degree of individualization in a reading program, the higher will be the students' motivation.

Population

Right

An ideal population would be all fourth grades in the United States. Because of different teacher-qualification requirements, different laws, and different teaching programs, though, such a generalization may not be justifiable. One that might be justifiable would be a population of all fourth-grade classrooms in the San Francisco-Bay Area.

Sampling

good sampling plan

random!! →

The study will be conducted in fourth-grade classrooms in the San Francisco-Bay Area, including inner-city, rural, and suburban schools. The sample will include at least one hundred classrooms. Ideally, the sampling will be done randomly by identifying all fourth-grade classrooms for the population described and using random numbers to select the sample classrooms. As this would require excessive amounts of time, this sampling might need to be modified by taking a sample of schools in the area, identifying all fourth-grade classrooms in these schools only, then taking a random sample from these classrooms.

Instrumentation

appears to have good logical validity. Items are consistent with definition

Instrumentation will include a rating scale to be used to rate the degree of individualization in the reading program in each classroom. A sample rating scale is shown below. Those items on the left indicate characteristics of classrooms with little individualization.

Should state how data on different days will be used. It can be used to check stability

Reliability: The ratings of the two observers who are observing separately but at the same time in the same room will be compared to see how closely the ratings agree. The rating scale will be repeated for each classroom on at least three different days.

Three days may not be sufficient to get reliable scores

Validity: Certain items on the student questionnaire (to be discussed in the next section) will be compared with the ratings on the rating scale to determine if there is a correlation between the degree of individualization apparently observed and the degree indicated by stu-

good

Can't use the same item for both variables!

dents' responses. In the same manner, responses to questions asked of teachers and parents can be used to indicate whether the rating scale is a true measure of the degree of individualization.

Would parents be qualified to judge this?

Another means of instrumentation to be used is a student questionnaire. A sample questionnaire is included. The following questions have as their purpose to determine the degree of motivation by asking how many books read and how the child indicates that he feels about reading: questions numbered 1, 4, 5, 6, 7, 9, 10, 11, 12, and 13. Questions 2, 3, 4, and 8 have as their purpose to help determine the validity of the items on the rating scale. Questions 14 and 15 are included to determine the students' attitudes toward the questionnaire to help determine if their attitudes are possible sources of bias for the study. Questions 8 and 9 have an additional purpose which is to add knowledge about the novelty of the reading situation in which the child now finds himself. This may be used to determine if there is a relationship between the novelty of the situation and the degree of motivation. ⟶ *But why?*

good

Most items appear to have logical validity but the lack of definition of motivation to read makes it difficult to judge

Good idea but may not be enough items to give a reliable index

To control novelty as an extraneous variable?

Good idea but maybe too few items to give a reliable index

RATING SCALE

1. Basal readers or programmed readers predominate in room.	1	2	3	4	5	There is an obvious center in the room containing at least five library books per child.
2. Teacher teaches class as a group.	1	2	3	4	5	Teacher works with individuals or small groups.
3. Children are all reading from the same book series.	1	2	3	4	5	Children are reading various materials at different levels.
4. Teacher initiates activities.	1	2	3	4	5	Student initiates activities.
5. No reading records are in evidence.	1	2	3	4	5	Children or teacher are observed to be making notes or keeping records of books read.
6. There is no evidence of book summarizing activities in the room.	1	2	3	4	5	There is evidence of book summarizing activities around room (e.g., student-made book jackets, paintings, drawings, models of scenes or characters from books, class list of books read, bulletin board displays about books read . . .).

RATING SCALE

7. Classroom is arranged with desks in rows and no provision for a special reading area.

1 2 3 4 5

Classroom is arranged with a reading area so that children have opportunities to find quiet places to read silently.

8. There is no conference area in the room for the teacher to work with children individually.

1 2 3 4 5

There is a conference area set apart from the rest of the class where the teacher works with children individually.

9. Children are doing the same activities at the same time.

1 2 3 4 5

Children are doing different activities from their classmates.

10. Teacher tells children what they are to read during class.

1 2 3 4 5

Children choose their own reading materials.

11. Children read aloud in turn to teacher as part of a group using the same reading textbook.

1 2 3 4 5

Children read silently at their desks or in a reading area or orally to the teacher on an individual basis.

Student Questionnaire

Is your intent here to get at socioeconomic level?

Age _____ Grade _____ Father's work _____

Mother's work _____

Appears valid 1. How many books have you read in the last month? _____

Appears valid 2. Do you choose the books you read by yourself? _____

If not, who does choose them for you? _____

Appears valid 3. Do you keep a record of what books you have read? _____

Does your teacher? _____

Appears valid 4. What different kinds of reading materials have you read this year?___

Questionable validity 5. Do you feel you are learning very much in reading this year? _____

Why or why not? _____

Some indication of the scoring system should be given. Open-ended questions must rely on content analysis of responses. You could use examples from your pilot study.

6. Complete these sentences:

   Books _____

   Reading _____   *How scored?*

7. Do you enjoy reading time? _____   *Appears valid*

8. Have you ever been taught reading a different way? _____   *Appear valid as indicators of novelty*

   When? _____ How was it different? _____

   _____

9. Which way of learning to read do you like better? _____

   _____ Why? _____

   Generally not a good idea to have one item (9) dependent on another item (8)

10. If you couldn't come to reading class for some reason, would you be   *Appears valid*

    disappointed? _____ Why? _____

11. Is this classroom a happy place for you during reading time? _____   *Appears valid*

12. Do most of the children in your classroom enjoy reading?   *Questionable validity*

    _____

13. How much of your spare time at home do you spend reading just for   *Appears valid*

    fun? _____

14. Did you like answering these questions or would you have preferred

    not to? _____

15. Were any of the questions confusing? _____

    Good idea

    If so, which ones? _____

    How were they confusing? _____

Student Questionnaire:

   Reliability: An attempt will be made to control item reliability by asking the same question in different ways and comparing the answers.   *Which items will be compared?*

   Validity: Validity may be questionable to some degree since school children may be reluctant to report anything bad about their teachers or the school. Observers will be reminded to establish rapport with children as much as possible before administering questionnaires and to assure them that the purpose of the questions does not affect them or their school in any way.   *Good point* *Good idea*

Why do you want this information?

A teacher questionnaire will also be administered. A sample questionnaire is included. Some of the questions are intended to indicate if the approach being used by the teacher is new to her and what her attitude is toward the method. These questions are numbered 1, 2, 3, and 4. Question 5 is supposed to indicate how available reading materials are so that this can be compared to the degree of student motivation. Questions 6 and 8 will provide validity checks for the rating scale. Question 7 will help in determining a relationship between socioeconomic levels and student motivation.

Why? how is this related to your hypothesis

May be too few items to give reliable index

Good

Incorrect. It is the reliability of information that counts. Persons may or may not be consistent in giving factual information. It does seem likely that these questions would provide reliable data.

Reliability: Reliability should not be too great a problem with this instrument since most questions are of a factual nature.

Validity: There may be a question as to validity depending upon how the questions are asked (if they are used in a structured interview). The way they are asked may affect the answers. An attempt has been made to state the questions so that the teacher does not realize what the purposes of this study are and so prejudice her answers.

Good

Teacher Questionnaire

Why include? As a means of controlling experience?

1. How long have you been teaching? _____

Why? to assess novelty?

2. How long have you taught using the reading approach you are now using? _____

Why?

3. What other approaches have you used? _____
_____

Why?

4. If you could use any reading approach you liked, which would you use?
_____

Why? _____

Why?

5. In what manner do you obtain reading materials? _____
_____

Where did you get most of those you now use? _____
_____

Appears valid for individualization

6. How often are the children grouped for reading? _____
_____

Under procedures, you explain that items 1–5 and 7 are intended as attempts to control extraneous variables. This is a very good idea but the purpose should be made clear earlier (in this section).

7. From what neighborhood or area do most of the children in this class

come? _____

_____

To assess socio-economic status

8. How do you decide when and how word recognition skills and vocabu-

lary are taught to each child? _____

_____

Appears valid for individualization

    If it were feasible, an excellent instrument would be a parent ques-
tionnaire. The purpose of it would be to determine how much the child
reads at home, his general attitude toward reading, and any changes in
his attitude the parent has noticed.

Good idea. Parents should be able to judge 'motivation to read'

Procedures

    Since the sample of one hundred classrooms is large and each
classroom will need to be visited at least three times for thirty minutes
to one hour during each visit on different weeks, quite a large team of
observers—probably around twenty—will be needed. They will work in
pairs observing independently. They will spend about one-half hour each
visit on the rating scale. The visits should take place between Monday
and Thursday, since activities and attitudes are often different on Fridays.
The investigation will not begin until after school has been in session for
at least six weeks so that all programs have had sufficient time to
function smoothly.

Good idea

    Control of extraneous variables: Sources of extraneous variables
might include that teachers using individualized reading might be the
more skillful and innovative teachers. Also, in cases where the individualized reading program is a new one, teacher enthusiasm for the new
program might carry over to students. In this case it might be the
novelty of the approach and teacher enthusiasm rather than the program itself that is motivating. An attempt will be made to determine if
there is a relationship between novelty and teacher enthusiasm and
student motivation by correlating the results of the teacher questionnaire
(showing newness of program and teacher preference of program), indications from questions on student questionnaire, and statistics on motivation in a scatterplot. The influence of student socioeconomic levels on
motivation will be determined by comparing the answers to the question
on the teacher questionnaire concerning what area or neighborhood
children live in, the question on parental occupations on the student

Good

Good

Good

o.k. but could be clearer

Good

This section does a good job of identifying and attempting to control variables likely to be detrimental to internal validity

Good but how will information be scored?

Isn't it likely that all classrooms would be affected the same? Further, it seems unlikely that your second variable (individualization) would be affected. If so, it's no problem so far as internal validity is concerned

Right

Delete. This is incorrect. Do you see why?

Unclear, delete

questionnaire, and student motivation. The amount and availability of materials may influence motivation also. This influence will be determined by the answers of teachers concerning where and how they get materials.

The presence of observers in the classroom may cause distraction and influence the degree of motivation. By having observers repeat procedures three or more times, later observations may prove to be nearly without this procedure bias. By keeping observers in the dark about the purpose of the study, it is hopeful that will control as much bias in their observations and question-asking as possible.

Will you use all of them?

Good idea. However, since they both observe (individualization) and administer your questionnaire (motivation) they may well figure out the hypothesis. If there is concern that this 'awareness' could influence their ratings and/or administration of the questionnaire, it would be preferable to have each instrument administered by different persons.

Data Analysis

Observations on the rating scale and answers on the questionnaires will be given number ratings according to the degree of individualization and amount of motivation respectively. The average of the total ratings will then be averaged for the two observers on the rating scale, and the average of the total ratings will be averaged for the questionnaires in each classroom to be used on a scatterplot to show the relationship between motivation and individualization in each classroom. Results of the teacher questionnaire will be compared similarly with motivation on the scatterplot. The correlation will be used to further indicate relationships.

But teacher questions lack logical validity as indicators of 'motivation.' Items 6 and 8 can check 'individualization' however.

PILOT STUDY

Procedure

The pilot study was conducted in three primary grade schools in San Francisco. The principals of each school were contacted and were asked if one or two reading classes could be observed by the investigator for an hour or less. The principals chose the classrooms observed. About forty-five minutes was spent in each of four third-grade classrooms. No fourth grades were available in these schools. The instruments administered were the student questionnaire and the rating scale.

Both the questionnaire and rating scale were coded by school and by classroom so that the variables for each classroom might be compared. The ratings on the rating scale for each classroom were added together then averaged. Answers on items for the questionnaire were rated "1" for answers indicating low motivation and "2" for answers indicating high motivation. (Note: Some items had as their purpose to test validity of rating scale or to provide data concerning possible biases, so these items were not rated.) Determining whether answers indicated high or low motivation created no problem except on Item #1. It was decided that fewer than eight books (two books per week) read in the past month indicated low motivation, while more indicated high motivation. The ratings for these questions were then added and averaged. Then these averaged numbers for all the questionnaires in each classroom were averaged. The results were as follows:

Room	Individualization	Motivation
#1	1.4	1.3
#2	2.1	1.6
#3	3.0	1.8
#4	3.2	1.7

SCATTERPLOT

Low ← Motivation → High

Low ← Individualization → High

   Although this pilot study could not possibly be said to uphold or disprove the hypothesis, we might venture to say that if the actual study were to yield results similar to those shown on the graph, there would be a strong correlation (estimate: $r = .90$) between individualization and motivation. This correlation is much too high to be attributed to chance with a sample of 100 classrooms. If these were the results of the study

random

described in the research proposal, the hypothesis would seem to be upheld.

Indications

Good observation

Right

Unfortunately, I was unable to conduct the pilot study in any fourth-grade classrooms which immediately throws doubt upon the validity of the results. In administering the student questionnaire, I discovered that many of the third-graders had difficulty understanding the questions. Therefore, the questioning took the form of individual structured interviews. Whether or not this difficulty would hold for fourth-graders, too, would need to be determined by conducting a more extensive pilot study in fourth-grade classrooms.

Right

It was also discovered that Item #7 in the rating scale was difficult to rate. Perhaps it should be divided into two separate items—one concerning desk arrangement and one on the presence of a reading area—and worded more clearly.

Item #8 on the student questionnaire seemed to provide some problems for children. Third-graders, at least, didn't seem to understand the intent of the question. There is also some uncertainty as to whether the answers on Item #15 reflected the students' true feelings. Since it was administered orally, students were probably reluctant to answer negatively about the test to the administrator of the test. Again, a more extensive pilot study would be helpful in determining if these indications are typical.

Right

Although the results of the pilot study are not very valid due to its size and the circumstances, its value lies in the knowledge gained concerning specific items in the instruments and problems that can be anticipated for observers or participants in similar studies.

Main Points of Chapter Eighteen

- A research proposal communicates a researcher's plan for a study.
- A research report communicates what was actually done in a study, and what resulted.
- The main body is the largest section of a proposal or a report and generally includes the problem to be investigated (including the statement of the problem or question, the research hypotheses and variables, and the definition of terms); the review of the literature; the procedures (including a description of the sample, the instruments to be used, the research design, the procedures to be followed, and a description and a justification of the statistical procedures used); and a budget of expected costs.
- The essential difference between a research proposal and a research report is that a research report states what was done rather than what will be done and includes the actual results of the study. Thus, in a report, a description of the findings pertinent to each of the research hypotheses or questions is presented, along with a discussion by the researcher of what the findings of the study imply for overall knowledge and current practice.
- Normally, the final section of a report is the offering of some suggestions for further research.
- All sections of a research proposal or a research report should be consistent with one another.

For Review

1. Review the problem sheets in Chapters 1–17 that you have completed to see how they correspond to the suggestions made in this chapter.

2. Review any or all of the critiques of studies included in Chapters 12–17 to see how they correspond to the suggestions made in this chapter.

For Discussion

1. To what extent should a researcher allow his or her personal writing style to influence the headings and organizational sequence in a research proposal (assuming that there is no mandatory format prescribed, by, for example, a funding agency)?

2. To what common function do the problem statement, the research question, and the hypotheses all contribute? In what ways are they different?

3. When instructors, in introductory research courses, evaluate research proposals of students, they sometimes find logical inconsistencies among the various parts. What do you think are the most commonly found inconsistencies?

4. Why is it especially important in a study involving a convenience sample to provide a detailed description of the characteristics of the sample in the research report? Would this be true for a random sample as well? Explain.

5. Why is it important for a researcher to discuss threats to internal validity in a) a research proposal? b) a research report?

Notes

1. Johnson, J. E. (1988). Bedtime routines: Do they influence the sleep of elderly women? *The Journal of Applied Gerontology, 7*:97–110.

2. Stiles, D. A., J. L. Gibbons, & J. Schnellman. (1987). The smiling sunbather and the chivalrous football player: Young adolescents' images of the ideal woman and man. *Journal of Early Adolescence, 7*:411–427.

3. Coleman, L. M., L. Jussim, & J. Abraham. (1987). Students reactions to teachers' evaluations: The unique impact of negative feedback. *Journal of Applied Social Psychology, 17*:1051–1070.

4. Levstik, L. S. (1986). The relationship between historical response and narrative in a sixth-grade classroom. *Theory and Research in Social Education, 14*(1):1–19. Reprinted with permission of the National Council for the Social Studies and the author.

5. Manning, B. H. (1988). Application of cognitive behavior modification: First and third graders' self-management of classroom behaviors. *American Educational Research Journal, 25*(2):194.

APPENDIXES

APPENDIX A
Table of Random Numbers

(a)	(b)	(c)	(d)	(e)	(f)	(g)	(h)	(i)
83579	83978	49300	01577	62244	99947	76797	00365	01172
51262	49969	56628	09946	78523	11984	54415	00641	07889
05033	90862	53849	93440	24273	51621	04425	23084	54671
02490	84667	67313	68029	00816	38027	91829	99524	68403
51921	09986	09539	58867	09215	97495	04766	21763	86341
31822	39187	57384	31877	91945	05078	76579	12364	59326
40052	40394	79717	51593	29666	35193	85349	22757	04243
35787	57263	95876	90361	89136	44024	92018	33831	82072
10454	46051	22159	54648	40380	72727	06963	55497	11506
09985	39854	74536	79240	80442	59447	83938	38467	40413
57228	04256	76666	95735	40823	82351	95202	87848	85275
04688	70407	89116	52789	47972	89447	15473	04439	18255
30583	58010	55623	94680	16836	63488	36535	67533	12972
73148	81884	16675	01089	81893	24114	30561	02549	64618
72280	99756	57467	20870	16403	43892	10905	57466	39194
78687	43717	38608	31741	07852	69138	58506	73982	30791
86888	98939	58315	39570	73566	24282	48561	60536	35885
29997	40384	81495	70526	28454	43466	81123	06094	30429
21117	13086	01433	86098	13543	33601	09775	13204	70934
50925	78963	28625	89395	81208	90784	73141	67076	58986
63196	86512	67980	97084	36547	99414	39246	68880	79787
54769	30950	75436	59398	77292	17629	21087	08223	97794
69625	49952	65892	02302	50086	48199	21762	84309	53808
94464	86584	34365	83368	87733	93495	50205	94569	29484
52308	20863	05546	81939	96643	07580	28322	22357	59502
32519	79304	87539	28173	62834	15517	72971	15491	79606
29867	27299	98117	69489	88658	31893	93350	01852	86381
13552	60056	53109	58862	88922	41304	44097	58305	10642
73221	81473	75249	88070	22216	27694	54446	68163	34946
41963	16813	31572	04216	49989	78229	26458	89582	82020
81594	04548	95299	26418	15482	16441	60274	00237	03741
27663	33479	22470	57066	31844	73184	48399	05209	17794
07436	23844	45310	46621	78866	30002	91855	14029	84701
53884	59886	40262	38528	28753	14814	71508	91444	94335
45080	08221	30911	87535	66101	95153	36999	60707	10947
42238	98478	80953	25277	28869	69513	93372	98587	64229
49834	43447	29857	75567	85500	24229	23099	96924	23432
38220	82174	85412	66247	80642	45181	28732	76690	06005
61079	97636	62444	07315	78216	75279	75403	49513	16863
73503	47241	61985	91537	25843	89751	63485	34927	11334
18326	96584	45568	32027	97405	06282	75452	26667	46959
89596	26372	01227	23787	33607	69714	28725	43442	19512
45851	81369	08307	58640	14287	10100	43278	55266	46802
87906	42482	50010	31486	23801	08599	32842	47918	40894
24053	02256	03743	26642	03224	93886	57367	78910	38915
20525	69314	34939	70653	40414	94127	99934	35025	50342
30315	62283	53097	99244	08033	97879	92921	68432	68168
69240	41181	08462	99916	88851	43382	28262	10582	25126
59159	99994	25434	73285	54482	91218	49955	01232	55104
33137	42409	49785	02790	98720	89495	00135	27861	39832

Table of Random Numbers (Continued)

(a)	(b)	(c)	(d)	(e)	(f)	(g)	(h)	(i)
03772	83596	01998	19683	03807	22324	16596	54549	15292
38223	26962	41821	84290	65223	83106	93175	24427	40531
38910	45316	82279	98066	67103	33755	85437	09309	75265
15780	60337	25069	47937	23687	40781	94043	74876	58012
59645	03262	42485	73462	41946	75704	61738	72335	96817
63333	68207	01070	92462	14781	82511	15065	46306	02456
85151	46866	48722	48086	20474	36574	69470	58413	37706
11531	34955	57169	04940	35640	98230	65837	36680	41477
96319	74374	15695	79458	31647	53067	13571	12179	99589
30134	59746	31665	13134	17529	39398	33946	73628	40643
04416	96960	85645	04216	28945	25137	60714	75168	83151
42928	79955	97819	45369	55359	17937	83239	11295	58130
52948	73337	82355	44257	52712	87726	91823	94251	98289
83365	12321	79618	53832	12536	21188	89557	96752	54411
17668	39848	04395	20304	74086	19150	86215	23346	84632
16488	84810	05643	70033	90915	95334	64949	45891	43946
87762	53973	04659	74735	31564	70225	76596	56131	90245
09545	67121	31566	88183	82886	45188	66813	56750	13472
50075	92832	23965	05293	84834	53872	13978	00210	77150
50014	56960	70470	84533	37605	35882	26829	09730	78137
27461	22430	70494	09014	81705	80986	72819	72797	20603
85455	36779	76804	65884	42010	20583	87053	01910	96843
46186	36401	36356	68021	41599	42851	79517	59232	37616
52865	88615	68405	17169	66648	89528	77078	45204	54016
19677	10382	66142	29876	62918	45150	73732	69810	82674
28445	84222	59854	57384	92011	14740	51517	21596	97755
80247	85449	88336	88043	86893	76735	08150	38847	06776
19069	16727	51768	37181	67709	08832	61876	83914	85457
07850	52649	32868	07651	77211	29598	13084	68633	88783
49746	61632	51796	53973	37340	46210	19822	28946	77191
32966	34486	41597	04154	32647	84479	92920	73104	97780
72920	05779	55936	34629	58795	95807	47141	57443	11846
96183	28273	32998	87991	37407	76595	49199	80466	75910
26410	63387	73201	37246	28831	18261	32480	95368	87073
25940	24468	45166	82520	94541	81832	56388	20212	81172
06149	87534	80183	38237	70561	15886	86544	56381	10014
07765	24744	91075	54307	72266	37821	89684	25908	17081
79930	48815	95288	00162	72993	37305	00922	57012	38192
86624	43304	96428	37148	61842	66107	26714	35042	33438
06874	26347	61749	34324	70973	00303	62882	70944	75589
22058	65172	55633	98434	63643	02538	79073	16385	44285
12825	40453	81056	09429	53089	47280	93450	25837	01359
09520	05545	62075	11026	92864	21694	94113	59588	07072
14123	63054	13983	27314	21748	26306	05480	58202	23461
07260	84731	51977	34707	40477	66515	42171	09292	43919
12494	23659	44181	58492	08178	20422	41828	73576	86239
82127	96579	74270	27091	21850	49286	75057	54749	66583
23184	99161	16549	28711	67847	90570	61705	02104	77154
55739	74047	33846	00562	85265	68479	28594	52163	79804
97799	90967	92906	67741	79498	76903	27121	32486	43435

APPENDIX B

Normal Curve Table

Column A lists the z-score values. Column B provides the proportion of area between the mean and the z-score value.

Column C provides the proportion of area beyond the z-score.

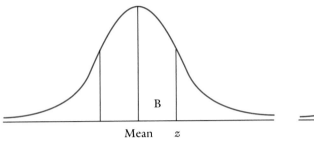

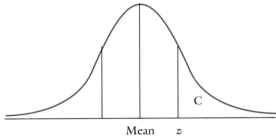

Note: Because the normal distribution is symmetrical, areas for negative z-scores are the same as those for positive z-scores.

(A)	(B) Area Between	(C)	(A)	(B) Area Between	(C)
z	Mean and z	Area Beyond z	z	Mean and z	Area Beyond z
0.00	.0000	.5000	0.25	.0987	.4013
0.01	.0040	.4960	0.26	.1026	.3974
0.02	.0080	.4920	0.27	.1064	.3936
0.03	.0120	.4880	0.28	.1103	.3897
0.04	.0160	.4840	0.29	.1141	.3859
0.05	.0199	.4801	0.30	.1179	.3821
0.06	.0239	.4761	0.31	.1217	.3783
0.07	.0279	.4721	0.32	.1255	.3745
0.08	.0319	.4681	0.33	.1293	.3707
0.09	.0359	.4641	0.34	.1331	.3669
0.10	.0398	.4602	0.35	.1368	.3632
0.11	.0438	.4562	0.36	.1406	.3594
0.12	.0478	.4522	0.37	.1443	.3557
0.13	.0517	.4483	0.38	.1480	.3520
0.14	.0557	.4443	0.39	.1517	.3483
0.15	.0596	.4404	0.40	.1554	.3446
0.16	.0636	.4364	0.41	.1591	.3409
0.17	.0675	.4325	0.42	.1628	.3372
0.18	.0714	.4286	0.43	.1664	.3336
0.19	.0753	.4247	0.44	.1700	.3300
0.20	.0793	.4207	0.45	.1736	.3264
0.21	.0832	.4168	0.46	.1772	.3228
0.22	.0871	.4129	0.47	.1808	.3192
0.23	.0910	.4090	0.48	.1844	.3156
0.24	.0948	.4052	0.49	.1879	.3121

From Table II of Fisher & Yates: *Statistical Tables for Biological, Agricultural and Medical Research*. Published by Longman Group Ltd. London (previously published by Oliver & Boyd Ltd. Edinburgh) and by permission of the authors and publishers.

Normal Curve Table   (Continued)

(A) z	(B) Area Between Mean and z	(C) Area Beyond z	(A) z	(B) Area Between Mean and z	(C) Area Beyond z
0.50	.1915	.3085	0.95	.3289	.1711
0.51	.1950	.3050	0.96	.3315	.1685
0.52	.1985	.3015	0.97	.3340	.1660
0.53	.2019	.2981	0.98	.3365	.1635
0.54	.2054	.2946	0.99	.3389	.1611
0.55	.2088	.2912	1.00	.3413	.1587
0.56	.2123	.2877	1.01	.3438	.1562
0.57	.2157	.2843	1.02	.3461	.1539
0.58	.2190	.2810	1.03	.3485	.1515
0.59	.2224	.2776	1.04	.3508	.1492
0.60	.2257	.2743	1.05	.3531	.1469
0.61	.2291	.2709	1.06	.3554	.1446
0.62	.2324	.2676	1.07	.3577	.1423
0.63	.2357	.2643	1.08	.3599	.1401
0.64	.2389	.2611	1.09	.3621	.1379
0.65	.2422	.2578	1.10	.3643	.1357
0.66	.2454	.2546	1.11	.3665	.1335
0.67	.2486	.2514	1.12	.3686	.1314
0.68	.2517	.2483	1.13	.3708	.1292
0.69	.2549	.2451	1.14	.3729	.1271
0.70	.2580	.2420	1.15	.3749	.1251
0.71	.2611	.2389	1.16	.3770	.1230
0.72	.2642	.2358	1.17	.3790	.1210
0.73	.2673	.2327	1.18	.3810	.1190
0.74	.2704	.2296	1.19	.3830	.1170
0.75	.2734	.2266	1.20	.3849	.1151
0.76	.2764	.2236	1.21	.3869	.1131
0.77	.2794	.2206	1.22	.3888	.1112
0.78	.2823	.2177	1.23	.3907	.1093
0.79	.2852	.2148	1.24	.3925	.1075
0.80	.2881	.2119	1.25	.3944	.1056
0.81	.2910	.2090	1.26	.3962	.1038
0.82	.2939	.2061	1.27	.3980	.1020
0.83	.2967	.2033	1.28	.3997	.1003
0.84	.2995	.2005	1.29	.4015	.0985
0.85	.3023	.1977	1.30	.4032	.0968
0.86	.3051	.1949	1.31	.4049	.0951
0.87	.3078	.1922	1.32	.4066	.0934
0.88	.3106	.1894	1.33	.4082	.0918
0.89	.3133	.1867	1.34	.4099	.0901
0.90	.3159	.1841	1.35	.4115	.0885
0.91	.3186	.1814	1.36	.4131	.0869
0.92	.3212	.1788	1.37	.4147	.0853
0.93	.3238	.1762	1.38	.4162	.0838
0.94	.3264	.1736	1.39	.4177	.0823

continued

APPENDIX B

Normal Curve Table (Continued)

(A) z	(B) Area Between Mean and z	(C) Area Beyond z	(A) z	(B) Area Between Mean and z	(C) Area Beyond z
1.40	.4192	.0808	1.85	.4678	.0322
1.41	.4207	.0793	1.86	.4686	.0314
1.42	.4222	.0778	1.87	.4693	.0307
1.43	.4236	.0764	1.88	.4699	.0301
1.44	.4251	.0749	1.89	.4706	.0294
1.45	.4265	.0735	1.90	.4713	.0287
1.46	.4279	.0721	1.91	.4719	.0281
1.47	.4292	.0708	1.92	.4726	.0274
1.48	.4306	.0694	1.93	.4732	.0268
1.49	.4319	.0681	1.94	.4738	.0262
1.50	.4332	.0668	1.95	.4744	.0256
1.51	.4345	.0655	1.96	.4750	.0250
1.52	.4357	.0643	1.97	.4756	.0244
1.53	.4370	.0630	1.98	.4761	.0239
1.54	.4382	.0618	1.99	.4767	.0233
1.55	.4394	.0606	2.00	.4772	.0228
1.56	.4406	.0594	2.01	.4778	.0222
1.57	.4418	.0582	2.02	.4783	.0217
1.58	.4429	.0571	2.03	.4788	.0212
1.59	.4441	.0559	2.04	.4793	.0207
1.60	.4452	.0548	2.05	.4798	.0202
1.61	.4463	.0537	2.06	.4803	.0197
1.62	.4474	.0526	2.07	.4808	.0192
1.63	.4484	.0516	2.08	.4812	.0188
1.64	.4495	.0505	2.09	.4817	.0183
1.65	.4505	.0495	2.10	.4821	.0179
1.66	.4515	.0485	2.11	.4826	.0174
1.67	.4525	.0475	2.12	.4830	.0170
1.68	.4535	.0465	2.13	.4834	.0166
1.69	.4545	.0455	2.14	.4838	.0162
1.70	.4554	.0446	2.15	.4842	.0158
1.71	.4564	.0436	2.16	.4846	.0154
1.72	.4573	.0427	2.17	.4850	.0150
1.73	.4582	.0418	2.18	.4854	.0146
1.74	.4591	.0409	2.19	.4857	.0143
1.75	.4599	.0401	2.20	.4861	.0139
1.76	.4608	.0392	2.21	.4864	.0136
1.77	.4616	.0384	2.22	.4868	.0132
1.78	.4625	.0375	2.23	.4871	.0129
1.79	.4633	.0367	2.24	.4875	.0125
1.80	.4641	.0359	2.25	.4878	.0122
1.81	.4649	.0351	2.26	.4881	.0119
1.82	.4656	.0344	2.27	.4884	.0116
1.83	.4664	.0336	2.28	.4887	.0113
1.84	.4671	.0329	2.29	.4890	.0110

Normal Curve Table   (Continued)

(A) z	(B) Area Between Mean and z	(C) Area Beyond z	(A) z	(B) Area Between Mean and z	(C) Area Beyond z
2.30	.4893	.0107	2.75	.4970	.0030
2.31	.4896	.0104	2.76	.4971	.0029
2.32	.4898	.0102	2.77	.4972	.0028
2.33	.4901	.0099	2.78	.4973	.0027
2.34	.4904	.0096	2.79	.4974	.0026
2.35	.4906	.0094	2.80	.4974	.0026
2.36	.4909	.0091	2.81	.4975	.0025
2.37	.4911	.0089	2.82	.4976	.0024
2.38	.4913	.0087	2.83	.4977	.0023
2.39	.4916	.0084	2.84	.4977	.0023
2.40	.4918	.0082	2.85	.4978	.0022
2.41	.4920	.0080	2.86	.4979	.0021
2.42	.4922	.0078	2.87	.4979	.0021
2.43	.4925	.0075	2.88	.4980	.0020
2.44	.4927	.0073	2.89	.4981	.0019
2.45	.4929	.0071	2.90	.4981	.0019
2.46	.4931	.0069	2.91	.4982	.0018
2.47	.4932	.0068	2.92	.4982	.0018
2.48	.4934	.0066	2.93	.4983	.0017
2.49	.4936	.0064	2.94	.4984	.0016
2.50	.4938	.0062	2.95	.4984	.0016
2.51	.4940	.0060	2.96	.4985	.0015
2.52	.4941	.0059	2.97	.4985	.0015
2.53	.4943	.0057	2.98	.4986	.0014
2.54	.4945	.0055	2.99	.4986	.0014
2.55	.4946	.0054	3.00	.4987	.0013
2.56	.4948	.0052	3.01	.4987	.0013
2.57	.4949	.0051	3.02	.4987	.0013
2.58	.4951	.0049	3.03	.4988	.0012
2.59	.4952	.0048	3.04	.4988	.0012
2.60	.4953	.0047	3.05	.4989	.0011
2.61	.4955	.0045	3.06	.4989	.0011
2.62	.4956	.0044	3.07	.4989	.0011
2.63	.4957	.0043	3.08	.4990	.0010
2.64	.4959	.0041	3.09	.4990	.0010
2.65	.4960	.0040	3.10	.4990	.0010
2.66	.4961	.0039	3.11	.4991	.0009
2.67	.4962	.0038	3.12	.4991	.0009
2.68	.4963	.0037	3.13	.4991	.0009
2.69	.4964	.0036	3.14	.4992	.0008
2.70	.4965	.0035	3.15	.4992	.0008
2.71	.4966	.0034	3.16	.4992	.0008
2.72	.4967	.0033	3.17	.4992	.0008
2.73	.4968	.0032	3.18	.4993	.0007
2.74	.4969	.0031	3.19	.4993	.0007

continued

Normal Curve Table   (Continued)

(A) z	(B) Area Between Mean and z	(C) Area Beyond z
3.20	.4993	.0007
3.21	.4993	.0007
3.22	.4994	.0006
3.23	.4994	.0006
3.24	.4994	.0006
3.30	.4995	.0005
3.40	.4997	.0003
3.50	.4998	.0002
3.60	.4998	.0002
3.70	.4999	.0001
3.80	.49993	.00007
3.90	.49995	.00005
4.00	.49997	.00003

Chi Square Distribution

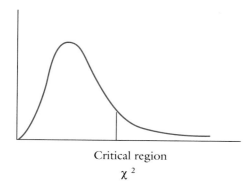

Critical region

χ^2

The table entries are critical values of χ^2

Degrees of Freedom (df)	Proportion in Critical Region				
	0.10	0.05	0.025	0.01	0.005
1	2.71	3.84	5.02	6.63	7.88
2	4.61	5.99	7.38	9.21	10.60
3	6.25	7.81	9.35	11.34	12.84
4	7.78	9.49	11.14	13.28	14.86
5	9.24	11.07	12.83	15.09	16.75
6	10.64	12.59	14.45	16.81	18.55
7	12.02	14.07	16.01	18.48	20.28
8	13.36	15.51	17.53	20.09	21.96
9	14.68	16.92	19.02	21.67	23.59
10	15.99	18.31	20.48	23.21	25.19
11	17.28	19.68	21.92	24.72	26.76
12	18.55	21.03	23.34	26.22	28.30
13	19.81	22.36	24.74	27.69	29.82
14	21.06	23.68	26.12	29.14	31.32
15	22.31	25.00	27.49	30.58	32.80
16	23.54	26.30	28.85	32.00	34.27
17	24.77	27.59	30.19	33.41	35.72
18	25.99	28.87	31.53	34.81	37.16
19	27.20	30.14	32.85	36.19	38.58
20	28.41	31.41	34.17	37.57	40.00
21	29.62	32.67	35.48	38.93	41.40
22	30.81	33.92	36.78	40.29	42.80
23	32.01	35.17	38.08	41.64	44.18
24	33.20	36.42	39.36	42.98	45.56
25	34.38	37.65	40.65	44.31	46.93
26	35.56	38.89	41.92	45.64	48.29
27	36.74	40.11	43.19	46.96	49.64
28	37.92	41.34	44.46	48.28	50.99
29	39.09	42.56	45.72	49.59	52.34
30	40.26	43.77	46.98	50.89	53.67
40	51.81	55.76	59.34	63.69	66.77
50	63.17	67.50	71.42	76.15	79.49
60	74.40	79.08	83.30	88.38	91.95
70	85.53	90.53	95.02	100.42	104.22
80	96.58	101.88	106.63	112.33	116.32
90	107.56	113.14	118.14	124.12	128.30
100	118.50	124.34	129.56	135.81	140.17

From Table VII (abridged) of Fisher & Yates: *Statistical Tables for Biological, Agricultural and Medical Research*. Published by Longman Group Ltd. London (previously published by Oliver & Boyd Ltd. Edinburgh) and by permission of the authors and publishers.

GLOSSARY

A-B-A-B design A single-subject experimental design in which measurements are repeatedly made until stability is presumably established (baseline), after which treatment is introduced and an appropriate number of measurements are made; the treatment phase is followed by a second baseline phase, which is followed by a second treatment phase.

abstract A summary of a study that describes its most important aspects, including major results and conclusions.

accessible population The population from which the researcher can realistically select subjects for a sample, and to which the researcher is entitled to generalize findings.

achievement test An instrument used to measure the proficiency level of individuals in given areas of knowledge or skill.

age equivalent score A score that indicates the age level for which a particular performance (score) is typical.

alpha coefficient See **Cronbach Alpha**

analysis of covariance (ANCOVA) A statistical technique for equating groups on one or more variables when testing for statistical significance; it adjusts scores on a dependent variable for initial differences on other variables, such as pretest performance or IQ.

analysis of variance (ANOVA) A statistical technique for determining the significance of differences among means; it can be used with two or more groups.

aptitude test An instrument used to predict performance in a future situation.

associational research/study A general type of research in which a researcher looks for relationships having predictive and/or explanatory power. Both correlational and causal-comparative studies are examples.

assumption Any important assertion presumed to be true but not actually verified; major assumptions should be described in the procedures section of a research proposal or report.

average A number representing the typical

473

score attained by a group of subjects. See **measures of central tendency.**

bar graph A graphic way of illustrating differences among groups.

baseline The graphic record of measurements taken prior to introduction of an intervention in a time-series design.

bias see **researcher bias**

case study An in-depth investigation of an individual, group, or institution to determine the variables, and relationship among the variables, influencing the current behavior or status of the subject of the study.

causal-comparative research Research that attempts to determine the cause for, or consequences of, existing differences in groups of individuals; also referred to as *ex post facto* research.

categorical data/variables Data (variables) that differ only in kind, not in amount or degree.

census An attempt to acquire data from each and every member of a population.

chi square (χ^2) A nonparametric test of significance appropriate when the data are in the form of frequency counts; it compares frequencies actually observed in a study with expected frequencies to see if they are significantly different.

closed-ended item A question and a list of alternative responses from which the responder selects; also referred to as a closed-form item.

cluster sampling/cluster random sampling The selection of groups of individuals, called clusters, rather than single individuals. All individuals in a cluster are included in the sample; the clusters are preferably selected randomly from the larger population of clusters.

coefficient of determination (r^2) The square of the correlation coefficient. It indicates the degree of relationship between two variables.

cohort study Longitudinal design (in survey research) in which a particular population is studied over time by taking different random samples at various points in time. The population remains conceptually the same, but individuals change (for example, graduates of San Francisco State University surveyed 10, 20, and 30 years after graduation).

comparison group The group in a research study that receives a different treatment from that of the experimental group.

concurrent validity (evidence of) The degree to which the scores on an instrument are related to the scores on another instrument administered at the same time, or to some other criterion available at the same time.

confidence interval An interval used to estimate a parameter that is constructed in such a way that the interval has a predetermined probability of including the parameter.

constant A characteristic that has the same value for all individuals.

constitutive defintion The explanation of the meaning of a term by using other words to describe concisely what is meant.

construct-related validity (evidence of) The degree to which an instrument measures an intended hypothetical psychological construct, or nonobservable trait.

content analysis The process of inductively establishing a categorical system for organizing open-ended information.

content-related validity (evidence of) The degree to which an instrument logically appears to measure an intended variable; it is determined by expert judgment.

contingency coefficient An index of relationship derived from a crossbreak table.

contingency question A question whose answer depends on the answer to a prior question.

contingency table See **crossbreak table.**

control Efforts on the part of the researcher to remove the effects of any variable other than the independent variable that might affect performance on a dependent variable.

control group The group in a research study that is treated "as usual."

convenience sample A sample that is easily accessible.

correlation coefficient (*r*) A decimal number between .00 and ±1.00 that indicates the degree to which two quantitative variables are related.

correlational research Research that involves collecting data in order to determine the degree to which a relationship exists between two or more variables.

counterbalanced design An experimental design in which all groups receive all treatments. Each group receives the treatments in a different order, and all groups are posttested after each treatment.

criterion The variable that is predicted in a prediction study; also any variable used to assess the criterion-related validity of an instrument.

criterion-referenced instrument An instrument that specifies a particular goal, or criterion, for students to achieve.

criterion-related validity (evidence of) The degree to which performance on an instrument is related to performance on other instruments intended to measure the same variable, or to other variables logically related to the variable being measured.

Cronbach alpha (α) An internal consistency or reliability coefficient for an instrument requiring only one test administration.

crossbreak table A table showing all combinations of two or more categorical variables, which portrays the relationship (if any) between the variables.

cross-validation Validation of a prediction equation with at least one group other than the group on which it was based.

cross-sectional survey A survey in which data are collected at one point in time from a predetermined population or populations.

curvilinear relationship A relationship shown in a scatterplot in which the line that best fits the points is not straight.

data Any information obtained about a sample.

data analysis The process of simplifying data in order to make it comprehensible.

data collector bias Unintentional bias on the part of data collectors that may create a threat to the internal validity of a study.

degrees of freedom A number indicating how many instances out of a given number of instances are "free to vary," that is, not predetermined.

dependent variable A variable affected or expected to be affected by the independent variable; also called "criterion" or "outcome variable."

derived score A score obtained from a raw score in order to aid in interpretation. Derived scores provide a quantitative measure of each student's performance relative to a comparison group.

descriptive research/study Research that attempts to describe existing conditions without analyzing relationships among variables.

descriptive statistics Data analysis techniques enabling the researcher to meaningfully describe data with numerical indices or in graphic form.

directional hypothesis A relational hypothesis stated in such a manner that a direction, often indicated by "greater than" or "less than," is hypothesized for the results.

discriminant function analysis A statistical procedure for predicting group membership (a categorical variable) from two or more quantitative variables.

distribution/distribution curves The real or theoretical frequency distribution of a set of scores.

ecological generalizability The degree to which results can be generalized to environments and conditions outside the research setting.

effect size An index used to indicate the magnitude of an obtained result or relationship.

empirical Based on observable evidence.

equivalent forms Two tests identical in every way except for the actual items included.

equivalent-forms method A method to obtain a reliability coefficient; a way of checking consistency by correlation scores on equivalent forms of an instrument. It is also referred to as alternate-forms reliability.

errors of measurement Inconsistency of individual scores on the same instrument.

Eta An index that indicates the degree of a curvilinear relationship.

ethnography/ethnographic research The collection of data on many variables over an extended period of time in a naturalistic setting, usually using observation and interviews.

experiment A research study in which one or more independent variables are systematically varied by the researcher to determine the effects of this variation.

experimental group The group in a research study that receives the treatment (or method) of special interest in the study.

experimental research Research in which at least one independent variable is manipulated, other relevant variables are controlled, and the effect on one or more dependent variables is observed.

experimental variable The variable that is manipulated (systematically altered) in an intervention study by the researcher.

external criticism Evaluation of the genuineness of a document in historical research.

external validity The degree to which results are generalizable, or applicable, to groups and environments outside the research setting.

extraneous event(s) See **history threat.**

extraneous variable A variable that makes possible an alternative explanation of results; an uncontrolled variable.

factor analysis A statistical method for reducing a set of variables to a smaller number of factors.

factorial design An experimental design that involves two or more independent variables (at least one of which is manipulated) in order to study the effects of the variables individually, and in interaction with each other, upon a dependent variable.

follow-up study A study conducted to determine the characteristics of a group of interest after some period of time.

frequency distribution A tabular method of showing all of the scores obtained by a group of individuals.

frequency polygon A graphic method of showing all of the scores obtained by a group of individuals.

generalizing See **ecological generalizability; population generalizability.**

grade equivalent score A score that indicates the grade level for which a particular performance (score) is typical.

Hawthorne effect A positive effect of an intervention resulting from the subjects' knowledge that they are involved in a study, or their feeling that they are in some way receiving "special" attention.

histogram A graphic representation, consisting of rectangles, of the scores in a distribution; the height of each rectangle indicates the frequency of each score, or group of scores.

historical research The systematic collection and objective evaluation of data related to past occurrences to determine causes, effects, or trends of those events that may help explain present events and anticipate future events.

history threat The possibility that results are due to an event that is not part of an intervention, but which may affect performance on the dependent variable, thereby affecting internal validity.

hypothesis A tentative, reasonable, testable assertion regarding the occurrence of certain behaviors, phenomena, or events; a prediction of study outcomes.

implementer threat The possibility that results are due to variations in the implementation of the treatment in an intervention study, thereby affecting internal validity.

independent variable A variable that affects (or is presumed to affect) the dependent variable under study and is included in the research design so that its effect can be determined; sometimes called the "experimental" or "treatment" variable.

inferential statistics Data analysis techniques for determining how likely it is that results based on a sample or samples are similar to results that would have been obtained for an entire population.

instrument Any procedure or device for systematically collecting data.

instrument decay Changes in instrumentation over time that may affect the internal validity of a study.

instrumentation The entire process of collecting data in a study.

instrumentation threat The possibility that results are due to variations in the way data are collected, thereby affecting internal validity.

interaction An effect created by unique combinations of two or more independent variables; systematically evaluated in a factorial design.

interjudge reliability The consistency of two (or more) independent scorers, raters, or observers.

internal criticism Determining if the contents of a document are genuine.

internal validity The degree to which observed differences on the dependent variable are directly related to the independent variable, not some other (uncontrolled) variable.

interval scale A measurement scale that, in addition to ordering scores from high to low, also establishes a uniform unit in the scale so that any equal distance between two scores is of equal magnitude.

intervening variable A variable that intervenes, or changes the relationship, between an independent variable and a dependent variable.

intervention A specified treatment or method that is intended to modify one or more dependent variables.

intervention study/research A general type of research in which variables are manipulated in order to study the effect on one or more dependent variables.

interview A form of research in which individuals are questioned orally.

item validity The degree to which each of the items in an instrument measures the intended variable.

Kruskal-Wallis One Way Analysis of Variance A nonparametric inferential statistic used to compare two or more independent groups for statistical significance of differences.

Kuder-Richardson approaches Procedures for determining an estimate of the internal consistency reliability of a test or other instrument from a single administration of the test without splitting the test into halves.

level of confidence The probability associated with a confidence interval; the probability that the interval will contain the corresponding parameter. Commonly used confidence levels in educational research are the 95 and 99 percent confidence levels.

level of significance The probability that a discrepancy between a sample statistic and a specified population parameter is due to sampling error, or chance. Commonly used significance levels in educational research are .05 and .01.

Likert scale A self-reporting instrument in which an individual responds to a series of statements by indicating the extent of agreement. Each choice is given a numerical value, and the total score is presumed to indicate the attitude or belief in question.

limitation An aspect of a study that the researcher knows may influence the results or generalizability of the results, but over which he or she has no control.

linear relationship A relationship in which an increase (or decrease) in one variable is associated with a corresponding increase (or decrease) in another variable.

literature review The systematic identification, location, and analysis of documents containing information related to a research problem.

location threat The possibility that results are due to characteristics of the setting or location in which a study is conducted, thereby producing a threat to internal validity.

longitudinal survey Study in which data are obtained on the same individuals two or more times during a period of time (usually of considerable length, such as several months or years).

manipulated variable See **experimental variable**

Mann-Whitney *U* test A nonparametric inferential statistic used to determine whether two uncorrelated groups differ significantly.

matching design A technique for equating groups on one or more variables, resulting in each member of one group having a direct counterpart in another group.

maturation threat The possibility that results are due to changes that occur in subjects as a direct result of the passage of time and that may affect their performance on the dependent variable, thereby affecting internal validity.

mean/arithmetic mean ($\overline{X}$) The sum of the scores in a distribution divided by the number of scores in the distribution; the most commonly used measure of central tendency.

measures of central tendency Indices representing the average or typical score attained by a group of subjects; the most commonly used in educational research are the *mean* and the *median*.

measures of variability Indices indicating how spread out the scores are in a distribution. Those most commonly used in educational research are the *range*, *standard deviation*, and *variance*.

median That point in a distribution having 50 percent of the scores above it and 50 percent of the scores below it.

mode The score that occurs most frequently in a distribution of scores.

moderator variable A variable that may or may not be controlled but has an effect in the research situation.

mortality threat The possibility that results are due to the fact that subjects who are for whatever reason "lost" to a study may differ from those who remain so that their absence has a significant effect on the results of the study.

multiple-baseline design A single-subject experimental design in which baseline data are collected on several behaviors for one subject, after which the treatment is applied sequentially over a period of time to each behavior one at a time until all behaviors are under treatment.

multiple correlation (R) A numerical index describing the relationship between predicted and actual scores using multiple regression. The correlation between a criterion and the "best combination" of predictors.

multiple regression A technique using a prediction equation with two or more variables in combination to predict a criterion ($y = a + b_1 X_1 + b_2 X_2 + b_3 X_3 \ldots$)

multiple-treatment interference The carryover or delayed effects of prior experimental treatments when individuals receive two or more experimental treatments in succession.

naturalistic observation Observation in which the observer controls or manipulates nothing, and tries not to affect the observed situation in any way.

negatively skewed distribution A distribution in which there are more extreme scores at the lower end than at the upper, or higher, end.

nominal scale A measurement scale that classifies elements into two or more categories, the numbers indicating that the elements are different, but not according to order or magnitude.

nondirectional hypothesis A prediction that a relationship exists without specifying its exact nature.

nonequivalent control group design An experimental design involving at least two groups, both of which are pretested; one group receives the experimental treatment, and both groups are posttested. Individuals are not randomly assigned to treatments.

nonparametric technique A test of significance appropriate when the data represent an ordinal or nominal scale, or when assumptions required for parametric tests cannot be met.

nonparticipant observation Observation in which the observer is not directly involved in the situation to be observed.

nonrandom sample/sampling The selection of a sample in which every member of the population does *not* have an equal chance of being selected.

norm group The sample group used to develop norms for an instrument.

normal curve A graphic illustration of a normal distribution. See **normal distribution.**

normal distribution A theoretical "bell-shaped" distribution having a wide application to both descriptive and inferential statistics. It is known or thought to portray many human characteristics in "typical" populations.

norm-referenced instrument An instrument that permits comparison of an individual score to the scores of a group of individuals on that same instrument.

norms Descriptive statistics that summarize the test performance of a reference group of individuals and permit meaningful comparison of individuals to the group.

null hypothesis A statement that any difference between obtained sample statistics and specified population parameters is due to sampling error, or "chance."

objectivity A lack of bias or prejudice.

observational data Data obtained through direct observation.

observer bias The possibility that an observer does not observe objectively and accurately, thus producing invalid observations and a threat to the internal validity of a study.

one-group pretest-posttest design A weak experimental design involving one group that is pretested, exposed to a treatment, and posttested.

one-shot case study design A weak experiment design involving one group that is exposed to a treatment and then posttested.

one-tailed test of statistical significance The use of only one tail of the sampling distribution of a statistic — used when a directional hypothesis is stated.

open-ended item A question giving the responder complete freedom of response.

operational definition Defining a term by stating the actions, processes, or operations used to measure or identify examples of it.

ordinal scale A measurement scale that ranks individuals in terms of the degree to which they possess a characteristic of interest.

outcome variable See **dependent variable.**

panel study Longitudinal design (in survey research) in which the same random sample is measured at different points in time.

parameter A numerical index describing a characteristic of a population.

parametric technique A test of significance appropriate when the data represent an interval or ratio scale of measurement and other specific assumptions have been met.

participant observation Observation in which the observer actually becomes a participant in the situation to be observed.

path analysis A type of sophisticated analysis investigating causal connections among correlated variables.

Pearson *r* An index of correlation appropriate when the data represent either interval or ratio scales; it takes into account each and every score and produces a coefficient between .00 and ± 1.00.

percentile rank An index of relative position indicating the percentage of scores that fall at or below a given score.

pie chart A graphic method of displaying the breakdown of data into categories.

pilot study A small-scale study administered before conducting an actual study—its purpose is to reveal defects in the research plan.

population The group to which the researcher would like the results of a study to be generalizable; it includes *all* individuals with certain specified characteristics.

population generalizability The extent to which the results obtained on a sample are generalizable to a larger group.

positively skewed distribution A distribution

in which there are more extreme scores at the upper, or higher, end than at the lower end.

posttest-only control group design   An experimental design involving at least two randomly formed groups; one group receives a treatment, and both groups are posttested.

prediction   The estimation of scores on one variable from information about one or more other variables.

prediction equation   A mathematical equation used in a prediction study.

prediction study   An attempt to determine variables that are related to a criterion variable.

predictive validity (evidence of)   The degree to which scores on an instrument predict characteristics of individuals in a future situation.

predictor variable(s)   The variable(s) from which projections are made in a prediction study.

pretest-posttest control group design   An experimental design that involves at least two groups; both groups are pretested, one group receives a treatment, and both groups are posttested. For effective control of extraneous variables, the groups should be randomly formed.

pretest-treatment interaction   The fact that subjects may respond or react differently to a treatment because they have been pretested, thereby creating a threat to internal validity.

primary source   Firsthand information such as the testimony of an eyewitness, an original document, a relic, or a description of a study written by the person who conducted it.

probability   The relative frequency with which a particular event occurs among all events of interest.

problem statement   A statement that indicates the variables of interest to the researcher and any specific relationship between those variables that is to be, or was, investigated; includes description of background and rationale (justification) for the study.

projective device   An instrument that includes vague stimuli that subjects are asked to interpret. There are no correct answers or replies.

purposive sample   A nonrandom sample selected because prior knowledge suggests it is representative.

qualitative research/study   Research in which the investigator attempts to study naturally occurring phenomena in all their complexity.

qualitative variable   A variable that is conceptualized and analyzed as distinct categories, with no continuum implied.

quantitative data   Data that differs in amount or degree, along a continuum from less to more.

quantitative variable   A variable that is conceptualized and analyzed along a continuum. It differs in amount or degree.

random assignment   The process of assigning individuals or groups randomly to different treatment conditions.

random numbers, table of   A table that provides the best means of random selection or random assignment.

random sample   A sample selected in such a way that every member of the population has an equal chance of being selected.

random sampling   The process of selecting a random sample.

range   The difference between the highest and lowest scores in a distribution; measure of variability.

ratio scale   A measurement scale that, in addition to being an interval scale, also has an absolute zero in the scale.

raw score   The total score attained by an individual on all of the items on a test or other instrument.

regression line   The line of best fit for a set of scores plotted on coordinate axes (a scatterplot).

regression threat   The possibility that results are due to a tendency for groups, selected on the basis of extreme scores, to regress toward a more average score on subsequent measurements, regardless of the experimental treatment.

relationship study A study investigating relationships among two or more variables, one of which may be a treatment (method) variable.

reliability The degree to which scores obtained with an instrument are consistent measures of whatever the instrument measures.

reliability coefficient An index of the consistency of scores on the same instrument. There are several methods of computing a reliability coefficient, depending on the type of consistency and characteristics of the instrument.

replication Refers to conducting a study again; the second study may be a repetition of the original study, using different subjects, or may change specified aspects of the study.

research The formal, systematic application of scholarship, disciplined inquiry, and most often the scientific method to the study of problems.

research bias see **threat to internal validity.**

research hypothesis A statement of the expected relationship between two or more variables, or other expected outcomes.

research proposal A detailed description of a proposed study designed to investigate a given problem.

research report A description of how a study was conducted, including results and conclusions.

researcher bias A situation in which the researcher's expectations concerning the outcomes of the study actually contribute to producing various outcomes, thereby creating a threat to internal validity.

sample The group on which information is obtained, preferably selected in such a way that the sample represents the larger group (population) from which it was selected.

sampling The process of selecting a number of individuals (a sample) from a population, preferably in such a way that the individuals represent the larger group from which they were selected.

sampling distribution The theoretical distribution of all possible values of a statistic from all possible samples of a given size selected from a population.

sampling error Expected, chance variation in sample statistics that occurs when successive samples are selected from a population.

sampling interval The distance between individuals chosen when sampling systematically.

sampling ratio The proportion of individuals in the population that are selected for the sample in systematic sampling.

scatterplot The plot of points determined by the cross-tabulation of scores on coordinate axes; used to represent and illustrate the relationship between two quantitative variables.

scientific method A way of knowing that is characterized by the public nature of its procedures and conclusions and by rigorous testing of conclusions.

secondary source Secondhand information, such as a description of historical events by someone not present when the event occurred.

sign test A nonparametric inferential statistic used to compare two groups that are not independent.

simple random sample See **random sample.**

simulation Research in which an "artificial" situation is created and participants are told what activities they are to engage in.

single-subject experimental designs Designs applied when the sample size is one; used to study the behavior change that an individual exhibits as a result of some intervention, or treatment.

skewed distribution A nonsymmetrical distribution in which there are more extreme scores at one end of the distribution than the other.

Solomon four-group design An experimental design that involves random assignment of subjects to each of four groups; two groups are pretested, two are not, one of the pretested groups and one of the unpretested groups receive the experimental treatment, and all four groups are posttested.

split-half procedure   A method of estimating the internal consistency reliability of an instrument; it is obtained by giving an instrument once but scoring it twice — for each of two equivalent "half tests." These scores are then correlated.

stability (of scores)   The extent to which scores are reliable (consistent) over time.

standard deviation (SD)   The most stable measure of variability; it takes into account each and every score in a distribution.

standard score   A derived score that expresses how far a given raw score is from the mean, in terms of standard deviation units.

standard error of the difference (SED)   The standard deviation of a distribution of differences between sample means.

standard error of estimate   An estimate of the size of the error to be expected in predicting a criterion score.

standard error of the mean (SEM)   The standard deviation of sample means which indicates by how much the sample means can be expected to differ if other samples from the same population are used.

standard error of measurement   An estimate of the size of the error that one can expect in an individual's test score.

standard error of a statistic   The standard deviation of the sampling distribution of a statistic.

static-group comparison design   A weak experimental design that involves at least two nonequivalent groups; one receives a treatment and both are posttested.

statistic(s)   Numerical index describing a characteristic of a sample.

statistical regression threat   See **regression threat.**

statistically significant   The conclusion that results are unlikely to have occurred due to sampling error or "chance"; an observed correlation or difference probably exists in the population.

stratified sampling   The process of selecting a sample in such a way that identified subgroups in the population are represented in the sample in the same proportion as they exist in the population.

subject characteristics threat   The possibility that characteristics of the subjects in a study may account for observed relationships, thereby producing a threat to internal validity.

survey study/research   An attempt to obtain data from members of a population (or a sample) to determine the current status of that population with respect to one or more variables.

systematic sampling   A selection procedure in which all sample elements are determined after the selection of the first element, since each element on a selected list is separated from the first element by a multiple of the selection interval. Example: every tenth element may be selected.

T score   A standard score derived from a z score by multiplying the z score by 10 and adding 50.

t test for correlated means   A parametric test of significance used to determine whether there is a significant difference between the means of two matched, or nonindependent, samples. It is also used for pre-post comparisons.

t test for independent means   A parametric test of significance used to determine whether there is a significant difference between the means of two independent samples.

target population   The population to which the researcher, ideally, would like to generalize results.

test of significance   A statistical test used to determine whether or not the obtained results for a sample are likely to represent the population.

testing threat   A threat to internal validity that refers to improved scores on a posttest that are a result of subjects having taken a pretest.

test-retest method   A procedure for determining the extent to which scores from an instrument are reliable over time by correlating the scores from two administrations of the same instrument to the same individuals.

threat to internal validity An alternative explanation for research results, that is, that an observed relationship is an artifact of another variable.

time-series design An experimental design involving one group that is repeatedly pretested, exposed to an experimental treatment, and repeatedly posttested.

treatment variable See **experimental variable.**

trend study Longitudinal design (in survey research) in which a general population is studied over time by taking different random samples at various points in time.

triangulation Cross-checking of data using multiple data sources or multiple data collection procedures.

two-tailed test of statistical significance Use of both tails of a sampling distribution of a statistic — when a nondirectional hypothesis is stated.

Type I error The rejection by the researcher of a null hypothesis that is actually true. Also called *alpha error.*

Type II error The failure of a researcher to reject a null hypothesis that is really false. Also called *beta error.*

unit of analysis The unit that is used in data analysis (usually a score for an individual or a group).

unobtrusive measures Measures obtained without subjects being aware that they are being observed or measured, or by examining inanimate objects (such as school suspension lists) that can be used in order to obtain desired information.

validity The degree to which correct inferences can be made based on results from an instrument; depends not only on the instrument itself, but also on the instrumentation process and the characteristics of the group studied.

validity coefficient An index of the validity of scores on an instrument; a special application of the correlation coefficient.

variability The extent to which scores differ from one another.

variable A characteristic that can assume any one of several values, for example, cognitive ability, height, aptitude, teaching method.

variance (SD^2) The square of the standard deviation; a measure of variability.

z score The most basic standard score that expresses how far a score is from a mean in terms of standard deviation units.

SUGGESTIONS FOR FURTHER READING

Chapter One
THE NATURE OF RESEARCH

Butterfield, H. (1960). *The origins of modern science.* New York: Macmillan.

Kuhn, T. S. (1970). *The structure of scientific revolutions.* Chicago: University of Chicago Press.

Nagel, E. (1961). *The structure of science: Problems in the logic of scientific explanation.* New York: Harcourt, Brace & World.

Phillips, D. C. (1987). *Philosophy, science, and social inquiry.* Elmsford, NY: Pergamon.

Shulman, L. S. (1988). Disciplines of inquiry in education: An overview. In R. M. Jaeger (Ed.), *Complementary methods for research in education.* Washington, DC: American Educational Research Association.

Stouffer, S. (1962). *Social research to test ideas.* New York: Free Press.

Chapter Two
THE RESEARCH PROBLEM

American Psychological Association. (1985). *Ethical principles in the conduct of research with human participants.* Washington, DC: American Psychological Association.

Campbell, J. P., Daft, R. L., & Hulin, C. L. (1982). *What to study: Generating and developing research questions.* Beverly Hills, CA: Sage.

Englehardt, H. T., Jr. & Callahan, D. (Eds.). (1980). *Knowing and valuing: The search for common roots.* New York: The Hastings Center.

Frankena, W. K. (1973). *Ethics* (2nd ed.). Englewood Cliffs, NJ: Prentice-Hall.

Kimmel, A. J. (1988). *Ethics and values in applied social research.* Beverly Hills, CA: Sage.

Milgram, S. (1963). Behavioral study of obedience. *Journal of Abnormal and Social Psychology, 67* (4), 371–378.

Reynolds, P. D. (1979). *Ethical dilemmas and social science research.* San Francisco: Jossey-Bass.

Chapter Three
VARIABLES AND HYPOTHESES

Blalock, H. J., Jr. (1982). *Conceptualization and measurement in the social sciences.* Beverly Hills, CA: Sage.

Ennis, R. H. (1964). Operational definitions. *American Educational Research Journal, 1*, 183–201.

Kaplan, A. (1964). *The conduct of inquiry.* (San Francisco: Chandler).

Scriven, M. (1988). Philosophical inquiry methods in education. In R. M. Jaeger (Ed.), *Complementary methods for research in education.* Washington DC: American Educational Research Association.

Tuckman, B. W. (1988). Identifying and labeling variables. In *Conducting educational research* (3rd ed.). San Diego: Harcourt, Brace and Jovanovich.

Chapter Four
REVIEWING THE LITERATURE

Cooper, H. M. (1984). *The integrative research review: A systematic approach.* Beverly Hills, CA: Sage.

Gover, H. R. (1981). *Keys to library research on the graduate level: A guide to guides.* Lanham, MD: University Press of America.

Woodbury, M. L. (1982). *A guide to sources of educational information* (2nd ed.). Washington, DC: Information Resource Press.

Chapter Five
SAMPLING

Bracht, G. H., & Glass, G. V. (1968). The external validity of experiments. *American Educational Research Journal, 5*, 437–474.

Cochran, W. G. (1977). *Sampling techniques* (3rd ed.). New York: John Wiley & Sons.

Jaeger, R. M. (1984). *Sampling in education and the social sciences.* New York: Longman.

Kalton, G. (1983). *Introduction to survey sampling.* Beverly Hills, CA: Sage.

Kish, L. (1965). *Survey sampling.* New York: John Wiley.

Williams, B. (1978). *A sampler on sampling.* New York: John Wiley & Sons.

Chapter Six
INSTRUMENTATION

Anastasi, A. (1982). *Psychological testing* (5th ed.). New York: Macmillan.

Andrulis, R. (1977). *A source book of tests and measures of human behavior.* Springfield, IL: Charles C. Thomas.

Miles, M. B., & Huberman, A. M. (1984). *Qualitative data analysis: A sourcebook of new methods.* Beverly Hills, CA: Sage.

Sawin, E. I. (1969). *Evaluation and the work of the teacher.* Belmont, CA: Wadsworth.

Sullivan, J. L., & Feldman, S. (1979). *Multiple indicators: An introduction.* Beverly Hills, CA: Sage.

Webb, E. T., Campbell, D. T., Schwartz, R. D., Sechrest, L., & Grove, J. B. (1981). *Nonreactive measures in the social sciences.* Boston: Houghton Mifflin.

Chapter Seven
VALIDITY AND RELIABILITY

Brinberg, S., & McGrath, J. E. (1985). *Validity and the research process.* Beverly Hills, CA: Sage.

Carmines, E. G., & Zeller, R. A. (1979). *Reliability and validity assessment.* Beverly Hills, CA: Sage.

Cronbach, L. J., & Meehl, P. E. (1955). Construct validity in psychological tests. *Psychological Bulletin, 52* (4), 281–302.

Kirk, J., & Miller, M. L. (1986). *Reliability and validity in qualitative research.* Beverly Hills, CA: Sage.

Chapter Eight
DESCRIPTIVE STATISTICS

Bruning, J. L., & Kintz, B. L. (1987). *Computational handbook of statistics* (3rd ed.). Glenview, IL: Scott, Foresman.

Jaeger, R. M. (1983). *Statistics: A spectator sport.* Beverly Hills, CA: Sage.

Rowntree, D. (1981). *Statistics without tears: A primer for non-mathematicians.* New York: Charles Scribner's Sons.

Schutte, J. G. (1977). *Everything you always wanted to know about elementary statistics (but were afraid to ask).* Englewood Cliffs, NJ: Prentice-Hall.

Chapter Nine
INFERENTIAL STATISTICS

Carver, R. P. (1978). The case against statistical significance testing. *Harvard Educational Review, 48* (3), 378–399.

Conover, W. J. (1971). *Practical nonparametric statistics*. New York: John Wiley & Sons.

Good, I. J. (1983). *Good thinking: The foundations of probability and its applications*. Minneapolis: University of Minnesota Press.

Hays, W. L. (1981). *Statistics* (3rd ed.). New York: Holt, Rinehart, and Winston.

Morrison, D., and Henkel, R. (eds.). (1970). *The significance test controversy*. Chicago: Aldine-Atherton.

Shaver, J. P. (1985). Chance and nonsense. *Phi Delta Kappan*, Part 1: *67*(1), 57–60; Part 2: *67*(2), 138–141.

Chapter Ten
STATISTICS IN PERSPECTIVE

Cohen, J. (1988). *Statistical power analysis for the behavioral sciences* (2nd ed.). Hillsdale, NJ: Lawrence Erlbaum Associates.

Glass, G. V., McGaw, B., and Smith, M. L. (1981). *Meta-analysis in social research*. Beverly Hills, CA: Sage.

Huff, D. (1954). *How to lie with statistics*. (New York: W. W. Norton).

Moore, D. S. (1985) *Statistics: Concepts and Controversies* (2nd ed.). New York: W. H. Freeman.

Chapter Eleven
INTERNAL VALIDITY

Barber, T. X. (1973). Pitfalls in research: Nine investigator and experimenter effects. In R. M. W. Travers (ed.), *Second handbook of research on teaching*. Chicago: Rand McNally.

Borg, W. R. (1984). Dealing with threats to internal validity that randomization does not rule out. *Educational Researcher*, *13* (10), 11–14.

Campbell, D. T., & Stanley, J. C. (1966). *Experimental and quasiexperimental designs for research*. Chicago: Rand McNally.

Jurs, S. G., & Glass, G. V. (1971). The effect of experimental mortality on the internal and external validity of the randomized comparative experiment. *Journal of Experimental Education*, *40*, 62–66.

Rosenthal, R., & Jackson, L. (1968). *Pygmalion in the classroom*. New York: Holt, Rinehart & Winston.

Shaver, J. P. (1983). The verification of independent variables in teaching methods research. *Educational Researcher*, *12* (8), 3–9.

Spector, P. E. (1981). *Research designs*. Beverly Hills, CA: Sage.

Chapter Twelve
EXPERIMENTAL RESEARCH

Campbell, D. T., and Stanley, J. C. (1963). *Experimental and quasi-experimental designs for research*. Chicago: Rand McNally.

Cook, T., D., and Campbell, D. T. (1979). *Quasi-experimentation: Design and analysis issues for field settings*. Chicago: Rand McNally.

Fisher, Sir R. A. (1935). *The designs of experiments*. New York: Hafner.

Phillips, D. C. (1981). Toward an evaluation of the experiment in educational contexts. *Educational Researcher*, *10* (6), 13–20.

Porter, A. C. (1988). Comparative experiments in educational research. In R. M. Jaeger (Ed.), *Complementary methods for research in education*. Washington, DC: American Educational Research Association.

Chapter Thirteen
CORRELATIONAL RESEARCH

Kenny, D. A. (1979). *Correlation and causality*. New York: John Wiley & Sons.

Kim, F. J., & Mueller, C. W. (1978). *Introduction to factor analysis: What it is and how to do it*. Beverly Hills, CA: Sage.

Liebetrau, A. M. (1983). *Measures of association*. Beverly Hills, CA: Sage.

Chapter Fourteen
CAUSAL-COMPARATIVE RESEARCH

Borg, W. R., & Gall, M. D. (1989). Exploring relationships between variables: The causal-comparative method. In *Educational research: An introduction* (5th ed.). New York: Longman.

Gay, L. R. (1987). The causal-comparative method. In *Educational research: Competencies for analysis and application* (3rd ed.). Columbus, OH: Merrill.

Platt, J. (1964). Strong inference. *Science*, *146*, 347–353.

Chapter Fifteen
SURVEY RESEARCH

Babbie, E. R. (1973). *Survey research methods*. Belmont, CA: Wadsworth.

Fink, A., and Kosecoff, J. (1985). *How to conduct surveys: A step-by-step guide*. Beverly Hills, CA: Sage.

Fowler, F. J., Jr. (1984). *Survey research methods*. Beverly Hills, CA: Sage.

Jaeger, R. M. (1988). Survey research methods in education. In R. M. Jaeger (Ed.), *Complementary methods for research in education*. Washington, DC: American Educational Research Association.

Chapter Sixteen
QUALITATIVE RESEARCH

Bernard, H. R. (1988). *Research methods in cultural anthropology*. Beverly Hills, CA: Sage.

Bogdan, R. C., and Biklen, S. K. (1982). *Qualitative research in education*. Boston: Allyn and Bacon.

Dobbert, M. L. (1982). *Ethnographic research: Theory and applications for modern schools and societies*. New York: Praeger.

Goetz, J. P., & LeCompte, M. D. (1984). *Ethnography and qualitative design in educational research*. San Diego, CA: Academic Press.

Jackson, P. W. (1968). *Life in classrooms*. New York: Holt, Rinehart, and Winston.

Spindler, G. (1982). *Doing the ethnography of schooling: Educational anthropology in action*. New York: Holt, Rinehart and Winston.

Wilson, S. (1977). The use of ethnographic techniques in educational research. *Review of Educational Research, 47*, 245–265.

Chapter Seventeen
HISTORICAL RESEARCH

Barzun, J., & Graff, H. F. (1985). *The modern researcher* (4th ed.). San Diego: Harcourt, Brace Jovanovich.

Carr, E. H. (1967). *What is history?* New York: Random House.

Tuchman, B. W. (1981). *Practicing history*. New York: Knopf.

Chapter Eighteen
WRITING A RESEARCH PROPOSAL OR REPORT

Behling, J. H. (1984). *Guidelines for preparing the research proposal* (rev. ed.). Lanham, MD: University Press of America.

Davitz, J. R., & Davitz, L. L. (1977). *Evaluating research proposals in the behavioral sciences*. New York: Teachers College Press.

Krathwohl, D. R. (1977). *How to prepare a research proposal* (2nd ed.). Syracuse, NY: Syracuse University Bookstore.

Locke, W. F., Spirduso, W. W., & Silverman, S. J. (1987). *Proposals that work: A guide for planning dissertations and grant proposals* (2nd ed.). Beverly Hills, CA: Sage.

INDEX

489